Scotland's Constitution:
Law and Practice

Scotland's Constitution: Law and Practice

Third Edition

C M G Himsworth
Emeritus Professor of Administrative Law,
University of Edinburgh

and

C M O'Neill
Chairman, Brodies LLP

Bloomsbury Professional

Bloomsbury Professional Limited, Maxwelton House, 41–43 Boltro Road, Haywards Heath, West Sussex, RH16 1BJ

© Bloomsbury Professional Limited 2015

A CIP Catalogue record for this book is available from the British Library.

ISBN: 978 1 78043 466 7

Typeset by Phoenix Photosetting, Chatham, Kent
Printed and bound in Great Britain by CPI Group (UK) Ltd, Croydon, CR0 4YY

Contents

Preface		*vii*
Table of Statutes		*ix*
Table of European Legislation		*xxiii*
Table of Statutory Instruments		*xxv*
Tables of Cases		*xxxi*
Bibliography		*xlvii*
1	Constitutions and Constitutional Law	1
2	Constitutional Law and Constitutional Values	23
3	The Scottish Constitutional Context	41
4	The Scottish Independence Referendum	69
5	The UK and Scottish Parliaments: the Institutional Framework	87
6	Law-making Competences for Scotland	125
7	The UK and Scottish Governments	177
8	Local Authorities and other Public Bodies	223
9	Law-making Procedures	245
10	The Parliamentary Accountability of Government	283
11	Public Finance	311
12	Courts and the Independence of the Judiciary	327
13	Citizen and State	359
14	Public Law Adjudication	407
Index		487

Preface

With its third edition in preparation, this book maintained a position of strict neutrality during the Scottish independence referendum campaign leading to the vote on 18 September 2014. It was aware, however, that, whatever the broader consequences for the country, the referendum result would affect its own identity and content deeply. If there had been a Yes vote, the book would have changed dramatically. The assumption of the first two editions – that Scotland's Constitution could be centred around the two levels of Parliament and Government operating under the Scotland Act 1998 – would have been displaced. An independence constitution would have been in preparation. On the other hand, a No vote would retain those institutions broadly in place, for the time being at least. The book's structure could be retained. It was a challengingly divergent prospect.

As things turned out, however, the book was offered the opportunity of a middle way. The introduction to the study of constitutional law in Chapter 1 through a hypothetical constitution for an independent Scotland could remain, with perhaps added poignancy. Much of the rest of the book has also moved forward into the new edition, but with much general updating but also specifically to take account of the impact of the Scotland Act 2012 and to anticipate the eventual impact of the Smith Commission recommendations.

But, because the referendum campaign, the result and its immediate aftermath have done so much to reframe the context within which Scottish constitutional law has now to be studied, a new Chapter 4 devoted to the referendum itself (the campaign, the result and events following) has been added. We were able, at the last minute, to add a brief reference to the UK Government's proposals (Cm 8990) for a new Scotland Act.

These changes have demanded more than usual amounts of support from our publishers for which we are very grateful, as we are too for the help and support of many individuals including, in particular, Professors Tony Bradley and Niamh Nic Shuibhne.

Chris Himsworth
Christine O'Neill
Burns Night 2015

Table of Statutes

[All references are to paragraph number]

Abolition of Poindings and Warrant Sales Act 2001 .... 6.12; 9.23
Act of Settlement 1700 .... 3.2; 5.7;
6.15; 7.2, 7.7
s III 5.7; 12.7
Act of Union 1706 *see* Union
with Scotland Act 1706
Act of Union 1707 *see* Union
with England Act 1707
Administration of Justice Act 1968
s 1 .... 5.13
Administration of Justice Act 1973
s 9 .... 12.10
Administration of Justice (Scot-
land) Act 1933
Pt III (ss 23–30) 6.15
Adoption and Children Bill
2001–02 .... 9.6
Agricultural Holdings (Scotland)
Act 2003 .... 13.11
s 72 .... 14.27
(10) 14.27
Agricultural Sector (Wales) Bill
2013 .... 14.25
Air Weapons and Licensing
(Scotland) Bill (2014–15) ... 6.17
Alcohol (Minimum Pricing)
(Scotland) Act 2012 .... 14.28
Antisocial Behaviour etc (Scot-
land) Act 2004 .... 13.19
Anti-terrorism, Crime and Secu-
rity Act 2001 .... 6.5; 13.5
Appellate Jurisdiction Act 1876.. 5.13
Appellate Jurisdiction Act 1887.. 5.13
Asylum and Immigration (Treat-
ment of Claimants etc) Act
2004 .... 13.3
Bankruptcy and Diligence etc
(Scotland) Act 2007
s 224(3) 9.34
(4)(b)(ii) 9.34
Bill of Rights 1689 .... 1.22; 3.2; 6.10
Borders, Citizenship and Immi-
gration Act 2009 .... 13.2

Breastfeeding etc (Scotland) Act
2005 .... 9.23
Bribery Act 2010 .... 12.10
British Nationality Act 1948 .... 13.2
British Nationality Act 1981 ... 1.22; 13.2
s 1(3), 94) 13.2
6 .... 13.2
40(2) 13.2
Sch 7 .... 5.7
British Nationality (Hong Kong)
Act 1997 .... 13.2
British Overseas Territories Act
2002 .... 13.2
Broadcasting Act 1990 .... 8.10
Budget (Scotland) Act 2014 .... 11.17
s 1–3, 5–7 .... 11.17
sch 1 .... 11.17
sch 2 .... 11.17
sch 3 .... 11.17
Buildings (Recovery of Expenses)
(Scotland) Act 2014 .... 9.23
Burrell Collection (Lending and
Borrowing) (Scotland) Act
2014 .... 9.27
Canada Act 1982 .... 6.5
preamble 6.5
Chequers Estate Act 1917 .... 7.4
Children and Young People
(Scotland) Act 2014 .... 8.3; 14.10,
14.28
Pt 4 (ss 19–32) 14.28
Children (Scotland) Act 1995 .. 9.34; 13.7
Children's Hearings (Scotland)
Act 2011 .... 8.2
Christmas Day and New Year's
Day Trading (Scotland) Act
2007 .... 9.23
City of Edinburgh Council
(Portobello Park) Act 2014: 8.3; 9.27
Civic Government (Scotland) Act
1982 .... 6.24; 8.3; 13.19
s 59 .... 13.18
63(3), (4), (11) 13.19
64, 65 .... 13.19

Civil Contingencies Act 2004
  s 1 .... 6.23
Civil Evidence (Scotland) Act
  1988 .... 6.5
Civil Partnership Act 2004 .... 14.17
Civil Service (Management
  Functions) Act 1992 .... 7.24
  s 1 .... 7.25
Civil Service (Special Advisers)
  Act (Northern Ireland) 2013: 7.23
Claim of Right 1689 .... 1.22; 3.2;
  .   6.23
Coal Industry Act 1994 .... 6.19
Coastguard Act 1925 .... 14.22
Comhairle an Eilean Siar (Eris-
  kay Causeway) Order Con-
  firmation Act 2000 .... 9.26
Commissioner for Children and
  Young People (Scotland)
  Act 2003 .... 9.24
Commissioners for Revenue and
  Customs Act 2005 .... 7.26; 11.14
Commonwealth Immigrants Act
  1962 .... 13.2
Communications Act 2003 .... 8.10; 14.17
Community Care and Health
  (Scotland) Act 2002 .... 10.14
Constitutional Reform Act 2005 .. 1.22;
  5.14; 7.7; 12.1,
  12.18, 12.19, 12.20;
  14.32
  s 3(1) 12.4
  24, 26 .... 12.5
  27, 38, 40 .... 14.32
  41 .... 14.21
  (1) 12.2
  (2) 12.2; 14.32
  42 .... 14.32
  137 .... 5.13
  Sch 9
    Pt I (paras 1–84) 14.32
Constitutional Reform and
  Governance Act 2010 ..... 1.22; 5.20;
  7.23; 14.2
  s 2–5 .... 7.2, 7.23
  6, 7 .... 7.2
  8 .... 7.2, 7.23
  9 .... 7.2
  10–16 .... 7.2, 7.23
  17, 18 .... 7.2
  42 .... 5.14
Consumer Insurance (Disclosure
  and Representations) Act
  2012 .... 9.4

Consumer Rights Bill (2014–15):   9.4
Contempt of Court 1981
  s 2 .... 10.6
Continental Shelf Act 1964 ....   6.5
Control of Dogs (Scotland) Act
  2010 .... 9.23
Convention Rights (Compliance)
  (Scotland) Act 2001 ..... 6.23; 14.17
  s 12 .... 9.34
Convention Rights Proceedings
  (Amendment)   (Scotland)
  Act 2009 .... 6.19; 7.26;
  14.30
  s 1 .... 14.30
Convention Rights Proceedings
  (Amendment)   Scotland)
  Bill 9.15
Council of the Law Society of
  Scotland Act 2003 .... 9.23, 9.25
Counter-Terrorism Act 2008 .... 13.5;
  14.13
Court of Session Act 1988 .... 14.12
  s 27A 14.12
  27B 14.12
  (1), (2) 14.12
  27C, 27D 14.12
Courts Reform (Scotland) Act
  2014 .... 12.1, 12.2, 12.4,
  12.5, 12.7, 12.10,
  12.19; 14.6,
  14.10
  s 14 .... 12.5
  16 .... 12.10
  (3) 12.10
  25 .... 12.7
  29 .... 12.4
  39 .... 12.1
  89 .... 14.10, 14.12
  120 .... 12.5
Criminal   Evidence   (Witness
  Anonymity) Act 2008 ....   9.4
Criminal Justice and Licensing
  (Scotland) Act 2010 ....   8.3
  s 3 .... 12.20
  5(1) 12.20
  38 .... 13.19
Criminal   Justice   and   Public
  Order Act 1994
  s 63–66 .... 13.19
Criminal Justice (Scotland) Act
  1980
  s 1, 2 .... 13.18
Criminal Justice (Scotland) Act
  2003 .... 8.9

Criminal Procedure (Legal Assistance, Detention and Appeals) (Scotland) Act 2010............................ 9.15; 13.18
s 1.. 13.18
Criminal Procedure (Scotland) Act 1995............................ 14.21
s 13... 13.18
(1)–(7)................................. 13.18
14.. 13.18
(1)–(8)................................. 13.18
18(2)–(7B)........................... 13.18
34, 35.................................... 13.18
170(1)................................... 12.11
288ZA............................ 14.1, 14.21
288ZB–288B........................ 14.21
Criminal Proceedings etc (Reform) Scotland Act 2007................. 12.2
s 45... 14.25
Crown Proceedings Act 1947...... 14.2
Crown Suits (Scotland) Act 1857....................................... 7.21
Damages (Asbestos-related Conditions) (Scotland) Act 2009.................... 2.8; 6.12; 14.10, 14.24, 14.26
s 1.. 6.12
(1), (2)................................ 14.26
2... 6.12
4(2)...................................... 14.26
Data Protection Act 1998........... 13.23, 13.24
s 1.. 13.23
(1).. 13.23
4(4)...................................... 13.23
6... 13.23
7... 13.23
13.. 13.23
27(2)..................................... 13.23
55A.. 13.23
Sch 7
para 3................................... 13.23
Data Retention and Investigatory Powers Act 2014
s 1.. 13.25
Debt Arrangement and Attachment (Scotland) Act 2002.............. 6.12; 9.23
Deregulation and Contracting Out Act 1994................. 6.23; 9.34
Development of Tourism Act 1969...................................... 8.12
Disabled Persons (Northern Ireland) Act 1989................ 6.5

Disabled Persons' Parking Badges (Scotland) Act 2014............ 9.23
Disabled Persons' Parking Places (Scotland) Act 2009........... 9.23
Diseases of Fish Act 1983........... 13.22
Dog Fouling (Scotland) Act 2003...................................... 9.23
Domestic Abuse (Scotland) Act 2011...................................... 9.23
Double Jeopardy (Scotland) Act 2011...................................... 12.12
Edinburgh Airport Rail Link Act 2007...................................... 9.27
Edinburgh Tram (Line One) Act 2006...................................... 9.27
Edinburgh Tram (Line Two) Act 2006...................................... 9.27
Education (Scotland) Act1973.... 2.8
Education (Scotland) Act 1980... 8.3
s 48A...................................... 13.7
Electoral Administration Act 2006: 5.7
s 17(1), (8)............................ 5.7
Electoral Registration and Administration Act 2013
s 1.. 5.6
6... 5.9
Electronic Communications Act 2000
s 8, 9..................................... 6.22
Emergency Powers Act 1920...... 6.23
s 1.. 6.23
Emergency Powers Act 1964...... 6.23
Energy Act 2008
s 18, 26.................................. 7.19
34.. 6.24
Environmental Protection Act 1990...................................... 7.19
Equality Act 2006....................... 13.14
s 2.. 13.14
4(1)...................................... 13.14
5(2)...................................... 13.14
Sch 1
para 2(3)............................. 13.14
16–23............................. 13.14
Equality Act 2010....................... 1.22; 13.2 14.2
s 7(1), (3)–(5)......................... 13.14
30(1), (2)............................... 13.14
Erskine Bridge Tolls Act 2001.... 2.8; 9.15
Ethical Standards in Public Life etc (Scotland) Act 2000.................................8.1, 8.17
s 1–3, 8, 17, 18, 22................. 8.17

European Communities Act
1972............................ 1.22; 3.12; 6.5,
6.6, 6.7, 6.8, 6.10,
6.19, 6.20, 6.24,
6.25; 13.9; 14.1
s 2.. 14.1
(1) 3.12; 6.7, 6.9
(2) 3.12; 6.7, 6.24
(3) 3.12
(4) 6.9, 6.10
3............................... 3.12; 6.7, 6.8
(2) 3.12
Sch 2.. 3.12
European Parliamentary Elections
Act 1978 .... 3.9
European Parliamentary Elections
Act 1999 .... 3.9; 9.7
European Parliamentary Elections
Act 2002 .... 3.9; 6.16
s 2... 5.8
European Union Act 2011...... 3.12, 3.15
s 2–4 .... 3.12; 6.9
18... 6.9
218... 3.12
Exchequer and Audit Departments
Act 1866
s 3... 2.5
Extradition Act 1989 ...... 6.5, 6.10; 14.32
Extradition Act 2003 .... 13.4
Pt 1 (ss 1–68A)....................... 13.4
s 2.. 13.4
10–21, 26 .... 13.4
67(1)(b)................................ 13.4
Pt 2 (ss 69–140A)................... 13.4
s 92, 94................................... 13.4
191 .... 13.4
216(9) 13.4
Factories Act 1961 .... 13.22
Fatal Accidents and Sudden
Deaths Inquiry (Scotland)
Act 1976................................ 7.22
Finance Act 2000 .... 7.26
Firearms Act 1968
s 44.. 14.6
Sch 5
Pt III
para 4............................... 14.6
Fixed-term Parliaments Act 2011:   5.4;
7.2, 7.3, 7.5,
7.12
s 1(2), (4)................................ 5.4
2(3) 7.5
3(1), (2)................................. 5.4
4.. 5.4

Food Standards Act 1999 ....   6.22; 8.9
Foreign Compensation Act 1950
s 4(4) 14.11
Forfeiture Act 1870
s 2.. 5.7
Forth Crossing Act 2011 .... 9.27
Forth Road Bridge Act 2013 .... 9.1
Freedom of Information Act
2000.................... 5.23; 8.16; 10.1;
13.22
s 36... 7.11
Freedom of Information (Amend-
ment) (Scotland) Act 2013:   13.22
s 1, 4....................................... 13.22
Freedom of Information (Scot-
land) Act 2002...... 5.23; 8.16; 9.10;
10.1; 13.21, 13.22
s 1(1) 13.22
2, 3, 5, 12–14......................... 13.22
Pt 2 (ss 25–41) 13.22
s 25–37................................... 13.22
38............................ 13.22, 13.23
42, 47, 51, 56, 59,
62, 64, 65, 65A 13.22
sch 1 .... 13.22
Further and Higher Education
(Scotland) Act 1992 .... 8.2, 8.9
Gaelic Language (Scotland) Act
2005....................................... 6.18
Ghana Independence Act 1957 ...   6.5
Glasgow Airport Rail Link Act
2007....................................... 9.27
Government of Ireland Act 1914:   9.7
Government of Ireland Act 1920:   1.20;
3.16, 3.19; 14.22
s 4.. 6.12
8(2) 7.19
Government of Wales Act 1998:   6.10,
6.20; 14.32
s 81, 108................................. 14.15
109 .... 14.1
Sch 8....................................... 14.1
Sch 9....................................... 14.15
Government of Wales Act 2006:   1.22;
3.19; 14.1,
14.18, 14.25
Pt 1 (ss 1–44) 3.19
s 4.. 3.19
22.. 3.19
32, 33..................................... 3.19
45–55..................................... 3.19
Pt 4 (ss 103–116) 3.19
s 93–102................................. 3.19
117... 3.19

Government of Wales Act 2006
– *contd*
s 149 .... 3.19; 14.1
Sch 2 .... 3.19
Sch 5 .... 3.19
Sch 7 .... 3.19
Sch 9 .... 3.19; 14.1
Government Resources and
Accounts Act 2000
s 27 .... 11.17
Greater London Authority Act
1999 .... 3.19
Greater London Authority
(Referendum) Act 1998 .... 3.19
Health and Safety at Work etc Act
1974 .... 13.22
s 14 .... 12.19
Health and Social Care Act 2008: 13.12
s 145 .... 6.19
Health Boards (Membership and
Elections) (Scotland) Act
2009 .... 7.1; 8.8
Health Service Commissioners
Act 1993 .... 10.11
Herring Fishing (Scotland) Act
1889 .... 6.5
High Hedges (Scotland) Act
2013 .... 9.23
House of Commons Disqualifica-
tion Act 1975 .... 5.7
s 2 .... 7.7
7 .... 14.1
Sch 1
para 1 .... 12.18
House of Commons (Removal of
Clergy Disqualification) Act
2001 .... 5.7
House of Lords Act 1999 .. 1.22; 5.6, 5.7,
5.13, 5.14; 6.6;
9.7
s 1, 2 .... 5.14
House of Lords Reform Act
2014 .... 5.14
House of Lords Reform Bill
2012 .... 9.5
Housing (Scotland) Act 2001
s 64 .... 6.17
sch 8 .... 6.17
Human Rights Act 1998 .... 1.22, 1.24;
2.1, 2.2, 2.7;
3.1; 6.2, 6.5,
6.10, 6.19, 6.20,
6.23; 8.16; 9.34;
12.3, 12.7, 12.11;

Human Rights Act 1998 – *contd*
13.5, 13.6, 13.9,
13.10, 13.11, 13.12,
13.13, 13.14, 13.15,
13.16, 13.24; 14.1,
14.2, 14.11, 14.15,
14.16, 14.17, 14.18,
14.19, 14.22, 14.24,
14.25, 14.30, 14.31,
14.32
s 1(1)–(3) 13.11
2 .... 13.17; 14.18
3 .... 13.12
(1) 14.17, 14.22
(2) 14.17
4 .... 6.20; 13.12; 14.17
(6) 14.1, 14.17
6 .... 8.16; 13.14; 14.17
(1) 13.12; 14.30
(3) 14.30
(a), (b) 13.12
(5) 13.12
7(1)–(3) 13.12
(5) 14.30
8 .... 12.11; 13.12
(3), (4) 14.30
9 .... 12.11
10 .... 9.34 14.17
12 .... 13.24
(2) 13.24
14, 15 .... 13.11
19 .... 14.17
(1)(a) 14.17
(2) 14.17
21(1) 14.17
Sch 1 .... 13.11
Sch 2 .... 14.17
Sch 3 .... 13.11
Sch 4
para 2(b) 14.17
4 .... 14.17
Hunting Act 2004 .... 6.5; 9.7
Immigration Act 1971 .... 13.2, 13.3
s 2 .... 13.3
3 .... 13.4
(2) 13.3
Immigration Act 1988
s 7 .... 13.3
Immigration Act 2014 .... 13.2
Immigration, Asylum and
Nationality Act 2006
s 56 .... 13.2
Insolvency Act 1986
s 427 .... 5.7

Intelligence Services Act 1994.... 13.25

Interests of Members of the
    Scottish Parliament Act 2006: 5.21;
    9.24

Interpretation Act 1978 .... 7.24

Interpretation and Legislative
    Reform (Scotland) Act 2010: 9.33,
    9.34

Pt 2 (ss 27–37) 9.31, 9.32

s 28 .... 9.34

Pt 4 (ss 48–53) 9.34

Jamaica Independence Act 1962.. 6.5

Judicial Pensions Act 1959 .... 12.7

Judicial Pensions Act 1981 .... 12.7

Judicial Pensions and Retirement
    Act 1993

s 26(7) 12.7

Sch 5.. 12.7

Judiciary and Courts (Scotland)
    Act 2008............... 8.9; 12.4, 12.5,
    12.8, 12.9

s 1 .... 12.4

Pt 2 Ch 2 (ss 4–8).................... 12.8

s 10.. 12.5

11(1) 12.5

12–16, 19, 20...................... 12.5

28–34 .... 12.9

46 .... 12.2

sch 2 .... 12.5

Land Reform (Scotland) Act
    2003....................................... 13.19

s 98 .... 7.19

Law Officers Act 1944

s 2(1) 7.20

Law Reform (Miscellaneous
    Provisions) (Scotland) Act
    1990....................................... 12.5

Learning and Skills Act 2000

s 104.. 6.22

Leasehold Casualties (Scotland)
    Act 2001................................ 9.23

Legal Profession and Legal Aid
    (Scotland) Act 2007

s 1.. 8.9

Legislative and Regulatory
    Reform Act 2006

Pt 1 (ss 1–20) 9.34

Licensing (Scotland) Act 2005.... 8.3

Life Peerages Act 1958 .... 5.13

Local Electoral Administration
    (Scotland) Act 2011

Pt 2 (ss 10–19) 6.13

Local Government Act 1988 .... 8.2

Local Government Act 1992 .... 8.2

Local Government Act 2000

Pt II (ss 10–48A)..................... 8.4

Local Government (Contracts)
    Act 1997............................... 2.7

Local Government etc (Scotland)
    Act 1994................... 3.2; 8.1, 8.2

Pt II (ss 62–126)..................... 8.2

Pt III (ss 127–138) 8.2

Local Government Finance Act
    1992...................................... 8.5

Sch 2.. 9.34

Local Government in Scotland
    Act 2003............................... 2.8

s 1 .... 2.8; 8.3

15, 20................................... 8.3

23–27................................... 2.8

35–39................................... 8.5

Local Government, Planning and
    Land Act 1980............... 6.19; 8.2

Local Government (Scotland)
    Act 1889............................... 8.2

Local Government (Scotland)
    Act 1929............................... 8.2

Local Government (Scotland)
    Act 1947............................... 8.2

Local Government (Scotland)
    Act 1973............................... 3.2; 8.2

Pt IIIA (ss 50A–50K)............. 13.21

Pt IV (ss 51–55) 8.2

s 56.. 8.4

69.. 8.3, 8.5

97, 99..................................... 8.5

201 .... 6.24; 9.29

202–204................................. 9.29

Local Government (Scotland) Act
    1975

Pt II (ss 21–32)........................ 10.11

Local Governance (Scotland) Act
    2004............................. 6.16; 8.2

Localism Act 2011 .... 8.4

Magna Carta 1215................. 1.22; 6.10

Marine and Coastal Access Act
    2009...................................... 6.13

Medicines Act 1968 .... 13.22

Meeting of Parliament Act 1694.. 5.4

Mental Health Act 1983

s 72, 73.................................... 14.17

Mental Health (Care and Treat-
    ment) (Scotland) Act 2005

sch 5 .... 6.22

Mental Health (Public Safety
    and Appeals) (Scotland) Act
    1999....................... 2.7; 6.23; 9.9,
    9.15, 9.18; 14.24

Mental Health (Scotland) Act 1984...................................... 2.7

Merchant Shipping Act 1988 ...... 6.9

Ministerial and Other Salaries Act 1975............................. 7.4, 7.7

Ministerial and Other Salaries Act 1997............................. 7.4, 7.7

Misuse of Drugs Act 1971 s 24..................................... 13.18

Mortgage Rights (Scotland) Act 2001...................................... 9.23

National Galleries of Scotland Act 2003.............................. 9.27

National Health Service (Scotland) Act 1972..................... 10.12

National Parks (Scotland) Act 2000.................................... 8.9
sch 2
para 8–10............................ 6.24

National Trust for Scotland (Governance etc) Act 2013: 9.27

Nationality, Immigration and Asylum Act 2002 .... 13.2

Nautical Assessors (Scotland) Act 1894............................ 14.32

Northern Ireland Act 1998 ..... 1.22; 3.12; 6.19, 6.20; 7.15; 14.1, 14.18, 14.24, 14.32
s 6... 14.15
7..................................... 6.19; 14.15
11... 14.1
16–20....................................... 3.19
24 ,71....................................... 14.15
79.................................... 14.1, 14.15
82... 14.1
Sch 10............................... 14.1, 14.15

Northern Ireland Act 2006 .... 3.19

Northern Ireland Constitution Act 1973........................ 1.20; 6.14
s 31... 3.16

Northern Ireland (Elections) Act 1998
s 2... 3.19

Northern Ireland (St Andrews Agreement) Act 2006.......... 3.19

Offences (Aggravation by Prejudice) (Scotland) Act 2009 ... 9.23

Offensive Behaviour at Football and Threatening Communications (Scotland) Act 2012: 13.19

Offices, Shops and Railway Premises Act 1963............... 13.22

Official Secrets Act 1911 .... 13.21

Official Secrets Act 1989 .... 13.21
s 1–4.. 13.21

Parliament Act 1911........ 1.22; 5.4, 5.13; 9.7, 9.34
s 2(1) 9.7

Parliament Act 1949....... 1.22; 5.4, 5.13; 6.5; 9.7, 9.34

Parliamentary Commissioner Act 1967.......................... 10.11, 10.13
s 1, 2.. 10.12
5(1)–(3)................................. 10.12
8, 10.. 10.12
12(3) 10.12
Sch 2.. 10.12
Sch 3.. 10.12

Parliamentary Constituencies Act 1986
s 2... 5.9
Sch 2.. 5.9

Parliamentary Costs Act 2006..... 9.4

Parliamentary Standards Act 2009
s 4A(6) 5.20

Parliamentary Voting System and Constituencies Act 2011 ..... 5.9

Partnerships (Prosecution) (Scotland) Act 2013.................... 6.5; 9.4

Peerage Act 1963 .... 5.13

Planning etc (Scotland) Act 2006............................. 8.3; 14.6

Plant Varieties Act 1997
Pt I (ss 1–41)............................ 6.14
Pt II (ss 42–46)......................... 6.14

Police Act 1997........................... 13.25

Police and Fire Reform (Scotland) Act 2012.............. 5.18; 13.18
s 19, 24, 44, 90....................... 13.18

Police, Public Order and Criminal Justice (Scotland) Act 2006: 13.19

Police (Scotland) Act 1967
s 26, 39, 41 .... 13.18

Political Parties, Elections and Referendums Act 2000........ 4.5; 5.8, 5.12; 7.26
s 1–3.. 2.5
12... 5.12
16... 5.9
Sch 1.. 2.5

Pollution Prevention and Control Act 1999
s 5(3) 6.24

Prevention of Terrorism Act 2005
s 11... 14.11

Prevention of Terrorism (Tempo-
rary Provisions) Act 1974 ...   5.12
Private Legislation Procedure
(Scotland) Act 1899 ....   9.26
Private Legislation Procedure
(Scotland) Act 1936 ......   6.19; 9.26,
                                    9.27
s 2 ....   9.26
Proceeds of Crime Act 2002 ....   6.5
Proceeds of Crime (Scotland) Act
1995 ....   6.19
Promissory Oaths Act 1868
s 5A 7.15
Property Factors (Scotland) Act
2011 ....   9.23
Protection from Abuse (Scotland)
Act 2001 ....   9.24
Protection of Wild Mammals
(Scotland) Act 2002 .....   9.23; 14.24
Provisional Collection of Taxes
Act 1968 ....   11.3
Provision of Rail Passenger
Services (Scotland) Bill 6.16
Public Appointments and Public
Bodies etc (Scotland) Act
2003 ....   8.15
s 2 ....   8.15
    (8) 8.15
4 ....   8.14
sch 2 ....   8.15
Public Bodies Act 2011 ....   6.24; 8.14;
                                    9.30
s 1–7 ....   8.14
8 ....   6.2; 8.14
9–12 ....   8.14
Sch 1 ....   8.14
Sch 2 ....   8.14
Sch 3 ....   8.14
Sch 4 ....   8.14
Sch 5 ....   8.14
Public Bodies (Joint Working)
(Scotland) Act 2014 ....   8.3
Public Finance and Accountability
(Scotland) Act 2000 ....   8.9, 8.16;
                                    9.15; 11.17, 11.18
s 1(3) 11.17
2, 3 ....   11.17
4 ....   6.12; 11.17
5, 8, 12 ....   11.18
13, 14 ....   11.18
15(3), (4) 8.16
    (8) 11.18
16, 19 ....   11.18
21–25 ....   11.18

Public Meeting Act 1908
s 1 ....   13.19
Public Order Act 1986 ....   13.19
s 1, 21 ....   3.19
11, 12 ....   13.19
    (1), (2), (4), (5), (11) 13.19
14 ....   13.19
14A 13.19
    (6)–(8) 13.19
14B 13.19
    (1), (2), (4) 13.19
14C 13.19
16, 18 ....   13.19
Public Service Pensions Act
2013 ....   7.4
Public Services Reform (Scot-
land) Act 2010 ....   8.9, 8.14;
                                    10.13
Pt 1 (ss 1–13) 8.14
Pt 2 (ss 14–30) 6.23; 8.14
s 25 ....   9.34
Pt 4 (ss 36–43) 8.14
Pt 5 (ss 44–107) 8.14
s 134 ....   8.14
Railtrack (Waverley Station) Order
Confirmation Act 2000 ....   9.26
Railways Act 2005
s 46 ....   6.24
Sch 9 ....   6.24
Reform Act 1832 ....   1.22; 3.1; 6.10
Regional Assemblies (Prepara-
tions) Act 2003 ....   3.19
s 1(4), (5) 3.19
Registration of Political Parties
Act 1998 ....   5.12
Regulation of Care (Scotland) Act
2001
sch 3
para 24 ....   7.26
Regulation of Investigatory Powers
Act 2000 ....   2.8; 13.25
s 22(2) 13.25
Regulation of Investigatory Powers
(Scotland) Act 2000 ....   2.8; 13.25
Representation of the People Act
1981 ....   5.7
Representation of the People Act
1983
s 1 ....   5.6; 13.19
2, 3 ....   5.6
3A 5.6
4 ....   5.6
5 ....   5.6
    (3)–(5) 5.6

Representation of the People Act
  1983 – *contd*
s 7, 7A–7C 5.6
  10ZC.................................... 5.6
  159...................................... 5.7
  160...................................... 5.6, 5.7
Representation of the People Act
  1985
s 1.. 5.6
Representation of the People Act
  2000..................................... 5.6
Revenue Scotland and Tax Powers
  Act 2014.............................. 11.14
s 4.. 11.14
  7... 2.5
  Pt 4 (ss 20–25) 11.14
Roads (Scotland) Act 1984 .... 8.3
Road Traffic Act 1988
s 6D...................................... 13.18
Road Traffic Offenders Act 1988: 14.25
  Sch 2
  Pt I..................................... 14.25
Robin Rigg Offshore Wind Farm
  (Navigation and Fishing)
  (Scotland) Act 2003 .... 9.27
St Andrew's Day Bank Holiday
  (Scotland) Act 2007 .... 9.23
Salmon and Freshwater Fisheries
  (Consolidation) (Scotland)
  Act 2003.............................. 9.16
Scotland Act 1978 .... 2.4; 3.18; 5.9;
              6.11, 6.14; 9.19;
              11.5, 11.6, 11.9
s 17(2) 6.22
  18.. 6.14
  63.. 6.14
  85.. 3.18
  Sch 2..................................... 6.15
  Sch 10.................................... 6.15
  Sch 11.................................... 6.15
  Sch 12.................................... 6.15
Scotland Act 1998 .... 1.20, 1.22; 2.7;
              3.1, 3.2, 3.12, 3.13,
              3.15; 4.14; 5.3, 5.9,
              5.18, 5.20, 5.21, 5.22,
              5.23; 6.2, 6.4, 6.5,
              6.9, 6.10, 6.11, 6.13,
              6.14, 6.15, 6.18, 6.19,
              6.22, 6.24; 7.1, 7.2,
              7.3, 7.8, 7.13, 7.14,
              7.15, 7.16, 7.17, 7.18,
              7.19, 7.21, 7.22, 7.26;
              8.1, 8.7, 8.8, 8.9,
              8.12; 9.2, 9.5, 9.6,

Scotland Act 1998 – *contd*
              9.7, 9.9, 9.17, 9.34,
              9.35; 10.11; 11.5, 11.9,
              11.17, 11.18; 12.4, 12.7,
              12.10; 13.6, 13.9; 14.1,
              14.14, 14.15, 14.16, 14.18,
              14.19, 14.20, 14.23, 14.24,
              14.25, 14.30, 14.32
s 1.. 5.9
  (2), (3)................................ 5.3
  2... 7.13
  (2) 5.4
  (3) 5.4; 9.17
  (5) 5.4
  3... 7.13, 7.15
  (1) 5.4
    (b).................................... 7.15
  (2)–(4)................................. 5.4
  5... 7.26
  6(2B)................................... 11.10
  7... 5.21
  9... 5.10
  10....................................... 5.10
  12....................................... 7.26
  13....................................... 5.10
  14....................................... 5.10; 14.30
  15....................................... 5.7; 9.35; 12.18
  19....................................... 5.22
  20....................................... 5.22
  21....................................... 5.22
  (1) 14.25
  22....................................... 5.22; 9.9
  23....................................... 8.11, 8.12; 10.10
  (2) 10.10; 11.9
  (6) 8.10; 11.9
  (7)–(9)................................. 10.10
  27....................................... 5.7; 7.21
  (3) 7.22
  28....................................... 4.3; 6.12, 6.15;
              14.19, 14.24
  (1) 6.11
  (2)–(4)................................. 7.13; 9.2
  (5) 6.11; 9.9; 14.25
  (6) 14.25
  (7) 6.11, 6.22; 7.26;
              8.9; 14.1, 14.25
  29....................................... 4.3; 6.12, 6.13,
              6.20, 6.24; 9.19;
              14.19, 14.24, 14.25
  (1) 6.11; 14.24, 14.25
  (2) 14.25
    (a).................................... 6.5, 6.13
    (b).................................... 6.14; 14.25
    (c).................................... 6.19

Table of Statutes

Scotland Act 1998 – *contd*

s 29(2)(d).................... 3.12; 6.9, 6.15,
                6.20; 14.15, 14.28
  (e)........................ 6.21; 7.22
  (3) 6.18, 6.19, 6.20;
              14.22, 14.25
  (4) 6.18; 14.22, 14.25
30...................... 6.17; 9.35; 13.23;
           14.19
  (1) 6.14
  (2) 6.17, 6.22, 6.23
  (3) 6.13
31(1), (2).................. 9.10; 14.19
32.................. 7.21; 9.2; 14.1, 14.19
  (1), (3)............................. 9.17
33............................ 7.21; 9.2, 9.17,
        9.19; 14.1, 14.19,
        14.22
34.......................... 9.2, 9.17; 14.1,
        14.19, 14.28
  (2) 9.18
35.......................... 6.15; 7.19, 7.26;
        9.2, 9.17, 9.19
  (4) 11.10
36.. 9.9
  (2) 9.14
  (3) 9.9, 9.14
    (c) 9.27
  (4)–(6)............................. 9.18
37.. 6.15
38.. 6.15
39.. 5.21
40................................. 5.22; 6.19
  (3) 14.19
41, 42........................ 5.21; 6.19
43.. 6.19
44(1) 7.14, 7.20
  (2), (3)........................... 7.14
45.. 5.7
  (1) 7.13, 7.15
  (2) 7.13, 7.15; 10.2
  (3)–(5).............................. 7.15
46(1) 7.15
  (2) 7.15
  (4) 7.15
47.. 5.7
  (1) 1.23; 7.13, 7.16
  (2) 10.2
  (3)(a), (b) 7.16
    (c)......................... 7.15, 7.16
    (d), (e) 7.16
48.. 5.7
  (1) 7.13
  (2) 7.20; 10.2

Scotland Act 1998 – *contd*

s 48(5) 6.21
 49(1) 7.17
  (4) 7.17
    (c)......................... 7.15; 10.2
51.. 6.15
  (1) 7.25
  (2) 7.25
  (5) 7.25
52.. 7.13
  (1) 7.14, 7.19
  (2) 7.19
  (3) 7.19, 7.21
  (6) 7.22
53.................................. 6.15; 7.13
  (1) 7.19
  (2) 6.15
    (a), (b) 7.19
  (3) 7.19
54.......................... 3.12; 6.24; 7.19;
        14.15, 14.30
56.. 7.19
  (1), (2)............................. 6.24
57............................ 14.15, 14.30
  (1) 6.15, 6.24; 7.19
  (2) 3.12; 6.15; 12.7;
        13.4
  (3) 6.15
58.......................... 6.15; 7.19, 7.26
59.. 5.9
60.. 6.15
61, 62.................................. 7.22
63.......................... 6.23; 7.19; 8.10
Pt III (ss 64–72) 6.19
s 64...................................... 11.5
  (1), (2)............................. 11.5
65............................ 11.5, 11.17
  (1)(c)............................. 11.17
69(1) 2.5; 11.18
  (2) 2.5
  (4) 11.18
70(1), (2), (9)...................... 11.18
Pt IV (ss 73–80) 6.16; 11.9, 11.10
Pt IVA (ss 80A–80K)............. 11.9
s 80B 11.9
 80C(1), (3)–(6), (8).............. 11.11
 80D–80F............................. 11.12
Pt IVA Ch 3 (ss 80I, 80J) 11.13
Pt IVA Ch 4 (s 80K)............... 11.13
s 81............................ 5.20; 7.16
84.. 5.10
  (4) 7.15
87.. 7.20
88.. 8.12

Scotland Act 1998 – *contd*

s 88(1)–(3)............................... 8.12
89.. 8.12
90............................. 6.15; 8.10, 8.12
92(2) 7.19
93.. 7.19
95.. 12.5
   (1)–(4)............................. 12.5
   (6)–(9)............................. 12.7
   (10)(a), (b) 12.7
96.. 7.26
98............................... 7.21; 14.1
99.. 7.26
   (1) 14.19
100........................... 14.24, 14.30
   (3) 14.30
   (3B)(a) 14.30
101 .... 14.15, 14.17, 14.22,
                        14.24
102...................................... 14.31
   (1), (3)–(7) 14.31
103(3)(c).............................. 9.18
104...................................... 6.22
107...................... 6.23; 7.26; 14.31
108...................................... 6.23
109...................................... 6.15
112–115 .... 6.24
116........................... 6.15, 6.24
117...................................... 6.24
118...................... 6.24; 9.33, 9.34
119(3) 12.10
121...................................... 6.24
126(1) 6.13, 6.19, 6.20
   (2) 6.13
   (3) 6.18
   (4) 6.18
   (5) 6.18; 14.25
   (6), (7)............................ 7.25
   (8) 7.25; 11.14
   (9) 6.20
   (10) 9.19
129(2) 6.20; 14.15
130...................................... 6.14
Sch 1.............................. 5.3, 5.9
Sch 2................................. 5.22
  para 2............................ 6.15
Sch 3................................. 5.22
  para 3, 4......................... 5.23
Sch 4................. 6.14, 6.17, 6.18,
              6.19, 6.23; 7.26;
              9.19, 9.35; 14.19,
              14.22, 14.25
  para 1(2)(a)..................... 6.15
      (f) 14.22

Scotland Act 1998 – *contd*

Sch 4 – *contd*

  para 2...................... 6.19; 14.25
    (1)............................... 14.25
  3(1), (2) 6.19
  4(1), (2) 6.19
    (3).....................6.19; 11.17
    (4)............................... 6.19
    (5)............................... 6.19
      (a).......................... 6.19
  5(a) 11.17; 12.10
  Pt II (paras 7–11) 6.19
  para 7........................ 6.19; 9.16
    12............................... 6.19
Sch 5........................... 4.4, 4.5; 6.14,
             6.15, 6.17, 6.18,
             6.19, 6.20, 6.21,
             6.22, 6.23; 7.26;
             9.19, 9.35; 14.19,
             14.22
Pt I 6.14, 6.15
  para 1................. 1.22; 4.3; 12.5
    (b).......................... 6.15
    (c) 6.15; 9.10
  2(3)(c)......................... 6.15
  3(1), (2) 6.15
    (3)(a) ,(b)............... 6.15
  4(1)............................ 6.15
  5................................... 6.15
  6................................... 6.15
  7(1)............................ 6.15
    (2)(a), (b)............... 6.15
  8......................... 6.15; 7.25
    (2)............................... 6.15
  9................................... 6.15
    (2)............................... 6.15
  10................................. 6.15
Pt II.................... 6.14, 6.15, 6.16;
             14.25
  para 2(1)–(4) 6.15
  Head A (paras A1–A5).... 6.16
    para A1 .... 6.18; 8.7;
             11.9, 11.13
  Head B (paras B1–B13).. 6.16
    para B1 .... 13.23
      B2................ 6.16; 14.28
      B3 .... 6.16; 8.7
  Head C (paras C1–C15).. 6.16
    para C9 .... 8.7
  Head D (paras D1–D5) ... 6.16
  Head E (paras E1–E5)..... 6.16
  Head F (paras F1–F4) 6.16
    para E3(a).................. 14.22
  Head G (paras G1–G3) ... 6.16

Scotland Act 1998 – *contd*
  Sch 5 – *contd*
    Pt II – *contd*
      Head H (paras H1–H3) ...   6.16
      Head J (paras J1–J5) 6.16
      Head K (paras K1–K4) ...   6.16
      Head L (paras L1–L7).....   6.16
        para L1 .... 6.15; 12.5, 12.10
        L2 ....   6.18
    Pt III 6.14; 8.7, 8.10
      para 2.............................   6.15
      5......................... 6.14, 6.16
  Sch 6...................... 7.21; 14.1, 14.20,
               14.21, 14.24, 14.29
    Pt I (paras 1, 2)......................   14.20
      para 1...............................   14.20
        (d)...........................   14.29
      2.................................   14.20
      4–12, 33–35.................   14.21
      36, 37..........................   14.21
  Sch 7....................... 6.23; 9.19, 9.35;
                          11.9
  Sch 8.............................   7.21
    para 5............................   9.26
    9(b)...............................   12.10
    15.................................   6.24
    33, 38–42, 75, 76.........   5.21
Scotland Act 2012......... 3.13, 3.16, 3.19;
                 4.10, 4.14; 6.14,
                 6.17, 6.18; 7.26;
                 8.10; 9.6; 11.1,
                 11.9, 11.16; 12.2;
                 14.19, 14.20
  s 6..............................   9.23, 9.27
  10...............................   6.17
  12............................... 1.8; 7.14; 9.10
  13...............................   5.7; 9.35
  14...............................   6.19
  16...............................   8.10
  19–22...........................   7.19
  25(3) 11.11, 11.12
  26(2) 11.10
  28–31 ....   11.13
  32.................................   11.15
  34.................................   11.16
Scottish Commission for Human
  Rights Act 2006...... 8.9; 9.11; 13.14
  s 2–6.............................   13.14
Scottish Independence Referen-
  dum Act 2013.....................   4.6
  s 1(2)–(4)..............................   4.6
  4, 5...............................   4.6
  11.................................   4.6
  26(1) 4.6

Scottish Independence Referendum Act 2013 – *contd*
  s 34, 35..................................   4.6
  sch 2.......................................   4.6
  sch 4.......................................   4.6
  sch 8.......................................   4.6
Scottish Independence Referen-
  dum (Franchise) Act 2013...   4.5
  s 2(1) 4.5
Scottish Local Government
  (Elections) Act 2002 ....   8.2
Scottish Local Government
  (Elections) Act 2009 ....   8.2
Scottish Parliamentary Commis-
  sions and Commissioners
  etc Act 2010 .... 5.21; 8.15; 9.24;
                          10.13
  s 1.......................................   5.21
  9....................................... 5.21; 8.15
    (4) 5.21
Scottish Parliamentary Pensions
  Act 2009.............................   9.24
Scottish Parliamentary Standards
  Commissioner Act 2002......   5.21;
                          9.24
Scottish Parliament (Constituen-
  cies) Act 2004 .... 5.3, 5.9
Scottish Public Services
  Ombudsman Act 2002... 6.23; 10.11,
                          10.13
  s 1.......................................   10.13
  2(2) 10.13
  5(1)–(3), (5)...........................   10.13
  7(9), (10)..............................   10.13
  15, 16, 16A–16G..................   10.13
  sch 1 ....   10.13
    para 4.......................................   10.13
      (1)(d) 2.5
Scottish Register of Tartans Act
  2008...............................   9.23
Scottish Qualifications Authority
  Act 2002...........................   8.9
Sea Fisheries (Shellfish) Amend-
  ment (Scotland) Act 2000 ...   9.23
Senior Courts Act 1981...............   12.7
  s 11...   12.7
    (3) 12.7
  31(3) 14.10
Senior Judiciary (Vacancies and
  Incapacity) (Scotland) Act
  2006............................... 9.15; 12.8
Septennial Act 1715.....................   5.4
Sexual Offences (Amendment)
  Act 2000...........................   9.7

Sheriff Courts and Legal Officers
(Scotland) Act 1927
   Pt I (ss 1–13) 6.15
Sheriff Courts (Scotland) Act 1907
   s 4 .... 12.10
Sheriff Courts (Scotland) Act
1971 .... 12.4, 12.7
   s 5(1) 12.5
   11 .... 12.7
      (2), (4) 12.7
Social Security Administration
Act 1992 .... 6.19
Social Work (Scotland) Act
1968 .... 8.3
Southern Rhodesia Act 1965 .... 6.5; 9.34
Sovereign Grant Act 2011 .... 7.2
Special Immigration Appeals
Commission Act 1997 .... 13.3
Standards in Scotland's Schools
etc Act 2000 .... 8.3
Statute Law (Repeals) Act 2004 .. 9.4
Statute Law (Repeals) Act 2013 .. 9.4
Statute of Westminster 1931 .... 1.22; 6.5
   s 4 .... 6.5
Statutory Instruments Act 1946 ... 9.31,
                        9.32, 9.33,
                             9.34
   s 3(2) 9.32
   4 .... 9.34
Stirling-Alloa-Kincardine Rail-
way and Linked Improve-
ments Act 2004 .... 9.27
Succession to the Crown Act
1707 .... 5.7
Succession to the Crown Act
2013 .... 7.2
Summer Time Act 1972 .... 6.16
Terrorism Act 2000 .... 13.5
   s 1 .... 13.19
   Pt II (ss 3–13) 5.12; 13.19
   s 11–13 .... 13.19
   41 .... 13.18
   Sch 2 .... 13.19
Terrorism Act 2006 .... 13.5
Terrorism Prevention and Investi-
gation Measures Act 2011 .. 13.5,
                             13.9
Terrorist Asset-Freezing etc Act
2010 .... 13.5
Tobacco and Primary Medical
Services (Scotland) Act
2010 .... 14.25
Tourist Boards (Scotland) Act
2006 .... 8.12

Town and Country Planning
(Scotland) Act 1997 .... 8.3
   s 47, 48 .... 14.6
   sch 4 .... 12.2
Transport and Works (Scotland)
Act 2007 .... 9.27
Tribunals, Courts and Enforce-
ment Act 2007 .... 14.5, 14.11
   s 1–3 .... 14.5
   13(8) 14.11
   20 .... 14.5
   21 .... 14.5
      (2), 93) 14.11
   44 .... 14.5
   Sch 1
      para 13 .... 14.5
   Sch 7 .... 14.5
Tribunals (Scotland) Act 2014 .... 12.2;
                             14.5
   s 1, 2, 4 .... 14.5
   8, 9 .... 14.5
   20, 23, 28, 57 .... 14.5
Union with England Act 1707 .. 1.22; 6.15;
                             7.2
   art XVIII 14.1
Union with Ireland Act 1800 .... 3.2
Union with Scotland Act 1706 .... 1.22;
                        6.10, 6.15
   s 6 .... 5.7
United Nations Act 1946
   s 1 .... 6.5
University of St Andrews (Post-
graduate Medical Degrees)
Act 2002 .... 9.23, 9.25
Ure Elder Fund Transfer and
Dissolution Act 2010 .... 9.27
Wales Act 1978 .... 2.4; 3.18
Wales Act 2014 .... 3.19
War Crimes Act 1991 .... 2.8; 9.7
War Damage Act 1965 .... 2.8
Water Industry (Scotland) Act
2002 .... 8.9
Water Services etc (Scotland) Act
2005 .... 8.9
Waverley Railway (Scotland) Act
2006 .... 9.27
Weights and Measures Act 1985 . 6.10
   s 1 .... 6.10
Welfare Funds (Scotland) Bill
   s 4 .... 10.13
Welfare Reform Act 2012 .... 5.18
Welfare Reform and Pensions
Act 1999 .... 6.19
Welsh Church Act 1914 .... 9.7

William Simpson's Home (Transfer of Property etc) (Scotland) Act 2010...................... 9.27

AUSTRALIA
COMMONWEALTH
Constitution
s 128 .... 14.1

CHINA
Constitution 1982......................... 5.12

FEDERAL REPUBLIC OF GERMANY
Constitution 1949......................... 3.1

FRANCE
Constitution.................................. 6.4

LESOTHO
Constitution 1966
  s 73(2) 1.23

MONTENEGRO
Constitution 2006......................... 3.1

SOUTH AFRICA
Constitution.................................. 2.1; 3.1
  s 26, 27.................................... 1.5

SOVIET UNION
Constitution 1936......................... 1.17
  Ch X... 1.17
  art 17 .... 1.17
Constitution 1977......................... 5.12

SPAIN
Constitution 1978......................... 3.1

UNITED STATES
Constitution 1787.................... 2.1, 2.5; 6.4
  art 1–3 .... 2.5

Table of European Legislation

[All references are to paragraph number]

AGREEMENTS, CONVENTIONS AND TREATIES

Agreement between the United Kingdom Government and the Scottish Government on a referendum on independence for Scotland (Edinburgh, 15 October 2012): 4.4, 4.13

Belfast Agreement (Belfast, 10 April 1998) 3.19

Charter of Fundamental Rights of the European Union (Nice, 7 December 2000) 3.14; 13.7, 13.8

  art 5(1) 3.14
    8, 16, 22 .... 13.8
    51(1) 13.8
  protocol 30 .... 13.8

Convention for the Protection of Human Rights and Fundamental Freedoms *see* European Convention on Human Rights

Convention for the Protection of Individuals with regard to Automatic Processing of Personal Data (Strasbourg, 28 January 1981) 13.23

Convention on Access to Information, Public Participation in Decision-Making and Access to Justice in Environmental Matters (Aarhus, 25 June 1998) 13.22; 14.11

Convention on Biodiversity (Rio de Janeiro, 4 June 1992) 14.24

Convention relating to the Status of Refugees (Geneva, 28 July 1951) 13.3

European Charter of Local Self-Government (Strasbourg, 15 October 1985) 1.11

  art 2 .... 1.11
    3(1) 1.11

European Convention on Human Rights (Rome, 4 November 1950) 1.20; 2.1, 2.2, 2.8; 3.1, 3.4, 3.14, 3.15; 6.5, 6.15, 6.19, 6.20; 7.19; 10.1; 12.2, 12.12, 12.16, 12.17; 13.1, 13.2, 13.5, 13.6, 13.7, 13.8, 13.9, 13.11, 13.12, 13.14, 13.15, 13.16, 13.17, 13.23, 13.24; 14.2, 14.9, 14.12, 14.13, 14.16, 14.18, 14.27, 14.32

  preamble 2.1
  art 2 .... 13.11
    3 .... 13.7, 13.11
    4 .... 13.11
    5 .... 13.11, 13.18, 13.19; 14.24
    (5) 12.11
    6 .... 2.8; 9.4, 9.10; 12.2, 12.3, 12.7, 12.13, 12.16; 13.11; 14.2, 14.9, 14.11, 14.20, 14.24, 14.26, 14.29
    (1) 12.7
    7 .... 13.11
    8 .... 13.11, 13.24, 13.25; 14.24, 14.30
    9 .... 13.11; 14.24
    10 .... 12.12, 12.18; 13.11, 13.19, 13.24; 14.24
    11 .... 13.11, 13.19; 14.24
    12 .... 13.11
    14 .... 13.2, 13.11; 14.24
    15 .... 13.11
  protocol 1
    art 1 .... 13.11; 14.24, 14.26, 14.27
    2 .... 13.7, 13.11
    3 .... 5.6; 13.11
  protocol 6
    art 1, 2 .... 13.11
    protocol 11 .... 13.7

European Convention on Human
Rights (Rome, 4 November
1950) – *contd*
protocol 6 – *contd*
protocol 14 .... 13.7
protocol 15 .... 13.7
protocol 16 .... 13.7
Good Friday Agreement *see* Bel-
fast Agreement
Harare Commonwealth Declaration (Harare, 20 October
1991) 2.1
Rio Declaration on Environment
and Development (Rio de
Janeiro, 3-14 June 1992) 14.24
Scottish Constitutional Conven-
tion (1989) 4.20
Treaty establishing the European
Coal and Steel Community
(Paris, 18 April 1951) 3.3
Treaty establishing the European
Community *see* Treaty on
the Functioning of the European Union
Treaty on European Union
(Maastricht, 7 February
1992) 3.3, 3.12, 3.15;
6.8, 6.25
art 4(3) 6.7
6 .... 3.14; 13.8
(2) 3.14
14(2) 3.9
15 .... 3.6
16 .... 3.7
(3), (7) 3.7
17 .... 3.8
(1), (3) 3.8
48(6) 3.12
Treaty of Lisbon amending the
Treaty on European Union
and the Treaty establish-
ing the European Commu-
nity (Lisbon, 13 December
2007) 3.3, 3.6, 3.14,
3.15; 13.8

Treaty on the Functioning of the
European Union (Rome, 25
March 1957) 3.3, 3.12
preamble 3.3
art 2, 4 .... 6.25
5 .... 6.7
20 .... 13.1
34 .... 14.28
226, 227 .... 3.9
234 .... 3.8
267 .... 3.10, 3.12
289, 294 .... 3.9
314 .... 3.9
352 .... 6.25
Treaty of Union between Scot-
land and England (London,
1 May 1706) 6.6; 14.1
art I-III VI, VII, XVIII 6.6
XIX 6.6; 12.5
XXII, XXV 6.6
United Nations Convention on
the Rights of the Child (New
York, 20 November 1989) ... 13.7
Universal Declaration on Human
Rights 1948 .... 14.24
United Nations International
Covenant on Civil and Po-
litical Rights 1966 .... 14.24
United Nations International
Covenant on Economic,
Social and Cultural Rights
1966 .... 14.24
Universal Declaration of Human
Rights (New York, 10 De-
cember 1948) 13.7
art 23, 24 .... 13.7

DIRECTIVES
Dir 95/46/EC 13.7, 13.23; 14.28
Dir 2000/78 .... 12.7
Dir 2003/4/EC 13.22
Dir 2003/35/EC 14.11

DECISIONS
European Council Decision
2013/312 .... 3.9

Table of Statutory Instruments

[All references are to paragraph number]

Act of Adjournal (Criminal Procedure Rules Amendment No 2) (Human Rights Act 1998), SSI 2000/315 .... 13.12

Act of Sederunt (Rules of the Court of Session Amendment No 5) (Public Interest Intervention in Judicial Review) 2000, SSI 2000/317 .... 14.10

Act of Sederunt (Rules of the Court of Session Amendment No 7) (Devolution Issues), SSI 2007/360 reg 58 .... 14.6

Act of Sederunt (Rules of the Court of Session Amendment) (Transfer of Functions of the Asylum and Immigration Tribunal Order 2010), SSI 2010/16 .... 14.11

Act of Sederunt (Transfer of Judicial Review Applications from the Court of Session) 2008, SI 2008/357 ...... 14.11

Adventure Activities (Licensing) (Designation) Order 2007, SI 2007/447 .... 8.12

Agricultural Holdings (Scotland) Act 2003 Remedial Order 2014, SSI 2014/98....... 14.17, 14.27

Al-Qa'ida and Taliban (United Nations Measures) (Channel Islands) Order 2002, SI 2002/258 .... 6.5

Asylum and Immigration Tribunal (Procedure) Rules 2005, SI 2005/230........................ 13.3

Census (Scotland) Order 2000, SSI 2000/68........................ 6.23

Civil Procedure (Amendment No 4) Rules 2013, SI 2013/1412: 14.12

Data Protection Act 1998 (Commencement) Order 2000, SI 2000/183 .... 6.16

Data Protection (Miscellaneous Subject Access Exemptions) Order 2000, SI 2000/419..... 13.23

Data Protection (Subject Access Modification) (Education) Order 2000, SI 2000/414..... 13.23

Data Protection (Subject Access Modification) (Health) Order 2000, SI 2000/413 .... 13.23

Data Protection (Subject Access Modification) (Social Work) Order 2000, SI 2000/415..... 13.23

Environmental Impact Assessment (Scotland) Regulations 1999, SSI 1999/1.......... 6.24; 9.32

Environmental Information (Scotland) Amendment Regulations 2013, SSI 2013/127:   13.22

Environmental Information (Scotland) Regulations 2004, SSI 2004/520............................. 13.22

Environmental Protection (Controls on Ozone-Depleting Substances) Regulations 2002, SI 2002/528 .... 7.19

European Communities (Designation) (No 5) Order 2010, SI 2010/2690 .... 5.9

European Parliamentary Elections (Franchise of Relevant Citizens of the Union) Regulations 2001, SI 2001/1184.................................... 5.6

European Parliament (Number of MEPs and Distribution between Electoral Regions) (United Kingdom and Gibraltar) Order 2008, SI 2008/1954 .... 5.9

First-tier Tribunal and Upper Tribunal (Chambers) Order 2010, SI 2010/2655............. 14.5
art 6 .... 14.5
art 7(a)(iii)............................... 14.5

First-tier Tribunal and Upper Tribunal (Chambers) Order 2010 – *contd*
art 10(a)(iii)............................. 14.5
   (b)(ii)............................. 14.5
Freedom of Information (Fees for Required Disclosure) (Scotland) Regulation 2004, SSI 2004/467 .... 13.22
Freedom of Information (Fees for Disclosure under Section 13) (Scotland) Regulations 2004, SSI 2004/376............. 13.22
Freedom of Information (Relaxation of Statutory Prohibitions on Disclosure of Information) (Scotland) Order 2008, SSI 2008/339............. 13.22
Freedom of Information (Scotland) Act 2002 (Designation of Persons as Scottish Public Authorities) Order 2013, SSI 2013/278....................... 13.22
Freedom of Information (Scotland) Act 2002 (Historical Periods) Order 2013, SSI 2013/365 .... 13.22
Human Rights Act 1998 (Commencement No 2) Order 2000, SI 2000/1851 .... 14.15
Human Rights Act 1998 (Commencement) Order 1998, SI 1998/2882 .... 14.15, 14.17
Human Rights Act 1998 (Designated Derogation) Order 2001, SI 2001/3644... 13.11
Human Rights Act 1998 (Jurisdiction) (Scotland) Rules 2000, SSI 2000/301
r 3 .... 13.12
Immigration (European Economic Area) Regulations 2006, SI 2006/1003............................. 13.3
Justice of the Peace Courts (Sheriffdom of South Strathclyde, Dumfries and Galloway) Order 2009, SI 2009/115 .... 9.34
Legislative Reform (Health and Safety Executive) Order 2008, SI 2008/960............... 6.17
Licensing of Venison Dealers (Application Procedures etc) (Scotland) Order 1984, SI 1984/922 .... 14.7

Local Government Elections (Changes to the Franchise and Qualifications of Members) Regulations 1995, SI 1995/1948 .... 5.6; 8.2
Local Government Finance (Scotland) Order 1999, SI 1999/364 .... 6.23
Local Government Finance (Scotland) Order 2014, SSI 2014/36 .... 8.5
National Assembly for Wales (Transfer of Functions) Order 1999, SI 1999/672..... 3.19
Northern Ireland Act 1998 (Devolution of Policing and Justice Functions) Order 2010, SI 2010/976............... 3.19
Offshore Installations (Public Inquiries) Regulations 1974, SI 1974/338......................... 12.19
Pet Travel Scheme (Scotland) Order 2003, SI 2003/229..... 6.13
Plant Health (Scotland) Order 2005, SSI 2005/613............. 6.13
Prisons and Young Offenders Institutions (Scotland) Rules 1994, SI 1994/1931
r 80 .... 14.20, 14.30
Protection of Wild Mammals (Scotland) Act 2002 (Commencement) Order 2002, SSI 2002/181 .... 14.24
Public Bodies (Abolition of Administrative Justice and Tribunals Council) Order 2013, SI 2013/2042............ 8.14; 14.5
Public Services Reform (Commissioner for Ethical Standards in Public Life in Scotland etc) Order 2013, SSI 2013/197............... 5.21; 8.15
Public Transport Users' Committee for Scotland Order 2006, SSI 2006/250...................... 9.34
Representation of the People (Scotland) (Description of Electoral Registers and Amendment) Regulations 2013, SI 2013/3206............. 5.11
Representation of the People (Scotland) Regulations 2001, SI 2001/497............... 5.11

Scotland Act 1978 (Repeal) Order 1979, SI 1979/928..... 3.18

Scotland Act 1998 (Agency Arrangements) (Specification) Order 1999, SI 1999/1512.................................... 7.19

Scotland Act 1998 (Agency Arrangements) (Specification) Order 2003, SI 2003/407.. 7.19

Scotland Act 1998 (Agency Arrangements) (Specification) Order 2000, SI 2000/745... 7.19

Scotland Act 1998 (Commencement) Order 1998, SI 1998/3178 .... 3.19; 6.14; 7.20; 12.7

Scotland Act 1998 (Concurrent Functions) Order 1999, SI 1999/1592 .... 7.19

Scotland Act 1998 (Consequential Modifications) (No 2) Order 1999, SI 1999/1820..................................... 10.12

Scotland Act 1998 (Cross-Border Public Authorities) (Adaptation of Functions etc) Order 1999, SI 1999/1747............. 8.12

Scotland Act 1998 (Cross-Border Public Authorities) (Specification) Order 1999, SI 1999/1319 .... 8.12

Scotland Act 1998 (Cross-Border Public Authorities) (Forestry Commissioners) Order 2000, SI 2000/746............... 8.12

Scotland Act 1998 (Functions Exercisable in or as Regards Scotland) Order 1999, SI 1999/1748 .... 6.13

Scotland Act 1998 (Modification of Schedule 4) Order 2009, SI 2009/1380 .... 6.19

Scotland Act 1998 (Modification of Schedule 5) Order 2001, SI 2001/1456 .... 6.17

Scotland Act 1998 (Modification of Schedule 5) Order 2013, SI 2013/242.................... 4.5; 6.17

Scotland Act 1998 (Modification of Schedule 5) Order 2014, SI 2014/1559....................... 6.17

Scotland Act 1998 (Modifications of Schedules 4 and 5) Order 1999, SI 1999/1749... 6.17, 6.19

Scotland Act 1998 (Modifications of Schedule 4) Order 2000, SI 2000/1831 .... 6.19

Scotland Act 1998 (Modifications of Schedule 5) (No 2) Order 2005, SI 2005/866.. 6.17

Scotland Act 1998 (Modification of Schedule 5) (No 2) Order 2013, SI 2013/192............... 6.17

Scotland Act 1998 (Modifications of Schedule 5) Order 2000, SI 2000/3252 .... 6.17

Scotland Act 1998 (Modifications of Schedule 5) Order 2002, SI 2002/1629 .... 6.17

Scotland Act 1998 (Modifications of Schedule 5) Order 2004, SI 2004/3329 .... 6.17

Scotland Act 1998 (Modifications of Schedule 5) Order 2005, SI 2005/865 .... 6.17

Scotland Act 1998 (Modifications of Schedule 5) Order 2006, SI 2006/609 .... 6.17

Scotland Act 1998 (Regulation of Care (Scotland) Act 2001) Order 2001, SI 2001/2478... 7.26; 14.31

Scotland Act 1998 (Transfer of Functions to the Scottish Ministers etc) (No 2) Order 1999, SI 1999/3321............. 7.19

Scotland Act 1998 (Transfer of Functions to the Scottish Ministers etc) (No 2) Order 2000, SI 2000/3253............. 7.19

Scotland Act 1998 (Transfer of Functions to the Scottish Ministers etc) (No 2) Order 2001, SI 2001/3504............. 7.19

Scotland Act 1998 (Transfer of Functions to the Scottish Ministers etc) (No 2) Order 2006, SI 2006/1040............. 7.19

Scotland Act 1998 (Transfer of Functions to the Scottish Ministers etc) Order 1999, SI 1999/1750 .... 7.19, 7.21; 8.10

Scotland Act 1998 (Transfer of Functions to the Scottish Ministers etc) Order 2000, SI 2000/1563 ...... 7.19

Scotland Act 1998 (Transfer of Functions to the Scottish Ministers etc) Order 2001, SI 2001/954 ...... 7.19

Scotland Act 1998 (Transfer of Functions to the Scottish Ministers etc) Order 2002, SI 2002/1630 ...... 7.19

Scotland Act 1998 (Transfer of Functions to the Scottish Ministers etc) Order 2003, SI 2003/415 ...... 7.19

Scotland Act 1998 (Transfer of Functions to the Scottish Ministers etc) Order 2007, SI 2007/2915 ...... 7.19

Scotland Act 1998 (Transfer of Functions to the Scottish Ministers etc) Order 2008, SI 2008/1776 ...... 7.19

Scotland Act 1998 (Transfer of Functions to the Scottish Ministers etc) Order 2014, SI 2014/2918 ...... 7.19

Scotland Act 1998 (Transitory and Transitional Provisions) (Complaints of Maladministration) Order 1999, SI 1999/ 1351 ...... 10.11

Scotland Act 1998 (Transitory and Transitional Provisions) (Finance) Order 1999, SI 1999/441 ...... 11.17, 11.18

Scotland Act 1998 (Transitory and Transitional Provisions) (Standing Orders and Parliamentary Publications) Order 1999, SI 1999/ 1095 ...... 3.19; 9.1, 9.9, 9.27

Scotland Act 1998 (Transitory and Transitional Provisions) (Statutory Instruments) Order 1999, SI 1999/1096... 9.32

Scottish Adjacent Waters Boundaries Order 1999, SI 1999/ 1126 ...... 6.13

Scottish Parliament (Constituencies and Regions) Order 2014, SI 2014/501 ...... 5.9

Scottish Parliament (Disqualification) Order 2010, SI 2010/ 2476 ...... 5.7

Scottish Parliament (Disqualification) Order 2003, SI 2003/ 409 ...... 9.35

Scottish Parliament (Elections etc) Order 2010, SI 2010/2999 ...... 5.11
art 88 ...... 5.4

Scottish Parliament (Letters Patent and Proclamations) Order 1999, SI 1999/737 ...... 9.17

Scottish Public Services Ombudsman Act 2002 Amendment (No 2) Order 2012, SSI 2012/85 ...... 10.13

Scottish Public Services Ombudsman Act 2002 (Amendment) Order 2002, SSI 2002/468 ...... 10.13

Scottish Public Services Ombudsman Act 2002 Amendment Order 2012, SSI 2012/43 ...... 10.13

Sexual Offences Act 2003 (Remedial) (Scotland) Order 2010, SSI 2010/370 ...... 14.17

Sexual Offences Act 2003 (Remedial) (Scotland) Order 2011, SSI 2011/45 ...... 14.17

Southern Rhodesia (Constitution) Order 1965, SI 1965/1952... 6.5

Terrorism Act 2000 (Remedial) Order 2011, SI 2011/631 ...... 14.17

Town and Country Planning (Determination of Appeals by Appointed Persons) (Prescribed Classes) (Scotland) Regulations 2010, SI 2010/ 467 ...... 12.2

Transfer of Functions (Lord Advocate and Secretary of State) Order 1999, SI 1999/678 ...... 7.21

Transfer of Property etc (Lord Advocate) Order 1999, SI 1999/ 1105 ...... 6.15

Transfer of Property etc (Scottish Ministers) Order 1999, SI 1999/1104 ...... 6.15

Transfer of Property etc (Scottish Parliamentary Corporate Body) Order 1999, SI 1999/ 1106 ...... 6.15

Wales Act 1978 (Repeal) Order
    1979, SI 1979/933 ....   3.18
Water Environment (Controlled
    Activities) (Scotland) Regu-
    lations 2005, SSI 2005/
    348 ....   14.25

Water Environment (Controlled
    Activities) (Scotland) Regu-
    lations 2011, SSI 2011/209 ..   14.25
Water Industry Commissioner
    for Scotland (Dissolution)
    Order 2007, SSI 2007/399 ..   8.9

Table of Cases

[All references are to paragraph number]

A

A v HM Treasury [2010] UKSC 2, [2010] 2 AC 534, [2010] 2 WLR 378........ 2.7
A v Secretary of State for the Home Department [2004] UKHL 56, [2005] 2 AC
 68, [2005] 2 WLR 87 .... 13.2, 13.3, 13.11
A v Scottish Ministers 2002 SLT (News) 71 .... 14.24
A v Secretary of State for the Home Department [2005] 2 AC 68, [2004] UKHL
 56, [2005] 2 WLR 87 .... 13.11
A v Secretary of State for the Home Department (2014) 18 Edin LR 395........ 14.11
A v United Kingdom (Application 3455/05) (2009) 49 EHRR 29, 26 BHRC 1 .. 13.11
A (respondent) v British Broadcasting Corpn [2014] UKSC 25, [2014] 2 WLR
 1243, [2014] 2 All ER 1037 .... 13.24
A-G v De Keyser's Royal Hotel Ltd *see* De Keyser's Royal Hotel, Re [1920]
 AC 508 .... 7.2
A-G v Jonathan Cape Ltd [1976] QB 752, [1975] 3 WLR 606, [1975] 3 All ER
 484... 1.23; 7.11
A-G v National Assembly for Wales Commission [2012] UKSC 53, [2013] 1
 AC 792, [2012] 3 WLR 1294 .... 14.22, 14.23
A-G v Wilts United Dairies (1921) 37 TLR 884 .... 11.2; 14.14
A-G for England & Wales v Counsel General for Wales [2014] UKSC 43,
 [2014] 1 WLR 2622, [2014] 4 All ER 789 .... 14.22
A-G of Hong Kong v Lee Kwong-Kut [1993] AC 951, [1993] 3 WLR 329,
 [1993] 3 All ER 939 .... 14.24
A-G of Hong Kong v Ng Yuen Shiu [1983] 2 AC 629, [1983] 2 WLR 735,
 [1983] 2 All ER 346 .... 14.13
A-G's Reference (No 3 of 1999) [2009] UKHL 34, [2010] 1 AC 145, [2009] 3
 WLR 142 .... 13.24
AXA General Insurance, Petrs [2011] UKSC 46, [2012] 1 AC 868, 2012 SC
 (UKSC) 122 .... 2.8; 5.1, 5.15; 6.5, 6.12; 13.11; 14.1,
                                                          14.10, 14.19, 14.23, 14.24,
                                                          14.26, 14.16
Abbas v Secretary of State for the Home Department 1993 SLT 502............... 14.9
Adair v McGarry 1933 JC 72, 1933 SLT 482..................................... 13.18
Adam (Derek) v HM Advocate [2013] HCJAC 14, 2013 JC 221, 2013 SLT
 235... 14.17
Adams v A-G 2003 SC 171, 2003 SLT 366, 2002 SCLR 881 .... 14.26
Adams v Scottish Ministers 2003 SC 171, 2003 SLT 366, 2002 SCLR 881 ...... 14.19,
                                                                          14.24
Advocate-General for Scotland v MacDonald [2001] 1 All ER 620, [2001]
 ICR 1, [2001] IRLR 748 .... 6.5
Advocate-General for Scotland v MacDonald 2002 SC 1, 2001 SLT 819, 2001,
 SCLR 795... 14.17
Agee v Lord Advocate 1977 SLT (Notes) 54..................................... 7.24
Agricultural, Horticultural & Forestry Industry Training Board v Aylesbury
 Mushrooms Ltd [1972] 1 All ER 280, [1972] 1 WLR 190 .... 14.14

Agricultural Sector (Wales) Bill, Re; A-G for England & Wales v Counsel
General for Wales [2014] UKSC 43, [2014] 1 WLR 2622, [2014] 4 All
ER 789 .... 14.25
Air 2000 Ltd v Secretary of State for Transport (No 1) 1989 SLT 698 .... 14.14
Åklagaren v Fransson (Case C-617/10) [2013] STC 1905, [2013] 2 CMLR 46,
15 ITL Rep 698 .... 13.8
Alili (Elyes) v HM Advocate [2008] HCJAC 3, 2008 SCCR 566, 2008 GWD
11-209 .... 13.4
Amendment of the Constitution of Canada, Re (1982) 125 DLR (3d) 1 .... 1.23
Anderson v Scottish Ministers 2001 SC 1, 2000 SLT 873, [2000] HRLR 450 .. 14.24
Anderson v Scottish Ministers [2001] UKPC 5, [2003] 2 AC 602, 2002 SC
(PC) 63 .... 14.9
Anisminic Ltd v Foreign Compensation Commission [1969] 2 AC 147, [1969]
2 WLR 163, [1969] 1 All ER 208 .... 12.2; 14.9, 14.11
Anwarm, Respondent [2008] HCJAC 36, 2008 JC 409, 2008 SLT 710.... 12.12; 14.10
Argyll & Bute Council v Scottish Public Services Ombudsman [2007] CSOH
168, [2008] SC 155, 2008 SLT 168 .... 10.13, 10.14; 14.1
Associated Provincial Picture Houses Ltd v Wednesbury Corpn [1948] 1 KB
223, [1947] 2 All ER 680, (1947) 63 TLR 623 .... 10.14; 14.9, 14.13, 14.24
Aston Cantlow & Wilmcote with Billesley Parochial Church Council v Wall-
bank [2003] UKHL 37, [2004] 1 AC 546, [2003] 3 WLR 283 .... 13.12
Austin v Commissioner of Police of the Metropolis [2007] EWCA Civ 989,
[2008] QB 660, [2008] 1 All ER 564 .... 13.19

B

BBC, Petitioners (No 2) 2000 JC 521, 2000 SLT 860, 2000 SCCR 533 .... 14.29
BH (AP) v Lord Advocate [2012] UKSC 24, [2013] 1 AC 413, 2012 SC
(UKSC) 308 .... 13.4
Baker v Carr 369 US 186 (1962) 14.1
Bank Mellat v Her Majesty's Treasury (No 2) [2014] UKSC 39, [2014] AC
700, [2013] 3 WLR 179 .... 14.13, 14.14
Barrs v British Wool Marketing Board 1957 SC 72, 1957 SLT 153 .... 14.9
Bates v Lord Hailsham of St Marylebone [1972] 3 All ER 1019, [1972] 1 WLR
1373, (1972) 116 SJ 584 .... 14.14
Beattie v Royal Bank of Scotland plc 2003 SLT 564, 2003 SCLR 352, 2003
GWD 11-301 .... 6.5
Beatty v Gillbanks (1881-82) LR 9 QBD 308, [1881-5] All ER Rep 559 .... 13.19
Beauregard v Canada [1986] 2 SCR 56, (1986) 30 DLR (4th) 481 .... 12.1
Beggs v Scottish Information Minister [2014] CSIH 10, 2014 GWD 5-113 ..... 13.22
Beggs v Scottish Ministers [2007] UKHL 3, [2007] 1 WLR 455, 2007
SLT 235 .... 7.25; 13.11
Belgian Linguistics Case (No 2) (1968) 1 EHRR 252 .... 13.2
Belize Bank Ltd v A-G of Belize [2011] UKPC 36 .... 14.1
Bellinger v Bellinger [2003] UKHL 21, [2003] 2 AC 467, [2003] 2 All
ER 593 .... 14.17
Blair v Lochaber DC 1995 SLT 407, 1994 SCLR 1070, [1995] IRLR 135 .... 14.8
Boddington v British Transport Police [1999] 2 AC 143, [1998] 2 WLR 639,
[1998] 2 All ER 203 .... 14.8, 14.14
Bolkiah v Brunei Darussalam [2007] UKPC 63 .... 14.1
Bowles v Bank of England [1913] 1 Ch 57 .... 6.5; 11.3
Bradford v McLeod 1985 SCCR 379, 1986 SLT 244, [1986] Crim LR 690 ...... 12.16
British Oxygen Co Ltd v Minister of Technology [1971] AC 610, [1969] 2
WLR 892, [1970] 3 All ER 165 .... 14.9
British Railways Board v Glasgow Corpn 1976 SC 24 .... 14.11

British Railways Board v Pickin [1974] AC 765, [1974] 2 WLR 208, [1974] 1
All ER 609, HL.. 6.5
Bromley London Borough Council v Greater London Council [1983] 1 AC
768, [1982] 2 WLR 92, [1982] 1 All ER 153 .... 14.9
Brown v Hamilton District Council 1983 SC (HL) 1, 1983 SLT 397, (1983) 133
NLJ 63... 14.9
Brown v Stott 2000 SLT 379, 2000 JC 328, 2000 SCCR 314 .... 6.2; 14.20, 14.24
Burden v United Kingdom (Application 13378/05) [2007] STC 252, [2007] 1
FCR 69, (2007) 44 EHRR 51.. 14.17
Burmah Oil Co (Burma Trading) Ltd v Lord Advocate [1964] AC 85, 1964 SC
(HL) 117, 1964 SLT 218.. 2.8
Burnett v Grampian Fire & Rescue Service [2007] CSOH 3, 2007 SLT 61,
2007 SCLR 192... 14.2
Bush v Gore 531 US 98 (2000.. 1.8

C

C's Application for Judicial Review, Re [2009] 1 AC 928 .... 13.25
CCSU v Minister for the Civil Service [1985] AC 374, [1984] 3 WLR 1174,
[1984] 3 All ER 935.. 6.23; 14.2, 14.9, 14.13, 14.26
CWS v Highland Council [2008] CSOH 28.. 14.12
Cadder (Peter) v HM Advocate [2010] UKSC 43, [2010] 1 WLR 2601, 2011
SC (UKSC) 13 .... 9.15; 12.3; 13.18; 14.20
Campbell & Cosans v United Kingdom (1982) 4 EHRR 293.................... 13.7, 13.11
Campbell v Mirror Group Newspapers Ltd [2004] UKHL 22, [2004] 2 AC 457,
[2004] 2 WLR 1232... 13.24
Carltona Ltd v Commissioners of Works [1943] 2 All ER 560 .... 7.24, 7.25; 14.9
Carroll v Scottish Borders Council [2014] CSOH 6, 2014 SCLR 532, 2014
GWD 4-94... 14.11
Central London Community Healthcare NHS Trust v Information Comr [2013]
UKUT 551 (AAC), (2014) 136 BMLR 61 .... 13.23
Chalmers v HM Advocate 1954 JC 66, 1954 SLT 177..................................... 13.18
Cheney v Conn [1968] 1 All ER 779, [1968] 1 WLR 242, 44 TC 217.............. 6.5
Christian Institute, The, Petrs [2015] CSOH 7, 2015 Fam LR 7, 2015 GWD
3-57 .... 14.10, 14.28
Clancy v Caird (No 2) 2000 SC 441, 2000 SLT 546, 2000 SCLR 526 ..6.2; 12.3, 12.7;
14.20, 14.29
Clark v Kelly [2003] 2 WLR 1586, [2003] 1 All ER 1106, 2003 SLT 308... 12.2; 14.21
Cocks v Thanet District Council [1983] 2 AC 286, [1982] 3 WLR 1121, [1982]
3 All ER 1135.. 14.8
Codona v HM Advocate 1996 SLT 1100, 1996 SCCR 300.............................. 13.18
Comhairle Nan Eilean Siar v Scottish Ministers [2013] CSIH 45, 2013 SC 548,
2013 SLT 687... 14.1
Commission v France [1997] ECR I-6569 .... 14.13
Common Services Agency v Scottish Information Commissioner [2008]
UKHL 47, [2008] 1 WLR 1550, 2008 SC (HL) 184 .... 13.22, 13.23
Congreve v Home Office [1976] QB 629, [1976] 2 WLR 291, [1976] 1 All
ER 697 .... 14.9
Corporate Officer of the House of Commons v Information Commissioner
[2008] EWHC 1084 (Admin), [2009] 3 All ER 403, [2008] ACD 71........ 13.22
Costa v Ente Nazionale per l'Energia Elettrica (ENEL) [1964] ECR 585,
[1964] CMLR 425... 6.8
Council of Civil Service Unions v Minister for the Civil Service [1985] AC
374, [1984] 3 WLR 1174, [1984] 3 All ER 935 .... 14.2

County Properties Ltd v Scottish Ministers 2002 SC 79, 2001 SLT 1125, [2002]
HRLR 11 .... 14.29
Craigdale Housing Association v Scottish Information Comr [2010] CSIH 43,
2010 SLT 655, 2010 GWD 18-363 .... 13.22, 13.23
Crocket v Tantallon Golf Club 2005 SLT 663, 2005 SCLR 657, 2005 GWD
16-265 .... 14.8
Cunningham v East Lothian Council [2011] CSOH 185, 2011 GWD 39-792... 14.9

D

D v Children's Reporter 2009 FLR 88, 2009 GWD 1-10 .... 13.24
D, Petr [2010] CSOH 28, 2011 SLT 101, 2010 Fam LR 47 .... 14.8
DPP v Hutchinson [1990] 2 AC 783, [1990] 3 WLR 196, (1991) 155 JP 71 ..... 14.14
DPP v Jones [1999] 2 AC 240, [1999] 2 WLR 625, [1999] 2 All ER 257 .... 13.19
DS v HM Advocate [2007] UKPC D1, 2007 SC (PC) 1, 2007 SLT 1026.......... 14.22
Dalziel Parish School Board v Scotch Education Department 1915 SC 234,
1914 2 SLT 449 .... 14.9
Davidson v Scottish Ministers (No 1) [2005] UKHL 74, 2006 SC (HL) 41,
2006 SLT 110 .... 2.7; 7.2
Davidson v Scottish Ministers (No 2) [2005] UKHL 34, [2005] 1 SC (HL) 7,
2004 SLT 895 .... 12.16, 12.17
Deakin v Milne (1882) 10 R (J) 22 .... 13.19
De Haes v Belgium (1998) 25 EHRR 1 .... 12.12
Department for Business, Innovation & Skills v Evans [2014] EWCA Civ 253 .. 13.22
Department of Health v Information Comr [2011] EWHC 1430 (Admin),
[2011] Info TLR 47, [2011] ACD 97 .... 13.23
Derbyshire County Council v Times Newspapers Ltd [1993] AC 534, [1993] 2
WLR 449, [1993] 1 All ER 1011 .... 14.16
Digital Rights Ireland Ltd v Minister for Communications, Marine & Natural
Resources (Case C-293/12) [2014] 3 WLR 1607, [2014] 2 All ER (Comm)
1, [2014] 3 CMLR 44 .... 9.4; 13.25
Dimes v Grand Junction Canal Proprietors (1852) 3 HL Cas 759, 10 ER 301 .. 12.15,
12.16; 14.9
Doherty v McGlennan 1996 SCCR 591, 1997 SLT 444 .... 12.16
Douglas v Hello! Ltd (No 1) [2001] QB 967, [2001] 2 WLR 992, [2001] 2 All
ER 289 .... 13.12, 13.24
Dumble v Borders Electoral Registration Officer 1980 SLT (Sh Ct) 60 .... 5.6
Dumfries & Galloway Council v Scottish Information Comr [2008] CSIH 12,
2008 SC 327 .... 13.22
Duncan v Jones [1936] 1 KB 218 .... 13.19
Dundee Harbour Trustees v Nicol *see* Nicol (D & J) v Dundee Harbour Trustees
Dunkley v Evans [1981] 3 All ER 285, [1981] 1 WLR 1522, (1981) 125
SJ 843 .... 14.14
Durant v Financial Services Authority [2003] EWCA Civ 1746, [2004]
FSR 28 .... 13.23

E

E (a child), Re [2008] UKHL 66, [2009] 1 AC 536, [2008] 3 WLR 1208 .... 13.14
E (a child) v Chief Constable of the Royal Ulster Constabulary [2008] UKHL
66, [2009] 1 AC 536, [2008] 3 WLR 1208 .... 14.10
EP (Zimbabwe) v Home Secretary [2014] CSIH 30, 2014 SC 706, 2014 GWD
13-239 .... 13.3
East Kilbride District Council v Secretary of State for Scotland 1995 SLT
1238 .... 14.14
Eastman v R [2000] HCA 29 .... 14.1

Eastwood v Royal Borough of Windsor & Maidenhead [2013] EWHC 3476
(Admin) 14.13
Eba v A-G for Scotland [2011] UKSC 29, [2012] 1 AC 710, 2012 SC
(UKSC) 1 .... 2.8; 12.2; 13.3; 14.9, 14.11
Edem v Information Comr [2014] EWCA Civ 92 .... 13.23
Ellen Street Estates Ltd v Minister of Health [1934] 1 KB 590 .... 6.5, 6.10
Entick v Carrington (1765) 19 State Tr 1029 1065, 95 ER 807, (1765) 2 Wls
KB 275 .... 2.7
Errington v Wilson 1995 SC 550, 1995 SLT 1193, 1995 SCLR 875 .... 14.9
European Commission v Hungary (Case C-286/12) [2013] 1 CMLR 44, [2013]
Eq LR 62, [2013]Pens LR 9 .... 12.7
European Commission v United Kingdom (Case C-530/11) [2014] QB 988,
[2014] 3 WLR 853, [2014] 3 CMLR 6 .... 14.11
Eweida v United Kingdom (Application 48420/10) [2013] IRLR 231, (2013)
57 EHRR 8, 34 BHRC 519 .... 13.11; 14.18

F

Ferris v Wallace 1936 SC 561, 1936 SLT 292 .... 5.6
Findlay v United Kingdom (1997) 24 EHRR 221 .... 12.17
Foley v Glen Golf Club [2012] COH 149, 2012 GWD 32-636 .... 14.8
Forbes v HM Advocate 1990 JC 215, 1990 SCCR 69 .... 13.18
Fotheringham (Wm) & Son v British Limousin Cattle Society Ltd 2004 SLT
485, [2004] Eu LR 786, 2004 GWD 12-255 .... 14.8
Fox v Stirk [1970] 2 QB 463, [1970] 3 WLR 147, [1970] 3 All ER 7 .... 5.6
Fraser (Nat Gordon) v HM Advocate [2011] UKSC 24, 2011 SC (UKSC) 113,
2011 SLT 515 .... 12.3; 14.20
Fraser v MacCorquodale 1992 SLT 229 .... 6.6
Freeburn (Samuel) v HM Advocate [2012] hcJAC 135, 2013 SLT 70, 2013
SCL 47 .... 13.18
Friend v Lord Advocate [2007] UKHL 52, 2008 SC (HL) 107, 2007
SLT 1209 .... 14.24

G

G v Secretary of State for the Home Department [2008] CSOH 115, 2008
GWD 34-517 .... 6.2
G v Watson [2014] CSIH 81, 2014 SLT 1030, 2014 GWD 32-621 .... 14.8
Gallagher v Lynn [1937] AC 863, [1937] 3 All ER 598 .... 14.22
Gerry Cottle's Circus Ltd v City of Edinburgh District Council 1990 SLT 235   14.9
Ghaidan v Godin-Mendoza [2004] UKHL 30, [2004] 2 AC 557, [2004] 3
WLR 113 .... 14.17
Gibbs v Ruxton 2000 JC 258, 2000 SLT 310, 2000 SCCR 136 .... 12.7
Gibson v Lord Advocate 1975 SC 136, 1975 SLT 134, [1975] 1 CMLR 563 .... 6.6;
14.1
Gillan v United Kingdom (Application 4158/05) (2010) 50 EHRR 45, 28
BHRC 420, [2010] Crim LR 415 .... 13.24
Gillies v Ralph 2008 SLT 978, [2008] HCJAC 55, 2008 SCCR 887 .... 13.18
Gillies v Secretary of State for Work & Pensions [2006] UKHL 2, [2006] 1
WLR 781, 2006 SC (HL) 71 .... 12.3, 12.16
Glasgow City Council v Scottish Information Comr [2009] CSIH 73, 2010 SC
125, 2010 SLT 9 .... 13.22
Goodes v East Sussex County Council [2000] 3 All ER 603, [2000] 1 WLR
1356, [2000] RTR 366 .... 14.2
Goodwin v United Kingdom (2002) 35 EHRR 447, [2002] IRLR 664 .... 13.11

Google Spain SL v Agencia Espanola de Proteccion de Datos (Case C-131/12) [2014] QB 1022, [2014] 3 WLR 659, [2014] 3 CMLR 50 .... 13.23

Greens v United Kingdom (Application 60041/08) (2011) 53 EHRR 21, [2010] 2 Prison LR 22, (2010) 160 NLJ 1685 .... 14.18

Greens, Petr [2011] CSOH 79, 2011 SLT 549, 2011 GWD 15-354 .... 13.11

Grieves v Everard & Sons Ltd sub nom Rothwell Chemical & Insulating Co Ltd & others [2007] UKHL 39, [2008] 1 AC 281, [2007] 3 WLR 876 ..... 14.26

Guzzardi v Italy (1981) 3 EHRR 333 .... 14.24

H

H v Lord Advocate [2012] UKSC 24, [2013] 1 AC 413, 2012 SC (UKSC) 308 .... 1.22; 7.19

HK (an infant), Re [1967] 2 QB 617, [1967] 2 WLR 962, [1967] 1 All ER 226 .... 14.9

HM Advocate v Campbell (Devolution Issues: Procedure) 1999 SCCR 980, 1999 GWD 37-1906 .... 14.29

HM Advocate v Hepper 1958 JC 39, 1958 SLT 160 .... 13.18

HM Advocate v Higgins (Lee Everton) 2006 SLT 946, 2006 SCCR 305, 2006 GWD 25-555 .... 13.25

HM Advocate v McLean (Duncan) [2009] HCJAC 97, 2010 SLT 73, 2010 SCL 166 .... 13.18

HM Advocate v Robertson (1870) 42 SJ 336, 1 Coup 404 .... 12.12

HM Advocate v Sinclair (Angus Robertson) [2014] HCJAC 130, 2014 SLT 1087, 2014 SCCR 545 .... 12.16

HM's Application for Judicial Review [2014] NIQB 43 .... 14.17

Haggart's Trustees v Lord President Hope (1824) 2 Sh App 125 .... 12.11

Hall v Bull [2013] UKSC 73, [2013] 1 WLR 3741, [2014] 1 All ER 919 .... 13.11

Hämäläinen v Finland (application No 37359/09) 37 BHRC 55 .... 13.11

Hamilton v Secretary of State for Scotland 1972 SC 72, 1972 SLT 233 .... 14.11

Handyside v United Kingdom (1979-80) 1 EHRR 737 .... 14.18

Helow v Home Secretary [2008] UKHL 62, [2008] 1 WLR 2416, 2009 SC (HL) 1 .... 12.16

Henderson (Alexander) v HM Advocate [2005] HCJAC 47, 2005 1 JC 301, 2005 SLT 429 .... 13.18

Hendrick v Chief Constable of Strathclyde [2014] CSIH 22, 2014 SC 551, 2014 SLT 382 .... 14.12

Highland Regional Council v British Railways Board 1996 SLT 274 .... 14.9

Hipperson v Newbury District Electoral Registration Officer [1985] QB 1060, [1985] 3 WLR 61, [1985] 2 All ER 456 .... 5.6

Hirst v United Kingdom (2006) 42 EHRR 41, 19 BHRC 546, [2006] 1 Prison LR 220 .... 5.6; 13.11; 14.18

Houston v Macdonald 2000 SLT 333, 1999 SCCR 605 .... 13.18

Hoekstra v HM Advocate (No 2) 2000 JC 391, 2000 SLT 605, 2000 SCCR 367 .... 12.16; 14.29

Hoffmann-La Roche (F) & Co AG v Secretary of State for Trade & Industry [1975] AC 295, [1974] 3 WLR 104, [1974] 2 All ER 1128 .... 14.14

Hyde Park Residence Ltd v Secretary of State for the Environment, Transport & the Regions [1999] 3 PLR 1, [1999] JPL 897 .... 6.5

I

IA (Iran) v Secretary of State for the Home Department [2011] CSIH 28, 2011 SC 625, 2011 SLT 706 .... 14.10

Imperial Tobacco v Lord Advocate [2012] UKSC 61, 2013 Sc (UKSC) 153, 2013 SLT 2 .... 1.22; 6.10; 14.25

Infant & Dietetic Foods Association Ltd, Petrs [2008] CSOH 87, 2008 SLT
  723, [2009] Eu LR 14 .... 3.13
Inland Revenue Commissioners v Barr 1956 SC 162, 1956 SLT 98, 49 R &
  IT 165 .... 14.9
Ireland v United Kingdom (1979-80) 2 EHRR 25 .... 13.11
Irvine v Royal Burgess Golfing Society of Edinburgh 2004 SCLR 386, 2004
  GWD 8-161 .... 14.8

J

James v United Kingdom (1986) 8 EHRR 123, [1986] RVR 139 .... 14.18
Jersild v Denmark (1995) 19 EHRR 1 .... 13.11; 14.18
John Muir Trust, Petr 2015 GWD 1-20 .... 14.11
Johnson v Johnson [2000] HCA 48, (2000) 201 CLR 488 .... 12.16
Joint Liquidators of the Scottish Coal Co Ltd v SEPA [2013] CSIH 108, 2014
  SC 372, 2014 SLT 259 .... 14.19, 14.25
Jolly (Andrew) v HM Advocate [2013] HCJAC 96, 2014 JC 171, 2013 SLT
  1100 .... 13.19
Jones v DAS Legal Expenses Insurance Co Ltd [2003] EWCA Civ 1071,
  [2004] IRLR 218, (2003) 147 SJLB 932 .... 12.17
Jones v HM Advocate [2007] HCJAC 35, 2008 JC 78, 2007 SLT 685 .... 13.18

K

K v Scottish Legal Aid Board 1989 SC 21, 1989 SLT 617, 1989 SCLR 144 ..... 14.9
KFTCIC v Icori Estero SpA (28 June 1991, CA Paris) 12.16
Kapri v Lord Advocate [2013] UKSC 48, [2013] 1 WLR 2324, 2013 SC
  (UKSC) 311 .... 13.4
Kaur v Lord Advocate 1980 SC 319, 1981 SLT 322, [1980] 3 CMLR 79 .... 6.5; 14.16
Kay v Metropolitan Commissioner [2008] UKHL 69, [2008] 1 WLR 2723,
  [2009] 2 All ER 935 .... 13.19
Kearney v HM Advocate [2006] UKPC D 1, 2006 SC (PC) 1, 2006 SLT 499 .. 12.7
Kennedy v Charity Commission [2014] UKSC 20, [2014] 2 WLR 808, [2014]
  2 All ER 847 .... 14.13
Kerr v Hood 1907 SC 895, (1907) 15 SLT 14 .... 14.14
Kilmarnock Magistrates v Secretary of State for Scotland 1961 SC 350, 1961
  SLT 333 .... 14.9
Kjelsden, Busk Madsden & Pederson v Denmark (1976) 1 EHRR 711 .... 13.11

L

L v Birmingham City Council [2007] UKHL 27, [2008] 1 AC 95, [2007] 3
  WLR 112 .... 13.12
Lafarge Redland Aggregates Ltd v Scottish Ministers 2001 SC 298, 2000 SLT
  1361, [2001] Env LR 27 .... 12.2; 14.29
Lawrie v Muir 1950 JC 19, 1950 SLT 37, 1949 SLT (Notes) 58 .... 13.18
Leech v Secretary of State for Scotland 1992 SC 89, 1993 SLT 365 .... 14.14
Liechtenstein v Guatemala (ICJ Rep 1955) 13.2
Lloyds Pharmacy Ltd v National appeal Panel for Entry to the Pharmaceutical
  Lists [2012] CSOH 22, 2012 GWD 8-137 .... 14.9
Locabail (UK) Ltd v Bayfield Properties Ltd [2000] QB 451, [2000] 2 WLR
  870, [2000] 1 All ER 65 .... 12.15, 12.16, 12.17
London & Clydeside Estates Ltd v Aberdeen District Council [1980] 1 WLR
  182, 1980 SC (HL) 1, 1980 SLT 81 .... 14.9

Lord Advocate's Reference (No 1 of 2000) 2000 JC 143, 2001 SLT 507, 2001 SCCR 296 .... 6.2

Lord Advocate's Reference (No 1 of 2001) 2002 SLT 466, 2002 SCCR 435, 2002 GWD 12-360.. 12.12

Lord Gray's Motion [2002] 1 AC 124, [2000] 2 WLR 664, 2000 SC (HL) 46 .. 5.14; 6.6

Lyons v Chief Constable of Strathclyde [2013]CSIH 46, 2014 SCLR 281, [2013] LLR 748 .... 13.23

M

M v Home Office [1994] 1 AC 377, [1993] 3 WLR 433, [1993] 3 All ER 537 .... 7.2

M v Law Society of Scotland [2013] CSOH 28, 2013 SLT 462, 2013 GWD 9-187.. 14.9

M v Scottish Ministers [2012] UKSC 58, [2012] 1 WLR 3386, 2013 SC (UKSC) 139 .... 9.34; 14.14

M's Guardian v A-G for Scotland [2009] CSOH 91, 2009 SC 643, 2009 SLT 831.. 14.17

MB v Secretary of State for Work & Pensions [2014] EWCA Civ 1112, [2014] ICR 1129, [2014] HRLR 27.. 13.11

MM v United Kingdom (The Times, 16 January 2013) 13.24; 14.18

McArthur v Lord Advocate 2006 SLT 170, 2006 SCLR 654, 2005 GWD 40-733 .... 14.11

MacCarthys v Smith [1981] 1 QB 180, [1980] 3 WLR 929, [1981] 1 All ER 111.. 6.9

McColl v Strathclyde Regional Council 1983 SC 225, 1983 SLT 616, [1984] JPL 351 .... 8.3; 14.9

MacCormick v Lord Advocate 1953 SC 396, 1953 SLT 255 .... 3.2; 6.6

McCue v Glasgow City Council [2014] CSOH 124, 2014 SLT 891, 2014 GWD 26-510 .... 14.11

MacDonald v Aberdeenshire Council [2014] CSIH 83, 2014 SC 114, 2014 SLT 2.. 14.2

McDonald v Secretary of State for Scotland 1996 SLT 16............................. 14.2

McGeoch v Lord President of the Council see R (on the application of Chester) v Secretary of State for Justice

MacGillivray v Johnston (No 2) 1994 SLT 1012, 1993 SCCR 772 .... 14.14

McGinty, Petr [2010] CSOH 5, 2010 GWD 15-289.................................... 14.11

McGonnell v United Kingdom (2000) 30 EHRR 289, 8 BHRC 56, [2000] 2 PLR 69 .... 12.17

McInnes v Onslow-Fane [1978] 3 All ER 211, [1978] 1 WLR 1520, (1978) 122 SJ 844.. 14.9, 14.13

Mackay & Esslemont v Lord Advocate 1937 SC 860, 1937 SLT 577 .... 12.7

MacManaway, Re [1951] AC 161, 66 TLR (Pt 2) 808, (1950) 94 SJ 687.......... 14.1

MacReath, Petr 2012 SLT 1195... 14.10

McTear v Scottish Legal Aid Board 1995 SCLR 611, 1997 SLT 108............... 14.9

Madzimbamuto v Lardner-Burke [1969] 1 AC 645, [1968] 3 WLR 1229, [1968] 3 All ER 561 .... 6.4, 6.5

Magnohard Ltd v United Kingdom Atomic Energy Authority 2004 SC 247, 2003 SLT 1083, [2004] Env LR 19... 14.8

Malloch v Aberdeen Corpn 1973 SC 227, 1974 SLT 253 .... 2.8

Malone v Metropolitan Police Commissioner (No 2) [1979] Ch 344, [1979] 2 WLR 700, [1979] 2 All ER 620...................................... 6.5; 13.6, 13.25

Manuel v Attorney-General [1983] Ch 77, [1982] 3 WLR 821, [1982] 3 All ER 822.. 6.5

Marbury v Madison 5 US (1 Cranch) 137 (1803).. 1.23; 6.4
Marcic v Thames Water Utilities [2002] EWCA Civ 64, [2002] QB 929, [2002]
    2 All ER 55.. 13.12
Marshall v Southampton & South West Hampshire Area Health Authority
    [1986] QB 401, [1986] ECR 723, [1986] 2 All ER 584 .... 6.9
Martin (Sean) v Most; Martin v HM Advocate [2010] UKSC 10, 2010 SC
    (UKSC) 40, 2010 SLT 412 .... 6.18, 6.19; 14.19, 14.20, 14.23, 14.25
Martin v O'Sullivan [1984] STC 258, 57 TC 709 .... 6.5
Medicaments & Related Classes of Goods (No 2), In re [2001] 1 WLR 700,
    [2001] UKCLR 550, [2001] ICR 564.. 12.16
Mellors, Petitioner 2003 SLT 479, 2002 SCCR 1007, 2002 GWD 33-1103...... 12.16
Millar v Dickson [2001] UKPC D 4, [2002] 3 All ER 1041, 2002 SC
    (PC) 30.. 12.7, 12.16
Miller v Thomson [2009] HCJAC 4, 2009 SLT 59, 2009 SCCR 179................. 13.19
Miln v Cullen 1967 JC 21, 1967 SLT 35, [1969] Crim LR 37 .... 13.18
Mitchell v Glasgow City Council [2009] UKHL 11, [2009] 2 WLR 481, 2009
    SLT 247... 14.2
Mitchell v North Lanarkshire Council [2007] CSOH 141, 2007 SLT 765,
    [2008] RA 41 .... 14.9
Mohammed v Ministry of Defence [2014] EWHC 1369 (QB) 13.13
Moncrieff v Lord Moncrieff (1904) 6 F 1021, (1904) 12 SLT 267 .... 14.9
Moohan v Lord Advocate; Moohan, Petr [2014] UKSC 67, [2015] 2 WLR 141,
    2015 SLT 2... 4.5
Moore v Clyde Pilotage Authority (1944) 77 LL Rep 138, 1943 SC 457, 1944
    SLT 111... 14.9
Morrow's Application, Re [2001] NI 261 .... 7.19
Mortensen v Peters (1906) 8 F(J) 93, (1906) 14 SLT 227 .... 6.5; 14.24
Mosley v Newsgroup Newspapers Ltd [2008] EWHC 1777 (QB), [2008]
    EMLR 20, (2008) 158 NLJ 1112.. 13.24
Mosley v United Kingdom (Application 48009/08) [2012] EMLR 1, [2012] 1
    FCR 99, (2011) 53 EHRR 30... 13.24
Moss' Empires Ltd v Glasgow Assessor 1917 SC (HL) 1, 1916 2 SLT 215...... 14.7
Muir v Magistrates of Hamilton 1910 1 SLT 164... 13.18
Murphy v East Ayrshire Council [2012] CSIH 47, 2012 SLT 1125, 2012 GWD
    19-391 .... 14.2
Murray v Rogers 1992 SLT 221 .... 6.6
Murray v UK (Application 14310/88) (1995) 19 EHRR 193............................. 14.24

N

NS v Secretary of State for the Home Department *see* R (on the application of
    NS) v Secretay of State for the Home Department (Case C-411/10)
Napier v Scottish Ministers 2005 1 SC 229, 2004 SLT 555, 2004 SCLR 558 ... 13.11
Neizer v Johnston 1993 SCCR 772, 1994 SLT 1012.. 14.14
Nicol (D & J) v Dundee Harbour Trustees [1915] AC 550, 1915 SC (HL) 7,
    1914 2 SLT 418.. 14.9, 14.10
Niemietz v Germany (1993) 16 EHRR 97... 13.11
North v Dumfries & Galloway Council [2013] UKSC 45, [2013] 4 All ER 413,
    2013 SC (UKSC) 298 .... 13.14
Norwood v United Kingdom (2005) 40 EHRR SE11 .... 13.11

O

O'Brien v Independent Assessor; R (on the application of O'Brien) v Indepen-
    dent Assessor [2007] UKHL 10, [2007] 2 AC 312, [2007] 2 WLR 544..... 11.2
O'Kelly v Harvey (1883) 14 LR 1R 105 .... 13.19

O'Moran v DPP [1975] QB 864, [1975] 2 WLR 413, [1975] 1 All ER 473 ...... 13.19
O'Neill v Scottish Joint Negotiating Committee for Teaching Staff 1987 SC 90,
    1987 SLT 648, 1987 SCLR 275 .... 14.11
O'Reilly v Mackman [1983] 2 AC 237, [1982] 3 WLR 1096, [1982] 3 All ER
    1124 .... 14.8
Office of Government Commerce v Information Comr [2008] EWHC 774 (Ad-
    min), [2010] QB 98, [2009] 3 WLR 627 .... 10.1, 10.5
Operation Dismantle v The Queen [1985] 1 SCR 441 .... 14.1
Osman v United Kingdom (2000) 29 EHRR 245, [1999] 1 FLR 193, (2000) 5
    BHRC 293 .... 14.2

P

P (a child) (adoption: unmarried couples), Re [2009] 1 AC 173 .... 14.22
Parliamentary Election for Bristol South East, Re [1964] 2 QB 257, [1961] 3
    WLR 577, [1961] 3 All ER 354 .... 5.13
Paterson v Harvie [2014] HCJAC 87, 2014 SLT 857, 2014 SCL 606 .... 13.19
Paton (John James) v Dunn [2012] HCJAC 49, 2012 SCL 802, 2012 SCCR
    441 .... 13.18
Paton v Ritchie 2000 JC 271, 2000 SLT 239, 2000 SCCR 151 .... 13.18
Peck v United Kingdom [2003] EMLR 15, (2003) 36 EHRR 41, 13 BHRC
    669 .... 13.24
Peebles v HM Advocate [2007] HCJAC 6, 2007 JC 93, 2007 SLT 197 .... 13.18
Peggie v Clark 1868 7M 89 .... 13.18
Pocock's Trustee v Skene Investment (Aberdeen) Ltd [2012] CSIH 61, 2012
    GWD 27-562 .... 14.12
Pollock v Secretary of State for Scotland 1992 SCLR 972, 1993 SLT 1173 ..... 14.11
Pollok School Co Ltd v Glasgow Town Clerk 1946 SC 373, 1946 SLT 365 ..... 14.9
Poplar Housing & Regeneration Community Association v Donoghue [2001]
    EWCA Civ 595, [2001] 4 All ER 604, [2002] QB 48 .... 13.12
Porter v Magill [2001] UKHL 67, [2002] 2 AC 357, [2002] 1 All ER 465 .... 12.16;
    14.9
Potter v Scottish Ministers [2007] CSIH 67, 2007 SLT 1019, 2008 SCLR 81 .. 13.11
Potter v Scottish Prison Service [2007] CSIH 67, 2007 SLT 1019, 2008 SCLR
    81 .... 13.24
Portobello Park Action Group Association v City of Edinburgh Council [2012]
    CSIH 69, 2013 SC 184, 2012 SLT 1137 .... 9.27
Pretty v United Kingdom [2002] 2 FLR 45, [2002] 2 FCR 97, (2002) 35
    EHRR 13.11
Pringle, Petitioner 1991 SLT 330 .... 6.6
Procola v Luxembourg (1996) 22 EHRR 193 .... 12.17

R

R v Bao (Chunxia) [2007] EWCA Crim 2781, [2008] 2 Cr Ap R (S) 10, [2008]
    Crim LR 234 .... 13.11
R v Birmingham City Council, ex p Ireland [1999] 2 All ER 609, (2000) 164 JP
    9, [1999] EHLR 243 .... 14.9
R v Bow Street Metropolitan Stipendiary Magistrate, ex p Pinochet Ugarte (No
    2) [2000] 1 AC 119, [1999] 2 WLR 272, [1999] 1 All ER 577 .... 12.13, 12.14,
    12.15, 12.16, 12.17; 14.9
R v Chayter (David) [2010] UKSC 52, [2011] 1 AC 684, [2010] 3 WLR 1707 ... 5.20
R v Chief Constable of Sussex, ex p International Trader's Ferry Ltd [1999] 2
    AC 418, [1998] 3 WLR 1260, [1999] 1 All ER 129 .... 14.13
R v Civil Service Appeal Board, ex p Cunningham [1991] 4 All ER 310, [1992]
    ICR 81, [1992] ICR 816 .... 14.9

R v Commissioner of Police, ex p Bennett [1995] QB 313, [1995] 2 WLR 598,
  [1995] 3 All ER 248 .... 6.6
R v Cotswold District Council, ex p Barrington Parish Council (1998) 75 P &
  CR 515, [1997] EG 66 (CS), [21997] NPC 70 .... 14.12
R v Criminal Injuries Compensation Board, ex p Ince [1973] 3 All ER 808,
  [1973] 1 WLR 1334, [1973] Crim LR 624 .... 14.9
R v DPP, ex p Kebilene [2000] 2 AC 326, [1999] 3 WLR 972, [1999] 4 All ER
  801 .... 14.18, 14.24
R v Davis [2008] UKHL 36, [2008] 1 AC 1128, [2008] HRLR 35 .... 9.4
R v Gough [1993] AC 646, [1993] 2 WLR 883, [1993] 2 All ER 724 .... 12.16
R v Higher Education Funding Council, ex p Institute of Dental Surgery [1994]
  1 WLR 242, [1994] 1 All ER 651, [1994] COD 147 .... 14.9
R v HM Inspectorate of Pollution, ex p Greenpeace Ltd (No 2) [1994] 4 All ER
  329, [1994] 2 CMLR 548, [1994] Env LR 76 .... 14.10
R v Hull Prison Board of Visitors, ex p St Germain (No 2) [1979] 1 WLR 1401,
  [1979] 3 All ER 545, [1979] Crim LR 726 .... 14.9
R v Jones (Margaret) [2006] UKHL 16, [2007] 1 AC 136, [2006] 2 WLR 772 ... 6.2
R v Race Relations Board, ex p Selvarajan [1975] 1 WLR 168, [61976] 1 All
  ER 12, [1975] IRLR 281 .... 14.9
R v Secretary of State for Employment, ex p Equal Opportunities Commission
  [1995] 1 AC 1, [1994] 2 WLR 409, [1994] 1 All ER 910 .... 6.9; 14.32
R v Secretary of State for Foreign & Commonwealth Affairs, ex p World
  Development Movement Ltd [1995] 1 WLR 386, [1995] 1 All ER 611,
  [1995] COD 211 .... 14.10
R v Secretary of State for Social Services, ex p AMA [1986] 1 WLR 1, [1986]
  1 All ER 164, (1985) 17 HLR 487 .... 14.14
R v Secretary of State for the Environment, ex p Hammersmith & Fulham Lon-
  don Borough Council [1991] 1 AC 521, [1990] 3 WLR 898,[1990] 3 All
  ER 589 .... 14.14, 14.26
R v Secretary of State for the Environment, ex p Nottinghamshire County
  Council [1986] AC 240, [1986] 2 WLR 1, [1986] 1 All ER 199 .... 14.14, 14.26
R v Secretary of State for the Environment, ex p Ostler [1977] QB 122, [1976]
  3 WLR 288, [1976] 3 All ER 90 .... 14.9
R v Secretary of State for the Home Department, ex p Bentley [1994] QB 349,
  [1994] 2 WLR 101, [1993] 4 All ER 442 .... 14.2
R v Secretary of State for the Home Department, ex p Brind [1991] 1 AC 696,
  [1991] 2 WLR 588, [1991] 1 All ER 720 .... 6.5; 14.13, 14.16
R v Secretary of State for the Home Department, ex p Fayed [1998] 1 WLR
  763, [1997] 1 All ER 228, [1997] INLR 137 .... 14.9
R v Secretary of State for the Home Department, ex p FBU [1995] 2 AC 513,
  [1995] 2 WLR 464, [1995] 2 All ER 244 .... 1.23
R v Secretary of State for the Home Department, ex p Northumbria Police
  Authority [1989] QB 26, [1988] 2 WLR 590, [1988] 1 All ER 556 .... 7.19
R v Secretary of State for the Home Department, ex p Oladehinde [1991] 1 AC
  254, [1990] 3 WLR 797, [1990] 3 All ER 393 .... 14.9
R v Secretary of State for the Home Department, ex p Simms [2000] 2 AC 115,
  [1999] 3 WLR 328, [1999] 3 All ER 400 .... 2.7
R v Secretary of State for Transport, ex p Factortame Ltd (No 2) [1991] 1 AC
  603, [1990] 3 WLR 818, [1991] 1 All ER 70 .... 6.9, 6.10; 14.26,
                                                                                          14.32
R v Secretary of State for Transport, ex p Factortame Ltd (No 5) [2000] 1 AC
  524, [1999] 3 WLR 1062, [1999] 4 All ER 906 .... 6.9, 6.10
R v Sheer Metalcraft Ltd [1954] 1 QB 586, [1954] 2 WLR 777, [1954] 1 All
  ER 542 .... 9.32

RB (Algeria) v Home Secretary [2009] UKHL 10, [2010] 2 AC 110, [2009] 2
WLR 512.. 2.8
R (on the application of Al-Fawwaz) v Governor of Brixton Prison [2001]
UKHL 69, [2002] 1 AC 556, [2002] 1 All ER 545 .... 6.5
R (on the application of Al-Jedda) v Secretary of State for Defence [2007]
UKHL 58, [2008] 1 AC 332, [2008] 2 WLR 31 .... 13.13
R (on the application of Al-Skeini) v Secretary of State for Defence [2007]
UKHL 26, [2008] 1 AC 153, 2007] 3 WLR 33 .... 13.13
R (on the application of Anderson) v Secretary of State for the Home Depart-
ment [2002] UKHL 46, [2003] 1 AC 837, [2002] 4 All ER 1089 .... 14.17
R (on the application of Bancoult) v Secretary of State for Foreign & Com-
monwealth Affairs (No 2) [2007] EWCA Civ 498, [2008] QB 365, [2007]
3 WLR 768.. 7.2; 14.14
R (on the application of Bradley) v Secretary of State for Work & Pensions
[2008] EWCA Civ 36, [2009] QB 114, [2009] QB 114............................. 10.14
R (on the application of Burkett) v Hammersmith & Fulham London Borough
Council [2002] UKHL 23, [2002] 1 WLR 1593, [2002] 3 All ER 97........ 2.8
R (on the application of Cart) v Upper Tribunal [2011] UKSC 28, [2012] 1 AC
663, [2011] 3 WLR 107 .... 14.11
R (on the application of Cavanagh) v Health Service Comr [2004] EWHC 1847
(Admin)... 10.14
R v (on the application of Chester) v Secretary of State for Justice [2013]
UKSC 63, [2014] AC 271 .... 13.17; 14.17
R (on the application of Chester) v Secretary of State for Justice; McGeoch v
Lord President of the Council [2013] UKSC 63, [2014] AC 271, 2014 SC
(UKSC) 25 .... 5.6; 13.17; 14.17
R (on the application of Corner House Research) v Secretary of State for Trade
& Industry [2005] EWCA Civ 192, [2005] 1 WLR 2600, [2005] 4 All
ER 1 .... 14.11
R (on the application of Countryside Alliance) v A-G [2007] UKHL 52, [2008]
1 AC 719, [2007] 3 WLR 922.. 14.26
R (on the application of Daly) v Secretary of State for the Home Department
[2001] UKHL 26, [2001] 2 AC 532, [2001] 3 All ER 433 .... 2.7; 14.13
R (on the application of E) v JFS Governing Body [2009] UKSC 15, [2010] 2
AC 728, [2010] 2 WLR 153.. 13.11
R (on the application of Edwards) v Environment Agency (No 2); Digital Satel-
lite Warranty Cover Ltd, Re [2013] UKSC 7, [2013] 1 WLR 605, [2013] 2
All ER 202 .... 14.11
R (on the application of Evans) v A-G [2014] EWCA Civ 254, [2014] QB 855,
[2014] 3 All ER 682... 13.22
R (on the application of Gentle) v Prime Minister [2008] UKHL 20, [2008] 1
AC 1356, [2008] 2 WLR 879.. 13.11; 14.14
R (on the application of H) v North & East London Region Mental Health
Review Tribunal [2001] EWCA Civ 415, [2002] QB 1, [2001] 3
WLR 512.. 14.17
R (on the application of HS2 Action Alliance Ltd) v Secretary of State for
Transport [2014] 2 All ER 109 .... 1.23; 3.12; 5.19; 6.9, 6.10
R (on the application of Hassan) v Secretary of State for Defence [2009]
EWHC 309 (Admin) 13.13
R (on the application of Heather) v Leonard Cheshire Foundation [2002]
EWCA Civ 366, [2002] 2 All ER 936, [2002] HRLR 30........................... 13.12
R (on the application of Holding & Barnes plc) v Secretary of State for the
Environment, Transport & the Regions [2001] UKHL 23, [2001] 2 All ER
929, [2001] 2 WLR 1389 .... 14.13

R (on the application of Infinis plc) v Gas & Electricity Markets Authority [2013] EWCA Civ 70, [2013] JPL 1037 .... 13.11

R (on the application of Jackson) v Attorney-General [2005] UKHL 56, [2006] 1 AC 262, [2005] 3 WLR 733 .... 6.5, 6.6; 14.1, 14.26

R (on the application of Javed) v Secretary of State for the Home Department [2001] EWCA Civ 789, [2002] QB 12, [2001] QB 129 .... 14.14

R (on the application of L) v Comr of Police for the Metropolis [2009] UKSC 3, [2010] 1 AC 410, [2009] 3 WLR 1056 .... 13.24

R (on the application of Laporte) v Chief Constable of Gloucestershire [2006] UKHL 55, [2007] 2 AC 105, [2007] 2 All ER 529 .... 13.19

R (on the application of McFetrich) v Secretary of State for the Home Department [2003] EWHC 1542 (Admin), [2003] 4 All ER 1093, [2003] Prison LR 361 .... 13.11

R (on the application of McIntyre) v Gentoo Group [2010] EWHC 5 (Admin), (2010) 154 (2) SJLB 29, [2010] 2 P & CR DG6 .... 14.8

R (on the application of Mohammed) v Foreign Secretary [2009] EWHC 152 (Admin), (2009) 159 NLJ 234 .... 2.7

R (on the application of Morgan Grenfell & Co Ltd) v Special Commissioner [2002] UKHL 21, [2003] 1 AC 563 [2002] 3 All ER 1 .... 2.7

R (on the application of NS) v Secretay of State for the Home Department; NS v Secretary of State for the Home Department R (Case C-411/10) [2013] QB 102, [2012] 3 WLR 1374[2012] 2 CMLR 9 .... 13.8

R (on the application of Nicklinson) v Ministry of Justice [2014] UKSC 38, [2014] 3 WLR 200, [2014] 3 All ER 843 .... 13.11

R (on the application of Northern Ireland Human Rights Commission) v Greater Belfast Coroner [2002] JRLR 35 .... 13.14

R (on the application of O'Callaghan) v Charity Commission for England & Wales [2007] EWHC 2491 (Admin), [2008] WTLR 117 .... 14.14

R (on the application of Osborn) v Parole Board; Reilly's Application for Judicial Review, Re [2013] UKSC 61, [2014] AC 1115, [2013] 3 WLR 1020 .... 13.17

R (on the application of Parish) v Pensions Ombudsman [2009] EWHC 32 (Admin), [2009] Pens LR 91 .... 10.14

R (on the application of Playfoot) v Governing Body of Millais School [2007] EWHC 1698 (Admin), [2007] 3 FCR 754, [2007] HRLR 34 .... 13.11

R (on the application of Pretty) v DPP [2001] UKHL 61, [2002] 1 AC 800, [2002] 1 All ER 1 .... 13.11

R (on the application of ProLife Alliance) v BBC, [2003] UKHL 23, [2004] 1 AC 185, [2003] 2 WLR 1403 .... 13.11; 14.18, 14.24

R (on the application of Quark Fishing Ltd) v Secretary of State for Foreign & Commonwealth Affairs (No 2) [2005] UKHL 57, [2006] 1 AC 529, [2005] 3 WLR 837 .... 7.2; 13.13

R (on the application of Reilly) v Secretary of State for Work & Pensions [2013] UKSC 68, [2014] AC 453, [2013] 3 WLR 1276 .... 13.11

R (on the application of S) v Chief Constable of Yorkshire Police [2004] UKHL 39, [2004] 1 WLR 2196, [2004] 4 All ER 193 .... 13.11

R (on the application of SB) v Govenors of Denbigh High School [2006] UKHL 15, [2007] 1 AC 100, [2006] 2 WLR 719 .... 13.11

R (on the application of Sacker) v HM Coroner for West Yorkshire [2004] UKHL 11, [2004] 1 WLR 796, [2004] 2 All ER 487 .... 13.11

R (on the application of Sandiford) v Secretary of State for Foreign & Commonwealth Affairs [2013] EWCA Civ 581, [2013] 1 WLR 2938, [2013] 3 All ER 757 .... 13.8

R (on the application of Spath Holme Ltd) v Secretary of State for the Environment & Transport [2000] 3 WLR 141, [2000] 1 All ER 884, (2000) 32 HLR 495.. 14.14

R (on the application of Sturnham) v Parole Board [2013] UKSC 47, [2013] 2 AC 254, [2013] 3 WLR 281... 13.17

R (on the application of T) v Chief Constable of Greater Manchester [2014] UKSC 35, [2015] AC 49, [2014] 4 All ER 159 .... 13.24

R (on the application of Ullah) v Special Adjudicator [2004] UKHL 26, [2004] 2 AC 323, [2004] 2 AC 323.. 13.17

R (on the application of Watkins-Singh) v Governing Body of Aberdare Girls' High School [2008] EWHC 1865 (Admin), [2008] 3 FCR 203, [2008] ELR 561 .... 13.11

R (on the application of Zagorski) v Secretary of State for Business, Innovation & Skills [2010] EWHC 3110 (Admin), [2011] Eu LR 315, [2011] HRLR 6... 13.8

Rangers Football Club plc, Petr [2012] CSOH 95, 2012 SLT 1156, 2012 GWD 20-402 .... 14.8

Rankin v Murray 2004 SLT 1164, 2004 SCCR 422, 2004 GWD 18-398 .... 13.19

Rape Crisis Centre v Secretary of State for the Home Department 2000 SC 527, 2001 SLT 389, 200 SCLR 807... 14.10

Rees v United Kingdom [1987] 2 FLR 111, [1993] 2 FCR 49, (1987) 9 EHRR 56... 13.11

Robbie the Pict, Petitioner (No 2) 2003 JC 78, 2003 SCCR 299, 2003 GWD 11-308 .... 12.3, 12.16; 14.14

Robinson v Secretary of State for Northern Ireland [2002] UKHL 32, [2002] NI 390 .... 7.15; 14.24

Rooney v Brown [2013] HCJAC 57, 2013 SCL 615, 2013 SCCR 334............. 13.19

Rooney v Strathclyde Police Joint Board [2008] CSIH 54, 2009 SC 73, 2009 SCLR 31.. 14.9

Roy v Kensington, Chelsea & Westminster Family Practitioner Committee [1992] 1 AC 624, [1992] 2 WLR 239, [1992] 1 All ER 705..................... 14.8

Ruddle v Secretary of State for Scotland 1999 GWD 29-1395 .... 2.7; 9.15

Rugby Football Union v Viagogo Ltd [2012] UKSC 55, [2012] 1 WLR 3333, [2013] 1 All ER 928... 13.8, 13.23

Russell v Dickson 1997 SC 269, 1998 SLT 96, 1997 GWD 22-1058............... 12.11

S

S v L [2011] CSIH 38, 2012 SC 8, 2011 SLT 1204 .... 14.19

S v United Kingdom (2009) 48 EHRR 50, 25 BHRC 557, [2009] Crim LR 355... 13.24

Salvesen v Riddell [2013] UKSC 22, 2013 SC (UKSC) 236, 2013 SLT 863 .... 13.11; 14.22, 14.27

Schechter Poultry Corp v United States 295 US 495 (1935.............................. 6.23

Scotch Whisky Association, Petrs [2013] CSOH 70, 2013 SLT 776, 2012 GWD 33-659 .... 14.10, 14.28

Scott v Phillips 1974 SLT 32, 1973 SLT (Notes) 75....................................... 5.6

Scottish Borders Council v Information Comr (unreported, 21 August 2013)... 13.23

Scottish Environment Protection Agency v Joint Liquidators of the Scottish Coal Co Ltd *see* Joint Liquidators of the Scottish Coal Co Ltd v SEPA

Scottish House Builders Association Ltd v Scottish Ministers 2002 SLT 1321, 2001 GWD 40-1531... 7.25

Scottish Ministers v Scottish Information Commissioner [2007] CSIH 8, 2007 SC 330, 2007 SLT 274.. 13.22; 14.1

Scottish Old People's Welfare Council, Petitioners 1987 SLT 179 .... 14.10, 14.14

Secretary of State for Education & Science v Tameside Metropolitan Borough
  Council [1977] AC 1014, [1976] 3 WLR 641, [1976] 3 All ER 665 .... 14.9
Secretary of State for the Home Department v F [2009] UKHL 28, [2009] 3
  WLR 74, (2009) 106 (25) LSG 14 .... 13.11
Sellar v Highland Railway Co 1919 SC (HL) 19, 1919 1 SLT 149 .... 12.14, 12.15; 14.9
Shahid v Scottish Ministers 2014 SC 490, 2014 SLT 335, 2014 GWD 6-131 ... 13.11
Singh v Secretary of State for the Home Department [1992] 1 WLR 1052, 1993
  SC (HL) 1, 1993 SLT 115 .... 12.2
Singh v Secretary of State for the Home Department (No 1) 1998 SLT 1370,
  1997 GWD 40-2095 .... 14.16
Smith v Donnelly 2002 JC 65, 2001 SLT 1007, 2001 SCCR 800 .... 13.19
Smith v Ministry of Defence [2013] UKSC 41, [2014] AC 52, [2013] 3
  WLR 69 .... 13.2, 13.11, 13.13
Smith v Nairn Golf Club [2007] CSOH 136, 2007 SLT 909, 2007 GWD
  25 420 .... 14.8
Smith v Scott [2007] CSIH 9, 2007 SC 345, 2007 SLT 137 .... 5.6; 14.17
Société Colas Est v France (2004) 39 EHRR 373 .... 13.11
Somerville v Scottish Ministers [2007] UKHL 44, [2007] 1 WLR 2734, 2008
  SC (HL) 45 .... 1.20; 6.19; 7.19, 7.25; 9.15; 14.9,
                                                              14.12, 14.20, 14.30
South Lanarkshire Council v Scottish Information Comr [2013] UKSC 55,
  [2013] 1 WLR 2421, 2014 SC (UKSC) 1 .... 13.22
St Johnstone Football Club v Scottish Football Association Ltd 1965 SLT 171   14.8
Stambuck v Germany (2003) 37 EHRR 1059, (2004) 77 BMLR 1 .... 13.11
Starrs v Ruxton 2000 JC 208, 2000 SLT 42, 1999 SCCR 1052 ... 6.2; 12.3, 12.7, 12.13,
                                                              12.14, 12.17; 14.15, 14.20
Stewart v Henry 1989 SLT (Sh Ct) 34 .... 6.6
Stewart v Secretary of State for Scotland 1996 SC 271, 1996 SLT 1203 .... 12.7
Stewart v Secretary of State for Scotland 1998 SC (HL) 81, 1998 SLT 385,
  1998 SCLR 332 .... 12.7
Swanson v Manson 1907 SC 426, (1907) 14 SLT 737 .... 14.10
Syme v Scottish Borders Council 2003 SLT 601, 2002 SCLR 1066, 2002 Rep
  LR 122 .... 14.2

T

T, Petr 1997 SLT 724, 1996 SCLR 897, [1997] Fam Law 225 .... 6.5; 14.16
TP & KM v United Kingdom [2001] 2 FLR 549, [2001] 2 FCR 289, (2001) 34
  EHRR 2 .... 14.2
Tesco Stores Ltd v Secretary of State for the Environment [1995] 2 All ER 636,
  [1995] 1 WLR 759, 93 LGR 403 .... 14.13
Tehrani v Home Secretary [2007] UKHL 47, [2007] 1 AC 521, 2007 SC
  (HL) 1 .... 13.3
Thoburn v Sunderland City Council [2002] EWHC 195 (Admin), [2003] QB
  151, [2002] 4 All ER 156 .... 1.22; 6.5, 6.10
Thomas v Sawkins [1935] 2 KB 249, [1935] All ER Rep 655 .... 13.19
Tyrer v United Kingdom (1979-80) 2 EHRR 1 .... 13.11

U

Uniplex (UK) Ltd v NHS Business Services Authority (Case C-40608) [2010]
  PTSR 1377, [2010] 2 CMLR 47 .... 14.12
Unison, Petrs [2006] CSOH 193 .... 14.12

V

Vakauta v Kellyy (1989) 167 CLR 568 .... 12.16

Valente v The Queen (1985) 24 DLR (4th) 161... 12.3
Vauxhall Estates Ltd v Liverpool Corpn [1932] 1 KB 733......................... 6.5, 6.10
Vervuren v HM Advocate 2002 SLT 555, 2002 SCCR 481, 2002 GWD 13-
  410.. 6.2

W

Wallace v East Lothian Council [2013] CSOH 195, [2013] JPL 813, 2013
  GWD 2-84.. 14.11
Walton v Scottish Ministers [2012] UKSC 44, [2013] PTSR 51, 2013 SC
  (UKSC) 67 .... 14.10
Wang v Commissioner for Inland Revenue [1994] 1 WLR 1286, [1995] 1 All
  ER 637, [1994] STC 753 .... 14.9
Watkins v Secretary of State for the Home Department [2006] UKHL 17,
  [2006] 2 AC 395, [2006] 2 WLR 807 .... 14.16
Watt v Lord Advocate 1979 SC 120, 1979 SLT 137.................................. 12.2; 14.9
Webb v R (1994) 181 CLR 41 .... 12.16
West v Secretary of State for Scotland 1992 SC 385, 1992 SLT 636, 1992
  SCLR 504.. 14.7, 14.8, 14.9
Westerhall Farms v Scottish Ministers 2001 GWD 14-537........................... 7.25
Whaley v Lord Advocate 2004 SC 78, 2004 SLT 425, 2003 GWD 2-651..... 1.20; 14.1,
  14.24
Whaley v Lord Watson of Invergowrie 2000 SC 125, 1999 GWD 39-1882 ...... 14.24
Whaley v Watson 2000 SC 340, 2000 SLT 475, 2000 SCLR 279.................. 5.1; 14.1
Wieser v Bicos Beteiligungen GmbH v Austria (2008) 46 EHRR 54 .... 13.11
Wildridge v Anderson (1897) 25 R (J) 27, (1897) 5 SLT 206 .... 12.15
Wille v Liechtenstein (2000) 30 EHRR 558, 8 BHRC 69 .... 12.18
Wilson v Robertson 1986 SCCR 700 .... 13.18
Winterwerp v Netherlands (1979-80) 2 EHRR 387.. 14.24
Wither v Reid 1980 JC 7, 1979 SLT 192.. 13.18
Wood v Commissioner of Police of the Metropolis [2009] EWCA Civ 414,
  (2009) 106 (22) LSG 24, (2009) 153 (21) SJLB 30 .... 13.24
Woods v Secretary of State for Scotland 1991 SLT 197................................. 14.9

Y

Young v Fife Regional Council 1986 SLT 331 .... 14.9

Z

Z v United Kingdom [2001] 2 FLR 612, [2001] 2 FCR 246, (2001) 34
  EHRR 3... 14.2

Bibliography

Adams, J, and Robinson, P, (eds) Devolution in Practice (2002)

Alston, P,(ed) The EU and Human Rights (1999)

Arthurs, HW, Without the Law (1985)

Bagehot, W, The English Constitution (1963) (Introduction by RHS Crossman)

Bamforth, N, and Leyland, P, (eds) Accountability in the Contemporary Constitution (2013)

Bamforth, N, and Leyland, P, (eds) Public Law in a Multi-Layered Constitution (2003)

Bankton, Lord, Institute of the Laws of Scotland (Stair Society, 1993–95)

Barker, A, (ed) Quangos in Britain: Government and the Networks of Public Policy-Making (1982)

Beard, CA, An Economic Interpretation of the Constitution of the United States (1913)

Bentham, J, Of Laws in General (HLA Hart (ed), 1970)

Bickel, AM, The Least Dangerous Branch (1962)

Bingham, T, The Rule of Law (2011)

Birkinshaw, P, European Public Law (2003)

Birkinshaw, P, Freedom of Information (4th edn, 2010)

Blair, S, Scots Administrative Law: Cases and Materials (1999)

Blaustein, AP, and Flanz, GH, (eds) Constitutions of the Countries of the World (1971–)

Bogdanor, V, Devolution in the United Kingdom (2001)

Bogdanor, V, The New British Constitution (2009)

Boyle, A, et al (eds) Human Rights and Scots Law (2002)

Bradley, AW, Ewing, KD,and Knight, CJS,(eds) Constitutional and Administrative Law (16th edn, 2014)

Calvert, H, Constitutional Law in Northern Ireland (1968)

Calvert, H, (ed) Devolution (1975)

Campbell, T, et al (eds) Sceptical Essays on Human Rights (2001)

Campbell, T, et al (eds) The Legal Protection of Human Rights (2011)

Clayton, R, and Tomlinson, H, The Law of Human Rights (2nd edn, 2009)

Cleland, A, and Sutherland, E, Children's Rights in Scotland (3rd edn, 2009)

Clyde, Lord, and Edwards, DJ, Judicial Review (2000)

Coppel, P, Information Rights (4th edn, 2014)

Craig, P and de Burca, G, EU Law (5th edn, 2011)

Craig, PP, Administrative Law (7th edn, 2012)

Crick, B, The Reform of Parliament (1970)

Daintith, T, and Page, A, The Executive in the Constitution (1999)

Dalyell, T, Devolution: The End of Britain? (1977)

De Lolme, JL, The Constitution of England (new edn, 1834)

De Smith, SA, Jowell, J, and Woolf, Lord, Judicial Review of Administrative Action (7th edn, 2013)

De Smith, SA, The New Commonwealth and its Constitutions (1964)

Dicey, AV, The Law of the Constitution (10th edn, by ECS Wade 1959)

Dicey, AV, and Rait, RS, Thoughts on the Union between England and Scotland (1920)

Douglas-Scott, S, Constitutional Law of the European Union (2002)

Duchacek, ID, Power Maps: Comparative Politics of Constitutions (1973)

Dunion, K, Freedom of Information in Scotland in Practice (2011)

Edward, D, and Lane, R, European Union Law (2013)

Ely, JH, Democracy and Distrust (1980)

Ewing, KD, and Dale-Risk, K, Human Rights in Scotland (2004)

Ferguson, PR, Breach of the Peace (2013)

Finnie, W, Himsworth, CMG, and Walker, N, (eds) Edinburgh Essays in Public Law (1991)

Forsyth, C, (ed) Judicial Review and the Constitution (2000)

Fraser, WIR, An Outline of Constitutional Law (2nd edn, 1948)

Gearty, C, and Douzinas,C, (eds), Human Rights Law (2012)

Gordon, GH, The Criminal Law of Scotland (3rd edn, 2001)

Grant, JP, (ed) Independence and Devolution: The Legal Implications for Scotland (1976)

Griffith, JAG, The Politics of the Judiciary (5th edn, 1997)

Hadfield, B, The Constitution of Northern Ireland (1989)

Hague, DC, Mackenzie, WJM, and Barker, A, (eds) Public Policy and Private Interests (1975)

Hailsham, Lord, The Dilemma of Democracy (1978)

Hall, W, and Weir, S, The Untouchables: Power and Accountability in the Quango State (1996)

Hanks, P, Constitutional Law in Australia (3rd edn, 2012)

Harden, I, and Lewis, N, The Noble Lie: The British Constitution and the Rule of Law (1986)

Harlow, C, and Rawlings, R, Law and Administration (3rd edn, 2009)

Hart, HLA, The Concept of Law (2nd edn, 1997)

Hartley, TC, The Foundations of European Union Law (8th edn, 2014)

Hazell, R, (ed) Constitutional Futures (1999)

Hazell, R, The English Question (2006)

Hazell, R, (ed) The State and the Nations (2000)

Hazell, R and Rawlings, R, (eds) Devolution, Law Making and the Constitution (2005)

Hewart, Lord, The New Despotism (1929)

Himsworth, CMG, and Munro, CR, Devolution and the Scotland Bill (1998)

Himsworth, CMG, and Munro, CR, The Scotland Act 1998 (2nd edn, 2000)

Himsworth, CMG, Local Government Law in Scotland (1995)

Hogg, PW, Constitutional Law of Canada (2008)

Hopkins, WJ, Devolution in Context: Regional, Federal and Devolved Government in the EU (2002)

Hume, D, Commentaries on the Law of Scotland Respecting Crimes (3rd edn, 1986)

Hunt, M, Using Human Rights Law in English Courts (1997)

Janis, MW, Kay, RS, Bradley, AW, European Human Rights Law: Text and Materials (3rd edn, 2008)

Jeffery, C and Mitchell, J, The Scottish Parliament 1999-2009 (2009)

Jennings, I, The Law and the Constitution (5th edn, 1959)

Jowell, J, and Oliver, D, (eds) The Changing Constitution (7th edn, 2011)

Keating, M, The Government of Scotland (2nd edn, 2010))

Keating, M, The Independence of Scotland (2009)

Kellas, JG, Modern Scotland (2nd edn, 1980)

Kellas, JG, The Scottish Political System (4th edn, 1989)

Kelsen, H, Pure Theory of Law (2nd edn, 1970)

The Laws of Scotland, Stair Memorial Encyclopaedia, Reissues 'Administrative Law' (2000), 'Constitutional Law' (2002)

Lester, A, Pannick, D and Herberg, J, (eds) Human Rights Law and Practice (3rd edn, 2009)

Loughlin, M, Foundations of Public Law (2010)

Loughlin, M, Legality and Locality (1996)

Loughlin, M, Sword and Scales (2000)

Loughlin, M, The British Constitution (2013)

Loughlin, M, The Idea of Public Law (2004)

Lynch, P, Scottish Government and Politics (2001)

MacCormick, N, Institutions of Law (2007)

MacCormick, N, Questioning Sovereignty:Law, State, and Nation in the European Commonwealth (1999)

MacCormick, N, (ed) The Scottish Debate: Essays on Scottish Nationalism (1970)

Macdonald, IA, and Webber, F, Immigration Law and Practice in the United Kingdom (6th edn, 2005)

Macdonald, J, Crail, R and Jones, C, (eds) The Law of Freedom of Information (2nd edn, 2009)

McFadden J, and Lazarowicz, M, The Scottish Parliament (4th edn, 2009)

McHarg, A and Mullen, T, (eds) Public Law in Scotland (2006)

Mackay, W et al, Erskine May's Treatise on the Law, Privileges, Proceedings and Usage of Parliament (24th edn, 2011)

Mackinnon, J, The Constitutional History of Scotland (1924)

Mackintosh, JP, The British Cabinet (3rd edn, 1977)

Mackintosh, JP, The Devolution of Power (1968)

McLean, I, Gallagher, J, and Lodge, G, Scotland's Choices (2nd edn, 2014)

MacPhail, ID, Sheriff Court Practice (3rd edn, Welsh, T, 2006)

MacQueen, HL, (ed) Scots Law into the 21st Century) (1996)

Milne, D, The Scottish Office (1957)

Mitchell, JDB, Constitutional Law (2nd edn, 1968)

Munro, CR, Studies in Constitutional Law (2nd edn, 1999)

Munro, J, Public Law in Scotland (2nd edn, 2007)

Norrie, KM, Children (Scotland) Act 1995 (Revised edn, 1998)

O'Neill, A, Judicial Review in Scotland (1999)

Oliver, D, Constitutional Reform in the UK (2003)

Paterson, AA, Bates, TStJN, and Poustie, MR, The Legal System of Scotland (4th edn, 1999)

Paterson, AA, Final Judgement: The Last Law Lords and the Supreme Court (2013)

Paterson, L, The Autonomy of Modern Scotland (1994)

Peers, S,Hervey, T, Kenner, J, and Ward, A, (eds) The EU Charter of Fundamental Rights: A Commentary (2014)

Quekett, AS, The Constitution of Northern Ireland (1928, 1933, 1946)

Rainey, B,Wicks, E,and Ovey, C,The European Convention on Human Rights (6th edn, 2014)

Rasmussen, H, On Law and Policy in the European Court of Justice (1986)

Rawlings, R, Delineating Wales (2003)

Reed, R, and Murdoch, J, A Guide to Human Rights Law in Scotland (3rd edn, 2011)

Seneviratne, M, Ombudsmen: Public Services and Administrative Justice (2002)

Stair, Viscount, Institutions of the Law of Scotland (1981)

Sunkin, M, and Payne, S, (eds) The Nature of the Crown (1999)

Supperstone, M, Goudie, J, and Walker, P, (eds) Judicial Review (5th edn, 2014)

Sutherland, E et al (eds), Law Making in the Scottish Parliament: The Early Years (2011)

Tierney, S, Constitutional Law and National Pluralism (2004)

Tierney, S, Constitutional Referendums (2012)

Tomkins, A, Public Law (2003)

Trench, A, Devolution and Power in the United Kingdom (2007)

Trench, A, (ed) The State of the Nations 2001 (2001)

Trench, A, (ed) The State of the Nations 2008 (2008)

Tribe, LH, American Constitutional Law (3rd edn, 2000)

Bibliography

Turpin, C, and Tomkins, A, British Government and the Constitution (7th edn, 2011)
Wade, HWR, and Forsyth, CF, Administrative Law (11th edn, 2014)
Walker, DM, The Scottish Legal System (8th edn, 2001)
Walker, N, Intimations of Global Law (2015)
Walker, N, (ed) MacCormick's Scotland (2012)
Walker, N, Policing in a Changing Constitutional Order (1998)
Weiler, PC, In the Last Resort: A Critical Study of the Supreme Court of Canada (1974)
Whatley, CA, Bought and Sold for English Gold? Explaining the Union of 1707 (2nd edn, 2001)
Wheare, KC, Federal Government (4th edn, 1963)
Wheare, KC, Government by Committee (1955)
Wheare, KC, Modern Constitutions (2nd edn, 1966)
White, RM, and Willock, ID,and MacQueen, HL The Scottish Legal System (5th edn, 2013)
Winetrobe, BK, Realising the Vision: a Parliament with a Purpose (2001)
Woolf et al, De Smith's Judicial Review of Administrative Action (7th edn, 2013)

Chapter 1

Constitutions and Constitutional Law

INTRODUCTION

1.1   This is a book about constitutional law and, in particular, about constitutional law in Scotland. Before we can embark on the project in detail, however, there is a need for an initial familiarity with the domain of study. The terminology and the language of constitutional law must also be acquired, together with some knowledge of its general ideas and the cultures and traditions within which those ideas are discussed. One must know what is important to constitutional lawyers and why; what it is that interests and even excites them; and what difficulties they encounter. One must learn how constitutional lawyers analyse existing constitutional situations; what assistance they derive from constitutional events in the past; and what guidance they may acquire from systems of constitutional law in other parts of the world. One must understand too how constitutional lawyers (joined by much of the Scottish population during the recent independence referendum period![1]) speculate about possible future developments in Scotland or elsewhere, how the law they study differs from other branches of the law; and how the approach to their subject of study tends to be different from that of political scientists, sociologists and others. This last distinction is not always straightforward or uncontroversial and although detailed discussion of the growing body of scholarship related to what might be described as inter-disciplinary approaches to law (including constitutional law) is beyond the scope of this book, that scholarship should not be overlooked.

How then to acquire the more traditional language and fundamental ideas of constitutional law rapidly? The method chosen in this introductory chapter is to enter the subject by way of discussion of a hypothetical written constitution for an independent Scotland. There is, of course, no such actual constitution because there is (at the time of writing) no independent Scotland – nor, in the light of the referendum outcome, an early prospect of an independent Scotland. It is, however, a useful exercise to make the imaginative leap required to consider what would be the principal component parts of such a written constitution. Because we know what other constitutions contain, we can engage in quite intelligent and informed speculation about a Scottish version. Because the referendum process produced some thinking about what an independence constitution might look like, we can also take some account of those proposals. Then, with the largely hypothetical model in mind, we can develop two useful lines of discussion. On the one hand, a process of comparison can do much to explain the function of constitutions in general, and to understand what influences the content of constitutional rules in different states. Secondly, we can compare and contrast the content of the hypothetical constitution with the continuing reality of constitutional law in Scotland today.

1 For discussion of the 2014 referendum, see ch 4.

1

A WRITTEN CONSTITUTION FOR SCOTLAND?

1.2　　While emphasising once again that, in this section, it is a hypothetical constitution for Scotland which is to be discussed, it should also be borne in mind that some individuals and organisations have made it a very practical task to draft a constitution for adoption by Scotland if it were to become an independent state. Such constitution-making is to be distinguished from the processes which have led to the establishment of a Scottish Parliament within the United Kingdom and which are considered in some detail later in this book. The drafting of potential independence constitutions for Scotland is a task which, in recent years, fell first to a campaigning organisation known as the Scottish Secretariat following the meeting of a provisional National Assembly in 1962[1] and latterly to the Scottish National Party ('SNP')[2]. A substantial contribution to the literature was added in 2011 by Elliot Bulmer's *A Model Constitution for Scotland*. Idiosyncratic in style and content, the draft constitution was accompanied by extensive annotations. In June 2014 the (SNP) Scottish Government published a draft Scottish Independence Bill, including a draft interim constitution[3]. The inspiration underlying these drafts has derived from a political impetus in the direction of an independent Scotland: the need for a new constitution would arise from Scotland's new status, once achieved. In this chapter, some of the provisions in such drafts have been taken into account but more dispassionately and without any underlying commitment to the desirability of any particular political future for Scotland. Ideas from these Scotland-based drafts are supplemented by others from draft models of a written constitution for the whole of the United Kingdom[4] and from the actual constitutions of other states. It is reasonable to assume that our hypothetical constitution for an independent Scotland might consist of, at least, the following ten different parts or chapters.

1 *A Constitution for Scotland* (1964). It was reissued with a new introduction in 1993.
2 For the text of the SNP draft and a commentary by Professor Neil MacCormick, see his 'An Idea for a Scottish Constitution' in W Finnie, C M G Himsworth and N Walker (eds) *Edinburgh Essays in Public Law* (1991). More recently, in September 2002, the SNP published a revised version: *A Constitution for a Free Scotland*. See also V S MacKinnon 'The Constitution of an Independent Scotland' in J P Grant (ed) *Independence and Devolution: The Legal Implications for Scotland* (1976).
3 http://www.scotland.gov.uk/Resource/0045/00452762.pdf. See para 4.14.
4 See, in particular, Institute for Public Policy Research *The Constitution of the United Kingdom* (1991) (hereafter '*IPPR Constitution*').

Part 1: A preamble

1.3　　A written constitution is first and foremost a legal document. It has authority in the country to which it applies and is binding on the people, the governing institutions and the courts of that country. Very often, however, legal documents contain a preface, frequently referred to as a preamble, which may or may not have the same binding force as the rest of the document but which, in an introductory fashion, explains who the parties to the document are, why they are creating the document and the principal purposes underlying the document. In the case of a constitution, the preamble will often explain that it is 'the People' who declare the constitution to be made in their name. Frequently a constitutional preamble will refer briefly to the circumstances under which the constitution was adopted – the collapse of the previous constitutional regime (whether or not in revolutionary circumstances) or the gaining or regaining of independence after a period of subordination to another power. It would not be surprising for a new Scottish constitution to explain in its preamble that it is being made by or on behalf of 'the Scottish People' at a time when independence, lost at the time of the Treaty of Union with England in 1707, was being regained[1]. The preamble might then refer to a number of values to which 'the People' and their constitution aspire. These would be expressed at this stage in very general terms and might include, for instance, the importance of the permanent independence of Scotland; some statement about the future relationship of Scotland to the former United Kingdom, to Europe and to other nations; the importance within Scotland of the freedom and equality of its people and of fairness, justice, democratic government and, to use a phrase to be discussed later, the rule of law. In other states, the preamble is often the place in which to declare the nation's attachment to a particular god or strand of religious teaching. The Irish constitution of 1937 is stated to be made by the people, but in the name of 'the Most Holy Trinity'. The Saudi Arabian constitution of 1992 declares the kingdom to be 'a sovereign Arab Islamic state, with Islam as its religion'.

1 The SNP draft of 2002 bypassed a preamble but, in art 1, asserted the absolute right of the people of Scotland to self-determination and to sovereignty over the territory and natural resources of Scotland. The Scottish Government's draft interim constitution of 2014 stated: 'In Scotland, the people are sovereign'.

Part 2: General

1.4   Many constitutions contain provisions which define the territory of the state – a feature which might be particularly important in a new constitution for Scotland which would, for instance, have to be quite clear about the boundary between Scotland and England, both on land and, perhaps more problematically, at sea[1]. The constitution might then appoint a particular city as the capital of the country. It might describe the national flag and provide for the national anthem. Constitutions are often used to identify the country's official language or languages – for Scotland, in all probability, Gaelic, Scots and English.

Another provision of the greatest importance in any modern constitution is that which defines the status of the constitution itself. The constitution of an independent Scotland would probably declare itself to be supreme; that its terms should be treated as having a higher status than ordinary law; and that, in the case of any discrepancy between the constitution and any other law, it should be the rule in the constitution that would prevail and the ordinary law would have no effect[2].

1 This is not a purely hypothetical issue: the extent of Scotland's territorial waters was a matter of some controversy in the context of the current devolution arrangements. See para 6.13. But the Scottish Government's draft interim constitution of 2014 stated simply that the territory of Scotland would be what formed the territory of Scotland immediately before independence day.
2 See para 1.23 below.

Part 3: Rights and freedoms

1.5   Nothing in this description of our hypothetical model constitution should suggest that, after the preamble and some general matters, the provisions should be set out in any particular order. There are, logically, many different possibilities. It may, however, be natural for constitutional drafters to place the matters they consider to be of greater political or social significance before matters of lesser significance. For many, this means that guarantees given to citizens and others that their fundamental rights and freedoms will be respected should appear at an early point in a written constitution. Such guarantees are often contained in what is popularly called a 'Bill of Rights' which typically consists[1] of a list of rights and freedoms[2] (eg the right to life; freedom from torture, slavery and forced labour; the right to liberty and security; the right to a fair and public hearing; the prohibition of retrospective criminal offences; respect for private and family life; freedom of thought and religion; the right to education; freedom of expression, of assembly and of association; and others). Each of these rights is briefly defined and is then followed, in most cases, by a reference to the limited circumstances (which have usually to be defined by another law) in which it is to be treated as justifiable to have a restriction placed on the original right. Thus, for example, a person has a right to his or her liberty – but not where it is taken away following conviction of a criminal offence by a court. There may also be other provisions offering rather softer guarantees of what are called 'social and economic rights' – eg rights to an adequate standard of living including adequate food, clothing and housing[3]; and sometimes a right of access to official information – thus providing 'freedom of information' – may be assured. In addition, there may well be further rules thought necessary to ensure the effective implementation and enforcement of the guaranteed rights. It should be remembered, however, that the constitution has already been stated to be the highest form of law in the country. The impact of that core characteristic of a written constitution is well illustrated by the support it provides for the upholding of basic rights and freedoms. They are 'fundamental' both in their intrinsic importance but also in the legal status guaranteed to them by the constitution. However, many constitutions do declare certain rights to be fundamental but then fail to provide mechanisms which are effective enough to sustain them. In such cases, the declarations amount to no more than that. They may be made in good faith or they may be made more cynically as window dressing but they can be expected to have little or no effect on the ground.

1 Quite apart from a list of rights specified in the constitution, it may be expected that an independent Scotland would be a party to the European Convention on Human Rights. This might have the effect of further expanding or strengthening the Bill of Rights. See also ch 13 below. For fuller discussion, see R Reed and J Murdoch *A Guide to Human Rights Law in Scotland* (3rd edn, 2011); A Boyle et al (eds) *Human Rights and Scots Law* (2002).

2 The list chosen is based on that in the *IPPR Constitution*.

3 The South African constitution provides that everyone has the right to have access to adequate housing (s 26) and to health care services, sufficient food and water, and social security (s 27). The Scottish Government's draft interim constitution of 2014 paid special attention to equality rights, the wellbeing of children and the right 'to live in a healthy environment'.

Part 4: Nationality

1.6   Although many of the provisions (including human rights provisions) of a written constitution will apply to anyone present in the country, constitutions do, for some purposes, make separate provision for those who 'belong' there and those who do not, for instance in relation to the right to vote in elections[1]. Typically, such 'belonging' will be defined in terms of a concept of nationality or of citizenship[2]. It would, therefore, be for our hypothetical constitution to say who is to qualify for Scottish nationality or citizenship – usually done by reference to some prior nationality and then to place of birth, parentage or a rule of naturalisation by residence. Also included might be an acknowledgment of a Scottish citizen's wider citizenship of the European Union and of the rights of citizens of other European states in Scotland.

1   The right to vote is not necessarily confined to citizens. For current rules in Scotland, see paras 5.5 and 5.6.
2   Although, for some purposes, fairly permanent residence in the country may be sufficient, perhaps in combination with citizenship of some other specified state. See, in relation to electoral registration, para 5.6 below. On UK citizenship in general see ch 13.

Part 5: Head of state

1.7   Our hypothetical constitution might now be expected to include a series of parts or chapters which deal with the composition and functions of the principal organs of government. In relation to these we have to make certain assumptions about what these might be in our imagined version of an independent Scotland.

As far as the head of state is concerned, it can probably be assumed that, at least for a while, Scotland would remain a monarchy, with the king or queen inheriting the title by succession. Provision would be made for this[1]. The alternative would be for Scotland to follow Ireland and become a republic, with provision made for the election of a president for a specific period of years. Symbolically, much might hang on the choice that is made. A switch to a republic might carry with it the impression of a more far-reaching break with a monarchical past in the United Kingdom. In other respects, however, the distinction between the republican and monarchical models is less than might be expected because an almost certain characteristic of either model would be to restrict very sharply the real power of the president or monarch. He or she would have a ceremonial role; would preside on great occasions of state; and might have restricted and residual powers to act in circumstances not fully foreseen by the constitution. He or she would have what the English nineteenth-century writer Walter Bagehot called a 'dignified' rather than an 'efficient' role[2]. There are other possibilities and it is well known, for instance, that the presidents of the United States and of France do exercise real political and constitutional power. In all probability, however, our hypothetical head of state of an independent Scotland might have many important governmental powers allocated to him or her but these powers would, in almost all cases, be stated to be exercisable only on the instruction

5

or recommendation of ministers who would be the people to whom most of the real powers are given.

1 The SNP's draft constitution of 1991 provided that Queen Elizabeth (and her successors) would remain head of state, 'until such time as the people of Scotland decide otherwise'. The Scottish Government's draft interim constitution of 2014 also proposed that the Queen would remain the Head of State.
2 *The English Constitution* (with introduction by R H S Crossman, 1963) p 61. See also paras 7.1 and 7.2 below.

Part 6: The Executive

1.8   This and the next two parts of the constitution would probably make clear the three-partedness, the 'tripartism'[1], of most contemporary Western constitutions. For reasons to be developed later, constitutions tend to allocate different types of governmental power (usually dubbed executive, legislative or law-making, and judicial power) to different types of institution – the executive, the legislature (parliament) and the judiciary (courts). There must be a 'separation of powers'.

This terminology is not without difficulties and these are explored at a later stage[2]. For present purposes, however, there should be no difficulty in recognising executive powers as the powers vested in those who 'drive' the state – those who make plans, devise policies, make decisions, take action and compel others to act. Sometimes the terms 'government' and 'governmental' are used in ways which embrace the whole of executive, legislative and judicial power. More narrowly, the term 'government' can be confined to the executive branch alone and it is in this sense that, in all probability, our hypothetical constitution would identify the Prime Minister (or perhaps First Minister) and other ministers, as the 'Executive'[3]. There might also be provision for a Deputy Prime Minister and also for a 'cabinet' of senior ministers. There might be specific provision for these to include a Minister of Finance (or Chancellor of the Exchequer), a minister responsible for foreign or international matters, and a Minister for Justice. There would be separate provision for officials (who might or might not be ministers) known as 'Law Officers'[4]. There would have to be provision for the means of appointment of the Prime Minister and other ministers and also for the termination of their appointments. Almost certainly, these would be closely related, in the constitutional model we are describing, to the acceptability of the Prime Minister to the parliament (or, if there are two houses or chambers in the parliament, to the directly elected house) and then the acceptability of other ministers to the Prime Minister and perhaps also the parliament. In other words, the Parliament would, directly or indirectly, choose the Prime Minister and dismiss the Prime Minister, along with other ministers, if they lost its confidence. The Prime Minister would have the power to appoint other ministers, probably with the agreement of the Parliament, and to dismiss them. The parliamentary connection would probably be continued in another constitutional rule which would require ministers including the Prime Minister to be accountable and responsible to the parliament[5]. This parliamentary model of government, including a close relationship between the membership and operation of the executive and the legislature (sometimes called the 'Westminster model') is, again, not inevitable. Many constitutions draw a much stronger line between the executive and legislative branches of government. Elections to each are separately organised. Each branch exercises powers separately from the other. Neither branch is directly accountable to the other, although there may be points at which the two can interact in a system of 'checks and balances'. The US constitution provides a well developed version of this model. Its presidential rather than parliamentary form of government is defined by its directly elected president[6] and the allocation of executive authority, including the office of commander-in-chief of the armed forces, directly to the president. Whichever general model of executive government is adopted, a constitution may make further provision for the public service, in part to give permanent civil servants some protection from political interference; there may be outline provision for the ways in which the government will be funded and its accounts independently audited; and there may be provision for the organisation and control of the armed forces.

1 I D Duchacek *Power Maps: Comparative Politics of Constitutions* (1973).
2 See ch 2.
3 There are further terminology problems specific to the executive branch under the current devolution arrangements in Scotland. It was, during the first eight years of devolution, known as the Scottish Executive but was in 2007 styled the Scottish Government by the incoming SNP administration. The term 'Scottish Government' was formally adopted by the Scotland Act 2012, s 12. See para 7.1 below.
4 Who, if the UK model were followed, would have formal responsibility for representing the government in legal proceedings and for providing government with authoritative legal advice.
5 What is meant by 'accountability' and 'responsibility' in this context is discussed in ch 10.
6 Actually, although the president is *separately* elected, the election is not wholly *direct*. Formally (and indeed in ways which have practical consequences), popular votes in states are for the membership of an electoral college which then elects the president. See US Constitution, art II and *Bush v Gore* 531 US 98 (2000).

Part 7: The Legislature or Parliament

1.9   As already mentioned, primary law-making powers are routinely allocated to a body which is different from the executive. This is the legislature or parliament. Under the parliamentary model of government, it is also usual to allocate to the same body powers of supervision and control of the executive, especially in relation to financial matters. Constitutions are typically designed to ensure that parliaments are representative of the people and, therefore, that their members are directly elected by the people. Essential to our hypothetical constitution, then, would be provisions determining the size of the parliament, how long each parliament would last between elections (and, therefore, the frequency of elections), who could vote in elections, and what the voting system and other arrangements would be. Quite separately, a decision must be made on whether a directly elected chamber would be supplemented by a second chamber constituted, probably, on a different basis. Some parliaments (including, of course, the present UK Parliament with both the House of Commons and the House of Lords) are made up in such a 'bicameral' way. However it is constituted, the functions of the second chamber and its relationship to the first chamber need to be defined.

Part 8: The judiciary

1.10 The third element in the tripartite structure is the judiciary. A constitution must make provision for judges (in particular, rules for their appointment, their tenure of office and termination of office) and for the structure of courts. On judges themselves, our hypothetical constitution may be expected to provide for appointments to the senior positions to be by head of state but on the recommendation of a minister (in some cases, the Prime Minister), perhaps after initial selection or screening by an independent body with special expertise. Importantly, the constitution would ensure that only in exceptional circumstances and by exceptional procedures could a senior judge be dismissed.

Part 9: Territorial division and local government

1.11 One typical feature unlikely to be adopted into a Scottish constitution would be the division of the country into a number of states or provinces, each with its own constitutionally guaranteed autonomy, territory and governmental powers. Almost certainly, however, a system of local government would be retained and its permanence assured[1]. Beyond that, however, although a federal system of government might be an appropriate model for a country the size of the United Kingdom, the small size of the territory and population would almost certainly preclude it for Scotland. Federal systems can, however, take a number of different forms[2] and, although classic models may be identified in, for instance, the United States or Canada, other models of federalism or quasi-federalism tending towards the form of devolution currently adopted in the United Kingdom are possible. On the other hand, there might, for instance, be a case for giving a constitutionally guaranteed autonomy to Orkney, Shetland or the Western Isles[3]. More generally, the territorial division of the country and the installation of locally elected units of government can be used to give expression to the principle of 'subsidiarity'. This has been given formal recognition in the constitutional arrangements of the European Union but is of wider application. It asserts the value of conducting government at a level as close as possible to the people – whether that be for different purposes at the level of the European Union, state level, sub-state or regional level, or at the level of local government.

1 The European Charter of Local Self-Government (1985), to which the United Kingdom and all of the 47 members of the Council of Europe are parties, requires that a 'substantial share of public affairs' should be entrusted to local authorities (art 3(1)) and that the 'principle of local self-government shall be recognised in domestic legislation, and where practicable in the constitution' (art 2). See also ch 8.
2 K C Wheare *Federal Government* (4th edn, 1963).
3 The Scottish Government's draft interim constitution of 2014 contained such a clause.

Part 10: Constitutional amendment

1.12 Two earlier features of the constitution make necessary this final part. One is the power of the parliament to make laws. The other is the provision in part 2 which has made the law in the constitution supreme over other laws. From this it may be deduced that the parliament cannot, in the ordinary way, make laws at variance with the rules in the constitution. The parliament cannot simply amend the constitution by ordinary legislation.

It may, on the other hand, be anticipated that circumstances could arise in which it would be widely thought to be desirable that a particular provision of the constitution be amended. The need for amendments to a constitution can be linked to the point made earlier that a written constitution can be viewed as an expression of a community's values. Technological or social change may, for instance, demand revision of the constitution from time to time and we should expect that our hypothetical constitution would include a mechanism to achieve it[1]. This would almost certainly enable the parliament to make the amendment but would also require it to adopt special procedures; or to proceed only if a special majority of parliament agrees; or only if the amending law is also approved by a majority of the population of Scotland in a referendum. Sometimes different procedures are required for different provisions in a constitution, depending on how fundamental and how unalterable they are thought to be. Some provisions may be considered to be so fundamental that they are not amendable in any circumstances at all, although this can be taken to undesirable extremes.

1 In some measure, constitutions are, in effect, also amended when courts make a decision to interpret and apply constitutional provisions in a different way. See ch 14.

VIRTUAL CONSTITUTION TO REAL CONSTITUTION

1.13   We should once again remind ourselves that the constitution whose terms we were quickly reviewing in this chapter was indeed a figment of our joint imagination, assisted by the thoughts of those who have prepared actual drafts. There has been no separate or independent Scotland since 1707. Scotland does not have its own written constitution. What the provisions of the hypothetical constitution should, however, assist us in doing is two things. The first is to think a little further about what constitutions are and what constitutions and constitutional law do. The second is to draw comparisons between the imaginary and the real, the better to understand the real constitution of Scotland.

Constitutions and their function

1.14   With our hypothetical constitution in mind, we should have no difficulty at all in making sense of some quite cryptic definitions of constitutional law. Thus, from one source, we are told that UK constitutional law is that part of the law which 'governs the system of public administration of the United Kingdom, and relationships between the individual and the state'[1]. Another informs that the 'constitution' means 'the set of laws, rules and practices that create the basic institutions of the state, and its component and related parts, and stipulate the powers of those institutions and the relationship between the different institutions and between those institutions and the individual'[2]. And another that 'the word "constitution" [is] used to refer to the aggregate of those laws in a state which are styled collectively the public law'[3]. The late Professor Sir Neil MacCormick wrote of 'how powers and functions of government are divided among different agencies, and how checks and controls are then maintained between and within different branches of government'[4].

1 Lord Lester of Herne Hill and D Oliver (eds) *Constitutional Law and Human Rights* (1997) p 7.
2 A W Bradley, K D Ewing and CJS Knight *Constitutional and Administrative Law* (16th edn, 2014) p 4, quoting from a report of the House of Lords Committee on the Constitution (HL Paper 11 (2001–02), ch 2).
3 C R Munro *Studies in Constitutional Law* (2nd edn, 1999) p 1, quoting from Jeremy Bentham *Of Laws in General* (H L A Hart (ed), 1970).
4 N MacCormick *Institutions of Law* (2008) ch 3 'Law and the Constitutional State' at p 45.

1.15   What these definitions have in common is, first of all, some idea of a state with a territory and people. Secondly, there is an assumption that such a state will have institutions whose purpose is to discharge the functions of the state – functions which impose important burdens on the state but which also require that substantial powers are exercised by the state's institutions. Thirdly, it is assumed that these state-related powers and responsibilities are different in character from the powers and responsibilities of individual people and non-state organisations such as businesses, partnerships and companies. Often the distinction is drawn between *public law* which governs relationships between such public bodies themselves and also between public bodies and private individuals and organisations and, on the other hand, *private law* which regulates relationships between individuals and private organisations. Fourthly, it is the constitution that regulates, or at least provides a framework for, these state-based or public law relationships. Our hypothetical Scottish constitution is full of examples of this. The parts on the head of state, the executive, the legislature and the judiciary consist largely of rules which define the composition of the different institutions and define how the separate elements within each relate to each other and then how they relate to the other principal institutions and also, bearing in mind the part on rights and freedoms, how the institutions of government relate to the people. Thus the part on the legislature has to contain rules dealing with the powers and procedures of the parliament. As we have seen, rules have to define the composition of the parliament; they must state whether it is to be unicameral or bicameral and, if bicameral, determine the relationship between the two houses; they must provide for the separate functions of the presiding officer or chair of (each house of) the parliament. But rules in that part and in the part dealing with the executive must also define the relationship between the actual government in the shape of the prime minister and other ministers and the parliament itself. They must determine how far ministers may or must also be members of the parliament. They must provide the powers and mechanisms to enable the parliament to supervise the work of the executive and to ensure, if this is intended, that ministers are accountable or responsible to the parliament. Within the chapter on the executive, rules must define the relationships between prime minister, other ministers, the cabinet and the public service.

Meanwhile, the part on the legislature must also contain the rules which relate the people to the parliament through the election process and also by the opportunities provided for members of the public to question executive decisions and action by invoking the help of members of the parliament. Similarly, an important function of the part on the judiciary is not only to establish the courts themselves but also to provide a framework within which members of the public may then use the courts to question the legal validity of things done or decided by the executive and, probably, the parliament too. Significant for all these processes are the provisions which provide rights of access to information for members of the public and the part on rights and freedoms. A right to free expression or a right to liberty which is declared to be protected from restriction by the executive or by parliament or to be capable of restriction only in limited circumstances clearly does much to regulate the relationships between executive, parliament and people. In so far as the courts have a role in resolving any disputes that may arise when the limits of the guaranteed rights are challenged by either side, that relationship between the courts, the other branches of government and the people being regulated by the constitution has to be established.

It is unsurprising, in the light of what has been said so far, that many constitutional lawyers find it helpful to think of constitutions as 'maps'[1]. What constitutions are doing is charting, within the political system of a state, the formal distribution of power and authority in different sites and then showing the connections between the sites. Such a map is intended to be an accurate description of the present location of constitutional authority but it is also intended to endure. A constitutional earthquake might in a wholly unpredictable way destroy the map. This might be caused by a revolution within the state which overthrows the existing constitutional order. There may be circumstances in which, by agreement of all those with map-making authority, the map may be redrafted in the form of amendments to the constitution and the relocation of some constitutional authority to a different site. But the map should not be alterable in matters of substance simply at the hand of those who exercise power at only one point on it. Those who exercise power should not be free unilaterally to amend the map by extending their boundaries and staking out new territory on it.

1 See, in particular, I D Duchacek *Power Maps: Comparative Politics of Constitutions* (1973).

1.16   For some, the analogy of the map may be to adopt too flat an image of the functioning of a constitution. They may prefer a more sophisticated model in which the different relationships between constitutional sites are represented in a multi-dimensional way. The idea, however, that what constitutions do is to define limits of constitutional space; that they separate some elements (whether institutions or functions) from others; that they allocate areas of free movement or autonomy to people or to institutions and restrain the invasion of that autonomy by others is certainly at the heart of most people's conception of a constitution. The strategies, the techniques and the mechanisms of constitutional law are, above all, concerned with the definition and protection of areas of constitutional space within which autonomous but constrained authority may be exercised.

There is a fifth assumption that underpins almost every conception of constitutional theory. This is that there is an underlying purpose to constitutions and to constitution-making. Constitutional techniques and mechanisms do not exist for their own sake. Constitutional mapping is not *merely* an exercise in geometry or surveying. What, for many of its devotees, provides the purpose and even the passion of constitutional law is a belief that important values can be injected into and sustained within a political system by constitutional means. This has two aspects. The first is the identification of the values themselves and frequently this is a cause of controversy. There is clearly no necessary reason to suppose that political and constitutional values will be identical across the great religious, cultural and ideological divides. If the same terminology is used, it may in fact relate to widely differing ideals. Even in the context of liberal democratic politics, the content of values such as equality, liberty, justice and democracy may be contested but it is, nevertheless, values such as these that constitutional lawyers usually have in mind at the point where they engage in constitutional redesign or in the evaluation of existing designs. These are matters to which we return (with more specific reference to Scottish, UK and European constitutional law) but it should at this stage be observed that it is probably three inter-linked groups of values that are most prominent: (1) those concerned mainly with the condition of the people in the state, including not only human rights, freedom, equality and procedural and social justice but also benefits such as shelter, education and a good environment; (2) those relating to the quality of government, for example that it be honest, fair, accountable, democratic and participatory but also efficient; and (3) those relating to the state itself, such as the wish that it be independent from or in closer union with other states or that it should operate in a highly decentralised way, with power formally and irrevocably divided between the institutions of the central and federal government and those of the states or provinces or, less rigidly, in a system of devolution; or, alternatively, in a much more highly centralised way. Choices (sometimes, of course, sharply constrained) have to be made as to both the ends and also the means to be adopted to achieve those ends but it is with considerations of these sorts in mind that constitutional lawyers will evaluate particular rules and the interrelationships between institutions and people.

The second consideration to be borne in mind in the pursuit of political and social values by constitutional means is the important question of the effectiveness of constitutions in achieving the purposes which they proclaim. What particularly prompts this question is the evident 'failure' of many constitutions worldwide. The list of twentieth-century failures was very long and failures in constitution-making have continued in the twenty-first century in, for instance, north Africa and Iraq. Constitutions do not always achieve for their people the freedom or justice they seek. They fail to restrain dictatorial executive power or they fail to achieve the democratic conditions to which, on their face, they aspire. Failing constitutions are sometimes described as merely 'paper' constitutions. The reasons for failure are many and not always easy to understand. Often they may be the same reasons that lead to the failure of other sorts of law. Just as a law against drug abuse does not always end abuse, so a constitutional guarantee may often be ineffective and sometimes the reason for ineffectiveness is not hard to discern. It may be that blame can be attached to a particular provision that was inadequately thought about in advance. Sometimes ineffectiveness may be the result of inept 'borrowing' from other systems or from inept draftsmanship. It may simply have been sloppily crafted. It may have been too general in its terms when greater specificity would have helped. In relation to constitution-making for former British colonies in the second half of the twentieth century, Professor S A de Smith wrote of the 'advantages of being explicit'[1]. On the other hand, there are strong arguments in favour of the use of general language (and, at the same time, fewer words) in constitutions, in contrast with other types of legal documentation. Constitutions intended to endure may be better written in general terms rather than in highly specific language which may date rapidly. Another factor to be taken into account at that point, however, is the role of the superior courts in their interpretation of the terms of the constitution. This will always have a bearing upon the practical application of the constitution and, therefore, upon its effectiveness in the light of the meaning attributed to its terms by courts. In principle, the more general the language of the constitution, the greater the scope of interpretative freedom, and therefore power, which rests with the courts[2].

1 S A de Smith *The New Commonwealth and its Constitutions* (1964) p 82.
2 See ch 14.

1.17　　Rather differently, another reason for failure may be that a constitutional provision has from the start been included as a mere token and with a cynical or negligent lack of concern for its effective implementation. In such a case the 'failure' cannot be attributed to any weakness in the text of the constitution itself but to more fundamental flaws in the motivations of those who designed and established it. The 1936 Constitution of the former Soviet Union is often held up as a good example of constitutional deceit and manipulation. The rights it proclaimed for the citizens of the Soviet Union were always illusory, as was the declared right of states to secede from the union if they wished[1]. Such deliberate cynicism may be unparalleled but it has also to be acknowledged that, whether as a result of flamboyant overstatement of objectives sincerely wished or of baser motivations, many constitutions in the world have expressed an aspiration to create institutions or achieve goals which, on a more sober assessment, were never likely to be attainable. In such a situation the 'failure' of the constitution is incorporated from the outset. Although most striking examples of dislocation between the declared and more covert aims of constitutions are to be found in more distant systems[2] – in part because, in contrast with the United Kingdom, they put their purposes on the formal record – any critical inspection of the UK constitution will reveal similar failings[3]. Any such analysis is, in any event, complicated by the tensions in any pluralist liberal democracy between political and, therefore, constitutional goals. Although it may sometimes be hoped and asserted that the constitutional order maintains an impartial overview of social and political difference, this is never achievable. Constitutions may be expected to sustain some purposes and values at the expense of others.

1 See ch X (fundamental rights and duties of citizens) and art 17 (right freely to secede).
2 For a classic dissection of the US constitution, see C A Beard *An Economic Interpretation of the Constitution of the United States* (1913).
3 See I Harden and N Lewis *The Noble Lie: The British Constitution and the Rule of Law* (1986).

1.18   There are also more subtle and elusive ways in which constitutions may be said to fail. Constitutions are constitutions of states. They are primarily concerned, as we have said, with the regulation of the exercise of state power. Constitutions are, therefore, dependent upon the existence of states and state power and their role becomes problematic in times when the idea of the state is itself challenged, as may be said to be the case in the contemporary condition of 'globalisation'. If the power of states, whether benign or threatening, is declining in the face of larger economic and political forces, so too does the underlying rationale for constitutions. State power and its regulation decline in significance. The limits of personal liberty are determined less by state authorities than by supranational forces. To the extent that these trends occur, so the importance of national constitutional orders will decline. This is a development which is distinguishable from situations where states, most notably today the member states of the European Union, resolve to bind themselves by treaty to collective undertakings and the surrender of their separate sovereignties. There, state power is asserted but shared in ways which produce constitutional consequences of their own[1]. The impact of 'globalisation', on the other hand, may be to force a reduction in the authority and significance of constitutions of any sort[2].

1 See ch 3.
2 See N Walker 'The Idea of Constitutional Pluralism' (2002) 65 MLR 317; C M G Himsworth 'In a State No Longer: the End of Constitutionalism?' [1996] PL 639; G Anderson 'Scottish Public Law in an Age of Constitutional Globalisation' in A McHarg and T Mullen (eds) *Public Law in Scotland* (2006); N Walker, *Intimations of Global Law* (2015).

Constitutional law in Scotland

1.19   The second introductory project within this section is once again to return to the hypothetical constitution for an independent Scotland and to rely on it to draw two rather obvious points of comparison and contrast between that imaginary model and the present reality of constitutional law in Scotland.

Scotland, the United Kingdom and the European Union

1.20   The first point is that, since constitutions are, for the most part, an aspect of statehood and Scotland is not an independent state but a part of the UK state, it is to the level of the United Kingdom that we have to look, for most purposes, for a 'national' constitution. That is not to say that it is wholly meaningless to talk about a Scottish constitution or Scottish constitutional law in conditions where national independence is lacking. Scottish constitutional law and public law in general have distinguishing features which have to be taken into account in any broader description of UK constitutional law. Since 1999 the most significant of these features has been devolved government under the Scotland Act 1998 (SA 1998) and, although this terminology is not widely used, that Act can quite reasonably be described as a constitution for Scotland[1]. In federations it is usual to have both a national constitution and then separate state or provincial constitutions at the local level. During the twentieth century, it was quite usual to acknowledge that Northern Ireland had a constitution of its

own within the United Kingdom. The Government of Ireland Act 1920, which
provided the basis of the Stormont Parliament and devolution in the Province
from 1922 to 1972, was frequently referred to as a 'constitution'[2] and, although
never fully implemented, it was the Northern Ireland Constitution Act 1973
which repealed much of the Government of Ireland Act 1920 and would have
provided a new 'constitution'. SA 1998 may be seen in a similar way and the
resulting constitutional context is further considered in Chapter 3 – as well as
in the rest of the book, as more specific topics are considered.

1 Indeed, SA 1998, read in combination with the ECHR and European Union law, has been
 described judicially as a 'mini constitution' (see *Whaley v Lord Advocate* 2004 SC 78, para 37
 (Lord Brodie)). It has also been said of SA 1998 that it 'may reasonably be expected therefore to
 contain everything that is needed by way of legislation for the proper working out of the system
 that it lays down' (*Somerville v Scottish Ministers* 2008 SC (HL) 45 per Lord Hope of Craighead
 para 17).
2 See, eg, A S Quekett *The Constitution of Northern Ireland* (1928, 1933, 1946).

1.21 There is another important way in which our model constitution for an
independent Scotland has to be contrasted with real constitutional conditions.
Not only has Scotland to be seen for most important purposes as a part of
the United Kingdom but the United Kingdom, along with the other 27 states
of the European Union, has been constitutionally affected by membership of
the Union. There is indeed a sense in which the treaties which establish the
Union and create its institutions, including the Court of Justice of the European
Union, serve as a constitution of the Union of which the United Kingdom
and the member states are simply parts. Although the parallel is resented
politically in many quarters, there are good reasons from a legal perspective
for comparing the European Union with federations such as the United States,
Canada or Germany. In those the federal constitution is the highest form of law
and the constitutions of member states are subordinate to it. The parallel with
the European Union, though not perfect, can readily be drawn and this and
related matters are further addressed in Chapters 3 and 6.

The unwritten constitution of the United Kingdom

1.22 There is another immediate contrast to be drawn once we begin to
look to the real United Kingdom constitution rather than the hypothetical
Scottish version. Probably the best-known single characteristic of the UK
constitution is that it is 'unwritten'. What this means is that there is, for the
United Kingdom, no single document of high authority which, in the manner
we have described, sets out the core rules of the British constitution. The United
Kingdom is unique among modern states in having no written constitution[1]
and the inconvenience of this situation is evident in compendia such as the
online *Oxford Constitutions of the World* where the editors struggle to find
for the United Kingdom the documentation readily available for other states.
Some would say that the lack of a written constitution is indeed merely an
inconvenience. If we wish to identify for the United Kingdom the documents
which, were we to assemble them in one place, would provide the equivalent
of a written constitution, we can indeed draw together some (mainly statutory)
material for the purpose. Candidates would include the (English) Magna Carta

1215, the (English) Bill of Rights 1689, the Scottish Claim of Right 1689, the Acts of Union 1706 and 1707, the Parliament Acts 1911 and 1949, the Statute of Westminster 1931[2], the European Communities Act 1972 (ECA 1972), the British Nationality Act 1981 and the Equality Act 2010, as well as SA 1998, the Government of Wales Act 2006 (GWA 2006), the Northern Ireland Act 1998, the Human Rights Act 1998 (HRA 1998) and the House of Lords Act 1999. There are, however, a number of problems with this. Because we lack a written constitution, we lack a definition of what counts as a constitutional statute or a constitutional document when drawn from another source. Some UK statutes such as the Constitutional Reform Act 2005 and the Constitutional Reform and Governance Act 2010 provide a clue in their titles. Beyond those, however, it is a question of what is important or significant enough to be included. Criteria for including some documents and excluding others have to be developed. One criterion might be the status or the degree of formal authority of one statute compared with others but, again, it is partly because of the lack of a written constitution that we also lack any formal hierarchical ordering of rules. In the case of *Thoburn v Sunderland City Council*[3], Laws LJ did find it useful to identify what he called 'constitutional statutes' and his list included Magna Carta, the Union with Scotland Act 1706, the Reform Acts 1832, the ECA 1972, HRA 1998 and as well as SA 1998 and the Government of Wales Act 1998[4]. That list is, however, in no sense formally definitive. It would presumably have to change over time and its content would, in any event, be contested[5]. There is one formal statutory source which does provide an account of what may be defined as the essential elements of the UK constitution: for the purposes of defining and limiting the legislative powers of the Scottish Parliament, SA 1998 describes what is meant by the 'reserved aspects of the Constitution'. These include '(a) the Crown, including succession to the Crown and a regency, (b) the Union of the Kingdoms of Scotland and England, (c) the Parliament of the United Kingdom, (d) the continued existence of the High Court of Justiciary, (e) the continued existence of the Court of Session'[6]. Clearly that list, assembled for a very limited purpose, does not, in itself, amount to a written constitution for the United Kingdom but it does suggest that, despite the difficulties of identification and selection, it may be argued that, once the choices have been made, the United Kingdom can muster a written constitution. The rules are not in a single document but they are written down. They may lack the coherence and convenience of a single text but the collected documents can perform the same function.

1 From time to time, of course, states may have only an 'interim' constitution prior to the adoption of a permanent constitution, as was the case in South Africa between 1994 and 1997. As mentioned above, an interim constitution for Scotland was proposed by the Scottish Government in 2014.
2 Creating a new constitutional basis for the Commonwealth.
3 *Thoburn v Sunderland City Council* [2003] QB 151. See too *Imperial Tobacco Ltd v Lord Advocate* [2012] UKSC 61 para 15 (Lord Hope); *H v Lord Advocate* [2012] UKSC 24, 2012 SC (UKSC) 308 para 30 (Lord Hope). See ch 6.
4 *Thoburn v Sunderland City Council* [2003] QB 151 at 186.
5 See ch 6.
6 SA 1998, Sch 5, Pt I, para 1.

1.23   However, this would, be an unhelpful analysis for at least four reasons:

(1)   First, a collection of statutes, however put together, leaves gaps in the UK constitution. Many rules which, because of their constitutional significance, would have to be included in a full account do not derive from any statute or other formal documents at all. Their origin lies in the unwritten rules of the 'common law' rather than statute ranging from many of the rules which define police powers and the liberties of individuals through to the special 'prerogative' powers, formerly exercised by the monarch but now in the main by ministers, such as the power to declare war and manage foreign affairs, as well as the power to summon and dissolve Parliament. The common law as a source of constitutional rules is dealt with in Chapter 6 but, for present purposes, it is quite easy to see that such rules are not readily defined as 'written' and yet they are important. It is true that rules of the common law may be articulated, developed or at least referred to in the written judgments of courts and such judgments are frequently cited as the written sources of the rules, but they would not lie easily alongside statutes as part of a written constitution.

(2)   The other principal omission from a documentary account of the UK constitution would be those rules or practices usually referred to as 'constitutional conventions'[1]. Many of these are central to the United Kingdom's institutional arrangements where formal legal rules are absent or provide only a partial picture. It may perhaps seem strange that key institutions such as the Cabinet and the Prime Minister are not formally established by law; the subordination of the Queen (despite possessing a range of formal legal powers) to the Prime Minister and other ministers is similarly unknown to the law; the relationship between ministers and Parliament is not legally regulated; and relationships between the two Houses of Parliament are only partially defined by legal rules. These are, however, institutions and relationships which are of sufficiently high constitutional importance to have been directly incorporated in the export version of the Westminster model when it travelled to former colonies in the second half of the twentieth century. To take one off the peg, the independence constitution of Lesotho in 1966 expressly provided that the Cabinet should be collectively responsible to the Houses of Parliament[2], a position which is regulated only by convention in the United Kingdom. When such provisions are indeed incorporated into a written constitution, their formal status as legal rules becomes clear[3]. It may be said that a similar but more partial process has occurred in the adaptation of Westminster-based procedures by SA 1998. This makes clear, for instance, that the Queen formally approves the appointment of members of the Scottish Government, made by the First Minister[4]. That power to appoint is now statute-based. On the other hand, the Queen's obligation to approve the names tendered to her probably remains based on convention.

At the UK level itself, the position is less clear and accounts vary. It is possible to say that all that happens in the British constitution which is not directly regulated by law is 'mere politics'. One can, in other words, *describe* politically created institutions and their relationships but such descriptions can have no normative force. There are practices but no rules. At the other end of the spectrum are accounts which insist that rules do operate in these areas[5]. Such rules are not legal rules – no legal rule prescribes whom the Queen must appoint as Prime Minister[6] – but, as conventional rules or constitutional conventions, they operate to similar effect, save only that they are, by definition, unenforceable by courts. Courts may acknowledge the existence of political relationships within the constitutional order where these may have a bearing on what a related legal rule is or should be. For instance, the rules governing the ways in which judicial control is exercised over administrative action may take into account the political accountability of ministers to Parliament[7]. The politically based idea of collective responsibility within a Cabinet may influence the legally enforceable rule of confidentiality of Cabinet proceedings[8]. Collective responsibility has also been recognised in judicial analysis of parliamentary procedure[9]. But courts will not adjudicate upon the substance of 'rules' which have only a political or conventional basis[10].

The answer to the question of whether conventional practice can be the source of rules (albeit non legal) probably lies at a point between the two more extreme positions. This acknowledges that, in the large area of political behaviour in the United Kingdom that currently lies beyond the reach of formal legal regulation, distinctions have to be drawn. In some areas, such as those which define the individual[11] and collective[12] responsibility of ministers, few 'rules' seem to operate beyond those determined by the flexible pressures of political power and survival. It is largely meaningless to characterise behaviour as constitutional or unconstitutional. In other areas, the most important of which determines the constraints on the Queen's behaviour vis-à-vis her ministers, it does make sense to describe her role as normatively constrained. There are rules which should be observed and the Queen would act unconstitutionally if she breached them. We shall find that a non-legal rule has already emerged to govern the circumstances in which the Westminster Parliament may use its power to make laws for Scotland in the areas for which the Scottish Parliament[13] has legislative competence. In accordance with what has been named the 'Sewel Convention', this should occur only with the consent of the Scottish Parliament. Although this could never be directly restrained by a court, an Act passed by Westminster without such consent might well be regarded as having been passed unconstitutionally.

(3)   The third objection to the idea that a group of statutory texts can be recognised in the United Kingdom as the equivalent elsewhere of a written constitution is that its lack of coherence, its lack of any statement of overall constitutional ideals and objectives and, above all, the fact that it has never been formally adopted into use mean that it has little chance of claiming the loyalty, and even the affection, of the people. It is not, it is true, a constitution imposed by a foreign power but it is a constitution which has been imposed by history and subjected to only incremental change. None of these objections has stood in the way of the production of 'restatements' of UK constitutional practice – merging

both law and convention – in a tolerably coherent form. A prime example has been the Cabinet Manual[14]. First produced as a partial draft by the Cabinet Secretary prior to the 2010 general election as a contribution to understanding best practice if the election produced an inconclusive result, the Manual was published as a complete draft for consultation in December 2010 and then, in its first edition proper, in October 2011. It was claimed to be[15] 'primarily a guide for those working in government', 'a guide to the operation of the Government itself', but also setting out – 'from the point of view of the Executive – the Government's place in the UK's parliamentary democracy'. After a brief introduction, it includes chapters on the Sovereign, elections and government formation, the Executive (Prime Minister and Ministers), collective Cabinet decision-making, the Executive and Parliament, the Executive and the Law, and Relations with the Devolved Administrations and local government. It is descriptive in tone – Prime Minister Cameron, in a foreword, portrayed it as 'a record of fact' – and, though public, it does have an internal house-keeping feel to it. The Manual provides a clear, coherent and yet concise (just over 100 pages) introduction to the institutions of the UK constitution and their inter-relationships. Despite its lack of 'official' status[16], its endorsement by the Cabinet gives it a high measure of predictive authority, especially in relation to the convention-regulated aspects of the constitution[17]. During 2014, the House of Commons' Political and Constitutional Reform Committee (PCRC) conducted a review of the Manual's contribution[18].

It was the PCRC itself which was the source of the other 'restatement'. In July 2014, the Committee published a report[19] whose primary aim was to consult on ways in which constitution-making might be taken forward[20]. In particular, the report offered three different options for the production of a codified constitution: (1) a constitutional code, sanctioned by Parliament but without statutory authority and which (not unlike the Cabinet Manual) would set out the essential existing elements and principles of the constitution and the workings of government; (2) a Constitutional Consolidation Act which would be a consolidation of existing laws and conventions of a constitutional nature in statute; (3) a full written constitution. The report offered illustrative blueprints.

(4)   The fourth objection is the most fundamental. One of the principal purposes of practically all modern written constitutions is to assert their own supremacy. This is not mere rhetoric. It is not supremacy for its own sake but rather a supremacy which creates a hierarchy in which constitutional rules are at the top and all other rules, including, most importantly, the laws made by the Parliament, are subordinated to them. Parliamentary laws which are not in accordance with the constitution are invalid – a proposition which, in turn, almost inevitably, demands that the courts (or a single court) must have the power to determine the validity or not of the laws made by the legislature[21].

It is this which makes the difference. It is the lack of supremacy of the constitution and, therefore, the lack of a judicial power to review the validity of Acts of Parliament which most sharply distinguish the United Kingdom's constitutional arrangements from almost all written constitutions. Instead of an ultimate rule of the constitutional order (for Hans Kelsen[22], the *grundnorm*) which directs courts to obey the constitution and thus, if necessary, to defy Acts of Parliament, there is, in effect, a *grundnorm* which directs courts to obey all Acts of Parliament without the option of defiance. In the United Kingdom, it is Parliament which is supreme, rather than a written constitution[23]. This has profound consequences for the UK constitutional order and the position of Scotland within it. Constitutional amendment becomes a matter for Parliament itself in the ordinary process of legislation rather than some special procedure under the supervision of a controlling court[24]. It is for this reason that if, failing a court, a 'constitutional long-stop' is sought for the protection of the constitution from manipulation by the party politically dominated House of Commons, this is, for some, to be found in the UK Parliament's second chamber, the House of Lords. Although the formal capacity of that House to restrain the law-making powers of the House of Commons has been very largely confined to a power of delay rather than of veto, the House of Lords, equipped with a Select Committee on the Constitution to assist it in the process, is widely seen to perform a 'long-stop' role[25].

1 The term is not to be confused with the 'constitutional convention' which is a meeting of worthy people convening for the purpose of devising the terms of a new constitution, such as that held in Philadelphia in 1787 – and perhaps the European Convention which met during 2002–03 to discuss the constitution of the European Union.
2 Constitution of Lesotho (1966), s 73(2).
3 Although there *may* still be doubt about the justiciability and, therefore, the enforceability of such rules in the courts.
4 SA 1998, s 47(1), and see para 7.13.
5 I Jennings *The Law and the Constitution* (5th edn, 1959) ch III.
6 See, para 7.5 below.
7 See, eg the speech of Lord Mustill (although a dissent) in *R v Home Secretary, ex parte FBU* [1995] 2 AC 513 at 567.
8 *A–G v Jonathan Cape Ltd* [1976] QB 752.
9 See *R(HS2 Action Alliance Ltd) v Secretary of State for Transport* [2014] 2 All ER 109 at paras 58, 66 and 70 (Lord Reed).
10 Although, in Canada, the Supreme Court did rule on whether there had been a breach of convention in *Reference re Amendment of the Constitution of Canada* (1982) 125 DLR (3d) 1.
11 See para 10.2.
12 See paras 7.10 and 7.18.
13 See para 6.12.
14 Cabinet Office, 2011.
15 According to the Preface by the Cabinet Secretary.
16 The Manual appears to have gone unremarked upon in UK courts.
17 See eg below at para 7.5 for its relevance to the 'rules' on government formation.
18 See HC 233 (2014–15).
19 *A New Magna Carta?*, HC 463 (2014–15).
20 In some respects expanding upon an earlier report, *Do we need a constitutional convention for the UK?*, HC 371 (2012–13).
21 For the confirmation of that power in the United States, see *Marbury v Madison* 5 US 1 Cranch 137 (1803).
22 *Pure Theory of Law* (2nd edn, tr M Knight, 1970).
23 See ch 6.
24 See discussion of this by the House of Lords Select Committee on the Constitution and its rejection of suggestions for the adoption of a special procedure for Bills of 'first class constitutional significance': *Changing the Constitution: The Process of Constitutional Change*, Fourth Report HL 69 (2001–02), paras 59–61.

25 See Report of the (Wakeham) Royal Commission *A House for the Future* (Cm 4543, 2000) ch 5; *Fifth Report of the House of Commons Public Administration Committee*, HC 49 (2001–02) paras 72–75; *First Report of the Joint Committee on House of Lords Reform*, HL 17, HC 171 (2002–03), p 10.

1.24   However, although it has generally been right to conclude that the British constitution is not one which has been policed by courts but has instead sought a political underpinning, things may now be in a state of flux. In ways to be discussed in Chapter 14, the courts have taken on a wider role, especially under HRA 1998 and the devolution Acts (with subsequent amendments) also of 1998, which may, for good or ill, expand into a broader capacity to undertake a form of constitutional review. It would be at that stage that, with an increasing part of the constitution committed to writing and a shift of final decision-making authority from the political to the judicial organs, the United Kingdom would become more closely aligned with other Western democracies. Until that stage is reached, however, constitutional developments will remain a matter, if not of political whim, of political debate and resolution.

Chapter 2

Constitutional Law and Constitutional Values

INTRODUCTION

2.1   It is often the case that written constitutions expressly incorporate a statement of principles or values which the constitution claims to uphold[1]. Such statements may take different forms – sometimes quite short and simple, sometimes more elaborate. Often the statement will not be included in the text of the constitution itself but will instead take the form of a preamble to the constitution which claims to declare in advance the goals which the constitution makers are seeking to achieve by the substantive rules which follow. A list of principles or values inserted in this way can include principles which are not strictly legal in character but which are more broadly social or political; they may be intended to be not directly enforceable by courts, while still available to aid courts where difficulties in the interpretation of specific clauses in the constitution arise; and they may be cast in very general terms. An example of a constitutional preamble of this sort which is frequently cited is that of the Indian Constitution of 1950. It is committed to securing for all citizens:

> JUSTICE, social, economic and political; LIBERTY of thought, expression, belief, faith and worship; EQUALITY of status and opportunity; and to promote among them all FRATERNITY assuring the dignity of the individual and the unity and integrity of the Nation.

The Constitution of the United States provides:

> We, the People of the United States, in order to form a more perfect Union, establish Justice, insure domestic Tranquillity, provide for the common defence, promote the general Welfare, and secure the Blessings of Liberty to ourselves and our Posterity, do ordain and establish this Constitution for the United States of America.

The South African Constitution proclaims that it was adopted to:

> Heal the division of the past and establish a society based on democratic values, social justice and fundamental human rights; Lay the foundations for a democratic and open society in which government is based on the will of the people and every citizen is equally protected by law; Improve the quality of life of all citizens and free the potential of each person; and Build a united and democratic South Africa able to take its rightful place as a sovereign state in the family of nations.

These constitutional texts all provide interesting examples of preambles designed to give specific recognition to the values intended to be sustained by the provisions which follow. Such preambles are not, however, an

23

inevitable element of a written constitution and, in many constitutions, they are omitted. Although the Indian Constitution did contain a substantial preamble, most of the other constitutions devised for newly independent states in the Commonwealth in the 1950s and 1960s did not[2]. This does not mean, however, that the constitution-makers involved were any less concerned to ensure that their constitutional texts reflected similar constitutional values. It was simply that their preferred drafting technique led them not to include formal statements but instead to leave any underlying principles or values to be deduced from the rules of the constitution actually laid down; implied from the text, rather than expressly stated. Most obviously, a written constitution which includes a Bill of Rights makes a strongly implied commitment to the underlying value to individuals of the rights and freedoms it contains. The incorporation of rules for the popular election of a Parliament may be taken to imply a commitment to principles of representative democracy. The adoption of a model of federal government which divides powers between central and regional authorities implies a commitment to the values of a democratic system which deliberately seeks to avoid the concentration of political power in a single central government. A constitution which expressly or impliedly confers strong powers on a constitutional court or on the judicial system in general demonstrates a preference – sometimes stronger, sometimes weaker – for the resolution of certain types of dispute by a court rather than by politicians.

Thus, the fact that a written constitution does not include a declaration of values and principles expressly articulated in a preamble to the main text should not at all be taken to mean that the constitution, taken as a whole, makes no commitment to a set of principles which inform its operation. Certain problems, however, attach to this process, whichever method is adopted. The principles asserted, whether expressly or impliedly, may not be all they seem. They may have a very vague and general character and they may not be intended to be directly enforceable by courts. This may easily lead to big differences between the principles proclaimed by the constitution on the one hand and their actual realisation in practice on the other. Whether intentionally or not, statements of principle tend to tell only a part of the story. They attempt to conceal contradictions between values; they select heavily in favour of those principles likely to show the constitution in a good light; they tend to be aspirational and ideological; and, at worst, they are a complete sham. Discrepancies between the assertion and reality of constitutional values and goals may be much greater[3].

When we come to examine the constitutions of Scotland and the United Kingdom, we find that the lack of a written constitution clearly rules out the possibility of any single authoritative statement of constitutional principles and values. Similarly, the opportunity is denied to derive from a single constitutional text a group of implied principles which might be said to underpin the constitutional order. However, this should not prevent us from describing the values which are claimed to be inherent in British constitutional arrangements. The lack of a single document may complicate this process a little and there is the added complication of the long period of historical development which is such an important feature of the UK constitution. This is also true, of course, of other enduring constitutions but it is certainly the case that accounts of the principles which underpin the UK constitution have changed over time and they continue to change. Just as statements contained in written constitutions will tend to be a response to conditions of the time of their making and will reflect the concerns and aspirations of that time, so too do statements about the unwritten British constitution. They vary over time, if only in the degree of emphasis given to different aspects from one commentator to another. There is nothing politically neutral about constitutional principles. In a UK context, a nationalist will attach great importance to the recognition given by the constitution to the separate 'nations' of the United Kingdom. A unionist will take a different view. Republicans and monarchists will disagree about the best form of the state. Different views will be taken of the value of human rights and their relative significance. Sometimes issues will divide the political left and right but, at other points, divisions will be along other lines. While such disagreements (whether about the principles themselves or the best means of pursuing them) are inevitable, they do nothing to diminish the need for any student of the constitution to have available a more or less coherent set of principles and standards against which the working of the constitution can be assessed and evaluated. They may not have any formal constitutional status but such principles and standards have an important bench-marking function as a tool of constitutional analysis. Thus, although the absence of a formal statement leaves us free to choose constitutional benchmarks of our own devising, there is merit in choosing standards associated with the liberal democratic tradition within which the UK constitution is claimed to operate and, if a written constitution were ever devised, would perhaps be asserted in its introductory preamble. For a start, despite the absence of a formal domestic constitutional statement, the United Kingdom has expressed itself bound by the standards imposed by many international documents. European Union law is of authoritative standing in the United Kingdom and it is the Treaty on European Union which, among other things, confirms in its preamble the Union's 'attachment to the principles of liberty, democracy and respect for human rights and fundamental freedoms and of the rule of law'. The United Kingdom is a party to the European Convention on Human Rights (ECHR) which has been applied by the courts in both the period before and since its 'incorporation' by the Human Rights Act 1998 (HRA 1998)[4]. In addition to the rights themselves, the preamble to the Convention commits members of the Council of Europe to the 'profound belief in those fundamental freedoms which are the foundation of justice and peace in the world' and reminds of the 'common heritage of political traditions, ideals, freedom and the rule of law'. And all 53 members of the Commonwealth, including the United Kingdom, committed themselves, in a 'Charter of the Commonwealth' (2013)[5] to upholding fundamental principles including democracy, human rights, the separation of powers, the rule of law and good governance.

With commitments such as these as a backdrop, this chapter focuses discussion on three areas:

(1) individual liberty and its protection (a short note only);
(2) standards of good governance, integrating within these the idea of the separation of powers;

(3)   the distinctive idea of accountability of government to the law, often referred to as the rule of law. Included in this account is discussion of the idea of a 'right to law'.

1 See para 1.3 above.
2 S A de Smith *The New Commonwealth and its Constitutions* (1964).
3 See the reference to the USSR at para 1.7 above.
4 See ch 14.
5 The Charter was assembled from a number of previous declarations (including the Harare Declaration of 1991) and statements of principles.

INDIVIDUAL LIBERTY AND ITS PROTECTION

2.2   There is little doubt that most people would proclaim the attainment of the liberty of the individual as one of the most fundamental purposes of a constitution. State institutions, whether in the form of kings or modern bureaucracies, have a tendency to oppress[1] and it should be the function of a constitution to protect individuals from that oppression. This is an imperative which has to be linked with the idea of good governance which is discussed below, at which point it will also be recognised that governments, while being restrained from oppression, must also be facilitated in the discharge of their lawful functions. The protection of individual liberty is also closely related to the idea of accountability to the law and the rule of law.

When indeed Professor Dicey propounded his analysis of the rule of law in 1885, he declared that it could at that time be said that the constitution was 'pervaded by the rule of law on the ground that the general principles of the constitution (as, for example, the right to personal liberty, or the right of public meeting) are with us the result of judicial decisions determining the rights of private persons in particular cases brought before the courts; whereas under many foreign constitutions the security (such as it is) given to the rights of individuals results, or appears to result, from the general principles of the constitution'[2]. For Dicey, personal liberty was very important. Whether or not he was right to say that it was better protected, as an aspect of the rule of law, by court decisions in their development of the common law than by express provision in a constitutional document is debatable. What is clear, however, is that, by the end of the twentieth century, there was a near consensus in the UK Parliament that this was insufficient, and the country's adherence from 1951 to the European Convention on Human Rights was relied on to provide the basis for the incorporation by HRA 1998 of a new system of rights protection. These developments are pursued further in Chapter 13.

1 Even though an important function of governmental institutions may be to shield a state's citizens from the ravages of markets.
2 A V Dicey *Law of the Constitution* (10th edn, 1959) p 195.

STANDARDS OF GOOD GOVERNANCE

Introduction

2.3   Constitutions are expected to deliver not only protection for the rights of individuals but, just as importantly, the conditions under which the institutions of government can secure social goods to the population at large. At some points the two objectives are entirely complementary. It is often through the delivery of public services that rights are also secured. At other points there is some tension between the two. The state acts in the general interest but only at the price of some interference with the rights of individuals. For many of its services, the state must have the power to obtain funding through the imposition of taxation. It must have the power to acquire land and to restrict the use of land and other property. The state also claims the power to license trades and professions and to regulate commercial and industrial activity in the interests of securing competitive conditions of operation, the health and safety of employees or the quality of the environment. In support of these powers, the state needs also to claim ancillary powers to enforce the governmental regimes that are established. At their most extreme, these involve imposing criminal penalties for non-compliance with the rules laid down. Thus, the administration and enforcement of governmental programmes often carry with them the danger of interference with the rights of individuals. The use of the state's powers and, even more, the abuse of those powers will always bring that possibility. And this is the case whatever the political tendencies of particular governments. The twentieth century saw fluctuations in the political programmes of governments including varying attitudes to how government in general should be conducted and the overall size of the government machine. But, whether one thinks of the period of nationalisation of industry after the 1939–45 war or of the Thatcherite determination to restrict the size and power of the state in the 1980s, similar questions are raised about how quality of governance is to be achieved. Nor is this merely a question of balancing public policy considerations against the rights of individuals, although that is clearly a matter of importance. Good governance also involves the attainment of standards of wider scope and it is these to which constitutions are also expected to aspire.

Traditionally, the emphasis in most accounts of constitutional values has been upon the dangers of abuse of governmental power and, therefore, upon the adoption of principles which might restrain those abuses. That approach remains important and some aspects of it are to be considered shortly. It is, however, important also to recognise that the point of restraining abuse of government is not ultimately to achieve no government at all but to achieve better government. This is not to suggest that there are objective criteria for the evaluation of particular governmental policies and programmes. These are matters on which, of course, reasonable people and, in particular, political parties, disagree. However, what can be agreed is that government should be enabled to be efficient and effective and a constitution which fails in this respect fails to meet the most important criterion of good governance. Beyond that, though, principles of good governance demand the injection of democracy; of decentralisation or subsidiarity[1]; of government which is free from corruption, unfair discrimination, illegality and maladministration; and of openness and transparency. Such a list is very general in nature and it is the stuff of constitutional debate to determine to what extent and in what ways these values should be represented in the institutions and procedures of a particular state. In the United Kingdom a particular focus has been placed in recent years upon the qualities which should be displayed by the public services. These have been expressed by the Committee on Standards in Public Life[2] as the 'Seven Principles of Public Life': selflessness, integrity, objectivity, accountability, openness, honesty and leadership. When the EC Commission published its White Paper on *European Governance* in 2001, its choice of 'principles of good governance' was openness, participation, accountability, effectiveness and coherence, all of which were stated to reinforce the further principles of proportionality and subsidiarity[3]. The UK Parliamentary Ombudsman has published *The Principles of Good Administration*[4].

1 See para 1.1 above.
2 First established in October 1994 and currently chaired by Lord Paul Bew.
3 COM (2001) 428 ch II.
4 Revised, 2009.

The principle of accountability

2.4   Above all else, good governance necessarily implies a commitment to the principle of accountability – a quality common to both the lists above[1]. This takes several different forms. Perhaps the most important is accountability of government to the law which, as the rule of law, is considered in the next section. The financial accountability of government is also important and is reflected in the audit and other mechanisms established with a view to securing financial propriety[2]. Accountability to ombudsmen in respect of maladministration has been developed across much of British public administration[3]. Overriding all these, however, in any liberal democracy is the claim made by institutions of government to be democratically accountable to the people. Such accountability is typified by the responsibility of ministers to the Westminster and Scottish Parliaments[4] but it is represented too in the accountability of elected local councils[5]. Neither of these models – central or local – provides the basis for a direct or 'pure' democracy in which the people themselves are seen to govern. Frequent elections combined with mechanisms of accountability between elections provide only an indirect form of democracy. The intermittent, though perhaps increasing, use of referendums to test public opinion on specific issues of importance[6] does not alter this position significantly. Another important feature of this constitutional order which gives general recognition to democratic principles is that it incorporates substantial variations in their application. In some areas democratic accountability is much more immediate and direct than in others. A lack of direct accountability may be the result of systemic failure and, as an example, the difficulties of giving effect to the principle of ministerial responsibility are considered in Chapter 10. At other points, however, the reduced application of democratic accountability is the result of deliberate decisions that this should be the case. For varying reasons, those bodies, grouped collectively as 'intermediate government' or 'quangos', are deliberately intentionally placed at arm's length from direct democratic control[7]. To an extent, the emergence of 'executive agencies' within UK government departments and the Scottish Administration has the same effect[8]. At all those points where general principles of open government give way to exceptional restrictions on public access, the scope for direct democratic accountability is reduced[9].

1 See D Oliver *Constitutional Reform in the UK* (2003) ch 3.
2 See para 11.14.
3 See para 10.11.
4 See para 10.2.
5 See ch 8.
6 Other modern instances have been the devolution referendums in Scotland and Wales in September 1997 (see para 3.19); and in Northern Ireland in 1998. A referendum might be held on the question of the UK's adoption of the euro currency. In 1975, a referendum was held on the UK's continued membership of the EC. In March 1979 referendums were held in Scotland prior to the (non-) implementation of the Scotland Act 1978 and the Wales Act 1978. More recently a UK-wide referendum was held in 2011 on the reform of the voting system (see para 5.7) and, most famously, there has been the Scottish independence referendum of 2014 (see ch 4).
7 See ch 8.
8 See ch 7.
9 See ch 10.

Separation of powers

2.5   Common to all relationships of accountability (democratic, legal and others) is the need to establish institutions whose membership, powers and procedures give them the degree of autonomy necessary to enable them to perform the function of holding to account which is allocated to them. To achieve the accountability of government to the law there must be a judiciary capable of acting sufficiently independently of the governmental bodies it is supposed to control. The principle of the independence of the judiciary, which is considered in Chapter 12, has a clear pre-eminence, despite its own complexities. That principle is, however, usually seen as one manifestation – and probably the most prominent manifestation – of a more general principle of the separation of powers. This is an idea of great antiquity in the history of thought about good governance – certainly one which predates modern conceptions of constitution-making and constitutionalism. Its age gives the doctrine of the separation of powers both its attraction as an honoured principle but also its crudeness as an analytical benchmark. Its limitations are particularly apparent in relation to constitutions based on the parliamentary form of government.

It is with the name of Montesquieu[1], the eighteenth-century French philosopher, that the doctrine of the separation of powers is principally associated. In his *De l'Esprit des Lois* (1748) he articulated a view of the British constitution as one which had achieved a separation of legislative, executive and judicial powers as the basis of securing the life and liberty of the subject. Even though a misleading description of the British constitution, then or now, the idea of the separateness of powers was enormously influential in constitution-making elsewhere, notably in the United States Constitution of 1787 whose opening articles are deliberately structured around the need for a separate legislature in the Congress[2], executive in the President[3], and judiciary in the Supreme Court and other federal courts[4]. Despite the superimposition on that division of institutions and functions of 'checks and balances' producing some interaction between the three sectors (eg the Senate's powers over presidential appointments to the Supreme Court and elsewhere) and the inevitable intermingling of party politics, the separation is real. The Supreme Court does have a large degree of independence and the separate elections to the presidency and the Congress ensure clear blue institutional water between the two. On the other hand, when export models of the UK constitution are committed to paper and also deal separately with the parliament, government and judiciary, the separateness is, beyond its presentational convenience, much less secure. In systems of parliamentary government, there *are* good reasons for insisting on a principled independence of the judiciary but the merger of powers and personnel between the executive and legislature means that any true separation of those branches of government is elusive. Legislative power is substantially shared between the parliament (whether, for instance, at Westminster or Holyrood) and the executive. Governments dominate primary law-making and have broad powers of secondary law-making[5]. The accountability of government to parliament on the one hand denies a separation between the two but, to an extent, insists upon it[6].

However, this does not mean that, viewed more broadly, respect is not paid to the value of institutional autonomy. Indeed, a complex and sophisticated pattern of autonomies is readily detectable. Apart from the functional autonomy sought on a territorial basis by the local government system[7] and by devolution itself, most examples are to be found in those bodies whose raison d'être is the scrutiny of the executive or where, for other reasons, it is thought desirable that a body should be free from direct control of ministers. The separation of powers becomes a principle which is much more significant as a basis for division of authority *within* the executive branch of government than between the executive and the legislature. This has been one of the justifications for the creation of many quangos[8] which then depend for their autonomy upon their separately conferred powers and protection from overt political control over appointments to and dismissals from the senior positions. In turn, this is what has driven the work of the Committee on Standards in Public Life and the Commissioner for Ethical Standards in Scotland when dealing with appointments to public bodies and, in the case of some high-profile bodies, statutory protections, similar to those afforded to judges, are built in. Thus the Scottish Public Services Ombudsman is appointed by the Crown but on the nomination not of the Scottish Ministers but of the Parliament. And he would be dismissible only following a resolution of the Parliament passed by a two-thirds majority of MSPs[9]. The Auditor General for Scotland is in a similar position[10]. In both cases, the official whose independence needs to be safe-guarded is protected from dismissal on the whim of the government. Similarly, because the supervision of elections is plainly a sensitive area, the Electoral Commissioners are appointed by the Queen but only on an Address from the House of Commons and then only with the agreement of the Speaker and following consultation with leaders of the political parties[11]. A dismissal would require a House of Commons Address preceded by a report from the Speaker's Committee[12] specifying the justification for the dismissal on limited statutory grounds[13]. In 2014, legislation created a new body to collect and manage devolved taxes in Scotland. The independence of Revenue Scotland is statutorily declared. Ministers are forbidden to seek to control it[14]. Another important area of institutional autonomy within the executive, and one of much greater antiquity, is that occupied by the law officers – members of the government itself and yet independent from government for the purpose of their major functions[15].

Separation of powers, broadly conceived, has also been important at the heart of central government itself. Differentiating clearly between the role of elected and politically driven ministers, on the one hand, and appointed, politically neutral civil servants, on the other, and then regulating relationships between the two groups, has long been a matter of constitutional concern[16]. There has to be a 'separation' between ministers and civil servants in general and then the creation of a relationship in which ministers can, subject to rules protecting their professional autonomy, direct civil servants in what they do. But, for some purposes, particular civil servants are given an enhanced autonomy enabling instead the scrutiny of ministers by them. This is the position of accounting or accountable officers whose duty it is to monitor the financial propriety of their own ministers[17]. Latterly, another element has been added – the civil servants who *do* have a political role or, as they have come to be known, 'special advisers' – and this has heightened the need for careful thought about appropriate relationships within government. The problems were nicely explored in a report, which explicitly incorporated the imagery of territorial relationships, of the Committee on Standards in Public Life[18]. Entitled *Defining the Boundaries within the Executive: Ministers, Special Advisers and the Permanent Civil Service*, the report discussed the boundaries and relationships, at one point the 'chemistry of relationships' (para 3.6), within the constitutional framework, the changing landscape of government and the need for the boundaries to be 'secured', principally by means of a new Civil Service Act[19].

A feature of that Standards Committee report is its insistence on the need for express regulation of a sector in which questions about boundaries had always been there but had not, until recently[20], been the cause of great concern. Things had, in the main, simply 'worked', despite some uncertainties and contradictions in the applicable rules. This reflects a wider approach in the United Kingdom to institutional analysis and reform of the 'If it ain't broke, don't fix it' school. There had been a tendency to try to leave unreformed those aspects of the constitution which, although on their face indefensible in principle, were nevertheless thought to 'work'. Nowhere was this more apparent than in the formerly combined roles of the Lord Chancellor – a senior minister who appointed judges and was the head of the English judiciary and 'convener' of the House of Lords – and, in particular, in the defence of those roles by a former holder of the office[21]; Lord Irvine of Lairg:

> We are a nation of pragmatists, not theorists, and we go quite frankly for what works. I would say that for countries emerging for the first time and trying to gain the attributes of a mature democracy, a much stricter doctrine of separation of powers would be appropriate than is appropriate for us who represent a very old and well-founded democracy in which those values are well understood and upheld ... We do not want to make changes for the sake of it or for academic reasons or to conform to some kind of universal paradigm of how we manage our affairs, but we should look to see what works[22].

But a more principled approach was shortly to prevail. The UK Supreme Court, in which the Lord Chancellor (no longer a judge or necessarily legally qualified) does not sit, was established[23]; and the Judicial Appointments Commissions/ Boards effectively became responsible for judicial appointments[24].

1   Charles de Secondat, Baron de Montesquieu.
2   US Constitution, art 1.
3   US Constitution, art 2.
4   US Constitution, art 3.
5   See ch 9.
6   See ch 10.
7   See ch 8.
8   See ch 8.
9   Scottish Public Services Ombudsman Act 2002, sch 1, para 4(1)(d).
10 Scotland Act 1998 (SA 1998), s 69(1), (2). The Comptroller and Auditor General is similarly protected. See Exchequer and Audit Departments Act 1866, s 3.
11 Political Parties, Elections and Referendums Act 2000 (PPERA 2000), ss 1 and 3.
12 The Speaker, two ministers, the chairman of the Political and Constitutional Reform Committee (all ex-officio) and five other MPs.
13 PPERA 2000, s 2 and Sch 1.
14 Revenue Scotland and Tax Powers Act 2014, s 7.
15 See N Walker '*The Antinomies of the Law Officers*' in M Sunkin and S Payne (eds) *The Nature of the Crown* (1999).
16 See para 7.23.
17 See para 11.14.
18 Ninth Report, (Cm 5775 (2003)).
19 For further discussion, see para 7.23.
20 See *Eighth Report of the House of Commons Public Administration Select Committee: Three Unfortunate Events* (HC 303) (2001–02).
21 Currently the role is combined with that of Secretary of State for Justice.
22 Evidence to the House of Commons Select Committee on the Lord Chancellor's Department, 2 April 2003 paras 28, 46. See also the evidence of Mr E Jurgens to the same Committee on 27 March 2003.
23 See para 12.2.
24 See para 12.5.

THE RULE OF LAW

Introduction[1]

2.6   Like the doctrine of the separation of powers, the rule of law is a long-standing concept in the history of constitutional theory. But, again, it is an idea whose meaning and utility have changed greatly over time. Aristotle's notion of government by laws being superior to government by men may carry little meaning today. On the other hand, Voltaire's preference for a land 'where men were ruled by law and not by caprice'[2] is wholly comprehensible. Professor Dicey gave a central position to his version of the rule of law but it is one which now has a much-reduced relevance. For him, the idea of the supremacy or the rule of law included at least three 'distinct though kindred conceptions'. It meant, first, that 'no man is punishable or can be lawfully made to suffer in body or goods except for a distinct breach of law established in the ordinary legal manner before the ordinary Courts'; second that 'not only … with us no man is above the law, but (what is a different thing) that here every man, whatever, be his rank or condition is subject to the ordinary law of the realm and amenable to the jurisdiction of the ordinary tribunals'; and, third, that 'the general principles of the constitution (as for example the right to personal liberty, or the right of public meeting) are with us the result of judicial decisions determining the rights of private persons in particular cases brought before the Courts'[3].

Over a century later, some aspects of this account still have attractions as a grounding for good governance. It is underpinned by assumptions that government should be conducted in accordance with the law; that the law should be administered by independent courts; and that the law should be administered in accordance with basic principles of equality. On the other hand, Dicey's insistence on a privileged but piecemeal role for the common law has lost its meaning today. His reliance on the 'ordinary' courts as the sole guardians of liberty needs much qualification, although the assurance of access to the sheriff court and Court of Session (and their equivalents in other parts of the United Kingdom) in civil actions against public bodies and on appeal or review from proceedings in tribunals remains important. Perhaps the least resonant aspect of Dicey's doctrine for the modern reader is his idea that governments and their officials should be made subject to the *same* law and, therefore, the *same* legal restrictions as the 'ordinary' citizen. Understandable as this may be as a first line of defence raised by a nineteenth-century commentator with a minimalist view of governmental power and who was worried about the growth of government with collectivist and interventionist tendencies, it appears too crude a response today. An expanded, complex and legitimate role for government demands a more subtle approach. It has also come to be recognised that the rule of law, while retaining its utility as a portmanteau concept, is easily capable of abuse as a mere political slogan and is certainly capable of attracting a variety of different meanings. What follows is a brief account which might capture mainstream views.

1 See J Jowell 'The Rule of Law and its Underlying Values' in J Jowell and D Oliver (eds) *The Changing Constitution* (7th edn, 2011).
2 Quoted by Dicey *Law of the Constitution* (10th edn, 1959) pp 189–190.
3 Dicey pp 188–205.

The principle of legality

2.7   In the first place, the rule of law represents and endorses a simple principle of legality[1]. Public bodies and their officials must act in accordance with the law as it is for the time being. For this purpose, it is irrelevant whether the relevant rules of law are 'good' or 'bad' rules, whether they are outdated and in need of reform, or whether they were made in accordance with procedures which, while legally unchallengeable, were unsatisfactory. All that is required is that the rules be valid in the system in which they are located. If they are, the rule of law, in this first aspect, insists that there is value in their being observed by and enforced against public bodies. Public bodies are as much bound by the law as anyone else and, unless specifically conferred, they have no power to suspend the application of the law in relation to themselves. They cannot make new law to benefit themselves or, indeed, for any purpose, without legal authority to do so. This idea of legality has a number of important consequences which serve to ensure the very high priority accorded to the rule of law. It secures the general liability of public bodies to actions arising out of a breach of contractual obligations or delict[2]. It is also the principle of legality and, in this sense, the rule of law which is sustained when the limits of the executive powers of the police or army or other public officials are tested in the courts. This was reflected in a statement by a former Minister for Justice to the Scottish Parliament when he said:

> This country does not operate by way of executive diktat. It is proper that [challenges on grounds of human rights] are a matter for the courts, despite the fact that the Executive may occasionally find itself on the wrong side of their decisions. That is part and parcel of belonging to a country in which the rule of law applies[3].

In particular, it is the principle of legality which is invoked in the process of judicial review where the courts' role is to assess the lawfulness of the act or decision of a public body by reference to the source of legal authority, usually statutory, on which the body purports to rely[4]. This may involve a difficult interpretative exercise but the point is to uphold the terms of the law as laid down.

Although these procedures are available not only to individuals but to other public bodies as well, it is the rule of law, in this initial sense, which has been regarded as the historic guardian of civil liberties. Until the more 'interventionist' approach to individual rights was adopted by HRA 1998 (and SA 1998), such rights were protected only to the extent that they were not reduced by the powers conferred on public bodies. In Dicey's day these limits were defined principally by common-law rules – a position well illustrated by the famous English case of *Entick v Carrington*[5] in which the court held unlawful a search of private premises which, though done under a warrant issued by a Secretary of State, had no legal justification in statute or in common law. A claim that 'state necessity' could legitimate the search was rejected. More recently, however, it is the limits of statutorily conferred powers which are more significant. To take an uncontroversial example, once the limits of the Mental Health (Scotland) Act 1984 had been clarified[6] it would have been unlawful, as the law then stood, for the Scottish Ministers to continue to detain a person who had murdered in the past, who might still be dangerous but whose condition was untreatable. It was, however, the Government's belief that the public interest demanded that such persons should be detained and the Mental Health (Public Safety and Appeals) (Scotland) Act 1999 was promptly passed by the Parliament in order to change the law to bring it into line with the demands of the policy.

A further minimum requirement of the rule of law as the principle of legality is its implementation by the courts. The law must be interpreted; it must be applied to the circumstances of particular cases; and it must, if necessary, be enforced. This requires courts which have the necessary skills but, more importantly, the ability to take an impartial and independent view of the facts and law before them. An independent judiciary, especially one which is not subordinated to the control of the executive, is an important ingredient of the rule of law. Without that, the principle of legality would unravel.

---

1 This is to be distinguished from the 'principle of legality' recently developed (though claimed to be of historic origins) in cases including *R v Home Secretary, ex parte Simms* [2000] 2 AC 115;

R (Daly) v Home Secretary [2001] 2 AC 532; *R (Morgan Grenfell Ltd) v Special Commissioner* [2003] 1 AC 563. See also *R (Mohammed) v Foreign* Secretary [2009] 1 WLR 2653 and *A v HM Treasury* [2010] UKSC 2, [2010] 2 AC 534. In these the rather narrower principle means that Parliament may derogate from fundamental principles of human rights only in express terms or by necessary implication.
2 Legally defined exceptions occur where, for instance, the Local Government (Contracts) Act 1997 overrode the general law on the validity of local authority contracts. The Crown Proceedings Act 1947 removed many earlier immunities attaching to the Crown, but leaves some in place. See also, however, *Davidson v Scottish Ministers* 2006 SC (HL) 41.
3 SP OR 11 November 1999, col 508, Jim Wallace MSP.
4 See ch 14.
5 (1765) 19 St Tr 1030.
6 *Ruddle v Secretary of State for Scotland* 1999 GWD 29-1395.

Beyond legality: the rule of law and justice

2.8   While it is difficult to overstate the value of the rule of law and the legitimacy which adherence to the law confers, it is plain that legality is not sufficient in itself to ensure a just society. It is, for this reason, that there is a reluctance to describe a state as complying with the rule of law if its laws are themselves manifestly unjust. Observing and enforcing the law then brings injustice rather than justice. Easy examples occur in manifestly dictatorial regimes where laws are made to suit the purposes of the dictator. The apartheid regime in South Africa prior to 1991 pretended an observance of the rule of law. There was a sophisticated legal system and a judiciary which could make claims to independence but many of the rules which were applied by the courts were not only undemocratic in origin but were deliberately discriminatory between the racial groups in the country. Huge injustices were done in the name of the law. Nearer to home, however, while the degree of systemic persecution may be less, similar complaints may be heard about recent terrorism legislation because of the breadth of the police powers conferred or indeed, earlier, about the Abolition of Domestic Rates etc (Scotland) Act 1987 which brought to Scotland the short-lived poll tax. The capacity, within the UK system of executive domination of a supreme Parliament, to produce laws which attract sharp and often widely shared criticism is apparent. It was in the face of the threat to the rule of law from 'elective dictatorship' that Lord Steyn once said that 'in exceptional cases...the rule of law may trump parliamentary supremacy'[1]. Nor is the Westminster Parliament alone in this. If Westminster can be criticised on 'rule of law' grounds for the authorisation of broader powers to intercept communications[2], so too can Holyrood[3]. Examples such as these have led to expanded views of the rule of law in perhaps three main directions. Most dominant has been a tendency to pack into the concept of the rule of law the whole gamut of human rights protection. Thus, legal rules which are profoundly and unjustifiably unequal in their terms or their impact are, like the apartheid rules, said to be contrary to the rule of law. But, similarly, rules which are in breach of other fundamental human rights, such as those articulated in the ECHR, are non-compliant. Beyond that, however, it may be argued that even more fundamental than those civil and political rights are the social and economic rights which guarantee education, employment, housing and an absence of poverty. The state which fails its citizens in these areas too may be regarded as failing to comply with the rule of law. Nor may the unequal protection of the rule of law be tolerated. 'That…is not the way the rule of law works. The lesson of history is that depriving people of its protection because of their beliefs or behaviour, however obnoxious, leads to the disintegration of society……The rights and fundamental freedoms that the [ECHR] guarantees are not just for some people. They are for everyone. No one, however dangerous, however disgusting, however despicable, is excluded. Those who have no respect for the rule of law – even those who would seek to destroy it – are in the same position as everyone else.'[4]

Secondly, the concept of rule of law can impose obligations on state institutions not only to respect the rights of citizens but also to obey wider obligations of 'institutional morality'[5] which would encompass qualities characterised in this chapter as 'good governance'. Principles of democracy, transparency and accountability can be restyled as aspects of the rule of law.

And, thirdly, the terminology of the rule of law is available to all those who, without any pretension at all to conceptual precision, will use the language of non-compliance with the rule of law to castigate a government or official for any extreme failure to act fairly or justly. This is especially the case where the threat of anarchy and lawlessness looms as, for instance, was the case when Keith Raffan MSP concluded a speech describing patterns of intimidation and electoral fraud in Zimbabwe by saying that '[i]nstead of the rule of law, there has been the rule of the mob'[6].

It is clearly impossible to define a single correct use of the concept of the rule of law. It can be used to refer to a number of specific qualities in a system of law or as an umbrella term to capture all that is good in a legal or political system. However, there is a strong case for saying that the rule of law may be best understood as a right to law – a right to the legal accountability of government. This is, in the main, to return to a narrow principle of legality but it is also to insist on the effective application and enforcement of laws by courts. There must be nowhere within the state to which the jurisdiction of the courts does not extend[7] – nor, for that matter, places beyond the limits of the state. There should, in principle, be no persons and no institutions who are immune from the law or the courts – even those at the highest level in the constitution[8]. Exceptionally, immunities or indemnities from the normal application of the law may be justified, as may, occasionally, the retrospective imposition of new legal vulnerabilities[9] but the standard expectation of the right to law is that the formal equality of subjection to, and treatment by, the law will prevail. This includes an understanding that review by courts is not excluded[10]; that governmental powers are not conferred in terms so broad that they are unreviewable by courts; and, as important as anything, that the law is enforceable. The former Scottish Executive said: 'Enforcement plays an important and integral role within the Scottish civil justice system. Without means to enforce them the orders of our civil courts would be but 'as bees without stings' and the rule of law could not be upheld.'[11] Not only should the law be enforceable but it should in fact be enforced, and enforced even-handedly. The legal system should be resourced adequately and access to the system must be assured, with the assistance of the legal profession as necessary. That, in turn, presupposes a measure of guaranteed independence for the profession itself. The Law Society of Scotland has said in evidence to the Justice 1 Committee of the Scottish Parliament: 'An independent Scottish solicitor profession is an important aspect of democracy and the Society believes that the independence of the legal profession is a central feature of the rule of law.'[12]

It may be contended that all these issues fall within the familiar territory of fundamental rights protection. The rights guaranteed by art 6 ECHR to a fair trial go a very long way to ensure a right to law. The right to law, however, should extend to beneficiaries beyond the 'victims'[13] recognised by the ECHR, including, in particular, public bodies themselves. Public bodies rely as much as anyone upon the power of the courts to enforce the law. They need to be able, in the public interest, to ensure that suspected criminals are prosecuted, that action is enforceable against those who breach licensing or other regulatory rules, and that taxes are gathered. It would be contrary to the rule of law if this enforcement power were abused but it would also be wrong if the power were not available. Equally, public bodies may need the law's protection from the unlawful acts of other public authorities. A power conferred by the Local Government in Scotland Act 2003 enables the Scottish Ministers to take steps to enforce a duty imposed on Scottish local authorities to secure 'best value' in the performance of their functions[14]. From a local authority point of view, it is important that they know that such enforcement action can be taken only within the limits of the rules laid down.

There are many other features of a 'right to law' which could be developed but one which is important relates to the timing of the operation of the law. It is often said that 'justice delayed is justice denied' and it is certainly true that the issue of delay in relation to legal proceedings can raise a range of (rule of law related) issues. Several were mentioned in the speech of Lord Hope in the English case of *R (Burkett) v Hammersmith and Fulham London Borough Council*[15]. First, he reminded that, until reforms in the 1980s, the Scottish procedure for judicial review of governmental action[16] 'was of little use in practice, as it took so long ... to obtain a decision of the court'[17]. Secondly, and conversely he dealt with the principle of 'promptitude' which demands that judicial review proceedings, in either Scotland or England, although the rules differ in detail between the two, should be brought without undue delay – mainly to protect the interests of the public authority concerned. Thirdly, however, those rules of 'promptitude' should themselves be sufficiently precise and certain to avoid the loss of a deserving action against a public authority because of confusion over the procedural rules to be applied[18]. It is in the texture of the rules which acknowledge procedural concerns such as these that respect for the rule of law can be said to be found.

Dominating all discussion of the rule of law since its publication in 2010 has been the late Lord Bingham's *The Rule of Law* (2011). Imbued with the unparalleled authority of the Senior Law Lord (prior to the creation of the UK Supreme Court) the book has become the primary point of reference in the field. Bingham eloquently identifies the 'core of the existing principle' as being 'that all persons and authorities within the state, whether public or private, should be bound by and entitled to the benefit of laws publicly made, taking effect (generally) in the future and publicly administered in the courts.' Careful to explain that the idea of the rule of law has evolved over time, he then proceeds to elaborate eight principles by which, in our own time, it may be recognised: (1) The law must be accessible and so far as possible intelligible, clear and predictable; (2) Questions of legal right and liability should ordinarily be resolved by application of the law and not the exercise of discretion; (3) The laws of the land should apply equally to all, save to the extent that objective differences justify differentiation; (4) Ministers and public officers at all levels must exercise the powers conferred on them in good faith, fairly, for the purpose for which the powers were conferred, without exceeding the limits of such powers and not unreasonably; (5) The law must afford adequate protection of fundamental human rights; (6) Means must be provided for resolving, without prohibitive cost or inordinate delay, bona fide disputes which the parties themselves are unable to resolve; (7) Adjudicative procedures provided by the state should be fair; (8) The rule of law requires compliance by the state of its obligations in international law as in national law.

Thus, it is the availability of law and the access to remedies in courts of law which are the essential ingredients of the rule of law. The courts must have an independence and impartiality discussed later in Chapter 12. They must have a range of powers – in turn opening up a range of legal avenues to those who access them – and these are addressed principally in Chapter 14. The courts offer, above all, the conditions of the legal accountability of government to complement the political accountability already discussed, and to be developed further in Chapter 10. It is the balance (or, at some points, the opposition) between the two – the one placing emphasis on political and democratic mechanisms and the other on judicial mechanisms – that best characterises the condition of the constitutional order. But, if that is the case, it is a contested balance and thus a contested constitutional order which is presented. And the rule of law is at the heart of the contest – in circumstances where the courts use the concept to assert the accountability not only of governments but of parliaments themselves and thus the subordination of parliaments to the jurisdiction of the courts. We shall find that, in *AXA General Insurance Ltd, Petitioners*[19], the UK Supreme Court has defined an unwritten limitation on the powers of the Scottish Parliament by reference to its obligation to observe the rule of law[20] and it has even been suggested, in a manner contested by Lord Bingham[21], that the courts can use rule of law principles to narrow the powers of the UK Parliament[22].

1   Attlee Foundation lecture, 11 April 2006.
2   Regulation of Investigatory Powers Act 2000. See eg Surveillance: Citizens and the State, 2nd report of the HL Committee on the Constitution (2008–09) HL Paper 18.
3   Regulation of Investigatory Powers (Scotland) Act 2000.
4   Lord Hope of Craighead, *RB (Algeria) v Home Secretary* [2010] 2 AC 110, para 210.
5   See eg, J Jowell 'The Rule of Law and its Underlying Values' in J Jowell and D Oliver (eds) *The Changing Constitution* (7th edn, 2011).
6   SP OR 13 March 2002, col 10206.
7   But, for an interesting exploration of this, see H W Arthurs *Without the Law* (1985).
8   For Crown immunity, see M Sunkin and S Payne (eds) *The Nature of the Crown* (1999). See also A Tomkins 'The Crown in Scots Law' in A McHarg and T Mullen (eds) *Public Law in Scotland* (2006).

9 But the War Damage Act 1965 operated retrospectively to undo the effect of *Burmah Oil Co (Burma Trading) Ltd v Lord Advocate* 1964 SC (HL) 117, as did the Education (Scotland) Act 1973 in relation to *Malloch v Aberdeen Corpn* 1974 SLT 253. The War Crimes Act 1991 has retrospective effect. See also the Erskine Bridge Tolls Act 2001 and the Damages (Asbestos-related Conditions) (Scotland) Act 2009 on which see *AXA General Insurance Ltd, Petitioners* 2012 SC (UKSC) 122 at paras 118–123 (Lord Reed).

10 Although review is sometimes excluded: see para 14.11.

11 *Enforcement of Civil Obligations in Scotland* (2002). 'Bees without stings' is attributed to Stair Institutions II, 4, 47.

12 *Report on Regulation of the Legal Profession Inquiry* SP Paper 700(2) 2002, Annex D.

13 See ch 14.

14 See Local Government in Scotland Act 2003, ss 1, 23–27.

15 *R (Burkett) v Hammersmith and Fulham LBC* [2002] 3 All ER 97. See also *Eba v Advocate General for Scotland* [2011] UKSC 29, 2012 SC (UKSC) 1, para 8 (Lord Hope).

16 See para 14.3.

17 [2002] 3 All ER 97 at 115.

18 [2002] 3 All ER 97 at 115–117.

19 2012 SC (UKSC) 1061.

20 See para 14.26.

21 See *The Rule of Law*, Ch 12.

22 See para 6.5.

Chapter 3

The Scottish Constitutional Context

INTRODUCTION

3.1   In Chapter 1 it became clear that the general function of all modern constitutions is the same. A constitution maps institutions and their interrelationships, and defines the position of individual citizens and others. Equally, in Chapter 2, the purposes and values promoted or permitted by constitutional orders, whether directly or indirectly, were seen to share a common core in the Western liberal tradition. But, within those very broad parameters, there is, of course, scope for very wide variations between one set of national constitutional arrangements and another. The constitution of the United Kingdom and then, within that, the constitutional position of Scotland have characteristics which, at a general level, are shared with other national constitutions but which also have peculiarities in their structure and content which are determined by the context in which they are situated.

The context within which a constitution is located is defined by reference to the complex interaction of the political, social and economic forces which shape the state to which the constitution relates. Sometimes these are fairly easily understood by reference to some recent event producing radical change and a new start. The current constitution of the Republic of South Africa was the product of deliberation over the period between 1990 and 1996 and the terms of the 1997 constitution clearly reflect the radically changed political circumstances in which it was born. Its preamble opens with a recognition of 'the injustices of the past'. But even that constitution was not written on a wholly clean slate and its terms also reflect some political and legal continuities in South Africa – for instance, the role of provinces in government, although in expanded numbers. The same is true of other states where circumstances have brought abrupt change but also a constitution which nevertheless owes something to the state's constitutional past, for example the constitution of the Federal Republic of Germany of 1949; the constitution of the Fifth French Republic of 1958; the post-Franco constitution of Spain of 1978 or the constitution of Montenegro after its separation from Serbia in 2006. In other states, such as the United Kingdom, where constitutional change has been more evolutionary, the continuities tend to overshadow the effect of the specific occasions where change has occurred. Our task is an understanding of the modern constitution but there is no avoiding the incorporation into a contemporary account of some of the features of its historical development where these continue to affect its current shape. For some, this points to the need for a substantial historical story and this was indeed the fashion in constitutional analysis at one time. But constitutional histories tend to distort. They give an illusion of constitutional continuity, of constitutional cause and effect, which ignores the much more significant impact of other changes over time. On the other hand, there are indeed some historical events which, though reshaped by the passage of time, still loom large in any modern account. It would be difficult to understand the modern constitutional situation of Scotland without absorbing the impact of the creation of the United Kingdom of Great Britain in 1707; the accession of the United Kingdom to the European Union[1] in 1973; and the launch of devolution and the Scottish Parliament under the Scotland Act 1998 (SA 1998). These three historical events and, in each case, their aftermath have had the greatest effect on defining the context in which we now study the constitutional law of Scotland. In subsequent sections of this chapter, each receives introductory treatment[2].

This is, of course, to be selective, and other choices might be made and added to the list. There is, for instance, no doubt that the United Kingdom's imperial past greatly affected its constitutional development and some might include modern Commonwealth relationships as one of the continuing defining characteristics of the modern UK constitution[3]. Some would attach particular significance to relationships between church and state as they have developed over time. Nor is there any doubt about the importance of the historical circumstances which brought the arrival of cabinet government in the eighteenth century or of a measure of democracy in the shape of the Reform Act 1832 and the extension of suffrage to women in 1918 and 1928. Another choice might be the United Kingdom's accession to the European Convention on Human Rights (ECHR) in 1951 or the passing of the Human Rights Act 1998[4] (HRA 1998). Certainly all these were events or circumstances of significance in their time and all have a continuing resonance. However, they lack the 'constitutive' impact for Scotland of the formation of the United Kingdom, accession to the European Union and devolution.

There are, of course, compelling arguments that what has most significantly framed the context of Scotland's constitution from 2014 has been the independence referendum of that year, its result and its aftermath. These arguments are acknowledged in Chapter 4 and in the references to the consequences of the referendum throughout the book.

1 Accession at that time was to the different 'Communities', subsequently known together as the European Union (see below).
2 For fuller treatment, see J Mackinnon *The Constitutional History of Scotland* (1924); J D B Mitchell *Constitutional Law* (2nd edn, 1968); J G Kellas *Modern Scotland* (2nd edn, 1980); J G Kellas *The Scottish Political System* (4th edn, 1989); L Paterson *The Autonomy of Modern Scotland* (1994); C R Munro *Studies in Constitutional Law* (2nd edn, 1999); SME Reissue Constitutional Law (2002).
3 A survivor has been the (declining) role of the Judicial Committee of the Privy Council as a court of appeal from certain Commonwealth countries, as to which see ch 14.
4 See ch 14.

The formation of the United Kingdom of Great Britain

3.2   The Westminster Parliament (to be) elected in May 2015 is the 56th Parliament of the United Kingdom. The numbering of Parliaments dates from 1801 when, by the Union with Ireland Act 1800, the United Kingdom of Great Britain and Ireland was formed. Prior to that, however, and more significantly from a Scottish point of view, it was in 1707 that the Articles of Union brought

Scotland, together with England and Wales[1], into the initial United Kingdom of Great Britain. The Articles laid down the terms on which the two countries – which had shared the same monarch (in 1707, Queen Anne) since the Union of the Crowns in 1603 – would come together. The Articles provided for a single flag combining the crosses of St Andrew and St George; for the succession to the throne to be to the House of Hanover as already determined for England by the Act of Settlement 1700; and for the United Kingdom to 'be represented by one and the same Parliament, to be styled, the Parliament of Great Britain'. There would be single systems of coinage and of weights and measures. Many of the other Articles dealt with the harmonisation of taxes and of the regulation of trade.

Clearly of momentous impact in its own time, the Treaty and the circumstances of its making might now be thought, some 300 years later, to be of very limited continuing significance. The Treaty did not create Great Britain as a federal state under which governmental responsibilities would be formally divided between London and Edinburgh, but it created instead the conditions under which London-based institutions could govern across an expanded territory. That would, however, be to underrate the Treaty's continuing relevance which might be summarised as follows:

(1)   In the first place, the very fact that in 1707 the new state of Great Britain was created by voluntary merger (but with consent perhaps corruptly obtained[2]) keeps alive arguments that, should it be the wish of the people of Scotland, a demerger could legitimately be negotiated, thus producing an independent Scotland once again. Such arguments are enhanced by claims that the original merger was based upon a distinct lack of democratic approval, and by the ease with which the territorial division between Scotland and England could be restored. It became the declared policy of the Scottish National Party that its victory in a Holyrood general election would trigger a popular referendum across Scotland on the issue of independence and that indeed produced, from 2011, the circumstances leading to the referendum of 18 September 2014[3].

(2)   An important consequence of the terms of the Union Treaty has been the survival of the separate legal system of Scotland. The Treaty, while establishing a single legislature at Westminster and thus enabling Parliament to amend the law of Scotland or to introduce new laws, did not itself make general amendments to the previously existing laws, except to the extent that they were contrary to or inconsistent with the Treaty itself. It did not, for instance, simply unify the legal systems by extending English law wholesale to Scotland. Indeed, the opposite was true. The continued existence and jurisdiction of the Court of Session and of the High Court of Justiciary were preserved (Art XIX) and the Treaty provided that, while Parliament might make laws 'concerning public right, policy and civil government' the same throughout the United Kingdom, no alteration could be made to 'laws which concern private right, except for the evident utility of the subjects within Scotland' (Art XVIII). In addition, the Treaty declared that 'no causes in Scotland [might] be cognoscible by the Courts of Chancery, Queen's Bench, Common Pleas[4] or any other court in Westminster Hall' (Art

XIX) although the impact of that provision was in effect undermined by the emergence, very soon after the Union, of the practice of taking civil appeals from the Court of Session to the House of Lords.

The principal effect of these Treaty provisions has nevertheless been to ensure the preservation of the 'mixed' (civilian and common law) system of private law in Scotland with clear continuing consequences, for instance, for property law. The divergence of public law rules may have been less noticeable but common law rules affecting, for instance, civil liberties and judicial review[5] have remained different from those in England. More prominently, the court systems themselves have remained quite distinct and rules relating to judicial tenure in Scotland trace back to the pre-Union Claim of Right (1689) rather than to the (English) Bill of Rights (1688) or the Act of Settlement 1700. Senior judges hold office *ad vitam aut culpam* (for life or until serious fault) although this is a position which has been substantially qualified by statute in recent years[6].

(3)   Extending beyond the legal system itself, the Treaty and the conditions under which the United Kingdom was created also influenced the general shape of governmental institutions in Scotland. The Treaty sought to preserve the position of the old royal burghs in the local government of Scotland (Art XXI) and, although much change was brought to them and surrounding institutions, they survived until 1975[7]. While their position was not directly protected by the Treaty, sheriffs exercised local administrative functions in addition to their dominant judicial role which, to a limited extent, they retain today[8]. More significantly, the eighteenth century brought the distinctive role of the Lord Advocate in Scottish government. Later, the conditions of 'board' government in the nineteenth century gave way to the Scottish Office, created in 1884. There also emerged the general practice of making separate legislation at Westminster in respect of the public administration of Scotland, which endured until the arrival of devolution in 1999.

(4)   Another, periodically revitalised, issue raised by the Treaty is its status as a written constitution, albeit only partial in its scope, for the United Kingdom. The case has been made[9] that, because the Articles of Union created a new state and one of its principal institutions – a *new* UK Parliament rather than merely an expanded English Parliament – the Treaty and the Acts of Union passed by the old Scottish and English Parliaments which implemented it should be regarded as *constitutive* of the new United Kingdom and not be treated as merely *legislative* in character. The point of seeking to establish a status of this sort for the Treaty is to establish also the basis for an argument that some, at least, of the terms of the Treaty are not, or should not be, amendable today simply by an Act of the Westminster Parliament. Put in this way, the argument for 'constitutional' status for the Treaty is an argument for its being treated as entrenched against incompatible legislation enacted by Westminster and, therefore, a challenge to that Parliament's claim to supremacy or sovereignty. Despite the apparent initial force of the arguments in support of the Treaty's special status, there are also formidable counter-arguments. These are addressed in Chapter 6.

These considerations taken together have placed Scotland in a constitutional relationship within the United Kingdom which must be unique in the world. It is a relationship which, since 1999, has been substantially restructured by the devolution arrangements introduced by the SA 1998 which are discussed in Chapters 5–7 below and indeed in most of the rest of this book. Important as these new arrangements are, however, they are heavily conditioned by the broader constitutional circumstances dating back to 1707. It is these which, though not creating a federation, permitted the United Kingdom to be called 'unitary' in only a highly qualified sense. Many have preferred the terminology of the 'union' state[10], acknowledge the special quality of Scotland's autonomy.

It is for similar reasons that, although Scotland has for many purposes, before and since devolution, been described as a 'region' of the United Kingdom, the title of 'nation', albeit a substate nation, has been preferred. This is, of course, to draw terminological distinctions which have a stronger political than purely legal resonance, but they have an important constitutional foundation.

1 Wales had been subject to the English Crown from 1283.
2 C A Whatley *Bought and Sold for English Gold? Explaining the Union of 1707* (2nd edn, 2001).
3 See ch 4.
4 The courts later to be reconstituted as the English High Court.
5 See ch 14.
6 See ch 12.
7 The Local Government (Scotland) Act 1973, subsequently overtaken by the Local Government etc (Scotland) Act 1994, removed the powers from the royal (and later statute-created) burghs.
8 See ch 12.
9 See especially N MacCormick 'Does the United Kingdom have a Constitution? Reflections on *MacCormick v Lord Advocate*' (1978) 29 NILQ 1.
10 See eg S Tierney 'Scotland and the Union State' in A McHarg and T Mullen (eds) *Public Law in Scotland* (2006).

THE EUROPEAN UNION

Introduction

3.3   On 1 January 1973, the United Kingdom, together with Ireland and Denmark, became members of three international organisations known as the European Coal and Steel Community, the European Economic Community (or Common Market) and the European Atomic Energy Community (Euratom). Already members since the foundation of the three Communities in 1951 and 1958 were Belgium, France, (West) Germany, Italy, Luxembourg and the Netherlands. In the period since 1973, membership has grown to a total of 28 with the addition of Greece in 1981, Portugal and Spain in 1986, Austria, Finland and Sweden in 1995, Cyprus, Estonia, Hungary, Latvia, Lithuania, Malta, Poland, Slovakia and Slovenia in 2004, Bulgaria and Romania in 2007, and Croatia in 2013. Over the same period, under changing treaty relationships negotiated between the parties, the principal Community, the European Economic Community, was restyled as the European Community to recognise an expansion of its competences beyond the merely economic and the European Union was created[1]. Both changes were made under the terms of the (Maastricht) Treaty on European Union 1992. Subsequently, the

Treaty of Lisbon of 2007 (effective from 2009) continued the reform of the Union, although not, as earlier planned, by means of a new 'Constitution'. The 'Community' terminology was ended but the Lisbon Treaty maintained the previous practice of having two principal treaties (The Treaty on European Union (TEU) and the Treaty on the Functioning of the European Union (TFEU)) rather than their integration into a single document. It is anticipated that membership of the Union may expand in the coming years. Negotiations for the admission of Macedonia (FYROM), Montenegro and Turkey are underway, although with different degrees of progress. At the time of their inception, the original Communities, as children of the post-Second World War European Movement, had the declared aims of laying the foundations of 'an ever closer union among the peoples of Europe'; ensuring 'the economic and social progress of their countries by common action to eliminate the barriers which divided Europe'; and 'pooling their resources to preserve and strengthen peace and liberty'[2]. Those broad aims have been retained but the aims of the Union have been greatly expanded to include the achievement of economic and monetary union, Union citizenship, and a common foreign and security policy[3].

1 In July 2002 the Treaty establishing the European Coal and Steel Community expired.
2 Preamble to the EEC Treaty 1957.
3 TEU, Preamble.

The United Kingdom and the European Union – a unique relationship

3.4   The European Union is one of the many international organisations of which the United Kingdom is a member under the terms of treaties into which it has entered. The United Kingdom is a member of the Council of Europe; it is a member of the Commonwealth and of the United Nations; and a member of countless other organisations conferring benefits but also imposing membership obligations in terms of their constituent treaties. The power to enter into such treaty relationships is clearly a significant aspect of the general governmental authority of the state. In a state such as the United Kingdom, which is generally to be regarded as 'dualist' rather than 'monist' (in that the terms of international treaties require specific legislation to implement their terms domestically rather than affecting the legal rights and obligations of those within the state automatically), many treaties do bring with them the need for an Act of Parliament to ensure that they work effectively and that the state's new obligations are met. For this reason, the treaty-making power has some constitutional significance. It is of importance to identify who has the power to bind the state in treaty obligations – in the case of the United Kingdom, a prerogative power of the Crown – and also to take account of the procedures necessary for their domestic implementation. Much more rarely, however, does the actual content of particular treaties or the organisations they create have substantial constitutional consequences[1].

There are, however, very good reasons for treating accession to the European Union as in a category of its own. The first of these derives from the unique strength and sophistication of its institutions. At the core of the Union, there are five principal bodies: the European Council; the Council (of the European Union), the Commission, the European Parliament and the Court of Justice of the European Union (including the Court of Justice and the General Court[2] – see below). While the Commission exercises important executive responsibilities in the Union, its functions are supplemented by a number of bodies, offices and agencies responsible for specific policy areas, including, for example, the Copenhagen-based European Environment Agency. Separately, there are the European Central Bank, the Court of Auditors[3] with audit responsibilities across the Union's institutions, and the European Ombudsman whose principal function is the investigation of complaints of maladministration. Another body, currently of greater potential than actual importance, is the Committee of the Regions which has consultative functions and is representative of the regions and local authorities of the Union. Scottish membership (four full and four alternate members) had earlier been drawn entirely from elected councillors but, since January 2002, representatives have been drawn from both the Scottish Parliament and local authorities.

1 But see the European Convention on Human Rights (ECHR), discussed in ch 13.
2 Also 'specialised courts' such as the Civil Service Tribunal.
3 Themselves both formally 'institutions' of the Union.

The institutions of the European Union

3.5   Returning to the principal institutions, they present a curiously idiosyncratic picture. Although, for some purposes, it is helpful, if also provocative, to compare the Union with a federal state and, therefore, tempting to compare its institutions with analogous federal bodies, such comparisons quickly break down. Mapping by reference to constitutional functions is difficult because, to an even greater extent than with domestic constitutions, the separation of legislative and executive powers is elusive – although judicial functions are, as one might expect, allocated to the Court of Justice and the General Court. The Union's institutions, although much changed over half a century, still largely retain the shape and division of functions originally appropriate for a small, limited-purpose, inter-governmental organisation. The institutions have a curious mix of functions and interrelationships both with each other, and then with the governments and peoples of the member states. In turn, this results in obscure lines of democratic accountability. The richness of this strange constitutional situation cannot be pursued here[1] but, in summary form, the principal institutions have the following membership and functions:

1 For a full account see D Edward and R Lane *Edward and Lane on European Union Law* (2013). See also S Douglas-Scott *Constitutional Law of the European Union* (2002); T C Hartley *The Foundations of European Union Law* (7th edn, 2010); S Weatherill *Cases and Materials on EU Law* (11th edn, 2014). See also P Craig and G de Burca *EU Law: Text, Cases and Materials* (5th edn, 2011).

The European Council

3.6   Only given a formal status by the Lisbon Treaty, the European Council comprises all the heads of state or government[1] who meet at summit conferences at least four times a year with the responsibility to 'provide the Union with the necessary impetus for its development and ... [to] define the general political guidelines thereof'[2]. The European Council elects its president, currently (from December 2014) Donald Tusk.

1 Together with its own President and the President of the Commission. The High Representative also takes part.
2 TEU, art 15.

The Council

3.7   Formerly known as (and still often referred to as) the Council of Ministers (and not to be confused with the European Council[1]), the Council is composed of a minister from each of the member states and is attended by the minister relevant to the subject matter of a particular meeting. The functions of the Council are defined as policy-making and coordinating[2] with the power to take decisions and confer powers of implementation on the Commission. The Council is the political power house of the Union. With membership drawn directly from the governments of the member states, the Council, overshadowed from time to time by the summits of the European Council, is the principal focus for political initiative and for political dispute. Such disputes take place in conditions of pressure, compromise and trade-off within a framework which assures individual states of a veto on a narrow category of important matters but otherwise permits majority voting, almost exclusively qualified majority voting (QMV). This model of voting lifts the curb on activity which a unanimity rule would impose but, subject to detailed adjustments incorporated over the years, gives added weight to national votes by reference to the population of each member state. Current rules, produce a situation in which voting strengths in the Council range from France, Germany, Italy and the United Kingdom with 29 votes each to Malta with 3 out of a total of 345, with 255 votes by a majority (sometimes a two thirds majority) of members constituting the qualified majority[3].

Very important to the practical working of the Council are the contributions of the Commission (below) and also of a body known as the Committee of Permanent Representatives (COREPER)[4]. This is an organisation which consists of senior members of the permanent missions maintained in Brussels by the member states and whose principal responsibility is preparing the Council's agenda. In practice, much of the burden on the Council is lifted by the prior discussion undertaken and agreements reached in COREPER. The Council is further assisted by its Secretariat-General, headed by the Secretary-General. One of the biggest curiosities of the organisation and working of the Council is its constantly changing presidency. A principal target for reform, the presidency – and, with it, the responsibility for setting the political agenda and for the management of meetings – rotates among member states at intervals of only six months. The Latvian presidency of January to June 2015 gives way to the Luxembourg presidency of July to December 2015 and thereafter to the Netherlands and then Slovakia. The next UK presidency is predicted from July 2017 – potentially including the period within which a referendum on the United Kingdom's membership of the Union might be held!

1 Nor, of course, with the *entirely* separate Council of Europe (based in Strasbourg) which has, among other things, responsibility for the administration of the European Court of Human Rights.
2 TEU art 16.
3 Art 16(3). There is also provision for blocking minorities for the protection of smaller states.
4 TEU art 16(7).

The Commission

3.8   Even with its Secretariat-General, the Council, as the principal policy- and decision-making body of the Union, could not undertake all the associated tasks of prior policy development and subsequent implementation. It would need additional administrative resources which, in state-based constitutions, would be represented by a permanent civil service. This function, at the Union level, is undertaken by the Commission but the Commission has an independence and significance which go far beyond the supporting role of a civil service. It is a distinctive Union institution, in that both its functions and composition are central to the working of the Union as a whole. The Commission is expected to promote the general interest of the Union and take appropriate initiatives to that end[1]. Its formal powers provide the authority for the Commission to play a primary role in policy initiative and to be the primary source of Union legislation[2], in that only the Commission may initiate legislative proposals even if, for the most part, their eventual approval becomes a matter for the Council and the Parliament. As the 'guardian of the treaties', it is also the body competent to take enforcement action against member states in the Court of Justice[3]. The autonomy of the Commission derives not only from its separately conferred functions but also from its membership. The Commission is currently a college of 28 Commissioners drawn from the member states, (currently Lord Hill of Oareford from the United Kingdom). Commissioners are appointed by means of a process involving nomination by member states, adoption of a proposed list of Commissioners (including a President) by the Council by QMV, and approval, following scrutiny, by the Parliament. The Parliament retains a power to dismiss the Commission by motion of censure[4]. Commissioners, assigned to different policy portfolios, have an obligation, despite the prior involvement of most in national politics, to act independently of political pressures. Their independence must be beyond doubt[5].

There is, of course, much more to the operation of the Commission than the collective work of the Commissioners themselves. The Commission is organised around sectoral Directorates-General and also by an elaborate system of committees, composed of member state representatives, in a process known as comitology. Although this has the capacity to contribute positively to the decision-making process, it also produces some confusion in lines of accountability within the Commission and a lack of transparency.

1 TEU, art 17.
2 Although much legislation is in practice generated by the Commission following a request by the Council.
3 TEU, art 17(1).
4 TFEU, art 234.
5 TEU, art 17(3).

The Parliament

3.9   It is the Parliament which injects an element of elected representative democracy into the working of the Union. The Parliament's role has been greatly strengthened since its early days as an Assembly whose members were not directly elected and, although its legislative functions as formally defined may still fall short of those attributed to national parliaments, it now has, in practice, powers both of legislation and administrative and financial scrutiny which are comparable, given the obvious institutional differences, with those of their national counterparts.

The Parliament is now directly elected by proportional representation on a five-year cycle in elections held on a national basis across the Union. Currently 73 MEPs (out of a total of 751) are elected from the United Kingdom[1] with the country divided for this purpose into 12 electoral regions. Scotland is defined as a single region for the election of six members. The European Parliamentary Elections Act 1999[2] which took effect for the elections held in that year provided for voting on the 'closed' regional list system with votes cast for political parties rather than for named individuals[3].

As we have seen, the principal law-making body of the Union is the Council. The Parliament's role is never formally to initiate legislation but it is involved in law-making- normally under the 'ordinary legislative procedure', involving the joint adoption by the Parliament and the Council of a regulation, directive or decisionon a proposal from the Commission[4].

In addition to its powers of intervention in the legislative process, the Parliament has formal powers in relation to the approval of the Union's budget and the scrutiny of expenditure[5]. It also imposes a measure of accountability on the Commission, both in respect of appointments (and, by censure, of dismissal) and by mandatory systems of reporting, and also, to a lesser extent, on the Council. The Parliament has the power to inject a further measure of democratic pressure into institutions – renowned for their general lack of democratic responsiveness – by the public conduct of its debates, its power to establish committees of inquiry to investigate 'alleged contraventions or maladministration in the implementation of Union law'[6], and by its system of public petitions under which individuals[7] may submit grievances in the hope of redress.

1 TEU, art 14(2) and European Council Decision 2013/312 OJ 2013 L181/57.
2 Amending the European Parliamentary Elections Act 1978 and since consolidated in the European Parliamentary Elections Act 2002.
3 With the exception of Northern Ireland which uses the STV voting system.
4 TFEU, arts 289, 294.
5 TFEU, art 314.
6 TFEU, art 226.
7 'Any citizen of the Union, and any natural or legal person residing or having its registered office in a member state' (TFEU, art 227).

The Court of Justice of the European Union

3.10   There are at present three courts of the Union which together comprise the Court of Justice of the European Union and which sit in Luxembourg – the

Court of Justice (ECJ) proper, the General Court (formerly the Court of First Instance (CFI)) which has a more limited jurisdiction (some of it concerned with enforcement actions against European institutions), and the Civil Service Tribunal, a 'specialised court' (per TEU, art 19) that deals with disputes between the Union and its employees and from which an appeal lies to the Court of Justice. The Court of Justice and the General Court are composed of judges appointed by the governments of the member states. Formally appointments are collective decisions but, in reality, they are on the nomination of each member state, albeit that a judge need not be a national of the nominating state. Appointments are for renewable periods of six years. Currently the UK judge at the ECJ is Christopher Vajda, and at the CFI, Nicholas Forwood. Both are English QCs. The ECJ is assisted by a team of eight Advocates General (also drawn from the member states) whose role, in most cases, is to assist the court by producing an often substantial written opinion on the arguments prior to the Court's own judgment.

The functions of the Court include adjudication upon challenges by member states and others to the validity of decisions by Union institutions, enforcement actions against member states, and references under TFEU, art 267 on points of Union law from national courts. The Court is required to provide its authoritative interpretation of the texts of the treaties and of Union legislation. It is also, however, a court which at some periods of its history has been viewed as a body with a strong integrationist agenda and has been subjected to a degree of criticism for that[1]. Inevitably, it has also been dubbed the 'constitutional court' of the Community or Union because of its role in the resolution of disputes between institutions and states, with the effect of strongly raising its profile among the Union's institutions.

1 See especially H Rasmussen *On Law and Policy in the European Court of Justice* (1986).

The European Union and the UK constitution

3.11 Even this summary account should be sufficient to reveal that the European Union is an organisation distinguished by the unique sophistication of its institutions. Other international organisations, notably the United Nations and the Council of Europe, have quite highly developed structures and, like the European Union, accommodate policy-making bodies, broadly representative assemblies, institutions for the implementation of policies and programmes and courts or tribunals for the adjudication of disputes. But, measured in terms of the financial and other resources devoted to it and the domestic impact of its policies, the European Union stands far ahead of any other international organisation. It is not for these reasons alone, however, that the European Union is accorded its very high constitutional significance. There are at least three further factors.

The treaties and the primacy of EU law

3.12 Much the most important is the status accorded to European Union treaties and legislation made under the treaties. It is a necessary aspect of the European project that European law should apply uniformly throughout the Union with predictable evenness, except in those situations where the institutions themselves have approved a lack of uniformity. There should, in principle, be a 'level playing field'. This demands that two main conditions be satisfied. In the first place, European law contained in the treaties, and the regulations, directives and decisions made under the treaties, has to flow into all the (member) states of the Union. Rules contained in the treaties and regulations are to be 'directly applicable' – without the need for separate legislation made by the parliaments of individual states – by all courts within the states. That is a position which has been strengthened by the ECJ which has held that even some of those rules contained in EU directives which, on their face, require domestic legislation for their implementation are nevertheless of 'direct effect' and must be enforced by domestic courts once the commencement date has passed, even though the implementing legislation has not been passed. This, in itself, means that the impact of the EU treaty regimes far exceeds that of any other international treaty.

It is, however, a position substantially reinforced by the other necessary consequence of the need for the uniformity of application of rules across the Union. The ECJ has also insisted on the 'primacy' of European law. Not only must the rules flow into the domestic legal systems and become enforceable by the courts of those systems, where appropriate, but they must also be given priority over any conflicting domestic law. Even if that domestic law is contained in a statute of the national parliament or (in the states other than the United Kingdom) in the written constitution, it is the European rule which must prevail and be enforced[1]. This is the position which has been adopted by the ECJ itself and which must be followed and applied by domestic courts. The mechanism which has particularly assisted the ECJ in the promulgation of this doctrine of primacy – and also of direct effect – has been the reference procedure under art 267 TFEU. This enables, and in the case of final courts in member states requires, a domestic court to request a ruling by the ECJ on any question relating to the interpretation of the Treaty or the validity or interpretation of acts of Union institutions which is necessary to enable judgment to be given. The Court's decision must then be applied and implemented. The power to respond to references under art 267 (and its predecessors) has given the ECJ the opportunity to dispense its views, with mandatory effect, across the Union. From a constitutional point of view, it is the impact of this new source of supreme law-making, backed by a court to enforce that supremacy, which has been the most significant legal consequence of EU membership.

The framework within which the status of European Union law has been achieved within the United Kingdom is to be found in the European Communities Act 1972 (ECA 1972)[2] and then, within Scotland, in SA 1998. ECA 1972 provides that '[a]ll such rights, powers, liabilities, obligations and restrictions from time to time created or arising by or under the Treaties[3] ... as in accordance with the Treaties are without further enactment to be given legal effect or used in the United Kingdom shall be recognised and available in law, and be enforced, allowed and followed accordingly'[4]. It also enables the implementation of EU obligations by delegated as well as by primary legislation[5]. Courts are required to take judicial notice of the Treaties and of 'any decision of, or expression of opinion by' the ECJ[6].

Of all ECA 1972's provisions, the most problematic has been s 2(4) which requires that 'any enactment passed or to be passed, other than one contained in this Part of this Act, shall be construed and have effect subject to the foregoing provision of this section'. From what has been said about the logic of the hierarchical demands of the European Union, there should be nothing surprising about a domestic UK provision which, when read with ECA 1972, ss 2(1) and 3, does appear to require a UK court to give precedence to European law where there is a conflict with a UK statute, even if that statute is of later date and thus, chronologically at least, in a position to displace the European provision. However, such a provision produces a conflict with a principle of the British constitution which, prior to ECA 1972, was assumed to be fundamental and inviolable – the legislative supremacy of the Westminster Parliament. On the face of it, that Parliament cannot be restricted in its law-making powers by previous laws from any source, including the terms of its own earlier Acts. The position has been made more problematic by the passing of the European Union Act 2011 (EUA 2011). The Act made two interventions affecting the relationship between the competing supremacy principles. A minor gloss on existing doctrine was introduced by s 18 which, in effect, restates that ECA 1972 is the basis of the status of EU law in the United Kingdom. Much more controversial however, are the provisions of ss 2–4 of the Act. Their potential impact is explored further in Chapter 6 but, in essence, they demand that, with certain exceptions, a referendum be held in all those circumstances where an Act of Parliament has approved a treaty amending (or replacing) the TEU or TFEU or a European Council decision to revise the TFEU[7]. If there is no referendum majority in favour of the amendment or revision, the relevant UK ratification or confirmation of the decision may not be made. These are not provisions which bear directly upon the competition for supremacy between EU law and the UK Parliament but they instead confront UK parliamentary supremacy by purporting to restrict the freedom of future UK Parliaments to legislate in the normal – referendum-free – manner.

In the meantime, the impact of SA 1998 is less momentous and less problematic. It reinforces the supremacy of European law by imposing upon the Scottish Parliament – a parliament which is, in any event, one of restricted competence – a prohibition on the making of any law which is incompatible with EU law[8]. The same restriction is applied to the Scottish Government[9].

1 For discussion of the ECJ case law in this area and the response of UK courts, see ch 6.
2 On which, see Lord Reed in *R(HS2 Action Alliance Ltd) v Sec of State for Transport* [2014] 2 All ER 109. See para 6.10 below.
3 Updated by successive amendments to ECA 1972, s 1.
4 ECA 1972, s 2(1).
5 ECA 1972, s 2(2) and Sch 2.
6 ECA 1972, s 3(2). ECA 1972, s 2(3) authorises expenditure on EU obligations to be charged on the Consolidated Fund. See para 11.2.
7 Under TEU, art 48(6). Later sections of EUA 2011 impose special procedural requirements on some other forms of decision-making in relation to the EU.
8 SA 1998, s 29(2)(d).
9 SA 1998, ss 54 and 57(2).

Ministerial accountability

3.13 Another consequence of the expansion of European Union activity, especially legislative activity, since the United Kingdom's accession in 1973 has been the growth of the involvement of government ministers in the making of legislation by the Council of Ministers and the promulgation of that legislation, as necessary, in domestic instruments. In turn, this creates a need for parliamentary scrutiny of that process[1].

These are functions which have taken on a new significance since the arrival of devolution in 1999. Ministerial representation at the Council of Ministers is a matter for the national level of government of the member state of the Union. It is a UK view of the policy under discussion – whether, for instance, energy, agriculture or fisheries – which has to be represented. Prior to devolution this did not at all stand in the way of some of the UK ministerial team being drawn from the Scottish Office, the UK department of government with Scottish responsibilities, where this was appropriate and especially where peculiarly Scottish interests (eg fisheries) were at stake. Since July 1999, it has continued to be possible for Scottish ministers – drawn from the Scottish Government rather than from a department of the UK government – to form part of the United Kingdom's team at Brussels[2]. It remains a single UK position which has to be represented, however, and this is a matter of some political sensitivity. There is a concern that Scottish interests, where different from UK interests taken as a whole, may be inadequately represented[3]. Implementation and enforcement of European law have become the responsibility of the Scottish Government within the devolved areas of government[4]. Responsibility for the parliamentary scrutiny of legislative proposals by the European Commission and Council has, again within the devolved areas, become shared between Westminster and Holyrood[5]. The scrutiny of implementing legislation made by the Scottish Government as Scottish statutory instruments is also a Holyrood responsibility[6].

One general consequence of these arrangements and of the introduction of devolution at a time when much of the control of important areas of national policy has been transferred from the United Kingdom to the European Union is that the formal scheme of devolution in SA 1998 (and SA 2012) does not tell the full story. That scheme is set out in Chapter 6 and it is a scheme under which, for example, agriculture and fisheries are matters devolved to the Scottish Parliament and Government. It will be apparent, however, that with both of these policy areas substantially 'devolved' to the EU and with UK control substantially exerted by UK ministers in the Council of Ministers, the effective extent of domestic devolution to Scotland is much diminished.

1 Scrutiny arrangements are in the hands of the House of Commons Select Committee on European Scrutiny and the House of Lords European Union Select Committee. The Commons Committee can refer EU documents for debate in an ad hoc European Committee (for reform proposals see HC 109 (2013–14) while the Lords Committee has six sub-committees.
2 This was anticipated in *Scotland's Parliament* (Cm 3658) ch 5.
3 In Nov 2014, there was resentment (*Scotsman* 11 Nov 2014) when a junior minister from the House of Lords was dispatched to a Fisheries Council meeting, rather than a Scottish minister.

The Smith Commission (see paras 4.20–4.21) recommended (para 31) (also in Nov 2014) that Scottish Government involvement in such EU decision-making be strengthened at all points.
4 See para 6.12.
5 For the UK Parliament, see n 1 above. In the Scottish Parliament, scrutiny is undertaken by the European and External Relations Committee.
6 See paras 9.28–9.34. Such implementation has been the subject of legal challenge: see *Infant and Dietetic Foods Association Ltd, Petitioners* 2008 SLT 723.

The EU Charter of Fundamental Rights[1]

3.14   Another quite different development has been the EU's 'solemn proclamation' of a Charter of Rights at the European Council in Nice in 2000[2]. Until the emergence of the procedure which led to the Charter, it had not been an express element in the project of the Community or Union to guarantee the rights of citizens. Many of the terms of the Treaties, though designed to establish the Common Market, did have a rights aspect to them – for instance, in the way they assured freedom of movement of persons or equality of treatment but there was no comprehensive rights agenda. This had been left to the quite separate institutions of the Council of Europe in Strasbourg, especially that Council's promotion of the ECHR and the European Social Charter. Thought had earlier been given to the possibility of the Community's own accession to the ECHR, but without, at that stage, a positive outcome[3]. More recently, a treaty commitment, though still not fulfilled, to accede has been adopted[4].

In the meantime, however, at European Council meetings in 1999 the proposal was made to establish a Convention[5] which would meet to develop a text of the Union's own making. The result was the Charter of Fundamental Rights proclaimed at Nice. Both its content and its status are important. The Charter consists of six chapters containing a total of fifty substantive articles, with a seventh chapter of general provisions. The substantive articles are spread across Dignity (including the right to life and the prohibition of slavery and forced labour); Freedoms (ranging through the right to liberty and security of the person, protection of personal data, freedom of thought, freedom of the arts and sciences, and freedom to conduct a business); Equality (including reference to the rights of the child, the elderly and persons with disabilities); Solidarity (workplace rights, social security, health care, environmental protection, and consumer protection); Citizens' Rights (the right to stand and vote in European Parliament and municipal elections, the right to good administration, the right to petition the Parliament); and Justice (fair trial and presumption of innocence). All the guaranteed rights derive from those assured by other international obligations common to the member states, especially the EU treaties, the ECHR and the European Social Charter[6]. The Charter is stated to be

> addressed to the institutions and bodies of the Union with due regard for the principle of subsidiarity and to the Member States only when they are implementing Union law. They shall therefore respect the rights, observe the principles and promote the application thereof in accordance with their respective powers[7].

Initially, the Charter was of only declaratory effect, a result of caution on the part of those nervous about making it legally binding. Eventually, however, the Charter was given a formally binding status under the Lisbon Treaty. TEU, art 6 now provides that the Charter 'shall have the same legal value as the Treaties'.

1 See para 13.8.
2 For a full account, see Edward and Lane ch 6.
3 The Constitution Treaty (and now the Lisbon Treaty) revived that option by requiring the Union to seek accession. It was the view of the ECJ (Opinion (ECJ) 2/94 [1996] ECR I–1759) that a Treaty amendment was required.
4 See TEU, art 6(2).
5 In the sense of a body meeting to establish a constitution. See para 1.23, n 1.
6 For an account of the background of each article, see the 'Explanations' published with the Charter.
7 Charter of Fundamental Rights, art 51(1).

The Future of the European Union and the United Kingdom and Scottish Relationship to it

3.15   Three strands in the recent history of the EU and the United Kingdom's relationship to it are of importance:

1   A Constitution for Europe?

A dominant theme in EU developments leading up to the Lisbon Treaty of 2007 was the project to strengthen the Union and its governance arrangements by means of the adoption of a constitution. It is not difficult to understand why many people are, in any event, inclined to describe the Treaties which establish the institutions and working of the European Union as a constitution. The Treaties allocate law-making functions to the Council and the Parliament; executive authority to the Commission; and judicial powers to the Court of Justice in ways which are analogous to those used in the constitutions of nation-states. The description of the Treaties as a constitution has become increasingly common and there have, for a long time, been those who are perfectly comfortable with the notion of the European Court of Justice as a constitutional court. Its powers to adjudicate on the compatibility of national laws with Union laws are entirely comparable with those of a constitutional court within a federation. Judges in the Court of Justice are making decisions similar to those made by constitutional judges elsewhere.

While the similarities of function between the Treaties and national constitutions may be admitted, however, there are objections to the comparison being pressed too far. For some, the idea of a constitution without an identifiable state or 'demos' is intrinsically unsound[1]. For others, it is the assumption that a constitution would formalise the creation of a state as the goal of the European project that is anathema. For 'Eurosceptics' the emergence of a federal state, a superstate, is to be resisted and talk of a constitution is, for them, a step in the wrong direction.

Be that as it may, the European Union did, in recent years, commit itself to a process intended to lead to the emergence of a more formal constitution. Responding to general pressures for institutional reform, a sense that public confidence in European institutions needs to be rebuilt[2] and the need to reform institutions in advance of the anticipated expansion of the Union, a White Paper on European Governance[3] was launched in July 2001 to pave the way for the European Council meeting held in Laeken, Belgium in December 2001. The White Paper contained the Commission's proposals for greater involvement and openness in the workings of the Union, better procedures for policy-making and policy delivery, better external relations for the Union and what it called 'refocused institutions' in the Union itself. It enunciated principles of good governance, and anticipated a wider process of constitutional reform to be initiated at Laeken. In due course, the Laeken Council did indeed establish a Convention on the Future of Europe under the chairmanship of former French President Valéry Giscard d'Estaing.

The Convention had 105 members, including representatives of all the governments of the member states and candidate states, representatives of national parliaments, and MEPs. It conducted its consultations and discussions until 12 June 2003 when it published its draft of a new Constitution Treaty[4] for presentation to the European Council and for eventual consideration by an Inter-Governmental Conference. For some, a bold new step in the development of the Union, for others a 'tidying-up' exercise, the draft contained much of interest. It proclaimed a commitment to a new restatement of values and objectives; a new legal personality for the Union; recognition of the Charter of Fundamental Rights; and a commitment to seek accession to the ECHR. It restated the principles of the primacy of Union law (and of the Constitution), the categories of exclusive and shared competence, and the principles of subsidiarity and proportionality. In a protocol on those principles, there was a commitment to consultation with national parliaments on EU legislative proposals, subject to the possibility of application to the ECJ for breach. The European Council would acquire a new President (for a maximum period in office of five years), thus ending the circulating presidency.

In due course, the Constitution Treaty was signed (in 2004) but the ratification process suffered a fatal set-back when the French and Dutch populations rejected the text in referendums in May and June 2005. Subsequently, further negotiations produced the successor Lisbon (initially dubbed the Reform) Treaty which drew heavily on the Constitution Treaty but deliberately omitted the language of the 'Constitution' as well as the more ambitious aims of the earlier text. As we have seen, however, the Lisbon Treaty did introduce changes to the powers and procedures of the Council and the Parliament and created the posts of President of the EU and High Representative for Foreign and Security Policy.

2   Euroscepticism in the United Kingdom

We have already taken note of one manifestation of UK euroscepticism in the European Union Act 2011 but it has since been apparent that it is by no means the end of the story. The eurosceptic wing of the Conservative Party has extracted from the Party an undertaking that, should it be returned with an overall majority in the general election of May 2015, the Government will seek renegotiation of the United Kingdom's terms of membership with the EU[5] and then an 'in/out' referendum on membership.

3   The Scotland-EU Relationship

For Scotland[6] the interest in EU reform has been two-fold. In the first place, there was the interest shared by the United Kingdom as a whole and by other member states in any new relationship between the states and the Union. Any tendency towards more formal federal-style arrangements would be watched closely by supporters and opponents alike[7]. Secondly, there is an interest in the reinforcement at the European level of the recognition of the principle of subsidiarity[8] at the substate level[9]. From the point of view of regions, the application of subsidiarity should be seamless and operate at all levels. In particular the threat that greater European integration may dilute the effect of domestic federalism or devolution should be reversed. Scotland participates in meetings of the presidential conferences of regions with legislative power. The TEU includes within its Protocol on subsidiarity not only an obligation to consult national Parliaments on legislative proposals but also a provision that those Parliaments should themselves 'consult, where appropriate, regional Parliaments with legislative powers'.

More recently, the independence referendum period saw the raising of questions about an independent Scotland's access to the EU[10] and its future relationship with the Union. In the aftermath of the referendum, there has been speculation about calls for a second independence referendum if 2017 were to bring a United Kingdom-wide decision to leave the EU, primarily on the strength of English eurosceptic votes.

1   For general discussion, see, eg, P Craig *'Constitutional Law, Constitutions, Constitutionalism and the European Union'* (2001) ELJ 125.
2   Especially in the light of the initial Irish 'no' vote on the Nice Treaty in June 2001.
3   *Enhancing Democracy: A White Paper on Governance in the EU* (COM (2001) 428).
4   CONV 797/1/03.
5   In July 2012, the Coalition Government initiated an inquiry into the 'balance of competences' between the United Kingdom and the EU. See Cm 8415.
6   For the views of the Scottish Parliament's European Committee at an earlier stage, see SP EU OR SP Paper 705, 2002.
7   In August 2014, the Scottish Government issued 'Scotland's Agenda for EU Reform'. See http://scotland.gov.uk/Resource/0045/00458063.pdf.
8   A principle operating mainly in the relationship between the states and the Union to ensure that, in the absence of an exclusive Union competence, the Union will act 'only if and in so far as the objectives of the intended action cannot be sufficiently achieved by the member states, either at central level or at regional and local level, but can rather, by reason of the scale or effects of the proposed action, be better achieved at Union level'.
9   In December 2002, the Committee on Constitutional Affairs of the European Parliament chaired by Giorgio Napolitano produced an important report on the role of regional and local authorities in European Integration which was adopted by the Parliament on 14 February 2003. The Parliament committed itself to the principle of bringing the European Union closer to its citizens through regional and local bodies.
10 See para 4.16.

DEVOLUTION AND THE SCOTLAND ACTS OF 1998 AND 2012

Introduction

3.16 Today the constitution of Scotland and of the United Kingdom as a whole would be incomprehensible without full account being taken of the pattern of arrangements for devolved government established not only in Scotland itself but also Wales, Northern Ireland and, indeed, in Greater London. An important issue in contemporary constitutional debate is where devolution goes from here. The biggest question in the last few years has been whether devolution in Scotland might give way to independence and the departure of Scotland from the United Kingdom. Because of its dominance of recent constitutional debate the independence referendum of September 2014 and its aftermath are given a chapter of their own. Other questions (inevitably now affected by events in Scotland) include whether the regions of England will join in. Will the devolved institutions grow in overall strength, in comparison with the central institutions in Westminster and Whitehall? Will there be a tendency to greater uniformity in the provision of devolution across the United Kingdom – perhaps in combination with a strengthening of devolution in the direction of a 'truly' federal model? Might an English Parliament be created? Will there, on the other hand, be a pattern of continuing divergence and asymmetry? What will be the continuing contribution of nationalist pressures, especially in Northern Ireland and in Scotland itself? Although none of these questions is wholly new, they have taken on a new vigour in the light of the Scottish referendum experience.

Prior to the developments of 1997–99, the British constitutional tradition was one which emphasised the unitary character of the state. The United Kingdom was a country with a single 'supreme' legislature at Westminster. The executive branch of government was, again, a single entity headed formally by the monarch but effectively driven by the Prime Minister and other ministers. Certainly a sharp contrast could be drawn between the unitary United Kingdom and federalist constitutions elsewhere. Dicey sang the praises of the unitary state and especially its sovereign Parliament. He elaborated their advantages over the divisions, weakness and litigiousness of federal government in the United States and elsewhere[1]. But Dicey's was an interpretation clouded by his staunch unionism. For him, the retention of Ireland within the United Kingdom was the political goal and essential to that project was a single supreme Parliament.

Whether or not distorted in this way, however, the legacy of the Diceyan unitary state and supreme Parliament came to dominate constitutional thought[2]. At the same time, the United Kingdom, while formally unitary in its structure, has always been a state with strong decentralising tendencies. Local government has traditionally been a great strength and, although the structure of the systems of local administration varied across the different parts of the United Kingdom and they varied over time, local bodies have borne many of the responsibilities of government which elsewhere have passed to the central state. Local government has acted as a counterweight to central government, in particular in the period since the democratisation of local councils in the late nineteenth century. In Scotland, the royal burghs first established in the 12th century, the parishes and sheriffs were joined by, and ceded power to, the elected country councils created in 1890 and then to the other local authorities established in successive reforms in the 20th century. Although local authorities would, at most, be described as junior partners in their relationship with central government, they have undoubtedly had an important decentralising influence.

Another significant challenge to the unitary model of the UK constitution was represented by the operation for half of the twentieth century of the Stormont system of devolved government in Northern Ireland from 1922 to 1972. This was not federalism in a classical form but the Parliament of Northern Ireland, although formally subordinate to Westminster and ultimately abolished by an Act of the Westminster Parliament[3], enjoyed very wide legislative powers. It was a substantial inroad into the unitary system. Stormont was created out of the special circumstances of Ireland within the United Kingdom, and pressures for independence or for home rule for the whole of Ireland. The Government of Ireland Act 1920 which was designed to devolve powers separately to the North and to the South of Ireland but its implementation was pre-empted by civil war and the creation of the Republic of Ireland in 1922. The struggle for home rule during the period from the 1880s to 1920 was not, however, a process wholly confined to Ireland itself and, for much of that period, there were parallel pressures in Scotland. There was a succession of home rule Bills and there was a joining of forces in 1913 for a Government of the United Kingdom Bill which would have brought 'home rule all round'[4].

Although these developments were ultimately abortive in that they did not bring a Parliament to Scotland at that time and significant moves in that direction were not to be revived until the 1970s, they were taking place against a background in which Scotland was, in other ways, acquiring distinctive institutions of government of its own. Indeed, from the time of the Union itself, the arrangements for the government of Scotland had their own character. The Union, even if it established a formally unitary state, never created a uniformity of provision and was the basis of much of the ensuing diversity.

Much of the government of Scotland fell to the Lord Advocate in the eighteenth century and then to appointed boards (eg the Board of Supervision (for poor relief) and the Prison Commissioners) in the nineteenth century. Later landmarks were the establishment of the Scottish Office under a Secretary for Scotland in 1885[5], the aggregation of functions in that Office which came to be headed by a Secretary of State in 1926, the physical relocation of much of the Scottish Office to St Andrew's House in Edinburgh in 1939[6], and the subsequent transfer to the Scottish Office of further powers (including, for instance, responsibility for major roads) in the 1950s[7].

1 Dicey, ch 3.
2 Including, for a long time, in Scotland. See W I R Fraser *An Outline of Constitutional Law* (2nd edn, 1948).
3 Northern Ireland Constitution Act 1973, s 31.
4 For an illuminating account of all the devolutionary proposals up to the 1970s see A G Donaldson 'Administrative and Legislative Devolution' in J P Grant (ed) *Independence and Devolution:*

The Legal Implications for Scotland (1976). See also J P Mackintosh *The Devolution of Power* (1968).

5 H J Hanham 'The Creation of the Scottish Office, 1881–7' 1965 JR 205; D Milne *The Scottish Office* (1957).

6 Committee on Scottish Administration (Gilmour Committee) (Cmd 5563, 1937). A London base was retained at Dover House, now the London home, within the Ministry of Justice, of the Scotland Office.

7 Royal Commission on Scottish Affairs (Balfour Commission) (Cmd 9212, 1954). See also report of the Royal Commission on the Constitution (Cmnd 5460, 1973) ch 4 and written evidence to the Commission by A W Bradley.

The home rule movement

3.17 As a background to this process of deconcentration of executive authority, political pressure for more radical change in the government of Scotland was building – especially at the hand of the Scottish National Party.

Founded in 1928 as the National Party of Scotland[1] the SNP grew in influence in the period after the 1939–45 war, with its Scottish Covenant of 1945 and subsequent victories in the polls. It was, in particular, the SNP's victory in the parliamentary by-election in Hamilton in 1967 that triggered the creation of the Royal Commission on the Constitution in 1969. The remit of the Kilbrandon Commission[2] was to examine the present functions of the central legislature and government in relation to the several countries, nations and regions of the United Kingdom; to consider, having regard to developments in local government organisations[3] and in the administrative and other relationships between the various parts of the United Kingdom, and to the interests of the prosperity and good government of Our people under the Crown, whether any changes are desirable in those functions or otherwise in present constitutional and economic relationships …'.

The Commission reported in 1973[4]. The enduring impact of the Commission's report has been, first, in its articulation of the late 20th-century case for constitutional change in Scotland. There was, above all, a case for an elected assembly or parliament in Scotland with law-making powers. The separate Scottish legal system and the tendency for Westminster to make much separate legislation for Scotland required a new legislature which should also have the important task of holding the Scottish Office to account. Secondly, however, the Commission legitimised, in modern times, a constitutional design for the United Kingdom which would recognise different needs for Scotland, Northern Ireland, Wales and the English regions and provide different responses for each[5]. It was unnecessary to contemplate a fully federal model of government – a solution firmly rejected by the Commission – and the preferred model of devolved government would clearly have to be asymmetric.

1 See D Young 'A Sketch History of Scottish Nationalism' in N MacCormick (ed) *The Scottish Debate: Essays on Scottish Nationalism* (1970).

2 Lord Kilbrandon succeeded to the chair of the Commission in 1972, on the death of Lord Crowther.

3 For Scotland, the (Wheatley) Royal Commission on Local Government in Scotland and, eventually, the Local Government (Scotland) Act 1973. See ch 8.

4 Cmnd 5460, 1973.

5 It was also, however, a Commission divided within itself. A strong dissent was recorded by two members.

The Scotland and Wales Acts of 1978

3.18   Growing political pressure on the returning Labour government in the 1970s led to its producing proposals for devolved government in Scotland and Wales[1]. A Scotland and Wales Bill[2] failed to make progress, however, and separate Bills were introduced and enacted, in due course, as the Scotland Act 1978 (SA 1978) and the Wales Act 1978. The latter contained a model of executive devolution (ie lacking primary law-making powers) to an elected assembly. On the other hand, SA 1978 would have produced an elected assembly with law-making powers and an executive (headed by a First Secretary) drawn from it. The assembly and executive were to be given a range of devolved powers spelled out in a Schedule to SA 1978. However, the two Acts of 1978 were never implemented. Lacking adequate political control over the House of Commons, the government had been forced to concede the need for the arrangements to be approved by a referendum held in the two countries affected and approved by not merely a majority of those voting but by at least 40 per cent of those entitled to vote[3]. Both referendums held on 1 March 1979 were lost[4] and, following the demise of the government itself in the general election of May 1979, the Acts were repealed[5]. The incoming Conservative government was hostile to devolution. It, and its successors, suppressed legislative proposals for devolution until their own demise in 1997. Politically, the Conservatives were in retreat in Scotland during this period, eventually returning no Scottish MPs at all in the 1997 general election. Constitutionally, they were prepared to 'take stock'[6] and made limited proposals for altering the handling of Scottish business at Westminster, including new rules for the Scottish Grand Committee of the House of Commons[7].

1   At that time England was quiescent and Northern Ireland in the midst of a series of constitutional experiments following the collapse of the Stormont Parliament in 1972 and its replacement by direct rule from London.
2   Following *Our Changing Democracy: Devolution to Scotland and Wales* (Cmnd 6348, 1975).
3   SA 1978, s 85.
4   In the case of SA 1978, a small majority of those voting were in favour of its implementation, but not enough to clear the 40% hurdle.
5   Scotland Act 1978 (Repeal) Order 1979, SI 1979/928; Wales Act 1978 (Repeal) Order 1979, SI 1979/933.
6   *Scotland in the Union: a Partnership for Good* (Cm 2225, 1993).
7   C M G Himsworth 'The Scottish Grand Committee as an Instrument of Government' (1996) 1 Edin LR 79.

The Scottish Constitutional Convention and subsequent developments in Scotland and the United Kingdom

3.19   Outside government, however, the flame of devolution was kept alive. In particular, a broad coalition, which had its origins in a body formed after the 1979 referendum and known as the Campaign for a Scottish Assembly, came together in 1989 as the Scottish Constitutional Convention, following the publication in 1988 of *A Claim of Right for Scotland*[1]. The Convention had a largely political membership drawn from Labour and Liberal MPs, MEPs and councillors and with representatives from other parties, though not the SNP. There was also a sprinkling of representatives from the Scottish Trades Union

Congress, the churches, ethnic minority communities and some others. In 1990 the Convention published a report, *Towards Scotland's Parliament*, containing initial proposals for a new Parliament. It went on to refine these in a final report, *Scotland's Parliament: Scotland's Right*, in 1995.

Although not presented in the form of a draft Bill and lacking some of the detail eventually needed, the Convention's report was highly influential as a blueprint for adoption by the Labour Government elected in 1997 with a manifesto commitment to legislate for a Scottish Parliament. The Government's plans were in the Queen's Speech delivered in the Westminster Parliament on 14 May 1997. Legislation was proposed for a devolved Scottish Parliament and also for a Welsh Assembly, and a directly elected authority for London. There was also a commitment to the need for referendum approval but, astutely, referendums were to be held not after the Acts were passed but before the Bills were even introduced into Parliament, in the light of legislative proposals to be published as White Papers. Public support in referendums would erode political opposition in Parliament. In the event, the referendum held in Scotland on 11 September 1997[2] saw the general question 'that there should be a Scottish Parliament' approved by 74.3 per cent of those voting and a second question 'that the Scottish Parliament should have tax-varying powers' approved by 63.5 per cent[3].

The Scottish White Paper *Scotland's Parliament*[4] to which approval had been given contained detailed proposals for the new arrangements for devolved government. It dealt with the composition and electoral arrangements for the new Parliament, an outline of how it would be expected to operate, the Parliament's relationship to a new Scottish Executive, financial arrangements and the relations between the devolved Scottish institutions and the European Union and other Scottish bodies such as local authorities. In December 1997, the government published its Scotland Bill[5], whose first clause read, in a way which retains a power to excite: 'There shall be a Scottish Parliament'. Thereafter, the Bill contained the provisions which, after some changes made during its parliamentary passage[6], form the basis of many of the later chapters of this book. SA 1998 reached the statute book on 19 November 1998 and was brought into effect in stages up to 1 April 2000[7]. In parallel with the passing of the Act itself, some important discussions were taking place within a body known as the Consultative Steering Group (CSG) on the Scottish Parliament[8]. This was set up by Donald Dewar MP, as Secretary of State for Scotland, in November 1997 with the task of reporting by the end of 1998 on its consideration of the operational needs and working methods of the Parliament and to produce proposals which would inform the preparation of the Parliament's initial standing orders. The CSG was chaired by Henry McLeish MP, at that time Minister of State at the Scottish Office, and contained representatives of all the main political parties as well as some former members of the Constitutional Convention. In December 1998, the CSG produced a substantial report, *Shaping Scotland's Parliament: Report of the Consultative Steering Group on the Scottish Parliament*, which was indeed highly influential in the making of the new Parliament's Standing Orders[9]. Perhaps of equal significance was the Group's generation of the four key principles which guided its own work and, as a manifestation of the 'new politics' intended to operate in devolved

Scotland, have had a lasting importance. In summary, the principles were that (1) the Parliament should embody and reflect the sharing of power between the people of Scotland, the legislators and the Scottish Executive; (2) the Scottish Executive should be accountable to the Scottish Parliament and the Parliament and Executive should be accountable to the people of Scotland; (3) the Parliament should be accessible, open, responsive, and develop procedures which make possible a participative approach to the development, consideration and scrutiny of policy and legislation; and (4) the Parliament in its operation and its appointments should recognise the need to promote equal opportunities for all. It was against the background of these principles that the Procedures Committee of the Parliament conducted its 'CSG inquiry' during 2002–03, leading to the publication of its report in March 2003[10]. The CSG principles have had an enduring appeal, featuring most recently in the work of the Calman Commission, see para 3.20. In addition to the creation of devolved government in Scotland there have been developments in Wales, Northern Ireland, London and the English regions. The emergence of a wider pattern of asymmetric devolution across the United Kingdom as a whole has provided the context within which Scotland's own arrangements have developed. The Government of Wales Act 1998 (GWA 1998)[11] provided a weaker form of devolution than that operating in Scotland. It created the National Assembly for Wales but gave it no primary legislative powers equivalent to those conferred on the Scottish Parliament. Instead, Wales became a country of 'executive devolution' by which it was meant that there were transferred to the Assembly[12] executive powers in defined areas[13] including education, social services, health services and agriculture, formerly exercised by the Secretary of State for Wales. These include powers to make delegated legislation[14]. All primary law-making authority for Wales remained at Westminster. Later, however, the Government of Wales Act 2006 (GWA 2006) was passed[15] to enhance (in two stages) the legislative powers of the Assembly; to reform its electoral arrangements; and to introduce a formal separation between the legislative and executive branches. As a result, the Assembly acquired wider powers to make subordinate legislation and the power to make Assembly measures within areas defined by Order in Council[16]. There were elections on a four-yearly cycle on the Additional Member System[17] and the Welsh Assembly Government (the Welsh Ministers) was established as a separate entity[18]. However, GWA 2006 also made provision for a referendum on the transfer to the Assembly of broader powers of law-making by way of Assembly Acts[19] and in October 2007 an independent All Wales Convention was established, under the chairmanship of Sir Emyr Jones Parry, to enquire into the strength of opinion in favour of such broader powers. The Commission reported in November 2009 with a strong recommendation for the implementation of Part 4 of GWA 2006 and the holding of a referendum which was duly held and the third phase of Welsh devolution began on 6 May 2011. Since that date, the National Assembly has enjoyed legislative powers in respect of matters enumerated in the 20 areas identified in Sch 7 to the Act – and, therefore, according to the 'conferred powers' model, as opposed to the more generous 'reserved powers' model of the Scottish Parliament[20]. Further changes are being made under the Wales Act 2014 which (tracking changes made for Scotland by the Scotland Act 2012) strengthen the financial powers of the National Assembly[21]. In March

2014, the (Silk) Commission on Devolution in Wales, appointed by the UK Coalition Government, made further recommendations for the strengthening of devolution, including the adoption of the reserved powers model of legislative competence[22].

The different arrangements in Wales produce somewhat different relationships between the National Assembly and the UK Government. The retention of primary legislative power at Westminster means that the continuing role of the Secretary of State for Wales (who, unlike his Scottish counterpart, is authorised to participate in Assembly debates[23]) and also of Welsh MPs is different. There is no immediate pressure to reduce Welsh representation in the House of Commons, but there is specific provision for the consultation of the Assembly by the UK Government on its legislative programme for Wales[24]. On the other hand, some of the other over-arching structures of devolution apply in the same way in Wales as in Scotland. Devolved government in Wales is financed by a grant under the same 'Barnett formula' arrangements[25] and 'devolution issues' raising questions about the lawfulness of the exercise of Assembly functions may be taken by reference or appeal to the UK Supreme Court[26].

Although Northern Ireland must be included within any contemporary survey of devolution within the United Kingdom and the institutions created under the Northern Ireland Act 1998 (NIA 1998) provide the basis for close comparison with those in Scotland, there are also difficulties which place such a study beyond the scope of this book[27]. The Assembly and Executive established under NIA 1998 and the powers potentially conferred produce a strong form of legislative devolution similar to that in Scotland. It is, however, a system strongly coloured by the previous history of devolution in the province (producing, for instance, a pattern of excepted, reserved and transferred powers reminiscent of that contained in the Government of Ireland Act 1920) and, more importantly, by the province's political history and present condition. NIA 1998 gives effect to the Belfast (or Good Friday) Agreement of April 1998[28] whose terms were subsequently approved by referendums held in both Northern Ireland and the Republic of Ireland. The Assembly is elected by the single transferable vote system[29] and the Executive is formed according to a sophisticated power-sharing formula[30]. However, progress towards the full implementation and operation of the Northern Ireland scheme of devolution initially became badly stalled because of substantial disagreements between the principal political parties on such fundamental issues as the decommissioning of arms. The Assembly was formally suspended for four periods during 2000 to 2003 following which the Northern Ireland Act 2006 created a non-legislative Assembly which was followed by a 'Transitional Assembly' established under the Northern Ireland (St Andrews Agreement) Act 2006. The devolution of policing and justice was implemented from April 2010[31]. Following a period of fundamental disagreement between the governing parties in Northern Ireland and of intense uncertainty about the future of devolution, on 23 December 2014 agreement was reached (the 'Stormont House Agreement') on some financial and welfare matters. Still unresolved at that point, however, were issues relating to 'flags, culture and tradition', parades, 'the past', and institutional reform. There was a commitment to the regular monitoring of progress towards the implementation of measures to deal with the outstanding issues.

It may be that, in due course, Scottish devolutionary arrangements will be as much affected by the development of regional government in England as by the current evolving settlements in Wales and Northern Ireland. The Greater London Authority Act 1999[32] created the London Assembly and the separately elected Mayor of London in 2000. In May 2002, the UK Government published its proposals for regional government in the rest of England[33]. These would enable the creation of directly elected assemblies in any or all of the eight regions outside London currently established for the purpose of decentralising governmental agencies. Nothing in the proposals, however, compelled the creation of an assembly in a particular region. That required a regional referendum on the issue held under the terms of the Regional Assemblies (Preparations) Act 2003. The Act enabled the Secretary of State to hold a referendum in a region where he had first 'considered the level of interest' in a referendum and he had also received recommendations on consequences for local government in the region[34]. If, as a result of these proposals and the testing of local opinion, regional government in England were to take off in a strong way, there would almost certainly be consequences for Scotland. In the longer term, assuming the continued existence of the United Kingdom, new possibilities for the redistribution of authority within the state might emerge, including perhaps renewed consideration of a federal solution and, less radically, other ways of representing the nations and regions in the UK Parliament[35]. It is also almost inevitable that regional government in England would compel the reconsideration of the financing of devolution across the United Kingdom[36] and might lead to wider reforms of intergovernmental relationships[37] but developments in this direction were wholly stalled in the light of the crushing defeat for the government's proposals for an assembly in north-east England in 2004. The outcome of the Scottish independence referendum of 2014 has, however, revived debate about a possible future for English devolution[38].

1   In due course the *Claim of Right* was formally 'received' by the Presiding Officer of the Scottish Parliament on 29 June 1999.
2   Referendums (Scotland and Wales) Act 1997; cf C R Munro 'Power to the People' [1997] PL 579.
3   For the tax-varying power as passed, see para 11.9.
4   Cm 3658, 1997.
5   See C M G Himsworth and C R Munro *Devolution and the Scotland Bill* (1998).
6   See C M G Himsworth and C R Munro *The Scotland Act 1998* (2nd edn, 2000) xiii–xvii.
7   Scotland Act 1998 (Commencement) Order 1998, SI 1998/3178.
8   See also P Grice 'The Creation of a Devolved Parliament' (2001) 7(3) *Journal of Legislative Studies* 1.
9   Initially contained in the Scotland Act 1998 (Transitory and Transitional Provisions) (Standing Orders and Parliamentary Publications) Order 1999, SI 1999/1095.
10 *The Founding Principles of the Scottish Parliament*, SP PR OR SP Paper 818 (2003).
11 Pursuant to proposals in *A Voice for Wales* (Cm 3718, 1997) and a referendum held on 18 September 1997.
12 GWA 1998, s 22 and then, principally by the National Assembly for Wales (Transfer of Functions) Order 1999, SI 1999/672.
13 GWA 1998, Sch 2.
14 Mainly as statutory instruments and published, unlike Scottish SIs, in the UK series.
15 This implemented proposals made in the (Richard) Report of the Commission on the Powers and Electoral Arrangements of the National Assembly for Wales (2004) and the White Paper 'Better Governance for Wales' (Cm 6582, 2005).
16 GWA 2006, ss 93–102 and Sch 5.

17 GWA 2006, Pt 1.

18 GWA 2006, ss 45–55.

19 GWA 2006, Pt 4.

20 For a useful account of the phases of Welsh devolution, see Lord Reed's judgment in *Agricultural Sector (Wales) Bill – Reference by the Attorney General for England and Wales* [2014] 4 All ER 789 at paras 18–29.

21 The Act (s 4) also formally amends the name of the Welsh Assembly Government to the Welsh Government, already informally adopted since 2011.

22 *Empowerment and Responsibility: Legislative Powers to Strengthen Wales* was the Commission's second report. See also the Commission's first report (Nov 2012) *Empowerment and Responsibility: Financial Powers to Strengthen Wales.*

23 GWA 2006, s 32.

24 GWA 2006, s 33.

25 GWA 2006, s 117 and see ch 11.

26 GWA 2006, s 149, Sch 9, and see ch 14.

27 On the situation prior to 1998, see H Calvert *Constitutional Law in Northern Ireland* (1968); B Hadfield *The Constitution of Northern Ireland* (1989). On more recent events, see B Hadfield 'The Implementation of the Belfast Agreement, in part or in whole' (2002) EPL 22.

28 Cm 3383, 1998.

29 Northern Ireland (Elections) Act 1998, s 2.

30 NIA 1998, ss 16–20.

31 SI 2010/976.

32 After a referendum held in May 1998 under the Greater London Authority (Referendum) Act 1998.

33 *Your Region, Your Choice: Revitalising the English Regions* (Cm 5511, 2002).

34 Regional Assemblies (Preparations) Act 2003, s 1(4), (5).

35 For proposals in relation to the House of Lords, see para 5.14.

36 See ch 11.

37 See para 7.26.

38 See para 4.21.

The Further Evolution of the Scottish Constitution

3.20   If recent years have been, by any standards, a period of rapid constitutional change in Scotland, the period since the formation of the minority SNP Government in 2007 and then of a majority SNP Government in 2011 has raised the most acute questions about Scotland's constitutional future. These have been most poignantly characterised by two, largely conflicting, constitutional projects. On the one hand there has been the Scottish Government's own independence project launched as its 'National Conversation' in August 2007[1]. This offered the prospect of a route to an independent Scotland by means of the opening of negotiations on independence with the UK government following approval in a national referendum. A draft Bill designed to establish the machinery for such a referendum was published[2] and there were discussions and meetings as a part of the Conversation, although in March 2009, the Parliament itself approved a motion urging that the Scottish Government should abandon its referendum plans[3]. In the meantime, however, from the 2007 Parliament itself, but with the support of the UK government, came the establishment in April 2008 of the Commission on Scottish Devolution chaired by Sir Kenneth Calman. This was given a remit to consider ways of changing present constitutional arrangements to enable the Scottish Parliament 'to serve the people of Scotland better'. In December 2008, the Commission published an interim report[4] in which it set out its provisional thoughts, to that point, on the emerging practice of devolution and on the powers and funding of the Parliament and in June 2009 it published its final report[5]. This provided a powerful restatement of the perceived advantages of the Union and of the benefits to Scotland of devolution. But devolution, though successful, was in need of further development. Most prominent were Calman's funding proposals. The financial accountability of the Scottish Parliament needed to be improved. There should be a new 'Scottish rate of income tax' to replace the existing, and unused, limited power to vary the UK rate; there should be additional devolved powers to tax; and provision for more to follow as required. These proposals were substantially adopted by the UK Government in a White Paper *Strengthening Scotland's Future*[6] and enacted in the Scotland Act 2012 (SA 2012)[7]. Calman also recommended small adjustments to the legislative competence of the Scottish Parliament (eg to regulate air guns)[8]; and various institutional reforms affecting the Scottish Parliament and the Scottish Government (including formally giving the Government that name) and the improvement of relationships between the Scottish and UK Governments and Parliaments[9]. Again, the substance of these proposals was carried forward, via the *Strengthening Scotland's Parliament* into SA 2012. Additionally, although Calman (pp164–5) made no recommendation and the issue had not been resolved by the time of the White Paper (p 69), SA 2012 contained important new provision for the handling of 'compatibility issues' by the UK Supreme Court[10]. Its content apart, however, the passing of SA 2012 was also an important aspect of the independence referendum story. The process bridged the Scottish Parliament general election of 2011 and thus the emergence of the SNP Government from minority to majority status. Inevitably, therefore, the unionist plans for their version of stronger devolution provided an opportunity for nationalist selection of which aspects of the Scotland Bill were acceptable and which not. This was manifested in the process of passing 'legislative consent motions' in respect of the Bill[11].

The ways in which independence referendum period has added to the further development of the constitution and shaped its future are considered in Chapter 4.

1   *Choosing Scotland's Future: A National Conversation.*
2   Ibid Annex B.
3   SPOR 5 March 2009, col 15578.
4   *The Future of Scottish Devolution within the Union: A First Report*, 2008.
5   *Serving Scotland Better: Scotland and the United Kingdom in the 21st Century.*
6   Cm 7973, Nov 2010.
7   See paras 11.5–11.9.
8   See para 6.17.
9   See para 7.26.
10 See paras 14.19–14.21.
11 See para 6.22.

Chapter 4

The Scottish Independence Referendum

INTRODUCTION

4.1   One phenomenon which, more than any other, serves to frame the context within which the contemporary Scottish constitution can be analysed has been the Scottish independence referendum. This culminated in the question being put to the people of Scotland on 18 September 2014: 'Should Scotland be an independent country?'. If the answer had been 'Yes', then Scotland would now be on its way to becoming a separate state, probably by 24 March 2016, and the content of this book would have been the subject of a total overhaul. In the event, however, the answer given to that question was an overall 'No'. There were 1,617,989 votes in favour and 2,001,926 against – a result which, on its face, simply left the existing devolution arrangements in place. But this would be wholly to misunderstand the impact on Scotland of the events of the period up to the referendum, the referendum campaign, and the conditions under which the result was decided. As we saw in Chapter 3, the Scottish Parliament general election of May 2007 produced a (minority) SNP Government in Edinburgh and that may be taken as the start of the referendum process. The SNP had been politically committed to an independent Scotland but it was the Party's election to Government which first signalled that, far from devolution killing Scottish independence stone-dead[1], the independence question would dominate the political and constitutional agenda of the country. Looking back in its aftermath, this chapter discusses the legal and constitutional events – conditioned by the historical backdrop of the Union of 1707 and the launch of devolution in 1999 – which led to the holding of the referendum and then its constitutional impact. Many of the referendum's more detailed consequences are spelled out at different points later in the book. But its impact overall is, at present, unknowable. Nothing, however, will be quite the same again!

1 A view expressed by Lord Robertson of Ellen in 1995.

THE POLITICAL CONTEXT

4.2   The general election to the Scottish Parliament of 2007 gave the SNP a governmental platform from which to launch their proposals for independence. From the start, these were to be progressed on the basis of a 'National Conversation' among the Scottish people. The Government published *Independence and Responsibility in the Modern World*[1]. At the heart of these proposals was a commitment to the holding of a referendum, in which the approval of the Scottish people would be sought. Such a referendum would be consultative in nature and a positive result would provide the basis for the Scottish Government opening negotiations with the UK Government on how independence might then be delivered. There had been a long-standing understanding on the part of successive UK Governments[2] that, should the SNP achieve a majority of the Scottish seats in the House of Commons or, latterly, a majority in the Scottish Parliament, the right to an independence referendum (and implementation, if affirmative) would be conceded.

If an SNP Government in 2007 was unexpected, the result of the 2011 general election was even more extraordinary. An assumed virtue of the Scottish Parliament's electoral system[3] had been that it would never deliver an overall majority to any single political party but this was exactly what was achieved by the SNP at the 2011 election. The party won a landslide victory and formed a majority Government, with the power and authority not only to argue for the holding of a referendum but also, all other things being equal, with a parliamentary majority enabling it to pass any legislation required for that purpose. After its election, that Parliament, initially expected to last until 2015, had its life extended, for unrelated reasons, to 2016[4].

In the meantime, at Westminster the general election of 2010 had replaced the previous Labour Government with a Conservative-Liberal Democrat Coalition. It became a matter of some significance during the referendum period that, at the UK level, the Government was Conservative-led. A strong element in the SNP campaign was to remind voters of the Thatcherite inheritance and to argue that Scotland should never again have a Conservative Government imposed by the predominantly English electorate. After the referendum, the Labour Party was blamed for its collaboration with the Conservatives during the campaign.

1 *Choosing Scotland's Future: A National Conversation – Independence and Responsibility in the Modern World* (2007).
2 See S Tierney *Constitutional Law and National Pluralism* (2004) p 323. That understanding of the Scottish people's right to decide (also reflected in the (Kilbrandon) Royal Commission Report (Cmnd 5460, 1973)) is often contrasted with the less accommodating approach of the Spanish Government to Catalonian aspirations. It should, however, be recalled that, until the closing days of the referendum campaign, there was always a widely-shared consensus that only a small minority of Scots would actually opt for independence and, therefore, that the understanding did not signify much.
3 See para 5.8.
4 See para 5.4.

THE LEGAL AUTHORITY TO HOLD A REFERENDUM

4.3   Whilst it may be open to any government to promote the idea of a referendum as a part of pursuing its overall policy objectives, it is almost inevitable that the actual holding of a referendum requires a legal basis deriving from legislation made by parliament. The referendum rules need to be formally adopted. In a Scottish context, this offered the choice of passing an Act by either the UK or the Scottish Parliament. But it was the very strong preference of the SNP Government that it should be the Scottish Parliament. As well as keeping the symbolic 'ownership' of the process within Scotland, rather than having it appear to be driven primarily from Westminster, this would keep most of the rule-making within the direct control of the Scottish Government and Parliament.

A further question was, however, bound to arise. Whatever the strategic preference of the Scottish Government, did the Scottish Parliament have the legal authority, the legal competence, to pass the necessary legislation? To understand this question and the answer to it, it is necessary, first, to understand that the Scottish Parliament is a Parliament of defined legislative competence[1]. It may pass Acts only if they are within its competence and it may not pass Acts outwith that competence. An attempt to do so will be prevented by the courts[2] and it is more than likely that, given the SNP's political dominance of the Parliament, in this case, the Unionist parties (or other opponents of independence) would have sought to challenge the terms of a referendum Bill devised by the SNP alone.

The rules on legislative competence are complex but, in a nutshell, the Scottish Parliament is *excluded* from making laws which 'relate to' matters reserved to the Westminster Parliament[3] which include, among many other things, 'the Constitution', which, in turn, is defined as including 'the Union of the Kingdoms of Scotland and England'[4]. During 2012, different views emerged as to whether the Scottish Parliament was thereby excluded from enacting a law providing for an independence referendum[5]. There were those, including the UK Government itself, who argued that such a referendum law would clearly 'relate to' the constitution and would be illegal[6]. There were, on the other hand, those, including the Scottish Government, who argued that a referendum Bill would survive any challenge[7]. In the event, the issue was never tested or finally resolved by a court. Instead both Governments were persuaded that a compromise position on the legislative route to be taken should be adopted.

1 See ch 6.
2 See chs 6 and 14.
3 SA 1998, ss 28, 29.
4 SA 1998, Sch 5, Part 1, para 1.
5 For a (not at all impartial) discussion, see House of Lords Select Committee on the Constitution, *Referendum on Scottish Independence* 24th Report (2010–12) HL Paper 263, ch 2.
6 *Scotland's Constitutional Future* Cm 8203 (2012).
7 In the second edition of this book, it was suggested that a referendum Act would 'almost certainly' be within the competence of the Parliament (see p 133).

THE EDINBURGH AGREEMENT

4.4   That compromise position was at the heart of a document signed by First Minister Salmond and Prime Minister Cameron on 15 October 2012 – a document which came to be known as the 'Edinburgh Agreement'[1]. The principal purpose of the Agreement (and its attached memorandum) was to record the parties' joint commitment to the promotion of an Order in Council under s 30 of SA 1998 – the mechanism used to amend Sch 5 to the 1998 Act to enable the Scottish Parliament to pass a law providing for a 'referendum on the independence of Scotland from the rest of the United Kingdom'. The referendum should thus be given 'a clear legal base'; it should also be 'conducted so as to command the confidence of parliaments, governments and people; and deliver a fair test and a decisive expression of the views of people in Scotland and a result that everyone will respect.' The referendum 'should meet the highest standards of fairness, transparency and propriety, informed by consultation and independent expert advice.' The poll had to be held no later than 31 December 2014. The Order in Council was also to make some other (limited) provision about the holding of the referendum and the memorandum recorded the Governments' agreement about some of the further rules to be laid down in the legislation to be passed by the Scottish Parliament. They should be in accordance with the principles underpinning the existing (UK) framework for referendums which regulates campaign finance and fairness. The referendum question itself was not determined by the Agreement but had to be 'fair, easy to understand and capable of producing a result that is accepted and commands confidence'. The wording of the question would be decided by the Scottish Parliament in a Bill introduced by the Scottish Government, and subject to the Electoral Commission's review process. In addition to anticipating the principal rules, the Agreement contained a commitment 'to working together on matters of mutual interest and to the principles of good communication and mutual respect'. The two Governments were further committed, in words which resonate strongly in the referendum's aftermath, 'to continue to work together constructively in the light of the outcome, whatever it is, in the best interests of the people of Scotland and of the rest of the United Kingdom' (para 30).

1 *Agreement between the United Kingdom Government and the Scottish Government on a referendum on independence for Scotland* (2012).

LEGISLATING FOR THE REFERENDUM

4.5   In the course of 2013, the legislation anticipated in the Edinburgh Agreement was passed. In the first place, the Order in Council, a draft of which had been approved by both Houses of the UK Parliament[1] and the Scottish Parliament[2] was made[3]. It duly amended Sch 5 to SA 1998 by excluding from the Act's 'constitution' reservation (and thus, in effect, permitting the Scottish Parliament to pass a law) a referendum on the independence of Scotland, provided that three conditions were met: the date of the poll was not to coincide with the date of any other referendum to be held under the Parliament's authority; the date had to be no later than 31 December 2014; and the referendum's ballot paper had to be restricted to only two responses[4]. This paved the way for the Scottish Parliament's own legislation and, because there was a degree of urgency formally to determine who would be entitled to be voters in the referendum, the first Act was directed towards that. The right to vote remained a controversial issue throughout the referendum process. There were those who argued that, as a matter so crucial to the future of Scotland and also of the United Kingdom, the franchise should, for instance, extend across the whole of the United Kingdom to include all resident citizens[5]. Others sought a vote for all 'Scots' (by birth or heritage) whether resident in Scotland, the rest of the United Kingdom or indeed anywhere in the world and challenges to the eventual rules laid down were thought possible. However, the SNP was committed to a referendum based on residence in Scotland, a position which could be grounded both in principle ('civic nationalism' rather than anything suggesting an ethnic basis for qualification) and in pragmatism. The use, as far as possible, of existing voters' rolls would be administratively very attractive and, by the time of the Edinburgh Agreement, it was settled (paras 9–11) that those entitled to vote in the referendum would be those already entitled to vote in Scottish parliamentary and local elections[6] – with one potential adjustment. The Scottish Government had been consulting on reducing the voting age to include 16 and 17 year-olds and, when the time came for legislation, this was the principal contribution of the Scottish Independence Referendum (Franchise) Act 2013[7]. It was a radical innovation in UK practice but was only lightly contested in the Scottish Parliament, in large measure on the grounds that the franchise should not be extended in this way on a one-off basis[8]. Another of the Act's provisions specifically excluded convicted prisoners from voting – a provision later unsuccessfully challenged in the courts[9].

1 HC Deb 15 Jan 2013 cols 742-840; HL Deb 16 Jan 2013 cols 694-756. See also the report of the HC Scottish Affairs Committee HC 863 (2012–13), 'The Referendum on Separation for Scotland: The Proposed Section 30 Order – can a player also be the referee?'.
2 SP OR 5 Dec 2012 cols 14376-14398 and 14410. See also the report of the Parliament's Referendum (Scotland) Bill Committee, SP Paper 221 (23 Nov 2012). The Committee had been established to scrutinise all the legislation implementing the referendum.
3 SI 2013/242, 12 February 2013.
4 The Order also extended to the referendum certain provisions of PPERA 2000, which regulate the holding of UK referendums and elections.
5 There was a prominent campaign by James Wallace (from Dumfries, but resident in London) given publicity by Elaine Murray MSP in a debate in the Scottish Parliament on 18 Jan 2012.
6 See para 5.6.
7 See s 2(1).
8 SP OR 27 June 2013 cols 21824-5.
9 *Moohan v Lord Advocate* 2015 SLT 2.

4.6   The other referendum legislation anticipated in the Edinburgh Agreement was enacted in a second Act of the Scottish Parliament – the Scottish Independence Referendum Act 2013[1]. Its most important provisions were s 1(4) which finalised the date of the referendum as 18 September 2014[2] and s 1(2), (3) and sch 1 which prescribed the content and form of the referendum ballot paper, with the instruction '**Vote (X) ONLY ONCE**' with **YES** and **NO** boxes for answering the question: 'Should Scotland be an independent country?'. That question was proposed by the Scottish Government after its earlier suggestion – Do you agree that Scotland should be an independent country? – had been criticised by the Electoral Commission[3] as insufficiently neutral. Even with the change made, however, the framing of the question in this way helped to characterise the Yes campaign as positive, in contrast with the No campaign's negativity – a phenomenon which, combined with other aspects of the No campaign, framed its presentation as inevitably much less radically progressive than the Yes campaign.

The Act then made administrative provision for the conduct of the referendum, including the appointment of the Chief Counting Officer[4] and her staff, and voting arrangements (s 4 and sch 2). The Chief Counting Officer was required to take whatever steps she considered appropriate to encourage participation in the referendum (s 26(1)). Section 34 of the Act confined any legal challenge (by judicial review[5]) to the counting of votes to a period of six weeks.

Potentially of greatest significance were the rules laid down by the Act (s 11 and sch 4)[6] to govern the conduct of the campaign (under the general supervision of the Electoral Commission) and especially those which governed campaign expenditure during the 'campaign period' of 16 weeks prior to the poll[7] – ie from 30 May 2014. In the event, despite the possibility of disputes over funding sources and levels during or after the referendum, this never became an area of contention.

1 It received Royal Assent on 18 Dec 2013.
2 Subject to the possibility of its deferral (to no later than 31 Dec 2014) by the Scottish Ministers.
3 *Referendum on Independence for Scotland: Advice of the Electoral Commission on the Proposed Referendum Question* (2013).
4 Defined by s 5 as the Chair of the Electoral Management Board for Scotland who is Ms Mary Pitcaithly.
5 See ch 14.
6 Substantially derived from PPERA 2000. See para 5.12.
7 Section 35 and sch 8.

THE REFERENDUM CAMPAIGN[1]

4.7   We have seen that the Edinburgh Agreement and the Referendum Acts of the Scottish Parliament which followed sought to lay down the ground rules for the referendum campaign. In doing so, however, they told only a very small part of a very much more complex story. In defining the period subject to campaign spending limitations, they failed to explain that the campaign was not waged over a mere 14 weeks but had begun, in effect, in 2007. Even if its start was defined by the launch of the 'Yes' and 'No'/'Better Together' campaigns in May and June 2013, this was a long period of contention. Campaign participants were not confined to those directly regulated by the Referendum Act. Nor were the campaign issues pre-defined. Although all were targeted on the question to be posed on 18 September, the actual issues raised during the campaign period ranged very widely. The modern politics of Scotland and of the United Kingdom as a whole has experienced nothing like it. For constitutional lawyers, it was a period of rich debate. Most campaign issues had a built-in constitutional aspect.

This is not the place for a blow-by-blow account of the referendum campaigns – the most prominent aspect of which were the two TV debates conducted by the two campaign leaders (Alex Salmond and Alistair Darling) on 5 and 25 August 2014 but in which there were also hundreds of meetings and debates across the country. Instead, there will be a brief listing of the principal participants and of their publications; and then of the principal constitutional issues raised in (and by) the campaigns.

1 For a valuable early analysis, see T Mullen 'The Scottish Independence Referendum 2014' (2014) 41 Jo Law and Soc 627.

Campaign Participants and their Publications

4.8   Taking a broad view, participants in the campaigns may be taken to include not only the core contenders – the Yes and No campaigns, the Scottish and UK Governments, the political parties, and the more loosely-defined groups in civil society which aligned themselves with one or other side in the debate;

but also others who, whilst deliberately avoiding taking sides on the issues, nevertheless contributed to, and thus participated in, the referendum process.

By far the largest single documentary contribution to the referendum debate was that of the SNP Government's White Paper *Scotland's Future: Your Guide to an Independent Scotland*. It was published in November 2013 and, at over 650 pages, was available online but also free, on application, in print to any UK address. Like all the other documents of its period, *Scotland's Future* was a campaigning document. Prefaced by a statement from the First Minister and concluding with 70 pages of annexes and endnotes, its meat was in Parts 1 (the case for independence), 2 (Scotland's finances), 3 (seven chapters on SNP policy proposals on the economy, health, education and others), and 4 (constitutional aspects under the heading of 'building a modern democracy'). Part 5 (Questions and answers) contained over 200 pages of 650 answers to 'questions about independence that have been asked of us'. A precise assessment of the document's impact would, of course, be elusive but its publication did herald a narrowing of the polls in favour of the Yes campaign. If *Scotland's Future* made an impact on public opinion it may be because it succeeded in contributing information and 'facts' to the debate. It was also, of course, a document of conviction and belief and, in this mode, relied principally upon the notion of independence bringing the opportunity for the people of Scotland to decide for themselves who should govern and formulate policies on their behalf. It very deliberately straddled the divide between the general advantages that independence would bring and then, on the other hand, the benefits of an SNP Government, were it to continue in power after independence. On specifically constitutional matters, *Scotland's Future* was important for its identification of 24 March 2016 as a 'realistic independence date' (pp 51 and 338), its account of what would occur in the transitional period between September 2014 and March 2016, and its proposals for constitution-making thereafter. The 'realism' of the independence date became controversial, especially as to the claim that it would permit sufficient time for negotiations with the UK Government, the European Union and other international partners and organisations. In due course, the constitutional proposals were to be fleshed out in a further Government paper[1] but *Scotland's Future* contained a sketch of the process whereby, in reliance on the Edinburgh Agreement, legislation by both the Scottish and UK Parliaments would establish a 'constitutional platform for independence' (pp 52 and 338) – although '[a]s with the referendum, independence will be made in Scotland' (p 338). There would also be the necessary transitional provision for Scottish institutions (including a Supreme Court) and laws in advance of the drafting in the post-independence period of a permanent written constitution by an independent, appointed convention. The Scottish Government declared its own commitment to the sovereignty of the Scottish people, the retention of the monarchy, but also to a ban on Scotland-based nuclear weapons. A commitment to local government and to reformed public services was asserted. Just about retaining the normal modulated tone of a Government White Paper, *Scotland's Future* also documented, with an eye to opponents in the campaign, the perceived disadvantages of a No vote (p 60) – the continuing control by Westminster and the lack of assurance of any increased powers for the Scottish Parliament. The risk would remain of a forced departure from the European Union, if a UK-wide referendum were held.

1 See para 4.14 below.

4.9   The UK Government's formal contribution took the form of a series of 15 documents published between February 2013 and June 2014[1] under the general heading of the 'Scotland Analysis Programme', opening with *Scotland analysis: devolution and the implications of Scottish independence*[2] which included a substantial Annex on international law aspects and closing with *United Kingdom, united future: Conclusions of the Scotland Analysis Programme*[3]. Documents in the series included the UK Government's views on currency and monetary policy, security, borders and citizenship, energy and work and pensions. The 'Conclusions' emphasised the success of the 300 years of Union and urged the merits of having 'the best of both worlds'.

1 https://www.gov.uk/government/collections/scotland-analysis
2 Cm 8554, 2013.
3 Cm 8869, 2014.

4.10   The other principal campaign documents came from the Unionist parties. An early feature of the campaign had been an absence of proposals from them as to Scotland's constitutional future in the event of a No vote[1]. They may have assumed that, whereas the Yes campaign had to make its case for change, the No campaign could content itself with simply opposing those arguments. In due course, however, political pressure compelled the No parties to describe their own versions of the future. It was already apparent that merely arguing for the status quo, even as already amended by SA 2012, simply would not suffice.

Following an interim report in April 2013, Scottish Labour's Devolution Commission produced its *Powers for a Purpose – Strengthening Accountability and Empowering People* in March 2014. There was a principal focus on the funding of devolution with a proposal to widen the Scottish Parliament's power to vary income tax levels from the 10p of the Scotland Act 2012 to 15p. The need for the core matters reserved by SA 1998 to be kept at the UK level was reaffirmed but certain powers (notably over housing benefit and attendance allowance) should be devolved. 'Double devolution' – the promise of greater powers for local authorities (and for the island authorities in particular) – should be assured.

Also in March 2014, the Scottish Liberal Democrats published a brief follow-up ('Campbell II') to their ('Campbell I') Report of the Party's Home Rule and Community Rule Commission: *Federalism: the best future for Scotland* (October 2012). It sought to address perceived weaknesses, at that stage, in the No campaign's case. On the one hand, it stressed the high degree of consensus across the No campaigners as to what should follow a No vote. Even with the Conservatives yet to report formally, it was possible to claim agreement on the expansion of the Scottish Parliament's tax-raising powers to enable it to fund a majority of devolved expenditure; and, deriving support from Gordon Brown's call for the Scottish Parliament to be 'indissoluble'[2], that the Scottish Parliament should be permanently 'entrenched'. The other need was to commit to a rapid response to a No vote (rather than the inactivity predicted in *Scotland's Future*), according to a timetable laid down. The Secretary of State for Scotland should convene a broadly-composed planning meeting within 30 days of the referendum, with a view to all parties including commitments to the implementation of strengthened devolution in their manifestos for the 2015 UK general election.

The Scottish Conservatives were the third of the main Unionist parties to declare their position by adopting the proposals of their (Strathclyde) Commission on the Future Governance of Scotland. That Commission's principal recommendations (published in May 2014) once again focused on funding, with a proposal that all the rates and bands of income tax in Scotland be decided by the Scottish Parliament. It acknowledged a case for devolving housing benefit (and attendance allowance) and a power to supplement welfare benefits. But the state pension should remain a UK matter. It also proposed reform of the scrutiny powers of the Parliament and of the senior civil service; greater decentralisation to local government; and the notion of a 'Committee of all the Parliaments and Assemblies of the United Kingdom'.

1 But see para 4.13 below.
2 See his book, *My Scotland, Our Britain* (Simon & Schuster, 2014).

4.11   A complete list of other (institutional) participants in the campaign(s) would be extremely long but selectively:

(a)   Other political parties included the Scottish Green Party and the Scottish Socialists who campaigned under the Yes Scotland banner.

(b)   Existing NGOs engaged in the debate, either to take sides or in a more impartial mode. So, for instance, the Electoral Reform Society produced its *Democracy Max: A Vision for a Good Scottish Democracy* (2013); the Institute for Public Policy Research (IPPR) promoted the concept of 'devo more'[1] through publications such as *Funding Devo More* (2013), *Devo More and Welfare* (2014), *Financing Devolution and the More or Less Federal Model* (2013) and *Divorcing a Nation: What Happens if Scotland Separates?* (2014).

(c)   Other (partisan) organisations spontaneously emerged. 'Lawyers for Yes', to which a number of academic and practising lawyers signed up, took a particular interest in legal and constitutional aspects of the Yes campaign. On the other side was 'Lawyers Together'.

(d)   A special category of participant were those whose primary concern was reconciliation after the event – see especially 'Collaborative Scotland'[2].

(e)   In another special category of 'participant' were the two Parliaments and their Committees. The House of Commons Scottish Affairs Committee and the House of Lords Constitution Committee intervened strongly on the No side. The Scottish Parliament's Referendum (Scotland) Bill Committee[3] was, of course, SNP controlled and the European and External Relations Committee also intervened on the matter of EU membership[4].

The UK perspective and the consequences of a Yes vote for the continuing United Kingdom were a particular focus of the House of Lords Constitution

Committee's Report on *Scottish Independence: Constitutional Implications of the Referendum* of May 2014[5]. The report laid an early emphasis on its conclusion, based on expert evidence that, in the event of separation[6], the United Kingdom would continue (as 'continuator state') whilst Scotland would have become a successor state, a fact that would have shaped the implications of independence. A Bill would need to be introduced to establish a negotiating team for the United Kingdom and to devolve a new power to the Scottish Parliament to establish Scotland's team.

One special intervention came from the independent Electoral Commission itself. In its 12-page *The 2014 Scottish Independence Referendum:Voting Guide* the Commission offered guidance on the voter registration and voting processes. It also offered brief statements from the two sides and then a joint statement from the two Governments – based on the consequences of a Yes or No vote. There was a focus on the formal consequences for the powers of the Scottish Parliament and Government.

1 As opposed to 'devo max' – taken to mean the devolution of all powers except defence and foreign affairs.
2 http://collaborativescotland.org/
3 From 29 October 2014, redesignated the Devolution (Further Powers) Committee.
4 http://www.scottish.parliament.uk/S4_EuropeanandExternalRelationsCommittee/Reports/euR-14-02w-rev.pdf
5 8th Report (2013–14) HL Paper 188.
6 'Separation' was the terminology preferred by the No campaign.

Campaign Issues

4.12   Those statements from the Electoral Commission may have captured the formal anticipated consequences of the vote. But they conceal both the richness and extent of other issues and also their relative prominence in the minds of voters. It was impossible to know how far issues of the heart – questions of belonging or identity – prevailed. Or whether issues of the mind – those which might have depended for their resolution upon the facts and figures of independence, as opposed to more devolution – were dominant. Or how far any issues at all, of either type, swayed voters over the referendum period. Until the closing stages, opinion polls moved little. There was a media assumption that the public wanted more 'facts' but how far these were ultimately relevant, even if forthcoming, is not easily knowable. Looming large in the course of the campaign were the issues of the future health of Scotland's economy, the future Scottish currency, access to the European Union – but with an emphasis (from the Yes side) on the freedom of the Scottish people to decide their own future, rather than governments (especially Conservative governments) elected from other parts of the United Kingdom.

Independence versus enhanced devolution

4.13   At the heart of the whole referendum process was, of course, the question put to the voters about their wish, or not, that Scotland be 'an independent country'. This apparently simple choice concealed other, more complex, considerations. In the first place, there was a widely felt regret that the vote offered no 'middle way'. Although, in the early stages of the process, it had appeared that a stronger form of home rule would be the preferred choice of most voters – rather than either independence or the status quo – this was not to be on offer. The SNP had originally preferred a straight yes/ no choice but had subsequently been persuaded that a third option should be made available. The UK Government had, however, insisted, at the time of the Edinburgh Agreement, that a clear two-way choice had first to be made. However, retaining a simple dichotomy in the question asked did not produce simplicity in debate. The prospects for independence and, on the other hand, for continued devolution had to be interrogated. Four features dominated.

First, the meaning of 'independence' turned out to be not as simple as might have been imagined. Scotland would take its own place on the international stage with its own seat in the United Nations. It would have its own constitution. But Scotland's would be an independence (sometimes categorised in derogatory terms as 'independence-lite') which, for the SNP, would have retained strong (and not merely social) ties to the United Kingdom – the Queen as head of state, the pound sterling as Scotland's currency (see below) and many services (initially at least) shared with the United Kingdom, especially, for instance, in relation to energy markets and power transmission networks[1].

Secondly, even if enhanced devolution was not itself to be an option on the voting paper, it came to be recognised by all the No political parties that their case depended on the coherence of their proposals for the strengthening of devolution in the event of a No vote and the credibility of the prospects for their adoption. Their broadly parallel offerings of more powers were followed, on the eve of the first television debate on 5 August 2014 by a consolidated undertaking to expand the powers of the Parliament, and then, in the closing days of the campaign (and at a time when the polls had briefly narrowed to give the No campaign only a very slight lead or no lead at all), by a joint 'Vow' published in a Scottish daily newspaper[2]. This was an agreement signed by the leaders of the three main UK political parties, inter alia, that the Scottish Parliament is permanent and that extensive new powers would be delivered. The 'Barnett allocation of resources'[3] would continue. It was a curiosity of a referendum in which a 'middle-way' question had been denied that a promised compromise of expanded powers came to be offered as the core element of the No package. As we shall see below, the 'Vow' had a profound post-referendum impact.

Thirdly, the meeting of the two campaigns on a shared middle-ground of better governance produced many overlapping issues. The best example is that of local government (including governance arrangements for the islands). Local government would continue, whatever the referendum result, but campaigners expressed views nevertheless (see para 4.15 below).

Fourthly, the debate over the choices between independence for Scotland or continued devolution (with the promise of expanded powers) prompted discussion, both within Scotland and in the United Kingdom as a whole, about the continued viability of its own constitutional order. This continued after the referendum.

1 Also eg DVLA.
2 *Daily Record*, 16 September 2014. http://www.dailyrecord.co.uk/news/scottish-news/daily-record-continues-set-agenda-4268950
3 See ch 11.

Constitutional design

4.14   But, returning to the core question of independence, a primary focus (although not on the streets!) was on the resulting need, if there were a Yes vote, for a written constitution for Scotland – uncharted waters in a UK context. The SNP had always made it clear that, in the event of independence, Scotland should have a new written constitution, a policy reiterated (see para 4.8 above) in *Scotland's Future*. These views were, however, expanded in a green paper – *The Scottish Independence Bill: A Consultation on an Interim Constitution for Scotland* – published in June 2014. The principal content of the paper was a draft Bill. The Independence Bill proper would be published and passed by the Scottish Parliament (by its normal process) with a view to its being in force from 24 March 2016 until replaced by a permanent constitution. The Act would not itself be entrenched but would be expected to have 'constitutional status'[1]. The draft Bill's principal content lay in Part 2, designated the interim constitution of Scotland. This made skeletal provision for the institutions of the new state, its territory, and citizenship. The draft also included reference to the court system, the EU, and the ECHR as well as equality, children's well-being, and nuclear disarmament. It also provided for the establishment of a Constitutional Convention to produce a new substantive constitution for independent Scotland.

Importantly, the Independence Act would 'sit alongside' (pp 22 and 50) the Scotland Acts (SA 1998 and SA 2012) which would be 'refreshed and rewritten'. Together they would be the 'constitutional platform'. Whilst many of the current rules establishing the Scottish Parliament and Government would be retained, it was anticipated that all those provisions enabling legislation for Scotland by the Westminster Parliament or a role for the UK Government or the UK Supreme Court would be removed. The modifications required would be enacted at Westminster, in the spirit, it was assumed, of the Edinburgh Agreement. Both the revised Scotland Act and the Independence Act would remain in force, along with other continuing laws, until subsequently modified by the (independent) Scottish Parliament and the constitution-making process itself (s 34).

What, of course, had to be recognised at the time of the publication of these proposals was that, although they were presented in the style of a legislative consultation with all the appropriate technicality of phrasing, they were nonetheless serving principally as a campaigning tool. The emphasis on the current Scotland Act 'restrictions' on the Scottish Parliament, and the incorporation of the 'sovereignty of the people' into the new constitutional dispensation prioritised change, whilst the insistence nevertheless on a degree of continuity of laws and institutions (notably the monarchy) sought to maintain a non-threatening approach. The inclusion of policy imperatives on child welfare, nuclear disarmament, and equality served clear campaigning purposes.

1 See para 6.10.

Double-Devolution, Local Government and the Islands

4.15   It is not surprising that the referendum process triggered interventions by other interested parties seeking solutions to problems of their own, whichever way the vote went on 18 September. Prominent among them were Scotland's local authorities and, as a special case within them, the Scottish islands authorities of Orkney, Shetland, and the Western Isles. The Convention of Scottish Local Authorities (COSLA)[1] established a Commission on Strengthening Local Democracy which reported in August 2014[2]. The Commission made no specific proposals for reform but offered a strong plea for real subsidiarity and for an end to central domination of local government. Meanwhile, the islands authorities combined to publish their *Our Islands – Our Future* in June 2013[3] seeking a special status for their areas, whatever the referendum outcome, which attracted undertakings by the Scottish Government in the form of its '*Lerwick Declaration*' of the following month. These were issues which were given a higher profile on the 'No' side, since a significant part of their case for a continued Union became a critique of 'centralism' by the SNP[4] and the need for much stronger decision-making at the local level.

1 See para 8.6.
2 *Effective Democracy: Reconnecting with Communities.*
3 There was also a petition in the Scottish Parliament (PEO 1516).
4 Especially the impact of the arrival of the national police force, Police Scotland. See para 13.18.

Membership of the European Union[1]

4.16   It might, at first sight, seem strange that Scotland's future membership of the European Union became a seriously contested issue in the referendum process. Polls suggested a more favourable view of EU membership in Scotland than in the United Kingdom as a whole. The issue would be unlikely to divide opinion in the principal campaigning groups. Complications arose, however, from two sources. First, the independence referendum process was being conducted against a background of a referendum on EU membership itself, promised by the UK Conservative Party for 2017, if it won the 2015 UK general election. Arguably, for Scotland to be sure of remaining in the European Union, Scots should first vote for independence[2].

But EU membership achieved its high profile mainly because of a dispute about an independent Scotland's probable route to EU accession. Concerned to downplay any possible difficulties, the SNP initially claimed that Scotland's membership would either be 'automatic' (because of Scotland's existing membership as a part of the United Kingdom and/or because of Scots' status as EU citizens) or (principally because of the presumed attractions to the European Union of Scotland's oil and other resources) at least unproblematic. Significant differences were, however, anticipated by the No side, producing a fierce debate, exacerbated by a row over the existence and content of legal advice, apparently relied on by the First Minister in a TV interview[3]. Muddying the debate further were conflicting views presented by legal experts as to the precise route to access that Scotland would be obliged to follow[4], an intervention by Jose Manuel Barroso, then President of the EU Commission[5]; and an awareness that, whether

81

Scotland might be generally welcomed or not, a procedure which, on any view, would require the assent of all other EU member states might take time. If an agreement were not, in fact, to be negotiated by March 2016, a membership 'gap', however short, might be very uncomfortable.

1 Although of lower political profile than the EU, it was also acknowledged that an independent Scotland would need to renegotiate treaties regulating other international relationships. See *Scotland's Future* ch 6. And see the UK Government's *Scotland Analysis:Devolution and the Implications of Scottish Independence* (Cm 8554, Feb 2013), *Scotland Analysis: EU and International Issues* (Cm 8765, Jan 2014).
2 *Scotland's Future* pp 216–7. A further specific matter of contention was the Scottish Government's declaration (at p 199) of its intention to continue its practice of charging fees for students from other parts of the United Kingdom at Scotland's universities.
3 For the First Minister's own explanation of the confusion see SP OR 23 Oct 2012.
4 The question was about whether the use of Art 48 or Art 49 TEU was appropriate.
5 16 Feb 2014.

The Scottish Currency[1]

4.17   It had to be a part of the SNP's campaign to demonstrate not only the positive case for independence but also that it had a clear vision of the consequences of independence and a strategy for handling them to Scotland's advantage, or at least with the avoidance of any significant disadvantages. One such consequence of independence would be the need for a Scottish currency and the options available were set out in *Scotland's Future* (pp 109–111). Drawing on the recommendations of its Fiscal Commission, the Scottish Government concluded that, rather than for example the creation of a new Scottish currency, membership of the euro or simply an (informal) continued use of sterling, the pound sterling should be retained (arguably also for the benefit of the United Kingdom as well) within a continuing formal monetary union. Avoiding here the merits of the economic arguments themselves (and also arguments about Scotland's future obligation to join the euro when admitted to the EU), the reason the currency issue became so hotly contested (including, most prominently, in the TV debates) was that the SNP's stance, requiring the consent of the United Kingdom to a continuing monetary union, was one which the United Kingdom appeared able to veto, raising questions about its viability. And the UK Government did indeed produce a response in *Scotland Analysis: Currency and Monetary Policy* (2013) which naturally expressed a preference for the current arrangements within the United Kingdom and ruled out their continuation if Scotland became independent. Thus, even if the currency proposed for an independent Scotland was unlikely to be a primary basis for the referendum decision of many voters, it may be that the prospect of an impasse (without, as Mr Darling demanded of Mr Salmond in the TV debates, a 'Plan B') and any resulting confusion may have been an issue for some.

1 For a brief discussion of this complex issue, see eg A Armstrong and M Ebell in C Jeffery and R Perman *Scotland's Decision* (2014) at pp14–17. *Scotland's Decision* was a publication funded by philanthropist Sir Tom Hunter which offered '16 Questions' to think about for the referendum, on the assumption that more 'facts' were required.

4.18   That listing of the principal participants, of their documentary contributions and of the principal political and constitutional issues on the referendum agenda, whilst they may provide a backdrop, can give no impression of the extent to which the referendum dominated the Scottish political scene during 2012–2014. 'Normal' politics was very substantially suspended and the referendum took over. To the (sometimes bemused) observer, there was a tendency for all aspects of political life (within Scotland and the United Kingdom but also, for alert campaigners, extending much more widely) to take on a referendum twist.

THE REFERENDUM RESULT AND THE CONSTITUTION[1]

4.19   Just as devolution had been embarked upon in 1999 with different motivations – Scottish Nationalists and Unionists had quite different constitutional projects in mind – so, in relation to the independence referendum, there were different ambitions. The SNP wanted a wholly new constitutional future for Scotland. The UK Government wanted to close down the debate for a generation.

In the result, neither side achieved its ambition. The Yes vote did not prevail and there is not to be a separate Scottish state. On the other hand, four features of the referendum outcome have ensured that there is to be no constitutional peace. First, although there was not a Yes victory, the fact that 1.6 million people (nearly 45% of all those voting) voted for independence meant that the question of radical constitutional change was not going to leave the political agenda. Secondly, the voter turn-out was very high at nearly 85% (much higher than normal general election figures) which may not only assist in keeping the cause of independence alive but also transform Scottish (and UK) politics more generally. The SNP has claimed a substantial leap in membership since the vote. Thirdly, the UK political establishment is, as a result of the 'Vow' to strengthen devolution, on a very tight timetable and under substantial pressure to deliver on the promises made. And fourthly, the promise of more powers for the Scottish Parliament accompanied by a promise, also contained in the 'Vow', of a sustained level of funding for Scotland by the UK Government and the retention of the Barnett formula prompted a fierce response from other parts of the United Kingdom (including the regions of England) to demand fairer treatment for them. Above all, it prompted demands for the immediate revisiting of the 'West Lothian Question' and, in particular, a demand from Conservative MPs, under pressure from the United Kingdom Independence Party (UKIP), for a guarantee of 'English votes for English laws' – ie the exclusion of extraneous Scottish MPs from voting in the House of Commons on domestic English issues.

1 See I McLean, J Gallagher, G Lodge *Scotland's Choices: The Referendum and What Happens Afterwards* (2nd edn, 2014).

4.20   The actual process for the 'implementation' of the 'Vow' was launched by the UK Prime Minister in Downing Street at 7am on Friday 19 September 2014. In addition to welcoming the referendum result, the Prime Minister offered a recommitment to the undertakings of the three pro-Union parties to a 'new and fair settlement for Scotland' and to additional powers for the Scottish Parliament over 'tax, spending and welfare'. The timetable proposed was abrupt. The process of reaching agreement (to be overseen by Lord Smith of Kelvin) on the devolution commitments was to be concluded by November 2014, with draft legislation to be published by January 2015. Actual enactment of legislation would be deferred until after the UK general election of May 2015, but, even so, the overall timetable for the implementation of major constitutional change (in contrast, for instance, with the Kilbrandon Royal Commission, the Scottish Constitutional Convention or the Calman Commission) was extraordinarily compressed. As the process came to be fleshed out, the Commission (consisting of Lord Smith and two representatives from each of the five Holyrood political parties (the SNP, Scottish Labour, the Scottish Liberal Democrats, the Scottish Conservatives and the Scottish Green Party))[1], after receiving written submissions from the UK Government[2], the Scottish Government[3] and others[4] was to report by St Andrew's Day, with the promised draft legislation to follow by Burns Night 2015.

If the work of the Smith Commission and the subsequent stages of implementation were to be intense, the position was further complicated by two other principal factors. In the first place, the Prime Minister threw into the ring, from the start, an insistence that a new and fair settlement for Scotland be accompanied by a new and fair settlement for all other parts of the United Kingdom as well. Without great difficulty (except perhaps in relation to funding levels) this would include further attention to devolution in Wales and Northern Ireland. But, much more problematically, he insisted that the 'West Lothian Question' (restated as 'English Votes for English Laws') required a 'decisive answer' and furthermore that 'all this must take place in tandem with, and at the same pace as, the settlement for Scotland'.The West Lothian Question, as a highly contested and intractable consequence of the currently asymmetric system of devolution across the United Kingdom is treated more fully later in this book[5]. It is an issue worthy of serious consideration but, in the context of the aftermath of the referendum result, it was also a mischievous contribution by the Prime Minister, concerned as much by placating his own party's right wing and providing a response to the threat from UKIP. In so far as the conjunction of the two distinguishable processes of implementing the 'Vow' and the resolution of the 'English votes' question as projects to be undertaken in tandem might have been fatally disruptive of the Scottish devolution project, that threat appeared to have been averted. The Smith Commission timetable would be maintained. However, as a wider contribution to an already messy constitutional and political environment, the insistence on 'English votes' made its presence felt.

And it is that political backdrop to the process which provides the second complicating factor, the second reason why the implementation of the 'Vow' would not be a merely technical exercise in constitutional redesign. In brief, the political opportunities and threats produced in Scotland by the referendum result, the divided population, the soaring membership claimed by the SNP, the unpromising fortunes of the Labour and Liberal Democrat parties, and the change in leadership of both the SNP (with Nicola Sturgeon succeeding as party leader on 14 November 2014 (and as First Minister on 20 November) Alex Salmond who resigned suddenly on 19 September) and of Scottish Labour (with Jim Murphy succeeding Johann Lamont on 13 December) all contributed. And, in the United Kingdom at large, the imminence of the general election of May 2015, the political vulnerabilities of all the major parties and the specific threat from UKIP made for an unsettled climate in which to produce new settlements of fraught constitutional issues. The prospect of a referendum on EU membership was disruptive – both at the general UK level, and also in respect of Scotland – following Ms Sturgeon's call on 29 October 2014 for a requirement that any overall vote to leave the EU be conditional on a vote to leave in all four constituent parts of the United Kingdom.

1 With terms of reference including to convene cross-party talks and to facilitate an 'inclusive engagement process' to produce Heads of Agreement, with recommendations for further devolution and more financial, welfare and taxation powers for the Parliament.
2 *The Parties' Published Proposals on Further Devolution for Scotland* Cm 8946 (Oct 2014) – a summary of the UK Government's commitments to the process and of the proposals previously made by the pro-Union political parties.
3 *More Powers for the Scottish Parliament* (Oct 2014).
4 In due course, the Commission reported that they had received '407 submissions from civic institutions, organisations and groups, and 18,381 from members of the public' (para 11 of the Report, see para 4.21 below).
5 See para 5.9.

4.21   The full outcome of the post-referendum phase of constitutional development remains uncertain. The Smith Commission published its proposals[1] on 27 November 2014. Although the consensus immediately began to unravel thereafter, all five political parties had agreed[2] to an extensive package of reforms, organised as three 'pillars' of their Heads of Agreement. Dominant was 'pillar 3', under which the Commission offered measures to strengthen the financial responsibility of the Scottish Parliament by devolving several tax-raising powers, including, most prominently most aspects of (non-savings and non-dividend) income tax; air passenger duty; and the aggregates levy (paras 75–91). The Barnett formula (for quantifying the block grant payable to the Scottish Government by the UK Government) would continue to apply (with adjustments to be agreed) and the Scottish Government would have strengthened borrowing powers. Under 'pillar 1' (to provide a durable but responsive settlement for the governance of Scotland), UK legislation would state that the Scottish Parliament and the Scottish Government are permanent and the Sewel Convention[3] would be put 'on a statutory footing' (paras 21, 22). The Scottish Parliament would have additional powers in relation to its own composition and functioning, including the power (if possible, with effect from the election of May 2016) to lower the voting age to 16. The machinery for inter-governmental relationships would be strengthened. Under 'pillar 2' were the Commission's proposals for the devolution of many 'welfare' benefits to the Scottish Parliament, along with the management of Scottish tribunals and with consideration to be given to the devolution of the power to regulate abortion. Although not included in the Heads of Agreement, Lord Smith added some recommendations of his own: he supplemented the agreement on inter-governmental machinery with a plea for a stronger relationship between Governments led by the Prime Minister and First Minister; he urged further devolution of powers *from* the Scottish Parliament to local communities; he encouraged the further improvement of the Scottish Parliament's oversight of the Government; and he urged the achievement of greater public awareness of the powers of the Parliament.

On 16 December 2014, William Hague, to whom, as First Secretary of State and Leader of the House of Commons, the Prime Minister had given the task of producing proposals on 'English Votes for English Laws', published a consultation paper[4]. This set out the current state of decentralisation in England, followed by a summary of the options for further devolution and decentralisation in England and of the impact of devolution across the United Kingdom on the Westminster Parliament and its implications. It referred to the possibility of a Convention to consider how to address these implications. Thereafter, the paper included two entirely separate sets of proposals on how each of the Coalition parties intended to proceed and, after inviting responses to the early sections of the paper, went on to invite, extraordinarily for a government publication, responses to the party proposals to be submitted to the parties themselves. The paper offered no timetable according to which responses might be made.

The next stage of the post-'Vow' developments came on 22 January 2015 (a few days ahead of the Burns Night target) when the UK Government published *Scotland in the United Kingdom: An Enduring Settlement* (Cm 8990), a consultation on proposals to implement the Smith Commission report to which were appended the promised 'Draft Scotland Clauses'. These included clauses (amending SA 1998 and other statutes) to recognise the Scottish Parliament and the Scottish Government as permanent; to recognise the Sewel convention; to amend existing provision for the arrangements for the Scottish Parliament and Government and for elections; to expand the Parliament's powers over income tax; and (immediately controversial between the parties) to devolve welfare benefits and employment support as well as to adjust other aspects of legislative and executive competence.

The further stages of the process towards the implementation of the Smith and Hague proposals were unknowable at the time this book went to press. What is apparent, however, is that, in addition to any lessons to be learned about the utility of the referendum mechanism itself as a contribution to the process of constitutional reform, the independence referendum will have had an impact on all aspects of Scotland's constitution. In terms of the effect on the content of this book, the subject-matter of virtually all chapters have faced and will continue to face a post-referendum impact. The structure, powers and operation of both Parliaments (Chapters 5, 6) are at the centre of implementing Smith and the resolution of the 'English votes' question. Reform of the House of Lords may yet return to the constitutional agenda. The powers of the two Governments and their inter-relationships (Chapter 7) and the position of local government in Scotland (Chapter 8) will continue to be scrutinised. Lord Smith's call for the improvement of the Parliament's accountability machinery may impact on Chapter 9. Public finance (Chapter 11) was at the heart of the Smith Commission recommendations and of their implementation. It is unlikely that the role of the courts (Chapters 12–14) will escape an impact, especially in the light of the near-federal UK structure now anticipated.

1 Report of the Smith Commission for further devolution of powers to the Scottish Parliament.
2 Members of the Commission explicitly agreed to refer to their proposals as 'the Smith Commission Agreement' (para 16).
3 See para 6.22.
4 *The Implications of Devolution for England*, Cm 8969.

Chapter 5

The UK and Scottish Parliaments: the Institutional Framework

INTRODUCTION

5.1   In any study of a parliament in a working constitution the main focus is inevitably on what that parliament actually does. Thus, in a system of parliamentary government, the role of parliament in the process of government formation and then in the process of holding governments to account are a central concern. So too are the parliament's legislative powers and the procedures by which laws are made, especially in so far as law-making is guided, or indeed dominated, by the executive. The ways in which the limits of the powers of the parliament may be tested in courts are also of great importance. These parliamentary powers and procedures and the involvement in them of the executive and the judiciary provide the defining characteristics of the constitution itself. For Scotland, since July 1999, those characteristics have included the phenomenon of two working parliaments and to the constitutional relationships already mentioned there has to be added the relationship which has been created and which continues to develop between them.

As a preliminary to the study of the workings of the UK and Scottish Parliaments, however, it is necessary to understand the rules governing their structure and composition. The ways in which their membership is defined and the rules by which they are brought into existence or may be terminated do much to establish whether they have the autonomy and legitimacy necessary to carry out effectively the functions constitutionally allotted to them. Particularly important in the assessment of the work of the two Parliaments is the question of how far they discharge their most distinctive function which is that of injecting the quality of democracy into the constitutional system as a whole. That, above all, is the task of parliaments and one to which other constitutional organs contribute much more weakly. The democratic benchmark is that against which parliaments are primarily to be tested.

It is for that reason that the main focus in paras 5.2–5.12 of this chapter is on the two elected chambers – at Westminster, the House of Commons and then the Scottish Parliament itself. At paras 5.13–5.15, however, there is brief coverage of the House of Lords and account is taken of the stage presently reached in the reform of that House. It has, for the last decade and a half, been the subject of considerable attention. The existence of the House of Lords has important consequences for the working of the Westminster Parliament: inevitably a bicameral parliament operates, and is intended to operate, differently from a unicameral parliament. In the Scottish Parliament the lack of a second chamber has consequences for its operation and, when compared with Westminster, it needs to look elsewhere for the performance of functions carried out there by the House of Lords. Some, however, have argued for a bicameral Scottish Parliament and brief discussion of that possibility concludes this section. At paras 5.16–5.18 is an introduction to parliamentary committees, although the main committee functions are dealt with in Chapters 9 and 10. For most purposes the Parliaments operate as collective bodies – whether as whole chambers or as committees of those chambers – but the status and function of individual members are also important. Paragraphs 5.20–5.21 concern such matters as pay and expenses – an area which has become one of the most controversial in British politics – and with the standards required of individual members and the privileges they claim, both individually and collectively. Paragraph 5.22 deals with the management and administration of the Parliaments. Finally, para 5.23 addresses, with particular reference to the Scottish Parliament, the question of public accessibility and openness.

It will be observed that this chapter involves – sometimes quite explicitly, sometimes implicitly – comparisons between the Westminster and the Scottish Parliaments. This is useful despite the obvious differences between the two. The Westminster Parliament is ancient while the Scottish Parliament is modern. The Westminster Parliament is bicameral and is much larger than its Scottish counterpart. The Westminster Parliament formally incorporates the Queen into its membership, whereas the Scottish Parliament does not. Many of those who campaigned for a Scottish Parliament had in mind that it should in no way become a mere replica of Westminster[1]. It was argued that it should be more responsive to the people, it should be less bound by ceremonial pomp and tradition, it should contain members who were less antagonistic to each other and less bound by party rivalry and discipline, and the Scottish Parliament should be more family friendly, especially in its working hours. A formal inquiry within which attempts were made to assess how the Scottish Parliament had 'measured up' to this agenda declared devolution a 'remarkable success' having heard praise for the 'transparency and openness' of the Scottish Parliament and its 'greater democratic scrutiny of public life in Scotland and of legislative proposals'[2]. This assessment is not universally accepted and there are many who would compare the Scottish Parliament unfavourably with Westminster[3]. Furthermore, for as long as the present devolutionary settlement subsists, there will be some ways in which formal comparisons between the Parliaments cannot truly be drawn. At the first meeting of the Scottish Parliament in May 1999, Winnie Ewing MSP said, when called upon to chair the initial proceedings, as the Parliament's most senior member, that she had always wanted either to say or to hear someone else say: 'the Scottish Parliament, which adjourned on 25 March 1707, is hereby reconvened'[4]. But, despite these brave words, the Scottish Parliament cannot readily be seen as the successor to the Parliament which went out of existence in 1707. It is not the Parliament of an independent Scotland. In all formal constitutional respects it is the statutorily created child of the Westminster Parliament – a point emphasised by Lord President Rodger in *Whaley v Watson*[5] when he referred to 'the fundamental character of the Parliament as a body which – however important its role – has been created by statute and derives its powers from statute. As such, it is a body which, like any other statutory body, must work within the scope of its powers'[6]. Although this may be unsurprising within the general context of devolution, it is, of course, also regarded as offensive by those who aspire to a greater autonomy for the Parliament. The ending of the formal subordination of the Scottish Parliament was a central plank in the Yes vote campaign in the 2014 referendum.

1 See the Scottish Constitutional Convention's Report, *Scotland's Parliament: Scotland's Right* (1995) p 24; *Report of the Consultative Steering Group on the Scottish Parliament* (1998) (*CSG Report*), section 2.
2 Commission on Scottish Devolution ('the Calman Commission'), *The Future of Scottish Devolution within the Union: a First Report* (2008) ('First Report'), para 4.6.
3 For further discussion see also Jeffery C and Mitchell J *The Scottish Parliament 1999–2009: The First Decade* (2009); E E Sutherland et al (eds) *Law-Making and the Scottish Parliament:The Early Years* (2011). An illuminating study was also provided by the Parliament's Conveners Group's Third Session 'Legacy Paper': http://www.scottish.parliament.uk/Committeeconvenersgroup/Conveners_Group_legacy_paper_-_Session_3.pdf
4 SP OR, 12 May 1999, col 5.
5 *Whaley v Watson* 2000 SC 340.
6 *Whaley v Watson* 2000 SC 340 at 348. The question of the Parliament's status and the grounds on which its legislation might be reviewed were considered in *AXA General Insurance Ltd, Petitioners* 2012 SC (UKSC) 122 at paras 42–52 (Lord Hope) and paras 135–154 (Lord Reed). See para 14.26.

THE ELECTED CHAMBERS

Structure and composition

5.2   The structure of the House of Commons and the Scottish Parliament is, in each case, determined by the rules which govern the number of members (MPs and MSPs), the election of members and the period for which the chambers are elected. These rules are, however, interrelated and the rules which apply to the Scottish Parliament are, to an extent, shared with those that apply at Westminster or are dependent upon them.

Elected members

5.3   Here the Scottish Parliament is taken first. The size of the Parliament is determined by reference to the number of constituencies (electoral areas) in Scotland – from each of which one MSP is elected – and the eight regions[1] – from each of which seven MSPs are elected[2]. The constituencies were identical to the Westminster parliamentary constituencies which existed when SA 1998 was passed, save that the Orkney Islands and Shetland Islands, which share a Westminster constituency, were separated to give each a constituency (and, therefore, a separate MSP) at Holyrood. There were 72 Westminster constituencies, producing 73 for Holyrood and, with 56 regional members, 129 MSPs in total. The mechanisms by which the constituency and regional MSPs are elected are considered below but it may be noted that the original provisions of SA 1998 tying the number of Holyrood constituencies to the number of Westminster constituencies (subject to the adjustment for Orkney and Shetland) would have had consequences going beyond mere administrative convenience in the management of elections – although that is, in itself, an important consideration. The reasons for the number of Westminster constituencies in Scotland having fallen in recent years (and, therefore, the number of Scottish

MPs) are discussed below but the impact on the size of the Scottish Parliament could not be justified on the same grounds. The case was made that the rules governing the size of the two Parliaments should be decoupled in the interests of maintaining the present size of the Scottish Parliament and, therefore, the same number of MSPs to serve on the Parliament's committees and to carry out its other functions[3] and the Scottish Parliament (Constituencies) Act 2004 gave effect to that change. The reduction in the number of Scottish Westminster constituencies to 59 as a result of the Fifth Periodical Review of the Boundary Commission for Scotland therefore had no impact on the number of MSPs[4].

The size of the House of Commons is a matter determined by reference to the number of single-member constituencies currently defined for electoral purposes. There are at present 650 parliamentary constituencies across the United Kingdom as a whole (including the 59 in Scotland referred to above) but this is a figure which is subject to variation[5].

1 The same as those formerly used as constituencies for elections to the European Parliament.
2 Scotland Act 1998 (SA 1998), s 1(2), (3) and Sch 1.
3 SP OR 27 March 2002, col 10653; Scottish Grand Committee 12 June 2000.
4 See Fifth Periodical Report of the Boundary Commission for Scotland, Cm 6427, 30 November 2004.
5 See para 5.9 below.

Parliaments and parliamentary sessions

5.4   Although the life of the Parliament elected in 2011 has been extended to five years[1], the normal length of each session of the Scottish Parliament[2] is four years. It is a fixed-term Parliament, with each general election falling four years after the last, on the first Thursday in May[3], the Parliament being dissolved 21 days before the election[4]. That is a rule which the Scottish Parliament cannot, yet[5], itself amend but it is subject to two exceptions, one of which is narrow and technical in nature but the other of wider constitutional importance. The Queen may, following a proposal by the Presiding Officer, by proclamation adjust the dates of the dissolution and the general election by no more than a month[6]. It is important that the power to propose such a change is to be exercised by the Presiding Officer and not by someone on behalf of the Scottish Government (or, indeed, by the opposition where a minority government might be put out of office): it should be exercised not for party political reasons but simply because the originally prescribed date was, for some reason, inappropriate. The other circumstance is where political paralysis has occurred and the Presiding Officer is required to shorten a session of the Parliament by proposing that the Queen dissolves the Parliament and calls a general election. Until the passing of the Fixed-term Parliaments Act 2011 (see below), one of the principal distinctions between the UK and the Scottish Parliaments was that, whereas the length of the Westminster Parliament was open-ended, subject to a maximum of five years, and could be dissolved, within that period, at any time by decision, in effect, of the Prime Minister, the Scottish Parliament must normally see out its fixed four-year session. The principal merit claimed for the fixed-term arrangement is that it reduces the power of the government to manipulate the date of general elections to party advantage by choosing a time favourable to itself and maintaining party discipline meantime – both of which used to be standard features of the Westminster Parliament. Having a fixed-term parliament forces its members to seek the resolution of political conflict (including conflict over the making and unmaking of governments) within its own membership and without recourse to an early general election and a probable change of membership. The disadvantage of a parliament of absolutely fixed terms is the risk that parliamentary and governmental activity could be brought to a complete halt if party political conditions prevented the formation (whether by coalition or otherwise) of a majority of members in support of a government and its policies. Political paralysis could indeed occur. This difficulty is met, in the case of the Scottish Parliament, by provisions which require the Presiding Officer to intervene where either (a) the Parliament with the support of two-thirds of MSPs resolves that it should be dissolved or (b) the Parliament fails to nominate a person for appointment as First Minister within the prescribed period and thus fails to allow a government to be formed[7]. In either of these circumstances an extraordinary general election is to be held. Such an extraordinary election does not disturb the normal four-year cycle of ordinary elections which remains in place, save that, if an extraordinary election takes place within six months of the date scheduled for the next ordinary election, that election does not take place[8].

As already mentioned, a fundamental difference between the two Parliaments, until 2011, was that, while the Scottish Parliament is (under normal circumstances) of fixed term, the Westminster Parliament was of variable length, subject only to a maximum duration of five years. That was a limit statutorily prescribed by the Parliament Act 1911, subject to adjustment only by another Act of Parliament. The 1911 Act had repealed an earlier seven-year limit[9] and was itself temporarily overridden to enable the extension of the length of the Parliaments during the two World Wars of the twentieth century[10].

The constitutional effects of the rules enabling (subject to the five-year limit) Parliaments of variable length were profound. They had, of course, an impact on Parliament itself – greatly affecting the political (especially the party political) dynamic of its operation. But they had an even greater effect on the processes of government formation and operation, the power and authority of the Prime Minister within government, and relations between government and Parliament. Arguably, the power of the Queen (in relation to the appointment of Prime Ministers[11] and the length of Parliaments) was also at issue. These effects all derived from a combination of legal and conventional rules under which it was understood that it was, at any point during the five-year period of a Parliament, competent for the Queen to dissolve that Parliament and thus produce the need for a general election. It was also understood, however, that, in dissolving Parliament, the Queen was always to act on the advice of the Prime Minister and, in modern times, always did so. It was this phenomenon which conferred the power on the political party currently in government (and especially the Prime Minister) to decide the date of the next general election. Although it could be overstated since political constraints also bore down on the Prime Minister, the rules gave a distinct advantage to the governing party over its political opponents and, within the governing party, a source of disciplinary power to the Prime Minister over his or her backbench MPs. They

91

could be threatened, if they collectively stepped out of line, with a dissolution which might bring an end to their political careers. It is not yet clear what the impact of an abrupt change to the rules has been. But abrupt change there was. Pursuant to the Coalition Government's *Progamme for Government*[12], the Fixed-term Parliaments Act 2011 (F-tPA 2011) was passed, with immediate effect. Instead of Parliaments lasting up to a maximum of five years, the five-year period (subject to two limited exceptions rather similar to those for the Scottish Parliament) is now fixed. This was done by prescribing (s 1(2)) the dates of the next general election (7 May 2015) and those thereafter – the first Thursday in May each fifth calendar year[13]. As mentioned, s 4 of F-tPA 2011 moves the date of the next general election for the Scottish Parliament to 5 May 2016, to avoid a clash on 7 May 2015[14]. The only two circumstances in which the date of a general election may be brought forward are (a) if the House of Commons (with a majority of two thirds of the number of seats) passes a motion that there shall be an early parliamentary general election; or (b) if the House of Commons passes a motion (not contradicted by a contrary motion within 14 days) of no confidence in Her Majesty's Government. Either motion would trigger a general election on a date appointed by a proclamation by the Queen on the recommendation of the Prime Minister. Subsequent elections are then programmed to follow in the May four or five years later (s 1(4)). The Act prescribes the date of the dissolution of Parliament as the 17th working day before the appointed polling day (s 3(1)). 'Parliament cannot otherwise be dissolved' (s 3(2)) – a rule which reconfirms the sweeping away of the previous practice of timetables decided by the Prime Minister and their presumed constitutional undesirability. New questions have arisen, however, about whether, for instance, the choice of the five-year fixed term was the right one.

1   See below.
2   In relation to 'sessions', terminology differs between the two Parliaments. At Westminster, a new Parliament is elected, following the dissolution of the last and the holding of a general election. Counting from 1801, the current Westminster Parliament (from 2010) is the 55th. The length of each parliamentary term is then divided into annual sessions, usually beginning and ending in November. In relation to the Scottish Parliament, the language of SA 1998 does not include reference to separate 'Parliaments'. Instead, the whole period between an election and the following dissolution is a 'session' of the Parliament. Since 2011, the Parliament has been in its fourth session. See the Standing Orders (SOs), r 2.1.
3   SA 1998, s 2(2).
4   SA 1998, s 2(3) and the Scottish Parliament (Elections etc) Order 2010, SI 2010/2999, art 88. Saturdays, Sundays and certain other holidays are disregarded in the calculation of the period.
5   The Smith Commission (see para 4.21 above) recommended that the Scottish Parliament should have responsibility for legislation on (most aspects of) elections and 'all matters relating to the arrangements and operations of the Scottish Parliament' (paras 23, 24, 26).
6   SA 1998, s 2(5).
7   SA 1998, s 3(1), (2). See para 7.5 below for the appointment of the First Minister.
8   SA 1998, s 3(3), (4).
9   Septennial Act 1715. Earlier there was a three-year limit: Meeting of Parliament Act 1694.
10 The length of a Parliament cannot be extended by an Act of Parliament passed by the House of Commons alone under the Parliament Acts 1911 and 1949. See para 9.7 below.
11 See para 7.5.
12 *The Coalition: Our Programme for Government* (2010).
13 And thus 7 May 2020, 1 May 2025 etc.
14 It seems, however, that a clash is in prospect for 2020.

ELECTIONS

Introduction

5.5   There is nothing more symbolically significant in a democracy than the ballot box[1]. The exercise of each individual's right to choose, in the secrecy of the voting booth, who should be his or her representative in an elected assembly is the guarantee which underwrites the democratic system. There is, however, nothing simple about the means of securing the working of fair and free elections in a sophisticated democracy dominated by political parties. This account focuses on elections to the Westminster and Scottish Parliaments but much of the UK electoral law relevant to national parliamentary elections is also used as the basis for the systems of election to local authorities and to the European Parliament. It covers entitlement to vote; entitlement to be a candidate and member; voting systems; candidates, political parties and constituencies; the tenure of members and the filling of casual vacancies; and a note on the conduct of elections themselves. There are some concluding remarks on parliaments and political parties.

1 Although even that symbol can be the subject of controversy: the use of 'cardboard' ballot boxes during the Scottish Parliament and Scottish local government elections of 2007 was one of many aspects of these elections which were the subject of criticism. The security of ballot boxes during those elections was also much debated: see Electoral Commission *Independent Review of the Scottish Parliamentary and Local Government Elections* (2007). N Ghaleigh, 'The Scottish Parliament elections 2007: what kind of hackery is this?' (2008) 12 Edin LR 2008 137.

Entitlement to vote[1]

5.6   An individual's entitlement to vote in an election depends on that person's name being on the electoral register for the area in which he or she intends to vote[2]. Registers are compiled by electoral registration officers throughout the United Kingdom and have to be available for an election called at any time, since the dates of elections to both Parliaments are not completely fixed and by-elections, at any level, are unpredictable. Since 2001, registers have been maintained as permanent records, with adjustments made on a 'rolling' basis reflecting day-to-day changes caused by people moving in or out of the area or coming of age[3]. For an individual, being on the register is absolutely essential to the right to vote in that area, although, in the case of absence from the address at the time of an election, it may be possible to vote by proxy or by post. Prior to 2001, electoral registers were compiled not on a rolling basis but annually and by reference to residence at an address on a particular date (10 October). Annual registers became out of date towards the end of their lives and, as a result, probably reduced voter participation. Although of less significance for the new rolling registers, an annual canvass of residents must still be carried out by registration officers, with 15 October as the operative date[4].

Admission to the electoral register depends on being resident in a constituency. RPA 1983, s 5 (as substituted by the Representation of the People Act 2000 (RPA 2000)), in which this test is laid down, does not, however, offer precise guidance on the meaning to be given to 'residence'. It does, on the other hand, seem clear that the physical quality of the fabric of the accommodation in which a person claims to reside may range widely. Certainly conventional bricks and mortar are not required and, in *Hipperson v Newbury District Electoral Registration Officer*[5], it was held that the tents and vehicles in which protestors at a peace camp slept would suffice. Certain other issues have been considered. RPA 1983 itself makes it clear that residence at an address will not be affected by temporary absence[6]. A person remains correctly registered at the home address rather than residence being interrupted temporarily by a holiday, business or educational absence. On the other hand, it has been recognised that, where a person acquires 'a considerable degree of permanence'[7] at some other address, residence there may also satisfy the test. In *Fox v Stirk*[8] it was held that university students could qualify at their university address. In *Hipperson* the protestors qualified at their peace camp, and in *Dumble v Borders Electoral Registration Officer*[9] weekend use of a cottage for political purposes sufficed. In *Scott v Phillips*[10], though, the summer use of a holiday cottage did not confer residence[11]. The idea of 'residence' has, at all events, acquired a special meaning in this electoral context. Physical presence[12] in a place is not the determining factor. The degree of permanence in a place (and more controversially its 'quality') is more significant.

The courts have created another dimension to the concept of residence, almost certainly not foreseen when it was first formulated and which is presumed to have survived the amendments of RPA 2000. This too derives from *Fox v Stirk* and is that a person may, in law, be resident in two places (and perhaps more) at once. Students may acquire a 'considerable degree of permanence' at both their university and 'home' addresses and this may apply to other voters as well. Dual registration does not confer the right to vote twice in a general election[13] but it does provide the option of voting in one place rather than another to groups whose numbers may be politically more significant in the more marginal of the two constituencies.

Special rules on residence apply to certain categories of potential voters. The right to vote is extended to British citizens now living overseas by permitting them to remain, for up to 15 years, on the register for the address at which they formerly resided[14]. Provision is also made for patients resident in mental hospitals except those who are detained offenders[15] and for prisoners held on remand[16]. Special provision is also made for certain homeless persons to make a 'declaration of local connection' to establish residence for electoral purposes[17]. Residence apart, admission to the electoral register depends upon the satisfaction of certain other criteria. Being on the register does not, however, guarantee a right to vote in all elections. Thus:

(1)   While persons aged 16 or over may be placed on the register, only those over 18 on the date of an election may vote[18].

(2)   Persons who are qualifying Commonwealth citizens (ie British citizens and citizens (with leave to enter the United Kingdom) of other Commonwealth countries) and citizens of the European Union may be registered[19]. However, only Commonwealth citizens and citizens of the Republic of Ireland may vote in elections to the House of Commons.

Citizens of all other states in the European Union may vote only in elections to the Scottish Parliament, in local government elections, and in elections to the European Parliament[20].

(3) Members of the House of Lords may be registered and may vote in all elections, except elections to the House of Commons. Prior to the House of Lords Act 1999, this exclusion extended to all hereditary peers. Since that Act, only those hereditaries who have retained their membership of the House of Lords are barred from voting in elections to the House of Commons.

(4) Despite registration, no person convicted and serving a sentence in prison may vote[21]. This blanket ban has been held by the European Court of Human Rights to be disproportionate to the UK's legitimate aim of encouraging 'responsible citizenship' and a breach of ECHR article 3 of Protocol 1 (re elections)[22]. In November 2012, the UK Government published a draft Voting Eligibility (Prisoners) Bill which was considered by an ad hoc joint parliamentary committee. The committee was sympathetic to the reform of the law to enable some categories of prisoner to vote and urged the introduction of the Bill[23]. No such Bill has yet been introduced.

(5) Persons convicted of corrupt or illegal practices at an election have restricted voting rights[24].

(6) People who are subject to a legal incapacity (eg serious mental impairment) may not vote[25].

1 If the Smith Commission recommendations are implemented (see para 4.21), power would be devolved to the Scottish Parliament to amend most aspects of election law affecting the Parliament, including a reduction of the voting age to 16. For entitlement to vote in the independence referendum see paras 4.5 and 4.6.
2 Representation of the People Act 1983 (RPA 1983), s 1.
3 Cut-off rules operate to crystallise the state of the register at the final date for nominations before elections. Individuals may appeal against their exclusion from the register to an Electoral Registration Court.
4 Since the implementation of s 1 of the Electoral Registration and Administration Act 2013 (inserting a new s 10ZC into RPA 1983) individual voter registration (rather than registration by household) was introduced from summer 2014.
5 [1985] QB 1060.
6 RPA 1983, s 5(3)–(5).
7 *Fox v Stirk* [1970] 2 QB 463.
8 *Fox v Stirk* [1970] 2 QB 463.
9 *Dumble v Borders Electoral Registration Officer* 1980 SLT (Sh Ct) 60.
10 *Scott v Phillips* 1974 SLT 32.
11 See also *Ferris v Wallace* 1936 SC 561.
12 Or 'actual residence', as RPA 1983 unhelpfully has it.
13 RPA 1983, s 1(2).
14 Representation of the People Act 1985, s 1.
15 RPA 1983, ss 3A and 7.
16 RPA 1983, s 7A.
17 RPA 1983, ss 7B, 7C.
18 RPA 1983, s 1(1).
19 RPA 1983, s 4.
20 RPA 1983, ss 1 and 2 and see SI 1995/1948; SI 2001/1184.
21 RPA 1983, s 3.
22 *Hirst v United Kingdom* (2006) 42 EHRR 41. See also *Smith v Scott* 2007 SC 345 in which the Court of Session sitting as the Registration Appeal Court made a declaration of incompatibility under HRA 1998 in relation to s 3 of RPA 1983. And see *McGeoch v Lord President of the*

Council 2014 SC (UKSC) 25, but in which it was also held that exclusion from the register could not be challenged under EU law.
23 See HL Paper 103, HC 924 (2013–14).
24 RPA 1983, s 160.
25 RPA 1983, s 1.

Entitlement to be a candidate and member

5.7   Until recently, there were no rules directly defining who might stand in an election to the House of Commons. However, there were rules which disqualified certain categories of person from membership and rules which might be used to exclude people who were subject to a disqualification, either at the point of election or subsequently. These rules remain and the same approach has been adopted for the Scottish Parliament, although with the use of a modified list of disqualifications. A consequence, however, of the introduction of the new voting system for the Scottish Parliament has been the need to introduce new rules directly governing candidature, and these are mentioned below[1]. The list of persons disqualified from membership of the House of Commons includes:

(a)   aliens but not those who are citizens of the Republic of Ireland or of Commonwealth countries[2];
(b)   persons under 18[3];
(c)   certain detained mentally ill persons;
(d)   members of the House of Lords[4];
(e)   undischarged bankrupts and persons against whom sequestration of their estate has been awarded[5];
(f)   those convicted of treason and serving a term of imprisonment of more than a year[6];
(g)   persons guilty of corrupt or illegal practices at elections[7].

It will be observed that these disqualifications are founded on a miscellany of historically based reasons[8], some of which are of dubious continuing constitutional legitimacy. Of more general importance, and invoking broader principles of constitutional propriety and the separation of powers, are rules which (a) disqualify certain persons holding positions in the public service and (b) restrict the number of holders of ministerial office who may be MPs. The ancestor of both rules was a section of the Act of Settlement 1700 which would have[9] barred all holders of an 'office of profit' under the Crown from membership of the Commons. As far as the holders of non-political office are concerned, the spirit of that restriction is maintained in the House of Commons Disqualification Act 1975 (HCDA 1975) which prevents all members of the civil service, the armed forces and any police force from being MPs. Equally, holders of judicial office including sheriffs principal, sheriffs and stipendiary magistrates are barred, as are a large number of holders of public offices specified in HCDA 1975[10]. These disqualifications sustain important elements of the principle of the separation of powers by drawing a line between the judiciary and large sectors of the executive on the one hand and the legislature on the other. In addition, there has been retained, as a device to enable an MP to resign his or her seat (for which no other direct provision is made[11]) certain disqualifying offices of profit under the Crown, notably the Stewardship of the Chiltern Hundreds, appointment to which has the indirect effect of a resignation.

However, the disqualifications do not extend to ministers of the Crown, which permits the constitutionally most important exception to any pure idea of the separation of powers. Ministers may, and according to convention must, be drawn from one or other House of Parliament, and with most of them from the House of Commons[12]. Notionally in the interests of restraining governmental dominance of the House of Commons, however, a limit is placed on the number of paid ministerial offices to be held at any one time in that House. HCDA 1975 and the Ministerial and Other Salaries Act 1975 together have the effect of restricting the number of ministerial offices in the Commons to 95 and also determine maximum numbers at prescribed salary levels in the Commons and Lords together.

Similar rules on disqualification and on ministerial offices apply in the Scottish Parliament. The general disqualifications are the same, save that there is no bar to membership of members of the House of Lords. Lord Steel of Aikwood, the Parliament's first Presiding Officer, Lord Watson of Invergowrie, and Lord Foulkes of Cumnock have all been MSPs[13]. Baroness Annabel Goldie is a continuing Member. Nor is there any formal bar on a person's combining membership of the Scottish Parliament with that of the House of Commons. Neither body has a disqualifying rule to this effect and that enabled several MPs elected in 1997 to the Westminster Parliament to be elected to Holyrood in 1999, including Donald Dewar and Jim Wallace. Although rules subsequently adopted by several parties forbade such 'dual mandates' the former First Minister, Alex Salmond, retained until 2010 the Westminster seat which he occupied before being (re) elected to the Scottish Parliament in 2007. Rules equivalent to those at Westminster bar certain office-holders from membership of the Scottish Parliament[14].

The inclusion of all ministers (with the exception of the two Law Officers[15]) as MSPs is a statutory, rather than a merely conventional, requirement at Holyrood[16] but there is no prescribed limit on the number of ministers in the Parliament.

1   The Political Parties, Elections and Referendums Act 2000 (PPERA 2000) as amended by the Electoral Administration Act 2006) also contains rules on the description of the party affiliation of candidates on ballot papers. See para 5.11.
2   Act of Settlement 1700, s III; British Nationality Act 1981, Sch 7. For fuller discussion of this and the other categories of disqualification, see *Erskine May's Parliamentary Practice* (24th edn, 2011) ch 3.
3   Electoral Administration Act 2006, s 17(1). Section 17(8) 'disapplies' s 6 of the (English) Union with Scotland Act 1706 which imposed a minimum age requirement of 21.
4   The terms of this disqualification were adjusted on the passing of the House of Lords Act 1999. Peers who are not members of the House of Lords are not disqualified. See para 5.13.
5   Insolvency Act 1986, s 427.
6   Forfeiture Act 1870, s 2; Representation of the People Act 1981 (RPA 1981).
7   RPA 1983, ss 159, 160.
8   Another was the disqualification of ordained clergy and (including Church of Scotland ministers), until lifted by the House of Commons (Removal of Clergy Disqualification) Act 2001.
9   But for its repeal by the Succession to the Crown Act 1707.

10 See the lists in the schedules to HCDA 1975 which are frequently amended.

11 Indeed, resignation from the English Parliament was prohibited by resolution of 2 March 1623.

12 See para 7.7.

13 In evidence to the House of Lords Committee on the Constitution, Lord Steel expressed his support for Presiding Officers of the Scottish Parliament (and also of the Welsh Assembly) being made peers: HL Paper 28 (2002–03).

14 SA 1998, s 15 and the Scottish Parliament (Disqualification) Order 2010, SI 2010/2476. SA 2012, s 13 has transferred the power to issue further such orders to the Scottish Government.

15 SA 1998, ss 27, 48.

16 SA 1998, ss 45, 47.

Voting systems: candidates, political parties and constituencies

5.8   Defining the electorate does not define the way in which they elect their representatives. That depends on how elections are organised; who may stand for election as a candidate; whether the electorate is divided into constituencies and, if so, whether one or more than one member are to be elected from each; how many votes each person has and how the votes are counted; and, perhaps most important of all, the ways in which voting for individual candidates is combined with a process of voting for political parties. As a result of a number of developments in recent years there are now four different types of voting system operating in the United Kingdom[1]. Elections to the Westminster Parliament are conducted on a constituency-based 'first past the post' (FPTP) system. Elections to the Scottish Parliament and the Welsh Assembly (and also the London Assembly) are held on the additional member system (AMS) which combines constituency-based FPTP with a system of electing additional regional members drawn from a party list[2]. Elections to the European Parliament are conducted on a regionally based 'closed list' system, except in Northern Ireland where the Single Transferable Vote (STV) system is used. This latter system has also been used for the election of the Northern Ireland Assembly and, since 2007, is also the system used for local government elections in Scotland. It is discussed in more detail below.

This diversity of practice has developed largely as a result of a long-standing dissatisfaction with the way in which FPTP has operated at Westminster. That system satisfies some of the widely accepted criteria for a good voting system but fails in other respects. The Labour government elected in 1997 had a manifesto commitment to a review which was conducted by the (Jenkins) Independent Commission on the Voting System, reporting in 1998[3]. It will be useful to consider the findings of that review and also the systems enacted for elections to the devolved Parliaments and the European Parliament but, as a starting point, the principal features of FPTP for the Westminster Parliament should be put in place. One of its claimed advantages is its simplicity: each constituency returns one MP; at each election (whether a general election or a by-election to replace an MP who has died or retired) voters have one vote which they cast for one candidate identified by name and, almost always, political party; the candidate with the largest number of votes wins and is returned as MP for the constituency. Counting in the constituencies is simple and the overall consequences of a general election are easily seen in the new membership of the House of Commons. All MPs have a formal equality of status and all voters know, or have the means of knowing, who their single elected representative is. These simplicities do, however, produce what is, for many, a profound unfairness represented by the inevitable tendency of a FPTP system to leave the many constituency voters (often a majority) who did not vote for the winning candidate feeling that they are without representation in Parliament and also to produce an overall pattern of representation skewed in favour of the party which happens to have come first most often, and against parties which may have attracted large number of votes but for candidates placed second or lower in their constituency contests. On the whole, smaller parties are disproportionately badly represented. In the 2005 general election the Labour Party won 356 seats (55 per cent) on 35 per cent of the total vote while the Liberal Democrats won 62 seats (9 per cent) on 22 per cent of the vote. On the other hand, FPTP produced a major surprise in the 2010 election, with no overall majority for any single party. The Liberal Democrats fell to 57 MPs but joined the Conservatives' 306 to enable the formation of the first peacetime coalition government in the United Kingdom since 1935[4]. The Labour Party had won 258 seats.

The overall lack of proportionality and the apparently unfair results it produces are not, for some, decisive. For them, the system's simplicity and straightforwardness of representative effect are important and these are coupled with its tendency (displaced, temporarily at least, in 2010) to produce a single overall winning party in the House of Commons which eases the process of government formation from that party and often, because of its distorted majority, 'strong' government thereafter. However, it is the arguments against the disproportionality of the FPTP system which have produced reforming proposals which have borne some fruit in recent years.

There have been three principal models of voting proposed to provide a solution to the perceived problems of FPTP. The first is the Single Transferable Vote (STV) system. This achieves its higher degree of proportional representation by (a) the creation of a small number of larger multi-member constituencies, with each returning, say, three or five or seven MPs and thus capable of ensuring that members of more than one significant party represent the constituency in Parliament; and (b) the opportunity for each voter to cast votes for the three, five or seven candidates, in order of preference, coupled with a counting system which gives weight first to first-preference votes and then to lower-preference votes. The capacity of this system for a higher degree of proportionality of outcome is obvious. Its disadvantages, when compared with FPTP, are its reduced capacity to deliver 'strong' government, with a greater possibility of the need for coalition rather than single-party governments; the loss of local representation because of the increased size of constituencies; the loss of personal directness of representation and accountability because of the multi-member team sent to Parliament; and the relative complexity of the voting and counting systems[5]. The second principal route to proportionality is by way of a 'list' system. In its purest form, this involves the abolition of separate constituencies, and in a single nationwide poll, the opportunity for all voters to cast votes for persons and/or parties on lists of candidates submitted (in the main) by political parties. The system operates to ensure, as precisely as possible, a matching of percentage support expressed by votes in the country against the percentage of representation in Parliament. In this, its purest all-

99

country version, local representation is entirely lost but may be reinstated to a degree by the organisation of elections on a regional basis; and it may admit to Parliament MPs representing tiny (and perhaps extreme) political parties, a feature which can be curbed by imposing a preliminary requirement to achieve a minimum (eg 5 per cent) of the total poll. The list system tends to lead to coalition governments. The system[6] deployed on a regional basis – with Scotland returning six[7] MEPs – is used for elections in the United Kingdom to the European Parliament. It is a modified list system which is used to provide the 'regional' members of the Scottish Parliament. At the third general election in May 2007 (which produced a far less 'diverse' Parliament than had the 2003 election) this enabled the Scottish Conservative Party to supplement its four constituency MSPs with thirteen regional members and, critically for the overall result, added 26 regional seats to the SNP's 21 constituencies. The system also produced two regional members for the Greens and one independent[8]. On the other hand, the Labour Party added only nine regional members to its 37 constituency MSPs and the Liberal Democrats added five to their 11. The 2011 result provided the biggest surprise. Despite the expectation that this model of proportional representation would produce coalition or minority governments for ever, the SNP did, in fact, with a landslide, dominate the Parliament. The Party had an initial 69 MSPs[9], with Labour back on 37 and the Conservatives on 15. The Liberal Democrats dropped to five and the Greens and independent MSPs[10] remained.

A third potential response came in the recommendations of the Jenkins Commission (above) which conducted a review of electoral systems as they might be applied to the House of Commons. The Commission expressed a preference for neither STV nor a list system as the primary means of reform. Instead, the Commission proposed a two-vote mixed system with the majority of MPs elected on an individual constituency basis, not by FPTP but by use of the Alternative Vote (which is not a means of achieving proportional representation but does offer voters the opportunity to express second and further preferences). Remaining MPs would be elected from open lists (ie lists giving the opportunity for the selection of individuals rather than simply of parties) based on small regions. There was, however, no immediate movement towards the adoption by government of the Jenkins proposals or, indeed, of any others, although in May 2009 Secretary of State Alan Johnson MP expressed his support for the 'AV plus' system and called for a referendum on electoral reform[11].

Ironically, therefore, the most recent (abortive) reform initiative came in the form of a national referendum held on 5 May 2011 on the question of whether the alternative vote (AV) system should replace FPTP. Provision for the referendum and for the scheme of AV to be adopted had been made in Part 1 of the Parliamentary Voting Systems and Constituencies Act 2011, pursuant not to any Labour Party initiative but to the Conservative-Liberal Democrat Coalition Agreement[12]. However, on a turn-out of 42.20%, a resounding majority of 67.9% voted No.

1   For a discussion of each and of the various reviews of the different systems which have taken place since 1997 see *The Government of Britain, Review of Voting Systems: The experience of new voting systems in the United Kingdom since 1997*, Cm 7304, 24 January 2008.

2 AMS systems are also be described, elsewhere in the world, as MMP (mixed-member proportional representation) systems.
3 Cm 4090.
4 The 'Lib-Lab pact' of 1977–79 aside.
5 As to which, and its consequences for the 2007 Scottish local government elections, see para 5.5, note 1.
6 'Closed list' rather an 'open list' which gives voters the choice of allocation of votes only by party rather than a named individual: European Parliamentary Elections Act 2002, s 2.
7 Reduced from eight by the European Parliament (Number of MEPs and Distribution between Electoral Regions) (United Kingdom and Gibraltar) Order 2008, SI 2008/1954.
8 *Report of the Independent Commission on the Voting System* (Cm 4090, 1998).
9 But by 2014 had lost three to become independents.
10 Later inflated by the former SNP members but then reduced by the loss of Margo MacDonald when she died on 4 April 2014.
11 The Times, 25 May 2009.
12 *The Coalition: Our Programme for Government* (2010) p 27.

Constituencies and their boundaries

5.9   Any electoral system short of one adopting a list-system vote across the entire territory of the nation relies upon the division of that territory into separate (and roughly equal-sized) constituencies and, because of the vagaries of population shifts, that division needs to be kept under review. The need for the division and review to be done scientifically and in the light of objective criteria in the interests of rationality and fairness suggests that the tasks should be allocated to bodies with a degree of independence from governments. That need for independence is enhanced by the peculiar susceptibility of constituency boundaries to party political manipulation. Especially in the constituencies required for the elections to the Westminster and Scottish Parliaments – small and, under FPTP, with single winners – quite slender boundary adjustments moving small populations of potentially friendly or hostile voters in or out of constituencies may produce quite different results. It is for this reason that the duty to review boundaries and to make recommendations for change has been placed in the hands of appointed boundary commissions for England, Northern Ireland, Scotland and Wales[1]. Although chaired *ex officio* by the Speaker of the House of Commons, the Boundary Commission for Scotland is, in practice, chaired by a Court of Session judge (currently Lord Woolman) with two other members appointed by the Secretary of State. The principal task of the Commission is to undertake periodic boundary reviews for both the Westminster and Scottish Parliaments. Its first periodic review of Scottish Parliament boundaries[2] produced recommendations which were implemented for the 2011 general election[3]. In advance of the next election in 2016, there has been a small interim review[4] which produced one marginal boundary change[5].

The overriding principle, so far as Westminster is concerned, has been to produce constituencies across Great Britain of equivalent size and thus with an electorate of about 70,000, but subject to special geographical considerations such as size, shape and accessibility as well as boundaries of local government areas[6]. A local inquiry may be held into the published provisional recommendations of the Commission which then submits its report in final form. It is then for the Secretary of State to lay the report before Parliament together with a draft Order in Council implementing the report, with or without modifications. As noted above[7], the 2006 Commission review of the Westminster constituencies was of much greater than usual significance because SA 1998, s 86 removed the long-standing statutory requirement that Scotland should be disproportionately well represented at Westminster with a minimum of 71 MPs. As a result of that review the number of Scottish MPs was reduced to 59. Since 2010, the UK Parliament boundary review process has been a victim of Coalition politics. Under the Parliamentary Voting Systems and Constituencies Act 2011, provision was made for a reduction in the overall size of the House of Commons to 600 members, with an accompanying anticipated redefinition and recalculation of constituencies under which, against the Labour Party, the Conservative Party was thought likely to benefit. The Act would have produced only 52 Scottish constituencies. However, the Boundary Commission Review (its sixth overall) which would have produced a report by 2018 was aborted (along with reviews across the United Kingdom) when implementation of the 2011 Act was blocked[8] by a rebellion by Liberal Democrat MPs at Westminster in defiance of any ministerial duties of collective responsibility[9] and in retaliation against the Conservatives' failure to progress the reform of the House of Lords[10]. There will be a return to the question of boundary reform, in one direction or another, after the 2015 general election.

THE WEST LOTHIAN QUESTION. There is one issue affecting the composition, and also the powers, of the two Parliaments which defies precise categorisation. It is captured by the question posed originally by Tam Dalyell (formerly MP for the West Lothian constituency and then for Linlithgow) at the time of the debate leading to the Scotland Act 1978[11] but which has a continuing relevance. As he put it, it was a question about why he, as a Westminster MP for a Scottish constituency, could legitimately be expected to participate in, or vote on, business in relation to Blackburn in the English county of Lancashire but not in relation to Blackburn in West Lothian because that business would, for Scotland, be devolved (and has now been devolved by SA 1998) to the Scottish Parliament. Dalyell viewed this as a fatal flaw in any system of devolution constructed on an asymmetrical basis. Forcing the Westminster Parliament to be both a UK Parliament dealing with 'reserved' matters across the whole country and also an English (and Welsh) Parliament in relation to the matters devolved to Scotland (and Northern Ireland) created inevitable and unacceptable tensions – in particular the possible use by a UK government to secure legislation for England by a Commons majority dependent upon Scottish MPs. This was a position exacerbated by the 'overrepresentation' of Scotland in the House of Commons, a matter now addressed by the boundary changes discussed above. Notwithstanding those changes, the West Lothian Question refuses to go away and has in recent years (and especially in the aftermath of the Scottish independence referendum) become a frequently kicked political football. Conservative Party policy in the period prior to the 2010 general election, for example, was to address the West Lothian question by giving English MPs a 'decisive say on laws that affect only England', by legislation in similar terms to Lord Baker of Dorking's Parliament (Participation of Members of the House of Commons) Bill – a private member's bill introduced in 2006 which would have given the Speaker discretion to exclude categories of MPs (including all Scottish MPs) from speaking and voting on a Bill. In its May 2009 report 'Devolution: A Decade On', the House of Commons Justice Committee recognised the force of the West Lothian Question but described the 'English question' as being about far more than voting by Scottish, Welsh and Northern Irish MPs on matters of importance only to England. Rather, it 'encompasses the wider issue of how England should be governed post-devolution'[12]. The Committee noted the range of possible solutions to the 'English question' depending on how that question is characterised:

'First, there are those solutions which seek to address the constitutional imbalance seemingly brought about by devolution, for example, through the creation of an English Parliament. Second, there are those solutions which seek to amend the role, practice and status of Westminster as a means of addressing the West Lothian Question, for example, schemes of English votes for English laws. However, others consider that the West Lothian Question could be best addressed by a change in the party political balance at Westminster, for example, through reform of the electoral system or a reduction in the number of MPs from Scotland and Wales. These approaches could be described as all-England solutions. The final category of solutions are those which attempt to tackle the centralised nature and relative size of England through decentralisation or devolution within England'[13].

Having identified this range of possible solutions, however, the Committee was unable to endorse any one of them. It expressed concern about the question of 'balance' which would arise in the event of the creation of a new English Parliament, given the 'sheer size of the English population'. The suggestion had been made to the Committee that in the context of what would have become a more explicitly quasi-federal structure it would be extremely unusual to see one federal unit representing 80% to 85% of the total population of the state. Limiting the right to vote on 'English-only matters including health and education, to MPs with English seats' would require more careful drafting of new legislation to isolate English provisions from those extending to other parts of the United Kingdom and would also demand reform of the current system of allocating public spending in terms of which funding allocations for Scotland, Wales and Northern Ireland are calculated by reference to the amount determined for England. Changes in the electoral system or a reduction in the numbers of 'devolved' MPs with seats at Westminster were felt not to address the issue of principle at the heart of this debate – i.e. what voting rights ought to be enjoyed by those MPs – while it was felt by the Committee that regional devolution within England would be unlikely to answer the demands of those who 'want an English solution to the West Lothian question'. The Committee concluded that there remained 'major political as well as constitutional questions which are for Parliament as a whole to consider. It is our belief that as devolved government in Scotland, Wales and Northern Ireland develops in profile and substance, Parliament will come under pressure to consider these questions'[14]. Meanwhile, north of the border the Calman Commission (see para 3.20) concluded that it was 'not for us to discuss where or how power might be decentralised or devolved in England...nor...how England's laws should be made'[15]. The 'West Lothian Question affects all of the UK, and is a matter for the UK Parliament, not a matter for the Commission'[16].

In the Conservative manifesto of 2010 and then in the Coalition Agreement which followed there was a commitment to action. The Agreement promised a commission to consider the West Lothian Question. However, two principal circumstances denied the opportunity for significant progress in the 2010–15 Parliament. The first was the dominance during the whole period of the independence referendum process. The second was that, although there were valuable informal contributions to the debate[17], the promised commission, when appointed in January 2012[18], was given a remit confined to 'how the House of Commons might deal with legislation which affects only part of the United Kingdom, following the devolution of certain legislative powers to the Scottish Parliament, the Northern Ireland Assembly and the National Assembly for Wales'. Thus, although the Commission touched the bases of a wider range of solutions, it could not stray beyond Commons procedures for those it adopted. The Commission was chaired by the former Clerk of the Commons, Sir William Mackay.

The Commission made two recommendations. First, the House of Commons should, by resolution, adopt the principle that: 'Decisions at the United Kingdom level with a separate and distinct effect for England (or for England-and-Wales) should normally be taken only with the consent of a majority of MPs for constituencies in England (or England-and-Wales)' (para 119). The principle should be supported by procedural changes to ensure greater clarity in the definition of the territorial scope of Bills and to establish, as necessary, public bill committees with an appropriate English or English-and-Welsh party balance – leaving nevertheless a power of override to the Commons as a whole. Secondly, there should be a new Devolution Committee to consider the cross-border effects of Bills[19].

No immediate action was taken in the light of the report, although the Government appeared, at one point, to favour an 'English-only' stage in the Commons, producing a 'fourth reading veto'[20]. Nothing of substance could be done prior to the independence referendum. But then, as soon as the referendum result came, answering the West Lothian Question (especially in the politically more compelling form of 'English votes for English laws') was immediately launched as the Conservative Party's response to the steps put in place to implement the 'Vow' to expand the powers of the Scottish Parliament[21]. In the light of opposing calls for the matter to be examined only in the context of a wider consideration of the governance of the United Kingdom, it is currently unclear how or when progress will be made.

1   Parliamentary Constituencies Act 1986 (PCA 1986), s 2. The Boundary Commission for Scotland is responsible for review of Scottish Parliament boundaries by virtue of s 1 and Sch 1 of SA1998, as amended by the Scottish Parliament (Constituencies) Act 2004. Statutory provision has been made for the transfer of the powers to the Electoral Commission (PPERA 2000, s 16) but this seems unlikely to affect the Scottish Commission for the foreseeable future.
2   *Report on the First Periodic Review of Scottish Parliament Boundaries* (2010).
3   SI 2010/2690.
4   *Report on Interim Review of Scottish Parliament Boundaries* (2013).
5   Implemented by SI 2014/501.
6   PCA 1986, Sch 2.
7   See para 5.3.
8   Reconfirmed thereafter by the Electoral Registration and Administration Act 2013, s 6.

9   See para 7.11.
10 See para 5.14.
11 T Dalyell *Devolution: The End of Britain* (1977) pp 245–251.
12 Devolution: A Decade On, Fifth Report of Session 2008–09, HC 529-I, para 158.
13 Ibid, para 163.
14 Ibid, para 230.
15 The Calman Commission, Serving Scotland Better: Scotland and the United Kingdom in the 21st Century ('*Serving Scotland Better*') (2009), para 2.13. For further discussion see R Hazell (ed), *The English Question* (2006) and The Constitution Unit, Towards a New Settlement? Report to the Commission, July 2008.
16 *Serving Scotland Better*, p 155, n 4.92.
17 Notably J Gallagher *England and the Union: How and Why to Answer the West Lothian Question* (2012).
18 In 2011, a private member's Bill (the Legislation (Territorial Extent) Bill) in the House of Commons failed to survive its 3rd reading vote. HC Debs 9 Sept 2011, col 710.
19 The Commission's proposal to give the Committee a supervisory role over Legislative Consent Motions ('LCMs') provided the opportunity for a critique of LCM procedures. See para 6.22.
20 Independent, 9 July 2013.
21 See para 4.20 and the reference there to the Hague proposals in Cm 8969.

The tenure of MPs and MSPs and the filling of vacancies

5.10   MPs and MSPs are elected for the period of the Parliament. In the Scottish Parliament, an MSP's term of office is stated to begin on the day on which the member is declared to be returned[1]. Before a member can take part in any proceedings of the Parliament he or she must take the oath of allegiance[2]. Thereafter, membership lasts until dissolution unless a member acquires a characteristic incompatible with membership[3] or dies or resigns. The device for enabling resignation from the House of Commons has been mentioned[4]. In September 2014, however, as a part of the continuing outwash from the 'expenses scandal'[5] a Government Bill (the Recall of MPs Bill) was introduced into the House of Commons. The Bill's provisions are complex but, at their heart, are rules enabling an MP to be removed where 10% of the electorate support a petition to do so, in circumstances where the MP has been found guilty of a serious criminal offence or subjected to a period of suspension by the House.

In the Scottish Parliament, resignation is by written notice to the Presiding Officer[6]. In both Parliaments, there is provision for the filling of casual vacancies. In the House of Commons, a by-election is held on the authority of a warrant issued by the Speaker, following a motion on behalf of the party which formerly held the seat[7]. In the Scottish Parliament, a 'constituency vacancy' is filled by a by-election held within three months on a date fixed by the Presiding Officer[8]. There cannot be the same option of a by-election in the case of a 'regional vacancy'. In the interests of maintaining proportionality of representation, the seat is to be filled by the person next in line at the last election on the relevant political party's regional list, who is willing and able to serve[9]. If the seat was held by an individual who is not a party representative, it is to remain vacant until the next general election[10].

1   SA 1998, s 13.
2   SA 1998, s 84.

3   See para 5.7.
4   The Stewardship of the Chiltern Hundreds see para 5.7.
5   See para 5.20.
6   SA 1998, s 14. The eventual resignation of Bill Walker MSP on 7 Sept 2013, following months
    of pressure after his (multiple) conviction for domestic violence prompted discussion of the
    need for a power to expel.
7   *Erskine May's Parliamentary Practice* (24th edn, 2011), p 25.
8   SA 1998, s 9.
9   To the end of 2014 there were ten such replacements.
10 SA 1998, s 10. This is what happened on the death of Margo MacDonald MSP on 4 April 2014.

The conduct of elections

5.11   Detailed rules for the conduct of elections are prescribed in regulations. For elections to the Scottish Parliament, rules about the registration of voters, registration appeals (to the sheriff and thence to a registration appeal court of three judges), the manner of voting (including absent and proxy voting), election campaigns (including election agents and the control of campaign expenses), the regulation of broadcasting during campaigns and the legal challenge of election results are contained in the Scottish Parliament (Elections etc) Order 2010[1].

1   SI 2010/2999. For UK parliamentary elections, the source of many of the equivalent rules is
    the Representation of the People (Scotland) Regulations 2001, SI 2001/497, as amended by SI
    2013/3206.

Parliaments and political parties

5.12   The written constitutions of the world do not have much to say about political parties[1]. They may take care to ensure that freedom of political thought and freedom of political association (including the right to form and belong to political parties) are guaranteed to citizens but, in the text of a constitution itself, few clues are given as to the dominant role of political parties in the actual working of constitutional rules. Political parties and even whole systems of party organisation may come and go while constitutions, remaining above the political fray, have an enduring character and display a neutrality and impartiality in their silence. Politics should be left to be conducted in the shadow of the constitution.

Historically, UK constitutional rules gave hardly any direct recognition to the participation by political parties in the system. Electoral candidates were permitted to identify their party affiliation on the ballot paper and, on the other hand, since 1974, certain political organisations have been proscribed (first under the Prevention of Terrorism (Temporary Provisions) Act 1974 and then under the Terrorism Act 2000, Pt II). For two main reasons, this situation has changed to produce the rules for the registration of political parties under PPERA 2000[2]. The introduction of proportional representation involving the use of lists of party candidates for the devolved assemblies and parliaments and for the European Parliament required official recognition for the parties. Secondly, registration was required by the wish to extend constraints on individual candidates in respect of election funding to constraints on parties as a whole; the wish to monitor donations to political parties; and the wish to facilitate (so far) limited public funding assistance for political parties. Since 1975, some funding assistance ('Short' money) has been made available to opposition parties at Westminster and this facility was extended to Holyrood at its inception, but additional forms of assistance required more formal structures. Under PPERA 2000, s 12 policy development grants are available to registered parties represented in Parliament. The Act also introduced mechanisms for the monitoring and control of donations to parties.

The changes introduced by PPERA 2000 serve only limited purposes, however, and go only a little way to regulate by law the party system which dominates the working of the Westminster and, in a different way, the Scottish Parliament. It is the ways in which parties determine who forms governments, how those governments are maintained in power and enabled to carry out their business, and the peculiar relationship of control and accountability between governments and Parliaments which loom largest but party domination of the electoral process is an essential initial element.

1 But the former Constitution (1977) of the USSR gave a leading role to the Communist Party. The current Constitution (1982, as amended) of the People's Republic of China continues such a tradition.
2 Originally under the Registration of Political Parties Act 1998.

THE HOUSE OF LORDS AND THE CASE FOR BICAMERALISM IN THE SCOTTISH PARLIAMENT

Introduction

5.13   The most obvious structural difference between the Westminster and Scottish Parliaments is that, in addition to its elected chamber, the Westminster Parliament includes the unelected House of Lords. It is bicameral rather than unicameral and this has clear consequences for law-making procedures at Westminster, and for government formation and accountability. The debate over the case for abolition of the House of Lords or for the reform of its composition and powers was an important element in constitutional discourse throughout the last century and, although several reforms were indeed made (including most recently the restrictions on membership by virtue of a hereditary peerage enacted by the House of Lords Act 1999), there is considered to be unfinished reforming business carried forward into the twenty-first century.

It may be helpful to begin with an account of the composition of the House of Lords before the recent reforms were launched following the election of the Labour Government in 1997. Much the largest single contingent was that of the hereditary peers and peeresses of whom there were about 759 (with nine of original creation and the remainder of the second or later generation). They would all have expected to retain membership for their lifetimes, with transmission to their successors[1]. Secondly, there were some 500 life peers created by virtue of the Life Peerages Act 1958. One question raised in the process of reform is whether all should be retained as members of the House of Lords for their lifetimes, with at least short- to medium-term consequences for the prospects of securing a reduction in total membership. Then in much smaller numbers, there were the Lords of Appeal in Ordinary (the senior judges who, until the advent of the Supreme Court (see para 14.31) sat in the Appellate Committee of the House of Lords and the Judicial Committee of Privy Council and, prior to 1958, the only 'life peers')[2] and retired Lords of Appeal, some 27 altogether. And finally, there were the 'Lords Spiritual': 26 archbishops and bishops of the Church of England.

The actual functions of the House of Lords are dealt with elsewhere in this book. The House of Lords participates in the making of Acts of Parliament but principally in a 'revising' capacity and subject ultimately to the discipline of the Parliament Acts 1911–49, according to which the will of the House of Commons prevails[3]. In the approval of secondary legislation, the Lords normally defer to the Commons but with occasional rebellions[4]. The Lords may hold individual ministers to account but they cannot bring down governments as a whole[5]. The Lords exercise their functions in a way which does not seriously challenge the primacy of the Commons, despite their being the 'Upper' House.

1 Prior to the Peerage Act 1963, the disclaimer of a title was not possible (*Re Parliamentary Election for Bristol South East* [1961] 3 WLR 577) but that Act enabled disclaimer for the lifetime of the incumbent, enabling, eg, Tony Benn and Sir Alec Douglas Home to become MPs.
2 Created under the Appellate Jurisdiction Acts 1876 and 1887 and the Administration of Justice Act 1968, s 1. Since the Constitutional Reform Act 2005, s 137, judges have been disqualified from sitting in the House of Lords.
3 See para 9.7.
4 See *A House for the Future* (Cm 4534) ch 7.
5 *The House of Lords – Completing the Reform* (Cm 5291) para 23.

The House of Lords: reform or abolition

5.14　If one were to start with a clean slate, the case for a bicameral (or even multicameral) legislature would be made in terms of a mixture of arguments concerning both the composition and functions of an additional chamber[1]. A second chamber designed to have weak, perhaps only advisory, functions attracts few serious questions about its membership. A second chamber designed to discharge important functions, including, for instance, the power to amend or veto legislative proposals, needs strong arguments for its very existence and provokes debate about its membership. Probably the most obvious justification for second chambers in general has been the wish to see state or provincial interests represented and given power in federal constitutions[2].

Whatever the general arguments, however, debate in the United Kingdom has never been permitted to start from a clean slate but has been conducted instead on the basis of more piecemeal reforms of the peculiarities of the historical heritage. The twin considerations of functions and membership have been important but they have been clouded by history, a commitment to the need for change to command broad support in Parliament, and political expediency. The starting point for the incoming Labour government in 1997 was a manifesto commitment to reform which was followed, in December 1998, by a White Paper outlining the way forward[3]. The first stage would be the removal of the right of all but a small number of hereditary peers to sit and vote in the House of Lords. This would produce a 'transitional' House which would be accompanied by a new independent Appointments Commission to recommend nonpolitical appointments to the transitional House. As far as longer-term reform was concerned this would be, as originally proposed in the manifesto, a matter for a Joint Committee of both Houses of Parliament but that Committee's work would be prefaced by a Royal Commission to consider possible alternatives for reform.

Thus, the next step taken was the passing of the House of Lords Act 1999 which provides that no one shall be a member of the House of Lords by virtue of a hereditary peerage, save for up to 92 hereditary peers for their lifetimes or 'until an Act of Parliament provides to the contrary'[4]. The government concession to allow some hereditary peers to remain was negotiated to prevent a stalling of the Bill by opposition in the House of Lords itself[5]. A non-statutory Appointments Commission was established with powers to recommend nonpolitical life peers and to vet all nominations.

By January 2000, the Royal Commission on Reform of the House of Lords, under the chairmanship of Lord Wakeham, had reported[6], with recommendations for a largely nominated membership and offering three different models for the election, on a regional basis, of the remainder. There would be a new Appointments Commission established by statute. At this point, however, the pace of reform slackened as it became apparent that a division of opinion was opening as to the way forward. In particular, the Royal Commission's preference for a mainly nominated membership of the reformed House was found to be unacceptable to many outside (and some inside) the government. It was not until after the May 2001 general election that the government itself provided a considered response to Wakeham. In *The House of Lords – Completing the Reform*[7], the government broadly accepted Wakeham but invited views on a number of outstanding issues. A very substantial contribution to the developing debate came from a report, in February 2002, of an inquiry held by the House of Commons Public Administration Committee[8] to which the government responded in April[9]. This was followed by the revival of the proposal, originally made in 1998 but thought to have been abandoned through the lack of sufficient parliamentary consensus, for a Joint Committee of both Houses on reform. That Committee (under the chairmanship of Jack Cunningham MP) met for the first time on 9 July 2002 and in December 2002 the Committee reported[10] that it was its view that there was broad agreement on the role, functions and powers of a reformed second chamber. The self-restraining conventions governing relations with the House of Commons should be continued as a vital part of any settlement. No new or additional powers should be conferred on the House of Lords but consideration would later need to be given to its treatment of secondary legislation. The composition of the House was the principal outstanding issue. There should be about 600 members, although with a larger number for a transitional period. Tenure for all members of 12 years was proposed and there would need to be further consideration of the position of bishops, the Law Lords, and the judicial function of the House of Lords. What was required before further progress could be made was a debate, and later a vote, in each House on the same list of seven options for the composition of a new House of Lords ranging from fully appointed to fully elected via different percentages of each. The debates were scheduled for 21 January 2003 and the votes on the options took place on 4 February. In the House of Lords there was a majority for a fully appointed House but for no other option. In the House of Commons, however, there was no majority for any of the seven options and there was a danger of paralysis once again.

In May 2003 the Joint Committee returned to the fray with the publication of a further report[11] summarising the extent of progress already made, the degree of consensus already achieved, even on some aspects of the future composition of the House, and the work still to be done. The report, from a divided Committee, concluded with an appeal to the government for an early response which could lead to an acceptance by both Houses that the work of the Committee should continue. That appeal went largely unheeded and such proposals as have been put forward by the government since 2003 for reform of membership of the Lords have failed to get off the ground[12].

The then Lord Chancellor Lord Falconer announced in September 2003 the government's intention to remove all remaining hereditary peers from the upper chamber but that proposal was not taken forward before the 2005 general election. Following the election, a cross-party group on Lords reform was established and its work led ultimately to the publication in February 2007 of a further White Paper – *The House of Lords: Reform*[13]. The White Paper described its role as being to 'set the stage for the free votes on the composition of a future House of Lords, promised in the Government's 2005 manifesto'[14]. It recommended a 'hybrid House' comprising a mix of elected and appointed members but offering a range of options on the precise balance of the two. A form of proportional representation would be introduced in relation to elected members, while appointees would be chosen by a statutory appointments commission reporting directly to Parliament. It was also proposed that at least 20% of the total membership of the Lords should be non party-political. Remaining life and hereditary peers would disappear but in a gradual way. There followed a government sponsored debate in the Commons on 7 March 2007[15] at the conclusion of which a large majority of MPs voted in favour of a wholly elected second chamber – only to be followed a week later by the Lords themselves voting against all options involving elections and favouring, instead, an all-appointed chamber[16].

Perhaps inevitably, this impasse was followed by the appointment of a further cross-party working group and the publication in July 2008 by the Ministry of Justice of another White Paper – *An Elected Second Chamber: further reform of the House of Lords*[17] – which advanced the case for a 100% or 80% elected chamber, with members serving a single term of between 12 and 15 years and being elected in 'thirds' with elections taking place on three electoral cycles. Hereditary peers would be removed, as would Church of England Bishops. It then appeared that reform was off the agenda until after the next general election. However, on 10 June 2009, Prime Minister Brown announced that 'The government will come forward with published proposals for the final stages of House of Lords reform before the summer break – including the next steps we can take to resolve the position of the remaining hereditary peers and other outstanding issues'[18].

At the 2010 general election, all three principal Westminster parties included Lords reform proposals in their manifestos and, after the election, the Conservative-Liberal Democrat Coalition Agreement contained a commitment to 'establish a committee to bring forward proposals for a wholly or mainly elected upper chamber on the basis of proportional representation' and, in May 2011, the Government was able to publish a draft Bill. That draft Bill was examined by a joint parliamentary committee which reported in March 2012[19]. It was, however, a badly divided committee and the resulting House of Lords Reform Bill (2012–13) was heavily contested. The proposed reformed chamber would (by 2020) have consisted of 240 elected members (rising from an initial 120); 60 appointed members (rising from 30); 16 bishops; and up to eight 'ministerial' members (to enable a ministerial presence and accountability). The Bill made no serious progress. Although it was given a second reading in the Commons, the programme motion (designed to secure timely progress on the Bill) was opposed by 91 Conservative MPs and the Bill was abandoned[20].

Although some minor adjustments were made by the House of Lords Reform Act 2014 (to enable peers to resign[21] and to secure their removal for non-attendance and for conviction of serious offences) it remains, as it was nearly 12 years ago when the first edition of this book was published, unclear when and how the process of reform of the Lords will be progressed and concluded. Unless the post-referendum period enables discussion of a new second chamber in some way representative of the nations of the United Kingdom, it seems that the intransigence of the current membership of the House of Lords and its allies will require a serious re-examination (in the interests of constitutional decency) of the option of simple abolition.

1   M Russell *Reforming the House of Lords: Lessons from Overseas* (2000); special issue of *Journal of Legislative Studies* (2001) vol 7 (Spring).
2   The US Senate performs that role on behalf of the states.
3   *Modernising Parliament: Reforming the House of Lords* Cm 4183, 1998.
4   House of Lords Act 1999, ss 1–2. The allocation of these peers was according to prior party strength in the Lords and the standing orders of the House contain the procedures for replacing deceased members. Since November 2002 this has been by election. The first election (of Lord Ullswater) was held in March 2003.
5   A challenge to the Bill in the House of Lords Committee for Privileges on grounds including an asserted obligation to protect Scottish hereditary peers under the Articles of Union failed. See *Lord Gray's Motion* 2000 SC 46 (HL) and paras 6.6.
6   *A House for the Future* (Cm 4534, 2000).
7   Cm 5291, November 2001.
8   *The Second Chamber: Continuing the Reform* (HC Paper 494 (2001–02)).
9   HC Paper 794 (2001–02).
10 HL Paper 17, HC Paper 171 (2002–03).
11 HL Paper 97, HC Paper 668 (2002–03).
12 A notable exception was the Constitutional Reform Act 2005 which focused on the judicial role of the Lord Chancellor and Lords of Appeal in Ordinary and created the new Supreme Court. Section 137 of the Act prevents members of the House from sitting while 'holding a disqualifying judicial office'.
13 Cm 7027.
14 Para 1.1.
15 HC Debs, 7 March 2007, Col 1524 *et seq*.
16 HL Debs, 14 March 2007, Col 741 *et seq*.
17 Cm 7438.
18 HC Debs, 10 June 2009, Col 798.
19 HL Paper 284.

20 With consequences for constituency reform. See para 5.9.
21 A small trickle of peers has begun to do so. It had already been possible to retire informally under a 'voluntary scheme' and, to maintain a foreign tax status, under s 42 of the Constitutional Reform and Governance Act 2010.

Bicameralism and the Scottish Parliament

5.15   Despite the occasional calls for abolition, the principal debate at Westminster has focused on the reform of the House of Lords. In relation to the Scottish Parliament, on the other hand, where a second chamber has been lacking from the start, there had been until recently virtually no serious discussion about creating one. It was not on the agenda of the Scottish Constitutional Convention nor did it appear in the process of the creation of the Parliament[1]. This is, arguably, for the good reasons that Scotland is a relatively small country; the range and volume of the Parliament's business were never likely to warrant its division across two chambers; there is no compelling reason for regional representation in Scotland beyond that provided in the first chamber; and there was no wish unnecessarily to incur the complexity and expense a second chamber would bring. Only two arguments in favour of the addition of a second chamber have been made. The first is that existing procedures, especially in the committees of the Scottish Parliament, are failing to provide a sufficiently strong 'revising' role on Bills. It is an argument which begs many questions about the meaning of both 'failure' and the legitimacy of a strong revising role for a chamber which might be largely unelected. The answers should almost certainly be sought instead by revision of the Parliament's existing procedures. The second argument derives, in effect, from a plea for the direct involvement in Scottish politics of the unelected great and good. The House of Lords provides a location (to include also ministers) for those who have retired (or been expelled) from elected politics or have never aspired to election, and a second chamber at Holyrood could perform a similar function. The democratic insistence on drawing only on elected politicians as ministers does, for better or for worse, restrict the field. Lord Steel, having been interpreted initially as proposing a second chamber, has instead suggested that there is a need for an 'external review panel', appointed by the Parliament to undertake a legislative scrutiny role[2]. The Calman Commission (see para 3.20) considered both these arguments and representations made to the Commission in favour of introducing a second chamber for the Scottish Parliament. It concluded, however, that those submissions did not provide 'the weight of evidence that would be required as a basis for serious contemplation of such a fundamental change'[3].

Two post-Calman developments, however, have affected the question of the legitimacy of the Scottish Parliament's reliance on a single chamber. The first was the unexpected emergence in 2011 of a (single-party) overall majority for the SNP Government and its potential consequences for its accountability to the Parliament, consequences noted by the UK Supreme Court[4]. And secondly, the Smith Commission, when it recommended that the Parliament should have the power to legislate to change 'the franchise, the electoral system or the number of constituency and regional members for the Scottish Parliament', also recommended that legislation in the Parliament would require a supermajority of two-thirds[5].

1 There was a second chamber in the (Stormont) Parliament of Northern Ireland. See A G Donaldson 'The Senate of Northern Ireland' [1958] PL 135.
2 Lecture on 'The State of the Nation', 29 January 2003. For consideration of the wider case for a second chamber proper, see H MacQueen 'The case for a second chamber' in *What Future for Scotland?* (2003) Policy Institute.
3 The SNP's proposals for an independence constitution prior to the referendum would have retained a single chamber. See para 4.14.
4 See *AXA General Insurance Ltd, Petitioners* 2012 SC (UKSC) 122 at para 51 (Lord Hope).
5 Para 27. For the Commission report generally, see para 4.21.

PARLIAMENTARY COMMITTEES

5.16   In a remarkable analysis of constitutional practice of 60 years ago, Sir Kenneth Wheare wrote that committees were such a familiar feature of both social and governmental organisations as to be part of 'the British way of life'[1]. Since then the popularity of committees in different aspects of governmental activity has been maintained, although their dominant role in local authorities may now be being questioned[2]. Certainly, however, the importance of committees in the Westminster Parliament has grown since Wheare's time and they have assumed a significant role at Holyrood.

The case for committees is largely based upon the simple proposition that some, at least, of a parliament's principal functions are not well discharged in a chamber of the whole membership of the House or Parliament, whether that be 650 MPs or 129 MSPs. The plenary session may serve well as the forum in which the great issues of the day can be debated by all members; where ministers can make significant statements and be questioned on them; where ministers can also be publicly questioned and harangued on matters chosen by members; and where the massed ranks of the political parties represented in a Parliament can be seen to confront each other. A plenary session lends itself to ceremony when this is called for and tends to demand a high degree of formality of procedure. If the principal functions of a parliament are to contribute to the enactment of legislation and to scrutinise the work of the executive, much of this can appropriately be done in plenary session. There are good reasons to expose Bills (and their proponents) to general debate and also to ensure that, if they are to pass, they do so at a meeting at which all members are entitled to be present and to vote. Equally, it is valuable to have ministers being called to account, from time to time, before meetings of the whole parliament. In the House of Commons, there are meetings in the chamber of the House every day. In the Scottish Parliament chamber meetings were raised from two a week to three from September 2012.

There are, on the other hand, reasons why, on some occasions, the handling of business in plenary sessions is inappropriate and the reference of such business to smaller groups is to be preferred. Detailed scrutiny of Bills is more efficiently done by a smaller group, whether the debate is then conducted by the members of the committee themselves in response to amendments proposed by them or, in investigative mode, by the interrogation of experts or other witnesses. Similarly, the detailed and systematic scrutiny of executive action is better conducted by committees with powers to call for relevant papers, to take evidence from ministers and other witnesses, and to sit in places other than the parliament building itself. Not only does the use of committees make these functions more efficient in themselves, by the use of smaller and more focused groups, but it also takes pressure off the House or Parliament as a whole. Committees can function, with different memberships, at the same time as other committees and even at the same time as plenary sessions.

1 K C Wheare *Government by Committee* (1955) p 1.
2 See para 8.4.

Westminster committees

5.17   At Westminster, the tradition of the House of Commons has been to draw a sharp line between the functions of *legislation* and *scrutiny of the executive*. A 'public bill committee'[1] is established for a Bill as it progresses through the House. Normally the powers of a public bill committee do not extend to taking evidence from external witnesses[2]. On the other hand, select committees are established for the full term of a Parliament and, with a remit covering a single government department, take on the functions of executive scrutiny and proceed in the main by investigations involving the taking of written and oral evidence[3]. The functions of the two sets of committees do not formally overlap, although proposals for the greater integration of select committees into the legislative process have been made[4]. There would be as many advantages in using the expertise of the policy-focused select committees in the scrutiny of Bills as in the scrutiny of the administrative activity of the department they monitor.

1 One category of 'general committees' (SO 84) which also includes the 'Grand Committees'.
2 But see para 9.6.
3 For details, see paras 10.8–10.9.
4 See *First Report of the Modernisation Committee: The Legislative Process* HC Paper 190 (1997–98) and more recently the *First Special Report of the House of Commons Modernisation Committee: Committee Stage of Public Bills: Consultation on Alternative Options* HC Paper 810 (2005–06).

Holyrood committees

5.18   From the outset, it was assumed that an integrated committee system would be adopted by the Scottish Parliament. Scotland's Parliament envisaged that the 'committees might for example initiate legislation, scrutinise and amend the Scottish Executive's proposals as well as having wide ranging investigative functions'[1]. The functions of the House of Commons' standing and select committees would be combined and allocated to a single set of 'subject committees' and provision for these was made in the Parliament's standing orders[2]. Such committees are established by resolution of the Parliament, on a motion of the Parliamentary Bureau. The precise nomenclature and remit of subject committees varies from Parliament to Parliament. Currently the Parliament has the following seven subject committees: Economy, Energy and

Tourism; Education and Culture; Health and Sport; Infrastructure and Capital Investment; Justice[3]; Local Government and Regeneration; and Rural Affairs and Climate Change. In addition, standing orders require the appointment of seven mandatory committees[4]. There must be a Standards, Procedures and Public Appointments Committee (dealing with compliance with the MSPs' Code of Conduct, practice and procedures of the Parliament and matters relating to public appointments in Scotland), a Finance Committee, Public Audit Committee (audit of public expenditure), a European and External Relations Committee (European Union and international matters), an Equal Opportunities Committee, a Public Petitions Committee and a Delegated Powers and Legislative Reform Committee (considering subordinate legislation and powers to make such legislation).

In addition to the mandatory and subject committees, the Parliament may appoint other committees. One special instance is the Conveners Group[5] which consists of the Presiding Officer and the conveners of all subject and mandatory committees. The Group has responsibility for the general operation of committees and collaborates with the Parliamentary Bureau in its decision-making. In September 2013, it initiated the practice of an annual informal meeting with the First Minister[6]. Other Committees are of an ad hoc nature. In the 2007–11 Parliament, the Review of SPCB Supported Bodies Committee was established to review the structure and functions of a number of bodies supported by the SPCB including the Scottish Public Services Ombudsman, the Scottish Information Commissioner and the Scottish Parliamentary Standards Commissioner. In the 2011–16 session there have been the Scotland Bill Committee (to consider the UK Bill which became the Scotland Act 2012[7]), the Referendum (Scotland) Bill Committee (which scrutinised the legislation to enable the holding of the independence referendum and, in September 2014, became the Devolution (Further Powers) Committee and the Welfare Reform Committee (to review the passage of the UK Welfare Reform Act 2012 and its implementation)[8]. It is also possible for the whole Parliament to sit as a committee for the consideration of Bills.

Appointments to membership of committees are made by the Parliament on a motion by the Parliamentary Bureau[9]. In proposing appointments the Bureau must have regard to the qualifications and experience of MSPs when they have expressed an interest in membership[10]. In the first two sessions, control by the Bureau and the Parliament led to a situation in which MSPs from one or other of the coalition Government parties had a majority on all committees although the non-Government parties were compensated by the allocation of a number of committee convenerships and deputy convenerships. The minority SNP administration of 2007–11 could not achieve the same dominance of committee membership and convenerships and deputy convenerships were divided fairly evenly amongst the main parties. On the other hand, since 2011, and the arrival of an SNP majority in the Parliament, the ruling party has taken nine convenerships and nine deputy convenerships across the 14 subject and mandatory committees, with an SNP majority on most but not all. Political control by Government parties does not, in itself, undermine the capacity of committees to act in a relatively impartial and cross-party way where the subject matter demands this (eg in relation to public audit, standards or petitions) but the political composition of committees is clearly an issue, whatever efforts are made to mitigate or suppress its effects, when, for instance, subject committees are considering Bills or scrutinising Government action[11].

The functions of the Parliament's committees are largely determined by reference to their specific remits. In addition, all committees have general functions including the consideration of the policy and administration of the Scottish Administration, the need for law reform in their area, and the power to initiate Bills[12]. It has already been mentioned that, in the closing stages of the first session of the Parliament, the Procedures Committee carried out its 'CSG Inquiry' and it is not surprising, in the light of the emphasis placed by the CSG on the potential contribution to be made by committees to the work of the Parliament, that large sections of its report[13] focused on how the committees had worked in practice. Notwithstanding discussion of a number of areas where improvement was thought possible, the inquiry report expressed satisfaction that, as committees had been expected to be a major component in the Parliament's mission to achieve the goals of accountability and power-sharing, they had indeed established themselves as a 'key part of the Parliamentary landscape'[14].

More recently, the Parliament's committee system was reviewed by the Calman Commission as part of its review of the operation of devolution. Like the earlier CSG inquiry, the Commission heard 'very considerable evidence … that the Scottish Parliament's committees generally work well'[15] but also found concerns raised about the effectiveness of committees in holding the government to account and, indeed, about the system of 'dual-purpose' committees which have been fundamental to the Parliament since its creation. In relation to this latter concern, the Commission observed that in order to fulfil this scrutiny role it was important for committee members to build up expertise in the subject area which, in turn, 'requires a relatively low rate of turnover of members'[16]. They wished to 'encourage' political parties to do what they could to minimise the 'churn' of committee members. Echoing concerns expressed elsewhere, the Commission also referred to the problem of 'legislative overload'[17] and while recognising that it was a difficult issue to address suggested more use of sub-committees and that the standing orders should no longer require sub-committees to have the approval of the whole Parliament[18]. In the closing days of the 2007–11 Parliament, the Conveners Group focused its 'legacy paper'[19] on reforming proposals for the committee system. A principal concern was the adequacy of provision for the scrutiny function[20] at times of high legislative activity.

Over and above the committees formally established under the Parliament's standing orders, there has also emerged a pattern of 'cross-party groups'. These provide an opportunity for MSPs of all parties and members of the public to discuss matters of shared interest. Although not created by the Parliament under its standing orders, such groups are subject to the supervision of the Parliament's Standards, Procedures and Public Appointments Committee and are regulated under the terms of the MSPs' Code of Conduct.

1   Cm 3658, para 9.10 and see also the *CSG Report*, section 2 'Sharing the Power: the Role of Parliamentary Committees' paras 9–16.

2   SOs, r 6.1.4.
3   There is also, at present, a Justice Sub-Committee on Policing to oversee the operation of the Police and Fire Reform (Scotland) Act 2012 as it relates to policing.
4   SOs, r 6.1.5. Reduced from eight in September 2007 by the merging of the functions of the Procedures Committee with those of the Standards Committee.
5   SOs, Ch 6A.
6   Reflecting the practice of the Liaison Committee of the House of Commons.
7   See para 3.20.
8   Also special private bill committees eg the City of Edinburgh Council (Portobello Park) Bill Committee.
9   SOs, r 6.3. For the Bureau, see para 5.22.
10 SOs, r 6.3.4.
11 *CSG Inquiry* para 584.
12 SOs, r 6.2.2.
13 *CSG Inquiry* para 830.
14 *CSG Inquiry* paras 596–658.
15 *Serving Scotland Better*, para 6.22.
16 Ibid, para 6.35.
17 Ibid, para 6.37.
18 Ibid, para 6.39.
19 http://archive.scottish.parliament.uk/s3/committees/committeeConvenersGroup/documents/ConvenersGrouplegacypaper-Session3.pdf
20 See para 10.10 below.

MPS AND MSPS[1]

General

5.19   It would be surprising if, in the examination of the work of a modern parliament, the institution were thought to be organised entirely on the basis of groups or blocks of members. Committees clearly perform an important role and political parties, although accorded a formally less significant position, give a structure and dynamic to the working of parliaments. Apart from key individuals such as the Presiding Officer of the Scottish Parliament and the Speaker of the Commons and perhaps the conveners of parliamentary committees, the role of individual members is diminished. For many parliamentary purposes, the member exists only as part of a party block; party discipline curbs the freedom to speak or vote as the member might wish; and opportunities for independence of action, or even of thought, may be few. This is particularly true of those MPs and MSPs who hold office in the UK or Scottish governments but the expectation of loyalty on the part of back benchers is almost as great. The party 'whips'[2] maintain a high degree of discipline[3]. That is much less true, of course, in the case of independent MSPs in the Scottish Parliament.

Even in the case of members of large party groups, however, the constitutional identity of individual MPs and MSPs is maintained, as well as some opportunities for individuality of function. At Westminster respect has been paid to the enduring theory that the role of an MP is that of a *representative* of his or her constituents rather than their *delegate*. An MP cannot be mandated to speak and vote simply as their constituents, or indeed any other organised group, might wish[4]. And, while party policy will usually dominate, opportunities for a 'free vote' on a matter of conscience do occur in both the House of Commons and the Scottish Parliament[5]. Equally, the chance to promote a (private) member's Bill is evidence of the possibility of some freedom of manoeuvre but, even there, unless the chosen subject matter of the Bill is genuinely nonpolitical, party pressures are not likely to be far away. Similarly, the opportunity to launch an adjournment debate in the Commons or a members' business debate in the Scottish Parliament and to ask parliamentary questions provide some scope for autonomous action. On the whole, the opportunity for such autonomy increases the further MPs or MSPs are from issues of high political concern and the nearer they are to personal or constituency matters. And, of course, it is in their constituencies, the correspondence and other work on behalf of constituents, and in the surgeries they hold that many MPs have traditionally found most fulfilment. This is not a wholly disinterested endeavour, however, and may, in marginal constituencies, be motivated as much by a concern for an MP's own re-election as for the welfare of his or her constituents. The same pressures are felt by MSPs and, although there might have been some expectation on the part of constituency members that this would be a role for them rather than their regional counterparts, both classes of MSP seem committed to 'constituency' work. Indeed this is a feature of the work of MSPs as a whole. There is less evidence than might have been expected of a two-tier membership, with the constituency MSP claiming to be the 'real' member. The Parliament's own *Code of Conduct* for Members insists that all MSPs have equal formal and legal status and provides guidance on relationships between them[6].

1 This section does not really deal with members of the House of Lords. Although there are many parallels, party discipline is less rigorous in that House and the position of individual members varies much more, according to their category of membership.
2 In the Scottish Government, the Minister for Parliamentary Business.
3 See *R(H2S Action Alliance Ltd) v Secretary of State for Transport* [2014] 4 All ER 109, paras 61–66 (Lord Reed).
4 On which, see para 5.21 below.
5 For instance, in the Scottish Parliament, on the Protection of Wild Mammals (Scotland) Bill (hunting): SP OR 19 September 2001, cols 2586, 2589; and on proceedings on the Marriage and Civil Partnership (Scotland) Act 2014 (same-sex marriage).
6 Rule 8.1.2. For the latest (5th) edition of the Code, see http://www.scottish.parliament.uk/ Parliamentaryprocedureandguidance/CodeofConduct-5thEdMay2014_3rdRevision.pdf

MPs' and MSPs' pay and allowances

5.20   The current rules on MPs' salaries and expenses (which are both set by the Independent Parliamentary Standards Authority (IPSA)) can be briefly stated. Annual salaries are fixed at £74,000 with effect from May 2015, subject to review by IPSA by September 2015[1] and to annual adjustment thereafter in accordance with the Office of National Statistics' rate of change of average earnings. Expenses are payable in respect of accommodation (when working from two locations), office support and travel and subsistence[2]. Such brevity, however, conceals the circumstances which gave rise to these arrangements and, in particular, to their supervision and control by a body independent of MPs themselves. The period between 2009 and 2015 has been one of attempting to cap the political volcano of the 'MPs' Expenses Scandal' and to restore trust in the former wholly discredited system which, following the revelation by the Daily Telegraph of an appalling range of inflated (and, in many cases, fraudulent) claims, several MPs resigned (including the Speaker) and a few were prosecuted[3]. SA 1998 gives the Scottish Parliament[4] the power to determine the salaries of MSPs (s 81) and, in March 2002, the Parliament accepted a recommendation[5] that salaries would be tied at 87.5% per cent of Westminster salaries[6], ie £54,093 from 1 November 2007. The Parliament also has a system for the payment of allowances.

1 See Parliamentary Standards Act 2009 s 4A(6) (as inserted by the Constitutional Reform and Governance Act 2010) and IPSA's *MPs' Pay and Pensions Final Report* (2013).
2 See *The MPs' Scheme of Business Costs and Expenses* (7th edn, 2015).
3 See *R v Chaytor* [2010] UKSC 52, [2011] 1 AC 684 for the lack of immunity of MPs to criminal prosecution. The effects of the scandal continued to be felt for many years, eg in the work of the Commons Committee on Standards (see para 5.21 below).
4 SA 1998, s 81, after initial arrangements made by SI 1999/1097.
5 SP OR 21 March 2002, col 10577.
6 SP OR Paper 554.

Standards and privileges

5.21   A feature of the historical development of the House of Commons has been the recognition that an efficient system of election is a necessary but not sufficient condition for the creation of a House able to discharge the functions assigned to it. Over the three centuries to the late twentieth century the principal object was to secure to parliamentarians the conditions of independence and freedom from interference necessary for the work of Parliament to be done. This originally derived from a continuing fear on the part of parliamentarians that the Crown would encroach upon their freedoms in an oppressive way and this is the fear still reflected in the ceremonial declaration of the privileges of the House of Commons which is made at the beginning of each Parliament. These privileges, represented in a special freedom of expression and freedom from arrest, have lost some their constitutional piquancy. Some are seen now as reflecting past battles fought and won on behalf of the House of Commons, although this by no means removes all continuing significance.

In the closing years of the twentieth century, however, there was an abrupt shift of emphasis. It became clear that the principal barriers to parliamentary business came not from threats to freedoms and privileges from outside but from misbehaviour and abuse of these privileges, or at least perceptions of misbehaviour and abuse within the House of Commons itself. There had always been a recognition that privileges could be abused by MPs and it was part of the task of the Privileges Committee to investigate such internal abuses. Now, however, there were calls for something much stronger and more positive to counteract the dangers of 'sleaze' and corruption to which some MPs had become vulnerable. The 'cash for questions' affair (of the mid-1990s) in which the Committee criticised the conduct of two MPs willing to accept up to £1,000 from a journalist pretending to be a businessman, in return for their asking a parliamentary question, led to the setting up of the Committee on Standards in Public Life under Lord Nolan. That committee produced a first report[1] which led to a strengthening of House of Commons procedures. The post of Parliamentary Commissioner for Standards was established and the former Committee on Privileges became the Standards and Privileges Committee, with a new remit. From the beginning of 2013, however, two separate committees were created once again, to enable the Standards Committee (to oversee the work of the Commissioner and to investigate complaints) to contain, uniquely[2] lay members in addition to MPs, whilst the Privileges Committee considers matters of privilege referred by the House[3].

'Standards' work of both the combined committee and now the separate committee has been dominated in recent years by the outwash of the 'expenses scandal' and other expenses issues[4]. Similar arrangements for standards and privileges exist in relation to the Scottish Parliament. SA 1998 makes no provision for the 'privileges' of the Parliament or its Members, save to protect in some measure proceedings of the Parliament and parliamentary papers from actions in defamation and in relation to contempt of court[5]. While the Consultative Steering Group did not address its attention to the privileges of MSPs[6], it did recommend that parliamentary standing orders should provide for a Standards Committee[7]. This recommendation was adopted in the making of the transitional standing orders and a Standards Committee was set up. That has now been replaced by the Standards, Procedures and Public Appointments Committee[8].

The Committee's remit, so far as standards are concerned, is to consider and report on (a) whether an MSP's conduct is in accordance with the Parliament's standing orders, (b) the Code of Conduct for Members[9] (the adoption, amendment and application of which is expressly placed within the Committee's remit), (c) matters relating to members' interests, and (d) any other matters relating to the conduct of members in carrying out their parliamentary duties[10]. The initial rules on the declaration of members' interests were laid down in an order made by the Secretary of State to meet the requirements of SA 1998, s 39[11] which was replaced by the Interests of Members of the Scottish Parliament Act 2006 (which began life as a Committee Bill promoted by the then Standards Committee). The Act puts on a statutory footing the Register of Interests of Members of the Scottish Parliament which is maintained by the Clerk of the Parliament. MSPs are required to register 'registrable interests' (a range of different financial interests including gifts, sponsorships and remuneration), they are also obliged to make an oral declaration prior to participating in proceedings of the Parliament, and there is a prohibition on paid advocacy. The Act provides for a range of sanctions, including measures to be taken by the Parliament itself to suspend or exclude MSPs who have breached the rules and, in some circumstances, criminal prosecution.

The Committee is not the only enforcer of standards of conduct for MSPs. The Scottish Parliamentary Standards Commissioner Act 2002 (SPSCA 2002) created the original Commissioner but, in a wider reform of 'standards' provision, the parliamentary duties were included in the remit of the Commissioner for Ethical Standards in Public Life in Scotland[12]. The Commissioner is appointed, for a single, non-renewable period not exceeding eight years, by the Parliamentary corporation with the agreement of the Parliament[13] and may be removed from office by the corporation only if the Parliament so resolves with not less than a two-thirds majority[14]. The functions of the Commissioner are investigating and reporting on complaints about the conduct of MSPs, his principal task being to decide whether the conduct complained about has been committed by the member and, if so, whether it has breached a 'relevant provision' of the Parliament's standing orders, the Code of Conduct or the members' interests rules.

Both the Committee and the Commissioner have been involved in dealing with a number of complaints against MSPs, perhaps none more controversial than those made against the then Scottish Labour leader Ms Wendy Alexander at the end of 2007[15]. The complaint, made by an SNP researcher, was that Ms Alexander had failed to register several 'gifts' – donations to help fund her campaign for leadership – in the register of interests. The complaint was first considered by the Commissioner who, amongst other things, reported the matter to the procurator fiscal in line with rules which require such reporting where the Commissioner reaches the view that the conduct complained of might constitute a criminal offence[16]. The fiscal having indicated that no prosecution would be brought, the Commissioner concluded his investigation and found that Ms Alexander's conduct constituted a breach of s 5 of the Interests of Members of the Scottish Parliament Act 2006. The Standards, Procedures and Public Appointments Committee considered the Commissioner's report and decided, but only by a majority, that it agreed with the Commissioner's findings. It was divided as to what if any sanction ought to be imposed on Ms Alexander but determined by division that she should be suspended from Parliament on the first Wednesday of the 2008–2009 parliamentary session. This determination, in July 2008, was regarded by many as being driven solely by political motives which, if it was, were satisfied by the resignation of Ms Alexander as Scottish Labour leader. However, the saga did not end there. On 4 September 2008 the Parliament debated the Committee's determination and voted to 'quash' the Committee's recommendation that Ms Alexander be suspended. In an acrimonious debate it was suggested by a number of MSPs that members of the Standards Committee had been influenced by party whips in reaching their verdict on Ms Alexander's conduct and on the sanction which should be applied[17]. This was undoubtedly a low point in the Committee's history and a reflection, perhaps of the fact that, as with all other activities of the Parliament, politics can never be removed entirely from the mix[18].

1   Cm 2850, 1995.
2   SO 149A.
3   The first business of the Committee since the separation related to an MP's complaint about an alleged contempt by the police. See HC 1021 (2013–14) and HC 588 (2014–15).
4   See eg HC 1179 (2013–14) (Maria Miller MP).
5   SA 1998, ss 41–42, Sch 8, para 33. See C Munro 'Privilege at Holyrood' [2000] PL 347.
6   Save again in relation to contempt and the need for a workable *sub judice* rule; see paras 38–42.
7   Paras 75, 76.
8   SOs, r 6.4.
9   See para 5.19.
10 SOs, r 6.4.
11 Since amended by SA 2012, s 7 to give the Parliament rather greater flexibility in making the rules. The Standards, Procedures and Public Appointments Committee is drafting a new Bill.
12 See the Scottish Parliamentary Commissions and Commissioners etc. Act 2010 (SPCCA 2010) and SSI 2013/197. See also para 8.17.
13 SPCCA 2010, ss 1, 9.
14 SPCCA 2010, s 9(4).
15 For a full account see the Sixth Report of the Standards, Procedures and Public Appointments Committee of 2007–2008, SP Paper 142.

16 Scottish Parliamentary Standards Commissioner Act 2002 (Procedures, Reporting and Other Matters) Directions 2002, issued by the then Standards Committee of the Parliament. In this case the 'potential' offence was the participation by Ms Alexander in proceedings of the Parliament while having failed to register registrable interests.

17 SP OR 4 Sept 2008, col 10439 *et seq.*

18 Although some 57 complaints against MSPs were lodged with the Commissioner for Ethical Standards during 2011–14, none was treated as admissible. See the Commissioner's *Annual Report 2013–14.*

THE MANAGEMENT AND ADMINISTRATION OF THE PARLIAMENTS

5.22   So far considered in this chapter have been the different elements of the parliamentary structure – chambers, committees and individual members – and the distribution of functions, to be dealt with in later chapters, between them. There is also a need in both Parliaments for some overall co-ordination, support and management to enable parliamentary purposes to be achieved. On the one hand, there is a need for the dispassionate and non-political assistance of officials whose job it is to hold the ring between the different interests represented and to ensure that they are provided with all the advice and administrative support necessary to discharge the individual and collective functions. On the other hand, it has also to be ensured that the work of a parliament is managed politically, broadly in accordance with the wishes of the political majority. At Westminster and, in particular, in the House of Commons, these are functions carried out by the Speaker, together with a substantial staff responsible to the Clerk of the House and, on the political front, largely through informal processes of mediation and control between the parties known as the 'usual channels'.

In the Scottish Parliament, there are slightly more formal arrangements which derive, in the first instance, from SA 1998 itself, including its specification of some of the content of the Parliament's standing orders[1]. On the 'non-political' side, the administration is headed by the Presiding Officer and two deputies elected by the Parliament at the first meeting of each session[2]. The elections are by secret ballot and there is a requirement that all three officers be not drawn from the same political party[3]. They must act impartially[4]. The Parliament's standing orders confer the general functions of the Presiding Officer which are to chair meetings of the Parliament, the Parliamentary Bureau and the Conveners Group as well as to determine and rule on questions arising under the standing orders. The Presiding Officer also represents the Parliament 'in discussions and exchanges with any parliamentary, governmental, administrative or other body, whether within or outwith the United Kingdom'. In parliamentary debates, the Presiding Officer does not normally vote but must exercise a casting vote in the event of a tie. Such occasions have caused occasional controversy where that vote has resulted in defeat for the government[5]. The Presiding Officer is a member (along with four other MSPs elected by the Parliament) of and chairs the Scottish Parliamentary Corporate Body (or Parliamentary corporation) which is established as a distinct legal entity with the functions of providing the Parliament with property, staff and services and representing the Parliament in legal proceedings by or against it[6]. It is also for the Corporate Body to appoint the Clerk of the Parliament[7] who acts as chief executive of the Parliament's administrative service.

On the 'political' side, the principal body is the Parliamentary Bureau[8] which has no statutory basis but, following recommendations of the Consultative Steering Group for a business committee, is established under standing orders[9] to make proposals to the Parliament for its business programme and for the remit and membership of committees. The Bureau's own membership comprises, in addition to the Presiding Officer, one member per political party[10]. The Parliamentary Bureau currently has four members, representing the SNP, Labour, Conservative and Liberal Democrat Parties[11]. Political control, however, derives from the voting system which gives each member a vote for each of the party's MSPs, thus normally ensuring a majority for the governing party or parties. The Presiding Officer has a casting vote, a privilege of no practical consequence[12]. It is the Bureau's ability to control the Parliament's programme, subject, of course, to any political majority in the Parliament itself, which ensures the government's broad control over the content and pace of the Parliament's agenda. The principal criticism of the CSG Inquiry was of the Bureau's lack of transparency[13].

1 Principally, SA 1998, s 22 and Sch 3. In the light of criticisms it received, the Calman Commission recommended a review of these constraints (rec 6.8). More importantly, the Smith Commission (see para 4.21) also recommended that 'UK legislation will give the Scottish Parliament powers to make decisions about all matters relating to the arrangements and operations of the Scottish Parliament' (para 26).
2 SA 1998, s 19.
3 SOs, r 3.3.7.
4 Lord Steel, the Parliament's first Presiding Officer, announced on 28 July 1999 that he had resigned from the Countryside Alliance.
5 When the Presiding Officer's vote defeated the SNP government's budget for 2009–10 (see SPOR 28 January 2009).
6 SA 1998, ss 21, 40 and Sch 2.
7 SA 1998, s 20.
8 The Bureau has an obligation to consult the Conveners Group on many matters. See SOs r 6A.2.
9 Ch 5.
10 Of five or more MSPs or group of smaller parties.
11 But, from November 2012 to April 2014, a Green/Independent group provided a fifth member. The death of Margo MacDonald MSP ended the arrangement.
12 As pointed out by the Presiding Officer in evidence to the Procedures Committee's *CSG Inquiry*, para 754.
13 *CSG Inquiry*, paras 743–783.

THE OPENNESS AND ACCESSIBILITY OF THE PARLIAMENTS

5.23   If maintaining high standards of conduct is an important precondition of a functioning Parliament, another general requirement is public access to the Parliament's deliberations and its papers. It has been largely uncontroversial that the work of the representatives of the people should be open to inspection by the people. Law-making should be done in public and scrutiny of an executive which may itself have tendencies to secrecy should, as a matter of principle, bring information into the public domain. In addition, the exposure of parliamentary business to scrutiny by the public and the press serves as an important check on standards of behaviour. There should at least be the right of public access and this has been ensured, formally at least, at Westminster by long-standing rules which ensure public rights of access to the two chambers and to committee meetings and which require the publication of (*Hansard*) reports of proceedings[1]. Increasingly, there has been pressure to extend this to a positive obligation to provide publicity and an important theme in the emergence of the Scottish Parliament was that of public involvement in the Parliament's work. One of the four guiding principles of the CSG was that of ensuring access and participation.

SA 1998 itself requires that proceedings of the Parliament (which includes committee proceedings) be held in public, except in circumstances provided for in standing orders[2]; and for the reporting of proceedings[3]. These requirements have been elaborated in standing orders giving unqualified rights of public access (subject to public order considerations) to the Parliament[4], but subject to permitted restrictions in the case of committees. There is a requirement for the Corporate Body to produce the Scottish Parliament Official Report[5]. The Parliament and the Corporate Body are, as public authorities, subject to the information regime provided by the Freedom of Information (Scotland) Act 2002[6]. In addition, provision may be made for the broadcasting of proceedings[7]. Both Parliaments stream proceedings (including committees) on the internet.

However, when the CSG urged that the Parliament should be accessible, open and responsive and that it should develop procedures which make possible a participative approach[8], it meant more than minimal guarantees of access to information and, in due course, the *CSG Inquiry*[9] was able to report on a large number of initiatives which have included the extensive use of an attractive website, the education service of the Parliament, and open days. Institutionally, the same spirit has been evident in the use by committees of their power, where resources permit, to meet outside Edinburgh and to involve members of the public in their inquiries. The petitions procedure[10] has also been considered to be important and so too has the encouragement given to the cross-party groups, many of which have sought to engage with the Scottish public.

1   But, for expressions of concern about participation in the UK parliamentary process, see reports of the House of Commons Public Administration Committee: HC Paper 373 (2000–01); HC Paper 334 (2001–02). See too the Hansard Society's annual *Audit of Political Engagement*. For discussion of the resistance of the Westminster Parliament to the coverage of its activity by the Freedom of Information Act 2000, see para 13.22.
2   SA 1998, Sch 3, para 3.
3   SA 1998, Sch 3, para 4.
4   SOs, r 15.2.
5   SOs, r 16.2.
6   See para 13.22.
7   SOs, r 16.4.
8   *CSG Report* (1998), section 2.
9   *CSG Inquiry*, paras 61–206.
10 See para 10.15.

Chapter 6

Law-making Competences for Scotland

INTRODUCTION

6.1   A primary function of any constitution is the identification of those bodies which are competent to change the law. This hardly requires explanation. It is the existing state of the law which defines the legal rights and obligations of individuals in all aspects of their lives. The law also defines relationships within and between bodies such as limited companies, partnerships and unincorporated associations. And it determines the functions of governmental bodies too. They, like individuals and companies, may act only within the limits of the law and the introduction of major new policies and programmes by public authorities, at whatever level, must normally be preceded by the making of new laws to confer new powers. New powers for ministers, or for local and other public authorities also frequently attract the need for new administrative bodies to be established; new procedures for implementing the policies concerned; new systems of enforcement, including the creation of new criminal offences for defaulters; and, perhaps above all, the authority to spend money. All of these require legal change and this makes the allocation of law-making power of prime importance. Above *all else*, the distribution of legislative power determines the constitutional character of the state. In a federal system it is the division of powers amongst the central legislature and the legislatures of the states or provinces that most clearly defines its structure. For Scotland, within the devolved structure of the United Kingdom and within the European Union, it is to the distribution of legislative power that one looks first as a guide to the working of the constitution as a whole.

The formal division of powers does not, of course, tell the whole story. As mentioned in Chapter 1, apparently autonomous states are subject to *external* influences which restrain their powers, including their law-making powers at all levels. These same influences also constrain the day-to-day operation of internal legal rules. Similarly, the activities of political parties across the constitutional order and the rules which govern access to and the distribution of public funding are just two of the many *internal* constraints on the exercise of legislative power. Above all, it is the conditions which determine *who* has effective control over the exercise of law-making power that also determine what new laws are produced. Formal legislative power may be vested in the Westminster or the Scottish Parliament but the operation of parliamentary government at Westminster has long served to transfer substantial control over the legislative programme from Parliament to ministers. The Scottish Government has also achieved a similar degree of control over Holyrood, albeit tempered, until 2011, by the constraints of coalition or minority government.

These are matters to which we return in Chapter 9 which deals with law-making procedures. In this chapter, the principal focus is on formal law-making competences. By way of introduction, however, para 6.2 provides a brief examination of the sources of law in Scotland before we consider how the existing body of law may be changed.

SOURCES OF LAW IN SCOTLAND

6.2 In this context, the 'law of Scotland' is to be understood as the law applied by the courts of the Scottish legal system[1]. It is the 'positive' law, as opposed to 'natural' or 'moral' law. Sources of law are 'the answer to the question: where do I find authoritative statements of the principles and rules which the courts must apply to determine my rights and duties, my remedies and liabilities, in various circumstances?'[2] They are, then, the documents[3], judgments[4] and principles[5] which courts treat as authoritative for the purposes of deciding cases brought before them. It is on the basis of legal propositions derived from such sources that cases are argued by counsel and that statements of the current state of the law are made by legal advisers and commentators. In situations in which the current law is uncertain, it is still to these formal sources of the law that lawyers must look in order to make their best predictions – sometimes, in truth, no more than a well-informed guess – as to what the law is or how it is likely to develop in the future. In other contexts, the terminology 'source of law' may be used in a less formal sense to denote, for instance, a historical event or document explaining the emergence of the present law; a religious or philosophical idea from which, arguably, the 'positive' law applied by the courts has been derived; or, in a comparative way, a related rule in another system of law which has had an influence on the way the law has developed in Scotland. Such 'non-formal' sources are not treated as strictly authoritative in Scottish courts but they are frequently called in aid to assist the reasoning process where formal domestic sources are lacking or are uncertain. This is particularly true in times of substantial legal change where new rules are introduced but the courts have little or no home-grown guidance on how to interpret them.

The experience of other jurisdictions where similar rules may have operated for a long time can be very helpful, although care must be taken to keep in mind not only the similarities but also the differences between the two systems. An example was the early use made of Canadian human rights cases in the Scottish courts following the coming into force of domestic protection for human rights by the Scotland Act 1998 (SA 1998) and the Human Rights Act 1998 (HRA 1998)[6]. Such cases may be helpful because they deal with similar facts and similar rules of law but they are not formally authoritative and they must be applied with great care by courts in Scotland[7]. Such examples nicely illustrate the difficulties often encountered in distinguishing between the formal and non-formal sources of law. The distinction is drawn and is important, especially in the lower courts of a hierarchical system. In the higher courts, however, where they are called upon to decide issues of great uncertainty and they have more freedom to select sources of guidance, the non-formal sources (in particular, rules from other systems) may have a greater influence.

It is appropriate to list the formal sources of authority for Scottish courts as a preface to considering the legislative bodies competent to make new law and to amend the existing law. No more than a snapshot of the sources of law can be provided, avoiding the many complexities which courts confront as they interpret rules from different sources and, in assessing the status of those rules, decide which to apply when conflicts arise. Essential to any account of sources of law is the notion of *hierarchy*: the degree of authority to be attributed to a rule of law derived from one source and the susceptibility of that rule to being overtaken or replaced by a rule deriving from another source. This question of hierarchy is explored below. A simple listing of sources produces, first, a distinction between the *'common law'*[8] developed at the hand of the courts, and, on the other hand, *statute law* – the product of a formally authorised legislature. The common law in Scotland is supplemented by the works of the *institutional writers*[9] (though with little direct impact upon contemporary public law) and, it seems, by customary *international law*[10]. Statute law comprises *Acts of the Westminster Parliament*[11], as supplemented, since 1999, by *Acts of the Scottish Parliament* and legislation made by others under the authority of such Acts. In a special category, since 1973, has been *European Union* (formerly *Community) law*.

1   Including some courts, eg the UK Supreme Court, located outside Scotland.
2   D M Walker *The Scottish Legal System* (8th edn, 2001) p 408.
3   For example, a written constitution or an Act of Parliament.
4   Of courts, tribunals and other bodies with the power to give authoritative decisions on legal questions.
5   Which may be derived from, for example, the work of institutional writers or from historical sources.
6   See, for example, *Starrs v Ruxton* 2000 SC (JC) 208 (discussed in more detail in ch 12); *Clancy v Caird* 2000 SC 441, *Brown v Stott* 2000 SLT 379 (Appeal Court of the High Court of Justiciary) and 2001 SC (PC) 43 (Privy Council) and *G v Secretary of State for the Home Department* 2008 GWD 34–517. Reference has been made also to South African and New Zealand jurisprudence, eg *Vervuren v HM Advocate* 2002 SLT 555.
7   'It is necessary, generally, to exercise considerable discretion in the application of decisions relating to different legal systems ... There is always an initial and possibly fundamental difficulty that one is unfamiliar with the legal systems involved and with the structure of the courts and the inter-relationships between the courts and other branches of government in the several countries in relation to which apparently similar issues have been considered:' *Clancy v Caird* 2000 SC 441 per Lord Penrose at 479.
8   This term is problematic. Here, it is used to mean court-made, non-statutory law in general and is a term shared by the Scottish and English legal systems. In other contexts, it is used as a term specifically to identify English common law and the common law world beyond in most of the United States and the Commonwealth and to be opposed to the 'civil law' in most jurisdictions of continental Europe. On this analysis, Scotland's system is often described as 'mixed'. See W D H Sellar 'Scots law: mixed from the very beginning? A tale of two receptions' (2000) 4 Edin LR 3; R Evan-Jones 'Receptions of law, mixed legal systems and the myth of the genius of Scots private law' (1998) 114 LQR 228; and C M G Himsworth 'Devolution and the mixed legal system of Scotland' 2002 JR 115.
9   See, for example, Stair's *Institutions of the Law of Scotland*; Bankton's *Institute of the Laws of Scotland*; and Hume's *Commentaries on the Law of Scotland Respecting Crimes*. For discussion see 22 *Stair Memorial Encyclopedia*; DM Walker *The Scottish Legal System* (8th edn, 2001); AA Paterson, TStJN Bates and MR Poustie *The Legal System of Scotland* (4th edn, 1999); R M White, I D Willock and HL MacQueen *The Scottish Legal System* (5th edn, 2013).
10 *Lord Advocate's Reference No 1 of 2000* 2001 JC 143 following the decision of Sheriff Gimblett at Greenock to acquit three anti-nuclear protestors of charges of malicious damage to a vessel used as part of the UK's Trident missile programme: 'A rule of customary international law is a rule of Scots law' (per Lord Prosser at 512). It was held by the Appeal Court of the

High Court of Justiciary that customary international law provided no justification for criminal damage to property even where that property was to be used for purposes which were 'illegal' under international law. See also S C Neff 'International law and nuclear weapons in Scottish courts' (2002) 51 ICLQ 171, C J Moxley 'The unlawfulness of the UK's policy of nuclear deterrence' 2001 JR 319 and *R v Jones (Margaret)* [2007] 1 AC 136.

11 And some still-surviving Acts of the Scottish Parliament passed before 1707.

THE WESTMINSTER PARLIAMENT

6.3   Despite the priority which courts have to give, in appropriate circumstances, to European Union law, it makes sense to most Scottish constitutional lawyers to consider first the powers of the Westminster Parliament. The powers of the Scottish Parliament, the delegated legislative powers of ministers and other bodies, and the law-making competences of the European Union are best understood by reference to those of Westminster. Treatment of those other sources of law-making power is therefore deferred until later sections of the chapter. On the other hand, the United Kingdom's accession to the European Union (then Communities) on 1 January 1973 brought profound consequences for the competence of the Westminster Parliament itself and these should be dealt with here. The only way to understand the consequences of EU accession is first to explain how things were prior to January 1973 and then the effect of accession.

Pre-1 January 1973

6.4   In the classic accounts of the UK constitution of the nineteenth and twentieth centuries, treatment of the powers of Parliament achieved a central position[1], and for good reason. In the absence of a written constitution, it was Parliament's apparently unconstrained law-making capacity which served as the ultimate source, the *fons et origo*, of the UK constitutional order. The condition which created this situation was the political victory of the English Parliament of the seventeenth century, a victory whose fruits were inherited by the combined UK Parliament from 1707. It was a victory over royal power, including royal law-making power, and it was a victory over any competing law-making or law-declaring power of the courts. The courts could still apply the common law but they were committed to a recognition that all other forms of law would yield to the superior statutory law of Parliament. Under a written constitution it is routinely the case that it falls to the courts – as they interpret the provisions of the constitution – to define the extent of the powers of the legislature[2]. Indeed, no working constitution, written or not, is entirely free from the interpretative hand of the courts as they shape the limits of legislative power.

In the United Kingdom, without any authoritative constitutional document conferring and defining law making powers, the responsibility for that definition fell even more squarely upon the courts and it was the courts which came to give recognition to Acts of Parliament as the highest form of law. There is something circumlocutory here: Parliament achieved pre-eminence in the constitutional order but relied on the courts to exercise a 'self-denying ordinance' to preserve that status[3]. The courts have in the past trenchantly defended this position:

> 'It is often said that it would be unconstitutional for the United Kingdom Parliament to do certain things, meaning that the moral, political and other reasons against doing them are so strong that most people would regard it as highly improper if Parliament did these things. But that does not mean that it is beyond the power of Parliament to do such things. If Parliament chose to do any of them the courts could not hold the Act of Parliament invalid ... Their Lordships in declaring the law are not concerned with [the political relationship between the United Kingdom and Southern Rhodesia]. They are only concerned with the legal powers of Parliament.'[4]

When we turn to consider the powers of the Scottish Parliament, we shall find that we start with certain provisions of SA 1998 which define those powers. It is plain that, when a new Parliament is established, it is necessary to lay down what its law-making powers shall be. SA 1998 serves as a constitution: it 'constitutes' the Scottish Parliament and defines its powers. In this respect, it performs a very similar function to that of a written constitution of a state, one of whose primary functions is to establish the legislature and then to set out its powers. The French Constitution defines the powers of the Assemblée Nationale[5]. The US Constitution establishes the Congress and then defines its powers[6]. One of the principal consequences of the lack of a written constitution for the United Kingdom is that there is no formal written definition of the powers of the Westminster Parliament[7].

How, then, do we know what its powers are? One simple answer is that we should take account of (a) the record of what Parliament has done and (b) the reaction of the courts to that record. Our concern is with the *legal* powers of Parliament and the primary test (the same test adopted under a written constitution) of the lawfulness of the exercise of law-making powers is how the courts react. Of course, we may, in any given case, question whether the courts have reacted correctly. There will be room for debate about how they would or should respond to some particular hypothetical Act of Parliament in the future. There is also room for discussion of whether the courts are now revising their view of some aspects of parliamentary power and, if so, in what direction. These considerations affect our assessment of the judicial record but they do not dislodge the courts as the ultimate authority on questions of interpretation of what the law is.

There are, however, two problems with a focus on courts and what they decide. In contrast with a general constitutional statement of the sort found in a written constitution, court decisions tend to be sporadic and issued only in reaction to particular cases raised. Courts are not usually called upon to provide systematic statements of the law and, if they do so, they may be accused of going beyond the sphere of their legitimate authority. Secondly, therefore, when courts do engage in general statements of the law, these are almost inevitably obiter (ie not decisive of the question at hand) and not strictly authoritative. We need to keep in mind what Parliament does as well as what courts do.

1 See, for example, A V Dicey *The Law of the Constitution* (10th edn, 1959); I Jennings *The Law and the Constitution* (5th edn, 1959).

2 See ch 1.
3 It was not a logical or even legal necessity which compelled the courts to adopt this position of subordination: the most oft-cited example of an alternative approach is *Marbury v Madison* 5 US (1 Cranch) 137 (1803) in which the US Supreme Court asserted its right to declare unconstitutional an Act of Congress.
4 *Madzimbamuto v Lardner-Burke* [1969] 1 AC 645 per Lord Reid at 723.
5 Title IV.
6 Art 1.
7 Equally, there is no formal constitution of Parliament itself.

Legislative supremacy of the UK Parliament[1]

6.5   With these considerations in mind, how do we describe the rules governing the legislative competence of the Westminster Parliament? The powers of the Scottish Parliament are defined by reference to a list of restrictions on its legislative competence. Even though no constitutional document defines such a list for the Westminster Parliament, could one be constructed from our knowledge of constitutional history and current practice? If so, it would be a much shorter list. The principal restrictions on the Scottish Parliament are defined by reference to subject matter: it may legislate on education but not energy; tourism but not trade. Subject, however, to possible exceptions mentioned below, there are no such restrictions on the Westminster Parliament. The Scottish Parliament's power to legislate has geographical limits: it may not legislate for a country or territory other than Scotland[2]. By contrast, the Westminster Parliament may legislate not only for the United Kingdom (either for the whole of the country or for some specified part[3]) but also for the Channel Islands and the Isle of Man[4]; it may legislate for the oil industry in the North Sea[5]; and, historically, it made laws for those parts of the world which formed the British Empire and, subsequently, the Commonwealth. For most former colonies, the final Act of the UK Parliament was that which conferred independence[6]. In the case of the former dominions, it has been assumed that, since the Statute of Westminster 1931, Westminster would not legislate for them except with the consent of the country concerned. This principle enabled the passing of the Canada Act 1982[7]. The same assumption that local consent would be required for legislation had been extended to the former colony of Southern Rhodesia (now Zimbabwe) but, in the circumstances of the Unilateral Declaration of Independence coup led by Ian Smith in 1965, the authority of the Westminster Parliament was asserted to make laws for Southern Rhodesia without the consent of its (illegal) government[8]. Such laws were accepted as having undoubted effect by the British courts[9] although they were not observed by the Southern Rhodesian courts[10]. The same principle applies where the UK Parliament passes laws creating criminal offences based on activities on the high seas or on the territory of other states[11]. Such laws bind UK courts but may be given little or no recognition in other parts of the world. It was Sir Ivor Jennings who wrote that the UK Parliament could, if it wished, ban smoking on the streets of Paris[12]. Subject to constraints possibly now imposed by EU law, that proposition remains true but now, as then, it is subject to the very real limitation that such a no-smoking law would have no noticeable impact on the French courts.

It is not difficult to see that examples such as these lead quickly to the proposition that the legislative competence of the Westminster Parliament is unlimited. It was the Swiss jurist J-L de Lolme who wrote that Parliament could do anything except make a woman a man or a man a woman[13]. He was distinguishing Parliament from the Roman jurisconsults who could call a daughter a son. Presumably, however, Parliament *could*, as a matter of law, do the same.

Any Act of Parliament – but not some lesser measure, even if approved by one or both Houses of Parliament[14] – will attract the loyal obedience of courts in the United Kingdom. The courts have considered it inappropriate to scrutinise the legislative procedure leading to the passing of an Act. Even if there have been allegations of fraud in that process, an Act of Parliament will be applied by the courts[15]. If an Act has reached the statute book, if it is on the parliamentary roll[16], it will be given effect by the courts.

Another clear proposition in the law of the United Kingdom is that Acts of the Westminster Parliament have the capacity to override rules of international law. 'Conventional' (treaty-based) rules of international law are not, in any event, accorded any formal status by UK courts[17], although their existence may be acknowledged as an interpretative aid. Acts of Parliament are frequently used to give domestic effect to the terms of treaties but, equally, Acts of Parliament may be passed in defiance of the United Kingdom's treaty obligations[18]. In the rather special case of the European Convention on Human Rights (ECHR) prior to its incorporation by HRA 1998, the English courts were inclined to take the terms of the Convention as an interpretative aid where a statute was thought to be ambiguous but, despite a presumption that Parliament would not intend to override the fundamental rights the Convention sought to guarantee[19], would acknowledge the superiority of a conflicting Act of Parliament where its terms were clear. The Scottish courts were initially reluctant to attribute any role to the Convention even as an interpretative aid[20] but later adopted a position in line with that taken in England[21]. The status conferred on Convention rights by HRA 1998 is considered in Chapter 13.

A further consequence of according an apparently unlimited competence to the Westminster Parliament is that, in principle, the Parliament of today (presumably like most other Parliaments) can always amend or repeal an Act passed by Parliament at any time in the past. Once again, questions of interpretation will arise. *Express* words of amendment or repeal will always prevail. Modification deriving from an *implied* intention to amend or repeal will depend upon a court's interpretation of the later Act. However, the general rule is clear: subject to consideration of the special case of the European Communities Act 1972 (ECA 1972)[22], Parliament cannot, in law, be constrained from amending or repealing earlier Acts[23]. There are some Acts whose amendment would, in practice, be highly improbable, except perhaps with the consent of those affected[24], but there would be no doubting, in the eyes of the UK courts, the formal competence of Parliament to make such amendments. Sometimes this principle is expressed in its inverted form – the rule that Parliament cannot 'bind its successors'. A provision in an Act of Parliament which purports to restrict the legislative freedom of a future Parliament is viewed as ineffective[25].

That, at least, is believed to be true of attempts to limit the *substantive* content of future legislation.

Questions have, however, been raised about the competence of an Act of Parliament to impose *procedural* conditions on the manner in which a future Parliament may repeal or amend its terms. Could an Act of Parliament impose conditions on a future Parliament requiring an amendment of that or other legislation to be made only following a positive referendum? Or by a procedure involving the two Houses sitting together? Or requiring special majority voting in both Houses?[26] While the arguments which have been made in favour of such limitations may be persuasive, they have not been founded on any clear and unambiguous support from the courts.

The most recent such attempt to challenge Westminster legislation on the grounds that procedural requirements had not been complied with also failed but provided the opportunity for the House of Lords to comment more generally on the concept of sovereignty of Parliament, particularly where that concept may appear to conflict with 'fundamental' principles of the common law. Before turning to the case itself, it may be useful to summarise the traditional approach of the courts to this issue. The recognition given by the courts to the apparently unlimited competence of the UK Parliament has led to the primacy of statute law over law from almost any other source. Thus, a provision in an Act of Parliament will always be accorded a higher status than a common law rule and it has been accepted that Parliament may amend or override the common law and courts will always give effect to such changes provided that they are made explicitly. The impact of a statutory provision on a common law rule will, however, always be a matter of interpretation for a court. The words of the Act, the presumed intention of Parliament and the impact – for example on personal freedom – of modifying the common law will all be relevant. In principle, the courts will acknowledge that, by express words, Parliament can make any change. They will be less inclined to accept that an important common law rule has been displaced if Parliament's intention to do so has not been made explicit and can be derived only by implication[27].

These principles were the subject of some discussion in *R (Jackson) v Attorney General*[28] which concerned a challenge to validity of the Hunting Act 2004 on the grounds that having been passed pursuant to the Parliament Act 1949 which was itself invalid the 2004 Act was also invalid. The arguments about the validity of the 1949 Act are discussed in more detail in Chapter 9[29] but in the course of rejecting the challenge a number of their Lordships made observations which cast doubt on the 'absolutist' view of parliamentary sovereignty described above. While Lord Bingham of Cornhill described 'the supremacy of the Crown in Parliament' as the 'bedrock of the British constitution' without departing from the traditional view, Lords Steyn and Hope of Craighead took different approaches. Expressing the view that 'we do not in the United Kingdom have an uncontrolled constitution', Lord Steyn referred to the impacts of Britain's membership of the EU – discussed below – and HRA 1998 and also noted that the supremacy of Parliament is 'a construct of the common law. The judges created this principle. If that is so, it is not unthinkable that circumstances could arise where the courts may have to

132

qualify a principle established on a different hypothesis of constitutionalism. In exceptional circumstances involving an attempt to abolish judicial review or the ordinary role of the courts, the Appellate Committee of the House of Lords or a new Supreme Court may have to consider whether this is a constitutional fundamental which even a sovereign Parliament acting at the behest of a complaisant House of Commons cannot abolish'[30]. Lord Hope's perspective was similar, observing in particular that the principle of absolute legislative sovereignty was an English one and that, in fact, 'the rule of law enforced by the courts is the ultimate controlling factor on which our constitution is based'[31].

Another inroad on supremacy has been made by the notion of the 'Constitutional statute'. This is discussed more fully below in the context of EU law[32] but it has a wider application. When, for instance, the Smith Commission[33] proposed that 'UK legislation will state that the Scottish Parliament and Scottish Government are permanent institutions' (para 21), apparently thus seeking to block their vulnerability to removal by repeal, the status of the Scotland Acts as constitutional statutes may be what was anticipated. That would imply that those provisions establishing the Parliament and Government and declaring them to be permanent could not be repealed by implication (most improbable, in any event) by a future Act of Parliament but would remain vulnerable to express repeal. To go beyond that and to *guarantee* that a future Act of Parliament could never repeal the declaration of permanence would imply the reversal of a foundational rule of the constitution – prompting a response by one commentator[34] that the declaration would be 'either meaningless fluff or a constitutional revolution'! Such a 'revolution' would indeed be required if the United Kingdom were, for instance, to adopt a truly federal constitution with the status of the constituent nations formally guaranteed.

Such developments apart, the idea of legislative supremacy as it was understood prior to EC accession in January 1973 remains very much intact. Legislative supremacy has never meant that Acts of Parliament are the only source of law: to the extent that they have not been displaced by statute, common law rules and, indeed, rules deriving from Scotland's institutional writers remain good law. Some common law rules, including those which define the royal prerogative, have significant constitutional effect. Similarly, rules made by authorities to whom power has been delegated by Parliament (including, indeed, powers to amend Acts of Parliament themselves[35]) are, of course, good law. Acts of the Scottish Parliament are, to take the most prominent example, becoming more and more important as sources of law in Scotland.

1   See A Bradley 'The Sovereignty of Parliament – Form or Substance?' in J Jowell and D Oliver (eds) *The Changing Constitution* (7h edn, 2011) and J Jowell 'Parliamentary Sovereignty under the New Constitutional Hypothesis' [2006] PL 562.
2   SA 1998, s 29(2)(a).
3   See, for example, the (pre-devolution) Civil Evidence (Scotland) Act 1988 and the Disabled Persons (Northern Ireland) Act 1989. See also the post-devolution Partnerships (Prosecution) (Scotland) Act 2013.
4   See, for example, the United Nations Act 1946, s 1 and the Al-Qa'ida and Taliban (United Nations Measures) (Channel Islands) Order 2002, SI 2002/258.
5   Continental Shelf Act 1964, and orders thereunder.
6   Eg Ghana Independence Act 1957; Jamaica Independence Act 1962.

7 The Preamble to the Canada Act 1982 stated that 'Canada has requested and consented' to the Act. A challenge to its enactment was brought by two representatives of Canadian 'aboriginal' [sic] communities who argued that certain provisions of the Act would prejudice their rights and that they had not given their consent. The Court of Appeal held that in order to comply with the requirement of consent in the Statute of Westminster, s 4 it was necessary only that there was an express declaration of consent in the legislation concerned and, if there was, the Court would not go behind that declaration: *Manuel v A-G* [1983] Ch 77. The Court did not rule on the question of whether the Canada Act 1982 would have been invalid had a declaration of consent been omitted altogether.

8 Southern Rhodesia Act 1965. The Southern Rhodesia (Constitution) Order 1965, SI 1965/1952 rendered null and void – at least so far as the UK was concerned – all laws passed by the new regime.

9 *Madzimbamuto v Lardner-Burke* [1969] 1 AC 645.

10 In *Madzimbamuto v Lardner-Burke* [1968] 2 SA 284 the High Court of Southern Rhodesia took the view that the Smith regime was unlawful but that as it was then the only effective government of Rhodesia, it was necessary to give effect to regulations made by it.

11 See *Mortensen v Peters* (1906) 8 F(J) 93 concerning the Herring Fishing (Scotland) Act 1889 and for more recent examples see the Proceeds of Crime Act 2002 (confiscation of property abroad), the Anti-terrorism, Crime and Security Act 2001 (extra-territorial effect of biological and nuclear weapons offences) and *R (Al-Fawwaz) v Governor of Brixton Prison* [2002] 1 AC 556 on the interpretation of the Extradition Act 1989.

12 I Jennings *The Law and the Constitution* (5th edn, 1959) pp 170–171.

13 *The Constitution of England* (new edn, 1834) p 117.

14 See *Bowles v Bank of England* [1913] 1 Ch 57. For statutory instruments approved by one or both Houses, see para 9.34.

15 *British Railways Board v Pickin* [1974] AC 765. Lord Denning, part of the Court of Appeal Bench whose decision was reversed by the Lords, had suggested that the question of whether (private) legislation had been obtained improperly was 'a triable issue' and that the court may, if it were to conclude that an Act had been so obtained, be under a duty to report the matter to Parliament's attention. He did not suggest that the Act could be struck down by the court ([1973] QB 219 at 230–231).

16 *Martin v O'Sullivan* [1984] STC 258.

17 See, for example, *Malone v Metropolitan Police Commissioner* [1979] Ch 344. However, it does appear to be accepted that customary rules of international law are part of the law of Scotland: cf para 6.2 above.

18 *Cheny v Conn* [1968] 1 All ER 779.

19 *R v Secretary of State for the Home Department, ex p Brind* [1991] AC 696

20 See especially Lord Ross in *Kaur v Lord Advocate* 1980 SC 319.

21 *T, Petitioner* 1997 SLT 724 and *Advocate General for Scotland v MacDonald* [2001] 1 All ER 620.

22 See para 6.9.

23 Or indeed authorising ministers to do so: see, for example, HRA 1998, s 10. However, a power to modify or repeal primary legislation which is conferred by secondary legislation will not be implied: there should be an express provision and this will be construed strictly and narrowly (*Hyde Park Residence Ltd v Secretary of State for the Environment, Transport and the Regions* [1999] 3 PLR 1).

24 For example, the Canada Act 1982, discussed above.

25 See *Vauxhall Estates Ltd v Liverpool Corpn* [1932] 1 KB 733; *Ellen Street Estates Ltd v Minister of Health* [1934] 1 KB 590; *Thoburn v Sunderland City Council* [2003] QB 151.

26 Requirements for special majority voting in the Scottish Parliament are included in SA 1998 (see para 5.4) but, as we shall see, the Scottish Parliament does not enjoy the same Westminster-style 'supremacy'.

27 See, for example, *Beattie v Royal Bank of Scotland plc* 2003 SLT 564.

28 *R (on the application of Jackson) v Attorney General* [2006] 1 AC 262.

29 See para 9.7.

30 [2006] 1 AC 262 at 302–303.

31 [2006] 1 AC 262 at 304. For similar views expressed by Lords Hope and Reed (but in relation to the review of an ASP, see *AXA General Insurance Ltd, Petitioners* 2012 SC (UKSC) 122.

32 See para 6.10.

33 See para 4.21.

34 C M O'Neill, *Scotsman* 4 and 15 Dec 2014.
35 For such powers, see para 6.9.

The Treaty of Union and the Westminster Parliament

6.6   Notwithstanding the comments of Lords Steyn and Hope in *Jackson*, what the concept of legislative supremacy *has* done in practice is to establish the UK Parliament as the *highest* source of law. It establishes that the highest rule known to a British court, the ultimate rule of recognition[1] or *grundnorm*[2] is that the law contained in the most recent Act of Parliament on a particular subject is to be obeyed. We turn shortly to examine whether, and to what extent, that position has been changed by ECA 1972. Before doing so, we should examine the one serious challenge to the doctrine of legislative supremacy which was launched much earlier. This is the challenge of the Articles (or Treaty) of Union concluded between Scotland and England in 1706 and enacted into law by the separate Parliaments of the two countries in 1707[3]. The arguments in favour of according higher law status to the Treaty are three:

THE 'CONSTITUTIVE' CHARACTER OF THE TREATY There are good reasons in constitutional logic to attribute a special status to the Treaty provisions. Although the Treaty was made in an age before written constitutions, as we would now understand them, were devised, there is no doubt that it had constitutive characteristics[4]. Article I provided for the two Kingdoms of Scotland and England to become united into one Kingdom of Great Britain. Article II provided for succession to the monarchy; and Article III for the United Kingdom to 'be represented by one and the same Parliament, to be styled the Parliament of Great Britain'. Article III is particularly important because it clearly points to the creation of a *new* Parliament and, therefore, one which should expect to operate subject to the terms laid down in the document by which it was created. At all events, the Treaty was certainly not itself a legislative product of the Parliament of Great Britain and has a strong claim, perhaps the strongest claim, to be a document which, unlike mere Acts of Parliament, could bind succeeding Parliaments.

THE LANGUAGE OF THE TREATY A separate argument in favour of the Treaty's status lies in the claims made by its own provisions. There is frequent use of the phrases 'for ever' and 'in all time coming'[5] subject to the qualification, in some articles, that alterations to the provisions laid down may be made by the Parliament of Great Britain. The Treaty concluded (in Art XXV) with a declaration that prior law and statutes which were contrary to or inconsistent with the Treaty would 'cease and become void'.

Two provisions have a special significance. One is Article XIX which provides for the Court of Session to 'remain in all time coming within Scotland as it is now constituted by the laws of that kingdom; and with the same authority and privileges as before the Union, subject, nevertheless, to such regulations, for the better administration of justice, as shall be made by the Parliament of Great Britain'. Its predecessor (Art XVIII) provides for laws in Scotland to remain in force 'but alterable by the Parliament of Great Britain; with this difference betwixt the laws concerning public right, policy, and civil government, and those which concern private right, that the laws which concern public right, policy and civil government may be made the same throughout the whole United Kingdom, but that no alteration can be made in laws which concern private right, except for evident utility of the subjects within Scotland'.

JUDICIAL RECOGNITION OF THE TREATY The third argument in favour of according the Treaty special status is the degree of recognition given to it by the courts[6]. The attitude adopted by courts is potentially, of course, of the highest importance. They have the authority to translate constitutional speculation into real rules. Unfortunately, however, there have been mixed signals given in the small number of cases (which have been prompted in the main by a wish for increased prominence for a political cause) that have come before the courts. Despite the passing of 60 years since it was decided, *MacCormick v Lord Advocate*[7] retains its iconic status for it was in that case, in which the title of the Queen as 'Elizabeth II' was challenged in the Court of Session, that Lord President Cooper gave significant support to the higher status of the Treaty. Referring to the principle of the unlimited sovereignty of Parliament as 'a distinctively English principle which has no counterpart in Scottish constitutional law'[8] he noted that the Treaty and the associated legislation, by which the Parliament of Great Britain was brought into being as the successor of the separate Parliaments of Scotland and England, contain some clauses which expressly reserve to the Parliament of Great Britain powers of subsequent modification, and other clauses which either contain no such power or emphatically exclude subsequent alteration by declarations that the provision shall be fundamental and unalterable in all time coming. He concluded that he had 'not found in the Union legislation any provision that the Parliament of Great Britain should be 'absolutely sovereign' in the sense that that Parliament should be free to alter the Treaty 'at will'. The significance of these dicta is, however, severely undermined by two further aspects of the case. In the first place, they are obiter and therefore lack any formal precedential authority because the case itself, dismissing the challenge, was decided on other grounds. Secondly, and more importantly from the point of view of the wider impact of Lord Cooper's opinion, what he gave with the right hand he took away with the left. Instead of moving forward from asserting the right and indeed the duty of the Court of Session to uphold and enforce the Treaty's pre-eminence against a future statute of the Westminster Parliament, he reverted to a position in which he declared: 'This at least is plain, that there is neither precedent nor authority of any kind for the view that the domestic Courts of either Scotland or England have jurisdiction to determine whether a governmental act of the type here in controversy is or is not conform to the provisions of a Treaty'[9].

By doubting the justiciability of the issue, Lord Cooper undermined the strength of his initial position on the status of the Treaty itself. Those doubts remain, along with rather more specific reservations about the justiciability of such terms in the Treaty as the 'evident utility of the subjects within Scotland'. Whether a court could be expected to determine the 'utility' of a measure (and, if so, according to what criteria) was doubted in the later case of *Gibson v Lord Advocate*[10] in which the pursuer claimed that an EC fishing regulation was contrary to the Treaty of Union. The court's rejection of the claim was on the ground that this was a question of public rather than private right and, therefore, that the 'evident utility' test was not engaged. In later cases arising out of challenges to the imposition of the poll tax in Scotland, attempts to invoke the Treaty failed but on grounds, inter alia, that it could not be used to question the validity of the statute under which the appeals were brought. There appeared to be a background assumption of the higher status of the Treaty, if only its terms could be successfully invoked[11].

That background assumption has not been completely dispelled by the most recent 'judicial' consideration of the status of the Treaty. Following the introduction of the House of Lords Bill[12] at Westminster in 1999 – intended to remove the rights of hereditary peers to sit and vote in the Lords – the House of Lords, on the motion of Lord Gray, referred to its Committee for Privileges the question: 'Whether the House of Lords Bill ... would ... breach the provisions of the Treaty of Union between England and Scotland'. It was argued on behalf of Lord Gray that the Bill would, if enacted, contravene Article XXII which provided, inter alia, that 16 of the peers of Scotland would be entitled to sit and vote in the House of Lords. The opinions of Lords Slynn, Nicholls and Hope of Craighead[13] deal with a wide range of matters including the existence of a 'Treaty'[14] of Union and whether, and by whom, the provisions of such a Treaty could be enforced given that neither of the contracting parties 'has existed as such since 1707'[15]. While their lordships were in agreement that the Treaty of Union, Article XXII had, in fact, been altered by subsequent Acts of the UK Parliament[16] and that Article XXII did not have the status of 'fundamental law' they were equivocal on the question of whether certain other articles might enjoy such status.

Lord Hope reviewed the earlier cases and noted that, rather than expressing any clear and unambiguous view on the capacity of the Treaty to bind the Parliament which it had created, each court faced with such a question 'has always been able to find another route for the disposal of the argument'[17]. His own view was that 'the argument that the legislative powers of the new Parliament of Great Britain were subject to the restrictions expressed in the Union Agreement by which it was constituted cannot be dismissed as entirely fanciful'. However, rather like the courts to which he had referred, Lord Hope did not think it necessary for the Committee to decide whether there might be circumstances in which 'the basic rule of legislative supremacy by qualified by judicial decision'[18]. That was a matter for the courts to decide.

As it stands, then, the debate as to the 'fundamental' nature of the Treaty of Union remains – at least at the level of constitutional theory – unresolved. While unwilling to concede that it imposes no limits whatsoever on the powers of the Westminster Parliament, it seems likely that the courts (and Parliament) will continue to deal with questions as to the Treaty's status in a pragmatic fashion by finding – in Lord Hope's words – an alternative route for their disposal[19].

1 H L A Hart *The Concept of Law* (2nd edn, Bulloch and Raz eds, 1997).
2 H Kelsen *Pure Theory of Law* (2nd edn, tr M Knight, 1970).
3 See the material referred to at para 3.2 and see also *SME Reissue* Constitutional Law paras 60–66; and JD Ford, 'The Legal Provisions of the Acts of Union' (2007) 66 CLJ 106.

4   N MacCormick 'Does the United Kingdom have a Constitution? Reflections on *MacCormick v Lord Advocate*' (1978) 29 NILQ 1.
5   See, for example, Arts I, II, VI, VII, and XIX.
6   In addition to the Scottish cases cited below, the relevance of the Treaty has been acknowledged in English cases. See, for example *R v Commissioner of Police, ex p Bennett* [1995] QB 313.
7   *MacCormick v Lord Advocate* 1953 SC 396.
8   *MacCormick v Lord Advocate* 1953 SC 396 at 411.
9   *MacCormick v Lord Advocate* 1953 SC 396 at 413.
10 *Gibson v Lord Advocate* 1975 SC 136.
11 *Pringle, Petitioner* 1991 SLT 330; *Murray v Rogers* 1992 SLT 221; *Stewart v Henry* 1989 SLT (Sh Ct) 34; *Fraser v MacCorquodale* 1992 SLT 229. See NC Walker and CMG Himsworth [1991] JR 45.
12 Now the House of Lords Act 1999.
13 *Lord Gray's Motion* 2000 SC (HL) 46. The Committee had a membership of seven but only the three 'Law Lords' gave written reasons for the unanimous decision of the committee to answer the question in the negative.
14 In the sense of a treaty binding on the two contracting states as a matter of international law rather than simply separate Acts of the independent Parliaments.
15 *Lord Gray's Motion* 2000 SC(HL) 46 per Lord Slynn at 49.
16 And eventually repealed by the Statute Law Revision (Scotland) Act 1964 and the Statute Law (Repeals) Act 1993.
17 *Lord Gray's Motion* 2000 SC (HL) 46 per Lord Hope of Craighead at 59.
18 *Lord Gray's Motion* 2000 SC (HL) 46 per Lord Hope of Craighead at 59.
19 In June 2003 Lord Hope was reported as having made comments to the effect that any new Supreme Court (as to which see ch 14) would require independent funding, management and accommodation to avoid breaching the Treaty of Union, Art XIX which prohibits the hearing of Scottish cases in 'the Courts of Chancery, Queen's-Bench, Common-Pleas or any other Court in Westminster-hall' *The Times*, 19 June 2003. See also Lord Hope's comments in *R (Jackson) v Attorney General* [2006] 1 AC 262 at pp 303–304.

Post-January 1973

6.7   In Chapter 3 it was explained that the United Kingdom's accession to the European Union has had a substantial impact on Scottish and UK constitutional law. The biggest single practical consequence is that, in line with the wider requirements of the Union, the European treaties as well as all the laws promulgated under the treaties as regulations and directives have to be given effect within the United Kingdom. They become part of UK law and must be implemented and enforced by UK courts. This, in itself, creates no major difficulties in principle and the incorporation of EU law was one of the main purposes of ECA 1972. ECA 1972, s 2(1) provided that all the then existing rights and obligations, and all *future* rights and obligations, 'created or arising by or under the Treaties ... are without further enactment to be given legal effect'. This was sufficient at the time to enable the United Kingdom to comply with the treaty requirement to 'take all appropriate measures to ensure fulfilment of the obligations arising out of this Treaty or resulting from action taken by the institutions of the Community'[1]. In addition, ECA 1972, s 3 required that UK courts should determine any question of the meaning or effect of any provision of EU law in accordance with the principles established by, and decisions of, the European Court of Justice.

But, of course, EU law changes and the treaties require that such changes must also be incorporated by member states. In the United Kingdom an Act of Parliament (or an Act of the Scottish Parliament) can be used to do this.

Alternatively, ECA 1972, s 2(2) provides for a special form
legislation by which ministers (UK or Scottish) may give effec
of an EU regulation or directive[2]. These procedures, taken a
straightforward enough to use although good questions can be a
sufficient democratic control can be maintained over the pro
given the sheer quantity of European legislation which has to be mee,
each year.

1 EC Treaty, art 5. See now TEU, art 4(3).
2 For delegated legislation generally, see paras 6.23–6.24.

Supremacy of EU law – the EU perspective

6.8   There is, however, a further requirement which the EU treaty
regime imposes. Not only must EU rules be incorporated but they must take
precedence over all other laws within the member state. The economic and
political reasoning behind this is clear: to achieve a common market and to
realise the other objectives of the Union, there is a necessity to achieve a high
degree of uniformity of legal provision. This was an imperative which the
European Court of Justice (ECJ) adopted with enthusiasm. In cases decided
before the UK accession, but whose principles have been reinforced repeatedly
ever since, the ECJ asserted a principle of supremacy designed to ensure that
the Court itself, and also all courts applying EU law in member states, will, in
the case of any conflict between EU and domestic rules, uphold and enforce
the EU rule:

> 'As opposed to other international treaties, the Treaty instituting the EEC
> has created its own order which was integrated with the national order of the
> member-states the moment the Treaty came into force; as such, it is binding
> upon them ... The transfer, by member-states, from their national order, in
> favour of the Community order of the rights and obligations arising from the
> Treaty, carries with it a clear limitation of their sovereign right upon which
> a subsequent unilateral law, incompatible with the aims of the Community,
> cannot prevail'[1].

1 *Costa v ENEL* [1964] CMLR 425 (at 455–456).

Supremacy of EU law – the UK perspective

6.9   In the United Kingdom, this supremacy rule is one which the courts
must apply, in accordance with ECA 1972, s 3 and, in many situations, this
need not cause any difficulty. The status of ECA 1972 itself ensures that the
rules which it incorporated at accession override any previous rule in UK law,
even if contained in an Act of Parliament. This, however, does not answer the
question of what a court must do if it confronts a situation, as is more likely 40
years after accession, in which an Act of Parliament is passed whose provisions
clash with EU law. If the Act is an Act of the Scottish Parliament there is,
as we shall find, no problem for the court: SA 1998 provides that EU law
must prevail[1]. However, in the light of our earlier discussion of the legislative
supremacy of Parliament, there would appear to be a greater problem if the Act

is an Act of the Westminster Parliament. We have concluded that the highest rule of law known to a UK court, the rule which defines the very basis of the UK constitution, is that the most recent Act of Parliament stating the law on any given subject must prevail over any other law from whatever source. This principle is, on the face of it, plainly at odds with the EU rule which requires EU law to prevail. The traditional pre-1973 theory of the authority of the UK Parliament left no room for compromise. The probable need for *future* compromise had, however, been anticipated by Parliament itself in ECA 1972, s 2(4) which provided that 'any enactment passed or to be passed, other than one contained in this part of this Act, shall be construed and have effect subject to the foregoing provisions of this section'.

It did not take long for the meaning of ECA 1972, s 2(4) to become the focus of judicial scrutiny as, inevitably, tensions between UK and EU law became the subject of litigation. Unsurprisingly, in light of the traditional approach to the legislative supremacy of Parliament, the courts were somewhat reluctant to adopt the ECJ's approach of subordinating national legislation to the rule of EU law. No doubt aware of the very difficult political and constitutional issues at stake, courts faced with an apparent conflict between domestic and European law preferred, at least initially, to recast the issue before them as one essentially of statutory interpretation: UK legislation would be given whatever (sometimes strained) construction necessary to give effect to EU law[2].

This approach to resolving differences between UK and EU law did not directly address the more fundamental issue at the heart of these disputes: which source of law would be accorded supremacy by the UK courts in the case of a clear conflict? An answer to *that* question was eventually given in 1990 following the challenge by a number of British companies – including Factortame Ltd – to the provisions of the Merchant Shipping Act 1988 (MSA 1988). It was argued that MSA 1988, by according certain benefits to companies which were owned and operated predominantly by British nationals, breached EU law prohibiting discrimination on grounds of nationality. The remedies sought by the applicants were a declaration that the provisions of MSA 1988, if applied, would contravene EU law and an order (including an interim order) prohibiting the Secretary of State from enforcing the UK legislation. The complex procedural history of the *Factortame* case cannot be fully described here but after an interim injunction was granted by the English High Court and then revoked in the Court of Appeal, the case reached the House of Lords. The Lords initially held that as a matter of UK law they had no power to suspend the operation of an Act of the UK Parliament but referred to the ECJ the question whether – in the case of a clear breach of EU law by domestic legislative provisions – the domestic courts were obliged or empowered to grant the remedy sought. The ECJ was unequivocal: 'a national court which, in a case before it concerning Community law, considers that the sole obstacle which precludes it from granting interim relief is a rule of national law it must set aside that rule'[3].

When the case returned from the ECJ to the House of Lords their Lordships granted the interim relief sought, thereby preventing the Secretary of State from invoking the provisions of MSA 1988. In explaining their decision to do so, their Lordships made clear their view that their decision in this case was a necessary consequence of Britain's accession to the European Union, and one which should have been anticipated by the Westminster Parliament:

> 'If the supremacy within the European Community of Community law over the national law of member states was not always inherent in the EEC Treaty it was certainly well established in the jurisprudence of the Court of Justice long before the United Kingdom joined the Community. Thus, whatever limitation of its sovereignty Parliament accepted when it enacted the European Communities Act 1972 was entirely voluntary. Under the terms of the 1972 Act it has always been clear that it was the duty of a United Kingdom court, when delivering final judgement, to override any rule of national law found to be in conflict with any directly enforceable rule of Community law.'[4]

However clear the duty of the court may have been thought to be, Lord Jauncey was rather more explicit about the significance of the decision. The court was, here, 'faced with the wholly novel situation of determining whether in the circumstances of this appeal interim relief against the application of primary legislation should be granted to the applicants'[5]. That it decided that such interim relief ought to be granted was, it has been suggested, a declaration that the ultimate rule of recognition – or *grundnorm* – of the UK legal systems had altered and to that extent at least the description of the *Factortame* decision as 'revolutionary' is an apt one. On the other hand, it is certainly arguable that the Lords in *Factortame* behaved in a manner entirely in keeping with their predecessors who, 300 years earlier, had recognised Parliament's position of constitutional pre-eminence and sought to ensure that the law reflected, and sustained, the political settlement reached within and beyond the state. Moreover, the revolution was only partial: while there was a clear modification of the traditional rule that the provisions of a later statute will impliedly repeal those of an earlier one, at least as far as ECA 1972, s 2(4) was concerned, there was no question of this marking the end of the supremacy of the UK Parliament. The effect of ECA 1972 was of that Parliament's doing and the ability of the same Parliament to undo ECA 1972 in its entirety was not questioned.

Since *Factortame*, the courts have been more willing to assert their right to review the compatibility of UK legislation with EU law[6] and to provide remedies where it is alleged that there is a breach of the latter by the former, even to the extent of finding those affected by the incompatibility of UK legislation with EU law entitled to damages directly caused by the breach[7].

As earlier noted[8], s 18 of the European Union Act 2011 (EUA 2011) restated the principle that, for the United Kingdom, ECA 1972 is the basis of the status of EU law – a position further affirmed by Lord Reed in *R (HS2 Action Alliance Ltd) v Secretary of State for Transport*[9]. The contribution of ss 2–4 of the Act, which are potentially of much greater general importance, will now be better understood. In relation to the EU treaty amendments to which they relate, what the Act claims to lay down is that their ratification by the United Kingdom is conditional upon the need for an authorising Act of Parliament *and* for that Act itself to provide for its coming into force to be dependent on approval by a referendum held across the United Kingdom (and Gibraltar). On its face, the Act binds successor Parliaments to a particular procedural route to the enactment of a certain class of legislation. As has to be the case where a 'fundamental' principle of the constitution appears to have been modified, it is, at the very least, unclear how the courts would react to an Act (and subsequent treaty ratification) achieved without satisfying the referendum condition laid down.

1 SA 1998, s 29(2)(d). See para 6.20 below.
2 See, for example, *MacCarthys v Smith* [1981] 1 QB 180; *Marshall v Southampton and South West Hampshire Area Health Authority* [1986] 2 All ER 584.
3 *Factortame Ltd v Secretary of State for Transport (No 2)* [1991] 1 AC 603 at 644.
4 *Factortame Ltd v Secretary of State for Transport (No 2)* [1991] 1 AC 603 per Lord Bridge of Harwich at 658–659.
5 *Factortame Ltd v Secretary of State for Transport (No 2)* [1991] 1 AC 603 at 676.
6 *R v Secretary of State for Employment, ex p Equal Opportunities Commission* [1995] 1 AC 1.
7 *R v Secretary of State for Transport, ex p Factortame Ltd (No 5)* [2000] 1 AC 524.
8 See para 3.12.
9 [2014] 2 All ER 109 at para 79.

The European Communities Act 1972 as a 'constitutional statute'

6.10   An interesting addition to the cases in which the status of EU law has been raised is *Thoburn v Sunderland City Council*[1]. There were, in fact, four different cases (all involving 'Metric Martyrs') of some complexity but each turned on the validity of regulations made in 1994 under ECA 1972, s 2(2) to outlaw the use of imperial (rather than metric) units of measurements of weight by amendment of the Weights and Measures Act 1985 (WMA 1985) and of other regulations, some of which were made under that Act itself. The principal argument raised by the Martyrs was that WMA 1985, s 1 which permitted the parallel use of imperial units of measurement, had, as a later statute, impliedly repealed ECA 1972, s 2(2) to the extent that it empowered the making of subordinate legislation that would be inconsistent with it. That argument was rejected by Laws LJ in the English Administrative Court. He took the view that (a) no such question of implied repeal could arise because there was no actual *inconsistency* between anything in WMA 1985, s 1 and ECA 1972, s 2(2) and that (b) there was no general limitation on the power of Parliament to confer a 'Henry VIII' power[2] to amend primary legislation which would be effective not only in respect of existing (in this case pre-1972) legislation but also later Acts. More importantly, however, he set out the proposition that ECA 1972 was a 'constitutional statute' which, in contrast with 'ordinary' statutes and by force of the common law, could *never* be impliedly repealed. It was a statute of the sort which either '(a) conditions the legal relationship between citizen and state in some general, overarching manner, or (b) enlarges or diminishes the scope of what we would now regard as fundamental constitutional rights'. To amend such a statute would require 'express words in the later statute, or ... words so specific that the inference of an actual determination to effect the result contended for was irresistible'[4]. In the light of that test, WMA 1985, s 1 (which was, in any event, a consolidation of an earlier pre-1972 Act) could never have impliedly repealed – and thereby restricted the effect of – ECA 1972, s 2(2).

Such a conclusion is not, in itself, surprising. The idea that an implied repeal might have occurred was highly improbable. Also within the mainstream of opinion on the status of the rules in ECA 1972 and of EU law within the United Kingdom was the view of Laws LJ that these were matters to be judged entirely by principles inherent in UK law itself. He was invited to adopt the view that it was now EU law itself that determined the legal relationship between the EU and the United Kingdom but such a proposition was, he said, false. The *grundnorm* had not, in other words, shifted: 'The conditions of Parliament's legislative supremacy in the United Kingdom necessarily remain in the United Kingdom's hands. But the traditional doctrine has in my judgement been modified. It has been done by the common law, wholly consistently with constitutional principle'[5]. However, as Laws LJ moves into the language of 'constitutional statutes'[6] in relation to ECA 1972, two rather different concerns arise. In this first place, it is not really clear what additional understanding it contributes. In particular, it appears to add little to the debate about how far ECA 1972 may 'bind successors'. At another part of the judgment, the traditional doctrine is invoked[7] but equally the force of *Factortame and R v Secretary of State for Employment, ex parte Equal Opportunities Commission* is sustained. The courts will uphold EU law against subsequent conflicting UK law and that, says Laws LJ, is to sustain the primacy of substantive EU provisions. But the limitation of sovereignty 'has no application where the question is, what is the legal *foundation* within which those substantive provisions enjoy their primacy, and by [sic] which the relation between the law and institutions of the EU law and the British state ultimate rests. The foundation is English law'[8]. This approach does not, however, answer the question about how a court would or should respond if ever there were to be a statute passed which was stated to be in conflict with EU law *and* 's 2(4) of the 1972 Act notwithstanding'.

The other problem with the constitutional statute and its status is that it is a category extended by Laws LJ to include such examples – it was not a definitive list – as Magna Carta, the (English) Bill of Rights 1689, the Union with Scotland Act 1706, the Reform Acts 1832, HRA 1998, SA 1998 and the Government of Wales Act 1998. The difficulty with such a listing is that, although the concept of the 'constitutional statute' may be useful for some purposes[9], in seeking to equate these other statutes with ECA 1972 important distinctions may be blurred. There has been no general avoidance of implied repeal of these measures in the past[10]. There would be difficulties in the identification of which provisions in them are protected. Not every provision in a statute claimed to have 'constitutional status' could be regarded as benefiting from that status.

There was a return to some of these questions in Lord Reed's judgment in *R (HS2 Action Alliance Ltd) v Secretary of State for Transport*[11] where, referring to a number of 'constitutional instruments' rather than 'constitutional statutes' to include a list very similar to Laws, LJ's, and also to certain principles 'fundamental to the rule of law' recognised by the common law, he described it as 'putting it at its lowest, certainly arguable' that there may be fundamental principles 'of which Parliament when it enacted ECA 1972 did not either contemplate or authorise the abrogation' (para 207) – raising interesting further questions about the relationships between one and another of those statutes or instruments dubbed 'constitutional'.

Further questions have been raised about SA 1998 as a 'constitutional statute'. In the First Division in *Imperial Tobacco Ltd v Lord Advocate*[12]. Lord Reed appeared to be dismissive of the notion of SA 1998 as a 'constitution' and thus attracting a more generous interpretation[13] and, in the UK Supreme Court[14] Lord Hope stated that 'the description of the Act as a constitutional statute cannot be taken, in itself, to be a guide to its interpretation' (para 15). On the other hand, Lord Hope, responding to an argument that express (and more restricted) rights of appeal under the Extradition Act 2003 had impliedly overridden rights of appeal to the UKSC (on 'devolution issues') against decisions by the Scottish Ministers, declared that express provision would be required 'because of the fundamental nature of the settlement that was achieved by the Scotland Act' (para 30).

1 *Thoburn v Sunderland City Council* [2003] QB 151.
2 See para 6.23 and G Marshall 'Metric measures and martyrdom by Henry VIII clause' (2002) 118 LQR 493.
3 *Thoburn v Sunderland City Council* [2003] QB 151 at 185.
4 *Thoburn v Sunderland City Council* [2003] QB 151 at 185.
5 *Thoburn v Sunderland City Council* [2003] QB 151 at 185.
6 See D Campbell and J Young 'The metric martyrs and the entrenchment jurisprudence of Lord Justice Laws' [2002] PL 399.
7 With reference to *Vauxhall Estates Ltd v Liverpool Corpn* [1932] 1 KB 733 and *Ellen Street Estates Ltd v Minister of Health* [1934] 1 KB 590.
8 *Thoburn v Sunderland City Council* [2003] QB 151 at 188.
9 This terminology is also used in the *First Report of the Joint Committee on House of Lords Reform* (HC Paper 171, HL Paper 17 (2002–03)) para 15 and in the report of the (Wakeham) Royal Commission on reform of the House of Lords (Cm 4534, 2000).
10 See the discussion of the Acts of Union at para 6.6 above.
11 [2014] 2 All ER 109.
12 2012 SC 297.
13 2012 SC 297 at paras 66–73.
14 2013 SC (UKSC) 153.

THE SCOTTISH PARLIAMENT

General

6.11   The creation of the Scottish Parliament by SA 1998 did not, of course, eliminate the Westminster Parliament as a law-making body for Scotland. From the discussion in the last section of the powers of the UK Parliament, it should be clear that, whatever powers Westminster confers on the Scottish Parliament, it retains its powers to legislate for Scotland – even in terms which contradict the (letter or) spirit of SA 1998[1]. That it remains formally competent to amend or even to repeal SA 1998 is a position which derives, regardless of any provision in SA 1998 itself, from the general theory of the supremacy of the Westminster Parliament, discussed above. Despite this, it is also explicitly stated in the section which confers general law-making authority on the Scottish Parliament that it 'does not affect the power of the Parliament of the United Kingdom to make laws for Scotland'[2]. The legal and political repercussions of the retention of these powers by Westminster – the constitutional consequences of a settlement which is devolutionary rather than federal in character – are considered below[3].

In the meantime, however, we should examine the law-making powers of the Scottish Parliament. In broad terms, it was the Blair government's intention to establish a Parliament which would extend democratic control over the widespread responsibilities then exercised on an administrative basis by the Scottish Office and other Scottish departments[4]. This in turn reflected the proposals earlier made by the Scottish Constitutional Convention[5] and was intended to confer rather broader powers than those which would have been devolved under the aborted Scotland Act 1978 (SA 1978). As we move on to consider the limits on the Parliament's legislative competence, however, we should bear in mind that these determine only what the Parliament may do in its *law-making* mode. They do not, dictate any general limits on what may be discussed by the Parliament, a fact which has sometimes been a matter of some sensitivity – for instance in the debate held on 16 January 2003 on the 'international situation' (Iraq)[6]. The Parliament has also held debates on the succession to the throne[7], the Scottish regiments[8] and repeatedly on the detention of illegal immigrants, particularly children, at Dungavel House Immigration Removal Centre in Lanarkshire[9]. In the period prior to, and since, the referendum of 2014 there has been constant discussion of the merits and demerits of (the reserved matter of) independence.

As to legislative competence itself, what was required was a statutory scheme which would enable the new Parliament to legislate for Scotland but which would then draw a line between the devolved matters on which the Scottish Parliament would be competent to legislate and, on the other hand, the reserved matters in respect of which Westminster would have sole legislative authority. The line would be drawn between devolved matters such as health, education, housing, economic development, the environment, agriculture and the police and, on the other hand, reserved matters relating to foreign policy, fiscal and social security policy and the constitution of the United Kingdom. It was the government's belief that reserving powers in those and other areas listed in their proposals would safeguard the integrity of the United Kingdom and produce the benefits for the United Kingdom – as a whole – of a consistent and integrated approach to those policy areas[10].

The translation of those political ambitions into the language of SA 1998 itself started simply but then became more complex. SA 1998, s 28(1) provides that the Scottish Parliament may make laws to be known as Acts of the Scottish Parliament (ASPs). Procedures in the Parliament leading to the passing of a Bill and its receiving the royal assent are considered in Chapter 9 but it should be noted here that, with a view to giving an ASP the same sort of protection from procedural challenge that the courts extend to Westminster Acts[11], SA 1998, s 28(5) provides that the validity of an ASP is not affected by any invalidity in the proceedings leading to its enactment[12].

That protection extends to certain procedural defects but it does not, of course, render immune to challenge an ASP whose provisions exceed the substantive limits of the Parliament's powers. On the contrary, the general law-making power in SA 1998, s 28(1) is stated to be subject to SA 1998, s 29 which provides that an ASP 'is not law so far as any provision of the Act is outside the legislative competence of the Parliament'[13]. Such a provision is unlawful and SA 1998 creates special procedures by which the validity of a provision suspected of being unlawful may be challenged in the courts[14].

1   Subject to what is said below (para 6.22) about putting the Sewel Convention 'on a statutory footing'.
2   SA 1998, s 28(7).
3   See para 6.22.
4   *Scotland's Parliament* para 2.1. For the background to devolution, see ch 3.
5   See *Towards Scotland's Parliament: a report to the Scottish people by the Scottish Constitutional Convention* (1990); and *Scotland's Parliament: Scotland's right* (1995).
6   SP OR 16 January 2003, cols 17013–17087 and, in relation to the Scottish Parliament's lack of legislative competence in this area, see the exchange between Tom McCabe MSP and Margo MacDonald MSP at col 17021.
7   SP OR 16 December 1999, cols 1633–1680: 'The Parliament is the voice of Scotland. If the voice of Scotland wishes to make its position plain, it should not consider itself silenced merely by virtue of the fact that our vote cannot change the law' (Roseanna Cunningham MSP, col 1680).
8   SP OR 31 May 2001, cols 1243–1258.
9   SP OR 11 September 2003, col 1582; SP OR 22 September 2005, col 19358 SP OR 5 September 2007, col 1413. On 25 Nov 2014, the Parliament discussed the Ukrainian famine of 1932–33.
10 *Scotland's Parliament* para 3.4.
11 See para 6.5.
12 See para 9.9.
13 SA 1998, s 29(1).
14 See para 14.19. There are also procedures for challenging provisions in Bills prior to enactment. See para 9.8.

The legislative competence of the Scottish Parliament – an outline

6.12   SA 1998, s 29 goes on to define the 'legislative competence' of the Parliament by listing a number of ways in which a provision in an ASP is outside that competence. In neither SA 1998, s 28 nor s 29 is there any positive qualification of the general power to 'make laws'. There is not, for instance, any statement that the Parliament's use of its legislative powers should be for the 'peace, order and good government' of Scotland – a formula which was often used in the definition of the powers of parliaments of newly independent states in the Commonwealth and also of the Stormont Parliament in Northern Ireland[1]. Rather, the definition of competence is entirely cast in negative terms by reference to matters which are outside competence. Foremost among the limitations on competence are those which were anticipated in the government's original proposals – an ASP must apply only to Scotland and must not relate to 'reserved matters'. The legislative competence of the Parliament is, however, also restricted in certain other ways and these are considered below.

Before moving on to these express *restrictions* on competence, however, it may be useful to mention certain implied positive aspects of that competence. First, it has been assumed that the power to make laws includes the power to delegate substantial law-making powers to others[2]. Second, the law-making power includes the power to amend or repeal provisions in Acts of the Westminster Parliament, whether made before or after 1 July 1999. Third, the power to make laws includes, of course, the power to amend and repeal the Scottish Parliament's own Acts[3]. It should be assumed that, like the Westminster Parliament, the Scottish Parliament cannot 'bind its successors' although it may enact the procedures which, subject to future modification, it expects the Parliament to adopt for legislating on certain matters in the future. For example, the Public Finance and Accountability (Scotland) Act 2000, s 4 authorises expenditure of sums allowed by the Budget Acts which have been passed annually since then[4] but this Act could not prevent the Parliament from adopting a different legislative device for the allocation of funds at a later date. Fifth, the Parliament's competence could, presumably, not be restricted by the terms of any agreement entered into between the Parliament and a third party. Such agreements are not likely to arise often, if at all, but it appears that the prospects for the Parliament's entering into a 'covenant' with Scottish local authorities during the first session may have foundered, in part, because of doubts about whether it would be appropriate for the Parliament to fetter, in any way, the freedom to use its law-making powers[5]. Finally, it appears that the Scottish Parliament has the power to legislate with retrospective effect[6] (including it appears with respect to events which may have taken place before 1 July 1999)[7].

1 Government of Ireland Act 1920, s 4.
2 See para 6.23.
3 See, for instance, the repeal of the Abolition of Poindings and Warrant Sales Act 2001 by the Debt Arrangement and Attachment (Scotland) Act 2002.
4 See para 11.17.
5 See 'Legacy Paper' of the Parliament's Local Government Committee, 25 March 2003. There was no such obstacle to the entering into a 'Concordat' between Scottish Government and COSLA in 2007: see para 8.7.
6 Erskine Bridge Tolls Act 2001.
7 See the Damages (Asbestos-related Conditions) (Scotland) Act 2009 which provides that ss 1 and 2 of that Act are 'to be treated for all purposes as having always had effect'. The validity of the Act was challenged (unsuccessfully and on other grounds) in *AXA General Insurance Ltd, Petitioners* 2012 SC (UKSC) 122.

Limitations on legislative competence – territory

6.13   Returning to SA 1998, s 29, the restriction of the Parliament's powers to apply to Scotland only may seem straightforward enough. It would, on the face of it, be surprising if the Scottish Parliament could legislate on matters outside Scotland and SA 1998 provides that a provision of an ASP is indeed outside the Parliament's legislative competence if 'it would form part of the law of a country or territory other than Scotland, or confer or remove functions exercisable otherwise than in or as regards Scotland'[1]. Although the reasons for this restriction may seem obvious, the result is that legislative proposals which require co-ordination with others for England or other parts of the United Kingdom may attract the need for legislation at Westminster rather than at Holyrood[2]. In addition, the need to define 'Scotland' for the purposes of conferring legislative competence in respect of the regulation of sea fishing was the cause of some difficulty and controversy[3]. It has also been interesting to see the use made, in some examples of delegated legislation to which the same territorial restriction applies[4], of the formula: 'Insofar as it extends beyond Scotland, this Order does so only as a matter of Scots law'[5]. There must be room for some doubt about how legislation admitted to extend beyond Scotland is permitted to do so 'as a matter of Scots law'[6].

1 SA 1998, s 29(2)(a).
2 See para 6.22. It seems, however, to be permissible for the Parliament to add to the functions of UK public bodies – see eg Pt 2 of the Local Electoral Administration (Scotland) Act 2011 (the Electoral Commission).
3 'Scotland' is defined to include 'so much of the internal waters and territorial sea of the United Kingdom as are adjacent to Scotland' (SA 1998, s 126(1)). An Order in Council may, however determine the boundaries of internal waters and territorial sea for this purpose (SA 1998, s 126(2)) and the lines drawn by the Scottish Adjacent Waters Boundaries Order 1999, SI 1999/1126 did cause political controversy. See SP OR 3 June 1999. An Order in Council may also be made to specify functions as being 'exercisable in or as regards Scotland' (SA 1998, s 30(3) and the Scotland Act 1998 (Functions Exercisable in or as Regards Scotland) Order 1999, SI 1999/1748). See also the Marine and Coastal Access Act 2009.
4 See para 6.24.
5 See, for example the Pet Travel Scheme (Scotland) Order 2003, SSI 2003/229 and the Plant Health (Scotland) Order 2005, SSI 2005/613.
6 For discussion, see SP Paper 504 (2002) para 12.

Limitations on legislative competence – reserved matters

6.14   The discussion in *Scotland's Parliament* of the need for SA 1998 to define the boundary between reserved matters and devolved matters has already been mentioned. The same document also gave an indication of how this was to be done. Put simply, the choice was between two possible mechanisms. Either SA 1998 should contain a list of all the matters to be devolved to the Parliament, stating also that anything not so specified was to be reserved; or it should specify the matters to be reserved, leaving all else devolved. Whichever mechanism was chosen, there would also be the question of the form the lists should take and the degree of detail they should contain. The argument in favour of some precision is that ambiguity and doubt should be avoided for the benefit of parliamentarians and citizens alike: uncertainty may give rise to unreasonable amounts of litigation in the courts. On the other hand, attempts at precision can themselves be the cause of great complexity and may in time produce more uncertainty and litigation.

The model for allocating powers in the SA 1978 was one which (a) listed devolved matters rather than reserved matters; and (b) did so in great detail and by reference to long lists of specific statutory provisions[1]. In 1997, when making their own proposals, the government was critical of the 1978 model. It thought that, because of its high level of specificity, the scheme would have required frequent updating and might have given rise to regular legal arguments about whether particular matters were or were not devolved. The objective of ensuring maximum clarity and stability was best served, in its view, by listing the matters to be reserved to the UK Parliament rather than specifying the devolved matters, an approach which had been adopted in the Northern Ireland Constitution Act 1973[2].

In SA 1998 itself, the scheme for defining the Parliament's law-making powers on this basis starts from s 29(2)(b) which states that a provision in an ASP is outside the Parliament's legislative competence if 'it relates to reserved matters'. The reserved matters themselves are set out in SA 1998, Sch 5[3] which is, as a result, at the core of the devolution settlement: by listing the reserved matters, its terms define the principal boundaries of the Parliament's powers. The government's explanation of the reasoning leading to the choice of the list of reservations was set out briefly in *Scotland's Parliament*: 'There are many matters which can be more effectively and beneficially handled on a United Kingdom basis. By preserving the integrity of the United Kingdom, the Union secures for its people participation in an economic unit which benefits business and provides access to wider markets and investment and increases prosperity for all. Scotland also benefits from strong and effective defence and foreign policies and a sense of belonging to a United Kingdom'[4].

This statement led fairly quickly to the identification of some subjects which should unproblematically be reserved. *Scotland's Parliament* listed such things as the constitution of the United Kingdom; UK foreign policy, defence and national security; and the stability of the United Kingdom's fiscal, economic and monetary system[5]. On the other hand, a test of what can be 'more effectively and beneficially handled on a United Kingdom basis' also leaves some matters unresolved. There are questions about what should logically fall on each side of the line. Should the National Health Service be reserved or not? Should legislation on social security policy be made at Westminster or Holyrood? And what about the police service? Or, in a different sector, broadcasting?

Another series of questions follows quickly behind. It might, for instance, be appropriate to reserve *some aspects* of a particular topic but to devolve others. In SA 1978, school education was devolved but university education was not. How were these to be treated in 1998? Could the universities still be handled more effectively and beneficially on a UK basis or should they join school education in being devolved? Transport, especially in respect of safety and regulation, may tend to attract the need for UK legislation but should not some aspects be devolved to Holyrood? Within the health sector, which might in general be devolved, should different considerations apply to abortion, human fertilisation, genetics, xenotransplantation and vivisection? It was the government's view that all of these special aspects should be reserved 'in view of the need for a common approach'[6]. It will not be surprising, however, that the content of SA 1998, Sch 5, in which all these borderline questions were exposed, was the focus of some of the most sustained debate as the Scotland Bill went through Parliament. The borderline between reserved and devolved was fraught with issues on which reasonable people would disagree and on which the differences between political parties would be substantial.

Another outcome of the process of demarcation between reserved and devolved matters is technical complexity. A simple listing of reserved matters in SA 1998, Sch 5 may have been the aim but the Schedule became a substantial document of reservations and exceptions to reservations (such exceptions being, of course, areas which are devolved to the Scottish Parliament[7]). Its terms are, in some respects, further complicated by SA 1998, Sch 4 which is considered below. SA 1998, Sch 5 itself is divided into three Parts. Part I contains what are called 'General Reservations' and Part II lists 'Specific Reservations', although it is not always obvious why each item falls into the category it does. The offence of treason is, for instance, listed as a 'general' reservation while the currency is listed as 'specific' in Part II. Schedule 5, Part III is headed 'General Provisions' but contains five paragraphs which supplement the provision already made in Parts I and II. Three of those paragraphs deal with 'Scottish public authorities' and 'reserved bodies'[8] and para 4 makes specific supplementary provision in relation to financial assistance to industry. Part III, para 5 provides an important interpretative aid relevant to Parts I and II: much of the detail in the lists of reserved matters in those Parts is provided by reference to the subject matter of a named Act of Parliament and para 5 confirms that such references are to be read as references to the subject matter of those enactments as at 1 July 1999[9].

It is explained below that the boundary between reserved and devolved matters defined in SA 1998 is not fixed and that it can be (and has been) amended, for instance by SA 2012. But from September 2014, in the light of the independence referendum result, the whole question of more powers for the Scottish Parliament by the further redefinition of the boundary between reserved and devolved matters has returned to the political and constitutional agenda. The recommendations of the Smith Commission have to be addressed and another Scotland Act is probable.

1 SA 1978, s 18 and Sch 2, s 63 and Schs 10–12.
2 *Scotland's Parliament* para 4.3. See also the Constitution Unit's *Scotland's Parliament: Fundamentals for a New Scotland Act* (1996) chs 3 and 4.
3 Given effect by SA 1998, s 30(1).
4 Para 3.2.
5 Para 3.3.
6 Para 3.3.
7 So, for example, while the broad subject area of intellectual property is reserved to Westminster, the exception to that reservation (and in relation to which Holyrood is competent to legislate) is the subject matter of the Plant Varieties Act 1997, Pts I and II (plant varieties and the Plant Varieties and Seeds Tribunal): SA 1998, Sch 5, Pt II, S C4.
8 On which see para 8.10.
9 Ie the 'principal appointed day' – see SA 1998, s 130 and SI 1998/3178. If the subject matter of an Act had ceased to have effect at any time between the passing of SA 1998 (ie 19 November 1998) and 1 July 1999, it should be read as a reference to the subject matter of the enactment immediately before that time.

Scotland Act 1998, Schedule 5, Part I – general reservations

6.15   Returning to the substantive provisions of SA 1998, Sch 5, Part I lists the general reservations under six headings: the constitution; political parties; foreign affairs; public service; defence; and treason.

THE CONSTITUTION A number of aspects of the constitution are declared to be reserved matters, beginning with the Crown, including succession to the Crown and a regency (although the Parliament has debated the question of the exclusion of Catholics from succession to the Crown by the Act of Settlement 1700, while acknowledging that any statutory change would be for Westminster)[1]. The general reservation of the Crown is qualified by other provisions in SA 1998, Sch 5 which produces a rather complex situation overall. Most importantly, though, SA 1998, Sch 5 recognises the position established elsewhere in the Act that the Scottish Government has had functions transferred to it which are within devolved competence and which are prerogative or other executive functions exercisable on behalf of the Queen[2]. Such functions are not, therefore, reserved by the reservation of the Crown[3]. On the other hand 'honours and dignities' are reserved, as are the functions of the Lord Lyon King of Arms so far as relating to the granting of arms but not his judicial functions which, like most aspects of the judicial system, are devolved[4]. The management of the Crown Estate is stated to be reserved[5] and the reservation of the Crown also reserves the functions of the Security Service (MI5), the Secret Intelligence Service (MI6) and the Government Communications Headquarters[6].

Another line which has to be drawn by SA 1998, Sch 5 lies between the reserved and devolved aspects of 'Crown' property. The general reservation of the Crown does not reserve 'property belonging to Her Majesty in right of the Crown' or belonging to any person acting on behalf of the Crown[7], although the compulsory acquisition of property held or used by a UK minister or government department[8] is reserved. On the other hand, the ultimate superiority of the Crown is not reserved[9], with the consequence that the Bill to abolish the feudal system was squarely within the Scottish Parliament's competence[10] and property held by the Queen in her private capacity is not reserved[11]. The hereditary revenues of the Crown *are* reserved[12], as are the royal arms and standard[13]. Finally, the Schedule reconfirms the non-reservation of the Scottish Seal[14].

Also reserved under the head of 'the Constitution' are the Union of the Kingdoms of Scotland and England[15]; and the Parliament of the United Kingdom. SA 1998 and the continued existence of the High Court of Justiciary and the Court of Session as, respectively, a criminal court and civil court of first instance and of appeal. This last reservation does, however, leave the Scottish Parliament free to legislate to amend the powers and procedures of the two courts and, of course, the Parliament has wider powers in relation to the lower courts[16] (although Sch 5, Pt II includes the reservation of judicial remuneration including that of sheriffs principal and sheriffs[17]). It is not clear whether it would be competent for the Parliament to legislate to curtail or abolish appeals to the UK Supreme Court: senior judicial opinion has been at odds with the views of the Parliament's Presiding Officer on the question[18].

POLITICAL PARTIES The second 'general reservation' made by SA 1998, Sch 5 is the registration and funding of political parties, although this is stated not to reserve the making of payments to parties for the purposes of assisting MSPs to perform their parliamentary duties[19].

FOREIGN AFFAIRS Thirdly, SA 1998, Sch 5 reserves 'foreign affairs', defined as international relations, including relations with the European Union and international organisations, the regulation of international trade and international development assistance[20]. The conduct of foreign affairs is a function readily associated with the United Kingdom as a whole rather than its constituent parts and joins the 'defence of the realm' (see below) as an obvious matter for reservation. International relations are to be conducted at the national level and this includes relations with the European Union. Despite argument that it would be appropriate for the Scottish Parliament and Government to have an autonomous representation in Europe, the formal line was held. On the other hand, the text of the reservation makes an exception of 'assisting Ministers of the Crown' in their conduct of international relations[21] which opens the door to Scottish participation in international and European negotiations including representation in the Council of Ministers[22]. Another exception recognises the dual character of international relations. While the negotiation and conclusion of treaty obligations is reserved, it is important that observing and implementing those obligations is not: within their own areas of competence, the Scottish Parliament and Government are not prevented from observing and implementing obligations deriving from international treaties, the European Convention on Human Rights (ECHR) and EU law[23]. In the case of the ECHR and EU law, this is reinforced elsewhere in SA 1998 by specific prohibitions against the Parliament and the Scottish Ministers legislating or acting incompatibly with Convention rights or EU law[24] and by the transfer to the Scottish Ministers of powers to implement EU law within their own areas of competence[25]. SA 1998 does not formally place the failure to observe other types of international obligations beyond the competence of the Scottish Parliament or Government, although the Secretary of State's powers of intervention under SA 1998, ss 35 and 58 may be used on those grounds[26].

PUBLIC SERVICE Further reserved by SA 1998, Sch 5 is the civil service of the state[27]. Separate provision is, however, made for appointments to the staff of the Scottish Administration and for other aspects of civil service management[28].

DEFENCE The general reservation of the 'defence of the realm' and related matters is not surprising[29]. All the armed forces (including reserve forces) are reserved matters, as are visiting forces, international headquarters and defence organisations, and trading with the enemy and enemy property. On the other hand, the exercise of civil defence functions (by persons other than members of the armed forces) is not reserved; nor is the conferral of enforcement powers in relation to sea fishing[30].

TREASON The final 'general reservation' is of the offence of treason[31].

1   SP OR 16 December 1999, cols 1633–1680.
2   SA 1998, s 53(2). See para 7.2.
3   SA 1998, Sch 5, Pt I, para 2(1). Similarly, a public authority which has no reserved functions does not become a reserved body simply by virtue of the reservation of the Crown: SA 1998, Sch 5, Pt III, para 2.
4   SA 1998, Sch 5, Pt I, para 2(2).
5   SA 1998, Sch 5, Pt I, para 2(3). The Smith Commission recommended (paras 32–35) the devolution of the Crown Estate.
6   SA 1998, Sch 5, Pt I, para 2(4).
7   SA 1998, Sch 5, Pt I, para 3(1). SA 1998 contains separate provisions for the transfer, by subordinate legislation, of property belonging to any Minister of the Crown or government department to the Scottish Ministers (SA 1998, ss 60, 90 and 109), the Lord Advocate (SA 1998, s 62) and the Scottish Parliament (SA 1998, Sch 2, para 2). See SIs 1999/1104, 1999/1105 and 1999/1106. SA 1998, s 116 also provides a mechanism by which ambiguities as to the transfer of property may be resolved by a certificate issued by the Secretary of State which is 'conclusive evidence' that a transfer has or has not taken place.
8   SA 1998, Sch 5, Pt I, para 2(3)(c).
9   SA 1998, Sch 5, Pt I, para 3(2).
10 See the Abolition of Feudal Tenure etc (Scotland) Act 2000, especially ss 58–61 and discussion at Stage 1 (SP OR 9 November 1999, cols 339–370) and Stage 3 (SP OR 3 May 2000 cols 213–357) of the Bill's progress.
11 SA 1998, Sch 5, Pt I, para 4(1).

12 SA 1998, Sch 5, Pt I, para 3(3)(a). Though not revenues from bona vacantia, ultimus haeres and treasure trove.
13 SA 1998, Sch 5, Pt I, para 3(3)(b).
14 SA 1998, Sch 5, Pt I, para 5. See also SA 1998, ss 28, 38.
15 SA 1998, Sch 5, Pt 1, para 1(b) and (c). The (English) Union with Scotland Act 1706 and the (Scottish) Union with England Act 1707 are declared to have effect subject to SA 1998, s 37, and see para 6.6 above. SA 1998, Sch 4, para 1(2)(a) also makes specific provision protecting the Union with Scotland Act 1706 and the Union with England Act 1707, Arts 4 and 6 from modification by the Scottish Parliament, so far as they relate to freedom of trade. The extent of the reservation was adjusted (see para 6.17 below) to enable the Scottish Parliament to legislate for the independence referendum of 2014.
16 See eg the Courts Reform (Scotland) Act 2014.
17 SA 1998, Sch 5, Pt II, Section L1.
18 Compare Lord Hope of Craighead 'Taking the case to London – is it all over?' 1998 JR 135 with the treatment of Adam Ingram MSP's Civil Appeals (Scotland) Bill discussed at para 9.10.
19 SA 1998, Sch 5, Pt I, para 6. And see para 5.20.
20 SA 1998, Sch 5, Pt I, para 7(1).
21 SA 1998, Sch 5, Pt I, para 7(2)(b).
22 See para 3.13.
23 SA 1998, Sch 5, Pt I, para 7(2)(a).
24 SA 1998, ss 29(2)(d), 57(2), (3).
25 SA 1998, ss 53, 57(1).
26 See paras 7.19 and 9.19. In debates on the Scotland Bill, the government argued that it would be inappropriate to make compatibility with international law a test of legislative or executive competence as this would present courts with issues inappropriate for resolution by them. See para 9.19.
27 SA 1998, Sch 5, Pt I, para 8. Paragraph 8(2) excepts from reservation the subject matter of the Sheriff Courts and Legal Officers (Scotland) Act 1927, Pt I and the Administration of Justice (Scotland) Act 1933, Pt III which are, respectively, concerned with the appointment of sheriff clerks and procurators fiscal, and officers of the High Court and the Court of Session.
28 See SA 1998, s 51 and para 7.25. The Smith Commission recommended that the Parliament should have 'powers to make decisions about all matters relating to the arrangements and operations of the Scottish Parliament and Government' (para 26).
29 SA 1998, Sch 5, Pt I, para 9.
30 SA 1998, Sch 5, Pt I, para 9(2). For other aspects of sea fishing, see para 6.13.
31 SA 1998, Sch 5, Pt I, para 10. The reservation includes constructive treason, treason felony and misprision of treason.

Scotland Act 1998, Schedule 5, Part II – specific reservations

6.16   Part II of Sch 5 to the Scotland Act 1998 contains a list of 'specific reservations'. They are arranged under a series of Heads from A to L as follows:

A   Financial and Economic Matters;
B   Home Affairs;
C   Trade and Industry;
D   Energy;
E   Transport;
F   Social Security;
G   Regulation of the Professions;
H   Employment;
J   Health and Medicines;
K   Media and Culture;
L   Miscellaneous.

Under each Head, the style of the Schedule is to include a number of Sections each of which contains a description of reserved matters either by reference to one or more subject areas (eg coinage, legal tender and bank notes) or by reference to the subject matter of a specific piece or pieces of UK legislation (either primary or secondary) or, in one case, an EC Directive[1]. Such specific statutory references make the Schedule vulnerable to change over time to reflect subsequent amendments[2] although the terms of the Schedule itself make clear that the subject matter of any enactment referred to is to be read as a reference to the subject matter as at 1 July 1999[3]. In the text of many of the reservations, the reservation itself is followed by one or more exceptions. Thus, in Section A1 there is a reservation of 'fiscal, economic and monetary policy, … taxes and excise duties' but there is an exception for 'local taxes to fund local authority expenditure (for example, council tax and non-domestic rates)'. The Scottish Parliament could not legislate to raise general taxes but it had available the tax-varying power under SA 1998, Pt IV[4] which is currently approaching repeal (with other powers to levy 'devolved taxes' added) by SA 2012[5]. The Parliament could legislate to amend or replace the council tax as a source of local authority revenue.

Other reservations imposed by SA 1998, Sch 5, Head A prevent the Parliament from legislating on the currency, financial services (but bank holidays *are* within the Parliament's competence), financial markets and money laundering. Head B (Home Affairs) reserves the misuse of drugs, data protection and elections for membership of the Scottish Parliament[6], the House of Commons and the European Parliament, although local government elections, with the exception of the franchise, are not reserved[7]. Also under Head B are reservations of firearms, entertainment (including video recordings and film classification), immigration and nationality, national security, gaming, emergency powers and extradition. Under Head C (Trade and Industry) are reserved business associations (but not charities), most aspects of insolvency, competition (but not the regulation of the legal profession), intellectual property, sea fishing outside the Scottish zone (except Scottish fishing boats)[8], consumer protection, most aspects of product standards and safety (excluding food), weights and measures, telecommunications, the Post Office and postal services, and the research councils.

A list of reservations under Head D (Energy) covers electricity, and most aspects of oil and gas, coal and nuclear energy. The reservation of Transport (Head E) includes most aspects of road traffic regulation, rail[9], marine and air transport. Practically all aspects of social security are reserved under Head F, while Head G reserves the regulation of architects, health professions and auditors. Head H reserves most of employment law and health and safety law[10]. While the provision of health services is not generally reserved, Head J (Health and Medicines) reserves abortion, xenotransplantation, embryology, surrogacy and human genetics as well as medicines[11]. Head K reserves broadcasting, including, controversially, the BBC itself[12] which is combined with lesser matters such as the public lending right under the general heading of Media and Culture. The list of reservations closes with Head L (Miscellaneous). This reserves the constitutionally significant matter of judicial remuneration[13] but that is joined by 'equal opportunities, the control of weapons of mass destruction, the Ordnance Survey and 'time'. By that is meant time scales and time zones[14] and the calendar, units of time and the date of Easter. On the other hand, the computation of periods of time and bank holidays and Quarter Days are not reserved. The regulation of activities in outer space is reserved[15].

1   See Section B2 (Data Protection), referring to Council Directive (EC) 46/95. For discussion of the legal challenge to the Children and Young People (Scotland) Act 2014 on grounds, inter alia, of intrusion into this reservation see para 14.28.
2   See, for example, the insertion of a new para (a) of Section B3 of Part II of Sch 5 by the European Parliamentary Elections Act 2002.
3   See SA 1998, Sch 5, Pt III, para 5. But see also Section B2 which provides, in relation to the reservation of the Data Protection Act 1998, that if any provision of the Act was not in force on 1 July 1999, it was to be treated as if it were. While parts of SA 1998 came into force at the date of royal assent (16 July 1998), the majority of the remaining provisions were brought into force on 1 March 2000 (SI 2000/183).
4   See para 11.9.
5   See para 6.17 below and para 11.9.
6   The Smith Commission recommended the devolution of powers in relation to elections to the Scottish Parliament (paras 23–25).
7   See the Local Governance (Scotland) Act 2004 for the introduction of STV voting.
8   See above.
9   The reservation concerning rail was the subject of amendment to increase the scope of rail powers devolved in Scotland (see below). Nevertheless, the Provision of Rail Passenger Services (Scotland) Bill which was introduced by Tommy Sheridan MSP in September 2006 was stated by the Presiding Officer to be outside legislative competence by virtue of the reservation of rail services. See para 9.10.
10 This reservation, somewhat controversially, led the Scottish Government to conclude in July 2006 the introduction of a new criminal offence of corporate homicide was a reserved matter: see the Corporate Manslaughter and Corporate Homicide Act 2007.
11 The Smith Commission recommended reconsideration of all aspects of this Head (paras 61, 62).
12 See also para 8.10.
13 See para 12.10.
14 Including the subject matter of the Summer Time Act 1972.
15 See below for the addition of 'Antarctica' as a new miscellaneous category.

Devolved and reserved matters: a flexible boundary

6.17   The list of reserved matters contained in SA 1998, Sch 5 is not fixed for all time. The Schedule can be amended by primary legislation passed at Westminster – see, in particular, SA 2012 (below). That is, however, a relatively cumbersome process and SA 1998 itself anticipated the need for a simpler method by secondary legislation, but with protection against its use simply to serve the interests of the UK government. Thus, SA 1998, s 30(2) enables Sch 5 (and also Sch 4) to be modified by Order in Council for purposes considered 'necessary or expedient' by Her Majesty but any such Order must first be approved in draft by resolution – not only of both Houses at Westminster but also the Scottish Parliament itself. The procedure has been used on a number of occasions to make amendments to the Schedule[1]. One Modifications Order[2] included the insertion of a new reservation of 'Access to information' but with an exception which paved the way for the Scottish Parliament to pass the Freedom of Information (Scotland) Act 2002. A subsequent adjustment of the transport reservation[3] enabled the grant of new railway services planning powers to local authorities by the Transport (Scotland) Act 2001 and another[4] permitted the introduction in the first session of the Stirling–Alloa–Kincardine Railway and Linked Improvements Bill. An adjustment to the insolvency reservation[5] enabled the Parliament to provide for the insolvency of social landlords[6]. General guidance has been issued to Whitehall departments on the use which may appropriately be made of SA 1998, s 30(2)[7]. It is suggested, for instance, that orders under the subsection should not routinely be used simply to resolve doubts about the precise boundaries of a reservation. That should generally be left to the courts but an exception might be where it is known that the Scottish Government has proposals to initiate legislation in an area and 'the [Scottish Government] and UK government see the risks and consequences of a successful legal challenge as being significant in the wider context'[8]. The most high-profile use of s 30 has been that enabling the Scottish Parliament to pass the legislation necessary for the holding of the independence referendum in September 2014. The order[9] enacted a conditional exception (including a time limit) to the 'Constitution' reservation in Sch 5. This was indeed an area in which the 'risks and consequences' were, by no means, negligible. Finally, it is to be noted that consequential amendments to Sch 5 have been made by 'ordinary' subordinate legislation made by the UK government[10]. An opportunity for broader-ranging change came with the report of the Calman Commission[11] which recommended a number of specific adjustments to the reserved/devolved boundary some of which were taken forward by the UK government[12] and included in SA 2012. As well as expanding the Parliament's powers of taxation (with a new income tax and amending the tax reservation to add a 'devolved taxes' exception[13]), the Act amended SA 1998, Sch 5 to permit the regulation of airguns[14].

It is, as yet, unclear how the recommendations of the Smith Commission[15] are to be implemented. No doubt some will require new primary legislation (presumably a new Scotland Act) but some might take the 's 30 order' route[16].

1   The Scotland Act 1998 (Modifications of Schedules 4 and 5) Order 1999, SI 1999/1749; and SI 2000/3252; SI 2001/1456; SI 2002/1629; SI 2004/3329; SI 2005/865; SI 2005/866; SI 2006/609; SI 2013/192; SI 2013/242; and SI 2014/1559.
2   SI 1999/1749.
3   SI 2000/3252.
4   SI 2002/1629.
5   SI 2001/1456.
6   Housing (Scotland) Act 2001, s 64 and sch 8.
7   Devolution Guidance Note 14.
8   Devolution Guidance Note 14, para 6 (ii).
9   SI 2013/242.
10 See the Legislative Reform (Health and Safety Executive) Order 2008, SI 2008/960.
11 Commission on Scottish Devolution, *Serving Scotland Better: Scotland and the United Kingdom in the 21st Century* (2009).
12 *Strengthening Scotland's Future*, Cm 7973, 2010. See para 3.20.
13 See para 11.9.
14 SA 2012, s 10. And see the Air Weapons and Licensing (Scotland) Bill (2014–15).
15 See para 4.21.
16 On 15 Dec 2014 it was announced that a s 30 order would enable the voting age for the Scottish Parliament to be reduced to 16.

Reserved matters: problems of interpretation

6.18   Although the line drawn by SA 1998, Sch 5 between devolved and reserved powers broadly achieved the political objectives of the UK government of 1998, the means by which this was done is not without difficulties. Some of these derive simply from the problems inherent in any attempt to define powers in the only way we have available – the use of language. Some are particularly associated with the adoption of the method of definition of powers by reference to reserved matters rather than by a listing of the devolved powers themselves. We might identify four particular difficulties:

(1)   At the most abstract level (and the level least likely to raise practical difficulties), one problem of definition by reservation is that, because there is no defined outer boundary of the limits of legislative power, reservations in SA 1998, Sch 5 have been chosen by reference to conventional categories of Westminster legislation, extended as an afterthought to such matters as time scales and the calendar. But what, for instance, of other matters of natural or scientific definition? Could the Scottish Parliament redefine for Scotland the periodic table of the elements; could it provide a new scale for the measurement of temperature or wind speed in Scotland; could it redefine categories of cattle or horses or cats or dogs? Less fancifully, could the Scottish Parliament intervene to legislate not only on the use of Gaelic or the resources to be allocated to it[1] but also on its orthography? And if on Gaelic, Lallans? And if on Lallans, the use of English in Scotland? Could the Scottish Parliament abolish the apostrophe?

(2)   Of more obvious practical application is the question of whether the line between the devolved and the reserved has been drawn correctly. The White Paper explained the case for reserving powers in these terms:

> 'There are many matters which can be more effectively and benefi-cially handled on a United Kingdom basis. By preserving the integ-rity of the UK, the Union secures for its people participation in an economic unit which benefits business and provides access to wider markets and investment and increases prosperity for all. Scotland also benefits from strong and effective defence and foreign policies and a sense of belonging to a United Kingdom'[2].

It is not difficult to see that many of these criteria for the reservation of particular areas to the Westminster Parliament are reflected in the terms of SA 1998, Sch 5. Most of the 'general' reservations can be seen to have a 'UK' aspect to them and, as long as the need for 'participation in an economic unit' taking the form of the United Kingdom is accepted, many of the 'trade and industry' and 'employment' reservations may be fairly unproblematic. But whether the same goes for other categories such as 'social security' and the 'financial and economic' matters is more debatable. More problematic still are reservations such as broadcasting and abortion. It is less clear that these are dictated by the criteria laid down. They were controversial at the time the Scotland Bill was debated in Parliament[3] and have remained so[4]. The controversy has extended much more broadly in the post-referendum period. The issue of the general dimensions of devolved power (and then the specific further competences which might be entailed by a new model) is at the heart of the renewed constitutional debate. As noted above, the Smith Commission[5] recommended reconsideration of the reservation of abortion.

(3)   Even if the boundaries between what is devolved and what is reserved were not themselves controversial, problems would remain for Parliaments and governments because, in many policy areas, there are inevitable overlaps between those parts which are reserved and those which are devolved. From the point of view of the Scottish Parliament, this makes it impossible for a wholly comprehensive and integrated policy position to be adopted, even in those areas which are, on the face of it, devolved. The education system, including universities, is devolved but the research councils and, therefore, research council funding of universities are currently not. Housing is generally devolved but housing benefit, upon which so much of contemporary housing policy depends, is, as an aspect of social security, has been a reserved matter – although some 'discretionary housing payments' are recommended for devolution by the Smith Commission (along with some other benefits)[6]. Environmental protection is generally devolved but most aspects of energy policy (including nuclear energy) and transport policy are not.

Some of the problems of overlap are addressed by means made available under SA 1998 itself or left for resolution by extra-statutory negotiation between the two tiers of government. SA 1998 makes provision for the 'executive' devolution of powers[7] which, for legislative purposes, are reserved. It also makes special provision for public bodies whose powers straddle the divide. The power retained by the Westminster Parliament to legislate in areas which have been devolved to Holyrood allows legislation to be enacted across the reserved–devolved boundary, although normally only with the consent of the Scottish Parliament[8]. One of the aims of the concordat regime between the Scottish and the UK governments has been to enable the co-ordination of policy[9].

One overarching overlap is represented by the reservation to Westminster of a near monopoly (until the changes brought by SA 2012) in matters of taxation. With the exception of the tax-varying power provided by SA 1998 itself[10] and the power of the Scottish Parliament to make laws on 'local taxes to fund local authority expenditure'[11], all the powers of the Parliament have to be read subject to the financial controls lying ultimately with Westminster and Whitehall[12]. Even if the extent of those powers is, despite the reservations in SA 1998, Sch 5, formally very broad, they are, in practice, exercisable only subject to external financial constraints. Expanded powers to tax (going well beyond those already provided for by SA 2012) appear to be on the way in the light of the Smith Commission report.

(4)   Finally, it has to be remembered that any exercise of legislative power by the Scottish Parliament is open to challenge in the courts. Such challenges in the early stages focused on human rights issues but several cases at

the reserved/devolved borderline have followed. The circumstances in which such challenges have arisen and the ways in which courts have handled them are considered later[13] but it should be noted that SA 1998 itself provided some interpretative assistance in s 29(3):

> 'For the purposes of this section, the question whether a provision of an Act of the Scottish Parliament relates to a reserved matter is to be determined, subject to subsection (4), by reference to the *purpose* of the provision, having regard (among other things) to its effect in all the circumstances'.

The importance of this subsection is that 'purpose' is prescribed as the defining test of whether a provision 'relates to' a reserved matter or not. It addresses the difficult question of overlap presented by any provision in an ASP which may 'affect' – to use a neutral term – both matters which are plainly not reserved but also, to an extent, some which are. SA 1998, s 29(3) states that a provision will not 'relate to' a reserved matter unless that is its purpose. This might be expected to save not only provisions which have a merely trivial impact on a reserved matter: even if the impact of a provision on a reserved matter is quite substantial it will be saved provided that its 'purpose' can be held to be within the devolved area. Of course, the purpose of a provision is itself to be determined with regard, 'among other things' to its 'effect in all the circumstances'. These supplementary tests are by no means wholly clear. Despite the centrality of 'purpose', how does one, for instance, determine the 'effect' of a provision in advance of its implementation[14]. What are 'all the circumstances' by reference to which one must judge the effect of a provision? What are the 'other things' to which one must also have regard?

From the start, difficulties of interpretation in these areas, were anticipated. Examples of legislation in overlapping areas were, however, provided by ministers at the time of debate on the (1998) Scotland Bill. As one example, Lord Sewel suggested that in a Bill which dealt in general with pollution control (a devolved area) but which also contained provisions dealing with water pollution from coal mines or dust from open cast mining, those provisions would be saved by their anti-pollution purpose despite their touching upon the reserved matter of coal mining. Similarly, a Bill dealing with local government reorganisation should be saved by its devolved purpose, despite its ancillary impact on the administration of local functions relating to reserved matters such as weights and measures and the provision of housing benefit. Until it became a political reality, a recurring hypothetical example with a high political profile was that of a Bill to authorise the holding of a referendum on independence for Scotland. Because its 'purpose' could be interpreted as the testing of opinion rather than the amendment of the constitution, it was always arguable that such a Bill would have been within the Parliament's powers, unaided by a s 30 order[15].

The ways in which these statutory provisions have framed the general approach of the courts to the determination of issues of legislative competence and then their handling of specific cases are considered in Chapter 14[16].

6.18 *Law-making Competences for Scotland*

In addition to the provision made by SA 1998, s 29(3), there is one particular category of overlapping provision which receives special treatment. SA 1998, s 29(4)[17] provides that a provision in an ASP which would *otherwise not relate* to reserved matters (ie on application, as necessary, of the test in SA 1998, s 29(3)) but makes modifications of *Scots private law* or *Scots criminal law*, as it applies to reserved matters, is normally to be treated as relating to reserved matters. As a general statement, this is, of course, unsurprising. Modifications of the law applying to reserved matters would be expected to 'relate to' reserved matters and thus be beyond the Parliament's competence. However, SA 1998, s 29(4), which has to be read with provisions in Sch 4 discussed below, is important for the exception to the general rule which it also contains. Thus, where the purpose of the provision is 'to make the law in question apply consistently to reserved matters and otherwise' that provision is *not* to be treated as relating to reserved matters.

The point here is to take account of the need to ensure that the Scottish Parliament is competent to take on the stewardship of the legal system of Scotland including the broad fields of private and criminal law. The division between devolved and reserved matters places some private and criminal law clearly within the Parliament's competence but some would plainly relate to reserved matters, for example the law of banking, insurance, consumer protection and employment or criminal offences relating to the misuse of drugs. A law whose purpose was to reform legal provision in those areas would plainly be beyond the competence of the Scottish Parliament. By virtue, however, of SA 1998, s 29(4), an ASP which, while modifying the law in those areas because it extended across the devolved/reserved divide, had, as its purpose, the making of 'consistent provision' across the divide, is to be saved. An ASP touching upon the general principles of contract (including those contracts which are reserved) or the general principles of delictual or criminal liability could be competent on the grounds of making 'consistent provision'.

To assist the interpretation of s 29(4); s 126(4) and (5) define the terms 'Scots private law' and 'Scots criminal law'. The former is defined to include the general principles of private law, the law of persons, the law of obligations, the law of property and the law of actions (including judicial review). 'Criminal law' includes criminal offences, jurisdiction, evidence, procedure and penalties and the treatment of offenders[18].

1 See, for instance, the Gaelic Language (Scotland) Act 2005.
2 Cm 3658, para 3.2.
3 See D Stockley 'The Increasingly Strange Case of Abortion: Scots Criminal Law and Devolution' HC Debs 31 March 1998, col 1093; HL Debs 3 November 1998, col 203. HC Debs 31 March 1998, (1998) 2 Edin LR 330–337 and the Scotland Bill debate on this issue.
4 For discussion of abortion issues and the reservation of abortion to Westminster see, for example, the Public Petitions Committee, SP PE OR, 6 November 2001, col 1396. First Minister Alex Salmond was reported in September 2007 to support the creation of a commission to consider whether abortion should cease to be a devolved matter.
5 See para 4.21.
6 Report, Pillar 2.
7 See para 7.19.
8 As to LCMs, see para 6.22.
9 See para 7.26.
10 As to which, see ch 11.

11 SA 1998, Sch 5, Pt II, S A1.
12 See ch 11.
13 See ch 14. See especially the treatment (para 14.22) of SA 1998, s 101.
14 In a slightly different but related context, s 126(3) of SA 1998 (concerning whether Scottish Government functions relate to reserved matters) uses the formula 'likely effects in all the circumstances'. Are 'likely effects' different from an 'effect'?
15 Not irrelevant, of course, to the purpose of a provision is any evidence of 'purpose' revealed in debates in the Parliament at the time of the passing of the Bill, reinforcing the statements of competence formally made by a minister and the Presiding Officer at the time of a Bill's introduction. See para 9.10. Note, too, that explanations of a Bill's competence are now attached to proposals from the Scottish Law Commission. A drafting technique which has been adopted in some ASPs has been to define terms by reference to the specific language of SA 1998, for example the Local Government in Scotland Act 2003, s 59 which defines 'equal opportunities' by reference to SA 1998, Sch 5, Pt II, S L2.
16 See para 14.22.
17 See also SA 1998, Sch 4, discussed below.
18 For the Supreme Court's interpretation of s 29(4), see *Martin v Most* 2010 UKSC 10 which is discussed at para 14.25.

Limitations on legislative competence: Scotland Act 1998, Sch 4

6.19   SA 1998, s 29(2)(c) provides that a provision in an Act of the Scottish Parliament is outside the Parliament's competence if it is in breach of the restrictions in SA 1998, Sch 4. As originally drafted, SA 1998, Sch 4 had a very simple purpose: it was designed to protect the Act itself from amendment by the Scottish Parliament. It would make a nonsense of a constitutional arrangement designed to structure the Parliament in a particular way, and to limit its powers, if the Parliament itself could amend SA 1998 at will. The terms of the Act needed to be 'entrenched'[1] against amendment, or at least, many of the Act's provisions require such protection – especially those which define the Parliament's powers. Arguably, other sections of SA 1998 need not be protected for all time. They provide some initial rules for devolved government which can quite reasonably be amended or repealed by the Scottish Parliament without jeopardising the integrity of the devolution scheme as a whole. Such qualified protection of SA 1998 is provided by Sch 4, para 4(1) which states that an 'Act of the Scottish Parliament cannot modify, or confer power by subordinate legislation to modify, this Act'. The paragraph goes on, however, to set out a list of exceptions to that prohibition[2]. Thus, for instance, the Scottish Parliament could, if it wished, modify[3] the rules governing legal proceedings against the Parliament itself, defamation and contempt of court in relation to proceedings of the Parliament and corrupt practices in the Parliament which are contained in SA 1998, ss 40, 41, 42 and 43 respectively[4]. Similarly, the Scottish Parliament is able to amend many of the financial provisions in SA 1998, Pt III. On the other hand, it is not permitted to amend core rules such as that which secures judicial salaries and thus assists in the protection of judicial independence[5]. Another specific protection given by SA 1998, Sch 4 is of the provisions under which by s 56 executive powers are reserved on a shared basis even though they would otherwise be wholly devolved to the Scottish Ministers[6]. Once again, the point here is to protect from amendment provisions which are fundamental to the devolution scheme itself.

The restrictions on the modification of SA 1998 were themselves amended to enable the Scottish Parliament to legislate in response to the decision of the House of Lords in *Somerville v Scottish Ministers*[7] which confirmed that the one year time limit under the HRA 1998 for bringing claims for breaches of Convention rights did not apply to claims brought for breach of Convention rights against the Scottish Ministers under SA 1998. The UK government made the Scotland Act 1998 (Modification of Schedule 4) Order 2009[8], extending the legislative competence of the Scottish Parliament in a very specific manner and this was followed by the passing by the Scottish Parliament of the Convention Rights Proceedings (Amendment) (Scotland) Act 2009, the terms of which mirrored that extension of legislative competence[9]. In addition to protecting most of SA 1998 itself from amendment by the Scottish Parliament, Sch 4 serves two other main purposes as a result of changes made during the passing of the Scotland Bill in 1998. First, it prevents the Parliament from amending certain other specified pieces of legislation. It entrenches provisions in the Acts of Union concerning freedom of trade, certain provisions of ECA 1972 and HRA 1998 as well as some other Acts of the UK Parliament[10]. Thus, although human rights are not a reserved matter under SA 1998, Sch 5, the particular mode of incorporation of the ECHR by HRA 1998 is protected by SA 1998, Sch 4[11]. The other main purpose of SA 1998, Sch 4 is to augment the provision made elsewhere in relation to reserved matters. As we have seen, SA 1998, Sch 5 identifies the reserved matters which are beyond the legislative competence of the Scottish Parliament and SA 1998, s 29(3) provides that the question of whether a provision of an Act of the Scottish Parliament 'relates to a reserved matter' is to be determined by reference to the purpose of that provision. This enables legislation to be passed by the Parliament which might well have an impact upon a reserved matter but, because its 'purpose' is to make law in a devolved area, the legislation will be competent. Now, however, SA 1998, Sch 4, para 2 adds a further restriction by protecting from modification 'the law on reserved matters' regardless of the 'purpose' of the Act of the Scottish Parliament. The 'law on reserved matters' – defined to include Acts of the UK Parliament, subordinate legislation or non-statutory rules of law (ie the common law) whose subject matter is reserved – is entrenched in much the same way as most of SA 1998 itself and the other enumerated Acts such as HRA 1998. Thus, to take an example mentioned earlier, an Act of the Scottish Parliament could legitimately affect coal mining, provided that its purpose is to prevent pollution. That Act could not, however, modify UK legislation whose subject matter is the coal industry. That general rule is subject to two qualifications. One allows a small exception in the case of modifications which are 'incidental to, or consequential on' provision made (by the same Act or another enactment) which does not relate to reserved matters. To be permissible, such modifications must not 'have a greater effect on reserved matters than is necessary to give effect to the purpose of the provision'[12]. Thus to stay with the mining example, an Act of the Scottish Parliament cannot in principle amend the Coal Industry Act 1994, even if the general purpose of the legislation is to prevent pollution. If, however, the amendment can be treated as merely 'incidental' and 'necessary' to achieve the pollution prevention purpose, such an amendment *is* permitted.

The other qualification raises once again the special status accorded by SA 1998 to Scots private law and Scots criminal law to take account of their inherent propensity to straddle the divide between reserved and devolved subject matter. Here in SA 1998, in Sch 4, the effect is to limit the restriction on the Scottish Parliament's powers to modify 'the law on reserved matters' where that law is such a rule of Scots private or criminal law[13]. If this is the case, the rule against modifying reserved matters applies only to the extent that the rule in question is *'special to a reserved matter'* or the subject matter of the rule is one of a defined list. That list[14] includes 'interest on sums due in respect of taxes or excise duties and refunds of such taxes or duties' and 'the obligations, in relation to occupational or personal pension schemes, of the trustees or managers'.

As to rules which are *'special to a reserved matter'* SA 1998, provides no further guidance. In parliamentary debate on the Bill, however, the Minister explained that it is 'important to ensure that the Scottish Parliament can legislate on the general rules of Scots private law and criminal law across the board and without fragmenting the general principles which distinguish Scots law as a separate system of law. The test in SA 1998, Sch 4 applies generally. In the case of Scots private and criminal law, however, it applies only to certain specified aspects of private law and to the rules of Scots private and criminal law which are special to reserved matters – those which result in a distinct and separate treatment of a reserved matter[15].

Three examples of rules 'special to a reserved matter' were suggested: the Copyright, Design and Patents Act 1988, s 90 which provides for assignation of copyright; the rule that gaming contracts cannot be enforced because they are *sponsiones ludicrae*; and the Proceeds of Crime (Scotland) Act 1995 which provides for confiscation of proceeds of drug trafficking. On the other hand, an example given of rules lacking such a 'special' character were those defining how a person may sign a document under Scots law – rules which may apply to both reserved and devolved areas.

The dividing line between the 'special' and the 'non-special' was not, however, going to be easy to discern and, as we shall see, it has atttarcted controversy and a deep division of opinion in the Supreme Court[16].

In addition to providing a form of protection for these three categories of 'entrenched' provisions – SA 1998 itself, the particular named enactments, and the law on reserved matters – Sch 4 makes two other types of provision. The first is to enact some general exceptions to the restrictions the Schedule has imposed on the powers of the Scottish Parliament. In particular, none of those restrictions prevents the Parliament from merely restating (eg by codification) the law in ways which would otherwise be prohibited by the Schedule[17]. The other set of provisions concern the transfer of *Scottish Government* powers. They permit powers to pass to the Scottish Ministers even though legislative power is prevented by SA 1998, Sch 4 from passing to the Scottish Parliament[18].

---

1   Not the language actually used in SA 1998 itself, but, in equivalent circumstances, the Northern Ireland Act 1998 does refer to 'Entrenched enactments' (see Northern Ireland Act 1998, s 7).

2   SA 1998, Sch 4, para 4(2)–(5), as modified by the Scotland Act 1998 (Modifications of Schedules 4 and 5) Order 1999, SI 1999/1749 and the Scotland Act 1998 (Modifications of Schedule 4) Order 2000, SI 2000/1831.
3   Including modification by amendment or repeal: SA 1998, s 126(1).
4   The Smith Commission recommended that the Scottish Parliament be given 'powers to make decisions about all matters relating to the arrangements and operations of the Scottish Parliament and Government'.
5   SA 1998, Sch 4, paras 4(3) and 5(a). See ch 12.
6   SA 1998, Sch 4, para 6. See para 7.19.
7   2008 SC (HL) 45 and see para 14.29.
8   SI 2009/1380.
9   For discussion of the Bill's designation as an emergency bill see para 9.15. The amendment to the Schedule and the Act were subsequently replaced by provisions in SA 2012, s 14.
10   Private Legislation Procedure (Scotland) Act 1936; Local Government, Planning and Land Act 1980; and Social Security Administration Act 1992.
11   See C Himsworth 'The Hamebringing: Devolving Rights Seriously' in A Boyle et al (eds) *Human Rights and Scots Law* (2002). The reservation did not prevent the Parliament from enacting the Scottish Commission for Human Rights Act 2006 (see para 13.14) but did apparently allow the UK Parliament to legislate in connection with the definition of public authority in the Human Rights Act 1998 without the need for a legislative consent motion: see Health and Social Care Act 2008, s 145.
12   SA 1998, Sch 4, para 3(1) and as to the assessment of what is 'necessary' to give effect to the purpose of a provision see SA 1998, Sch 4, para 3(2).
13   Whether contained in a statute or the common law.
14   This list was expanded by the Scotland Act 1998 (Modifications of Schedule 4) Order 2000, SI 2000/1831 to take into account of the Welfare Reform and Pensions Act 1999. All relate to aspects of fiscal, pension and social security regimes reserved by SA 1998, Sch 5.
15   HL Debs 21 July 1998, col 821.
16   See *Martin v Most* 2010 SC (UKSC) 40 and the discussion at para 14.25.
17   SA 1998, Sch 4, para 7. In addition, other provisions of SA 1998, Sch 4, Pt II permit the Parliament to change the titles of judges and certain public officials and to change procedures for the making of subordinate legislation.
18   SA 1998, Sch 4, para 12.

Limitations on legislative competence: Convention rights and EU law

6.20   In addition to the restraints imposed by SA 1998, Sch 5 on legislation relating to reserved matters (as elaborated by s 29(3)) and Sch 4 in relation to private and criminal law, there remain three further limitations on legislative competence imposed by s 29 itself. Two are prescribed by SA 1998, s 29(2)(d) which states that a provision in an ASP is beyond the competence of the Parliament if it is incompatible with any of the Convention rights[1] or with EU law[2].

The justification for these constraints, against the wider background of the incorporation of the ECHR by HRA 1998[3] and of the implementation of EU law in the United Kingdom by ECA 1972 is quite straightforward. Both regimes demand a subordination of UK law-making to the 'higher' rules they introduce and, although difficulties have been encountered on the road to accepting the subordination of UK Acts to EU law[4] and UK Acts are given a form of protected status under HRA 1998[5], there is no doubt about the obligation to read the terms of ASPs subject to rules of the two European regimes. In the case of HRA 1998, ASPs are specifically defined as 'subordinate legislation', which parallels the effect of SA 1998, s 29(2)(d): there is room for an argument that ASPs, as the product of a parliament rather than merely the decisions of public officials, should have been treated more like Westminster Acts[6] but the enacted rules reject that.

1 Defined by s 126(1) as having 'the same meaning as in the Human Rights Act 1998'. It was intended that there would be symmetry between SA 1998 (and indeed the Northern Ireland Act 1998 and the Government of Wales Act 1998) and HRA 1998. The latter defines 'Convention rights' as those described in articles of the ECHR set out in HRA 1998, Sch 1.
2 Defined by SA 1998, s 126(9) as '(a) all those rights, powers, liabilities, obligations and restrictions from time to time created or arising by or under the Community Treaties, and (b) all those remedies and procedures from time to time provided for by or under the Community Treaties'.
3 In fact, however, HRA 1998 was not fully implemented until 2 October 2000, over a year after the Scottish Parliament acquired its powers on 1 July 1999. Provision was made in SA 1998 itself for relevant provisions (including s 29(2)(d)) to have effect during that period, despite the non-implementation of HRA 1998 upon which they relied SA 1998, (s 129(2)). For discussion of activity during 1999–2000 and the relationship between the two Acts, see I Jamieson 'Relationship between the Scotland Act and the Human Rights Act' 2001 SLT (News) 43; C Himsworth 'Rights versus Devolution' in T Campbell et al (eds) *Sceptical Essays on Human Rights* (2001); C Himsworth 'Human Rights at the Interface of State and Sub-State: The Case of Scotland' in T Campbell, KD Ewing and A Tomkins (eds), *The Legal Protection of Human Rights* (2011); and C Himsworth, 'Devoluted Human Rights' in C Gearty and C Douzinas (eds), *Human Rights Law* (2012). See also para 14.15 below.
4 See paras 6.8–6.10.
5 HRA 1998, s 4 enables a 'declaration of incompatibility' to be made in respect of 'primary legislation' (the definition of which excludes ASPs) but does not empower the courts to 'strike down' an Act of the UK Parliament which is incompatible with Convention rights. See para 14.17.
6 See C Himsworth 'Rights versus Devolution' in T Campbell et al (eds) *Sceptical Essays on Human Rights* (2001). For litigation which has challenged ASPs on grounds of incompatibility with Convention rights see para 14.19.

Limitations on legislative competence: the position of the Lord Advocate

6.21   The final restriction on the legislative competence of the Parliament relates specifically to the position of the Lord Advocate. It should be noted that, although the Lord Advocate is a member of the Scottish Government and he is competent to exercise powers allocated collectively to the Scottish Ministers[1], he also has quite separate functions to be exercised independently[2]. These are the decisions made in the Lord Advocate's capacity as head of the systems of criminal prosecution and investigation of deaths in Scotland in which his independence[3] and freedom from political interference are at a premium. By SA 1998, s 29(2)(e), the Lord Advocate's independence is also placed – with a prominence which would not have been achieved by its inclusion simply as a reserved matter in Sch 5 – beyond the legislative reach of the Parliament. However, while the general justification for the protection of the Lord Advocate's powers may be clear, it might stand in the way of the adoption of a policy to confer a power to prosecute statutory offences on certain regulatory authorities – an area in which there is currently a marked difference between Scotland and England[4].

1 See para 7.20.
2 SA 1998, s 48(5).

3 See ch 2.

4 In environmental matters, for instance, the Environment Agency can prosecute while the Scottish Environment Protection Agency must refer potential prosecutions to the procurator fiscal.

WESTMINSTER LEGISLATION ON DEVOLVED MATTERS

6.22   It has already been pointed out that SA 1998 expressly preserves the power of the Westminster Parliament to make laws for Scotland[1] which includes the possibility of laws which are within the legislative competence of the Scottish Parliament. As former First Minister Dewar stated, 'in a devolved system, it could not be otherwise'[2]. This rightly implies that Westminster could, in theory, use its powers either to reform the structure of devolved government or, leaving that in place, to make legislation which could override the wishes of Holyrood. It was, however, explained, as the Scotland Bill proceeded through Parliament, that the UK government did not expect that the powers would be used other than with the Scottish Parliament's consent[3]. It was assumed that a convention would be established to that effect. In accordance with such a convention it might, for instance, be convenient to use Westminster legislation to incorporate the terms of an international treaty which covered both reserved and devolved matters[4].

Since the setting up of the Scottish Parliament, this approach has been reaffirmed in both Parliaments and the 'Sewel convention' has become an established part of the architecture of devolution. In particular, First Minister Dewar restated the understanding that the UK government would not introduce proposals to legislate, without consent, on devolved matters and would oppose any private member's Bill which sought to do so[5]. Any UK government proposal would have to be placed before the Scottish Parliament and Westminster business adjusted accordingly. An initial example of such legislation which was immediately taken forward on that basis was the Food Standards Act 1999[6], the justification being that a single regime of regulation across the United Kingdom would be appropriate. Consent is given by the Scottish Parliament by passing a 'legislative consent motion'[7]. A legislative consent motion (LCM) is debated following the lodging by the Scottish government of a legislative consent memorandum which summarises the provisions and policy objectives of the UK Bill in question, specifies those provisions which are within the competence of the Parliament or the Scottish Ministers and explains why it is thought appropriate for the Bill to make such a provision. A legislative consent memorandum is also required in relation to the UK Bills which include such provisions even where the Scottish Government does not intend to lodge an LCM. In relation to delegated legislation made in respect of Scotland by UK ministers, there is no general requirement to obtain the consent of the Scottish Parliament, although such orders or regulations may sometimes require the consent of the Scottish Ministers before they can be made[8]. However, the UK Public Bodies Act 2011 (itself passed with an LCM because it enables the abolition of bodies with devolved powers in Scotland) created a special style of order which, by statute (s 8 of the 2011 Act) rather than convention, requires a consent motion in the Scottish Parliament[9].

It remains open to the Scottish Parliament to amend or repeal measures enacted by Westminster pursuant to a legislative consent motion so far as they fall within the Parliament's competence. There can, in other words, be no question of inferring that an encroachment by Westminster into the devolved area produces a permanent enlargement of the reserved matters and an implied amendment of SA 1998, Sch 5. The terms of SA 1998, s 28(7) plainly accommodate the possibility of such Westminster legislation within the devolution settlement's own terms[10].

There has been greater use of the Sewel convention than might have been anticipated and a considerable amount of debate about that use within the Scottish and UK Parliaments[11] and elsewhere. So, for example, early research showed that in the period to 30 April 2002 30 LCMs were debated in the Scottish Parliament to approve the extension of provisions in Westminster Bills to Scotland in areas of devolved subject matter[12]. Perhaps ironically, though early LCMs provided a ready target for the (SNP) opposition in the Scottish Parliament[13] on the basis that they demonstrate a dependence on Westminster and a surrender of autonomy inappropriate to the devolution scheme, during the SNP administrations, the third and fourth sessions of the Parliament have seen a continuing steady use of the procedure[14].

The use of LCMs raises interesting questions relevant to the overall relationship of 'partnership' between Edinburgh and London. They are part of the regime of co-operation under the Memorandum of Understanding and concordats established between the UK and devolved governments[15] and may be understood as part of that wider pattern of inter-governmental relationships. There remains, however, a legitimate interest in (1) the extent and purposes of the use of LCMs; (2) an explanation of why they have occurred so often; and (3) an understanding of the problems raised by their use. As to (1), the extent of use has been mentioned. While the types of legislation for which such motion may be used would include legislation to alter the legislative competence of the Scottish Parliament[16] or the competence of the Scottish Government[17], the main purpose has been that originally conceived – to legislate for devolved purposes. In turn, this last category subdivided, in the early analysis of Alan Page and Andrea Batey[18], into five suggested justifications: to include Scotland in UK-wide reforms; to implement international obligations; to enable Scottish participation in UK arrangements; to give UK bodies the same powers (or constraints on powers); and to give Scottish bodies the same powers as those enjoyed elsewhere in the United Kingdom.

On (2), explanations for frequency of use, Page and Batey saw these principally in terms of a higher-than-predicted quest for uniformity of provision, whether because of high electoral expectation of similar rules, the need for regulatory equivalence, or (during the first two Holyrood sessions) because of the similarity of political commitment of governments in Edinburgh and London. Even these rationales for uniformity do not necessarily, however, justify legislation at Westminster rather than Holyrood where the explanation derives from a preference for immediate action on a Westminster initiative rather than a probable delay while a Holyrood Bill is drafted and enacted; a wish to avoid disruption of the Scottish Government's own legislative programme; and perhaps to avoid challenge in the courts (whether by an individual or even the UK government) to a Scottish Bill close to the limits of legislative competence.

Even if the use of LCMs to enable legislation at Westminster is justifiable or, at least, explicable in these ways, it does not mean that the practice is free from difficulties[19]. At a purely practical level, the frequent use of Westminster legislation is aggravating the problems of a divided statute book. Reserved matters quite apart, even law on devolved matters is uneasily split between UK Acts and ASPs. More important is the surrender of scrutiny of 'Sewel' Bills to the Westminster Parliament[20] where they may receive little attention from a specifically Scottish perspective. And there are also problems with the LCM procedure itself. At the time a motion is passed in the Scottish Parliament, it may be unclear what exactly is being approved and difficulties have arisen, unsurprisingly, over the extent to which an LCM can be taken to accommodate significant changes at Westminster to the Bill as first conceived. Although primarily directed towards the West Lothian Question, the Mackay Report[21] commented on LCM procedures including those arising out of amendments to Bills as they proceed at Westminster[22] and made some reforming proposals (paras 263–274) for consideration by a new Devolution Committee of the House of Commons. The Commission was concerned, in particular, that LCMs should be accorded a more formal status at Westminster and MPs should be better informed about the content of LCMs (actual or proposed) as Bills proceed.

A more recent intervention came with the Report of the Smith Commission in November 2014[23] which proposed, rather baldly, that the 'Sewel Convention will be put on a statutory footing' (para 22). The mechanism whereby that would be achieved was not at that stage discussed. To put it mildly, the convention's conversion to a statutory base may create problems with accommodating the supremacy of the Westminster Parliament.

1   SA 1998, s 28(7) and para 6.11.
2   SP OR 9 June 1999, col 358.
3   HL Debs 21 July 1998, col 791 (Lord Sewel).
4   *Scotland's Parliament* para 4.4.
5   SP OR, 9 June 1999, col 358. See also House of Commons Procedure Committee Fourth Report, *The Procedural Consequences of Devolution* HC Paper 185 (1998–99).
6   For the Sewel motion see SP OR 23 June 1999, col 675.
7   This terminology was introduced in 2005 following an inquiry conducted by the Parliament's Procedures Committee, see SP Paper 428 (2005) and SOs Chapter 9B.
8   See para 7.19.
9   See para 8.14. It may also be observed that one of the Conservative options in Cm 8969 (para 4.21) for the solution of the 'English Votes for English Laws' question was a system of LCMs granted by English MPs.
10 For a contrary view see N Burrows 'This is Scotland's Parliament; let Scotland's Parliament legislate' 2002 JR 213, based on the assumption that, '[i]t is outwith the competence of the Scottish Parliament to amend UK legislation' (p 236). For examples of such amendments, including amendment of post-devolution UK legislation, see the Mental Health (Care and Treatment) (Scotland) Act 2003, sch 5. Interestingly, SA 1978, s 17(2) had provided expressly that 'A Scottish Assembly Act may amend or repeal a provision made by or under an Act of Parliament'.
11 See the Procedures Committee report referred to at note 7 above; the report of the House of Lords Select Committee on the Constitution *Devolution: Inter-Institutional Relations in the UK* HL Paper 28 (2002–03); the report of the House of Commons Scottish Affairs Committee on The Sewel Convention: the Westminster perspective HC (2005–06) 983; A Page and A Batey 'Scotland's Other Parliament: Westminster Legislation about Devolved Matters in Scotland Since Devolution' [2002] PL 501, (upon which this section draws heavily); B K Winetrobe 'Counter-Devolution? The Sewel Convention on Devolved Legislation at Westminster' 2001

SLPQ 6(4) 286; J Munro, Thoughts on the Sewel Convention, 2003 SLT News 194; *CSG Inquiry* and SP OR 11 June 2002, col 1620.

12 Page and Batey, p 503.

13 See for example K MacAskill and M Curran, 'Is Holyrood passing the buck' 2005 JLSS 50(3) 20.

14 In 2012–13, there were 13 LCMs and in 2013–14, 11.

15 See para 7.26. LCM procedures are set out in Devolution Guidance Note No 10 – 'Post-Devolution Primary Legislation Affecting Scotland'. Note also the use of SA 1998, s 57(1) to implement EU obligations. See para 6.24.

16 Not so far done, except by the alternative route of an Order in Council under SA 1998, s 30(2).

17 See the Learning and Skills Act 2000, s 104 and the Electronic Communications Act 2000, ss 8–9.

18 See n 11 above.

19 A special instance of LCM practice occurred in relation to the Bill leading to SA 2012. Though qualified in certain respects the initial LCM passed under the minority SNP administration on 10 March 2011 became a much more restricted motion at the hand of the SNP majority on 18 April 2012.

20 Including, for instance, scrutiny of delegated powers which would normally be undertaken by the Delegated Powers and Law Reform Committee at Holyrood.

21 Report of the Commission on the Consequences of Devolution for the House of Commons, March 2013. See para 5.9.

22 Noting also other circumstances in which other cross-border effects of legislation may arise (including SA 1998, s 104). See paras 80–103.

23 See para 4.21.

SUBORDINATE LEGISLATION MADE BY MINISTERS AND OTHERS

General considerations

6.23   It has been a well-known feature of law-making at the UK level that far more legislation is made each year by ministers than by Parliament. In purely quantitative terms, ministers[1] (mainly as 'the Secretary of State') make many more rules, regulations, schemes, orders and other forms of subordinate legislation – a great range of terminology is used – than is made by Parliament as Acts of Parliament. Some powers are formally exercisable by 'Her Majesty by Order in Council' but effective power lies, of course, with ministers[2]. In 2013, the number of statutory instruments, which include almost all subordinate legislation made by UK ministers, was nearly 3300 whereas the number of Public Acts of the Westminster Parliament was 33. Ministers make virtually all subordinate legislation under powers delegated to them (hence 'delegated legislation') by Parliament, although, in a very small number of cases, the authority derives from the royal prerogative[3]. It is, of course, fundamental to the idea of the rule of law that there should be such a primary source of authority for any rule-making power of ministers and it would be considered intolerable if ministers were to purport to make rules or regulations, other than in the exercise of powers conferred upon them. This was an abuse ended when completely discretionary law-making powers were wrested from the Crown and its ministers in the seventeenth century[4]. Today, the courts take a strict view of ministers who purport to exercise powers they do not have[5]. On the other hand, the courts cannot question the authority of Parliament to delegate law making powers to ministers if it chooses to do so. Under the terms of a written constitution, a legislature may be constrained in the powers it delegates[6] but the 'supreme' Westminster Parliament is not.

The question has still to be asked why the Westminster Parliament, even with the authority to do so, chooses to give legislative powers to ministers to produce delegated legislation on the scale already indicated. Why should Parliament wish to appear to breach the principle of the separation of powers by conferring legislative powers on the executive to such an extent? In part, the answer is technical in that what is formally promulgated as delegated *legislation* is frequently no more than a series of executive decisions. Each year until 1999, ministers[7] made a Local Government Finance (Scotland) Order[8] which allocated an amount of grant to each local authority in Scotland. This was really executive decision-making but it took the form of delegated *legislation*. In most other cases, however, subordinate legislation is more clearly *legislative* in character. Ministers are entrusted with powers to make rules and this requires some justification. The official explanation has remained broadly the same since the early part of the twentieth century and dates back to the Report of the Committee on Ministers' Powers in 1932[9]. In the period following the 1914–18 war, there developed a panic about what was perceived to be the rapid and uncontrolled expansion of executive power. Lord Hewart, the Lord Chief Justice of England, published his polemic *The New Despotism* in 1929 and the (Donoughmore) Committee on Ministers' Powers was set up in response. While making a number of proposals for the reform of governmental procedures, the Committee did acknowledge that executive power was not simply going to go away. The process of delegated law-making could be better structured and ministers could be made more accountable to Parliament but the case for extensive powers of delegated legislation had to be recognised. Central to that case was the argument that Parliament had no alternative but to delegate. The sheer quantity of the legislation required would be unmanageable if it had to be treated as primary legislation and taken as Bills through all their parliamentary stages. There would simply not be sufficient time. As we shall find[10], some delegated legislation does attract the need for limited parliamentary supervision but this is much less than would be required if it all made its way through Parliament as Bills. Other justifications which were offered by the Ministers' Powers Committee for bypassing full parliamentary scrutiny included the technicality of the subject matter of much delegated legislation, which made it less appropriate for discussion by parliamentarians and the need for flexibility. It is impossible for any government, when introducing primary legislation, to tie up every detailed aspect of its operation for all time. Occasions will arise when further changes to the law will be required to alter rules in response to events; to alter the terms of earlier legislation which may affect the operation of the new rules in unexpected ways; and to alter the pace of introduction of the new rules. One way in which this is done is by making the operation of most primary legislation dependent upon the making of commencement orders by ministers to bring them into effect, often in a number of separate stages according to a timetable which can be adopted and amended, as required, after the primary legislation itself has been passed. A special need for flexibility justifies the conferring of particularly wide powers on ministers in times of emergency. Parliamentary procedures do permit the accelerated passage of Bills and this is sufficient to meet the needs of some forms of emergency situation[11] but more aggravated civil emergencies may demand a response which is even more rapid. This is an area which has seen significant legislative activity recently. The Emergency Powers Act 1920[12] which empowered the Queen to make a *proclamation of emergency* when, or when it is anticipated that, 'events of such a nature as to be calculated, by interfering with the supply and distribution of food, water, fuel, or light, or with the means of locomotion, to deprive the community, or any substantial portion of the community, of the essentials of life'[13] was replaced with the Civil Contingencies Act 2004 which imposes duties and confers powers to deal with events or situations which threaten serious damage to 'human welfare in a place in the United Kingdom', 'the environment of a place in the United Kingdom' or 'war or terrorism which threatens serious damage to the security of the United Kingdom[14].

Despite the substantially changed circumstances of British government in the 80 years or so since the 1932 Report, broadly the same justifications for the use of delegated legislation tend to be offered today. One consequence of this has been that, when the Scottish Parliament was proposed and thought given to how its business would be done[15], the assumption was made that the delegation of law-making powers to the Scottish Ministers would be a necessary part of the package[16]. Certainly, no doubts were ever expressed that the general legislative competence of the Parliament included the power to delegate to ministers, although there was discussion of the use to which the powers might be put[17].

This continued acceptance of the case for subordinate legislation at both the UK and Scottish levels does not mean, however, that some of the explanations for the need for ministerial law-making power should not be looked at quite sceptically by each generation. Ministers will always tend to be attracted by this relatively uncontrolled power and the Westminster Parliament and the Scottish Parliament have shown themselves to be alert to some of the dangers. The sheer quantity of delegated legislation is a principal concern while powers given to ministers to amend primary legislation cause a particular constitutional frisson. Such powers have been dubbed 'Henry VIII clauses' at Westminster because of the potential threat they present, but they vary greatly in significance. At one end of the scale they are a necessary and merely technical adjunct to major new primary legislation. Powers to make delegated legislation are required to enable ministers to amend existing statutes to allow full effect to be given to the new provisions. At the other end of the scale are the very substantial powers which were conferred by, for instance, the Deregulation and Contracting Out Act 1994, the Convention Rights (Compliance) (Scotland) Act 2001, and Part 2 of the Public Services Reform (Scotland) Act 2010.

Another area of sensitivity is the delegation of powers which might release direct parliamentary control of financial matters. There has been a reluctance to delegate powers to vary rates of taxation and, at Holyrood, the power of the Scottish Ministers to authorise appropriations under the Public Finance and Accountability (Scotland) Act 2000 by Budget Acts raised rather similar concerns[18]. It was eventually accepted that, once initial appropriations had been made in the annual Budget (Scotland) Act, variations could be made by order by the Scottish Ministers. Other concerns can arise in relation to the use of subordinate legislation with retrospective effect or in such a way as to exclude review by the courts.

Another principal concern at Westminster and Holyrood has been the tendency for primary legislation to delegate to ministers not only matters of detail but also matters of core legislative provision. The Scottish Parliament's Education (Graduate Endowments and Student Support) (Scotland) Act 2001 made provision, in one section, for the endowment scheme itself and left all else to regulations to be made by the Scottish Ministers. SA 1998 itself provides several examples of potentially wide-ranging law making powers delegated to ministers which might, on their face, by vulnerable to abuse. The power in SA 1998, s 30(2) to amend, by Order in Council, the terms of Schs 4 and 5[19] avoids the need for primary legislation but gives substantial power to UK ministers. The powers contained in SA 1998, ss 63 and 108 to transfer executive functions from UK ministers to the Scottish Ministers and vice versa[20] are also significant; and the power in SA 1998, s 107 'to remedy ultra vires acts' of the Scottish Parliament or the Scottish Government is another[21]. These and many others are listed in SA 1998, Sch 7 but what is also important about the Schedule is that it prescribes the model of parliamentary scrutiny (mainly at Westminster but, in some cases, also at Holyrood) for each class of instrument. It is this parliamentary accountability, discussed in Chapter 9, and also the legal accountability (Chapter 14) of delegated law-making which lift some of the constitutional concern which would otherwise attach to the allocation of broad powers to ministers.

1 For executive powers in general, see ch 7.
2 The number of *devolved* powers exercisable by Order in Council is not large but, for instance, the Census (Scotland) Order 2000, SSI 2000/68 is an example. New powers to legislate by Order in Council conferred by ASPs have, again, not been numerous but the power in the Scottish Public Services Ombudsman Act 2002, s 3 to amend the Ombudsman's jurisdiction is an example.
3 As explained in para 7.23, until recently one continuing prerogative legislative power was that used to regulate the civil service. It was an instruction made under the Civil Service Order in Council that was unsuccessfully challenged in *CCSU v Minister for the Civil Service* [1985] AC 374.
4 See Claim of Right 1689.
5 See ch 14 below.
6 In the United States, see inter alia *Schechter Poultry Corp v United States* 295 US 495 (1935).
7 From 2000, the Scottish Ministers: see below.
8 See Local Government Finance (Scotland) Order 1999, SI 1999/364.
9 *Report of the Committee on Ministers' Powers* (Cmd 4060).
10 See ch 9.
11 See, for example, the Mental Health (Public Safety and Appeals) (Scotland) Act 1999 and para 9.15.
12 As amended by the Emergency Powers Act 1964.
13 EPA 1920, s 1.
14 Civil Contingencies Act 2004, s 1.
15 As earlier explained it can be argued that all ASPs are themselves subordinate legislation of a sort. HRA 1998, for its purposes, does so classify them and ASPs are judicially challengeable, although on grounds different from rules made by ministers (see ch 14). For present purposes, ASPs are better regarded as primary legislation.
16 See the *Report of the Consultative Steering Group on the Scottish Parliament* (1998), paras 27–33.
17 See C Himsworth 'Subordinate Legislation in the Scottish Parliament' (2002) 6 Edin LR 356.

18 See SP SL or SP Paper 69 (2000).
19 See para 6.17.
20 See para 7.19.
21 See para 7.26.

Delegated law-making powers in Scotland

6.24   The implementation of SA 1998 created a situation in which there are now four broad categories of ministerial subordinate legislation in relation to Scotland:

(a)   *Subordinate legislation made by Ministers of the Crown* (including legislation made as Orders in Council) in relation to reserved matters. Existing powers of UK ministers continue in relation, for instance, to social security.

(b)   *Subordinate legislation by the Scottish Ministers under powers conferred by Acts of the Scottish Parliament.* Many such ASPs have been passed. There is no doubt about the formal competence of the Parliament to delegate law-making powers to the Scottish Ministers and to others, provided, of course, that the powers would, in other respects, be within the Parliament's legislative competence. It is not competent for the Parliament to purport to enable others to legislate on matters on which the Parliament itself could not legislate[1]. It might further be speculated that an ASP which was itself skeletal but which conferred extremely wide powers on ministers might be challengeable – in a way that a Westminster Act would not – on the ground that the Parliament was failing to perform the duty to 'make laws' laid down by SA 1998, s 28(1).

(c)   *Subordinate legislation under powers transferred from UK ministers to the Scottish Ministers under SA 1998.* Many of the powers exercisable by the Scottish Ministers are not powers conferred directly by the Scottish Parliament but are the powers transferred, within 'devolved competence', from UK ministers under SA 1998, ss 53–54[2] and also those transferred, as additional Government powers, under SA 1998, s 63. This pattern extends to powers of delegated law-making (including legislation by Order in Council), most of which has so far been made under the transferred powers. These include the power, under ECA 1972, s 2(2)[3] to implement EU law in Scotland[4]. The very first Scottish Statutory Instrument – the Environmental Impact Assessment (Scotland) Regulations 1999, SSI 1999/1 – was such a measure.

There is no general power retained by UK ministers to exercise lawmaking functions in the areas transferred to the Scottish Ministers (and, therefore, no scope for a general equivalent of the Sewel convention[5] to govern when that retained power might be exercised) but it should be recalled that certain specified powers[6], including some powers of delegated law-making, are shared powers which may be exercised by ministers at both levels. A special instance of shared power is that conferred on UK ministers, as well as the Scottish Ministers, by SA 1998, s 57(1) to implement EU obligations. The agreed use of this power by UK ministers is often,for instance, because the impact of an instrument would be minor and technical, or because there is no particularly Scottish interest in it.

(d)   A final category of ministerial subordinate legislation includes *powers conferred directly on the Scottish Ministers by post-devolution Acts of the Westminster Parliament.* Examples include the powers conferred by the Energy Act 2008, s 34[7], enabling the Scottish Ministers to transfer functions relating to the licensing of carbon capture and storage schemes to another body (eg SEPA). Although the most important powers to make delegated legislation (both in constitutional and purely quantitative terms) are those exercisable by ministers, other public bodies enjoy *byelaw-making powers* to enable them to carry out their functions. Scottish local authorities have general powers (subject to confirmation by the Scottish Ministers) to make byelaws under the Local Government (Scotland) Act 1973, s 201 for the 'good rule and government' of their areas and for the 'prevention and suppression of nuisances' and they have certain, more specific, powers under the Civic Government (Scotland) Act 1982[8]. The national park authorities have powers to make byelaws and management rules[9] and bodies such as rail operators[10] also have byelaw-making powers.

1   That is a consequence expressly prohibited by, for example, SA 1998, ss 29, 54.
2   Most such powers are contained in 'pre-commencement enactments', a category which may be extended to include powers in post-devolution UK Acts which expressly declare themselves to be such 'pre-commencement enactments'. See, for example, Pollution Prevention and Control Act 1999, s 5(3).
3   See SA 1998, Sch 8, para 15 which amends ECA 1972 for this purpose. Although the generally implied assumption in SA 1998 that any Orders in Council in devolved areas would be made on the advice of Scottish (rather than UK) ministers, para 15 does make specific reference to Orders 'made on the recommendation of the First Minister'.
4   See para 3.13.
5   See para 6.22, including discussion of the (statutory) consent motions under the Public Bodies Act 2011.
6   SA 1998, s 56(1), (2).
7   Such powers are to be distinguished from those transferred under 'pre-commencement enactments'. See above.
8   SA 1998, ss 112–118 (management rules), 121 (byelaws to control seashore).
9   National Parks (Scotland) Act 2000, sch 2, paras 8–10.
10 Railways Act 2005, s 46 and Sch 9.

THE EUROPEAN UNION

6.25   The impact of the European Union upon law-making in the United Kingdom has already been noted in earlier sections of this chapter. EU law has successfully asserted superiority over Acts of the UK Parliament[1] and, as a result, the most fundamental rule of the constitution has been changed. It is also clear that all legislation made by the Scottish Parliament and by the Scottish Ministers is subordinate to EU law but that Acts of either Parliament or delegated legislation by UK ministers or the Scottish Ministers under ECA 1972 are used to implement EU rules. The superior status of EU law should not, however, lead us to conclude that the Community can issue legislation on any subject whatever. The Union's lawmaking competence is bounded by the terms of the Treaty on European Union (TEU)[2] and the tasks of the Court of Justice include ruling not only on the compatibility of national law with EU law but also on the compatibility of EU legislation with the Treaties.

The treaties allocate powers to the Union in both fairly specific and more general terms[3]. A limited number of competences are exclusive to the Union. Others are competences shared between the EU and the Member States. Among the exclusive competences are powers in relation to the common commercial policy (towards third countries), the customs union, and some aspects (marine biological resources) of the common fisheries policy. Shared competences include those in relation to the internal market, agriculture and fisheries, transport, energy, social policy, the environment and consumer protection[4]. These are supplemented by a clause which enables the Council to take 'appropriate measures' to attain the objectives of the EU for which no specific power has been provided by the treaties[5]. The Union's powers also extend to competences in relation to the common foreign and security policy[6].

1 See paras 6.8–6.10.
2 See para 3.3.
3 For discussion, see *Edward and Lane on European Union Law* (2013) ch 7.
4 A restated list of these competences appears in the Treaty on the Functioning of the European Union (TFEU) art 4.
5 TFEU art 352.
6 See para 3.3 above and TFEU art 2.

Chapter 7

The UK and Scottish Governments

INTRODUCTION[1]

7.1   The Scottish campaign for devolution in the 1980s and 1990s was primarily a campaign for a Scottish Parliament. Although the language was that of '*self-government*', the principal focus was on establishing an elected assembly or parliament. Politically, that was what would make a difference. A parliament is a powerful symbol and, if given sufficient law-making competence, could bring real change. But parliaments, contrary to some generally held beliefs, do not govern. Parliaments do not, on the whole, have policies or programmes – although they may have some power to influence or control those who do. Parliaments do not themselves even implement policies and programmes. They do not, in the main, make decisions directly affecting the lives of individuals – although they may make the laws which provide the framework within which such decisions are made. Parliaments do not spend money – although, once again, they may give the authority to spend to those who do.

Those who make and implement policies; who make decisions; and who spend money are the holders of the executive powers of the state. The importance of these functions and, therefore, of the executive branch is self-evident and it is perhaps surprising that, in the run-up to constitutional reform in Scotland in 1998, the emphasis was so strongly upon the new Parliament rather than upon the new institutions of executive government that would also have to be created. In part, this is to be explained by the commitment simply to replicate for Scotland the model of parliamentary government already operating at the United Kingdom level rather than to create an executive on a presidential model with a much sharper differentiation of institutions and a stronger commitment to the separation of powers. Had a presidential model been sought, much more attention would have been paid to procedures for the election of a Scottish president, the powers of that president and the president's relationship to the Parliament. The adoption instead of a parliamentary model of government meant that the institutions required could be taken, with necessary modifications, from the Westminster peg. This is, on the other hand, no reason for belittling the significance of the executive branch of government on the parliamentary or Westminster model. Despite the absence of the formal prominence which would be given to a president, it is often the case that a government on the parliamentary model has greater overall power. In the relationship between government and Parliament, the balance tends to tip in favour of the government. Constitutional formalities apart, the principal political driving force lies in the executive branch. An account of parliamentary government is one in which the executive is viewed as central, with parliament as a, sometimes supporting and sometimes restraining, secondary force[2].

The subject matter of this chapter is, in brief, the executive at the UK level and then, more substantially, the executive in Scotland. The principal focus is, therefore, upon the teams of ministers and supporting civil servants headed by the UK Prime Minister and the Scottish First Minister. However, this focus has, to be qualified in two ways. In the first place, it has to be recognised that at neither the UK nor the Scottish level is all executive authority concentrated at the centre. Much executive power is dispersed to other bodies. Local authorities have extensive executive authority within their localities. Their responsibilities for matters such as school provision and social work are directly conferred on them by statute. In addition, a large number of executive functions are distributed at an 'intermediate level' (ie between central and local government) to public bodies – frequently dubbed 'quangos'. Some of these, such as health authorities, have local responsibilities. Traditionally, the primary distinction between local authorities and quangos is that members of local councils are elected while members of the governing boards of quangos are appointed[3]. Other quangos have a national remit. Both local authorities and quangos are dealt with in Chapter 8.

The other qualification to an account of executive authority which places the primary focus upon ministers and their civil servants is that the constitution continues to accord functions to the Sovereign (or to the 'Crown'). This may seem to be a strange way to introduce a person and institution whose formal role is often described as the head of state and the fount of executive authority. It was, however, the 19th-century commentator Walter Bagehot who, in 1867, provided us with a useful distinction in our analysis of the constitution which is nowhere better illustrated than in relation to the Queen. That was the distinction between the 'efficient' and, on the other hand, the merely 'dignified' aspects of the constitution[4]. The efficient aspects are those which are based on the actual working of the constitution. They reflect actual power and authority. The dignified aspects, on the other hand, are those which have a purely formal character in the modern constitution. Typically, they derive from historically founded constitutional relationships which were once real and efficient but have long since ceased to be so. The functions of the Queen may be described today as almost entirely dignified rather than efficient but no account can completely ignore the very limited efficient aspects. Nor can one ignore the contested nature of the account at some points. There is some debate about what the working rules of the constitution actually are. There is also debate about what they *should* be. Some would argue strongly for a greater reduction of the real power and authority of the Queen and, in some cases, ultimately in the direction of a republic. Others would argue for a retention and even expansion of monarchical power, as a check on the power of politicians.

At all events, it is necessary in this account of executive government in the United Kingdom and in Scotland to start with some remarks on the role of the monarch. Thus comments on the Queen and the UK government (para 7.2) precede observations on the UK government itself (paras 7.3–7.12) and on the Queen and the Scottish Government (para 7.13) precede those on Scottish Government itself (paras 7.14–7.18). Paragraph 7.19 deals with sources of executive power and paras 7.23–7.25 deal with government departments including, in particular, the Scottish Administration. Paragraph

7.26 addresses relations between Whitehall (the London home of much of the UK government) and St Andrew's House (the building in Edinburgh where the Scottish Government has its principal offices[5]).

1 Terminological difficulties arise immediately and should be acknowledged. SA1998 recognised and defined both the 'Scottish Executive' and 'Scottish Administration' but not the 'Scottish Government'. During the first two terms of the Scottish Parliament, the governing coalition was known in Scotland and elsewhere, colloquially, as 'the Executive'. When the SNP took office in 2007 it styled itself – to the consternation of some – as the Scottish Government. By virtue of s 12 of SA 2012, however, the title 'Scottish Government' was officially conferred. In this book 'Scottish Executive' is used only in an historical context but, of course, 'the executive' is retained in relation to both the Scottish and UK Governments (and others) as the generic category. Problems are still encountered with the use (or not) of the upper case in relation to the Governments.
2 The centrality of the executive is well recognised and explored in T Daintith and A Page, *The Executive in the Constitution* (1999).
3 That distinction was briefly blurred by the passing of the (since repealed) Health Boards (Membership and Elections) (Scotland) Act 2009 which provided for the experimental election of some members of health boards. The experiment was a failure.
4 W Bagehot, *The English Constitution* (1963) p 61.
5 The term 'St Andrew's House' is, for this reason, generally adopted in this book, although 'Victoria Quay' (Leith) does have a competing claim to provide the name for the Government's principal home.

THE QUEEN AND THE UK GOVERNMENT

7.2   It has been mentioned that discussion of the role of the monarch is complicated by the effect of history largely to 'hollow out' that role in such a way as to remove from it virtually all effective constitutional authority. In broad terms, rules relating to the monarch may be divided into three categories[1]:

In the first place, certain 'efficient' rules define who shall be king or queen. The Act of Settlement 1700 and the Acts of Union 1707 confirmed the line of succession to the House of Hanover and thence, eventually, to the House of Windsor and Queen Elizabeth II. The right of males to succeed to the throne in preference to females was removed, as was the barring of those married to Roman Catholics, by the Succession to the Crown Act 2013. However, the right to succeed remains barred to Roman Catholics themselves[2]. Funding of the monarchy is provided (since 2012) by a 'sovereign grant' (calculated by reference to the value of Crown estate income) voted annually by Parliament[3]. Similarly efficient rules include the Queen as part of the UK (but not the Scottish) Parliament and, in both Parliaments, require her assent to legislation: an Act of either Parliament is not valid without that assent. In law, ministers are appointed by the Queen. Efficient rules also define the composition of the Privy Council and prescribe the requirement that certain measures be formally made or agreed by the Council[4]. Secondly, however, a long list of powers formally vested in the monarch are best described as merely dignified because the substantive power to decide is, for all efficient purposes, transferred elsewhere. Thus, while the Queen's assent to Bills passed by the Houses of Parliament *is* required before they become law as Acts of Parliament, the Queen must not withhold that assent[5]. The Queen makes virtually no contribution to the appointment or dismissal of ministers, beyond a formal involvement. The Queen must approve measures placed before the Privy Council. And the same applies to virtually all other powers vested by statute in the Queen. The Queen plays no 'efficient' part in the appointment of judges[6], the Parliamentary Ombudsman or the Scottish Public Services Ombudsman[7]. The Queen cannot, at her own hand, dismiss ministers even though they 'hold office at Her Majesty's pleasure'.

Similarly, the Queen does not, in an 'efficient' way, exercise any of the great range of powers vested in her not by statute but by virtue of what is called the royal prerogative[8]. Formally the Queen makes war and peace and conducts relations with foreign countries[9]. Such powers are mostly ancient in origin and are the survivors, often heavily modified and circumscribed by statute[10], of a much longer list of genuinely monarchical powers. Even the survivors, however, are only in a dignified sense powers of the Queen. Like the statutory powers, prerogative powers have become a part of the efficient powers of ministers[11]. Ministers are the ones who make the choices and the decisions for which they subsequently take responsibility[12]. A web-based document issued by the Scottish Government used to refer to some public appointments being made 'by the Queen on behalf of Ministers', which captures nicely both the formal primacy but also the practical subordination of the Queen's position. One constitutional consequence of the elision of the functions of ministers and monarch (whether involving total transfer of functions – statutory or prerogative – to ministers or the Queen acting wholly on ministerial advice), and also of the vagaries of language and conceptual imprecision over time, has been the emergence of the concept of the 'Crown'[13]. Sometimes a term used to refer simply to the person of the sovereign, sometimes to the sovereign as an institution of government and sometimes to the entire collectivity of sovereign and ministers (of the Crown), the concept of the 'Crown' has been useful in defining a distinct governmental entity for legal purposes – although an entity which is divisible between the tiers of government, hence the acknowledgment by the Scotland Act 1998 (SA 1998) of both 'the Crown in right of Her Majesty's Government in the United Kingdom' and also 'the Crown in right of the Scottish Administration'[14]. Confusion has arisen over the extent to which immunities from legal proceedings possessed by the sovereign personally[15] extend also to ministers[16] and what remedies may be available against the Crown in legal proceedings[17].

Thirdly, in a few very limited respects, however, the general transfer of effective power to ministers has to be qualified. The Queen does, it is believed, retain a personal power of decision-making in relation to members of the royal household and certain honours such as appointments to the Orders of the Garter and the Thistle and the Order of Merit. In addition, it was declared by Bagehot that the Queen had the right to 'be consulted, the right to encourage and the right to warn' her government[18]. Although that position has not since been seriously contradicted, it probably amounts to an overstatement of the Queen's power in the 21st century. Of greater constitutional significance, it is arguable that the Queen retains a residual power of choice of a new Prime Minister which might be exercisable in the conditions of a hung Parliament. Prior to the passing of the Fixed-term Parliaments Act 2011, it used to be suggested that the Queen retained a power to refuse a Prime Minister's request to dissolve Parliament or even to dissolve Parliament on her own initiative[19].

1   Many other models of analysis are, however, possible. See eg R Brazier 'Constitutional Reform and the Crown' in M Sunkin and S Payne (eds) *The Nature of the Crown* (1999) (Sunkin and Payne).
2   Act of Settlement 1700.
3   Sovereign Grant Act 2011.
4   For the Order in Council as delegated legislation, see para 6.23.
5   See para 9.6. On the other hand, the requirement of 'Crown consent' to certain Bills (in both Parliaments) has been a matter of controversy because of the 'real' decisions it may involve. See 11th Report of the HC Political and Constitutional Reform Committee (2013–14) HC 784.
6   See ch 12.
7   See ch 10.
8   In March 2004, the Public Administration Select Committee of the House of Commons published its report 'Taming the Prerogative: Strengthening Ministerial Accountability to Parliament (HC 422, 16 March 2004) in which it examined the range of prerogative powers exercised by ministers and recommended legislation first to list, and thereafter to put in place safeguards to apply to the use of, those powers. The Governance of Britain Green Paper (Cm 7170, 2007) proposed a number of reforms relating to the use of prerogative powers by ministers, including in some cases placing those powers on a statutory footing and in others giving Parliament a more formal role (for example in relation to decisions to deploy the armed forces). The 2009 draft Constitutional Renewal Bill (Cm 7342, 2009) included provisions relating only to the ratification of treaties and not to the other prerogative powers discussed by the Select Committee and in the Green Paper. See the Constitutional Reform and Governance Act 2010.
9   Only recently did the regulation of the civil service become a statutory rather than a prerogative function. See Constitutional Reform and Governance Act 2010, ss 2–18.
10 *A-G v De Keyser's Royal Hotel Ltd* [1920] AC 508.
11 *Re R (Bancoult) v Secretary of State for Foreign and Commonwealth Affairs (No 2)* [2007] EWCA Civ 498, [2008] QB 365 Sedley LJ paras 31–36.
12 In the case of the declaration of war and other hostilities, there appears, to be an emerging convention (normally) requiring parliamentary approval. See 8th Report of the HC Political and Constitutional Reform Committee HC 923 (2010–12), especially in the light of the Coalition Government's failure to secure approval for an intervention in Syria on 29 August 2013 and the debate on an intervention in Iraq on 26 September 2014.
13 For constructive criticism of the treatment of this subject in the first edition of this book, and for more detailed discussion than space here permits, see A Tomkins, 'The Crown in Scots Law' in A McHarg and T Mullen (eds), *Public Law in Scotland* (2006). See also Sunkin and Payne.
14 See A Twomey, 'Responsible Government and the Divisibility of the Crown' [2008] PL 742 and its discussion of *R (Quark Fishing Limited) v Secretary of State for Foreign and Commonwealth Affairs* (No 2) [2006] 1 AC 529.
15 Even these deserve critical scrutiny. See D Pannick [2003] PL 201.
16 *M v Home Office* [1994] 1 AC 377.
17 But see *Davidson v Scottish Ministers* 2006 SC (HL) 41.
18 *The English Constitution* p 111.
19 See para 5.4.

THE UK GOVERNMENT

7.3   Turning now from the almost entirely 'dignified' to the 'efficient', the essence of parliamentary government on the Westminster model is to be found in an executive consisting of a team of ministers, headed by the Prime Minister and drawn from the party (or parties) which has (or have) secured political domination of the House of Commons. The most senior ministers are appointed as Secretaries of State[1] and junior ministers are styled Ministers of State and Parliamentary Under-Secretaries. Governmental powers are mainly vested (principally by statute but also by virtue of the royal prerogative) in the Secretaries of State and are exercisable by them and the junior ministers allocated to their departments. Certain powers and responsibilities are also vested directly in the Prime Minister[2]. The separateness of the exercise of these powers is, however, heavily modified in practice by a collectiveness of governmental activity imposed upon senior ministers by their membership of the Cabinet; by a wider notion of political and perhaps constitutional collective responsibility which touches all ministers; and then by the control exercised by the Prime Minister over the entire government. Governmental activity at ministerial level is assisted and implemented by the civil service distributed between departments and executive agencies[3].

What follows is a short summary of the current practice of government formation at the United Kingdom level. Until recently, it was, in many respects, an account of a system which had, in its most important aspects, remained reasonably stable for over a century. It should, however, be borne in mind that many of the rules and practices were heavily dependent upon wider constitutional and political conditions. In particular, they depended upon the rules which govern the composition of Parliament – including the composition of the House of Lords and the system of elections to the Commons – and the relationship, expressed in terms of both control and accountability, between government and Parliament. Since 2010 the system has had to confront a situation in which the elected House of Commons has been unable to deliver the conditions necessary for single-party majority government and the only option has been the novelty of coalition government. In addition, the Fixed-term Parliaments Act 2011 (F-tPA 2011) has produced consequences which are just as important for the executive as for Parliament itself.

1 And occasionally there may be a 'First Secretary of State', the title being honorific and denoting the political weight carried by its holder. Lord Mandelson served as First Secretary of State during 2009–10; and William Hague during 2010–15.
2 See eg the Prime Minister's power under SA 1998, s 95 to recommend the appointment of Scotland's two most senior judges.
3 See below para 7.24.

The Prime Minister

7.4   The position of Prime Minister is central to the functioning of British government. Constitutionally and politically, the Prime Minister is head of government. Prime Ministers have powers of appointment, patronage and leadership in government which place them head and shoulders above their political colleagues. However, this is a position which is achieved more by the operation of politics and constitutional practice than as a result of specific legal rules. Indeed, the office and powers of the Prime Minister receive only very sketchy recognition from the law. Legal provision is made for pay, pension[1] and house in the country[2] and certain of the Prime Minister's powers of appointment are specified in statute but these are marginal considerations. The prominence of the Prime Minister derives much more from his or her political profile as leader of the majority party; the power to hire and fire fellow ministers; and his or her presence in Parliament, the country, in the European Union and abroad.

1 Ministerial and Other Salaries Act 1975 (as amended by the Ministerial and Other Salaries Act 1997) and the Public Service Pensions Act 2013.
2 Chequers Estate Act 1917.

Appointment of the Prime Minister

7.5   A new Prime Minister is needed whenever the post falls vacant. The circumstances in which a vacancy may occur vary widely but they may be broadly grouped under two heads: (a) circumstances where the majority political party (or coalition) retains its support in and control of the House of Commons but the Prime Minister dies or resigns on grounds of illness or other personal or political reasons (Churchill (1955), Eden (1957), Macmillan (1963) Wilson (1976) and Blair (2007)) or because of loss of support of or dismissal by the ruling party (Thatcher (1990)). The party continues in control but the leader has to be replaced.

On the other hand, (b) following the dissolution of Parliament and loss of the ensuing general election. Until F-tPA 2011 these events were triggered by the Prime Minister's decision to request of the Queen a dissolution of Parliament, whether forced to do so by severely adverse conditions in the House of Commons such as loss of a vote of confidence, or alternatively for tactical reasons usually associated with his or her assessment of the prospects of success in an early election.

Since F-tPA 2011, however, and for as long as it remains on the statute book, the circumstances in which a dissolution of Parliament and general election can occur have been narrowed sharply and, in particular, to remove the Prime Minister's option of the tactical dissolution. Now, in only exceptional circumstances, are Parliaments not likely to run their prescribed five years. What has not, though, been changed by the new Act is that, following a dissolution and election, it is the outcome of the election which decides whether a prime ministerial resignation and replacement are necessary. Until the result is known, the Prime Minister and the government as a whole remain in office and, if their party wins the election, they continue to do so. There is at no stage a vacancy in the office of Prime Minister and the incumbent continues (Wilson (1966), Thatcher and Blair (both twice)). If, however, the incumbent Prime Minister loses the election, his or her position becomes politically and constitutionally untenable and resignation must follow (Douglas Home (1964), Wilson (1970), Heath (1974), Callaghan (1979) and Major (1997)). A rule, derived from recent practice and which is expressed in terms of 'winning' and 'losing' elections, works clearly where election outcomes are, themselves, clear but might, of course, present difficulties where the outcome is a more finely balanced House of Commons. In the last half century, the only problematic outcome, in this respect, was when, in 1974, Mr Heath lost his own overall Conservative majority but Labour too had failed to win overall. It was not considered constitutionally improper, in those circumstances, for Heath briefly to explore the prospect of securing an arrangement for support by the Liberals before, on failing to secure that support, offering his resignation. Indeed, such suspension of decision-making might reasonably be carried forward, if necessary, to a testing of the Prime Minister's continuing support at an early meeting of the new Parliament. In 2010, Mr Brown failed to secure a majority for the Labour Party in the general election of 6 May but continued in office as Prime Minister until, by 11 May, it had become clear that negotiations to form a Labour-Liberal Democrat government could not succeed and that a Conservative-Liberal Democrat coalition was confirmed. It is likely that such problematic election outcomes and, therefore, uncertainties as to the obligations of Prime Ministers to resign will increase if British politics ceases to be a mainly two-party affair and a third significant party or group of parties gains a significant and lasting foothold. Such uncertainties aside, however, this account of the circumstances which produce a vacancy in the office of Prime Minister and the need for a successor are seen to be underpinned by two main principles. The first is that, purely personal conditions such as health apart, a Prime Minister's tenure is dependent upon political support in the House of Commons and the second that, although as a matter of law the Queen has the power to appoint and dismiss her ministers including the Prime Minister, that power is wholly subordinated to the party political imperative and must be exercised in deference to it. Short of the sort of crisis unknown in the working of the modern constitution, there is no room for an independent discretionary power to dismiss her Prime Minister.

The same principles are carried forward into the appointment process itself. The formal appointment of a Prime Minister occurs when he or she receives the Queen's warrant but the rules which propel the appointee into the Queen's presence are political. Thus, in the circumstances grouped under (a) above – ie conditions in which the ruling party remains in control but its leader has to be replaced, it is entirely for the internal electoral procedures of the party to produce the name of the successor[1]. Interim arrangements can be made. In circumstances (b), where a general election has produced the need to replace a defeated Prime Minister, the leader of the party now commanding an overall majority in the Commons must be invited by the Queen to be Prime Minister and to form a government. Questions similar to those raised above about the consequences of an election which produces uncertainty have provided much scope for debate among commentators despite, or perhaps because of, the absence of any such live instances. If the largest post-election party lacks an overall majority but appears able to secure the support of a smaller party, it seems clear (Wilson (1974)) that the leader of that largest party should be appointed as Prime Minister. Even in the absence of such a coalition or pact, the same person should be invited to form a government.

These principles are largely unaffected by the enactment of F-tPA 2011, save that the Act removes the possibility, in the situation of a hung Parliament of a Prime Minister's being appointed in the hope that he may survive but with the option, open to a Prime Minister prior to the Act, of seeking a second dissolution if things do not work out. The Act also produces the newly prescribed circumstances where a government has been defeated in a vote of no confidence, following which, if no government can regain the confidence of the House of Commons, a dissolution must follow[2]. The *Cabinet Manual* (whose arrival in its initial form[3] was prompted, in part, by the prospect of a hung Parliament in 2010) provides guidance on government formation, both in situations of uncertainty after an election and, in the intermediate situation, after a vote of no confidence[4]. In both cases, it is primarily for the political parties to hold discussions (with the assistance of the civil service, if sought (through the Cabinet Secretary and with the Prime Minister's authority), and with the Palace kept informed but otherwise uninvolved) in search of a government which might be formed in the circumstances.

1 In the case of Prime Minister Brown, his succession to Mr Blair was the result of an unopposed candidature for leadership of the Labour Party in 2007.
2 F-tPA 2011, s 2(3). See para 5.4.
3 See para 1.23.
4 Paras 2, 12–2.20.

Prime Minister's functions

7.6   Once appointed, the Prime Minister has the following principal functions:

(a)   To form a government by the appointment of ministers, a process discussed below and one which the Prime Minister may have to repeat following decisions to dismiss or relocate ministers in subsequent 'reshuffles'.

(b)   To make many other public appointments responsibility for which, whether authorised by statute or in the exercise of the prerogative, is allocated to the Prime Minister.

(c)   To lead and co-ordinate the functions of government as a whole, including the chairmanship of the Cabinet and many of its committees[1].

(d)   To be the principal representative of the government in the House of Commons, the country, the European Union and abroad.

(e)   To lead his or her political party in Parliament and in the country and, in particular, to play a leading role in elections.

1 See paras 7.10–7.12.

The Cabinet and other ministers

7.7   Although all ministers are, like the Prime Minister, formally appointed by the Queen, and are formally dismissible by her, the choice of who should join and, in due course, be removed from the government is one for the Prime Minister. However, it is very much a constrained choice. The Prime Minister will be seeking the best team available: people who are politically able, who have the qualities necessary to present and defend policies in Parliament and in the country, people who will not be vulnerable to personal attack (perhaps on grounds of earlier misdeeds) or otherwise be damaging to the government as a whole. Politics dominates the choice and, with occasional exceptions to the rule, it is almost inevitable that ministers will be members or supporters of the governing party or parties. Within the party or parties[1], appointees are likely to be political allies and friends but with room for some former opponents, perhaps to forestall any opposition on the government's back benches. If the Government is a Coalition (as during the 2010–2015 Parliament), there is inevitably a need for the fair distribution of posts between the parties of Government – from the Deputy Prime Minister down – and probably with a degree of formal adoption of the principles to apply, as the Coalition's years in Government proceed[2]. There may be a need for balance between left and right, 'pro-European' and 'Euro-sceptic', old and young, male and female, black and white, and between the nations and regions of the United Kingdom. There is also, however, an overriding constitutional constraint which insists that all ministers must be drawn from one or other House of Parliament[3]. This is what is meant by parliamentary government. Inevitably, most ministers will be MPs rather than peers because the House of Commons, despite proposals for the reform of the Lords (as to which see Chapter 5), remains the constitutionally and politically dominant House and expectations of appointment are high among MPs who are members of the majority party. It would be unthinkable for the Chancellor of the Exchequer to be anywhere but the Commons, and, although in recent years a number of other Secretaries of State have been drawn from the Lords, that may still be regarded as an exception to the general rule.

As a consequence of the Constitutional Reform Act 2005 it is no longer essential that the Lord Chancellor be a member of the House of Lords[4] but it remains necessary for the conduct of the government's business in the House of Lords to have ministers located in that chamber[5]. The Lords is, in any event, a source of party allies, often with previous government experience in the Commons. Another reason for drawing some ministers from the Lords is that there is a statutory numerical cap on numbers of ministers in receipt of a salary who may be members of the House of Commons. The House of Commons Disqualification Act 1975, s 2 currently restricts that number to 95[6] whereas recent governments have tended to consist of about 115 ministers. Ministers are allocated to their departmental portfolios by the Prime Minister and the distribution of posts can provide him or her with the opportunity to reorganise the departmental conduct of business[7].

Ministers hold office on an 'open-ended' basis and their period of office may be brought to an end by death; their removal by the Prime Minister, whether to move to another post or to leave the government altogether; or their resignation, which might be on grounds of health or other personal reasons, or in response to adverse political pressure, or a mixture of these. In some cases, resignation may be to forestall dismissal by the Prime Minister or may be the consequence of a strong Prime Ministerial suggestion. During their period of office, ministers discharge the functions deriving from either statute or the royal prerogative which are either directly conferred on them (although few modern statutes do identify a specific minister, with a preference instead for the generic formula 'Secretary of State'), or are, less formally, allocated to ministers, including junior ministers, by the Prime Minister. Thus, typically, executive powers (including powers to make subordinate legislation) relating to social security (eg the jobseeker's allowance or income support) are conferred by legislation on the 'Secretary of State'; they are, therefore, exercisable, by the Secretary of State for Work and Pensions but with many responsibilities delegated in practice to the relevant junior minister – for example, the Minister of State for Employment.

For their services, ministers are rewarded by salaries on a statutory scale[8]. There is, however, a category of ministerial assistants to whom no salary is paid. These are the parliamentary private secretaries who hold office under conditions prescribed by the *Ministerial Code*. As a form of trainee ministers, they are MPs who, in terms of the demands of political discipline, occupy a position half-way between that of minister and back-bencher. Their equivalent at Holyrood is the parliamentary liaison officer[9].

1 It is usual, but not inevitable, that governments be composed of party members. Prime Minister Gordon Brown included several ministers who were not Labour Party members in his Cabinet in 2007.
2 See *Coalition Agreement for Stability and Reform* (May 2010).
3 But ministers remain in office after the dissolution of Parliament and a short-term absence from Parliament pending election to the Commons may be tolerated. A standing *exception* to the general rule prior to devolution was the Scottish Solicitor-General who was frequently a member of neither House. The usual means by which 'outsiders' are brought into the government is by conferring a life peerage on them.
4 The current incumbent is Chris Grayling MP who is also Secretary of State for Justice.
5 Although, not necessarily in the Cabinet. Following the ministerial reshuffle of July 2014 there was no peer in the Cabinet. See House of Lords Constitution Committee 5th Report (2014–15) HL Paper 41.
6 This provision has its origins in the Act of Settlement 1700 which, if implemented, would have excluded all ministers.
7 For departments in general, see paras 7.23–7.25 below.
8 Ministerial and Other Salaries Act 1975 (as amended by the Ministerial and Other Salaries Act 1997 which ties ministerial salaries to civil service salaries).
9 See para 7.17.

Law Officers of the Crown

7.8 In a special category as ministers are the three UK Law Officers: the Attorney General for England and Wales, the Solicitor General[1] and the Advocate General for Scotland. Although owing a political loyalty to the government, the Law Officers are obliged to adopt a more dispassionate stance in their roles of providing legal advice to government, representing the government in court and, in the case of the Attorney General and the Solicitor General, in their overarching responsibility in England and Wales for the independent Crown Prosecution Service, headed by the Director of Public Prosecutions. The Advocate General for Scotland is a position created at the time of devolution in 1999 when the original Scottish Law Officers, the Lord Advocate and the Solicitor General for Scotland, were transferred to the Scottish Government[2]. The Advocate General advises the UK government on matters of Scots law and has special functions under SA 1998 in relation to 'devolution issues'[3].

1 J LL C J Edwards *The Law Officers of the Crown* (1964); N Walker 'The Antinomies of the Law Officers' in Sunkin and Payne.
2 See para 7.20. There is also a separate Attorney General for Northern Ireland.
3 See para 14.19. L Clarke 'The Role of the Advocate General for Scotland' in A Boyle et al (eds) *Human Rights and Scots Law*; 2002 SLT (News) 139.

Ministerial conduct

7.9   How ministers conducted themselves in office was once a matter simply for administrative regulation by the Prime Minister. An internal document, *Questions of Procedure for Ministers*, gave guidance on a number of managerial matters, including some which touched on ministerial behaviour. The 1990s brought publication of the document as the *Ministerial Code* but also, with the creation in 1994 of the Committee on Standards in Public Life, a much higher profile for questions of conduct. The content of the *Code* has, from 1999, been substantially reproduced in the *Scottish Ministerial Code*, discussed below[1]. In so far as either Code requires enforcement, this remains a matter for the Prime Minister or First Minister, a perceived weakness in the system of enforcement which has led to criticism.

In response to these criticisms and in partial implementation of recommendations made by the (Wicks) Committee on Standards in Public Life Prime Minister Brown announced changes in July 2007[2] including the appointment of a new independent adviser who, at the Prime Minister's request, can investigate alleged breaches of the Code[3].

1 See para 7.18.
2 The Governance of Britain, Col 7170.
3 See HC Public Administration Committee 22nd Report (2010–12) HC 1761.

Cabinet government

7.10   An idea central to the concept of parliamentary government is its collective character. In contrast with, for example, the United States government in which executive power is constitutionally concentrated in the President and all other executive members have a deliberately subordinate role, the emphasis in the historical emergence of the parliamentary Westminster model has been on the executive's functioning as a collectivity. This is the yardstick against which modern governments are measured and, though they may be found to be wanting, it endures. The principal emblem of the collective nature of parliamentary government is the Cabinet. The Cabinet retains some of the functions of Bagehot's 'hyphen' – joining executive and Parliament – but has become even more strongly the 'board of control'[1], the executive committee of the government. Like other boards of directors and executive committees, its work may be sidelined to an extent by a strong chairman or chief executive in the form of the Prime Minister but its position at the centre remains important. All senior ministers (including the Secretary of State for Scotland and the other 'territorial' Secretaries of State) are members of the Cabinet which meets weekly at the centre of a network of Cabinet committees in which much of its work is done. Once protected by secrecy, the remits and membership of Cabinet committees (including, for instance, those responsible for the government's legislative programme) are now well publicised. The Cabinet is serviced by the Cabinet Office, headed by the Cabinet Secretary who is also the Head of the Home Civil Service[2].

A frequently asked question is whether the collective style of government is, in practice, maintained, and much depends here on political contingency, varying according to general political conditions and the temperament of the Prime Minister. The model of Cabinet government enables but does not guarantee collective decision-making. It also enables or, at least, does not prevent prime ministerial government. Three closely related factors (much affected by the conditions of coalition government since 2010) contribute to an assessment:

(a)   the collective responsibility of ministers;

(b)   the dominance or not of the Prime Minister;

(c)   the relationship of ministers to Parliament and especially the relationship of accountability. This last aspect is something treated separately in Chapter 10 but the others may be addressed here.

1 *The English Constitution* pp 67–68.

2 During the period Jan 2012 to Sept 2014, the two offices were split. From Sept 2014, a new position of Chief Executive of the Home Civil Service was also created.

Collective responsibility[1]

7.11   There are strong pressures within a system of parliamentary government for ministers, whether in the Cabinet or not, to act collectively. Sometimes these pressures are elevated by commentators to the status of a constitutional convention or doctrine of 'collective responsibility' but they derive almost entirely from political expediency. Ministers may enjoy separately conferred statutory powers. They may operate in separate departmental units for most policy-making and policy-implementing purposes. Ministers may have the distinctive status of MP or peer, or prestige within their party. Personally, they may have large egos and career ambitions which involve the displacement, if the opportunity presents, of their senior ministerial colleagues. And yet, it will almost always be advantageous to almost all members of a government to be collectively loyal to the team they have joined for the time being. This implies a degree of pooling of information and discussion prior to the making of important decisions[2]; the opportunity for that information and discussion – especially where it involves dissent on controversial matters – to be kept secret; and, perhaps above all, a commitment on the part of all ministers publicly to defend decisions when made and to present a united front to Parliament and to the public, whatever the degree of earlier anguish and dissent. Sometimes it will suit a government's purposes to depart from this model of internal secrecy and external unity. It may be useful for some ideas under discussion to be 'leaked' by one means or another to test public reaction prior to a final decision or to soften up public opinion for bad news (perhaps not as bad as the version which was leaked) to be announced later. Sometimes the impression of a lively debate between ministers rather than that of sullen acquiescence may be advantageous instead of destructive. To have a minister who briefly appears 'greener' than most[3] or appears more sympathetic to the plight of underfunded university students[4] is not necessarily harmful. Publicly declared differences – agreements to disagree – may occasionally be the best that can be achieved without total collapse of the government[5].

For the most part, however, it is the need for solidarity which dominates and it is team discipline which keeps in place the package of obligations associated with 'collective responsibility'. Ministers must remain 'on message'. Ministers who step out of line, especially by publicly revealing dissent on important issues without authority to do so, may expect to be reprimanded or to lose their jobs. However, it will be open to the Prime Minister to be more tolerant of misdemeanours if personal or political considerations demand. In all important respects, these 'rules' of political solidarity apply as much to the principal opposition party as to the party in government. The shadow team of ministers is almost as much concerned to present a united front as the government[6]. Sanctions are applied to dissidents in the same way and this reinforces the political rather than any constitutional underpinning of the concept of collective responsibility. Political expediency keeps both teams together. It is true that some aspects of governmental collective responsibility are given structure by the *Ministerial Code*[7]. It is also true that the parliamentary device of the motion of 'no confidence in Her Majesty's Government' reinforces the collective nature of the sanction invoked. Either the government falls or it survives as a whole. And the idea of collective responsibility was given some recognition as the basis of the English High Court's decision to uphold the confidentiality of Cabinet business in the 'Crossman diaries' case in 1976[8].

These phenomena do not, however, deny the political character of collective responsibility itself – a feature clearly illustrated by events at the time of the Iraq war of 2003. Because of his disagreement with the government's decision to commit forces, Robin Cook MP resigned from his ministerial position as Lord President of the Council (Leader of the House of Commons). On the other hand, the International Development Secretary, Clare Short MP, first described her own government's policy in the lead-up to the conflict as 'reckless' but neither resigned, nor was dismissed by the Prime Minister. Nor did Ms Short resign as the war began or, at a later stage, when she was again critical of the government's aid policy on Iraq. Eventually, however, she did resign and, amid great acrimony, used her resignation speech on 12 May 2003 to condemn the state of Cabinet government as she saw it. In Bagehot's terms, the Cabinet had become, like the Privy Council, merely a 'dignified' part of the constitution. In her words there was 'no collective responsibility because there is no collective, just diktats from the Prime Minister'[9]. Whatever the rights and wrongs of this judgment, there is no doubt that events surrounding the Iraq crisis posed many questions about the condition of Cabinet government.

The statements of principle about the notion of collective responsibility and the illustrations, just cited, of its operation in practice are drawn from the conditions of majority single-party government which have dominated UK practice in modern times. What concerned commentators during the 2010–15 period, however, were the consequences for collective responsibility of two-party government under the Conservative/Liberal Democrat Coalition. On the face of it, one might have expected the required collectiveness of ministerial spirit to falter under conditions of some presumed political antagonism. As we shall find, however, the starting normality of coalition governments in Scotland did not herald the demise of the operation of collective responsibility. And this was also the formal starting point of the UK coalition government. The Ministerial code continued with an unamended reassertion of its principles[10].

On the other hand, it was also recognised in the *Coalition Agreement for Stability and Reform* (May 2010) that, whilst collective responsibility would continue to apply (para 2), there would be acknowledged exceptions (identified in an 'Agreements Reached' document of 11 May 2010 and in *The Coalition: Our Programme for Government*) in relation to positions to be taken on the proposed referendum on electoral reform (AV)[11], higher education funding, the renewal of Trident, nuclear power and a married couples tax allowance, These special 'agreements to differ', however, could never have captured the degree of political difference with which the parties had to live[12] especially in the Coalition's final months. It was never credible that ministers notionally bound to solidarity in government and yet preparing and presenting policies for a divergent future beyond the next general election could maintain a united front. Much deviation from any such united front was tolerated, but also actively provoked, on both sides of the coalition. At the time of the Chancellor's Autumn Statement in November 2014, the two parties' representatives came together to defend what had been done under the Coalition, but promptly divided sharply on future economic policy. As earlier noted[13], the Government was, in December 2014, wholly unable to maintain a united response to the question of 'English Votes for English Laws'. In the report of a House of Lords Committee, however, a firm line was maintained:

'77. Collective responsibility has served our constitution well. It promotes collective decision-making and ensures Parliament is able to hold the Government effectively to account for its actions, policies and decisions. It should continue to apply when there is a coalition government.

78. We recognise that the parties in a coalition government will not automatically agree on everything; from time to time they will differ. However, it is incumbent on ministers to seek to reach a collective view on issues wherever possible. Having reached a collective view, it is essential that they can be held to account for it. Given its constitutional importance, the setting aside of the convention of collective responsibility should be rare, and only ever a last resort.

79. Where it is clear that no collective position can be reached on an issue, a proper process should be in place to govern any setting aside of collective responsibility. Such setting aside should be agreed by the Cabinet as a whole and be in respect of a specific issue. Ordinarily it would be for a specified period of time; rules should be set out by the Prime Minister governing how ministers may express their differing views. This process should be drawn up by the Prime Minister and Deputy Prime Minister for the remainder of this Parliament, and should be set out in future coalition agreements.'[13].

1   For a discussion of the history and content of the concept see O Gay 'The collective responsibility of Ministers' HC Research Paper 04/82 2004.
2   In June 2003, the consultation document accompanying the draft Civil Contingencies Bill (Cm 5843) explained that powers formally exercisable by a single Secretary of State 'would be exercised by Ministers in accordance with the normal principles of Cabinet collective responsibility' (p 29).

3 Eg the Environment Secretary, Michael Meacher MP at the time of a Johannesburg climate change summit in August 2002.
4 Clare Short MP, November 2002.
5 The best example of this being the presentation by the Labour government in 1975 of separate options on whether or not to withdraw from the EC. But see also below for the stresses imposed by coalition government.
6 For example, Kenneth Clarke MP, as shadow business secretary, caused embarrassment to the Conservative opposition in March 2009 by appearing to depart from party commitments on reform of inheritance tax, leaving the party leadership to 'restate' their official position.
7 It should also be noted that 'collective responsibility' has received statutory recognition in the Freedom of Information Act 2000, s 36 and the Freedom of Information (Scotland) Act 2002, s 30.
8 *A-G v Jonathan Cape Ltd* [1976] QB 752.
9 HC Debs, 13 May 2003, col 38.
10 Para 2.1.
11 See para 5.8.
12 A useful survey was provided in the 5th Report 'Constitutional Implications of Coalition Government', of the House of Lords Constitution Committee HL Paper 130 (2013–14), esp in ch 4.
13 See para 4.21. See note 12 above.

Prime Ministerial government

7.12   As already indicated, an important question about the modern functioning of Cabinet government in the United Kingdom relates specifically to the role of the Prime Minister. No one would seriously suggest today that he or she is merely *primus* or *prima inter pares*, the 'first among equals'. The political dominance of the Prime Minister within the governing party; the Prime Minister's leading role on the government's behalf in Parliament and the media; the role as statesman abroad; ultimate responsibility for the use of nuclear weapons; and certainly the Prime Minister's power (subject to any constraints of coalition) to hire and fire ministers are all factors which give the Prime Minister an inevitable pre-eminence. Until the enactment of the F-tPA 2011, there was, in addition, the power to exert pressure on ministerial colleagues and MPs by the right to decide the date of the next general election. And yet, the idea of the Cabinet as a team lingers[1]. There is a widespread belief – one that goes back many years[2] – that the Prime Ministerial position is open to abuse and that it is, in fact, abused by some incumbents. Prime Ministers may use technical tricks to dominate colleagues – by determining the agenda, length and content of the minutes of Cabinet meetings and Cabinet committees. They may hector and bully. They may snub and sideline and use their substantial powers to 'spin' information. They may demean colleagues by assuming lead responsibility for *their* functions – whether health, or education or foreign affairs. They may dominate party campaigns, especially at general elections. Such features tend to be accompanied by others which suggest that Prime Ministers – especially those with large and virtually unassailable majorities in the Commons – not only dominate Parliament but may also be tempted to ignore it. Together, these produce the apprehension that Cabinet government has been replaced not merely by prime ministerial government but by presidential government. Most frequently, such suggestions are merely political rhetoric intended both to charge Prime Ministers with abuse of power and shedding their accountability to party, Parliament and people and, on the other hand, to deride other senior ministers for their feeble subordination. On the other hand, the charge of presidentialism has sometimes to be taken seriously as a critique of the operation of the modern constitution. The manner in which executive power is exercised *is* important and it is especially important to be aware of the consequences of any change for the accountability of government to Parliament and the people. We may provisionally conclude that, while modern technology and communications and a heightened sensitivity of Prime Ministers to changing expectations of the media and the general public have undoubtedly affected prime ministerial behaviour, most of the institutional rules forcing a dependence upon party support and electoral success (even if, in both cases, on the basis of a coalition government divided into its separate party components) ensure a continuing distinction between prime ministerial and presidential government.

1 Harold Wilson's description, in the 1960s, of his ministers as a football team with himself as a centre half has become more than a little quaint.
2 J P Mackintosh *The British Cabinet* (3rd edn, 1977).

THE QUEEN AND THE SCOTTISH GOVERNMENT

7.13   SA 1998, s 45(1) provides that '(t)he First Minister shall be appointed by Her Majesty and ... shall hold office at Her Majesty's pleasure'. The section goes on to make provision for the First Minister's resignation – to be tendered to Her Majesty[1] – and subsequent sections require the approval by the Queen of the appointment of the other ministerial members of the Scottish Government[2]. It is to the Queen that recommendations are to be made for the appointment (and removal) of the Lord Advocate and Solicitor-General for Scotland[3]. On the face of it, therefore, SA 1998 confers very substantial constitutional powers on the Sovereign. As already explained, it is, however, one of the best known features of the UK constitution that the involvement of the Sovereign at this and many other points is more apparent rather than real. It is formal rather than substantive. Hers is the role of the figurehead or, more dismissively, the rubber stamp. In some instances, this is made clear by the statutory context in which the powers are conferred. There is no doubt, for instance, that the rules on the formation of the Scottish Government are intended to confer the substantive powers to choose on the Parliament (subject to political forces within it) and (once appointed) on the First Minister and to leave the Sovereign with only the formal role of accepting the recommendations made to her. It would be unconstitutional for her to do otherwise. The same position is reached in the non-statutory procedure for the appointment of the UK government, as already described[4]. The principle that the Sovereign's role should be merely formal applies, with only very limited exceptions, across the full range of the functions conferred upon her, whether by statute or by virtue of the prerogative.

Certain 'dignified' functions are assured by SA 1998 itself. Not only are the First Minister, other members of the Scottish Government and junior ministers formally appointed by the Queen but their functions are formally exercised on behalf of the Queen[5]. In relation to the Parliament, the Queen is formally empowered in defined circumstances to order a dissolution and require a poll and subsequent meeting[6]; and a Bill, when passed by the Parliament, becomes an Act when it has received Royal Assent[7]. While not deriving from SA 1998, the Queen attended the opening ceremony of the first Parliament on 1 July 1999, and attended a Kirking Service in St Giles' Cathedral on the previous day. The Queen addressed the Parliament when it met in Aberdeen in May 2002, her jubilee year[8], and she addressed the Parliament again after the beginning of the second session in June 2003[9], its third session in June 2007[10], on the tenth anniversary of its opening on 1 July 2009, and again at the beginning of the fourth session in July 2011. The practice of using a 'Queen's Speech' has not been adopted and the First Minister has simply presented the Scottish Government's legislative programme to the Parliament[11]. It has become the practice of the Privy Council to involve Scottish Privy Counsellors, in particular the First Minister, in business including the making of Orders in Council required by the Scottish Government[12] and it is an indication of the formality of these proceedings that Orders in Council promoted by either the UK or the Scottish government may be conducted in the presence of ministers from both administrations.

Arrangements are made for the Queen to receive papers from the Scottish Cabinet[13] and there has emerged a practice of meetings between the Queen and the First Minister, although these have not achieved the frequency or regularity of the Prime Minister's audiences[14]. It is, therefore, acknowledged that the Queen has the right to be informed about Scottish government. Whether, in line with Bagehot's formula, she has a right to advise or warn has yet to emerge.

1   SA 1998, s 45(2).
2   SA 1998, s 47(1).
3   SA 1998, s 48(1).
4   See paras 7.5 and 7.7.
5   SA 1998, ss 52–53.
6   SA 1998, ss 2–3.
7   SA 1998, s 28(2)–(4).
8   SP OR 28 May 2002, col 12125.
9   SP OR 3 June 2003, col 317.
10 SP OR 30 June 2007, col 3.
11 See para 9.9.
12 But there is no rule about this. Many 'Scottish' Orders in Council are approved in the presence of UK ministers only.
13 *Guide to Collective Decision Making*, para 4.25. For the *Guide* more generally, see below.
14 First Minister McConnell said that he had 'audiences with Her Majesty the Queen from time to time' (SP OR S2W-1283, 28 July 2003) and many such audiences with First Minister Salmond were also reported. First Minister Sturgeon had her first audience with the Queen on 10 December 2014.

THE SCOTTISH GOVERNMENT[1]

7.14   SA 1998 creates a Scottish Government[2] , the members of which are (a) the First Minister; (b) ministers appointed by the First Minister; and (c) the two Scottish Law Officers, the Lord Advocate and the Solicitor General for Scotland[3]. SA 1998 further states that the 'members of the Scottish Government are referred to collectively as the Scottish Ministers'[4] and the 'Scottish Ministers' is the term used elsewhere in SA 1998 to describe the body in which statutory powers are vested[5]. A person who 'holds a Ministerial office' (ie a UK government minister) may not be a member of the Scottish Government[6].

1 It may be borne in mind that the Smith Commission (see para 4.21) recommended in November 2014 that UK legislation should state that the Scottish Government is a permanent institution'(para 21).
2 See para 7.1 and note 1 for discussion of the replacement of 'Executive' by 'Government' by SA 2012, s 12.
3 SA 1998, s 44(1), as amended.
4 SA 1998, s 44(2).
5 SA 1998, s 52(1).
6 SA 1998, s 44(3).

Appointment and tenure of the First Minister

7.15   SA 1998 has established a parliamentary form of government similar to that at the United Kingdom level, in that the First Minister and the Ministers he or she then appoints are drawn from the membership of the Scottish Parliament itself. They owe their appointment and subsequent retention of office to the political support they have in the Parliament. In a purely formal sense, however, the appointment of the First Minister is made by the Queen by royal warrant. He or she is to be 'appointed by Her Majesty from among the members of the Parliament and shall hold office at Her Majesty's pleasure'[1]. However, SA 1998 makes it clear that the Queen does not have a free choice in her selection of the First Minister. She receives a recommendation from the Presiding Officer of the Parliament and that recommendation must, in turn, be of the person nominated by the Parliament itself[2]. On appointment, the First Minister must take the official oath, tendered by the Lord President at a sitting of the Court of Session[3].

There was more use of these procedures in the early years of the Parliament than might have been expected. The initial appointment of Donald Dewar as First Minister in May 1999 was followed, on his death, by the appointment of Henry McLeish in October 2000 and then, on his resignation, by the appointment of Jack McConnell in November 2001. In each case, the nomination was contested, producing a vote and victory for the Labour/Liberal Democrat partnership candidate. At the beginning of the second session, Jack McConnell was renominated as First Minister against opposition from candidates from the SNP, the Conservatives, the Greens and the Scottish Socialists as well as Dennis Canavan MSP and Margo MacDonald MSP[4]. The third session of Parliament produced, for the first time, a First Minister leading a minority government. Alex Salmond faced opposition from the Conservatives, Labour and Liberal Democrats but secured the nomination when the two Green MSPs elected in May 2007 voted with the SNP block[5]. Following the general election of May 2011 in which the SNP won a clear overall majority, there was no doubt about the (unopposed) re-nomination of Mr Salmond as First Minister[6]. After his own resignation (intimated immediately after the independence referendum result on 19 September 2014) and the subsequent election of Nicola Sturgeon as its leader by the SNP, she became the Parliament's nominee as First Minister (after defeating Ruth Davidson (the Conservative leader) by 66 votes to 15) on 19 November 2014.

Once an appointment has been made, the First Minister holds office until one of four events occurs:

(1)   The First Minister may at any time voluntarily tender his or her resignation[7]. This is what brought Mr McLeish's tenure to an end on 8 November 2001. SA 1998 does not indicate in so many words whether the Queen is obliged to accept the First Minister's tendered resignation. However, it may be assumed that she must do so in all imaginable circumstances[8]. The sort of circumstances in which a First Minister might resign are also not expressly anticipated in SA 1998 but clearly they include personal circumstances such as illness. They would also include circumstances in which the First Minister feels[9] that his or her own conduct or personal responsibility for the failures of the Government requires resignation or where, in any event, the pressure to resign from colleagues (including fellow members of the Government) or from the Parliament becomes irresistible. One thing not made completely clear in SA 1998 is whether, in the case of a 'voluntary' tendering of resignation, that resignation must take immediate effect[10].

(2)   If the degree of dissatisfaction felt by the Parliament towards the First Minister and the Scottish Government reaches the level at which the Parliament formally 'resolves that the Scottish Government no longer enjoys the confidence of the Parliament', then the First Minister has no option. The First Minister must tender his or her resignation to the Queen[11] and, in such an event, all ministers in the Scottish Government must also resign[12]. So too must the junior Scottish Ministers[13]. It is assumed that, in the case of such an involuntary tendering of resignation, it would have to take immediate effect.

(3)   SA 1998 also provides that the nomination procedure is triggered if the office of First Minister becomes vacant, otherwise than in consequence of a resignation. This is what happened in the sad circumstances of Donald Dewar's death on 11 October 2000.

(4)   Finally, SA 1998 formally assures adherence to the parliamentary model of government by providing that, if a First Minister should cease to be an MSP (other than by dissolution of the Parliament), the Parliament must nominate a successor. In the more routinely predictable circumstances of the dissolution of the Parliament, dissolution does not, of itself, bring to an end a First Minister's tenure of office. The First Minister (and the rest of the Scottish Government) may remain in office through the period of the dissolution and subsequent general election. The First Minister's fate hangs on the result of the election and then of the process of nomination which the Parliament must undertake thereafter. If the First Minister is renominated (as Mr McConnell was in May 2003 and Mr Salmond in May 2011), he or she is to be reappointed. If not, and some other person is nominated for appointment, the existing First Minister ceases to hold office once his or her successor is actually appointed[14].

In some of these circumstances where a vacancy produces the need for the nomination of a new First Minister, there will also be the need for a temporary replacement, as was the case on Donald Dewar's death and the resignation of Henry McLeish. In such circumstances, First Ministerial functions are to be exercised by a person designated by the Parliament's Presiding Officer. Such an Acting First Minister must be an MSP or, if the Parliament has been dissolved, someone who was an MSP prior to the dissolution[15]. In both instances mentioned, Jim Wallace, who served as Deputy First Minister throughout the first session of the Parliament but, as leader of the junior partner, was not a candidate for the First Ministership itself, was so designated. An Acting First Minister may also be designated if the First Minister, while still in office, is 'for any reason unable to act'. It may be, however, that there will in practice be very little use of this option. There is no elaboration of what is meant by the First Minister's being 'unable to act'. Presumably, a short-term illness, acknowledged by the First Minister to be disabling, might be a relevant condition – although Donald Dewar's heart surgery and recuperation in the summer of 2000 did not prompt the need for a formal replacement. Jim Wallace stood in on an informal basis.

These general rules are supported by the procedural requirement that, if one of four specified events occurs, the Parliament must make its nomination within a period of 28 days beginning with the date of the event[16]. The four events are: (1) the holding of a poll at a general election; (2) the First Minister's tendering of his or her resignation; (3) a vacancy in the office of First Minister, other than by resignation; and (4) the First Minister's ceasing to be an MSP (other than by dissolution of the Parliament itself). There is, however, provision for the period of 28 days to begin to run again if another 'event' occurs. The running of time would be brought to a halt if the Parliament used its exceptional power under SA 1998, s 3 to pass a resolution for its own dissolution[17] but with the procedure triggered once again by the poll at the ensuing general election. In the unlikely event that, for whatever reason, the Parliament fails to make a nomination for appointment as First Minister within the statutory period, the Presiding Officer must initiate a dissolution and general election[18].

1 SA 1998, s 45(1).
2 SA 1998, s 46(1), (4).
3 SA 1998, s 84(4); Promissory Oaths Act 1868, s 5A.
4 SP OR 15 May 2003, col 18.
5 SP OR 16 May 2007, col 20.
6 SP OR 18 May 2011.
7 SA 1998, s 45(2).
8 An assumption reinforced by SA 1998, s 46(2)(b).
9 As in the case of Mr McLeish.
10 In the case of Mr Salmond's resignation in 2014, that was not formally tendered until 18 November 2014.
11 SA 1998, s 45(2).
12 SA 1998, s 47(3)(c).
13 SA 1998, s 49(4)(c).
14 SA 1998, s 45(3). As happened to Mr McConnell on 16 May 2007, some two weeks after the general election in which the SNP secured the largest number of seats in the Parliament.
15 SA 1998, s 45(4), (5).
16 Although 28 days may be enough for most appointments where a party leader is already available, it puts great pressure on the ruling party, in the case of a death or resignation, to elect a successor.
17 See para 5.4.

18 SA 1998, s 3(1)(b). The categorical terms of the section appear to impose an absolute duty on the Presiding Officer, although in the different rules of the Northern Ireland Act 1998 under which the Assembly must elect a First Minister and deputy First Minister within six weeks and in the different political conditions in the Province, a majority in *Robinson v Secretary of State for Northern Ireland* [2002] NI 390 held that the Secretary of State did not act unlawfully in not dissolving the Assembly, despite breaching the deadline by a few days.

Government formation by the First Minister

7.16   Once appointed, the most important initial task of the First Minister is to form a government by appointing the other members of the Scottish Government (including the Law Officers[1]) and the junior Scottish Ministers. It may, of course, be the case that, as with Mr McConnell in May 2003 or Mr Salmond in 2011, a First Minister is reappointed following success in a general election and, with many ministers continuing in office during the election period, will have few adjustments to make to the original team, as was the case in May 2011, when ministers simply continued in office and only the new entrants to the Government required parliamentary nomination[2]. The same can happen, following the retiral of a First Minister, as with the retiral of Mr Salmond in November 2014. On that occasion, ministers stayed in office through the period of Ms Sturgeon's nomination to the First Ministership, until she announced her own ministerial team which required the nomination (and approval by the Parliament) of three new ministers[3].

Whether starting with a clean slate or with a partially formed group of ministers, it is for the First Minister to appoint the further ministers required, such appointments being made with the formal approval of the Queen[4]. Ministers must all be drawn from the membership of the Parliament[5] – it is, again, a government on the parliamentary model which is being formed – and, in addition, the Parliament maintains further controls over the appointments process, some more formal than others. Most prominent is a formal requirement that the Parliament should agree to each appointment of a minister. This is a form of parliamentary involvement which does not apply at Westminster. There it is for the Prime Minister to make his or her own selection of ministerial colleagues, without the need for ministerial appointments to be approved by Parliament. The requirement in SA 1998 that such approval should be obtained derives from the recommendations of the Constitutional Convention[6]. It should be borne in mind, however, that the formal rule requiring parliamentary approval of appointments is to be understood within the broader operation of the party system in the Parliament. The First Minister may have emerged from a particular alignment of political parties, acting as a coalition. The same coalition of forces may, at the same time, impose conditions on the party balance to be achieved in the subsequent appointment of the Government and indeed upon the choice of individual ministers[7]. In the course of the minority SNP administration of 2007–2011, the other main parties did not support Mr Salmond's ministerial choices but did not use their voting power to frustrate him[8]. The Parliament cannot itself determine the allocation of portfolios to ministers, although views may be expressed to the First Minister[9]. On appointment, a minister must take the official oath. Although the terminology is not used in SA 1998, the Scottish Government has, from the start, adopted the language of 'the Cabinet'[10] for meetings of the Government[11]. Since 2007, as we have seen, ministers have been styled 'Cabinet Secretaries'.

In formal terms, a minister holds office, like the First Minister, at Her Majesty's pleasure[12] but SA 1998 also provides that a minister may be removed from office by the First Minister[13] and such removals from office are not required to have the consent of the Parliament. The First Minister has a freer hand at the point of dismissal than on appointment. On the other hand, if the ministry as a whole loses political support and the Parliament resolves that the Scottish Government no longer enjoys its confidence, then all ministers must resign[14]. At any other time, a minister may resign[15] and, whatever the circumstances of a resignation, the minister ceases to hold office immediately[16]. A minister also ceases to hold office if he or she ceases to be an MSP 'otherwise than by virtue of a dissolution'[17]. Like the First Minister, ministers do not immediately go out of office once a dissolution has occurred prior to a general election. They remain in office to perform the functions of the Scottish Government until a successor First Minister and ministry are appointed – with the exception of any minister who has lost his or her own seat in the Parliament. Such a minister may be expected to resign, as did Iain Gray after failing to be re-elected on 1 May 2003[18].

Ministers are paid at rates approved by the Parliament under the authority of SA 1998, s 81. Different rates have been set for ministers and junior ministers but the prescribed rates are stated to be maxima and lower salaries may be paid[19].

1   The Law Officers are dealt with separately below.
2   See SPOR 25 May 2011.
3   And five new junior ministers – see below.
4   SA 1998, s 47(1).
5   SA 1998, s 47(1).
6   *Scotland's Parliament: Scotland's Right* (1995) p 25.
7   For the formation of the first Executive in 1999, subsequent developments and the formation of the second Executive in 2003, see para 7.18 below.
8   See SP OR 17 May 2007, col 37. The two Green MSPs in the Parliament supported the First Minister while all other parties (and the sole independent MSP) abstained.
9   See eg the discussion by the Transport and Environment Committee of the desirability of a *separate* minister for the environment, 4 April 2001.
10 See the *Scottish Ministerial Code* and *Collective Decision Making* below.
11 Rather anomalously, the Scottish Cabinet has 'sub-committees' (rather than 'committees') – currently a Legislation Sub-committee and a Resilience (civil contingencies etc) Sub-committee.
12 SA 1998, s 47(3)(a).
13 SA 1998, s 47(3)(b).
14 SA 1998, s 47(3)(c).
15 SA 1998, s 47(3)(c).
16 SA 1998, s 47(3)(d).
17 SA 1998, s 47(3)(e).
18 A resignation might be thought unnecessary. Had he not now ceased to be an MSP 'otherwise than by virtue of a dissolution'? Perhaps not, because his ceasing to be an MSP occurred at the date of the dissolution? But, in that case, perhaps his departure from office could not have been enforced, save by the First Minister?
19 SP OR 21 March 2002, cols 10577, 10596; resolution adopting SP Paper 554. Subsequent salary increases have been in line with the scheme adopted in 2002.

Junior Scottish Ministers

7.17   SA 1998 enables the First Minister to appoint what it dubs 'junior Scottish Ministers' – although they are, in current practice, described as ministers (in contrast to ministers who are, as noted above, currently known as Cabinet Secretaries). Such appointments are to be made with the approval of Her Majesty and, like their senior colleagues, the candidates must be MSPs[1] and must be agreed by the Parliament. Once appointed, junior Scottish Ministers have the same formal tenure of office as their seniors[2]. They may be removed by the First Minister. SA 1998 states that junior Scottish Ministers are 'to assist the Scottish Ministers in the exercise of their functions'. They often act formally on behalf of the Scottish Ministers (eg by signing statutory instruments) and answer oral questions in the Parliament. Ministers are further assisted in their duties by 'Parliamentary Liaison Officers' (PLOs). These were previously known as 'ministerial parliamentary aides' and have a role equivalent to that of parliamentary private secretaries at Westminster[3]. Like them, they are unpaid and are required to assist Cabinet ministers in the discharge of their parliamentary duties. Appointments require the approval of the First Minister.

1 SA 1998, s 49(1).
2 SA 1998, s 49(4).
3 *Scottish Ministerial Code* paras 4.6–4.11.

Scottish Cabinet government

7.18   The provisions of SA 1998 just described provide the formal framework within which the Scottish Government must be constituted. However, they do not tell the whole story. SA 1998 is silent on the matter of party political representation in the Government which is something left to be determined in the light of political conditions in the Parliament. It is, moreover, only a skeleton of legal rules which needs to be fleshed out with the combination of non-legal rules, guidance and practice which are adopted by First Ministers and the Government as a whole, as they take office. After 16 years of devolved government in Scotland, it is possible to draw upon the experience of the formation of the first four Scottish Governments in 1999, 2003, 2007 and 2011. These are illustrative of the ways in which SA 1998's provisions can be applied in the formation and operation of government within quite different political conditions.

An expectation, in the light of the parliamentary election system based upon proportional representation, was that, in contrast with the historic pattern at Westminster, an outright general election win for any single political party was unlikely. And, true to that expectation, the result of the general election held on 6 May 1999 produced the conditions for the first 'Partnership Government' in which a coalition drawn from the Scottish Labour Party and the Scottish Liberal Democrats took office. Unable to command the support of an overall majority in the Parliament from the membership of his own party, Donald Dewar sought agreement with Jim Wallace, leader of the Scottish Liberal Democrats, under which ministerial offices would be shared, following commitment to a programme of policies as a basis for joint working. Such an agreement was by no means an inevitable outcome; an all-Labour Government with only minority support in the Parliament being another possibility, as occurred in the early days of the Welsh Assembly.

The *Programme for Government* agreed between the leaders of the two parties included a list of 'principles' and 'initiatives' across a range of policy areas such as education, health, enterprise and justice. There was a declared commitment to building communities, enhancing rural life and integrating principles of environmentally and socially sustainable development into all government policies. Scotland's culture would be promoted. One controversial policy matter was admitted to divide the parties – that of student tuition fees. There was a commitment to set up a Committee of Inquiry[1] and to consider the evidence and conclusions of the Committee. The Liberal Democrat members of the Government would not be 'bound in advance'. Elsewhere, however, the parties declared a commitment to introducing a 'new style of politics based on partnership and consensus building'. There were commitments to local government, equal opportunities, strong and independent parliamentary committees and the development of the 'Civic Forum'. The Parliament's tax-varying power would not be used. There were commitments to collective responsibility and to the nomination of Jim Wallace as Deputy First Minister. The allocation of ministerial portfolios between the two partners would be agreed by the party leaders and appointments would be made by the First Minister, following consultation with his Deputy.

It was on the basis of this partnership agreement that the appointments of ministers and junior ministers were made in May 1999. In addition to being Deputy First Minister, Jim Wallace became Minister for Justice. Another Liberal Democrat was appointed as Minister for Rural Affairs and two others became deputy ministers. All other positions – another seven ministers, eight junior ministers and the two Law Officer posts – were held by Labour Party nominees. In the course of the first session of the Parliament, the principal reshuffle of ministers occurred following the appointment of Jack McConnell as First Minister.

In May 2003, the political balance in the Parliament produced a situation in which the Labour Party and the Liberal Democrats were again attracted to the negotiation of a coalition agreement. The Labour Party had only 50 seats (compared with 56 prior to the dissolution) but the Liberal Democrats had increased their representation to 17. Negotiations were rather more protracted than in 1999 but were completed, in the shape of *A Partnership for a Better Scotland*, between the election on 1 May and the nomination of Jack McConnell as First Minister on 14 May with the support of both parties. The new *Partnership* document was longer and more sophisticated than its predecessor but it served similar purposes. It listed a substantial number of policy commitments, including the commitment not to use the Parliament's tax-varying power and, more controversially, the undertaking to introduce proportional representation (by single transferable vote) in local government. The principles of collective responsibility were reaffirmed and there was a commitment to update and publish the *Scottish Ministerial Code* and the

Guide to Collective Decision Making. On ministerial portfolios, the Liberal Democrats would have a share at least equal to their share of partnership MSPs. The roles of the (Labour) First Minister and the (Liberal Democrat) Deputy First Minister were spelled out, with other appointments by the First Minister, subject to consultation with and, in the case of a Liberal Democrat minister, nomination by the Deputy First Minister. Nominations of the Law Officers had to be *agreed*. A substantial section of the document reinforced the mechanisms designed to strengthen support for the Government by the partnership MSPs. In the first session of the Parliament it had been a recurring concern in the Labour Party that Liberal Democrat MSPs had lacked discipline in maintaining support for the coalition. It was on the strength of *A Partnership for a Better Scotland* that the First Minister brought forward his proposals for the new ministerial team. With most former members of the Government and deputy ministers continuing in office, there was a need on 21 May 2003 for the Parliament to approve the appointment of only three new ministers and two junior ministers.

The May 2007 general election produced, for the first time, a Scottish Government formed from a single 'minority' party in the Parliament. As in the 1999 and 2003 elections, no single party secured an overall majority but, in a change from the first two sessions of Parliament, the distribution of seats was such that the 'traditional allies' of Labour and the Liberal Democrats combined could not achieve such a majority and the SNP was, by a single seat, the largest single party. Following several days of discussions the SNP secured limited support from the Scottish Green Party but fell short of a formal coalition with them or any other parties. The First Minister therefore appointed a ministerial team from amongst the SNP's 47 MSPs. Making a virtue out of necessity, Mr Salmond reduced the number of Cabinet Ministers – to be known from then on as Cabinet Secretaries – from nine to five and appointed a further ten junior ministers (to be known simply as ministers)[2].

In May 2011, the expectation of minority or coalition government in Scotland was abruptly challenged with the arrival of majority SNP government. A similar pattern of appointments was maintained, but with the number of Cabinet Secretaries rising to nine by 2014. Since the formation of Ms Sturgeon's government in November 2014, the Cabinet has comprised the First Minister, Nicola Sturgeon and nine Cabinet Secretaries: for Finance, Constitution and Economy; Infrastructure, Investment and Cities; Fair Work, Skills and Training; Education and Lifelong Learning; Health, Wellbeing and Sport; Social Justice, Communities and Pensioners' Rights; Justice; Rural Affairs, Food and Environment; and Culture, Europe and External Affairs. Until November 2014, Ms Sturgeon had held office (from May 2007) not only as a Cabinet Secretary but also (unofficially) as Deputy First Minster, a position held previously by the Liberal Democrat leader in the Labour-Liberal Democrat coalitions. From November 2014, John Swinney, in addition to being Cabinet Secretary for Finance, was appointed Deputy First Minister.

In the course of the early months of the first government, two new procedural guides were developed and in August 1999 a *Scottish Ministerial Code* and a *Guide to Collective Decision Making* were published. These have been updated and re-issued a number of times, the *Code* most recently in December 2011 and the Guide in November 2008. The *Code* in large measure replicates for the Scottish Government the *Ministerial Code* developed by the UK government and contains a mixture of administrative guidance and guidance on propriety. At its core is a statement of principles of ministerial conduct: the principle of collective responsibility must be upheld; Ministers have 'a duty to the Parliament to account, and be held to account, for the policies, decisions and actions taken within their field of responsibility'; they must give accurate and truthful information to the Parliament – 'Ministers who knowingly mislead the Parliament will be expected to offer their resignation to the First Minister'; openness is encouraged; and Ministers must ensure that conflicts of interest are avoided. These principles are then spelled out further in sections dealing with the conduct of government business; ministers and the Parliament (including the priority to be given to making public announcements first to the Parliament); ministers and their responsibilities, including the use of special advisers (currently 14 in all[3]) and the making of appointments; and procedures governing the party interests of ministers, ministerial visits, the presentation of policy and ministers' private interests. Guidance is given on the need to dispose of any financial interest giving rise to an 'actual or perceived conflict' of interest or to take alternative steps to prevent it. Although it need not do so, the *Code* reminds Ministers that they must also comply with the Interests of the Members of the Scottish Parliament Act 2006[4]. A criticism that had been made of the *Ministerial Codes* is that enforcement procedures, over which the Prime Minister and First Minister ultimately preside, are weak. The UK government response to these criticisms is described above (para 7.9). Since June 2008, the Scottish Ministerial Code has made provision for the First Minister as 'ultimate judge of the standards of behaviour expected of a Minister' to refer matters, as he deems appropriate, to a panel of independent advisers on the Code[5]. The advisers were initially two former Presiding Officers and their first inquiry related to a complaint that the First Minister himself had misled Parliament. The panel's principal conclusion was that he had not[6]. More recently, two former Lords Advocate became advisers and they have been followed by Sir David Bell[7] and James Hamilton (a former Irish DPP).

The need to observe collective responsibility is elaborated first in the *Code* and then in the *Guide*. These largely repeat principles contained in the equivalent UK documentation[8]. The *Guide* states that:

> 'the Scottish Government operates on the basis of collective responsibility and every effort must normally be made to ensure that every Minister with an interest in an issue is kept fully informed and has a chance to have his or her say – in an appropriate forum or manner – before a decision is taken. Collective responsibility also means that, once a decision has been announced, all Ministers are required to abide by it and to defend it as necessary. The doctrine of collective responsibility bites after a decision has been reached; it does not mean that there must be unanimity (or even consensus) beforehand. Ministers can express their views frankly in internal discussion of an issue, but their membership of the Government requires them to maintain a united front once decisions have been reached. This isto ensure that the privacy of opinions expressed in internal discussions

is maintained and to ensure that the internal processes through which a decision has been made are not disclosed'[9].

It was on the basis of these rules that the Partnership Executive operated during the first session of the Parliament – symbolically most prominently, perhaps, in its survival of two votes of no confidence, first on the handling of management of the Scottish Qualifications Authority in December 2000[10] and then on road transport policy in February 2001[11]. A collective solidarity was generally maintained on Executive policies although it was noticeable that, perhaps because of the special circumstances of the case, there was no uniformity of response on the (reserved) issue of the Iraq war[12]. When Tavish Scott resigned as a Deputy Minister in March 2001 because he disagreed with the fisheries policy then being pursued, he said: 'Let me be clear: when one is a minister, one supports the Government. If one cannot support the Government, one resigns'[13]. Cabinets since have continued to observe the convention. The vulnerability of government and individual ministers to a successful vote of no confidence might, initially, be thought to be greatly increased where – as was the case between May 2007 and May 2011 – that government represented a minority within the Parliament. Paradoxically, though, the minority government may have been more secure than its predecessors given that all concerned understood that a successful vote of no confidence would require the formation of a new administration, which failing an extraordinary general election[14].

1   In due course, the Cubie Committee Inquiry into Student Finance. See *Student Finance: Fairness for the Future* (1999).
2   Although a new Solicitor General was appointed, perhaps unusually, the Lord Advocate was not replaced by Mr Salmond. Elish Angiolini eventually stepped down at the 2011 general election and was replaced by Frank Mulholland.
3   See para 7.23 below.
4   See para 5.21.
5   See the *Scottish Ministerial Code* para 1.6.
6   Report, March 2009.
7   Whose report cleared Mr Salmond again (on a self-reference relating to legal advice on EU membership for an independent Scotland) in Jan 2013. At that time, Mr Salmond expressed his delight that in all 6 cases referred for investigation, the minister had been cleared.
8   Ministerial Code section 2 'Ministers and the Government'.
9   Paras 2.1–2.2. For consideration of the situation which arose in the special circumstances of Northern Ireland in which certain ministers had specifically declared themselves not to be bound by collective responsibility, see *Morrow's Application* [2001] NI 261.
10 SP OR 13 December 2000, col 841. On the SQA, see also para 10.10.
11 SP OR 15 February 2001, col 1279.
12 See SP OR 16 January 2003, col 17013.
13 SP OR 15 March 2001, col 601.
14 For further discussion see para 5.4.

SOURCES OF EXECUTIVE AUTHORITY

General

7.19   Ministerial functions must have a basis in legal authority[1]. It is a characteristic of modern government that the majority of functions exercised by UK ministers derive their legal authority from statute. Indeed the principal purpose of much legislation is to confer new powers on ministers or to modify existing powers. This includes the grant of extensive powers to make subordinate legislation[2]. As already mentioned, however, ministers may also derive powers from the common law which include those special powers originating in the royal prerogative but also powers enjoyed by ordinary persons, such as powers to enter into contracts, to employ staff and to convey property. In this respect, ministers exercising powers of the Crown are, again like ordinary persons, permitted in principle to do all those things which are not prohibited by law[3]. Ministers, unlike statutory bodies, are not restricted to the exercise of powers positively conferred by statute.

Although the powers of the Scottish Government are similarly based, they are moulded by SA 1998 to suit the devolution settlement. SA 1998 provides for functions to be conferred on the Scottish Ministers, except for those conferred specifically upon the First Minister[4] or the Lord Advocate[5], and that statutory powers of the Scottish Ministers are exercisable by any member of the Scottish Government[6]. This method of conferring powers collectively upon the Scottish Ministers[7], rather than upon individual ministers, has consequences which are discussed below[8].

The actual powers exercisable by the Scottish Ministers fall into four main categories[9]. In the first place, they may be given powers by the Scottish Parliament itself. Over time and if devolved government endures, this may be expected to be much the largest group of powers and many of the Acts of the Parliament have already conferred powers on ministers. Nevertheless it probably remains true to say that most of the functions exercisable by the Scottish Ministers fall into the second category and are those devolved to them at the launch of devolved government on 1 July 1999. Just as law-making powers were devolved, within limits defined by SA 1998, to the Parliament[10], executive powers were transferred to the Scottish Ministers. Thus functions which had previously been exercised by Ministers of the Crown (ie Ministers in the UK government and especially the Secretary of State for Scotland) were transferred to be exercisable *instead*[11] by the Scottish Ministers 'so far as they are exercisable within devolved competence'[12]. The functions may be either statutory[13] or from a prerogative (or other common law) source[14] but, just as the powers of UK ministers are nearly all statute-based, so too were the powers transferred to the Scottish Ministers. Common law powers such as the Crown's power to contract, are, however, available and so are any of the remaining prerogative powers exercisable within devolved competence[15]. 'Devolved competence' is defined by reference to the legislative competence of the Parliament. Those things which are beyond the Parliament's legislative competence are prima facie beyond the executive competence of the Scottish Ministers. Thus, it is stated to be 'outside devolved competence' to make subordinate legislation if it would be outside the Parliament's competence, if the power were included in an Act of the Scottish Parliament (ASP); and, in the case of other types of function, if a provision of an ASP conferring the function would be outside the competence of the Parliament[16]. There are certain additional categories of functions which were devolved to the Scottish Government from 1 July 1999 but which are hidden from sight because of their conventional rather than legal basis. These occur in those areas where the Queen must receive ministerial advice on the making of appointments and where no statute prescribes who should offer the advice, and on the use of the royal prerogative. In such areas, advice would formerly have been given by the Prime Minister or another UK minister but now this falls to the First Minister, not by virtue of any formal order but by virtue of administrative arrangement announced by the Prime Minister in June 1999[17]. Thus, in respect of functions within devolved competence such as the royal prerogative of mercy or the appointment of regius professors in Scottish universities, the Queen is advised not by the Secretary of State but by the First Minister. Advice on many other appointments is similarly transferred[18], as well as certain other functions, including the issue of congratulations on 100th and succeeding birthdays[19]. It was, at the same time, indicated that, in respect of some appointments, advice would continue to be given by the Prime Minister or another UK Minister but that the First Minister would be consulted[20]. Guidance was also given on the submission of ministerial advice in relation to Scottish business of the Privy Council. Much of that relates to the making of subordinate legislation by Order in Council[21] but certain other functions, relating, for example, to universities and special bank holidays, are also transferred.

Returning to the transfer of competences under SA 1998, it was the UK government's intention to base the boundaries of executive competence on the legislative powers of the Scottish Parliament but then to extend them further. The Scottish Ministers should be able to discharge some statutory functions which, as reserved matters, remained within the legislative competence of the Westminster Parliament[22]. Thus, the third category of powers are those transferred to the Scottish Ministers under SA 1998, s 63[23]. That section enables the transfer (by Order in Council approved by both Parliaments) of further functions 'so far as they are exercisable by a Minister of the Crown in or as regards Scotland'[24] and the power was used to make a substantial transfer with effect from 1 July 1999[25]. Subsequent transfers have been made[26]. Large numbers of powers in relation, for instance, to the interception of communications, extradition, road traffic regulation, abortion (approval of clinics) and many others have been transferred to the Scottish Ministers. The fourth, and final, category of powers are those which have been directly conferred on the Scottish Ministers in post-devolution primary legislation at Westminster. Some have been ad hoc[27]. There was a more general shift of executive competences when SA 2012 transferred responsibilities for the control of drug misuse, and the setting of drink-driving limits and of speed limits[28]. The Smith Commission[29] recommended in November 2014 that a number of other functions be transferred.

The functions of the Scottish Ministers are declared to be 'exercisable on behalf of Her Majesty'[30] and to be exercisable by any member of the Scottish Government[31]. Powers may be exercised by junior ministers and, in principle, by civil servants on behalf of the Government[32]. But UK ministers are not permitted to discharge the functions of the Scottish Ministers. For them to purport to do so would be an abuse of power[33]. However, there are three qualifications which have to be made to this general position. First, SA 1998, s 58 does provide the UK government with specific powers to intervene to prevent or, indeed, to require action on the part of the Scottish Government. It has some parallels, as a constitutional longstop, with SA 1998, s 35 which enables the UK government to intervene in the law-making process[34]. One ground of intervention is to secure compliance with international obligations (other than EU or ECHR obligations) and if the Secretary of State has reasonable grounds to believe that it is required he or she may order that action proposed by the Scottish Government be not taken; or direct that action should be taken; or he may revoke subordinate legislation. Such an order must be reasoned and would be subject to annulment by either House of the Westminster Parliament. The other circumstance in which a revocation order could be made is where a provision in subordinate legislation makes 'modifications of the law as it applies to reserved matters and which the Secretary of State has reasonable grounds to believe have an adverse effect on the operation of the law as it applies to reserved matters'. No such orders have been made so far.

The second qualification to the general rule against intervention by Whitehall ministers is that certain functions are deliberately stated to be shared between the two levels of government. SA 1998, s 56 lists a number of powers including powers to give financial assistance to industry and to others which, while devolved to the Scottish Ministers, may continue to be used by UK ministers[35]. Of greater significance is the specific power conferred by SA 1998, s 57(1) which declares that, despite the general transfer to the Scottish Ministers of functions within devolved competence, 'in relation to observing and implementing obligations under EU law', the functions continue to be exercisable by UK ministers. Although measures to implement EU directives are, in practice, almost entirely made by the Scottish Ministers, a few are made, with the agreement of the Scottish Government, by UK ministers where, for instance, uniformity of provision is sought or no Scottish interest is affected. An additional rationale for the availability of the power in SA 1998, s 57(1) is that it is ultimately for the UK government itself to ensure the full implementation of EU measures and any penalty imposed by the Union for non-compliance would fall, in the first instance, on the United Kingdom as the member state[36].

The third general qualification arises where, under SA 1998, s 93, 'agency arrangements' are made between the two governments for specified functions to be exercised by one on behalf of the other. Such arrangements have been made for administrative transfers in both directions[37]. In contrast with SA 1998, s 63, they do not have the effect of transferring the function itself. It is expressly stated that an agency arrangement 'does not affect a person's responsibility for the exercise of his functions'[38].

1   For the need for authority for expenditure, see para 11.4.
2   See para 6.23.
3   This is sometimes known as the 'Ram doctrine', after Grenville Ram, First Parliamentary Counsel, whose memorandum of 2 November 1945 was published in January 2003 – see HL Debs, 22 January 2003, col (WA) 98. See also A Lester and M Weait [2003] PL 415.
4   See eg the powers to recommend the appointment of ministers and judges (paras 7.16 and 12.5).
5   See para 7.22 below.
6   SA 1998, s 52(1)–(3).
7   In some instances, Acts of the Scottish Parliament have, in fact, conferred powers simply on 'Ministers', a term then defined to mean the Scottish Ministers. See eg the Land Reform (Scotland) Act 2003, s 98.

8   At para 10.2.
9   There are also certain 'shared' and other powers. See below.
10 See para 6.11.
11 It is the entire competence which is transferred. With the exception of the few instances of expressly shared competence (see below), the UK minister retains no continuing competence in the devolved area.
12 SA 1998, s 53(1). All functions of the Scottish Government must be exercised in accordance with the ECHR and EU law. For important consequences of that requirement, see *H v Lord Advocate* 2012 SC (UKSC) 308 (see para 13.4).
13 Ie conferred by a 'pre-commencement enactment', a term defined in SA 1998, s 53(3) to include mainly Acts passed before it. Some subsequent Westminster Acts and Orders have, however, defined themselves as a 'pre-commencement enactment' in order to ensure the distribution of powers to the Scottish Ministers. See, for example, The Environmental Protection (Controls on Ozone-Depleting Substances) Regulations 2002, SI 2002/528 made under the Environmental Protection Act 1990.
14 '[T]hose of Her Majesty's prerogative and other executive functions' or functions conferred by a prerogative instrument: SA 1998, s 53(2) (a), (b). The formula 'prerogative or other executive power' was the means used for the statutory transfer of common law powers in the Government of Ireland Act 1920, s 8(2).
15 Eg the power to arm and supply police forces in order to keep the peace. See *R v Home Secretary, ex parte Northumbria Police Authority* [1989] QB 26.
16 SA 1998, s 54. For analysis of the concept of devolved competence see in particular *Somerville v Scottish Ministers* 2008 SC (HL) 45, discussed in more detail in ch 14.
17 HC Debs 30 June 1999, cols 215–216 (WA). The announcement was repeated in the House of Lords at HL Debs 1 July 1999 cols WA 50–51.
18 Eg H M Inspectors of Fire Services and of Constabulary.
19 Also 60th and certain succeeding wedding anniversaries (on application to National Records of Scotland).
20 Eg Lords Lieutenant and members of the (since abolished) Royal Commission on Environmental Pollution and the Forestry Commission.
21 See para 6.24.
22 *Scotland's Parliament* para 2.7.
23 SA 1998, s 108 provides for a 'reverse' redistribution, ie the allocation, subject to the agreement of both Parliaments, from the Scottish Ministers to a UK minister.
24 Powers may also be transferred to the Scottish Ministers to be exercised concurrently with a Minister of the Crown or may be left with a Minister of the Crown but subject to the agreement of, or consultation with, the Scottish Ministers.
25 Scotland Act 1998 (Transfer of Functions to the Scottish Ministers etc) Order 1999, SI 1999/1750.
26 Including SIs 1999/3321, 2000/1563, 2000/3253, 2001/954, 2001/3504, 2002/1630, 2003/415, 2006/1040, 2007/2915, 2008/1776, 2014/2918.
27 Eg Energy Act 2008, ss 18, 26.
28 SA 2012, ss 19–22.
29 See para 4.21.
30 SA 1998, s 52(2).
31 SA 1998, s 52(3). The subsection refers to 'statutory functions', ie 'conferred by virtue of any enactment' (subs (7)). Even if not conferred by virtue of an enactment, the transferred prerogative and other executive powers are also exercisable on behalf of Her Majesty.
32 See paras 7.24–7.25 below.
33 And challengeable as a 'devolution issue' under SA 1998, Sch 6.
34 See para 9.19.
35 See also the Scotland Act 1998 (Concurrent Functions) Order 1999, SI 1999/1592 (as amended).
36 But the penalty might be recovered from the Scottish Government. See *Scotland's Parliament* para 5.8.
37 Eg SIs 1999/1512 and 2000/745 both of which included the specification of certain environmental functions for discharge by UK departments. SI 2003/407 specified housing mobility functions.
38 SA 1998, s 92(2).

The Scottish Law Officers

7.20   The two Scottish Law Officers, the Lord Advocate and the Solicitor General for Scotland, are members of the Scottish Government[1]. They are appointed (and are removable) by the Queen on the recommendation of the First Minister, with the agreement of the Parliament[2]. A Law Officer may resign at any time and must do so, like other members of the Government, if the Scottish Government loses the confidence of the Parliament. Law Officers must, by virtue of the demands of their offices, be legally qualified. Historically, both offices were occupied by advocates but the Elish Angiolini who was Lord Advocate from October 2006 to April 2011 was the first solicitor to have held successively both posts[3].

The two Law Officer positions are of long standing[5], but their functions underwent a significant transformation on the implementation of devolution[6]. Until the implementation of SA 1998, they were the Scottish Law Officers of the UK government. Since then, they have been the Law Officers of the Scottish Administration and a new Scottish Law Officer of the UK government, the Advocate General for Scotland, was appointed[7]. The Lord Advocate and the Solicitor General[8] have two broad areas of responsibility:

1 SA 1998, s 44 (1). The Solicitor General is not, however, a member of the Cabinet. The Lord Advocate ceased to be a voting member of the Cabinet from November 2001. The *Guide to Collective Decision Making* provides that the Lord Advocate does not 'normally' attend Cabinet Meetings (para 4.2).
2 SA 1998, s 48(2).
3 But created a QC on appointment as the Solicitor General in 2001.
4 See *SME Reissue* Constitutional Law, paras 425–436.
5 For the purposes of their 'retained functions' (see below), the transfer of powers was on 20 May 1999 rather than 1 July 1999. See SI 1998/3178.
6 SA 1998, s 87.
7 The Solicitor General may perform 'functions authorised or required, by any enactment or otherwise, to be discharged by the Lord Advocate': Law Officers Act 1944, s 2(1).

Legal advice

7.21   As members of the Scottish Government, the Law Officers act as the Government's most senior legal advisers and provision is made in the *Scottish Ministerial Code* and the *Guide to Collective Decision Making* to ensure that the law officers are 'consulted in good time before the Government is committed to critical decisions involving legal considerations'. Normally their opinion is to be obtained on a reference from the Scottish Government Legal Directorate[1]. There is no requirement that the Law Officers be MSPs but, to the extent permitted by standing orders, they may participate in its proceedings (but not vote)[2] and, exceptionally, to make statements to Parliament about specific prosecutions which may have given rise to public debate[3]. In this way, a Law Officer may represent the Government in answering questions or in support of a Bill, although it should be borne in mind that, in relation to the presentation of broader aspects of policy, the Cabinet Secretary for Justice has a general responsibility. The Lord Advocate has a role in judicial appointments[4] and SA 1998 gives him or her specific responsibilities in relation to the reference of

Bills to the Supreme Court[5] and devolution issues[6] and compatibility issues[7]. The Lord Advocate is also the representative of the Crown in legal proceedings brought by or against the Scottish Administration[8]. As members of the Scottish Government, the Law Officers are formally entitled to exercise any of the functions vested in the Scottish Ministers[9]. At the time of the implementation of SA 1998, many functions formerly allocated directly to the Lord Advocate became exercisable instead by the Scottish Ministers[10]. These functions largely involve appointments or rule-making (sometimes simply in a consultative role) for tribunals with responsibilities in Scotland and (it may be assumed that) the Law Officers have retained a lead responsibility in these areas.

1   *Code* paras 2.30–2.35; *Guide* Annex B. It is stated that the expectation is that the written opinions of the Law Officers, unlike other ministerial papers, will generally be made available to succeeding administrations. But the fact and content of their opinions must not be disclosed publicly without the authority of the Law Officers.
2   SA 1998, s 27. See also SOs, r 4.5.
3   Elish Angiolini, as Lord Advocate, for example, made a statement defending the Crown's decision to bring prosecutions in the 'World's End' case which collapsed when the trial judge Lord Clarke determined that there was 'no case to answer'. This statement provoked an unusual public exchange between the Lord Advocate and the Lord Justice General. See SP OR 13 September 2007 col 1763 and Lord Hamilton's letter to the Lord Advocate of 26 September 2007. See also para 12.12.
4   See para 12.5.
5   SA 1998, ss 32, 33. See para 9.18.
6   SA 1998, s 98 and Sch 6. See para 14.19.
7   See para 14.19.
8   Crown Suits (Scotland) Act 1857, as amended by SA 1998, Sch 8.
9   SA 1998, s 52(3).
10 This was achieved in a two-stage process. Powers were first transferred by the Transfer of Functions (Lord Advocate and Secretary of State) Order 1999, SI 1999/678, and then secondly by the general transfer of functions by SA 1998, ss 53 or 63 and the Scotland Act 1998 (Transfer of Functions to the Scottish Ministers etc) Order 1999, SI 1999/1750.

Retained functions

7.22   The second group of Law Officers' functions are different in that they are reserved entirely to them and not shared by other members of the Scottish Government. SA 1998 refers to these as the 'retained functions' of the Lord Advocate[1]. They are the functions left to the Lord Advocate after the transfer of others to the Scottish Ministers, and are exercisable exclusively by the Law Officers[2]. They are the functions of the Lord Advocate as head of the systems of criminal prosecution and investigation of deaths in Scotland[3] and SA 1998 goes to some lengths to preserve the Law Officers' independence in these areas. The powers must be exercised separately to avoid political interference and the importance of this principle is recognised by the protection of the Lord Advocate's position against amendment by Act of the Scottish Parliament[4]. This independence is important at both the Scottish and UK levels because the Lord Advocate prosecutes in relation to criminal offences within the legislative competence of both Parliaments. In addition, the Scottish Parliament's powers of scrutiny of the Lord Advocate and the Solicitor General in relation to particular legal cases is restricted[5]. In operational terms, the process of criminal prosecution is the responsibility of the Crown Office. The investigation of deaths is a responsibility assigned to sheriffs in fatal accident inquiries[6].

1 SA 1998, s 52(6).
2 Specific provision is also made for property and liabilities to be transferred to the Lord Advocate in respect of these functions. See SA 1998, ss 61, 62.
3 The formula used in SA 1998, s 29(2)(e).
4 SA 1998, s 29(2)(e). See para 6.21 above.
5 SA 1998, s 27(3).
6 In terms of the Fatal Accidents and Sudden Deaths Inquiry (Scotland) Act 1976. A Scottish Government sponsored review (chaired by Lord Cullen) of the operation of the Act reported in November 2009. In July 2014, the Government launched a consultation into proposals for reform.

UK GOVERNMENT DEPARTMENTS AND THE SCOTTISH ADMINISTRATION

7.23   Ministers are appointed and given their powers in the ways already explained. It is, however, self-evident that these Ministers, whether at the UK or the Scottish level of government, cannot act alone in carrying out the great range of responsibilities allocated to them. The answer lies in the core institutions of executive government which combine ministers, in whom powers are formally vested, with a civil service whose numbers and organisation are intended to enable the functions to be discharged. It is a combination of the political ministers with the non-political civil servants: the public and high-profile with the, relatively, anonymous. It combines those whose tenure of office depends on the will of the relevant Parliament and Prime or First Minister with those whose tenure, as part of the 'permanent' civil service, is more secure.

Two main purposes are intended to be achieved by these arrangements. The first, as already implied, is operational efficiency. By providing ministers with the resources of expert guidance and advice and then the means to put into effect the ministers' policy programmes and to provide the machinery that all governments need, the civil service is an essential element of the primary function of government, which is to govern. Second, this combination of ministers with civil servants is fundamental to the principal mechanisms relied on to provide accountability in government. Inevitably, most things done by governments are done by civil servants. As a practical matter, it would be impossible for things to be otherwise. On the other hand, it is also a system which, for almost all important purposes, insists that ministers remain legally and politically responsible for acts and decisions (and omissions to act or decide) across the board. The ways in which these lines of responsibility or accountability operate, and with what measure of success, are considered in Chapter 10.

The degree of autonomy sustained by the modern civil service in making its particular contribution to government is as difficult to analyse and explain as it is important. The absence of a written constitution, here as in other sectors, brings a situation in which there are no formal constitutional guarantees of the relative independence and impartiality which have been achieved. Concerns about this state of affairs, particularly in light of what was described as New Public Management (one aspect of which was the creation of next steps agencies (see para 7.24 below)), led to calls for a Civil Service Act to remove its prerogative basis[1] and to establish a statutory framework for the public service[2]. The case for such an Act was accepted by the Labour government as long ago as 2002[3] but it was not until the passing of the Constitutional Reform and Governance Act 2010 that (very skeletal) provision was made to place civil service appointments (under a statutory Civil Service Commission) and management[4] on a statutory basis and to require a code of conduct for the civil service[5] regulation of 'special advisers'[6]. Current versions of the Civil Service Code[7] focus on the need for integrity, honesty, objectivity and impartiality in the civil service. 'Special advisers' are rather cryptically defined in the Act as persons appointed to assist a Minister of the Crown or the Scottish Ministers after being selected by the Minister personally (and approved by the Prime Minister) or, in the case of appointments to the Scottish Government, by the First Minister personally. Currently, in the Scottish Government, there are 14 special advisers. Because such personnel are civil servants but are not subject to the same rigours of appointment on merit and of impartiality of operation their role has been controversial[8].

1 The Civil Service Order in Council 1995.
2 For a useful discussion of the background and issues see G Drewry, 'The Executive: Towards Accountable Government and Effective Governance?', in J Jowell and D Oliver (eds) *The Changing Constitution* (7th edn, 2011).
3 HC Debs, 22 May 2002, cols 279–280. See also HL Debs, 1 May 2002, col 691 et seq.
4 Constitutional Reform and Governance Act 2010, ss 2–4, 10–14.
5 Constitutional Reform and Governance Act 2010, s 5.
6 Constitutional Reform and Governance Act 2010, ss 8, 15, 16. See also the Civil Service (Special Advisers) Act (Northern Ireland) 2013.
7 Laid before the UK Parliament on 11 November 2010 and, in the case, of the Scottish Government version, before the Scottish Parliament on the same day.
8 See Drewry, op cit.; *'Special Advisers: Boon or Bane' Fourth Report of the HC Public Administration Committee* (HC Paper 293 (2000–01)); (HC Paper 463 (2001–02)) (government's response); and HC 122 (2007) op. cit. See also Sixth Report of the Public Administration Select Committee HC 134 (2012–13).

UK government departments

7.24   At the level of UK government, the structure which has come to encapsulate the combination of ministers and civil servants has been the government department. Ministers, as already discussed, do operate collectively as a team, whether at the centre of government as the Cabinet or, more broadly, as the ministry as a whole. Civil servants are part of a unified Civil Service[1] subject to centralised regulation[2]. For the purpose of the conduct of government business, however, a minister (or a small group of ministers) combines with civil servants to carry out functions within a specific sector. Together, as a department, they carry out the functions assigned to the Cabinet (or sometimes more junior) minister at their head. Thus the Secretary of State for the Home Department, with a team of junior ministers (Ministers of State or Parliamentary Secretaries), heads the Home Office with responsibilities including immigration in respect of the whole United Kingdom, and prisons in respect of England and Wales. The Foreign Secretary heads the Foreign and Commonwealth Office; the Secretary of State for Transport heads the Department for Transport; the Chancellor of the Exchequer heads the Treasury; and so on.

Importantly, from the point of view of the government of Scotland, there continues to be a Secretary of State for Scotland although the arrangements for the administration of that Minister's responsibilities have been the subject of regular change over the past ten years. Until 1999, the Scottish Secretary headed the Scottish Office and was responsible for the administration of a very substantial part of Scottish public affairs[3] and, in the period immediately prior to devolution, for all the legislative and administrative reforms required. From 1999[4], the office of Secretary of State was retained but with the name of the department changed to the Scotland Office and, since most of the former responsibilities had been devolved to the Scottish Ministers, with a much smaller range of functions. Elections and the electoral system in Scotland (in respect of both Holyrood and Westminster) are reserved matters and, therefore, part of the Secretary of State's remit[5]. Other reserved responsibilities for Scotland, however, remained with other UK departments, such as the Department for Work and Pensions and, in relation to immigration, the Home Office. In June 2003, these arrangements were shaken up. In the ministerial reshuffle of 12 June, Mrs Liddell resigned and was replaced as Secretary of State by Alistair Darling. Mr Darling, however, did not become a full-time Secretary of State for Scotland but combined the post with his existing post of Secretary of State for Transport. From the same time, Peter Hain combined the posts of Leader of the House of Commons and Secretary of State for Wales. Alongside the ministerial changes, the Scotland Office[6] and also the Wales Office ceased to exist as separate departments of government but were subsumed within the new Department for Constitutional Affairs, created mainly out of the former Lord Chancellor's Department and headed by the Secretary of State for Constitutional Affairs. In further changes in May 2007, the Department for Constitutional Affairs was itself abolished and its functions transferred to the Ministry of Justice. These were later transferred to the Cabinet Office; the Scotland Office was reinstated as a ministerial department; and the Secretary of State for Scotland revived as a stand-alone Cabinet post, occupied during the Coalition years by Liberal Democrat MPs (with Alistair Carmichael replacing Michael Moore in October 2013). The Secretary of State (along with a Parliamentary Under-Secretary) represents Scottish interests in the House of Commons while the Scotland Office's official spokesperson in the House of Lords has been Lord Wallace of Tankerness (the Advocate General for Scotland).

Some of the other UK departments have long histories, with functions changing only to reflect changes in the emphasis of government policies and programmes. Others are of more recent creation, to reflect changing views of whether large departments are to be preferred over small departments and, if large, then representing which preferred combinations of functions. Whatever the particular structure of government departments has been, however, the principal characteristics of departments have, subject to what is said below about executive agencies, remained the same. They are established as separate entities and with separate functions assigned to each. There are formal lines of demarcation between departments which bring the strengths of concentration on certain defined areas of government activity but also the weaknesses of heightened departmental rivalries in their competition for funding and other resources such as access to parliamentary time for their legislative programmes.

Such departmental demarcation tends to undermine the co-ordination of government programmes and to prevent what is today called 'joined-up government'. This division of governmental activity is not greatly affected by the modern practice of designating most ministerial heads of department as Secretaries of State. If a function is allocated by statute to 'the Secretary of State', any person so designated may, in law, exercise the function[7]. This has certain procedural benefits but has little impact on departmental practice. Decisions are made by the minister responsible for the relevant department, or rather, in the case of most decisions, by civil servants in that department. The law recognises that functions vested in ministers may be competently exercised by their civil servants[8].

Probably the most significant adjustment to the department-based architecture of the Civil Service in management terms has been the creation, within the domain of most departments, of 'executive agencies'. Pursuant to recommendations originally made in a report by Sir Robin Ibbs, *Improving Management in Government: The Next Steps* (1988), the delivery of services has been separated from policy formulation and placed in the hands of agencies, each of which is headed by a chief executive and is subject to performance targets defined annually under the terms of framework documents issued by the department. It is a means of seeking to achieve a degree of efficiency in service provision short of privatisation and in a way which also stops short of the further degree of 'hiving off' which is achieved by the creation of a separately constituted non-departmental public body or quango[9]. One consequence of keeping the agencies within the overall direction and control of existing departments is that, in contrast with quangos, they remain formally within the area of accountability of ministers, although the heightened profile of agency chief executives has given rise to some adjustments of practice and perhaps also a contribution to the wider case for seeking a distinction between ministerial accountability and responsibility[10].

1   The Home Civil Service. Organised separately are the Northern Ireland Civil Service and the Diplomatic Service.
2   Although much diversity is achieved under the Civil Service (Management Functions) Act 1992.
3   See para 3.16.
4   For an assessment, see 'Devolution: Inter-Institutional Relations in the United Kingdom' *Second Report of the House of Lords Select Committee on the Constitution* (HL Paper 28 (2002–03)) paras 54–78.
5   See, for instance, the debate about the future size of the Scottish Parliament at para 5.3.
6   Linked to the Scotland Office is the Office of the Advocate General for Scotland.
7   See Interpretation Act 1978 and *Agee v Lord Advocate* 1977 SLT (Notes) 54.
8   *Carltona v Commissioners of Works* [1943] 2 All ER 560.
9   See ch 8.
10 See para 10.2.

Scottish Administration departments/directorates

7.25   Devolved executive government in Scotland has been established on a rather different legal basis and, for reasons of the scale and scope of functions exercised, it will never be possible to make precise comparisons between St Andrew's House and Whitehall. Historically, the Scottish

Office, as a territorially rather than functionally defined department of the UK government, was always different from most of its Whitehall cousins[1]. The creation of the Scottish Administration[2] has at the least emphasised the distinct identity of the Scottish Government. Powers are conferred collectively on the Scottish Ministers and we have already noted the ways in which these powers have been distributed between ministers currently appointed to the Scottish Government. In the first two sessions of the Scottish Parliament the responsibilities of the senior ministers (as members of the Scottish Cabinet) were reflected in the work of the six departments mirroring in general terms the Westminster model of matching Ministers with departments. Since then, however, the SNP administrations have adopted a rather different model. Beginning by defining the remit of each Cabinet Secretary, there has been created a large number of 'Directorates' for which each Cabinet Secretary is responsible. (Overall management of the Directorates is allocated to six 'Directors-General' who, together with the Permanent Secretary (currently Sir Peter Housden) the Chief Scientific Adviser, the Chief Economic Adviser, the Chief Executive of the Crown Office and Procurator Fiscal Service, and three Non-Executive Directors, comprise the Scottish Government's Strategic Board). So, for example, the Cabinet Secretary for Justice, is supported by the Director-General for Learning and Justice, Leslie Evans, who has responsibility for five Directorates including the Justice Directorate itself. These directorates are different from the departments established at Whitehall. They are created not by any statutory order but simply by administrative decision (of the Scottish Ministers). Civil servants within the Scottish Administration are members of the Home Civil Service[3] and the civil service is a reserved matter[4]. The general rules, including those in the *Civil Service Management Code* and the *Civil Service Code* (in its Scottish Government version – see above), therefore extend to the staff of the Scottish Administration[5] but with the appointment function and, as with UK departments, many management functions delegated to the Scottish Ministers[6]. Some consequences of the current accommodation of the Administration's civil servants within the Home Civil Service, rather than the adoption of the Northern Ireland model of a separate service, are considered below in discussion of relations between St Andrew's House and Whitehall[7]. The Scottish National Party had called for a separate Scottish civil service before it took office, although since forming its first administration in 2007 the issue appears to have lost a degree of urgency for the SNP – perhaps because in practice Scottish civil servants have proved themselves more independent from their UK colleagues than the government anticipated.

1 D Milne *The Scottish Office* (1957).

2 A term used to include ministers, 'office-holders' and their civil servants: SA 1998, s 126(6)–(8).

3 SA 1998, s 51(2). Although see below for discussion of recent proposals for reform of that status.

4 SA 1998, Sch 5, Pt I, para 8. The Smith Commission Report (see para 4.21) included a recommendation that 'UK legislation will give the Scottish Parliament powers to make decisions about all matters relating to the arrangements and operations of the Scottish Parliament and Scottish Government' (para 26) but it was unclear whether this was to be interpreted as a recommendation to remove this reservation.

5 See also the extension of the *Carltona* principle by *Scottish House Builders Association Ltd v Scottish Ministers* 2002 SLT 1321; *Westerhall Farms v Scottish Ministers* (25 April 2001, unreported) and the limitations of the principle explored in *Beggs v Scottish Ministers* 2007 SLT 235. See also *Somerville v Scottish Ministers* 2008 SC (PC) 45.

6 SA 1998, ss 51(1) and (5), extending powers under the Civil Service (Management Functions) Act 1992, s 1.
7 See para 7.26. See also the *CSG Inquiry* consideration of civil servants' relations with the Parliament, at paras 513–548.

RELATIONS BETWEEN ST ANDREW'S HOUSE AND WHITEHALL

7.26   In this concluding section of the chapter we draw together some of the material already considered and try to assess how the Scottish and UK governments relate to each other under the devolution settlement established by SA 1998[1]. Politically, it is, of course, a relationship much affected by the independence referendum and its aftermath. The future of the relationship is still being worked out. At the core of the legal relationship between the two governments, however, is the framework for the allocation of legislative powers to the Scottish Parliament to which the Scottish Government has access and, on the other hand, the powers retained as 'reserved matters' to the Westminster Parliament[2]. Similarly, there is the statutory scheme for the division of executive powers. The powers transferred to the Scottish Ministers by SA 1998 itself, by transfer of functions orders or by agency agreements have already been considered and so too have the powers shared between the two governments and the powers which require consultation between governments before they can be exercised[3]. The creation of the two, constitutionally distinct, governments or administrations[4] and the formal division of powers between them provide the principal foundations of the intergovernmental relationship.

But the initial allocation of powers is only a starting point. SA 1998 contains many other provisions which define the way in which the two tiers of authority share in the government of Scotland. Most tend to confer powers of scrutiny and control upon UK ministers, although, as we have seen, adjustments of the powers of the Scottish Parliament or the Scottish Ministers do require the formal agreement of *both* Parliaments[5]. UK departments scrutinise Bills in the Scottish Parliament with, in the background, the possibility that the Law Officers might initiate a challenge by way of reference to the Supreme Court[6]. The Secretary of State also has the power under SA 1998, s 35 to intervene to block the progress of a Bill[7], and, as earlier noted[8], similar powers under SA 1998, s 58 to prevent or require action by the Scottish Government.

The Secretary of State's powers under SA 1998, ss 35 and 58 are potentially very intrusive. They may have been considered a necessary element in a system of devolution which might require central government rather exceptionally to assert its authority in support of some wider UK interest. However, the powers take on a restraining and even disciplinary aspect when seen from the point of view of the Scottish Government. There is another provision in SA 1998 which enables UK ministers to make subordinate legislation to make provision considered necessary or expedient in consequence of (a) an Act of the Scottish Parliament which is not, or may be, within its legislative competence or (b) any purported exercise by a member of the Scottish Government of functions 'which is not, or may not be, an exercise or a proper exercise of those functions'[9]. Because of its potentially very broad application, this power too could be very intrusive although to date it has been used only once to make a minor technical adjustment[10]. Nor are the powers which could be available to the UK government confined to those set out in SA 1998. SA 1998, s 28(7) reminds of the continuing power of the UK Parliament to make laws for Scotland. On the initiative of UK ministers, the Westminster Parliament can, for instance, amend SA 1998 itself[11] and it did so, most prominently, to enact SA 2012.

Most of these powers may be seen as available for use only in exceptional circumstances. If used at all, other than with the consent of the Scottish Government and Parliament, it would probably be in circumstances of crisis or feared breakdown of government. Much more routinely, however, the UK government continues to exert a measure of control over Scottish government. It can exert its powers in reserved areas (such as taxation or social security) in ways which affect devolved government and, very importantly, it retains the power to regulate the financing of the work of the Scottish Government and Parliament. Finance is a principal determinant of the reality of power[12].

But, even when all the statutory rules are taken into account, the legal framework still tells only a part of the story of inter-governmental relationships. That framework is a necessary, but far from sufficient, condition of good governance. Devolution also demands good practical relations between governments. As it was put in *Scotland's Parliament*, the 'Scottish Executive will need to keep in close touch with Departments of the UK Government'[13]. There would be a need to 'develop mutual understandings covering the appropriate exchange of information, advance notification and joint working'[14].

The extent to which these mutual understandings and joint working have in fact developed has been considered, formally, several times during the period since 1999. Early on, the House of Lords Select Committee on the Constitution considered the impact of devolution on inter-institutional relations in the UK while, more recently, the House of Commons Justice Committee and the Calman Commission have considered the first ten years of devolution from a whole UK and a Scottish perspective respectively[15]. The Smith Commission's deliberations in the wake of the independence referendum and the 'Vow' provided another significant forum[16] for the discussion of intergovernmental matters and the Commission itself made recommendations for the strengthening of the mechanisms of the relationship[17].

Of undoubted importance is the maintenance of good working relations between officials of the two administrations. We have already noted suggestions for a separate Scottish civil service (para 7.25) but there has also been support from other quarters for the continuation of a single Home Civil Service to which all belong. The House of Lords Select Committee on the Constitution considered the consequences of a single civil service for inter-institutional relations and the arguments for separation and concluded that retention of the single service strengthened the guarantee of civil service impartiality; provided a 'brand' recognised within and beyond the service; provided opportunities for interchange and linkage between staff; and enabled close working and a ready flow of information[18]. More recently, the House of Commons Justice

Committee recognised that reform of the civil service to give greater recognition to the demands of devolution may be inevitable but concluded that there was an 'overwhelming case for a more systematic programme of secondments between Whitehall, Cardiff and Edinburgh' which would help raise awareness of devolution, promote best practice and allow for shared learning across all three administrations[19]. The Calman Commission found that the 'evidence on the civil service has overwhelmingly been to retain a unified service' with '[c]ommon working practices, staff secondments and ease of communication' being cited in support of the status quo[20]. Of greater importance are the relationships between ministers, the political representatives of the two governments. Here, party political considerations loom large, particularly where, as now, the two governments are not only of different political persuasions but also of wholly different views as to the future governance of Scotland. As a result of the independence referendum campaign, 'normal' relationships between the governments have been substantially suspended and it is currently not known whether and, if so, when normal relationships may be resumed. During the period prior to 2007, however, understandings about how relations between the two tiers of government were developed and even during and since the referendum campaign many of these understandings have endured. It has suited neither party to have any sort of breakdown.

One feature of the relationship between the Scottish and UK governments from the outset was that it developed partly on an incremental basis in response to events – an example of the constitution being simply what happens – but partly also on the basis of more structured agreement between the parties. The original White Paper proposals for devolution recognised that, at points where the interests of the two governments would most obviously overlap – for instance at the margin between reserved and non-reserved matters, and where European Union and international relations were at issue – there would be a need for special arrangements to be made[21]. As the Scotland Bill proceeded through Parliament, the UK government indicated that these arrangements would take the form of a Joint Ministerial Committee[22] and a series of agreements as to working relationships in the form of 'concordats'[23].

The initial arrangements were published on 1 October 1999[24]. There was an overarching Memorandum of Understanding agreed by the UK government, the Scottish Ministers and the Cabinet of the National Assembly for Wales (now the Welsh Ministers) which contained the general arrangements. There was then a series of supplementary agreements to establish the Joint Ministerial Committee; a concordat on co-ordination of European Union policy issues (including separate sections on Scotland and Wales and with a common annex); a concordat on financial assistance to industry; a concordat on international relations (again with separate sections on Scotland and Wales and a common annex); and a concordat on statistics. The document also anticipated that UK government departments would be entering into bilateral concordats with their counterparts in Scotland and Wales[25].

The Memorandum of Understanding describes itself as 'a statement of political intent, and should not be interpreted as a binding agreement. It does not create legal obligations between the parties. It is intended to be binding in honour only'[26]. The Memorandum then sets out the main principles on which it and the dependent concordats are based – the need for good communication and consultation (especially on policy proposals); the importance of co-operation; the need for the exchange of information, statistics and research; and also, to a degree, the need for confidentiality in the handling of official information. Meetings of Joint Ministerial Committees, under the terms of the Memorandum, have been held to discuss common issues in the fields of education, local government, transport and crime, and sub-committees have been established on matters such as health and European policy. The Scottish Government has concluded a large number of bilateral concordats with individual UK departments. These too emphasise their non-legal character and the need for good communications and then pick out specific policy areas in which co-operation is expected. To supplement the Memorandum and the concordats there have been published a series of Devolution Guidance Notes. These start with a general Note on 'Common Working Arrangements' and then deal with rather more specific matters such as the handling of parliamentary business and the attendance of UK ministers at committees of the devolved legislatures.

Several attempts have been made to assess the contribution made by the concordat regime to relations between the different administrations. In 2002 the House of Lords Committee noted that 'although the value of having the concordats is unquestioned, their usefulness in practice is more questionable'[27]; and that it had been suggested that the UK government's view was that 'the chief value of the concordats is the process of making them, rather than actually using them to facilitate intergovernmental relations'[28]. It was the Committee's own view that concordats should, in the future, be renegotiated on a fixed-term basis and that the Prime Minister's annual statement about intergovernmental relations should be accompanied by a full list of agreements concluded during the previous 12 months or in force at the date of the annual plenary meeting of the Joint Ministerial Committee[29].

The House of Lords Committee's recommendations were not, in fact, taken forward and the Calman Commission noted that there had been no plenary meetings of the Joint Ministerial Committee between 2003 and 2008[30]. The Commission cited several reasons for the irregularity of JMC meetings including the fact that for the first eight years of devolution in Scotland the same party was in government at Westminster and at Holyrood, leading to a situation where 'informal and party-level contacts, and pre-existing relationships, shouldered the burden that would otherwise have relied on more formal arrangements'[31]. This hints at the explanation for the timing of the meeting which took place in June 2008: it followed a formal request to the Prime Minister (and to the Secretary of State for Scotland) by First Minister Salmond[32]. The meeting, held in London and attended by representatives of the UK government, Welsh and Northern Irish assemblies and Scottish Government, was widely regarded as having been a success: both the Calman Commission and the House of Commons Justice Committee noted its contribution to the reaching of an agreement on a UK wide approach to marine planning, an area which spans the devolved/reserved boundary in complex ways[33]. More recently and despite the surrounding referendum environment, meetings of the JMC appear to have stabilised. A plenary meeting was held on 19 September 2012 (to discuss the economy and public finances, and aviation policy) and another on 16 October 2013 (covering, again, the economy and then migrants' access to public services, and major sporting events). Nor does the plenary JMC activity tell the whole story. There are also Joint Ministerial Committees dealing with specific policy areas including finance, European issues. A special area of ministerial interaction has focused on the arrangements made by both Governments to implement the tax reforms enacted by SA 2012[34]. The overall future of JMC activity will plainly depend greatly on the future of devolution itself. In the meantime, at the JMC plenary meeting of 15 December 2014, it was resolved that, because 'the constitutional landscape has changed fundamentally' since 2000, the Memorandum of Understanding should be revised.

1 In the discussion which follows, the focus is almost exclusively upon inter-governmental relationships. Including, as necessary, reference to executive access to the Parliaments for legislation and other authority for use of powers, it is these which define the working conditions of the devolution settlement. The theory and practice of relationships between *Parliaments* are much more problematic. For earlier discussion of relations between Holyrood and Westminster, see 'Devolution: Inter-Institutional Relations in the United Kingdom' *Report of the House of Lords Select Committee on the Constitution* (HL Paper 28 (2002–03) hereafter 'Inter-Institutional Relations') and Appendix 5 (B Winetrobe) and the UK government response to the report, Cm 5780 (2003). More recently, this area was also considered by the House of Commons Justice Committee in *Devolution: A Decade On* (House of Commons Justice Committee, Fifth Report of Session 2008–09, HC 529, ch 6 – hereafter, *Devolution: A Decade On*) and by the Calman Commission in *Serving Scotland Better* (Final Report of the Calman Commission, 15 June 2009, Part 3 – hereafter, *Serving Scotland Better*).
2 See ch 6.
3 See para 7.19.
4 For the purposes of giving formal recognition to their separate rights and liabilities and enabling proceedings between them, the 'Crown in right of Her Majesty's Government in the United Kingdom' and the 'Crown in right of the Scottish Administration' are identified by SA 1998, s 99.
5 See para 6.17.
6 See para 9.18.
7 SA 1998, s 35. See para 9.19 below.
8 See para 7.19.
9 SA 1998, s 107.
10 The Scotland Act 1998 (Regulation of Care (Scotland) Act 2001) Order 2001, SI 2001/2478 which repealed Regulation of Care (Scotland) Act 2001, sch 3, para 24, which sought to amend the Finance Act 2000.
11 Apart from the orders to amend SA 1998, Schs 4, 5 (see ch 5), SA 1998 has been amended in small ways to update it in the light of other developments, eg the amendment of SA 1998, ss 5 and 12 by the Political Parties, Elections and Referendums Act 2000 and the repeal of s 77(8) (relating to the mechanism for accounting for additional Scottish income tax where the Parliament has resolved to raise the basic rate) by the Commissioners for Revenue and Customs Act 2005. It was also amended, perhaps more fundamentally, by the Scottish Parliament itself by the Convention Rights Proceedings (Amendment) (Scotland) Act 2009 – see para 14.29.
12 See ch 11 below.
13 Cm 3658, para 4.13.
14 Cm 3658, para 4.13. SA 1998, s 96 gives the Treasury the statutory power to require information from the Scottish Ministers.
15 See *Inter-Institutional Relations; Devolution: A Decade On*; and *Serving Scotland Better*.
16 See para 4.20.
17 To which Lord Smith added his own personal reinforcement. See the *Report* paras 28–30 and Foreword.
18 *Inter-Institutional Relations*, ch 5.
19 *Devolution: A Decade On*, paras 77 to 87.
20 *Serving Scotland Better*, paras 4.91 to 4.94.
21 *Scotland's Parliament* (Cm 3658) paras 4.12 to 4.21 and ch 5.

22 HL Debs 28 July 1998 col 1487.
23 See eg HC Debs, 31 March 1998, col 1158.
24 SE/99/36; Cm 4444. Subsequent versions have been published as Cm 4806 (2000) and Cm 5240 (2001), mainly to take account of the varying situation of Northern Ireland within the arrangements. The current version was published in October 2013.
25 For general discussion see R Rawlings 'Concordats of the Constitution' (2000) 16 LQR 257; J Poirier 'The Functions of Intergovernmental Agreements: Post-Devolution Concordats in a Comparative Perspective' [2001] PL 134; A Scott 'The Role of Concordats in the New Britain: Taking Subsidiarity Seriously?' (2001) 5 Edin LR 21.
26 Para 2. The Memorandum of Understanding was approved by the Scottish Parliament on 7 October 1999.
27 *Inter-Institutional Relations*, para 38.
28 Para 40.
29 Paras 43 and 45. For the government's response, see Cm 5780.
30 *Serving Scotland Better*, para 4.28.
31 *Serving Scotland Better*, para 4.120. The Commission also noted that some departmental concordats were 'clearly out of date and may not properly reflect the political or administrative changes since they were agreed' and that the regular reviews of concordats which were envisaged had not taken place.
32 *Devolution: A Decade On*, para 111.
33 See *Serving Scotland Better*, para 4.29 and *Devolution: A Decade On*, para 112.
34 See para 11.16.

Chapter 8

Local Authorities and other Public Bodies

INTRODUCTION

8.1   Central government – government, that is, by ministers and civil servants – has never been the whole of executive government in Scotland or the United Kingdom at large. In particular, local authorities have been responsible for much of the planning and delivery of public services and their importance continues. The legal status of local authorities has changed since David I first established burghs in Scotland by charter in the early 12th century. They once had a legal and constitutional autonomy[1] which has become more precarious today. The structure of local government was changed at many points during the 19th and 20th centuries and the responsibilities of local authorities have, similarly, been modified to reflect the changing needs of increasing urban populations and changing perceptions of the appropriate balance to be achieved between the functions of central and local government. The structure and responsibilities of the 32 councils established by the Local Government etc (Scotland) Act 1994 (LG(S)A 1994) with effect from 1 April 1996 are sketched at paras 8.2–8.4. The passing of the Scotland Act 1998 (SA 1998) and the implementation of devolved government from 1 July 1999 did not, in themselves, bring major change to local government. It was, however, anticipated that the new powers of the Scottish Parliament and the Scottish Government would have important consequences for local authorities and, in particular, their relationship with the new forms of central government[2]. Those consequences, and their treatment by a Commission on Local Government and the Scottish Parliament under Neil McIntosh, are considered at para 8.7.

Occupying a sort of middle ground between central and local government, there is what has been called 'intermediate government' (para 8.8). This consists of a somewhat chaotic grouping of bodies which (a) are mainly created by statute but some by virtue of the prerogative or, more informally, by decision of central government; (b) are not a part of central government in that, unlike 'executive agencies', they are not contained within central departments but are 'non-departmental public bodies'[3]; (c) do, for the most part, have executive (ie decision-making) functions but some have an adjudicatory, advisory or consultative role; and (d) are headed not by ministers who are members of an elected government nor by elected local councillors but by persons, typically constituting a 'board', appointed by ministers. Such bodies have been established for a variety of different reasons and with different justifications for their independence from direct political accountability – often, but not always, based on reasons of commercial efficiency. In many individual instances this type of government has been unproblematic but the lack of direct accountability, the risks of abuse of patronage that appointment by ministers can bring, and the secrecy that sometimes accompanies their operation have all meant that government by 'quango' has acquired many negative attributes. Intermediate government has attracted close scrutiny by the Committee on Standards in Public Life[4] and also by the House of Commons Select Committee on Public Administration[5]. Paragraphs 8.9–8.12 of the chapter consider the consequences of devolution for intermediate government. As with local authorities, many quangos with responsibilities in Scotland were initially unaffected by the implementation of SA 1998, save that some are now within the competence of the Scottish Parliament and Government. Others remain United Kingdom-level institutions. Some, however, have functions that straddle the line between reserved and non-reserved matters and there has been the need to create a new category of 'cross-border public authority' to which special rules apply. Paragraphs 8.13–8.16 are headed 'Reforming intermediate government' and deal, inter alia, with the supervision of appointments procedures. Finally, at para 8.14, the Ethical Standards in Public Life etc (Scotland) Act 2000 (as amended), which applies to both local government and other public bodies, is considered.

1 Articles of Union, Art XXI (royal burghs).
2 *Scotland's Parliament* (Cm 3658) ch 6.
3 For a listing see *Public Bodies 2012* (Cabinet Office). See too https://www.gov.uk/government/organisations.
4 *Standards Matter: A Review of Best Practice in Promoting Good Behaviour in Public Life* (Jan 2013).
5 '*Mapping the Quango State*', *Fifth Report* (HC Paper 367 (2000–01)); '*Government by Appointment: Opening up the Patronage State*' *Fourth Report* (HC Paper 165 (2002–03)). More recently the Committee's output has declined but see eg '*Smaller Government: Shrinking the Quango State*' Fifth Report (HC 537 (2010–11)).

SCOTTISH LOCAL GOVERNMENT SINCE 1996

Introduction

8.2   Although the present structure of local government in Scotland dates back only to April 1996, it is a system whose principal formal characteristics remained broadly the same throughout the 20th century[1]. The period to 1975 saw the long rise of the county councils, from their statutory creation in 1890, alongside the burgh authorities which were mostly of much earlier date[2]. Local authorities were elected; they were multipurpose bodies rather than existing simply for the discharge of a single function; they were financed from both grants from central government and from rates collected locally; and decision-making was mainly by committees of the authority. Following the 1939–45 war, the range and importance of the services provided by local authorities increased. New responsibilities for town and country planning and social work combined with expanding responsibilities for education, housing, roads, water and sewerage to give local authorities a very substantial role. At the same time, however, their structure and organisation were failing to keep pace. In the view of the Wheatley Royal Commission which reported in 1969, something was seriously wrong[3]. There were too many authorities (some 643) and of too many (5) different types. This led to inefficiencies which could be remedied only by reform implemented, in due course, in May 1975 under the terms of the Local Government (Scotland) Act 1973. With the declared aim of achieving both greater democracy and greater effectiveness, the number of authorities was greatly reduced. Across mainland Scotland a two-tier structure was created. There were nine regional councils, taking responsibility for functions including education, social work, roads, structure planning and water supply; then 56 district councils, with responsibility for housing, environmental health and local planning. This, it was believed, would be a system coming closest to providing authorities of a size appropriate to the efficient delivery of the different services while, at the same time, linking the authorities to identifiable communities across the country. In the three islands areas of Orkney, Shetland and the Western Isles, however, single-tier authorities were created, with responsibility for all local functions save that they were amalgamated with the Highland Region for the provision of police and fire services. It was interesting that, whereas prior to the 1975 reorganisation the all-purpose authorities had been in the four major cities, after that reorganisation all-purpose authorities shifted to the islands. In the next reorganisation, however, single-tier authorities were introduced uniformly across Scotland.

The reorganisation of 1996 took place in very different circumstances from that of 1975. In the earlier period, there was an acknowledgment that the organisation of local government needed a substantial overhaul but there was no serious challenge to the idea of local government itself. Local self-government was essential to the delivery of local services and the structures had to be reformed to sustain the ideal. There were tensions between central government and local authorities, in relation to the funding of local government in particular, but it was still credible to refer to the relationship between the two as a 'partnership'. By the early 1990s, however, these conditions had changed substantially. From 1979, in particular, the Thatcher governments were less tolerant of the political independence of local authorities; they sought to restrict the authorities' freedom to spend money; and they removed many local authority powers. In the privatising ideology of the times, local authorities came to be viewed not as the essential providers of local services but as enablers of service provision. This led, for instance, to the removal of local authority responsibility for further education in 1992[4] and, at the point of reorganisation in 1996, of responsibility for water and sewerage services and the Children's Reporter service[5]. Just as importantly, however, central government imposed on local councils an expanding regime of 'compulsory competitive tendering' (CCT)[6] under which councils were required to compete with private-sector providers in the supply of services.

This approach to local government as a whole produced a different approach to how to achieve its most desirable structure. The big regional authorities, especially Strathclyde Regional Council and Lothian Regional Council in the central belt, had become symbolic of old-style big government and, particularly since they tended to be controlled by central government's political opponents, could readily be dispensed with. Two-tier local government, it was argued, was, in any event, confusing and unnecessary and produced uncertain lines of accountability. There was no involvement of a Royal Commission or other equivalent of the earlier Wheatley Commission but instead a direct move to consultation papers[7] and the Bill which became LG(S)A 1994. Leaving the three islands' councils intact, LG(S)A 1994 replaced the 9 mainland regions and 53 districts with 29 councils – roughly replicating the number of pre-1975 county councils but without the added complications of burgh or district councils. Subject to initial transitional arrangements, elections were originally to be held on a three-yearly cycle with effect from May 1999. Since then, however, these arrangements have been changed in two ways. First it was decided to synchronise local elections with those for the Scottish Parliament, and the Scottish Local Government (Elections) Act 2002 introduced a new four-yearly cycle with effect from May 2003. Later the local elections were disengaged from the parliamentary cycle by the Scottish Local Government (Elections) Act 2009 which provided for elections in 2012, 2017 and then every fourth year after that. Since the implementation of the Local Governance (Scotland) Act 2004 in 2007, elections have been held using the single transferable vote system of proportional representation[8] with council areas divided into multi member wards for the purpose. The electorate is the same as for elections to the Scottish Parliament and the European Parliament and thus includes members of the House of Lords and citizens of EU countries, provided that they are resident and on the electoral roll[9]. Since 1975, and surviving the reorganisation of 1996, there have also operated in Scotland bodies known as community councils[10]. These have no executive powers but consist of local people, mainly elected, whose task is consultative, especially on planning matters.

1   For a fuller account, see C M G Himsworth *Local Government Law in Scotland* (1995): C Himsworth, 'Local Government in Scotland' in A McHarg and T Mullen (eds) *Public Law in Scotland* (2006). See also *SME Reissue* Local Government; and *SME Reissue* Constitutional Law, paras 438–467.

2   Local Government (Scotland) Act 1889; Local Government (Scotland) Acts 1929 and 1947.

3   Cmnd 4150, paras 1, 2.

4   Further and Higher Education (Scotland) Act 1992.

5   LG(S)A 1994, Pts II, III. The Children's Hearings system has since been reformed with the Scottish Children's Reporter Administration responsible for the principal reporter's functions and Children's Hearings Scotland responsible for the administration of the hearings system itself: see Children's Hearings (Scotland) Act 2011.

6   Local Government, Planning and Land Act 1980; Local Government Act 1988; Local Government Act 1992. See now the obligation to secure 'best value' para 8.3 below.

7   *The Structure of Local Government in Scotland: The case for change, principles of the new system* (1991) and *Shaping the New Councils* (1992).

8   The Executive appointed the (Kerley) Renewing Local Democracy Working Group which reported in June 2000 – with a majority of the Group recommending the adoption of the single transferable vote (STV) system of election from multi-member constituencies. Subsequently, the Executive consulted further and, after it renewed its commitment in principle in September 2002, proposals for the introduction of STV were included in the draft Local Governance (Scotland) Bill published in February 2003. A commitment to proportional representation was included in the Liberal Democrat manifesto prior to the general election of May 2003 and, although the Labour Party manifesto expressed a preference for no change, the agreed coalition document, *A Partnership for a Better Scotland,* of May 2003, contained a promise to introduce, by the time of the 2007 elections, the STV system with multi-member wards of either three or four members, depending on local circumstances.

9   Local Government Elections (Changes to the Franchise and Qualifications of Members) Regulations 1995, SI 1995/1948.

10 Local Government (Scotland) Act 1973 (LG(S)A 1973), Pt IV.

Powers

8.3   Local authority powers derive from statute[1], as passed mainly by the Westminster Parliament but increasingly by the Scottish Parliament. In the British tradition of local government, powers tend to be conferred in quite specific terms and this means that the legal authority for most local authority functions is contained in statutes which deal with a particular functional area. Thus, local authorities derive their powers in relation to schools from the Education (Scotland) Act 1980 and subsequent legislation[2]; their powers to construct and maintain roads from the Roads (Scotland) Act 1984; their social work functions from the Social Work (Scotland) Act 1968 and the Children and Young People (Scotland) Act 2014; their planning powers from the Town and Country Planning (Scotland) Act 1997[3], and so on. Other powers are contained in statutes such as the Civic Government (Scotland) Act 1982 which provides for certain licensing and public order functions[4] and some are conferred by the Local Government Acts themselves.

The tradition of conferring powers by specific statutory provision has meant that, until very recently, local authorities have not had general or residual powers to do things of their choice for the good of their local communities. They have not had a 'general competence'. Their only flexibility has derived from two rather restricted sources. The LG(S)A 1973, s 69 confers a power on authorities 'to do any thing ... which is calculated to facilitate, or is conducive or incidental to, the discharge of any of their functions'[5]. Then, LG(S)A 1973, s 83 conferred what was, at first sight, a much wider power. It permitted any authority to incur expenditure which in its opinion is in the interests of its area (or any part of it) or all or some of its inhabitants. The apparent breadth of that power was qualified in a number of ways but it was, in any event, replaced by the Local Government in Scotland Act 2003 (LG(S)A 2003), s 20. Responding to the calls for a power of general competence, s 20 conferred a new power to do anything which a local authority considers is likely to promote or improve the well-being of its area and/or persons within that area). Local authorities were also given the duty to adopt a leadership role (community planning) within their areas in the shape of an obligation to maintain and facilitate a process by which public services are planned for and provided (LG(S)A 2003, s 15). Authorities were subjected to a new duty to secure 'best value', ie the 'continuous improvement in the performance' of their functions (LG(S)A 2003, s 1). Two further ASPs are to change things further for local authorities[6]. The implementation of the Public Bodies (Joint Working) (Scotland) Act 2014 will bring substantial changes to local authority practice as their services are 'integrated' with those of health boards. And, if the current Community Empowerment (Scotland) Bill is enacted, there will be further, and more general, reform as the compulsory participation in a strengthened form of community planning partnerships is introduced. It is unclear, as these developments proceed, how far the distinctive role of elected and autonomous local government will survive the process.

1 Including private legislation (see para 9.25) eg the City of Edinburgh Council (Portobello Park) Act 2014.
2 See, for example, the Standards in Scotland's Schools etc Act 2000.

3 As amended by eg the Planning (Scotland) Act 2006.
4 See also the Licensing (Scotland) Act 2005, as amended by the Criminal Justice and Licensing (Scotland) Act 2010.
5 But see *McColl v Strathclyde Regional Council* 1983 SC 225.
6 Both in consequence, in particular, of the (Christie) Report of the Commission on the Future Delivery of Public Services.

Internal structure and organisation

8.4   The powers of a local authority are almost exclusively vested in the elected council itself[1]. Traditional British practice has not been to adopt a model of local government involving an elected council or assembly and then, separately, an elected provost or mayor in whom some or all of the powers of the authority are vested. Local government has not had a 'presidential' character of this sort. Equally, there has not been a practice of conferring powers on a 'Cabinet' of senior politicians forming an administration separate from, but accountable to, the council at large. Nor has there been a tradition of conferring powers upon a 'manager' or chief executive as the head of the paid service of the council. Rather, the principal model for local government administration has been one giving pre-eminence to government by committee. Until recently most local authority decision-making was by committees organised on functional lines (ie with an education committee, a planning committee etc) and controlled politically by the party having a majority on the council itself. Since the 1975 reorganisation, most councils have also had a co-ordinating committee of senior councillors – typically a policy and resources committee; and many took some advantage of a power to delegate decision-making to officers[2].

Developments since devolution have brought change to the management of local authorities. It was a concern of the McIntosh Commission[3], followed up in the report of the (MacNish) Leadership Advisory Panel[4], that government by committee had become inefficient and unaccountable. The option of directly elected mayors or provosts which has been permitted (subject to local referendum) in England[5] has not found favour in Scotland, but many councils have modified their structures to produce a form of 'Cabinet' decision-making. Powers are formally exercised by an executive committee of senior councillors, with other committees assuming a more advisory or scrutinising role.

1 Exceptionally, powers are vested directly in an officer, for example assessors for the purposes of valuation for rating and the council tax.
2 LG(S)A 1973, s 56.
3 See para 8.7 below.
4 *Scottish Local Government's Self-Review of its Political Management Structures: Report of the Leadership Advisory Panel* (April 2001).
5 Local Government Act 2000, Pt II. See also the Localism Act 2011.

Local government finance

8.5   The continuing commitment to entrusting large volumes of local service provision to elected local authorities makes the work of those authorities expensive (in 2013, nearly £21 bn across Scotland as a whole[1]) and the question of funding them important. Authorities must have sufficient funds to meet their needs but they should also be funded in a way which preserves a degree of autonomy in their decision-making and which encourages local accountability.

Local councils are funded today in three principal ways[2]. A small amount of revenue derives from charges made for services provided. Secondly, councils impose a local council tax on domestic properties, based largely on the value of the property concerned. Thirdly, councils receive from central government (since 1999, the Scottish Government) annual grants allocated according to formulae designed to reflect their needs, by reference principally to their population (adjusted to take account of its special features) and to their own tax-raising capacity. Although certain grants attach to specific services (for example, in respect of certain housing expenditure), most grant funding is general and, notionally at least, may be spent in accordance with a council's own priorities. The general grant funding is provided in terms of an annual Local Government Finance (Scotland) Order[3] under the authority of the Local Government Finance Act 1992 and consists of two elements. The *revenue support grant* is funded from the Scottish Government's general revenues while the second element, the proceeds of *non-domestic rate* income, redistributes to local authorities the sums initially collected by them from commercial ratepayers at a level fixed by the Scottish Ministers. The funding of local government – not only in terms of overall levels but also the lack of robust and buoyant sources under the control of local authorities and, therefore, their heavy dependence upon central grants – has been a matter of controversy for many years. Central government has been reluctant to make radical reform, for instance in the direction of a local income tax which was an option considered positively by the Layfield Committee on local government finance as long ago as 1976[4]. There was also the grave error made in the poll tax experiment of the Thatcher government from 1989 to 1991[5] which left much bitterness.

Expenditure by local authorities and their accounts in general are audited by the Accounts Commission for Scotland[6]. Auditors are required to monitor for good accounting practice but also for illegal expenditure and good value for money[7].

1 The figure published in the Accounts Commission's '*An Overview of Local Government in Scotland 2014*'.
2 Discussion here is of the funding of recurrent or revenue expenditure. Councils may also fund capital expenditure by borrowing. See LG(S)A 1973, s 69 and Local Government in Scotland Act 2003, ss 35–39.
3 For 2015–16, see SSI 2014/36.
4 Cmnd 6453.
5 Himsworth *Local Government Law in Scotland* (1995) pp 113–115.
6 LG(S)A 1973, s 97 (as amended).
7 LG(S)A 1973, s 99.

Central–local relations

8.6   The most important constitutional issue in local government is the relationship which exists between local authorities, both individually and collectively (principally in the form of the Convention of Scottish Local Authorities (COSLA)), and central government. The reason for this is that the point of local government – the justification for the delivery of local services by way of independently elected local authorities rather than field administration by local offices of central government – lies in its freedom to act autonomously on behalf of local people. Local authorities could never be wholly independent, of course. Equally, however, they should not be mere pawns in the hands of central government. An appropriate balance must be struck and frequently the preferred language to describe the relationship has been one of 'partnership'[1]. Essential prerequisites of that partnership are that local authorities do have substantial powers vested in them; that, as we have seen, they have the financial and other resources to discharge their functions; and that they are not subjected to unnecessary supervision and control by central government.

Although there was much room for disagreement, it was generally conceded that in the final quarter of the 20th century the status of local government in Scotland, in common with conditions elsewhere in Great Britain[2], was in decline. In particular, the Conservative governments from 1979 had removed functions from local government[3]; they had reorganised local government in ways likely to weaken it[4]; and had mismanaged local finance, especially during the poll tax experiment. On the local government side of the relationship, there had built up substantial anger and resentment – not ideal conditions under which to launch the devolution project in 1997.

1 See (Wheatley) Royal Commission Report (Cmnd 4150, 1969).
2 In Northern Ireland, the loss of many local services from local authorities to unelected boards in the 1970s had produced an ever starker picture.
3 For example, water services and the Children's Reporter service in 1996.
4 Again, in Scotland, in 1996. In England and Wales, the Greater London Council and the metropolitan counties were abolished in 1986.

LOCAL GOVERNMENT AND DEVOLUTION[1]

8.7   SA 1998 did not in itself bring immediate change to local government. It did not reorganise the structure; nor did it adjust the functions or financing of local government. However, it did bring with it the prospect of future change and, in particular, of a changed relationship with central government which, for these purposes, has now become the Scottish Government.

Local government is not, in the terms of SA 1998, a reserved matter. Nor are practically all the functions discharged by local authorities[2]. This means that it is within the legislative competence of the Scottish Parliament to reorganise local government or take away or add to the functions of local authorities[3]. Although the Parliament cannot in general legislate on matters of taxation, it can legislate for 'local taxes to fund local authority expenditure'[4]. The Scottish Parliament can also amend the system of local elections, although not the franchise[5]. Similarly, the Scottish Government took over the former functions of the Secretary of State for Scotland in relation to local authorities, including the determination of levels of financial assistance through grant.

Anticipating these transfers of power, the White Paper *Scotland's Parliament*[6] foresaw that they might produce the undesirable consequence that the Scottish Parliament would take the opportunity to accumulate a range of new functions at the centre which should instead continue to be more appropriately and efficiently delivered by other bodies, especially local authorities. The principle that decisions should be made as close as possible to the citizen (ie the principle of subsidiarity) held good *within* Scotland as it did *between* Scotland and the UK government. The UK government had just signed the Council of Europe Charter of Local Self-Government and the Scottish people would be served best by the Scottish Parliament and Executive working closely with strong democratically elected local government. That relationship with local authorities was particularly crucial to the good governance of Scotland and the effective provision of services to its people[7].

To assist the emergence of this relationship, the UK government established a Commission on Local Government and the Scottish Parliament under the chairmanship of Neil McIntosh. It had a remit to consider (a) how to build the most effective relations between local government and the Scottish Parliament and Scottish Executive and (b) how councils could best make themselves responsible and democratically accountable to the communities they served. The Commission carried out a substantial consultation exercise and reported in June 1999 to recommend that central and local government should commit themselves to joint agreements setting out working relationships. Rather like the concordats agreed between the Scottish and UK ministers[8], there should be a 'covenant' between the Scottish Parliament and the 32 local councils, supported by a standing joint conference to consider matters of mutual concern. There should be a separate formal agreement between local government and the Scottish Ministers. In addition, the Commission recommended a new statutory power of general competence for local authorities; a review of local government finance; the reform of election arrangements and the electoral system; the review by councils of the way in which they conduct their business, including the formalisation of political leaderships as council executives; and the strengthening of community councils.

Some of these recommendations were carried forward. A Partnership Framework between the Scottish Executive and the Convention of Scottish Local Authorities was agreed in May 2001. This was a document based on 'parity of esteem and the principles of subsidiarity underlying the European Charter of Local Self-Government'[9] and which committed the Executive to consultation, the exchange of information and meetings on matters of local government concern. In the Scottish Parliament, the first substantive policy debate was on local government[10] and the Parliament's Local Government Committee devoted some time in the 1999–2003 session to the discussion of a covenant between the Parliament and local government. A draft was prepared which provided, as with the Partnership Framework, for consultation in a relationship which was to be 'effective and meaningful'. A Standing Joint Conference would be established to undertake periodic reviews of the relationship and of the working of the covenant. However, the covenant was not concluded in the first session because of a number of unresolved difficulties. While the committee thought it possible that its successor in the second session might wish to pursue the matter further, it also thought that events had demonstrated that the Parliament was not, in practice, likely to 'absorb' local government powers. Perhaps more fundamentally, following legal advice, it referred to the retention of the Parliament's powers to legislate on local government matters 'irrespective of the views of local government representatives, or others. Any covenant could not alter this fundamental legislative position'. The committee was questioning the case for a covenant purporting to bind the Parliament. On the other hand, the Local Government Committee, in the face of Executive reluctance to set up a general inquiry into local government finance at that time, conducted its own inquiry – making recommendations that the balance between central and local funding of local government should be put on a 50:50 basis rather than 80:20; that properties should be revalued regularly for council tax purposes; that the non-domestic rate should be returned to local control; and that a further inquiry should be held into the feasibility of introducing a local income tax[11]. The coalition document of May 2003 committed the Executive to establishing an independent review of local government finance[12]. In due course, the report of the (Birt) Committee[13] was published but its findings (including the recommendation of a new local property tax) were rejected by the Executive. When the SNP Government entered into its concordat with COSLA in November 2007 the principal focus was on the important issue of local government finance. In return for a 'freeze' on council tax levels during the years to 2010–11 (and extended to the present), the Government, in recognition of 'the unique position held by local government in the governance of Scotland', would seek to ensure a general increase in funding with less 'ring-fencing' of specific grants. At the same time, however, a Single Outcome Agreement[14] committing to specified policy objectives would be negotiated with each authority. A related SNP initiative[15] to abolish the council tax altogether and to replace it with a local income tax – at a single rate fixed nationally across the country and thus leaving authorities with no discretionary tax rate of their own – was subsequently abandoned because of lack of parliamentary support from other parties[16]. On 26 November 2014, First Minister Sturgeon included in her *Programme for Government* a commitment (in partnership with COSLA) to an independent commission to find a replacement for the council tax and report by Autumn 2015.

There has been a Scottish Government commitment not to engage in an early reorganisation of local government. Whilst the independence referendum period brought a flurry of proposals from the Scottish Government about the future of local government and its constitutional status in an independent Scotland[17] it is unclear whether the current SNP Government will have any reforming proposals under continuing devolution. For its part however, COSLA established a Commission on Strengthening Local Democracy, which reported in August 2014[18] with proposals focusing principally on increased community involvement but also seeking greater local financial accountability. When the Smith Commission[19] reported in November 2014, it was one of Lord Smith's personal recommendations that there should be 'devolution from the Scottish Parliament' – the Scottish Government should work with the Parliament, civic Scotland and local authorities to set out ways in which local areas could benefit from the powers of the Scottish Parliament[20].

1   For a recent analysis see J Gallagher et al *Rethinking Central Local Relations in Scotland: Back to the Future?* (David Hume Institute, 2007).

2   An exception is weights and measures: SA 1998, Sch 5, Pt II, S C9.
3   See SA 1998, Sch 5, Pt III.
4   SA 1998, Sch 5, Pt II, S A1.
5   SA 1998, Sch 5, Pt II, S B3.
6   Cm 3658.
7   Cm 3658, ch 6.
8   See para 7.6.
9   Under that Charter (of 1985) periodic national monitoring reports and recommendations are issued by the Congress of Local and Regional Authorities of Europe. See eg the report and recommendation on the United Kingdom of 2014.
10 SP OR, 2 July 1999, col 878.
11 SP Paper 551, Session 1 (2002).
12 *A Partnership for a Better Scotland* p 46.
13 *A Fairer Way*, November 2006.
14 See *Single Outcome Agreements: Guidance, format and indicators* issued by COSLA, the Scottish Government and others in February 2008. But see too *Single Outcome Agreements: Guidance to Community Planning Partnerships* (Dec 2012).
15 *A Fairer Local Tax for Scotland*, March 2008.
16 For their discussion of the proposal, see the proceedings of the Local Government and Communities Committee of 28 May and 25 June 2008.
17 See *Scotland's Future* (2013) pp 366–68 and *The Scottish Independence Bill: A Consultation on an Interim Constitution for Scotland* (2014).
18 See '*Effective Democracy: Reconnecting with Communities*'.
19 See para 4.21.
20 *Report*, Foreword.

INTERMEDIATE GOVERNMENT

8.8   In Chapter 1 we were introduced to the idea of constitutions as maps on which are located a state's institutions and their interrelationships. In the territory of intermediate government, map-making has been only partial and, therefore, unreliable. As we have seen, starting descriptions are negatively cast. Intermediate government occupies that space not occupied by central government or elected local authorities. Prior to devolution, 'central departments' were all located at the UK level. Post-devolution, 'central government' must include the 'devolved administrations' since it would be inappropriate to relegate elected assemblies or bodies accountable to elected assemblies and parliaments into intermediate government. The definition of what, therefore, constitutes central departments is tolerably clear, although 'department' is not a term of art and central departments collectively are far from monolithic. Non-ministerial departments and offices[1] and executive agencies are part of a varied pattern. But then, even with central government identified, the negative style of definition breaks down in that it does little to help identify the field of intermediate government nor, more importantly, to categorise its occupants[2]. A simple listing of bodies would be possible but not very enlightening. Analysis could be chronological – certainly, some bodies have a much longer history than others – but, again, to little analytical effect. Classification by function is more useful – bodies may be categorised as having adjudicative, regulatory, supervisory, licensing, advisory, service provision or other characteristics – but this can obscure more important distinctions. Similarly, classification by reference to the supposed rationale for the creation and continued existence of public bodies separated from central and local government may be only fairly helpful. It is true that most justifications for intermediate government may be offered by reference to the need for efficiency (for example, the reason for giving the (decreasing numbers of) nationalised industries a commercial independence from government); or the need for a higher degree of independence from political control and political accountability in the provision of certain services (such as the BBC, the NHS or Scottish Water or the Scottish Court Service (soon to be the Scottish Courts and Tribunals Service) in its support of the judiciary); or the need for a quasi-judicial independence for licensing or regulatory bodies (such as the Scottish Environment Protection Agency) and for those who have to scrutinise the functions of government itself (such as the National Audit Office and Audit Scotland). But objective classification on this basis would be elusive. The present pattern of public bodies owes much to the contingencies of history – whether the rise and fall of nationalisation and privatisation; the politics of health care provision; varying climates of friendliness or hostility to local government; or variations in views on the optimum size of the 'state' – and to political expediency.

Probably the most useful guides to the field are those which facilitate contemporary constitutional analysis. This tends to focus on the efficacy of governmental processes (such as economic regulation), accountability (whether of public bodies themselves or of those whom they hold to account), transparency, and the vulnerability of intermediate government to abuse, especially political patronage by ministers in the appointments process. Concerns about quango[3] government and successive promises, in response, from politicians to launch 'bonfires of quangos' are mainly located in these areas. Thus certain potential admissions to the field of intermediate government are fairly quickly excluded. The armed forces, though interestingly different from standard government departments, remain within central government. The police service, on the other hand, is now to be seen, since the creation of Police Scotland, as a form (though a special form) of intermediate government. Courts of law are excluded, because they lack 'governmental' characteristics. On the other hand, tribunals, whose functions and composition may be very similar, would probably be included. Ombudsmen would probably be excluded, like courts, on functional grounds – although, from the point of view of the risk of abuse of political patronage, their position may not be immediately distinguishable from some others. Universities vary in their formal status and, although probably not immediately recognisable as quangos, they are 'public bodies' in receipt of substantial public funding. Certainly their function as education providers does not exclude them. Colleges (formerly 'further education colleges') are more easily grouped as quangos[4] and so are the Scottish Funding Council (further and higher education) and the research councils[5]. Regulators such as those dealing with the privatised industries (for example, the Office of Rail Regulation, OFGEM (gas and electricity)), the Drinking Water Quality Regulator for Scotland, SEPA and the Electoral Commission are within the sector. Service providers including the remaining nationalised industries (such as CalMac Ferries Ltd), Scottish Water and, above all, the health boards[6] and other bodies within the National Health

Service are certainly within intermediate government. Purely advisory bodies such as the (Scottish) Judicial Appointments Board or the Scottish Law Commission, whose situations, because lacking executive powers and serious public funding, are less exposed, would also be included.

One constitutionally distinct group which may be identified are the bodies who are appointed by the Queen on the nomination of the Scottish Parliament rather than of ministers and are supported by the Scottish Parliament Corporate Body. They are the Commissioner for Children and Young People in Scotland, the Scottish Public Services Ombudsman, the Scottish Information Commissioner, the Commissioner for Ethical Standards in Public Life in Scotland[7] and the Scottish Commission for Human Rights.

1 For example, those identified by SA 1998 as 'offices in the Scottish Administration which are not ministerial offices'.
2 For one attempt at definition and classification, see Sixth Report of the Public Administration Committee (HC Paper 209-I (1989–99)) paras 8–25. See also the Scottish Government's Guide to Public Bodies in Scotland (2011) Annex B.
3 The term originated misleadingly as an acronym for 'quasi non-government organisation'. For discussion, see A Barker 'Governmental bodies and the neutral of mutual accountability' in A Barker (ed) *Quangos in Britain: Government and the Networks of Public Policy-Making* (1982). See also D C Hague, W J M Mackenzie and A Barker (eds) *Public Policy and Private Interests* (1975); W Hall and S Weir *The Untouchables: Power and Accountability in the Quango State* (1996); and D Oliver *Constitutional Reform in the UK* (2003) ch 17.
4 See *Governance and Accountability in the Further Education Section* (Scottish Executive, May 2002).
5 For example, the Economic and Social Research Council (ESRC).
6 See Health Boards (Membership and Elections) (Scotland) Act 2009.
7 See paras 8.15–8.17 below.

PUBLIC BODIES AND DEVOLUTION (INCLUDING CROSS-BORDER PUBLIC AUTHORITIES)

8.9   The implementation of SA 1998 brought important changes to the constitutional position of intermediate government and many of the consequences of those changes are still being worked out. The allocation of legislative powers to the Scottish Parliament meant that, for the future and within the limits of those powers, the Parliament could decide whether or not to establish new public bodies; their powers; their membership; and their methods of working. Questions of whether to allocate such new business to local authorities, to the Scottish Ministers or to a quango are for the Parliament to decide. Since 1999, the Parliament has created a number of bodies including Audit Scotland[1], the national park authorities[2], the Care Inspectorate[3], a Risk Management Authority[4], the Scottish Commission for Human Rights[5], the Scottish Legal Complaints Commission[6] and others. The former three separate water authorities have been merged into Scottish Water[7]; predecessor bodies were merged into the Scottish Further and Higher Education Funding Council (commonly known as the Scottish Funding Council)[8] and the constitutions of the Scottish Qualifications Authority[9] and the Scottish Court Service were adjusted[10]. Similarly, new bodies, which can appropriately be established by means other than primary legislation by the Parliament, may also be created. The use of the prerogative, for instance, to establish a new royal commission to inquire into some problem or the appointment of a commission or committee on a more informal basis is within the competence of the Scottish Ministers[11]. By the same token, it remains competent for the Westminster Parliament and UK ministers to establish new public bodies with responsibilities in relation to reserved matters affecting Scotland and, at the same time, decide whether or not to involve the Scottish Ministers, for example by specifying that they will be consulted on certain appointments[12]. It should also be borne in mind that the Westminster Parliament retains the power to legislate on any matter, reserved or not[13], and it could use this power to create a new authority with responsibilities which include devolved matters. It is unlikely that this power would be used other than with the consent of the Scottish Ministers and the Scottish Parliament[14] and an early example was the setting up of the Food Standards Agency in 2000. It would have been within the powers of the Scottish Parliament to establish such a body separately for Scotland but, by agreement, this was done for the United Kingdom as a whole[15]. This was, however, rather a special 'transitional' case, in that preparations for the Agency were already under way prior to devolution.

A rather more complex position presented itself (and with continuing effects) in relation to those public bodies which were *already in existence* prior to 1 July 1999. The main questions raised are (i) how far the Scottish Parliament may affect such bodies by amending or repealing the legislation under which they operate; (ii) what involvement the Scottish Ministers have in relation to appointments or other aspects of the operation of these bodies, including their financing; and (iii) what influence the Scottish Parliament and its committees have on their operation. For these purposes, existing public bodies may be divided into three broad categories:

1   Public Finance Accountability (Scotland) Act 2000.
2   National Parks (Scotland) Act 2000.
3   Public Services Reform (Scotland) Act 2010.
4   Criminal Justice (Scotland) Act 2003.
5   Scottish Commission for Human Rights Act 2006.
6   Legal Profession and Legal Aid (Scotland) Act 2007, s 1.
7   Water Industry (Scotland) Act 2002. See also the dissolution of the Water Industry Commissioner by the Water Services etc (Scotland) Act 2005 and SSI 2007/399.
8   Further and Higher Education (Scotland) Act 2005.
9   Scottish Qualifications Authority Act 2002.
10 Judiciary and Courts (Scotland) Act 2008.
11 See, for example the Report of the (Cubie) Independent Committee of Inquiry into Student Finance, *Student Finance: Fairness for the Future* (1999); and the Reports of the Jandoo and Campbell Inquiries into the Chhokar Affair (SP Papers 424 and 425 (2001)); the Report of the (Crerar) Independent Review of Regulation, Audit, Inspection and Complaints Handling of Public Services in Scotland 2007; the Report of the (Sutherland) Review of Free Personal Care 2008; the (McCluskey) Review Group on the relationship between the High Court of Justiciary and the Supreme Court in criminal cases 2011; and the (Carloway) review of corroboration 2011.
12 Or, as in the case of OFCOM under the Communications Act 2003, s 20, the establishment of advisory committees for different parts of the United Kingdom.
13 SA 1998, s 28(7), and see para 6.22 above.
14 See para 6.22.
15 Food Standards Act 1999. The current Food (Scotland) Bill would establish Food Standards Scotland.

(a) Public bodies with responsibilities entirely connected with reserved matters

8.10   A large number of public bodies, whose responsibilities fall outwith the legislative competence of the Scottish Parliament, are within this category[1]. They include such bodies as the BBC, the Independent Television Commission, the Health and Safety Executive, the Office of Rail Regulation and the Equality and Human Rights Commission. Such bodies are beyond the legislative competence of the Scottish Parliament. At first sight, they would also be wholly beyond the competence of the Scottish Ministers but some adjustments have been made in the process of expanding executive competence under SA 1998, s 63[2]. In, for instance, the field of broadcasting, the powers to make payments to the Gaelic Media Service[3] for the financing of programmes in Gaelic was transferred to the Scottish Ministers[4]. Despite the reservation of the functions of these bodies, the Scottish Parliament's powers to monitor their activities has been a live question since the proceedings on the Scotland Bill at Westminster, especially in relation to such institutions as the BBC. The Scotland Act 2012 (SA 2012) now requires the agreement of the Scottish Ministers to the appointment of a Scottish member of the BBC Trust[5] and strengthens funding and accountability arrangements for the Gaelic Media Service. SA 1998 does not confer any power on the Parliament to demand documents or the presence of witnesses in relation to a reserved body[6] but witnesses may be invited to attend on a voluntary basis. The Smith Commission[7] made a number of recommendations (eg in relation to the BBC, OFCOM and the Maritime and Coastguard Agency) with a view to strengthening the role of the Scottish Government.

1 A small number of these are specifically identified as 'reserved bodies' in SA 1998, Sch 5, Pt III but the category extends much more broadly than that.
2 See para 7.19.
3 Under the Broadcasting Act 1990 but now under the Communications Act 2003.
4 Scotland Act 1998 (Transfer of Functions to the Scottish Ministers etc) Order 1999, SI 1999/1750.
5 Section 16, inserting a new s 90 in SA 1998.
6 SA 1998, s 23(6).
7 See para 4.21.

(b) Public bodies with responsibilities within the competence of the Scottish Parliament

8.11   Again, a very large number of bodies fall into this category. It includes, for instance, the health service bodies, the water authorities (which became Scottish Water) and many others mentioned above. A list was attached as Annex A to the White Paper *Scotland's Parliament*[1]. For these bodies the Scottish Parliament has full legislative competence and their powers could be amended or the bodies themselves could be abolished by the Parliament and their powers ended or transferred elsewhere. In those cases where the bodies exist by virtue of administrative decision only, the same powers to amend or abolish are now held by the Scottish Ministers – to whom have also been transferred the powers to appoint, to give directions and to provide funding that were previously within the responsibility of UK ministers[2]. As far as the scrutiny function of the Parliament is concerned, the power to call for the necessary witnesses and documents is provided[3]. One of the highest-profile investigations of the first session of the Parliament was that conducted by the Enterprise and Lifelong Learning Committee and the Education, Culture and Sport Committees into mismanagement at the Scottish Qualifications Authority[4].

1 Cm 3658.
2 For the general transfer of executive responsibilities, see para 7.19 above.
3 SA 1998, s 23.
4 See para 10.10.

(c) Public bodies with mixed responsibilities

8.12 This is the most complex group because the mixture of functions within the remit of a single existing body causes inevitable problems for the working of the devolved scheme of government, although some of the problems are only transitional and will be gradually removed over time. Bodies may have mixed functions in two different ways. They may be based entirely in Scotland and yet have responsibilities which are both reserved and devolved. It appears that hardly any of these remain[1]. The other form of mixture of functions occurs where bodies have responsibilities in both Scotland and other parts of the United Kingdom and these responsibilities include devolved matters, whether or not also in combination with some reserved matters. This is a much longer list and includes such bodies as the British Tourist Authority, the Criminal Injuries Compensation Authority[2], the Forestry Commissioners and many others[3].

In the case of all these bodies, it is, in principle, open to the Scottish Parliament to make new provision for them within its legislative competence[4]. As with Scottish local authorities, the Parliament could carry out substantial adjustments to their structure and it could abolish functions or transfer them elsewhere. However, in order to make that process work more smoothly and also to regularise the running of most of these mixed authorities (for which administrative responsibility has, in some way, to be shared between Scottish and UK ministers), SA 1998 created the new category of 'cross-border public authority' (CBPA)[5]. With effect from 1 July 1999, CBPAs[6] were specified in an Order in Council[7]. Others have since been designated as CBPAs on their creation[8]. Then, in relation to those specified CBPAs, the standard rules transferring executive responsibilities, within devolved competence, to the Scottish Ministers are disapplied, leaving responsibilities with UK ministers who are required to consult the Scottish Ministers in matters of appointments and the exercise of functions affecting devolved matters on Scotland[9]. Reports relating to CBPAs must be laid before the Scottish Parliament as well as the UK Parliament and the rights of the Scottish Parliament to call for witnesses and documents in relation to CBPAs are established[10]. In order to fine-tune these arrangements and, in particular, to define which ministerial responsibilities are allocated to which ministers (whether on a separate or shared basis or involving consultation), further provision has been made to adapt the functions of some CBPAs and ministers[11]. The specification of a body as CBPA does not prevent the Scottish Parliament from legislating to remove a function from a CBPA (in so far as exercisable in Scotland), perhaps in order to establish a separate body in Scotland. SA 1998 does, however, make provision for the property consequences of such a change[12] if it is made.

1 SI 1999/1319 (below) listed several but it seems that only the Scottish Traffic Commissioner survives. Another originally listed was the Scottish Consumer Council, subsequently Consumer Focus and then Consumer Futures before its abolition in 2014.
2 The earlier Compensation Board was abolished from 1 April 2000.
3 Also listed in SI 1999/1319.
4 The Tourist Boards (Scotland) Act 2006 changed the name of the Scottish Tourist Board to Visit Scotland but retained its connection with the British Tourist Authority under the Development of Tourism Act 1969.
5 SA 1998, ss 88–90. See *Scotland's Parliament* (Cm 3658, paras 2.8–2.11).
6 Which may include not only the quangos we have been discussing but also other government departments, offices and office-holders.
7 SA 1998, s 88(5), (6). See Scotland Act 1998 (Cross-Border Public Authorities) (Specification) Order 1999, SI 1999/1319.
8 On the other hand, the pre-devolution Committee on Standards in Public Life and the post-devolution Electoral Commission have not been designated.
9 SA 1998, s 88 (1), (2). See eg SI 2007/447.
10 SA 1998, s 88(3) and s 23.
11 SA 1998, s 89 and see the Scotland Act 1998 (Cross-Border Public Authorities) (Adaptation of Functions etc) Order 1999, SI 1999/1747. Particularly extensive provision was made in relation to the Forestry Commissioners (SI 2000/746).
12 SA 1998, s 90.

REFORMING INTERMEDIATE GOVERNMENT

8.13   Under this heading it is appropriate to return to some of the constitutional concerns which have been associated with intermediate government and to take account of some of the measures taken to address them. The main emphasis here is upon initiatives taken by the Scottish Government and Parliament since 1999 but the underlying issues have been familiar for much longer and they continue to be addressed with some vigour at the UK level. One such initiative has focused upon the question of maintaining ethical standards in public bodies and that is considered, along with parallel developments in local government, at para 8.17 below.

Otherwise, the main political and constitutional concerns have been with other possible forms of abuse of the quango system. What they have in common is the fear that quangos may be created and funded, and appointments made, not to serve the public interest represented by the ostensible purposes of the bodies themselves but to serve much narrower political purposes. The concerns which have arisen may be divided under three broad heads. There may, firstly, be questions about whether certain quangos are needed at all. Could they not be abolished and their functions given either to a merged quango or to central or local government? Secondly, and perhaps most prominently, there is the vexed question of appointments. There is a long-standing fear that appointments by ministers to quangos may be used as an improper form of political patronage. Thirdly, there are questions about the accountability of bodies whose very justification is based in part upon a wish to avoid direct political accountability but which must nevertheless be kept within some reasonable boundaries of supervision and control.

These concerns have been joined by a cruder concern from a different quarter. Especially in the years since the financial crisis of 2007, quangos have come under assault from governments anxious to cut spending and to limit the size of the public sector[1]. In Scotland, it was the need to make 'efficiency savings' that underpinned the work of the (Christie) Commission on the Future Delivery of Public Services which reported in 2011.

1 See *Public Bodies 2012* (Cabinet Office).

The need for quangos

8.14   The extent of Scottish government by quango was the subject of some attention by the Executive during the first parliamentary session. In January 2001, a review of public bodies was launched. It was concluded in June with the publication of *Public Bodies: Proposals for Change*. This report surveyed a field of some 180 public bodies; it sought to generate principles according to which their continued existence (and the creation of other bodies) should be judged; and made proposals for a number of abolitions and mergers, and, in some cases, for further review. The principles adopted by the Executive started from the need for ministers to be directly accountable to the Parliament for the overall policy and strategic framework within which all devolved functions were carried out. Functions such as giving specialist advice and making quasi-judicial decisions apart, only where it was clear that ministers should be distanced from the execution of a function should it be allocated to some body outwith the Executive, and then only when subject to clear strategic direction. Bodies had to be properly run, efficient and effective. Overall the review produced proposals for the abolition or merger of 52 bodies and the more detailed review of a further 61. Seventy bodies were to be retained. The Public Appointments and Public Bodies etc (Scotland) Act 2003, s 4 dissolved five quangos, including the Ancient Monuments Board for Scotland and the Scottish Conveyancing and Executry Services Board. More recently, the SNP Governments have had a commitment to reducing the number of public bodies in Scotland through a programme of 'Simplifying Public Services' launched in January 2008. The Public Services Reform (Scotland) Act 2010 paved the way for substantial changes to the organisation of public service delivery, first by the reform of specific sectors (including the dissolution (and simplification) of a number of named bodies (Pt 1), the establishment of Creative Scotland (Pt 4) and the reform of the delivery of social care and social work (Pt 5)) and, secondly, by the creation of ministerial order-making powers to improve efficiency, effectiveness and economy or to 'remove or reduce burdens'(Pt 2). The powers are cast extremely broadly, although accompanied by procedural protections, including the need for affirmative procedures in the Scottish Parliament. The powers (unless extended by order) expire in August 2015[1].

At the UK level, the Public Bodies Act 2011 conferred similarly very broad powers on ministers to abolish, merge or otherwise modify the working of a large number of scheduled public bodies[2]. The procedure is by consultation, draft order (and explanatory document), and approval by both Houses of Parliament prior to the making of the final order, but with the possibility, at the instance of either House, of additional representations to the minister before the final order is made[3]. Because such orders (eg to abolish a public body) may have an impact on devolved matters in Scotland, any orders which would be within the legislative competence of the Scottish Parliament or which modify the powers of the Scottish Ministers require the consent of the Scottish Parliament[4] – a form of statutorily ordained legislative consent motion, many of which have, indeed, since been approved by the Parliament[5].

1 Public Services Reform (Scotland) Act 2010, s 134.
2 Public Bodies Act 2011, ss 1–12 and Schs 1–5.
3 Public Bodies Act 2011, s 11.
4 Public Bodies Act 2011, s 9.
5 For example, to consent to the Public Bodies (Abolition of Administrative Justice and Tribunals Council) Order 2013, SI 2013/2042.

Appointments to quangos

8.15   On appointments to public bodies, the starting point was an extension to devolved public bodies in Scotland of the regime created for UK public bodies under the Commissioner for Public Appointments. That office was created by (prerogative) Order in Council following a recommendation by the Committee on Standards in Public Life[1]. When the UK Government published *Scotland's Parliament*, it included the commitment that the Scottish Executive would be required to put arrangements in place to ensure that appointments to Scottish public bodies were subject to independent scrutiny and conform to the Commissioner's *Code of Practice*[2]. The *Code* laid down certain general principles the ultimate responsibility for appointments resting with ministers; selection on merit; appointment panels including an independent assessor; and the observance of principles of equal opportunity, probity, transparency and proportionality. There was no statutorily imposed obligation to adhere to these standards, but the 1999 coalition document, *Partnership for Scotland* contained a commitment to 'encourage the Parliament to review and monitor public appointments' and, in the meantime, the pre-devolution arrangements for public appointments were retained and extended to include appointments made by the Scottish Government. The Commissioner for Public Appointments continued, therefore, to have a UK-wide role and the Scottish Ministers followed the Commissioner's guidance when making appointments[3]. In February 2000, the Minister for Finance launched a review of the system and, in due course, the Executive brought forward proposals not for a prerogative-based Commissioner but for a statutory solution in the form of the legislation enacted just before the end of the first session of the Parliament in March 2003 as the Public Appointments and Public Bodies etc (Scotland) Act 2003 (PAPB(S)A 2003). It established the office of Commissioner for Public Appointments in Scotland. More recently, under the Scottish Parliamentary Commissions and Commissioners etc Act 2010 (SPCCA 2010)[4], that office was combined with that of the former Public Standards Commissioner[5] to create, from July 2013, the Commissioner for Ethical Standards in Public Life in Scotland. The Commissioner is appointed by the Parliamentary Corporation with the agreement of the Parliament. Appointments are for periods of up to eight years and Commissioners are removable only if the Corporation (supported by a resolution of the Parliament) is satisfied that the Commissioner has breached his terms and conditions and should be removed; or the Parliament passes a vote of no confidence in the Commissioner. In either case, the Parliament's vote must be supported by a two-thirds majority [6]. The principal duty of the Commissioner is to prepare and publish a code of practice for appointments to be made by the Scottish Ministers to any of a scheduled list of offices and bodies[7]. It is then for the Commissioner to examine the appointments methods and practices employed by the Government and to investigate complaints. Ultimately the Commissioner is required to report failings under the code to the Parliament, with a related power to direct ministers to refrain from making an appointment subject to investigation 'until the Parliament has considered the case'[8].

1 *First Report* (Cm 2850, 1995).
2 Cm 3658, para 6.8.
3 *Appointments to Public Bodies in Scotland: Modernising the System* (Scottish Executive, February 2000) para 1.8.
4 As amended by the Public Services Reform (Commissioner for Ethical Standards in Public Life in Scotland etc) Order 2013, SSI 2013/197.
5 See para 8.17 below.
6 SPCCA 2010, s 9.
7 PAPB(S)A 2003, s 2 and sch 2. The current version of the Code came into force in October 2013.
8 PAPB(S)A 2003, s 2(8).

Accountability and control of quangos[1]

8.16   As to questions of the supervision, control and general accountability of public bodies, many of the mechanisms[2] applicable to the Scottish Administration have been extended to them. Scottish quangos have been made subject to the audit arrangements introduced under the Public Finance and Accountability (Scotland) Act 2000. Accountable officers must be designated within each body[3]. Intermediate government is also subject to the ombudsman regime. Practically all devolved Scottish bodies are within the jurisdiction of the Scottish Public Services Ombudsman[4]. Most reserved bodies and cross-border public authorities with executive powers remain within the jurisdiction of the UK Parliamentary Ombudsman. Reserved bodies are included within the scope of the Westminster Freedom of Information Act 2000 and devolved bodies fall under the Freedom of Information (Scotland) Act 2002[5]. As with local authorities, another significant change in the legal environment of quangos (both reserved and devolved) was brought about with the implementation of the Human Rights Act 1998 (HRA 1998)[6]. For the purposes of that Act, they are 'public authorities' and they must, therefore, act in a manner compatible with the (ECHR) Convention rights[7]. Bodies with regulatory powers, in particular, found it necessary to adjust the ways in which they implement and enforce the statutory regimes they supervise. Overarching this catalogue of ways in which the accountability of intermediate government is established and maintained is the role of the two Parliaments. We have taken note of their formal legislative powers and the division of responsibility between them. The structure and operation of devolved bodies and, if they are dissolved, the devolved elements of CBPAs are for the Scottish Parliament. Reserved bodies remain the responsibility of Westminster. But what should be the role of the Parliaments in the routine monitoring of public bodies? There are, of course, strong arguments in favour of a very limited role. The point of intermediate government in the first place is to put it at arm's length from ministers and, therefore, to exempt it from the normal rigours of ministerial responsibility to Parliament. Equally, as a practical matter, it would be simply impossible, even if desirable, for the Parliaments to take a close supervisory interest in quangos. It is true that, at Westminster, select committees of the House of Commons include departmentally related quangos within their remit and some investigations have necessarily centred on these. The same possibilities are open to the Scottish Parliament, as evidenced by the SQA inquiries, but it would be impossible to maintain a regime of systematic scrutiny. This was a point powerfully made in the report of the House of Commons Public Administration Committee in November 1999[8]. On the other hand, conditions in the Scottish Parliament may yet turn out to be rather different. There may be both a willingness to take on a broader remit and, subject to other pressures, the scope to do so in practice[9].

1 See R Parry, ' Quangos, Agencies and the Scottish Parliament' in C Jeffery and J Mitchell (eds) *The Scottish Parliament 1999–2009* (2009).
2 See chs 10 and 11.
3 Public Finance and Accountability (Scotland) Act 2000, s 15(3), (4). For fuller discussion of audit arrangements, see para 11.18.
4 See para 10.13.
5 See para 13.22.
6 See para 13.10.
7 HRA 1998, s 6.
8 'Quangos', *Sixth Report* (HC Paper 209 (1998–99)) para 41.
9 For discussion, see Procedures Committee *CSG Inquiry*, paras 549–557. In the Scottish Executive's consultation paper *Appointments to Public Bodies in Scotland* in February 2000, ch 7 was devoted to the Parliament's potential role. Committees do consider the work of quangos from time to time. Currently the Education and Culture Committee is inquiring into Creative Scotland's 'Time to Shine' Strategy.

ETHICAL STANDARDS IN LOCAL GOVERNMENT AND PUBLIC BODIES

8.17   Another early initiative of the Scottish Executive was to introduce the Bill enacted as the Ethical Standards in Public Life etc (Scotland) Act 2000 (ESPL(S)A 2000). With origins first confined to local government, the Executive's proposals were expanded to embrace other public bodies and took forward the non-statutory codes of practice which the UK government had developed in response to proposals from the (Nolan) Committee on Standards in Public Life[1].

The Executive took the view that, although a statutory method of regulation of public bodies had been rejected by Nolan, such a system would now be appropriate. The principle that the highest standards of conduct should apply across the public service was paramount and there was no reason to believe that people genuinely committed to public service values would be deterred by a statutory system. Indeed a clear and strong framework of control, backed up by transparent and readily understood sanctions, would offer assurance to members of public bodies themselves[2].

Thus ESPL(S)A 2000 extends not only to all Scottish local authorities but also to a scheduled list of executive public bodies (including NHS bodies), but not advisory bodies or bodies such as local enterprise companies, university courts and nationalised industries. These were all thought to be sufficiently regulated in other ways[3]. The Scottish Ministers were required to issue a code of conduct for councillors[4] and, separately, a model code of conduct for members of devolved public bodies[5]. Both had to be approved by the Parliament by resolution and, in the case of the model code, each public body was required to submit for approval by the Scottish Ministers its own version of the code to be applied to it[6]. Both codes of conduct urge general principles of selflessness, integrity, openness, honesty and others; there are 'general conduct' rules on, for instance, compliance with regulations on allowances, accepting gifts and hospitality; rules on the registration and declaration of interests; and on lobbying of councillors and members. The councillors' code concludes with an additional section on dealing with quasi-judicial or regulatory business, including planning applications. The machinery provided for the enforcement of the codes of conduct is in the hands of the Standards Commission and the Commissioner for Ethical Standards in Public Life in Scotland[7] who is given extensive powers to investigate and report on alleged contraventions of the codes. Such reports may lead to a hearing before the Commission which has the power to impose sanctions ranging from censure, through suspension, to disqualification[8]. An appeal is available to the sheriff principal and thence to the Court of Session[9]. In practice, most complaints and investigations have related to the activities of local councillors.

1 First Report on Standards in Public Life (Cm 2850, 1995); *Guidance on Codes of Practice for Board Members of Public Bodies* (Cabinet Office, 1997).
2 *Standards in Public Life* (November 1999).
3 *Standards in Public Life* (November 1999).
4 ESPL(S)A 2000, s 1. The 3rd edition of the Councillors' Code was published in 2010.
5 ESPL(S)A 2000, s 2. The current code dates from 2002.
6 ESPL(S)A 2000, s 3.
7 ESPL(S)A 2000, s 8. The Commissioner also has, since creation in July 2013, responsibilities for public appointments (see para 8.15 above, where the Commissioner's mode of appointment and dismissal is discussed) and for parliamentary standards (see para 5.20 above).
8 ESPL(S)A 2000, ss 17, 18
9 ESPL(S)A 2000, s 22.

Chapter 9

Law-making Procedures

INTRODUCTION[1]

9.1   An essential part of the devolution project was to deliver a Scottish Parliament which not only had substantial law-making powers but which would also be in a position to use these powers to good effect. Its location in Scotland and its ability to focus entirely on Scottish issues, in a way that Westminster plainly could not, would provide the separate legal system of Scotland with a legislature dedicated to its needs. But more was required. It was hoped that the opportunity would also be taken to improve on Westminster's performance. Law-making should become a more open and accessible process; and it should involve more consultation on the terms of proposed legislation, both in the Parliament itself and in the stages prior to its introduction into the Parliament. There should be less governmental domination of legislation and more opportunity for back-bench participation; and many of the time constraints and technicalities of procedure at Westminster should be avoided. Much of this depended on devising appropriate procedures and recommendations on the legislative process were an important element of *Shaping Scotland's Parliament*, the report of the Consultative Steering Group, in 1998. The Parliament's original standing orders[2] reflected many of those recommendations. Over the past 15 years, as the Parliament has become well established as a law-making body[3], those original standing orders have been subject to review and revision[4]. The procedures of the Scottish Parliament have become, like those of Westminster, the focus of inquiry and debate inside and outside the Parliament[5]. The largest section of this chapter (paras 9.2–9.20) is devoted to a comparative discussion of the procedure on Government Bills in the Westminster and Scottish Parliaments[6]; paras 9.21–9.24 deal with members' Bills and, in the Scottish Parliament, committee Bills; and paras 9.25–9.27 with private Bills. Paragraph 9.28 provides a brief note on post legislative scrutiny and paras 9.29–9.35 cover procedures for the making of subordinate legislation.

1 For an outline of EU law-making procedures, see paras 3.7–3.9.
2 Initially the Scotland Act 1998 (Transitory and Transitional Provisions) (Standing Orders and Parliamentary Publications) Order 1999, SI 1999/1095, replaced by the Parliament's own standing orders in December 1999.
3 The Forth Road Bridge Act 2013 was the 200th Act of the Scottish Parliament (ASP).
4 The current version of the standing orders is the 4th Edition (as since revised) of April 2011.
5 For internal inquiries see example the Procedures Committee's 6th Report of 2004, a New Procedure for Members' Bills, SP Paper 193 and for external debate see the work of the Calman Commission (para 3.20).
6 Some procedural aspects of 'Sewel' or 'legislative consent' motions are dealt with in ch 6.

GOVERNMENT BILLS

General

9.2   This section describes the essential elements of legislative procedure at Westminster and then, by way of comparison, looks at the procedures adopted in the Scottish Parliament. However, this is not without difficulties. In neither Parliament do the formal procedural rules tell the whole story. Much depends on their practical application in conditions dominated by party politics. Comparisons are further complicated because Westminster and Holyrood procedures are subject to revision in light of the particular needs of each and without necessary reference to the other.

Common to the process of legislation in both Parliaments, however, are procedures intended to subject legislative proposals to successive stages of debate. Some stages are designed to encourage debate and decision-making on the principles of the proposals, their general desirability or undesirability. Other stages are designed to encourage detailed scrutiny. If the proposals are approved at all relevant stages, they then require the formal approval of the Queen (royal assent) to become an Act[1]. In both Parliaments the legislative proposals, once introduced into the Parliament, are known as Bills[2]. Prior to their introduction they may have taken the form of a 'draft Bill'.

In other respects, the legislative procedures in the two Parliaments necessarily diverge. Most significantly, there are the complications at Westminster produced by the need to involve and, if necessary, to resolve differences between, both Houses of Parliament, rather than within a single chamber as at Holyrood. In the Scottish Parliament there are the special forms of procedure laid down by the Scotland Act 1998 (SA 1998) to enable challenge, if appropriate, to the validity of a Bill when passed by the Parliament but prior to its submission for royal assent[3].

1 For Acts of the Scottish Parliament (ASPs), see Scotland Act 1998 (SA 1998), ss 28(2)–(4), 32.
2 For ASPs, SA 1998, s 28(2).
3 SA 1998, ss 32–35 and see paras 9.17–9.19 below.

The passing of a public Bill at Westminster

9.3   Bill procedure at Westminster takes a variety of different forms. It is useful to consider first the course of one which may be regarded as of 'standard' form. This would be a 'public' Bill – one of general application (even if confined to specific subject matter and perhaps to only certain parts of the United Kingdom), rather than a 'private' Bill restricted in its application to particular persons or bodies or places[1]. It would be a public Bill introduced by a minister as a member of the government, rather than by a 'private member'[2]. It would be a Bill introducing new law (while also amending or repealing existing law) rather than consolidating existing law scattered over a number of statutes. It would be a Bill introduced first into the House of Commons, although others start their procedural life in the Lords.

One of the curiosities of legislative procedure at Westminster is the terminology used to describe the stages through which a Bill must pass in both Houses. The stages of a Bill are marked by a series of 'readings', usually taken in plenary session on the floor of the House, supplemented by a committee stage, usually taken away from the floor of the House but sometimes not, and a report stage at which the outcome of that committee stage is 'reported' to the House. 'Readings' are not, however, occasions on which a Bill is actually read. Instead they mark the points at which the House authorises further procedural progress – usually after a vote (division) which, in turn, usually follows a debate[3].

1 See paras 9.25–9.27.
2 See paras 9.21–9.23.
3 For detailed treatment see *Erskine May's Parliamentary Procedure* (24th edn, 2011) Part 4.

First reading

9.4   The first reading stage of a Bill is, however, an exception. In Westminster practice, this is the stage at which a Bill is introduced. A motion that the Bill be read for a first time is formally moved by a minister in the case of a government Bill. There is no debate. The procedure takes only a few seconds but it provides authority for the Bill to be published and it may also be the occasion for intimating the date of the next stage, the second reading. Although the first reading of a Bill is the occasion on which the House receives formal notice of the Bill and, shortly afterwards, its contents, the Bill's introduction will not usually be a surprise. The government's intention to introduce the Bill in that annual session of Parliament will usually have been announced in the legislative programme set out in the Queen's Speech at the beginning of the session. Since 2012, sessions have run from May to May. In turn, that announcement will usually be consequential upon statements of the government's commitment to the policy programme from which the Bill derives, often contained in the governing party's manifesto prior to the previous general election (or, in the case of the 2010 coalition, the coalition agreement[1]) and for which it will, therefore, claim to have a democratic mandate to enact into legislation. Not all of a government's Bills, however, will have their origin in an election manifesto. Often a government will adopt new policies as the life of the Parliament proceeds and these too will require new legislation to bring them to fruition. At other points, a government will simply be responding to events, sometimes with an element of emergency. The Criminal Evidence (Witness Anonymity) Act 2008 was a response to the judgment in *R v Davis*[2] in which the House of Lords held that the use of anonymous witness evidence could be a breach of art 6 ECHR[3]. The Data Retention and Investigatory Powers Act 2014 was a sudden (although delayed and controversial) response to an ECJ decision[4]. Other government Bills include measures to implement law reform proposals from the Law Commissions[5] (the independent bodies established to make proposals for law reform[6]) and the enactment of annual financial legislation[7].

Whatever the origins of a Bill, the traditional position at Westminster is that its content, especially its detail, will not be well known to parliamentarians or the public prior to its formal introduction at first reading. The Bill will usually, of course, have been subject to much discussion in the government department from which it originates. There will have been consultation between policy-makers, ministers, legal advisers, draftsmen and, where necessary, other departments which may be affected. Decisions on the co-ordination and timetabling of the government's legislative programme will have been made by the relevant Cabinet committees. There is, however, no formal obligation on governments to expose their legislative proposals to wider scrutiny by the public or by affected interests until a Bill's formal introduction, although *some* consultation may be undertaken informally and there is a developing practice of publishing draft Bills (often announced in the Queen's Speech) well in advance of their formal introduction.

1 See para 7.11 above.
2 [2008] 1 AC 1128.
3 See para 13.11.
4 *Digital Rights Ireland Ltd v Minister for Communications, Marine and Natural Resources* [2014] 3 CMLR 44. And see para 13.25.
5 For the special procedure to be adopted, see para 13.25. Since the creation of the Scottish Parliament, the implementation of Scottish Law Commission proposals at Westminster has been very infrequent, the only examples since 1999 being the Statute Law (Repeals) Act 2004, Parliamentary Costs Act 2006, the Consumer Insurance (Disclosure and Representations) Act 2012 and the Statute Law (Repeals) Act 2013, all of which resulted from joint reports of the Law Commission and the Scottish Law Commission. The Consumer Rights Bill 2014–15 derived in part from joint Law Commission recommendations. The Partnerships (Prosecution) (Scotland) Act 2013 derived from Scottish Law Commission recommendations.
6 Law Commissions Act 1965.
7 See ch 11.

Second reading

9.5   The giving of approval in principle occurs at the 'second reading' of a Bill. On the motion that it 'be read a second time', a minister from the relevant department introduces the Bill; outlines its clauses; and commends its merits to the House. In a debate which will usually last some four or five hours, the views of leading spokespersons of the opposition parties as well as some backbench MPs will be heard before a division in which MPs usually vote strictly along party lines. The government (even if a coalition government), therefore, almost always wins and it would indeed be a set-back probably sufficient to prompt resignation or consequential recourse to a vote of confidence in the government if it did not[1].

The standing orders of the House of Commons do permit the possibility of holding the equivalent of a second reading debate in a committee rather than on the floor of the House. This is an opportunity infrequently taken but the rule is indicative of the desirability, where appropriate, of lifting the pressure on plenary sessions in the House, a feature of much debate on procedural reform. A special instance of the use of a 'second reading committee' was the use made in relation to exclusively Scottish legislation, before SA 1998, of the Scottish Grand Committee, despite the problems with its political composition (ie its Labour majority) in the period 1979–97[2].

1 Even a win at second reading may, in special circumstances, be insufficient to ensure that a Bill proceeds. See eg the House of Lords Reform Bill 2012 (see para 5.14).
2 C M G Himsworth 'The Scottish Grand Committee as an Instrument of Government' (1996) 1 Edin LR 79. Because it was a Scottish Law Commission Bill, the Partnerships (Prosecution) (Scotland) Bill (which became the Act of 2013) was considered by a second reading committee. For Law Commission Bills, see para 9.16.

Committee stage

9.6   The next stage in the progress of a Bill through the Commons is when it is sent to a committee for detailed scrutiny. Typically, this stage is taken in a public bill committee (formerly known as a 'standing committee'), consisting usually of about 20 MPs reflecting the party balance in the House. It is a committee formed specifically for the consideration of a particular Bill (and given the name of the Bill) but, although it will include the relevant junior minister, opposition spokespersons and perhaps a few other MPs with a known interest in the Bill's subject matter, the membership of a public bill committee is predominantly non-specialist in character. The business of a public bill committee is the detailed consideration of the clauses of a Bill. Often misleadingly called 'line-by-line' scrutiny of a Bill, debate is given a structure by a focus on amendments proposed (usually by opposition members of the committee) to individual clauses and then on the approval of each clause taken as a whole. The political composition of public bill committees means that amendments are rarely made without the approval of the government majority[1]. In a small number of cases, the committee stage of a Bill may be taken on the floor of the House. This occurs where Bills are brief and uncontroversial and a separate committee stage is unnecessary. At the other end of the scale, it also occurs on Bills of high constitutional importance, such as the two Scotland Bills which became SA 1998 and the Scotland Act 2012 (SA 2012), where the Bill justifies the attention and time of the whole House. Previous restrictions on the power of the former standing committees to hear evidence from outside Parliament led to provision being made, though rarely used in practice, for the committal of Bills to a 'special' standing committee which had the power both to debate amendments in the ordinary way but also, in advance of that, to hear evidence for and against the Bill's provisions[2]. Following changes to the Parliament's standing orders in 2006 a Bill may be referred to a select committee, a joint committee of both Houses or to a public bill committee with the power to take written and oral evidence ('to send for persons, papers and records'). These variants on the standard public bill committee procedure are almost never used[3] although many public Bill committees do invite written submissions from the public.

At the end of the committee stage, the Bill proceeds to report stage back on the floor of the House. This stage provides another opportunity for debate on proposed amendments, often including amendments proposed by the government in the light of developments since the Bill was introduced or in the light of undertakings given in committee to amend the Bill in response to criticisms at that stage. The report stage usually leads straight on to the third reading which is a last opportunity for the House to debate and vote on the general acceptability of the Bill before it proceeds to the House of Lords.

Procedures on a Bill in the Lords follow the same overall pattern as in the Commons. The principal formal difference is that there is no general use of public Bill committees in the Lords, although it has become more common in recent years to refer a Bill to a public Bill committee which sits away from the chamber of the House itself but which all peers remain eligible to attend. Following a Bill's approval by the House of Lords, the Bill must still receive royal assent before it becomes an Act. If, however, the Bill has been amended in the Lords, royal assent must be postponed until both Houses have approved it in precisely the same terms. For this purpose, the Bill must first return to the Commons where either the Lords amendments are accepted, in which case royal assent can follow, or if they are rejected, the Bill must go back to the Lords, with the possibility of further 'ping-pongs' between the two Houses before a final text is agreed by both. When parliamentary proceedings on a Bill are complete, royal assent is given under the terms of the Royal Assent Act 1967. As noted earlier[4], this is, in modern times (ie since 1708), a purely formal matter.

1 For one such rare occasion, see Small Business, Enterprise and Employment Bill, HC Debs 18 Nov 2014 col 196.
2 A special standing committee was used for the Adoption and Children Bill in 2001–02.
3 An exception is the use of select committees for the five-yearly Armed Forces Bills.
4 See para 7.2.

House of Commons and House of Lords

9.7   The procedures sometimes required to obtain the agreement of both Houses to a single text of a Bill prior to royal assent are only one illustration of the complexity caused by having a bicameral legislature in which the mix of political composition and constitutional status of one House is very different from that of the other and in which legislative activity must usually to be conducted within the confines of annual parliamentary sessions.

However, one effect of bicameralism with straightforward consequences is that a Bill may start life in either House. Governments use this facility to distribute business between the two Houses at the beginning of the session, though usually taking care not to introduce Bills first in the Lords which, constitutionally or politically, it would be more appropriate to start in the Commons. Bills of 'first class constitutional importance', finance Bills and politically controversial Bills would not start life in the Lords. The different composition and traditions of the two Houses then affect procedures on Bills. In the House of Commons, the government will usually be able to secure a majority in all divisions on a Bill by applying the discipline of the party whip to its own MPs. This applies to divisions on substantive motions but it also applies to divisions on procedural matters. In particular, the government often uses its Commons majority to impose a timetable on a Bill according to which progress must be made at committee or report stage, failing which the 'guillotine' falls and large blocks of the Bill are formally approved with either very little debate or none at all. The restriction of debate by use of a timetable motion has consequences for the quality of scrutiny of a Bill and it routinely attracts accusations from the opposition that democracy is being suppressed, however much opposition MPs may themselves have been guilty of obstruction by earlier time-wasting! Such business management by use of the government party majority does ensure that government Bills make progress through the Commons. In the House of Lords, however, governments cannot always rely upon the same degree of cooperation – a situation which has not changed greatly since the reforms of the House of Lords Act 1999.

It is indeed in the legislative process that the problematic relationship between the two Houses of Parliament[1] is most apparent. In purely formal terms, the Houses have an equality of status and it might even be conceded that the House of Lords, as the 'upper' House, is superior. It is there that the Queen's Speech is delivered at the beginning of each session and MPs are merely summoned to attend. On the other hand, the Commons has an undoubted political pre-eminence. In some respects, this disjunction need not be a cause of difficulty. Peers recognise, for instance, that Bills which they introduce in their own House may make very little progress in the Commons. However, tension can arise around the handling of the government's own Bills. Sometimes the existence of the second chamber serves the government's purposes very well. The introduction of some Bills in the House of Lords before going to the Commons eases the government's programme, and the facility of the House of Lords as a revising chamber is of as much benefit to the government as others: they have the opportunity to revise their own Bills by proposing amendments in the Lords.

On the other hand, the formal requirement that Bills do need the approval of both Houses, including that of the Lords where the government's enemies may outnumber its friends – and even its friends are not subject to the same discipline as MPs – does provide the House of Lords with the opportunity to threaten to withhold its consent and to disrupt the government's programme. Although, by the end of the 19th century, it was generally accepted by the Lords that they should not play their joker to thwart the intentions of a government seeking to implement its democratic mandate – the Salisbury (or Salisbury-Addison) convention[2] – it was the actual resort to the threat in the early twentieth century that prompted a formal amendment of the rules[3]. The Parliament Act 1911 (PA 1911) provided that a public Bill could reach the statute book without the need for the approval of the House of Lords if certain conditions were met. A 'money Bill' (a Bill certified as such by the Speaker of the Commons) may be passed, after only a month's delay in the Lords, by the Commons alone – a rule which reflects the special position of the Commons on financial matters. Then, in relation to all other Bills (except a Bill to extend the maximum length of a Parliament beyond five years), PA 1911 (as since amended by the Parliament Act 1949 (PA 1949)[4]) enables a Bill which has been passed by the Commons in two successive sessions to proceed to royal assent without the consent of the Lords, provided also that a period of 12 months has passed between the initial second reading and the second third reading stages in the Commons. In recent years, the Parliament Acts have been invoked to pass the War Crimes Act 1991, the European Parliamentary Elections Act 1999 and the Sexual Offences (Amendment) Act 2000. The most recent use of the Acts – to pass the Hunting Act 2004 – provoked litigation which resulted in the examination by the House of Lords of the validity of the 1949 Act itself. In *Jackson v Attorney General*[5] opponents of the 2004 Act – which banned hunting with dogs – argued that it was 'not of legal effect' because it had been made using the 1949 Act which, it was said, was itself invalid. This was because the 1949 Act had been made using the procedures contained in the 1911 Act whereas – so it was contended – the 1911 Act could be amended only with the consent of the Lords. Sitting as a panel of nine, the Lords rejected this novel attempt to strike down an Act of the Westminster Parliament holding that s 2(1) of the 1911 Act, which allowed the amended procedure to be used in relation to 'any public Bill' (other than a money Bill), was wide enough in application to comprehend an Act which amended the 1911 Act itself. On the broader question of the legitimacy of the 1911 and 1949 Acts, Lord Bingham of Cornhill observed that:

> 'It has been a source of concern to some constitutionalists…that the effect of the 1911, and more particularly the 1949, Act has been to erode the checks and balances inherent in the British constitution when Crown, Lords and Commons were independent and substantial bases of power, leaving the Commons dominated by the executive, as the ultimately unconstrained power in the state. There is nothing novel in this perception. What, perhaps, is novel is the willingness of successive governments of different political colours to invoke the 1949 Act not for the major constitutional purposes for which the 1911 Act was invoked (the Government of Ireland Act 1914, the Welsh Church Act 1914, the 1949 Act) but to achieve objects of more minor or no constitutional import (the War Crimes Act 1991, the European Parliamentary Elections Act 1999, the Sexual Offences (Amendment) Act 2000 and now the 2004 Act). There are issues here which merit serious and objective thought and study. But it would be quite inappropriate for the House in its judicial capacity to express or appear to express any opinion upon them, and I do not do so'[6].

One reason perhaps for what Lord Bingham notes as the relatively scare use of the Parliament Acts is that they clearly do not remove all problems for a government faced with a rebellious House of Lords. It may be very inconvenient to have to contemplate the year's delay and in a system which, at present, usually requires Bills to be passed within a single annual session[7], the government's opponents in the House of Lords may be in a position to force the government to the brink[8] and extract concessions in return for their approval of a Bill.

1 At the heart of the reform proposals discussed in ch 5.
2 Doubts have been expressed about the survival of the convention under coalition government but see the statement of Lord Strathclyde at HL Deb 20 Jan 2011 cc 596–601.
3 And also the wider process of House of Lords reform. See ch 5.
4 By PA 1949 (itself enacted under the terms of PA 1911), the original period of two years' delay was reduced to the present one year.
5 [2006] 1 AC 262. The case is also discussed at para 6.5 in the context of the legislative supremacy of the Westminster Parliament.
6 Ibid pp 286–287.
7 Running, since 2012, from May to May.
8 SA 1998 itself was subject to brinkmanship of this sort, on the matter of the Presiding Officer's power to pronounce on the legislative competence of a Bill.

Modernising legislative procedures at Westminster

9.8   When the former Modernisation Committee of the House of Commons issued its report on the legislative process in 1997, it acknowledged that much work on the subject had been done by others in the past[1]. The Committee noted a number of perceived defects in the process which had become familiar. There was too little consultation on the content of Bills prior to their formal introduction; communication between the government, MPs and interested persons outside Parliament was patchy and spasmodic; ministers had become so dependent on Bills being approved largely unchanged that there was an inevitable disposition to resist alteration; committee stages of Bills were failing to be an occasion for constructive and systematic scrutiny but rather for politically partisan debate and struggles to extend or curtail discussion, leading to the use of the guillotine and a failure to consider large parts of a Bill; special standing committees were rarely used because of the perception, perhaps misconceived, that the extra time they required put additional pressure on the legislative timetable; report stages were frequently unconstructive, with the opposition using proposed amendments as pegs on which to hang debates on politically controversial issues and the government sometimes tabling hundreds of amendments, both technical and substantive, often to correct initial drafting faults; there was a marked imbalance in legislative activity at different times in the session, producing unacceptable pressures early in the year for the Commons and then, at the end of the year, for the Lords; and the absolute cut-off on the progress of public Bills imposed by prorogation at the end of the session frequently produced chaos amid the attempts to complete the government's legislative programme, and consequent scope for confusion and error.

The Committee's criticisms could easily have been expanded into an even longer list of failings in the Westminster legislative process, especially in the House of Commons. Viewed dispassionately, many existing procedures are inefficient and irrational. Time is wasted and the task of detailed scrutiny often goes undone. Government appears sometimes to treat as important only the stages of the legislative process after the introduction of a Bill into Parliament. There has been governmental resistance to the intrusion of extra-parliamentary views by extending the government's own consultative processes into pre-legislative hearings or by the expanded use of the opportunities offered by special standing committees. There has been a government intolerance of criticism, backed by the assumption made by both government and opposition that weakness in the face of criticism quickly becomes a matter of confidence. Progress on long and complicated Bills has been marred by technical defects requiring correction by substantial numbers of amendments, sometimes not introduced until the Lords stages and, therefore, with the capacity to cause confusion in the closing stages in the Commons.

The weight of tradition has made reform difficult. Entrenched attitudes and practices are difficult to displace, especially when they continue to reflect the systemic balance of power and authority[2]. Reforming proposals need to take account of how far they seek to disturb that balance or how far, on the other hand, they seek to be accommodated within it. In ways which anticipated procedures to be adopted later by the Scottish Parliament, the Modernisation Committee's original proposals ranged widely and many have since been implemented, at least in part[3]. The Committee proposed more pre-legislative scrutiny of draft Bills and, by November 1999, was able to record six instances of drafts referred to select committees, ad hoc committees or joint committees of both Houses. The Committee urged the greater use of the then special standing committees and later noted the reference of the Immigration and Asylum Bill in 1998–99 to such a committee; and also the greater use of committee stages split between a Committee of the Whole House and standing committees (used for the Greater London Authority Bill and the Sexual Offences (Amendment) Bill, as well as for Finance Bills). All Bills should be accompanied by full explanatory notes written in plain English[5], a recommendation adopted from the start of the 1998–99 session[6]. There should be more use of agreed motions to programme Bills[7], rather than having guillotines imposed; and the possibility of the 'carry over' of certain Bills from one session to another should be explored[8].

The Committee revisited these issues in 2006, producing reports on the legislative process generally and, in a special report, on the committee stage of public Bills[9]. In the former, the Committee focused on recommendations which would make it easier for the general public, representative bodies and other stakeholders to become more involved in the drafting and passing of legislation. It noted that pre-legislative scrutiny of Bills had proved 'one of the most successful Parliamentary innovations of the last ten years' and recommended that this should become more widespread – which has indeed occurred. More recently, however, with the exception of some attention to private members' Bills (see below) the thirst for reform appears to have abated[10].

1   See *The Legislative Process* (HC Paper 190 (1997–98)) para 2.
2   See B Crick *The Reform of Parliament* (1970).
3   The Modernisation Committee's First Special Report of 1998–99 (HC Paper 865), issued in November 1999, recorded progress on the implementation of proposals for the reform of legislative and other procedures to that date.
4   HC Debs, 20 May 2003, col 842.
5   *Second Report* (HC Paper 389 (1997–98)).
6   Following enactment, the explanatory notes are revised and published on the HMSO website.
7   The first Bill subject to an (unofficial) programme motion was the Scotland Bill. Standing orders have since made provision for such motions which are now normal on Government Bills.
8   *Third Report* (HC Paper 543 (1997–99)). Carry-over has become a frequent occurrence. Six Bills were carried over between the 2013–14 and the 2014–15 sessions, one of which was the Consumer Rights Bill (see above).
9   HC 1097, HC 810 (2006).
10 One area of discussion at Westminster (as at Holyrood – see para 9.28) has been 'post-legislative scrutiny'. This has formally become a responsibility of select committees – see para 10.9.

A public Bill in the Scottish Parliament

9.9   The absence of the need to accommodate the wishes of a second chamber is what most distinguishes legislative procedure in the Scottish Parliament. However, it was recognised in advance that the lack of a revising chamber would place higher obligations of scrutiny upon the Parliament itself[1].

It was also assumed that Bills would be more widely consulted on in draft form prior to their introduction to the Parliament and more information about the purposes of a Bill and explanation of its content would be supplied[2].

SA 1998 itself made only outline provision for the stages of Bills, leaving the details to be supplied by the Parliament's standing orders[3]. During the early months of the Parliament, however, procedure was governed by temporary standing orders made by the Secretary of State in advance of the Parliament's first meeting[4]. These were replaced by the Parliament's own standing orders (SOs) in December 1999[5] (most recently updated in above). Although the rules contained in the standing orders are, of course, expected to be followed by the Parliament, a breach of the procedural rules will not usually be fatal. Indeed, SA 1998, s 28(5) specifically provides that '[t]he validity of an Act of the Scottish Parliament is not affected by any invalidity in the proceedings of the Parliament leading to its enactment'[6]. However, it is not clear that SA 1998, s 28(5) could save from invalidity a Bill which the Parliament failed to pass in accordance with the procedures laid down by SA 1998 itself – for example, the requirements of stages of Bills in SA 1998, s 36.

As at Westminster, the rules in the Scottish Parliament assume that most legislation will be introduced by the government as Government Bills but separate provision is also made for members' Bills (the equivalent of Private Members' Bills at Westminster)[7]; for committee Bills introduced on the initiative of a committee of the Parliament[8]; budget Bills (the equivalent of Consolidated Fund (or Appropriation) Bills at Westminster[9]); and private Bills[10]. There are also special rules for consolidation Bills, codification Bills, statute law repeals Bills and statute law revision Bills[11]. Recently added has been the additional category of Scottish Law Commission Bills[12]. Finally, there are emergency Bills[13]. It may now be regarded as a historical curiosity that the very first Bill introduced in the Scottish Parliament was the Bill which became the Mental Health (Public Safety and Appeals) (Scotland) Act 1999: this was an Emergency Bill and was dealt with under the special rules[14].

Such emergencies apart, Government Bills are usually drawn from the Government's previously announced legislative programme. There is no provision for a 'Queen's Speech' to be used as a vehicle for announcing the programme. Nor, in the Scottish Parliament, is the programme tied to the annual timetable which, at present, imposes (despite 'carry-over') a specific time discipline on proceedings at Westminster. At Holyrood, a 'session' of the Parliament is the full period of the Parliament up to its dissolution[15]. Nevertheless, there is now a fairly well established practice of First Ministers making annual announcements as to the Government's legislative intentions for the forthcoming year. On 26 November 2014, First Minister Nicola Sturgeon MSP announced a modest programme of 12 Bills, including Bills on land reform, carers, the reform of succession law and fatal accident inquiries[16].

1 *CSG Report* section 3.5 para 3. Concerns about the extent to which the Parliament has discharged those obligations were reflected most recently in submissions to the Calman Commission (see para 3.20) suggesting the establishment of an unelected 'senate' to provide 'detached and expert scrutiny of legislation'. The prospect of an elected or unelected second chamber was rejected by the Commission in its first report. (*The future of Scottish Devolution within the Union: A First Report*, December 2008, para 8.14).

2   *CSG Report* section 3.5 paras 4–7.
3   SA 1998, ss 22, 36.
4   Scotland Act 1998 (Transitory and Transitional Provisions) (Standing Orders and Parliamentary Publications) Order 1999, SI 1999/1095.
5   The standing orders are supplemented by the more informal *Guidance on Public Bills* (and also *Guidance on Private Bills*) prepared by the Parliament's officials.
6   See the Presiding Officer's announcement in the Parliament's Business Bulletin 106/2000 of 21 June 2000 acknowledging an earlier breach of the rules on 'manuscript amendments' at Stage 3.
7   See para 9.23.
8   See para 9.24.
9   See para 11.17.
10 See para 9.27.
11 SA 1998, s 36(3) and SOs, rr 9.18–9. 20.
12 SOs, r 9.17A.
13 SOs, r 9.21.
14 A more recent example was the Bill for the Criminal Procedure (Legal Assistance, Detention and Appeals) (Scotland) Act 2010 which was, controversially introduced as an Emergency Bill following the *Cadder* case. See paras 9.15 and 14.20.
15 SOs, r 2.1.
16 One of the list of Bills in 2014 was the Community Charge Debt (Scotland) Bill (to end the collection of community charge/poll tax debts) which originated in First Minister Salmond's commitment announced on 2 October 2014.

Introduction of a Bill

9.10   A Bill formally starts life on introduction to the Parliament[1]. A Bill's structure and style must be in line with rules laid down by the Parliament's Legislation Team[2] and it must be accompanied by a number of other documents:

PRESIDING OFFICER'S STATEMENT OF COMPETENCE. A written statement signed by the Presiding Officer, as required by SA 1998, s 31(2), declaring whether or not, in his or her view, the Bill's provisions would be within the legislative competence of the Parliament. If any provision is declared not to be competent, reasons must be given[3]. Negative statements, while rare, have been made. On 21 September 2006 the Presiding Officer made a statement that a large number of the provisions on the Civil Appeals (Scotland) Bill – a members' Bill introduced by Adam Ingram MSP which was intended to abolish the final right of appeal to the House of Lords in Scottish civil cases – were outside the legislative competence of the Scottish Parliament. The Presiding Officer was of the view that the majority of provisions related to reserved matters, ie 'the Constitution', by virtue of SA 1998, Sch 5, paragraph 1(c). One further provision was in his view incompatible with art 6 ECHR[4].

As a direct consequence of the Presiding Officer's statement the lead committee considering the Bill – the Justice 2 Committee – recommended that the Bill's general principles not be agreed to and the Bill fell on 20 December 2006 when that recommendation was accepted by the whole Parliament[5].

FINANCIAL MEMORANDUM. A financial memorandum, containing estimated costs of the Bill's proposals[6]. In the case of a Government Bill, there must also be:

GOVERNMENT STATEMENT OF COMPETENCE. A statement by the person[7] in charge of the Bill that the provisions of the Bill would, in his or her view, be within the Parliament's legislative competence, as required by SA 1998, s 31(1).

EXPLANATORY NOTES which 'summarise objectively' the effects of the Bill.

POLICY MEMORANDUM policy memorandum which sets out the Bill's policy objectives, any alternative strategies considered, consultations undertaken and an assessment of the Bill's effects on equal opportunities, human rights, island communities, local government, sustainable development and any other matters the Scottish Ministers consider relevant. Once introduced, the Bill and its accompanying documents are to be printed and published. The Bill then embarks on the procedure consisting of three stages (not confused by Westminster's language of 'readings') as required by SA 1998, s 36(1) and elaborated in the Standing Orders. The three stages are: Stage 1 for the consideration of a Bill's general principles (equivalent to a second reading at Westminster); Stage 2 for the consideration of details (a committee stage); and Stage 3 for final consideration and a decision on whether the Bill is to be passed (a third reading at Westminster). There follows the royal assent, with the possibility, however, of a reference to the Supreme Court or intervention by the Secretary of State, discussed further below.

The Bill's stages proceed according to a timetable laid down in the business programme of the Parliament, although the Standing Orders provide for standard minimum periods of 12 sitting days between Stages 1 and 2 and 10 sitting days between Stage 2 and Stage 3. The business programme is itself a matter for the Parliament to decide, on a motion from the Parliamentary Bureau[8].

1 SOs, r 9.2.
2 See *Guidance on Public Bills*, Annex A.
3 The terms of SA 1998, s 31(2) were a matter of controversy during the passage of the Scotland Bill. For debate at the final stage, see HL Debs, 17 November 1998, cols 1171–1175.
4 For the treatment of Mr Ingram's request, under the Freedom of Information (Scotland) Act 2002, for details of the legal advice given to the Presiding Officer in relation to his statement see Decision 209/2007 of the Scottish Information Commissioner.
5 SPOR 30 December 2006, col 30752 et seq. This was not the first occasion on which the Presiding Officer had made such a statement. He had done so earlier the same year in relation to the Provision of Rail Passenger Services (Scotland) Bill. For a discussion of both see CMG Himsworth, 'Presiding Officer Statements on the Competence of Bills', (2007) 11 Edin LR 397.
6 In the case of a Bill which would charge expenditure on the Scottish Consolidated Fund, there must also be a report by the Auditor General for Scotland.
7 Extended to cover any (non-governmental) promoter of a Bill by SA 2012, s 12. See also para 9.24.
8 SOs, r 5.4.

Stage 1

9.11 The principal decision to be made by the Parliament at Stage 1 is whether it agrees to the general principles of the Bill and whether it should, therefore, proceed. The debate and decision on this take place on the floor of the Parliament but they may do so only after the Bill's provisions have been considered by an appropriate committee (the 'lead committee') of the Parliament (and, if necessary, the Delegated Powers and Law Reform Committee[1] and any 'secondary' committee or committees[2]). The lead committee must provide a report on the Bill and (in the case of Government Bills) on the policy memorandum for the assistance of the Parliament. For that purpose it may proceed by discussion but also by the taking of evidence.

The Stage 1 reports of lead committees have proved influential particularly in highlighting to the promoter parts of a Bill which the Committee would expect to see improved by amendment at Stage 2. Lead committees have on occasion been unwilling or unable to endorse the general principles of a Bill. In the case of the Scottish Commissioner for Human Rights Bill the Committee was divided on which of three options ought to be pursued in order to fulfil the policy objective of the Bill. Because 'none of these options enjoys the support of a majority of Members of the Committee' the Committee was not 'in a position to recommend to the Parliament whether the general principles of the Bill should be agreed to or not'[3]. The Bill was nevertheless passed – as the Scottish Commission for Human Rights Act 2006. Even where a committee recommends agreement to the general principles of a Bill, it may not secure the support of the whole Parliament. The Creative Scotland Bill was the first Government Bill to fall at Stage 1, the Parliament having agreed its general principles but not the financial resolution ancillary to the Bill (see SP OR 18 June 2008, col 9842).

1 See para 5.18.
2 SOs, r 9.6.
3 Justice 1 Committee, 1st report, 2006, SP Paper 508.

Stage 2

9.12   If the Parliament agrees to the general principles of the Bill at Stage 1 and the Bill has, if necessary, been the subject of a financial resolution to approve any expenditure it may impose on the Scottish Consolidated Fund[1], the Bill proceeds to Stage 2 which is usually to be taken in the same 'lead committee' as at Stage 1 but may, on a motion of the Parliamentary Bureau, be taken, in whole or in part, by some other committee or by a Committee of the Whole Parliament, chaired by the Presiding Officer. Stage 2 of all emergency Bills (see below) must be taken by a Committee of the Whole Parliament. If Stage 2 is taken in a normal committee, other MSPs may attend, and propose and debate amendments but may not vote. Procedure is by debate on a section-by-section[2] basis, triggered by the proposal of amendments as at Westminster, except that amendments, though they may be grouped to assist debate, are not subject to selection by the convener.

1 For the role of the Finance Committee in relation to such resolutions, see para 11.17.
2 Not 'clause-by-clause' as at Westminster.

Stage 3

9.13   Following Stage 2, the Bill, if amended, is reprinted[1] and proceeds to Stage 3 which takes place in the full Parliament and a decision must be made, following debate, on whether the Bill is passed. At this stage, however, amendments may still be proposed or, on the motion of the member in charge of the Bill, it is possible for a Bill to be sent back for further Stage 2 consideration in committee. If, on the other hand, amendments are made at Stage 3 it is open to that member to propose an adjournment of the proceedings to another day before a final decision on the passing of the Bill is made. These are procedural devices intended to prevent insufficiently scrutinised provisions from reaching the statute book but they have not been regarded by all as having fulfilled that purpose effectively[2].

1 Together with any revised or supplementary Explanatory Notes and revised or supplementary Financial Memorandum: SOs r 8A, 8B and 8C.
2 The Calman Commission recommended a further Stage 4 but this was not proceeded with.

Special forms of public Bill in the Scottish Parliament[1]

9.14   While the standard procedure described may serve well across the generality of public Bills promoted by governments, whatever their particular subject matter, certain Bills demand a different procedure[2]. In the standing orders of the Scottish Parliament, special provision[3] is made for the following categories of Bill:

1 Members' Bills are also public Bills but are dealt with separately below, at para 9.23.
2 Recognised, in relation to the Scottish Parliament, in SA 1998, s 36(2), (3).
3 See also the provision made for Budget Bills: ch 11.

Emergency Bills[1]

9.15   Where urgency is required, the Scottish Government may propose that a Bill be treated as an emergency Bill. If that motion is agreed by the Parliament, all stages of the Bill are to be taken in a single day[2]. Such an abbreviation of normal procedures carries risks, of course, but sometimes a particularly rapid response to a problem is necessary. The Parliament's very first Bill, which became the Mental Health (Public Safety and Appeals) (Scotland) Act 1999, was an emergency response to a significant court decision[3]. Emergency Bill procedure was invoked in respect of the Senior Judiciary (Vacancies and Incapacity) (Scotland) Act 2006 (allowing for the functions of the Lord President and the Lord Justice Clerk to be carried out by others should either be incapacitated by reason of ill health or their office be vacant). The procedure also used in February 2009 to enable the (eventual) speedy passage of the Budget (Scotland) Act 2009 one week after the minority administration's Bill had been rejected on the casting vote of the Presiding Officer[4]. Failure to secure the passage of the Bill would have led to the provisions of the Public Finance and Accountability (Scotland) Act 2000 for emergency funding being invoked[5]. Controversially, the Emergency Bill procedure was used in June 2009 when the Convention Rights Proceedings (Amendment) (Scotland) Bill was dealt with by the Parliament in a single day. The Cabinet Secretary for Justice, Kenny McAskill, explained that the Bill was intended as a response to the decision of the House of Lords in *Somerville v Scottish Ministers*[6] and would impose a one year limit on the bringing of claims for breach of Convention rights against the Scottish Ministers[7]. Mr McAskill observed that the decision had created uncertainty and had led to tens of millions of pounds being set aside to meet possible compensation claims arising as a result of the decision. He stated that it was 'generally agreed that the situation needs to be resolved as quickly as possible'[8] but gave no explanation for the fact that the 'emergency' to which the Bill was responding was a judgment handed down some 20 months earlier – indeed, he observed (in explaining why there had been no public consultation on the proposed new legislation) that the government had 'stated publicly our desire for a change in the law as long ago as November 2007, so the change should not come as a surprise to anyone' (col 18521). There was further concern when, following the UK Supreme Court decision in *Cadder v HMA*[9], the Criminal Procedure (Legal Assistance, Detention and Appeals) (Scotland) Act 2010 was passed[10].

1   SOs, r 9.21.
2   Extendable, as in the case of the Mental Health (Public Safety and Appeals) (Scotland) Act 1999, on a motion by the Parliamentary Bureau: SOs, r 19.21.2.
3   *Ruddle v Secretary of State for Scotland* 1999 GWD 29-1395.
4   See SPOR 4 February 2009 col 14644.
5   See also the Erskine Bridge Tolls Act 2001 (correcting an administrative error which had removed the power to levy tolls on the bridge).
6   2008 SC (HL) 45.
7   For further discussion of the case see para 14.29.
8   SP OR 18 June 2009, col 18517.
9   [2010] UKSC 43, 2011 SC (UKSC) 13.
10   See para 14.20.

Scottish Law Commission and related Bills[1]

9.16   Special provision was made (in 2013) for Bills to implement all or part of a report of the Scottish Law Commission. Instead of being considered by a subject committee, such Bills go to the Delegated Powers and Law Reform Committee[2]. The Legal Writings (Counterparts and Delivery) (Scotland) Bill was the first to be introduced under the new rule. Of longer standing are consolidation Bills whose purpose is to restate existing law. This may involve the merging and reordering of existing statutes or the codification of the common law. In either case, some degree of amendment of existing law is permitted, on the recommendation of the Scottish Law Commission[3]. Such Bills go to a special consolidation committee, instead of a subject committee[4]. Amendments to consolidation Bills are confined to those necessary to achieve an accurate restatement of the law (or to implement the Law Commission recommendations). Only one consolidation Bill has reached the statute book: the Salmon and Freshwater Fisheries (Consolidation) (Scotland) Act 2003.

1   SOs, r 9.18. See also the provision made in SOs, rr 9.18A, 9.19–9.20 for Codification Bills, Statute Law Repeals Bills and Statute Law Revision Bills. For the competence of Acts restating the law, see SA 1998, Sch 4, para 7 and para 6.19 above.
2   SOs, rr 6.11(1)(g) and 9.17A.
3   Or joint recommendation from the Scottish Law Commission and the (England and Wales) Law Commission.
4   In the Westminster Parliament, a joint committee of both Houses is used.

Royal assent and pre-assent challenge to Bills

9.17   To become an Act, a Bill which has been passed by the Parliament needs to receive the royal assent. SA 1998 makes provision for this and states that '[a] Bill receives Royal Assent at the beginning of the day on which Letters Patent under the Scottish Seal signed with Her Majesty's own hand signifying Her Assent are recorded in the Register of the Great Seal'[1]. Beyond that formal stipulation, the Act is silent on the Queen's role but it has to be assumed that the Queen has no discretion as to whether to grant or withhold assent. If there is a discretion, it should be exercised on the advice of the First Minister.

SA 1998 does, however, specify that it is for the Parliament's Presiding Officer to submit Bills for royal assent[2], and this is important. The Presiding Officer's duty to submit a Bill arises once it has been passed but, in the ordinary way, he or she must delay the submission for a period of four weeks because it is within that period that an intervention may be made by either a Law Officer to secure a reference to the Supreme Court (formerly the Judicial Committee of the Privy Council) or by the Secretary of State to prohibit the submission of the Bill for assent[3]. Neither of these procedures has any counterpart at Westminster as both derive from the Scottish Parliament's status as a Parliament of restricted competence. The power to refer to the Supreme Court the question of whether a Bill (or any provision of a Bill) is within the legislative competence of the Parliament at this pre-assent stage complements the other procedures available under SA 1998 to ensure compliance[4]. Pre-assent challenge does not provide the last word on legislative competence since an ASP may be reviewed by the courts at a later stage. There have been a number of this latter type of challenge to ASPs[5] but, so far, no pre-assent references[6].

1 SA 1998, s 2(3), (4) and the Scottish Parliament (Letters Patent and Proclamations) Order 1999, SI 1999/737.
2 SA 1998, s 32(1).
3 SA 1998, ss 32(2), (3); 33–35.
4 See the obligations imposed on those introducing Bills and on the Presiding Officer at a Bill's introduction at para 9.10 above.
5 See para 14.23.
6 Although, from Wales, there have been three: *Local Government Byelaws (Wales) Bill 2012* [2013] 1 AC 792, *Agricultural Sector (Wales) Bill 2012* [2014] 4 All ER 789; *Recovery of Medical Costs Asbestos Diseases (Wales) Bill 2013* [2015] UKSC 3.

References to the Supreme Court

9.18   A reference may be made by either the Advocate General or the Attorney-General on behalf of the UK government or by the Lord Advocate on behalf of the Scottish Government. The possibility of a reference by one of the UK Law Officers might arise in circumstances where their government doubts the competence of the Bill. This was, unlikely up to 2007 in relation to a Government Bill where broad political partnership between the two governments existed and prior consultation on the terms of Scottish Bills was routine. Even where, as has been the case since the Scottish general election of 2007, no such political partnership exists, such a reference would be an exceptional step. The reference of a member's Bill passed by the Parliament without Government support might, on the other hand, be more likely. The reference of a Bill by the Lord Advocate, unless also in relation to a member's Bill, is unlikely in practice although a 'friendly' reference of a Bill to clarify a point of interpretation, perhaps in consequence of an Government undertaking to do so as the Bill was debated, would not be unthinkable. Whatever the motivation of the reference, it proceeds under rules laid down under SA 1998[1]. If the Supreme Court decides that a Bill (or one of its provisions) would not be within the competence of the Parliament[2], the Bill cannot proceed to royal assent in its initial form. There is, however, provision[3] for a 'reconsideration' stage in the Parliament[4]. If the Bill is passed by the Parliament, and subject to the possibility of a further Law Officer reference to the Supreme Court, it may be submitted for royal assent. If the Supreme Court decides that the Bill is not outwith the legislative competence of the Parliament, the Bill may proceed to royal assent[5]. Whatever the Supreme Court's decision, this reference procedure may be the cause of some delay in securing the final enactment of an ASP and, as already noted, royal assent must usually be delayed, in any event, for the four-week period within which a reference is competent. The only circumstance in which the four-week period may be shortened is if all the Law Officers (and also the Secretary of State[6]) have given the Presiding Officer notice of their intention not to exercise their powers under SA 1998[7].

1 SA 1998, s 103(3)(c).
2 For discussion of how courts including the Supreme Court approach questions of legislative competence, see para 14.23 below.
3 SA 1998, s 36(4)–(6) and SOs r 9.9.
4 A Bill may also be reconsidered if, having been referred by the Supreme Court to the ECJ, the Parliament itself resolves to reconsider rather than await the outcome. See SA 1998, s 34(2).
5 Where Bills are passed by the Parliament immediately prior to a dissolution, royal assent can, of course, be expected only after the dissolution. But could any 'reconsideration' stage, if one were required, take place in the next session of the Parliament?
6 See below.
7 As was the case, for example, with the first ASP. The Mental Health (Public Safety and Appeals) (Scotland) Act 1999 was passed by the Parliament on 8 September and received the royal assent on 13 September 1999. Similarly, the Senior Judiciary (Vacancies and Incapacity) (Scotland) Act 2006 was passed by the Parliament on 15 June and received the royal assent on 27 June 2006.

Intervention by the Secretary of State

9.19   The Secretary of State's power under SA 1998, s 35 (unused since the creation of the Parliament) is very different from that of the Law Officers under SA 1998, s 33. Described there as a 'Power to intervene in certain cases', it is a power to make an order prohibiting the Presiding Officer from submitting a Bill for royal assent. The 'certain cases' are not cases of suspected legislative incompetence and it is for this reason that a power of control by United Kingdom ministers over the Scottish Parliament – compared by some with the powers of a colonial Governor General[1] – is a matter of some sensitivity. On the other hand, the three circumstances in which the Secretary of State – any Secretary of State, not just the Secretary of State for Scotland – may intervene are quite narrowly defined and it may, in any event, be assumed that the power is a long-stop, to be used extremely sparingly if at all[2]. Prior consultation between the two governments will in most cases have removed provisions which might attract intervention. The first situation for intervention under the section is where the Secretary of State has reasonable grounds to believe that provisions in a Bill would be incompatible with any of the United Kingdom's 'international obligations'. These are defined[3] to include obligations *other than* those arising under the EU treaties or the ECHR (incompatibility with which would, in any event, take the Scottish Parliament beyond its competence). Incompatibility with any *other* international obligations may be restrained by the power under SA 1998, s 35: in the drafting of the Act, it had been thought more appropriate to leave judgments in this area to ministers rather than to courts. Secondly, the Secretary of State may intervene on grounds of incompatibility with 'the interests of defence or national security'; and the third power to intervene is closely interwoven with the rules in SA 1998, s 29 and Schs 4 and 5 which define the competence of the Scottish Parliament by reference to reserved matters[4].

Although the Parliament is, in general, restrained from enacting legislation which relates to reserved matters, those provisions do enable incursions into reserved matters where, for instance, the 'purpose' of the legislation is to deal with devolved matters. However, if a Bill does make modifications of the law as it applies to reserved matters and the Secretary of State has reasonable grounds to believe that it 'would have an adverse effect on the operation of the law as it applies to reserved matters', he may order that the Bill be not submitted for royal assent. The timetable for a Secretary of State intervention is similar to that for Supreme Court references – it must be made within four weeks of the passing of the Bill or, if the Bill is referred to the Supreme Court, within four weeks of a determination of that reference. The order prohibiting submissions for royal assent must not only identify the offending provisions but also state the Secretary of State's reasons for making the order. Such orders are subject to annulment in either House of the Westminster Parliament[5] and would also be subject to challenge by judicial review[6].

1 An image carried over from the event stronger powers which would have been available under SA 1978, s 19.
2 See para 7.26.
3 SA 1998, s 126(10).
4 See para 6.14.
5 SA 1998, Sch 7. For annulment procedures, see para 9.34.
6 See ch 14.

Procedures Committee (and latterly the Standards, Procedures and Public Appointments (SPPA) Committee) reviews of the legislative process

9.20   In the first decade of the Scottish Parliament's life the procedures and processes which it has adopted in making new laws have been the subject of scrutiny by the Parliament's own procedures committee. A number of inquiries have been conducted and reports produced – leading in many cases to revision of the Parliament's standing orders. So for example, at a relatively early stage, the legislative process received attention in 2002–03 from the Procedures

Committee in its CSG Inquiry[1]. The Committee did not report comprehensively at that time but recommended that a further review of all aspects of both primary and subordinate legislation procedures should be undertaken by the Committee in the next session[2]. It did, however, respond to some concerns which had been expressed and most of these focused on Executive Bills although it did also refer to an expectation that the balance between Executive and non-Executive Bills should shift in favour of Members' and Committee Bills[3]. Such Bills should be further supported with time and resources.

The principal concerns about Executive Bills were directed towards the severe timetabling pressures which had been imposed, especially but not exclusively in committees. There was a perception of there being too little time allocated for outside consultation before and during the legislative process and too little time for the proper consideration of amendments to Bills. Research had indicated average times spent on Executive Bills as 33 days for Stage 1; and 8 days for Stage 2 (with an average gap between those Stages of 14 days); and the gap between Stages 2 and 3 about 12 days[4]. But principles for time allocation were unclear and the Committee made a series of recommendations that the periods allocated during and between stages should be increased. Special care should be taken to ensure proper opportunities for debate at Stage 3, the last opportunity to amend a Bill[5]. If necessary, more time should be allocated and timetables extended to afford proper speaking opportunities for members[6]. These themes were taken up by Committee again in session 2 when it conducted a major inquiry into Timescales and Stages of Bills. In its subsequent report[7] a number of recommendations for changes to the standing orders were made to allow greater time for scrutiny of Bills, many of which recommendations have been implemented[8] and the increase in the minimum number of sitting days between stages 1 and 2 from seven to eleven (SO r 9.5.3A). Since then the Procedures Committee has conducted inquiries into a number of other areas including private legislation[9], consolidation Bill procedure[10] and circumstances in which it might be appropriate for an MSP who has introduced a Bill to be a member of a committee considering that Bill[11]. More recently, the SPPA Committee has reviewed the 'hybrid' Bill procedure (see below).

1   *The Founding Principles of the Scottish Parliament* SPPR OR SP Paper 818 (2003). See para 3.19.
2   SP Paper 818, Recommendation 37.
3   SP Paper 818, paras 305 and 695–714.
4   SP Paper 818, para 343.
5   SP Paper 818, para 357.
6   SP Paper 818, paras 358–362.
7   7th report, 2004: Timescales and Stages of Bills, SP Paper 228.
8   See for example the recommendation that a minimum period of one week should elapse between publication of the Stage 1 report and the stage 1 debate (SO r 9.6.3A).
9   SP Paper 334 (2005).
10 SP Paper 676 (2006).
11 SP Paper 652 (2006).

MEMBERS' BILLS

9.21   Although it is an almost inevitable feature of the 'Westminster model' of parliamentary government that the legislative programme of the Parliament is dominated by government Bills, the opportunity must be given to individual members to introduce Bills of their own. That opportunity reflects an assertion of autonomy on the part of the Parliament and of its individual members. The Parliament is not merely at the beck and call of the executive branch but may also initiate legislative proposals of its own. Such freedom represents an important principle and has great symbolic significance. In practice, however, the principle is much eroded, at Westminster at least, by executive pressure.

Private Members' Bills at Westminster[1]

9.22   In the House of Commons, 13 Fridays are allocated in each session to private members' business. That time is given initially to second reading debates on Bills whose promoters have won a high place in a ballot of MPs held at the beginning of the session[2]. Successful MPs use the opportunity to introduce a Bill on a topic of their choice, often one prepared in advance by a pressure group waiting for its chance for legislative reform. Such Bills are usually short, single-issue measures which, while not attracting governmental hostility, might never acquire sufficient priority for adoption into the government's own programme. However, governments do frequently support private members' Bills by the offer of drafting assistance, sometimes to the extent of a complete remodelling of the Bill. Conversely, government opposition to a Bill, or indeed resistance from any individual MP, will usually be fatal to a private member's Bill. Without the discipline of an assured majority or timetable motions, private members' Bills are vulnerable to being simply 'talked-out' at second reading, in which case, although they may be reintroduced, they lose their place in the queue. As with practically all other public business[3], private members' Bills lapse at the end of the session. They cannot be 'carried over'.

Those private members' Bills which survive the second reading stage are committed to a public bill committee (selected to ensure a majority in favour of the Bill) from which they return for remaining stages during Friday business before moving on to the Lords.

1 During 2013–14, the House of Commons Procedure Committee made extensive proposals for the amendment of private member's Bills procedure, including their rebranding as 'bankbench Bills' – see HC 188 (2013–14).
2 An alternative procedure for airing a proposal for a Bill is under the 'ten minute rule'.
3 Although promoted by private members, these Bills are 'public' Bills. For private Bills, see para 9.23.

Members' Bills in the Scottish Parliament

9.23   The Consultative Steering Group (CSG) was clear in its report on the need for MSPs to be enabled to make proposals for legislation which, if they had the support of a minimum number of members – the CSG suggested 10 per cent of the total – could then be brought forward as Bills. The Group recommended that no member should be able to introduce more than two Bills in any four-year parliamentary session[1]. These recommendations have been carried forward into the standing orders of the Parliament which contain provision for what are known at Holyrood as 'members Bills', as opposed to the *private* members' Bills at Westminster[2]. Following the launch of the Parliament in July 1999, there was some enthusiasm for the initiation of Bills by MSPs. In the course of the first session some 45 proposals for Bills were lodged, but most did not proceed to formal introduction. There was a decline, towards the end of the session, in the numbers of supported proposals taken forward to the stage of introduction into the Parliament as a Bill. Only one proposal for a Bill introduced after the end of 2001 was enacted. In all, eight Members' Bills reached the statute book. The first Act was the Sea Fisheries (Shellfish) Amendment (Scotland) Act 2000. Although it was very brief and it made only a small technical amendment to earlier legislation, it was hailed as a triumph for the Parliament. It managed very quickly to make a small but locally much-appreciated change in the law without fuss and without the opportunity for the procedural blockages which had earlier thwarted attempts at Westminster to achieve similar legislative change. No single MSP could simply shout 'Object' in the Scottish Parliament[3]. The second member's Bill to reach the statute book was that introduced by Tommy Sheridan MSP and which became the Abolition of Poindings and Warrant Sales Act 2001. That too was hailed as a parliamentary triumph over the preferred position of the Scottish Executive on debt enforcement. The Government had, however, managed to ensure the inclusion of a section delaying implementation of the Act for nearly two years, before which it was repealed by the Executive's own Debt Arrangement and Attachment (Scotland) Act 2002. Other members' Bills which were successfully introduced and carried through to the statute book became the Protection of Wild Mammals (Scotland) Act 2002[4], the Leasehold Casualties (Scotland) Act 2001, the Mortgage Rights (Scotland) Act 2001, the Dog Fouling (Scotland) Act 2003, the University of St Andrews (Postgraduate Medical Degrees) Act 2002 and the Council of the Law Society of Scotland Act 2003. The apparent enthusiasm with which MSPs embraced members' bills did, however, give rise to cause for concern in some quarters. In 2004 the Procedures Committee conducted an inquiry into the use of the mechanism, driven in large part by evidence that the ease with which members could introduce bills was putting pressure on the Non-Executive Bills Unit[5] and supported by the Parliamentary Bureau. The Committee's subsequent report[6] led to changes to the standing orders which appeared at first to have played at least a part in reducing the number of members' bills being introduced. In session 2 only three members' bills made it to the statute book[7]. But then in session 3 there were the Disabled Persons' Parking Places (Scotland) Act 2009, the Scottish Register of Tartans Act 2008, the Offences (Aggravation by Prejudice) (Scotland) Act 2009, the Control of Dogs (Scotland) Act 2010, the Domestic Abuse (Scotland) Act 2011 and the Property Factors (Scotland) Act 2011. In session 4 there have been the High Hedges (Scotland) Act 2013, the Buildings (Recovery of Expenses) (Scotland) Act 2014, and the Disabled Persons Parking Badges (Scotland) Act 2014. There may yet be an Assisted Suicide (Scotland) Act[8].

An MSP who is not a member of the Scottish Government[9] and wishes to introduce a member's Bill must first lodge with the Clerk a 'draft proposal' consisting of the proposed short title of the Bill and a brief explanation of its purposes together with either a consultation document which will form the basis for a public consultation on the policy objectives of the draft proposal or a written statement of reasons why, in the Member's opinion, a consultation is unnecessary. The draft proposed must be published in the Business Bulletin with details of the consultation period or, alternatively, information about the statement of reasons for not having consulted. The draft proposal is then referred to an appropriate committee of the Parliament which can require the lodging of a consultation document within two months, which failing the Bill falls. Thereafter the member must lodge a 'final proposal' together with such consultation responses as have been received. The final proposal is published in the Business Bulletin for a month, during which time any other member may notify the Clerk of his or her support. If, by the end of the prescribed month, at least 18[10] other members (which number includes members of at least half of the political parties represented in the Parliamentary Bureau) have notified support for the final proposal, the Bill may be introduced. If, on the other hand, insufficient support is forthcoming, the proposal falls and no proposal in the same or similar terms may be made by any member within the succeeding six months. As recommended by the CSG, a member is restricted to a maximum of two Bills per session[11]. When a member's Bill is introduced, it follows the same procedural track as a standard (Government) Bill[12]. An important facility available to MSPs as they prepare their Bills is the Parliament's Non-Government Bills Unit (NGBU) which offers procedural advice and arranges for the drafting of Bills by experts recruited for the purpose. The NGBU offers similar facilities for committee Bills (see below).

1   *CSG Report*, para 3.5.21.
2   SOs, r 9.14.
3   See SP OR 28 September 2000 cols 829–834.
4   See para 14.24.
5   Now the Non-Government Bills Unit. See below.
6   SP Paper 193 (2004).
7   The Breastfeeding etc (Scotland) Act 2005, the St Andrew's Day Bank Holiday (Scotland) Act 2007 and the Christmas Day and New Year's Day Trading (Scotland) Act 2007.
8   After previous unsuccessful attempts to achieve such legislation under the formidable leadership of the late Margo Macdonald MSP who introduced a Bill on 13 November 2013.
9   Apparently a (junior) minister is not formally excluded.
10 Increased from eleven as a result of the Procedures Committee's recommendations.
11 Including for this purpose, a Bill deriving from a draft proposed by an MSP but then adopted as a Committee Bill – see below.
12 SA 2012, s 6 extended the need for the person introducing a member's Bill to provide a statement of legislative competence.

COMMITTEE BILLS IN THE SCOTTISH PARLIAMENT

9.24   A special feature of procedure in the Scottish Parliament is the power given to committees of the Parliament to initiate legislation. The standing orders provide for what are known as 'committee Bills'[1]. At Westminster, it is often the case that select committees of the House of Commons make recommendations for the introduction of legislation and it is open to the government, if it accepts the recommendation, to introduce a Bill. Similarly, individual MPs, whether members of the committee or not, could take the initiative[2]. At Holyrood, however, it was envisaged from the outset, that, as part of the overall strategy to give committees a strong role in the work of the Parliament, the committees themselves would have the power to introduce Bills[3]. The CSG developed the idea with recommendations that committees of the Parliament should be able to conduct inquiries into the need for legislation in any area within their terms of reference and take proposals to the Parliament[4]. The CSG's views were incorporated into the standing orders.

A committee may make a proposal for a Bill. This might arise out of the committee's own business but standing orders also permit any MSP to submit, via the Parliamentary Bureau, a draft proposal for consideration by a relevant committee. Prior to making a proposal for a Bill (which may contain a draft of the Bill itself) the committee may hold an inquiry into the need for a Bill. The proposal must be accompanied by an explanation of that need. If the Parliament accepts the proposal, the Scottish Government has the opportunity to indicate that it will introduce a Bill to give effect to that proposal. If, on the other hand, no such indication is given within five sitting days, then the convener of the originating committee may introduce the Bill. Thereafter, a committee Bill follows normal procedures, save that, at Stage 1, it may be referred directly to the Parliament for consideration of its general principles without the need for any additional report from a committee.

The committee Bill procedures have not been extensively used but the initiative was taken in January 2001 when the first formal proposal for a Bill – subsequently the Protection from Abuse (Scotland) Act 2001 – was considered by the Parliament[5]. The proposal was supported by the Executive and the debate was dubbed 'a testament to the flexibility and power of our new Parliament and its procedures'[6]. Other committee Bills which have been enacted include the Scottish Parliamentary Standards Commissioner Act 2002, the Commissioner for Children and Young People (Scotland) Act 2003, the Interests of Members of the Scottish Parliament Act 2006; the Scottish Parliamentary Pensions Act 2009; and the Scottish Parliamentary Commissions and Commissioners etc Act 2010[7]. There have, therefore, been only six ASPs passed by this method in the history of the Parliament. There have been no committee Bills at all in the (current) fourth session of the Parliament. But a further Interests of MSPs Bill is anticipated[8].

1 SOs, r 9.15.
2 Bills promoted by committees are not a feature of legislative practice at Westminster.
3 *Scotland's Parliament* (Cm 3658) para 9.10.
4 Section 3.5, paras 18–20.
5 SP OR 24 January 2001, col 510.
6 Col 515.
7 Most of these Bills were considered at Stage 2 by specially established committees. The Protection from Abuse (Scotland) Bill, promoted by the Justice 1 Committee, was considered by the Justice 2 Committee. The Act of 2010 was considered, as a Bill, by the Finance Committee.
8 See para 5.21.

PRIVATE LEGISLATION AT WESTMINSTER AND HOLYROOD

9.25   The purpose of the legislation discussed so far is to make changes – by new law or by the amendment or repeal of existing law – to the general law of the land. A piece of legislation of this type is referred to, in both the Westminster and Scottish Parliaments, as a *public* Act. It is a public Act regardless of who initiated the Bill from which it emerged, whether a minister, an MP or MSP or, in the case of the Scottish Parliament, a committee. It is also a public Act, even though the generality of its application is qualified by its subject matter or by the territory to which it applies. Thus, a Fisheries Act or a Schools Act is a public Act, even though its subject matter is confined to fish and fishermen or to schools, pupils and teachers respectively. Such Acts have general (public) effect across the classes of person or organisation to which they apply. Similarly, a UK Act confined in its application to Wales or Scotland is a public Act despite the territorial or jurisdictional restriction. The Scottish Parliament could pass an Act restricted to the islands areas of Scotland but it would not thereby cease to be a public Act[1].

Both Parliaments do, however, recognise the need for another type of legislation and for a different procedure by which it should be handled. The distinction is drawn between the public legislation described above and *private* legislation. Private legislation is sought by persons or organisations whose aim is not to change the general law but instead to achieve a change in the law specifically in relation to them. They might want to be excused from the application to them of a particular restrictive rule. Thus, two individuals forbidden to marry under the general law because of the closeness of their relationship would need a change in the law, confined to them alone, to permit them to marry. More usually, a local authority might seek special powers, over and above those generally available, to control a nuisance or to impose a new parking regime within their area. Similarly, a public body, or indeed a commercial company, may seek powers to acquire land compulsorily to enable a particular development to take place.

All such legislation is different from public legislation because of the very specific results sought for the benefit of its promoters. Procedurally, this has two main consequences. First, the promoter has to be given access to parliamentary procedures which are usually restricted to the Parliament's own members. Secondly, the procedures for consideration of a private rather than a public Bill have to be designed to ensure not only that the promoter has the opportunity and responsibility for establishing the need for legislative change but also that any opponents of the proposal, who may have very substantial reasons to object because their property or other interests are affected, have a clear opportunity to have their day in court. In debate on a public Bill, the primary responsibility for testing its merits falls on parliamentarians, even if, in some cases (and especially in the Scottish Parliament), they may call upon external experts to give evidence. In the case of private legislation, members are required to adopt a more dispassionate, 'quasi-judicial' role and to decide on a Bill's merits in the light of arguments presented for and against. Of course, in some instances, private Bills may attract no objections and be unopposed, in which case the task of the parliamentarians is more straightforward.

---

1 The University of St Andrews (Postgraduate Medical Degrees) Act 2002, the Council of the Law Society of Scotland Act 2003 and the National Library of Scotland Act 2013 derived from public Bills.

Private legislation in the Westminster Parliament

9.26   The Westminster Parliament has evolved two distinct approaches to private legislation. Neither can be dealt with comprehensively here and, since July 1999, the Westminster procedures have less relevance to Scotland because most potential private legislation is within the competence of the Scottish Parliament. Prior to 1999, however, Scottish business had a substantial impact on Westminster procedures.

The primary response of the Westminster Parliament to the special requirements of private legislation has been to adapt the standard committee stage on public Bills to enable an inquiry into the need for the powers or exemption sought in a private Bill. The promoter and objectors have the opportunity to call and to cross-examine witnesses. Private Bill procedure is inevitably an expensive matter for the parties and it was largely with a view to abating the expense for Scottish promoters that an alternative procedure was developed. The need to attend committee inquiries at Westminster was removed and the opportunity to have substitute inquiries conducted in Scotland was provided by the Private Legislation Procedure (Scotland) Act 1899, replaced later by an Act of the same name in 1936 (PLP(S)A 1936). While leaving open the option of standard private legislation procedure for Bills which 'raise questions of public policy of such novelty and importance[1]' that they ought to be dealt with in that way, PLP(S)A 1936 requires applicants for private powers to petition the Secretary of State (on 27 March or 27 November in any year) requesting the issue of a 'provisional order'. Once issued, the order is appended to a brief 'confirmation' Bill which is introduced into Parliament and usually passed without substantive debate[2]. The real debate takes place at the stage prior to the making of the provisional order when an inquiry is held (usually in Scotland) by four commissioners, normally two MPs and two peers. Since the arrival of the Scottish Parliament, it has been very unlikely that there will be much demand for private legislation relating to Scotland at Westminster[3]. There have been only two confirmation Acts since 1999[4] – both in the very early days of the Scottish Parliament. Westminster procedures do also give recognition to 'hybrid Bills' – Bills which are predominantly public in character but which touch upon particular private interests by, for instance, providing for the acquisition of specific land. Such Bills attract special procedures in committee to enable evidence to be heard for and against those provisions[5].

1 PLP(S)A 1936, s 2.
2 But not always. For discussion see the *Report of the Joint Committee on Private Bill Procedure* (HL Paper 97, HC Paper 625 (1987–88)).
3 PLP(S)A 1936 was amended by SA 1998, Sch 8, para 5 to exclude its use to confer powers wholly within the legislative competence of the Scottish Parliament.
4 Comhairle Nan Eilean Siar (Eriskay Causeway) Order Confirmation Act 2000 and Railtrack (Waverley Station) Order Confirmation Act 2000.
5 *Erskine May's Parliamentary Practice* (24th edn, 2011) chs 44, 45. A recent high-profile example of a hybrid Bill has been the High Speed Rail (London to West Midlands) Bill 2014 – the 'HS2' Bill.

Private legislation in the Holyrood Parliament

9.27   The Scottish Parliament's procedures for consideration of private Bills have been the focus, over the past decade, of what might at first seem like a surprising amount of attention. That attention is a reflection, however, of the significant part which private Bills have played in delivering major public infrastructure projects in Scotland. Recent reforms – principally the enactment of the Transport and Works (Scotland) Act 2007 – should reduce the role which private legislation might be expected to play in Scotland and we may expect rather less of a focus on the procedures which are in place to deal with private bills. Early recognition of the need for procedures to handle private legislation was provided by SA 1998, s 36(3)(c) which enabled the making of special standing orders for private Bills. The initial versions of the Parliament's standing orders did contain such provision[1] but that was very much a holding measure, pending full consideration by the Parliament itself of how best to deal with private legislation in the longer term. The rules were a curious procedural mix, providing for special consideration by committees but, from PLP(S)A 1936, retaining a provision restricting the introduction of private Bills to 27 March and 27 November each year. While this might be appropriate to the provisional order procedure under PLP(S)A 1936, its purpose in the Scottish Parliament was not obvious. At all events, private legislation became an early topic for review by the Procedures Committee of the Parliament and, following investigation by a Private Bill Working Group, the Committee reported in November 2000 with recommendations including proposals for new standing orders[2]. The rules were subsequently adopted as Chapter 9A of the Parliament's standing orders. No private Bills had been introduced under the original rules. An important preliminary question for the Procedures Committee had been which approach to private legislation to adopt. Should it be similar to the standard in-house procedure used at Westminster for almost all private Bills, except those relating to Scotland? Or should it be a simplified version of the provisional order procedure in PLP(S)A 1936, with functions split between the Parliament and the Scottish Government? In the Committee's view, a 'Parliament-led' system was preferable, as it was more accessible and participative. The Parliament was directly involved throughout. Because the wholly parliamentary approach needed only a change of standing orders rather than new legislation, it could also be adopted quickly. In the event, practical experience of dealing with private Bills led to re-consideration of that Parliament-led system as the most appropriate mechanism for authorising 'public works'. Following an inquiry in 2005, the Procedures Committee noted that the system had come under a great deal of strain (particularly in terms of parliamentary resources) because of the large number of transport infrastructure bills which had been introduced in the preceding three years. The Committee recommended that the government take forward legislation to enable such projects to be dealt with under a procedure which was driven by ministers (rather than Parliament) and which had greater similarities to the process for obtaining planning consent for major developments (see SP Paper 334, 4 May 2005). The Committee's recommendations were in due course taken forward in the shape of the Transport and Works (Scotland) Act 2007, the consequence of which is that very few major transport projects would now be taken forward by primary legislation of the Parliament. One exception was the Bill to authorise a new Forth Crossing[3], for which purpose (amongst others) the SPPA Committee recommended changes to the standing orders to allow for hybrid bills to be introduced in the Parliament[4].

The Private Bill rules provide for the introduction of a Bill on any sitting day of the Parliament. It must be lodged with the Clerk along with accompanying documents including a statement by the Presiding Officer as to whether the Bill is within the legislative competence of the Parliament, explanatory notes and a promoter's memorandum setting out the Bill's objectives, alternatives considered, consultation undertaken, and the promoter's own statement of legislative competence[5]. Other documents are to include a funding statement and a promoter's statement concerning affected heritable property and an undertaking to pay the fee determined by the Parliamentary corporation[6]. Private Bills and their accompanying documents are printed and published[7]. Within 60 days of the introduction of a Bill, objections may be lodged by those who consider that their interests would be adversely affected, and a list of objectors is published[8].

On the introduction of a private Bill, the Parliament establishes a private Bill committee of not more than five members. Special rules exclude members resident in, or who represent, an area affected by the Bill and provide that members may be absent from meetings in exceptional circumstances only[9]. Private Bill procedure is divided into three stages. The preliminary stage involves consideration of the general principles of the Bill by the committee and preliminary consideration of the objections, following which the Parliament decides whether the Bill should proceed[10]. If the Bill proceeds, it is referred back to the private Bill committee for detailed examination at the consideration stage[11]. Where the Bill is a 'works Bill'[12] or a Bill which would confer powers of compulsory purchase the Bill Committee can direct the Parliamentary corporation to appoint – for the purposes of the consideration stage – an 'assessor' to consider and report to the Committee on outstanding objections (SOs r 9A.8.2A). The role of the assessor is akin to that of a reporter at a planning inquiry, taking evidence and producing a report for the Parliament[13]. Where an assessor is appointed, the promoter and objectors (who may be grouped for the purpose) are to be invited to attend to give evidence or to provide written evidence or both. Standing orders make no detailed provision for how private Bill committees should conduct the evidence-taking proceedings but the Procedures Committee assumed that promoters and objectors should be able to lead evidence and to cross-examine witnesses on the other side[14]. Legal representation would be permitted and, although the Committee did not accept that parties (especially objectors) would necessarily be disadvantaged by the lack of legal representation, the Procedures Committee proposed that the Scottish Government should be invited to consider extending the legal aid scheme to these inquiries[15]. After the taking of evidence, the consideration stage on a private Bill follows a similar procedure – consideration of amendments and sections – as that adopted for public Bills. The same is true of the third and final stage at which the Parliament decides whether a private Bill is to be passed[16] and there is equivalent provision too for matters such as reconsideration by the Parliament following reference of a Bill to the Supreme Court[17].

A private Bill introduced in one session falls if it has not been passed before the end of that session. The Bill may, however, be introduced within 30 days of the beginning of the next session and, if the consideration stage has been completed, in the terms agreed at the end of that stage[18].

Private legislation passed by the Parliament includes the National Galleries of Scotland Act 2003, the Robin Rigg Offshore Wind Farm (Navigation and Fishing) (Scotland) Act 2003, the Stirling-Alloa-Kincardine Railway and Linked Improvements Act 2004, the Edinburgh Tram (Line One) and (Line Two) Acts of 2006, the Waverley Railway (Scotland) Act 2006, the Glasgow Airport Rail Link Act 2007, the Edinburgh Airport Rail Link Act 2007, the William Simpson's Home (Transfer of Property etc) (Scotland) Act 2010, the Ure Elder Fund Transfer and Dissolution Act 2010, the National Trust for Scotland (Governance etc) Act 2013, the City of Edinburgh Council (Leith Links and Surplus Fire Fund) Act 2014, the City of Edinburgh Council (Portobello Park) Act 2014[19], and the Burrell Collection (Lending and Borrowing) (Scotland) Act 2014.

1 See both SI 1999/1095 and the December 1999 version of the Parliament's standing orders, r 9.17.
2 *Second Report of the Procedures Committee* SP Paper 204.
3 See the Forth Crossing Act 2011.
4 SP Paper 299, 16 June 2009. And see SOs Chapter 9C. The Forth Crossing Act 2011 was passed under the new procedures. Subsequently the SPPA Committee reviewed the hybrid Bill procedures, leading to new *Guidance on Hybrid Bills* (June 2014).
5 This requirement was extended to all Bills (ie in addition to Government Bills) by SA 2012, s 6.
6 SOs, rr 9A.1, 9A.2. At the time of writing, the standard fee is £5000, with a reduced fee for Bills relating to 'charitable, religious, educational ,literary or scientific purposes whereby no private profit or advantage is derived' or is 'promoted by a person other than a local authority, and is one from which the Promoters appear unlikely to derive substantial personal or corporate gain' (guidance on Private Bills, Annex J).
7 SOs, r 9A.4.
8 SOs, r 9A.6.
9 SOs, r 9A.5.
10 SOs, r 9A.8. There is provision also for a Bill to be referred back for further consideration in committee.
11 SOs, r 9A.9.
12 See above.
13 An assessor was appointed to consider objections to the Glasgow Airport Rail Link Bill and to the Edinburgh Airport Rail Link Bill.
14 *CSG Inquiry* para 70.
15 *CSG Inquiry* para 76.
16 SOs, r 9A.10.
17 SOs, r 9A.11.
18 SOs, r 9A.7.5–11.
19 Required in consequence of *Portobello Park Action Group Association v City of Edinburgh Council* 2013 SC 184.

POST-LEGISLATIVE SCRUTINY

9.28   In October 2013 the SPPA Committee of the Scottish Parliament published a report on Post-Legislative Scrutiny[1] – whose title suggests that the work of parliaments should not end with the making of legislation itself. It is a thought which has also been expressed in the Westminster Parliament[2] and has indeed been formally introduced as a new task for select committees[3]. Following suit, the SPPA Committee made some rather half-hearted proposals for the review of the implementation of legislation by subject committees at Holyrood[4]. The study of some aspects of legislative technique apart, however, these initiatives seem to be misplaced. Parliaments are unlikely to be the best judges of the effectiveness of their own products.

1 SP Paper 410.
2 See especially a report of the HL Constitution Committee, HL 173 (2003–04).
3 See para 10.9.
4 *Post-legislative Scrutiny*, 8th Rpt, 2013.

THE MAKING OF SUBORDINATE LEGISLATION BY MINISTERS

Introduction

9.29 The rationale for delegated law-making by ministers has already been explained in Chapter 7[1]. So too have the forms that such delegated legislation may take and the tension that it produces between the demands for the effectiveness of government and, on the other hand, maintaining some measure of democratic control. That tension is nowhere better reflected than in the procedures adopted for the actual making of delegated legislation. Most of the point of delegating powers to ministers is to exempt them from the degree of scrutiny and control that both Parliaments try to exercise in relation to primary legislation. There is a will to surrender much of that control but, on the other hand, both Parliaments are reluctant to release ministers from all supervision of the exercise of their powers[2]. This reluctance is demonstrated at two, quite different, points.

1 Delegated legislation may also, of course, be made by bodies other than ministers. The procedures required for the making of local authority byelaws are laid down in the Local Government (Scotland) Act 1973, ss 201–204.
2 For parliamentary scrutiny of proposed EU legislation, see para 3.15.

Control of legislation conferring powers on ministers

9.30 The first is at the stage when the relevant Parliament is considering a Bill which contains provisions for the delegation of power to ministers. Such provisions come under the scrutiny of the Parliament, especially in committee (Westminster) or at Stage 2 (Holyrood), and members will wish to establish whether the delegation of power to ministers is justified at all and, if so, whether the powers are cast too broadly, leaving the Bill itself a mere 'skeleton'; whether the powers include 'Henry VIII' clauses to amend primary legislation; whether there are sufficient requirements to consult affected persons prior to the making of the regulations; and whether the provisions for parliamentary scrutiny of the delegated legislation[1] are sufficient. To assist in this process of Bill scrutiny prior to conferring delegated powers, both Parliaments have specialised committees. At Westminster, there is the Deregulated Powers and Regulatory Reform Committee in the House of Lords[2] and, in the Scottish

Parliament, this is one of the functions of the Delegated Powers and Law Reform (formerly Subordinate Legislation) Committee[3].

In a category of their own are orders made by UK ministers under the Public Bodies Act 2011, eg to abolish named public bodies exercising devolved functions. These are subjected to legislative consent motions in the Scottish Parliament[4]

1 See below.
2 On the origins of the Committee, see C M G Himsworth 'The Delegated Powers Scrutiny Committee' [1995] PL 34. Such a committee was first recommended in the report of the (Scott/ Donoughmore) Committee on Ministers' Powers (Cmd 4060, 1932).
3 See C Himsworth 'Subordinate Legislation in the Scottish Parliament' (2002) 6 Edin LR 356 for the work of the Committee in its first three years. See also CT Reid (2002) 6 Edin LR 380 and (2003) 24 Stat LR 187.
4 See para 6.22.

Control of ministers' exercise of powers

9.31   The second point at which both Parliaments demonstrate a wish to impose a measure of supervision and control over the delegated law-making process is when the orders or regulations have been made, or have at least been published in draft form. Here, parliamentary scrutiny takes different forms. In the first place, ministers are subject to the general principles of accountability and are answerable to their respective Parliaments for the making of delegated legislation, or for the failure to make it. They are answerable for the subsequent impact of delegated legislation. Questions may be asked by MPs or MSPs; parliamentary debates may be initiated; and inquiries may be conducted by parliamentary committees which have the impact (or anticipated impact) of delegated legislation as their main focus. It should be borne in mind too that these standard parliamentary mechanisms for scrutiny and control are accompanied by the standard mechanisms for the judicial control of ministerial activities. The making of delegation legislation is subject to judicial review in much the same way as other executive acts[1]. Thus, even if no special steps were taken to scrutinise the making of delegated legislation, the ordinary principles of parliamentary and legal accountability would apply.

However, special steps have also been taken. Some apply to delegated legislation at large. Others, while made available in standard form, need to be applied to particular rule-making powers by the primary legislation (sometimes called the 'parent Act') which confers them. In the first category are rules contained in the Statutory Instruments Act 1946 (SIA 1946) which regulate most delegated law-making by UK ministers and these have been extended to the Scottish Ministers by Part 2 of the Interpretation and Legislative Reform (Scotland) Act 2010 (ILR(S)A 2010). Also in this first category is the provision made by both Parliaments for the 'technical' scrutiny of delegated legislation made by ministers. In the second category are the rules laid down in many Acts of Parliament and now in Acts of the Scottish Parliament which require that the delegated legislation which they authorise must be brought to the attention of the relevant Parliament by being 'laid' before that Parliament (at Westminster, either the Commons alone or both Houses) and, in most cases, is also made subject to an approval procedure.

1 See para 14.3.

Statutory Instruments Act 1946 and the Interpretation and Legislative Reform (Scotland) Act 2010

9.32 To take these measures in order, the principal contribution of SIA 1946 was to adopt recommendations made 14 years earlier by the Committee on Ministers' Powers[1]. That Committee had complained about the confusing range of types of ministerial order then available and the varying degrees of formal publication required. The variety of practice impeded knowledge of the orders in force and endangered the rule of law. In response, SIA 1946 created the device of the 'statutory instrument' and then attached to all such instruments certain standard characteristics. It was not intended to affect the content of instruments promulgated nor their overall quality or quantity, but to impose proper procedural controls. The rules in SIA 1946 apply to statutory instruments including, since July 1999, those instruments which extend to Scotland but which continue to be made by the Secretary of State for Scotland or other UK ministers in the exercise of powers which have not been devolved to the Scottish Ministers.

As noted earlier[2], most statutory powers to make delegated legislation take one of two forms. The first is, as a matter of legal form, conferred on the Queen in Council and exercisable by Order in Council. The second is conferred directly upon a minister, typically in the style of 'the Secretary of State', who is authorised to make the rules, regulations or order permitted by the parent Act. In either case, the Act may have imposed some prior procedural requirement including, for instance, the obligation to consult other persons or organisations. The contribution of SIA 1946 is to add further procedural requirements to a process which would otherwise be complete once the Order in Council or rules have been formally made. The Act applies to all statutory Orders in Council and also to all legislative powers delegated to ministers and stated to be exercisable by statutory instrument. Standard requirements are laid down for the numbering; printing and publishing (by the Queen's Printer); and citation of all statutory instruments. Certain instruments may be exempted from the need for publication. Despite the standard requirement of publication, it was held, in an early case under SIA 1946, that, even without publication, an instrument is nevertheless valid once made and, if this is required by the parent Act, laid before Parliament[3]. However, SIA 1946 does itself provide a defence in criminal proceedings involving an alleged breach of a statutory instrument where it is proved (a) that a statutory instrument has not been issued by the Stationery Office unless, on the other hand, it is proved (b) that reasonable steps have been taken to bring the instrument to the notice of the public or of persons likely to be affected or of the person actually charged[4]. As respects delegated legislation made by the Scottish Ministers, after initial transitional provision[5], Part 2 of ILR(S)A 2010 made very similar provision for the numbering and printing of instruments ('Scottish Statutory Instruments') made by a member of the Scottish Government[6] or by any other person with power to do so, within devolved competence, under an Act, whether of the UK or the Scottish Parliament, a definition which includes Orders in Council made within devolved competence. The Act requires that, immediately after it is made, a Scottish statutory instrument must be sent to the Queen's Printer for Scotland for numbering (SSI 1999/1 and so on) and for printing and sale. Local instruments may be exempted. The limited defence to criminal proceedings provided by SIA 1946 is extended to Scottish statutory instruments and there is provision for the preparation and publication of an annual edition of Scottish statutory instruments.

1 Cmd 4060, 1932.
2 See para 6.23.
3 *R v Sheer Metalcraft Ltd* [1954] 1 QB 586.
4 SIA 1946, s 3(2).
5 Scotland Act 1998 (Transitory and Transitional Provisions) (Statutory Instruments) Order 1999, SI 1999/1096.
6 Or by a Scottish public authority with mixed functions or no reserved functions.

Technical scrutiny

9.33   Another important procedure in the Westminster Parliament which has been modified for adoption at Holyrood is that known as the 'technical' scrutiny of delegated legislation. Practically all statutory instruments and some other types of rules and orders are required to be laid before Parliament at the time of their making or sometimes in draft, prior to their formal making. This is not a requirement of SIA 1946 (or of ILR(S)A 2010) but it is routinely imposed by Acts which provide the delegated powers. The laying of an instrument brings it formally to the notice of the Parliament in which it is laid and this is a procedure frequently, but not necessarily, linked to an opportunity (which may, in practice, also be merely formal) given to that Parliament to approve or reject the instrument (see below). In the Westminster Parliament, the requirement is most commonly to lay an instrument before *both* Houses, although some instruments of a financial character are required to be laid only in the House of Commons. In the Scottish Parliament, there is not the complication of two chambers and the rules on laying are straightforward where they derive from Acts of the Scottish Parliament. Many such requirements have already been imposed and the standing orders of the Parliament make the necessary procedural provision[1]. However, many powers now vested in the Scottish Ministers derive from Acts of the Westminster Parliament and, for these, the original obligation to lay an instrument before one or both Houses at Westminster has been translated into an obligation to lay it before the Scottish Parliament[2].

Once laid, instruments fall within the scrutinising jurisdiction of committees in the two Parliaments. At Westminster there is a Joint Committee on Statutory Instruments which considers instruments laid before both Houses and a Commons Committee for instruments laid only before that House. They share the same terms of reference which require the Committees to draw instruments to the special attention of Parliament on any of a number of specified grounds or on any other ground which does not impinge on the merits of the instrument or on the policy behind it. The specified grounds are that the instrument imposes a charge on public revenues; that it is excluded from challenge in the courts; that it purports to have retrospective effect; that there has been unjustifiable procedural delay; that there are doubts about whether it is intra vires; that it requires elucidation; or that its drafting appears defective[3].

In the Scottish Parliament powers virtually identical to those of the Westminster Committees have been given to the Delegated Powers and Law Reform Committee[4], the committee already charged with the scrutiny of Bills in the Parliament which contain proposed powers to make delegated legislation[5].

1 SOs, ch 14.
2 SA 1998, s 118.
3 HC standing orders , r 151.
4 With the additional ground that an instrument raises a devolution issue.
5 SOs, r 10.3. For the Committee's powers to scrutinise Bills, see para 9.30.

Merits scrutiny

9.34   It has been the usual practice of the Westminster Parliament, when conferring powers to make delegated legislation, to go further than to require merely that instruments should, when made, be laid before Parliament. An Act of Parliament may, as mentioned earlier, impose requirements on ministers to consult with bodies outside Parliament before making delegated legislation. With or without such a statutory requirement, ministers will, in any event, usually engage in extensive consultation with relevant interest groups. Much more frequently, however, statutes reserve the possibility of additional scrutiny by Parliament itself and it has already been pointed out that the question of whether scrutiny should be required is an important question for Parliament and, in the House of Lords, the Delegated Powers and Regulatory Reform Committee checks this aspect of a Bill as it proceeds. The same question now arises in the Scottish Parliament and in its Delegated Powers and Law Reform Legislation Committee.

The way in which the scrutiny of instruments is sought is by one of two main procedural devices. The first is for the Act which confers the delegated lawmaking power to provide that any orders or rules made are subject to annulment by resolution of either House of the Westminster Parliament (or of the Commons only) or, as the case may be, by resolution of the Scottish Parliament. While the power to annul has to be conferred by the empowering Act itself, further contributions have been made by SIA 1946 and by ILR(S)A 2010. Those Acts provide that, where an enactment requires a statutory instrument to be laid before Parliament, the instrument must be laid before the date on which it is to come into force[1]. It also standardises the period during which resolution to annul may be passed at 40 days[2]. Conventional practice at Westminster then supplements the requirements of SIA 1946 to ensure that ministers will lay an instrument not less than 21 days before it is to come into force. This is intended to provide a real opportunity for a negative resolution to be considered before the instrument takes effect. In the Scottish Parliament, ILR(S)A 2010 goes further, however, by giving legal status to the convention, with the laying period extended to 28 days[3].

Sometimes the legislature goes beyond the negative resolution procedure and provides instead that an instrument cannot be brought into effect at all unless the instrument (or a draft of the instrument) has been positively approved by resolution. Once again, at Westminster this is a requirement normally attached to both Houses and an affirmative resolution from each is needed before an instrument can come into force or, if approved in draft, before the final version of the instrument can be made. Such requirements in pre-SA 1998 legislation have the effect, in relation to orders to be made in devolved areas, of requiring the approval of the Scottish Parliament[4].

These standard procedures, now established in both Parliaments, provide, on their face, a clear hierarchy of scrutiny and control. Wishing to retain some measure of supervision of a process which they recognise must largely be driven by ministers, the Parliaments have reserved the right to be informed (by laying only); the right to annul (by negative resolution); and the right to withhold consent (by use of the affirmative resolution procedure). The idea of a formal hierarchy has been broadly recognised in practice by the allocation of a procedure appropriate to the significance of the power delegated. Thus, the negative resolution procedure is effectively treated as standard and is widely deployed at both Holyrood and Westminster. The requirement merely to lay is used more sparingly in situations where no further degree of control is sought. Perhaps paradoxically, this has been taken to include commencement orders even though the impact of the use or non-use of such orders may, of course, be considerable[5]. The Delegated Powers and Regulatory Reform Committee of the House of Lords has expressed concern about one aspect of this – the quantity of unimplemented legislation on the statute book[6] – and has sought to monitor the situation. At the other end of the scale, there has been a recognition of the desirability of subjecting particularly important instruments to the affirmative resolution procedure. Many financial measures are included in this category for instance the annual finance orders distributing funds to local authorities[7]. Sometimes an order which establishes a new administrative scheme from a very skeletal statute may be subject to the affirmative resolution procedure in the first instance, but with succeeding orders subject to only the negative procedure[8]. In the construction of its budget procedures, the Scottish Parliament paid special attention to the control appropriate to the modification of the terms of Budget Acts by order[9] and care was taken to impose the affirmative resolution procedure in respect of orders to amend such Acts. A 'super affirmative'[10] level of control, under which an order is not only subjected to be affirmative resolution procedure but is also required to be put out for wider consultation prior to the resolution, was attached to powers to designate parks under the National Parks (Scotland) Act 2000[11]. Despite the apparent rationality underlying the imposition of these form of control, all is not what it seems. Effective scrutiny in all degrees is subject to restrictions not apparent on the face of the rules formally laid down. At Westminster there have been three main impediments to serious control. First, the domination of party politics extends from procedures on primary legislation into those on secondary legislation. Despite the formal opportunities for the rejection of a statutory instrument, whether by annulment or by withholding approval, it would be almost unthinkable for a government with a stable majority in the House of Commons to 'lose' an instrument in this way. Options in the House of Lords are, of course, different but, in practice, that House has acted with great restraint[12]. There is no equivalent to the 'Parliament Acts' procedure for the overriding of resistance by the Lords but consideration has been given to such procedures in the context of House of Lords Reform[13]. At Holyrood, a majority loyal to the Government (with the exception of the period 2007–11, see below) has largely prevented upsets, although substantial pressure brought undertakings for change when a draft Census Order was considered by the Parliament. As one MSP said, 'It might not yet be all power to the committees but it is some power'[14]. The second barrier to serious scrutiny and control is more technical. With very limited exceptions, an instrument may be only either entirely approved or entirely rejected. This is a situation which could be changed and suggestions have indeed been made at Holyrood that the Parliament's capacity to amend instruments could be enhanced. In the meantime, however, the limitations of an all-or-nothing vote do restrict mature scrutiny of an instrument which even the Opposition would not wish to reject as wholly unwanted but would simply like to amend. The third obstacle at Westminster has been the lack of available parliamentary time. A back-bench MP might put down a motion to annul an instrument but time for a debate on the motion will not be allocated. This is a situation which has been alleviated somewhat by the practice of referring such motions to delegated legislation committees (but these committees cannot pass or even recommend a motion to annul[15]) and then, since 30 November 1999, the expansion of Commons business into Westminster Hall. At Holyrood the consideration of instruments falls in the main to the subject committees. Although occasionally threatened even under majority coalition governments[16], there has not been a motion to annul an instrument on the floor of the chamber. The minority SNP Government avoided such motions by opting to revoke orders recommended for annulment in committees[17].

1 SIA 1946, s 4.
2 SIA 1946, ss 5–6; ILR(S)A 2010 s 28.
3 ILR(S)A 2010 s 28.
4 SA 1998, s 118.
5 For a difficult example of the effect of commencement, see *R M v Scottish Ministers* [2012] UKSC 58, 2013 SC (UKSC) 139. And see C Himsworth (2014) 18 Edin LR 109.
6 *First Report of Select Committee on Delegated Powers* (HL Paper 9 (1993–94)), paras 11–12.
7 Local Government Finance Act 1992, Sch 12, the powers under which are now exercised by the Scottish Ministers. See para 8.5.
8 See, for example Bankruptcy and Diligence etc (Scotland) Act 2007, s 224(3), (4)(b)(ii).
9 See para 11.17.
10 The term was first used to describe the scrutiny attached to the extremely wide powers delegated by the Deregulation and Contracting Out Act 1994.
11 See also the special procedures under the Human Rights Act 1998, s 10; the Convention Rights (Compliance) (Scotland) Act 2001, s 12; the Legislative and Regulatory Reform Act 2006, Pt 1; the Public Services Reform (Scotland) Act 2010, s 25; and the 'special procedure orders' under ILR(S)A, Pt 4.
12 There have, however, been occasional exceptions, where the House of Lords has refused to comply – in relation to sanctions under the Southern Rhodesia Act 1965 in 1968; and the Greater London Council election rules in 2000.
13 HC Public Administration Committee (HC Paper 494 (2001–02)).

14 SP OR 16 Feb 2000, col 1100. See also, on an order under the Children (Scotland) Act 1995, the Education Culture and Sport Committee, 29 January 2002.

15 A Beith 'Prayers unanswered' (1981) 34 *Parl Affs* 165.

16 See, for example Education, Culture and Sport Committee, 22, 29 January 2002 and, in connection with the Public Transport Users' Committee for Scotland Order 2006 (SSI 2006/250) see SP OR 13 June 2006, col 3878.

17 See eg the Justice of the Peace Courts (Sheriffdom of South Strathclyde, Dumfries and Galloway) Order 2009 where a motion to annul was passed by the Justice Committee on 5 May 2009. The Committee was unhappy about the proposals for closure of certain Justice of the Peace (formerly District) Courts within that sheriffdom.

Subordinate legislation under SA 1998

9.35   Finally, and as a little appendix to the consideration of instruments by one or other Parliament, a note should be added on the exceptional case of the subordinate legislation introduced by SA 1998 itself which requires some special forms of scrutiny for certain devolution-related orders. Some instruments to be made by Order in Council, such as those amending SA 1998, Sch 4 or 5 (competence of the Scottish Parliament) require approval in draft not only by both Houses of the Westminster Parliament but also by the Scottish Parliament[1]. An Order in Council to prescribe the list of offices disqualifying the holder from membership of the Scottish Parliament needs the approval of that Parliament[2]. Although the general constitutional justification for these approvals may be clear, they create a situation in which orders promoted, in effect, by UK ministers require approval by the Parliament of which they are not themselves members[3].

1 SA 1998, s 30 and Sch 7.

2 SA 1998, s 15 and Sch 7.

3 For discussion, in relation to the Scottish Parliament (Disqualifications) Order 2003, SI 2003/409, see SP OR 9 January 2003. But see now SA 2012, s 13.

Chapter 10

The Parliamentary Accountability of Government

INTRODUCTION

10.1   In the White Paper *Scotland's Parliament* it was stated that '(t)he Scottish Parliament will hold the Executive to account for its actions'[1] and it was one of the 'key principles' adopted by the Consultative Steering Group in *Shaping Scotland's Parliament* that 'the Scottish Executive should be accountable to the Scottish Parliament and the Parliament and Executive should be accountable to the people of Scotland'[2].

These statements reflect two important ideas. The first is the general principle of the accountability of governments. The primary purpose of governments is, of course, to govern. They must also ensure the adequate financing of their operations. They must, if necessary, obtain legal authority for their actions by promoting the passing of new legislation. It has, therefore, to be an important role of constitutions to assist in bringing about the conditions under which governments can discharge these functions efficiently on behalf of the people they are elected to serve. It is, however, of equal importance that the powers of government should not be unconstrained and that those in power should be accountable for their actions. They should be in a position in which they can be held responsible for what they do. In some measure, this may be seen as a means to ensure the greater effectiveness of governments. Governments which know that they are subject to scrutiny and that they may be called to account for their failings may be expected to try to maintain or improve their standards. The merit of accountability is also, however, to be seen in terms of the need for the deliberate control of executive power. Whether one has in mind the behaviour of Scottish or English monarchs prior to the 17th century or the tendencies to abuse of power by modern governments, it is assumed to go without saying that governments must be held to account. In democracies, this has to imply an ultimate accountability to 'the people' but it is also recognised that this may need to be operationalised by a variety of different means and that some of these may be rather indirect. The ballot box may be an important symbol of direct democratic accountability but in representative democracies it has required substantial supplementation. There is in the United Kingdom a reliance on the differentiation of both the principles and also of the methods of accountability. The task of maintaining the legal accountability of government and the rule of law has been substantially, but not exclusively, allocated to the courts[3]. Such legal accountability has broadened to embrace accountability to the standards imposed by the European Convention on Human Rights, with a reliance, but again not exclusively, on the courts. The creation and expansion of the powers of ombudsmen have, to an extent, separated off the accountability which is maintained by the insistence on standards of good administration in government[4]. Similarly, the imposition and the monitoring of standards of ethical conduct operate as a distinct mechanism of accountability. For much longer, there have been forms of financial control over government and, in particular, procedures for the audit of government accounts which also operate to strengthen the general process of accountability[5].

All these forms of accountability involve, in addition to the separate roles of courts, ombudsmen and auditors, a strong role for Parliament. However, the aspiration contained in the opening statements of this chapter – that the Scottish Government should be accountable to the Scottish Parliament – refers not so much to these specific accountabilities but more to that form of general political accountability which is represented by the principle that ministers are, at Westminster, responsible to Parliament for their actions. The UK Government's aim was to see this position replicated in Scotland. 'The relationship between the Scottish Executive and the Scottish Parliament will be similar to the relationship between the UK Government and the UK Parliament'[6]. Just how far that aim has been fulfilled is a matter for debate, but certain comparisons can be made between the rules applicable in the two systems. Paragraph 10.2 sets out, in summary form, the present theory and practice of ministerial responsibility. In paras 10.3–10.10 the forms of procedure designed to maintain accountability in both Parliaments are discussed. Paragraphs 10.11–10.14 deal with the role of ombudsmen and para 10.15 deals specifically with the Scottish Parliament and its public petition procedure. The separate rules on financial accountability and on legal accountability are dealt with in Chapters 11 and 14 respectively.

Since access to relevant information is a vital component of maintaining accountability, the implementation of the Freedom of Information Act 2000 and the Freedom of Information (Scotland) Act 2002 have been of great importance. These Acts are discussed in Chapter 13 below but their provisions supporting individual citizen access to information and, indirectly, MP and MSP access to information through parliamentary channels should be borne in mind[7].

Although the parliamentary accountability of the Scottish Government was not a principal point of concern during the independence referendum period, it was raised in the Report of the Smith Commission in November 2014[8]. Under the heading of 'Parliamentary and independent oversight', it was one of Lord Smith's personal recommendations that the Scottish Parliament's powers of oversight should be strengthened.

1 Cm 3658, 1997, para 4.7.
2 Section 2, para 2.
3 See ch 14.
4 See below.
5 See ch 11.
6 *Scotland's Parliament* para 2.6.
7 For discussion of the impact of the 2000 Act on parliamentary questions see Fifth Report of the Public Administration Committee (2004–05) HC 449-1, para 6 and the case of *Office of Government Commerce v Information Commissioner* [2008] EWHC 774 (Admin), [2010] QB 98.
8 See para 4.21.

MINISTERIAL RESPONSIBILITY – AN INTRODUCTION

10.2 First a word on terminology. In the discussion so far, the ideas of 'accountability' and 'responsibility' of ministers have been used more or less interchangeably and this practice will continue. Plainly, the two words can be used in contexts which make one preferable rather than the other. Equally, however, the meanings elide in general usage and a choice is often made simply on grounds of elegance. Ministers have duties and responsibilities and, whilst it would be clumsy to speak of a responsibility to Parliament for their responsibilities, it is perfectly acceptable to speak of accountability without change of meaning. The current *Civil Service Code* refers to ministers being 'accountable to Parliament'[1] and the current UK *Ministerial Code* states that 'Ministers have a duty to Parliament to account, and be held to account, for the policies, decisions and actions of their departments and "next steps" agencies'[2]. 'Accountability' here embraces both the idea of giving an account of policies, decisions and actions and of being held responsible for them. However, it has to be acknowledged that, for the purpose of restricting the scope of responsibility and especially the scope of blameworthiness, distinctions have sometimes been drawn between the broader obligations of accountability and the narrower or more focused obligations implied by responsibility. It is a distinction to which we should return while, in the meantime, continuing to use the terminology more or less interchangeably. It is, in any event, not merely questions of language which make a principle routinely stated to be fundamental to the working of the constitution so uncertain in its content. It would be surprising if a principle which is described as constitutional, but which is so intimately bound up in the workings of politics, were not of disputed content.

However, some things are clearer than others. Firstly, it is *ministers* who are described as responsible. This has three main consequences. The first is that the principle of ministerial responsibility is designed to protect those over whom the minister presides – the departmental civil servants – from the obligation publicly to defend the actions of the department. There is nothing very exceptional in this. In most organisations, those who lead find it operationally necessary or desirable to represent the organisation publicly, whether to take praise or blame and without regard to the steps which may be taken *internally* to attribute responsibility where it more accurately lies. Constitutionally, however, this principle also operates to distinguish the publicly accountable politician from the unaccountable and often 'anonymous' civil servant[3]. An exception is the special role of the 'accountable officer'[4]. Secondly, the principle distinguishes ministers from other, non-departmental, holders of public office. Ministers are responsible to Parliament but chief constables (in Scotland, the single chief constable) and chairs of quangos (formally, at least) are not[5]. Thirdly, ministers are responsible only in respect of those matters which are within their departmental remit. This may be broad – and the Prime Minister's remit may be interpreted *very* broadly[6] – but it does impose limits. Similarly, it is a responsibility owed to *Parliament*. This has consequences not only for the nature of the obligations of accountability themselves but also for their priority over obligations to others. Ministers must, for instance, ensure that the most important announcements of government policy are made, in the first instance, in Parliament[7]. Beyond this, however, there is much indeterminacy, an indeterminacy which arises out of the twin circumstances which underpin the constitutional situation of governments on the Westminster model. On the one hand, they owe their very existence to the will of Parliament and can be removed by it[8]. On the other hand, governments are in a position to impose a considerable degree of discipline and control on a majority of Parliament's members. Governments are, therefore, at the same time, both acutely vulnerable to Parliaments but also protected from them. The position of individual ministers is further shaped by the solidarity (formally described as 'collective responsibility') which is extended to and demanded of them[9]. Except in circumstances where the alleged failing of a minister relates directly to a question of personal behaviour, whether by virtue of unacceptable personal relationships or of dishonesty, a Prime Minister will tend always to extend the cloak of protection, at least for a while. The political backdrop also produces a starker and more restricted range of outcomes. In particular, the idea of responsibility has been overlaid by the rather absurd notion that proof of error will always demand a resignation. Resignation may be too severe a penalty for mistakes apparently made blamelessly, at least from the point of view of the affected minister. Unrepentant denial of responsibility may be the only practical alternative and it is not surprising when, for instance, prisons prove to be insecure[10] ministers react very defensively.

In the modern working of the UK constitution, there are two principal questions which remain unresolved. The first is how the rhetoric of the asserted responsibility to Parliament of ministers for the entire working of their departments and executive agencies can be reconciled with the practical reality that ministers cannot possibly be directly involved in, or even know about, the vast range of actings and decision-making in their departments. Doctrine demands that it is *ministers* who must indeed be responsible, in the main because doctrine also demands that civil servants should be protected. But common sense, not just the common sense of ministers but also of parliamentarians and outsiders, tells us that the responsibility of ministers across the entire range of activities, especially if it carries with it the risk of blame and sanctions, perhaps to the extent of loss of office, is impractical and illusory. There is a circle here which cannot be squared. However, successive attempts at a reconciliation have been made and this is what prompted the reformulation of the doctrine following the Crichel Down affair of over 60 years ago when, following the resignation of the Minister of Agriculture because of the mistakes and inefficiency of his officials in the handling of the return to farmers of requisitioned land, the Home Secretary of the time (Sir David Maxwell Fyfe) sought to distinguish between situations with varying degrees of ministerial involvement – ranging from a civil servant's carrying out a ministerial order to a civil servant's taking action completely unknown to the minister – to determine the appropriate degree of responsibility. The Home Secretary's analysis also incorporated varying degrees of seriousness of the decisions made and of the fault of the civil servant so that no clear conclusions can be drawn beyond the bald statement that ministers are indeed constitutionally responsible to Parliament and that they must 'render an account' of their stewardship[11]. There have been attempted distinctions between matters of 'policy' for which ministers have a responsibility, and matters of 'administration' for which they have, at most, a reduced level of responsibility[12]. This is a distinction which acquired a higher profile after the arrival of executive agencies and the special relationship between ministers and their chief executives[13]. Most prominently, reliance has been placed on a distinction, already mentioned, between 'responsibility' for some matters and, on the other hand, 'accountability', an obligation merely to inform and give an account, for the rest[14]. Another distinction has been drawn between 'constitutional accountability', as delivered through the convention of ministerial responsibility and 'managerial accountability'[15]. While none of these accounts[16] supplies a wholly persuasive reconciliation of the dilemma, it does also appear that an accommodation of a sort has been reached. The element of responsibility which involves an obligation to provide information, as we shall see when considering parliamentary mechanisms below, has been strengthened. On the other hand, political responsibility (in the sense of ministerial vulnerability to Parliament) has become marginalised as a serious element of governmental accountability as a whole. As long ago as 1956, Professor SE Finer reduced questions of responsibility to the political relationship between a minister, the Prime Minister and their party[17] and nothing much seems to have changed there. The weakness of crude political responsibility need not necessarily be a cause of distress if greater confidence can be placed in the other structures of accountability which have been built around it. If this is the case, ministerial responsibility as vulnerability to raw political pressure in Parliament can safely take on a more residual role.

The second, and related but also more subversive, question is whether the ministerial responsibility which does survive beyond the obligation to inform is really best seen as a responsibility to *Parliament* at all or whether instead it is better seen as a responsibility to the public, in relation to which Parliament exercises, along with other institutions, only a facilitative role. There are, of course, no formal constitutional rules to guide us here. We are in the domain of convention and such 'rules' as there are must derive from today's observable practice – not from statements in classic texts, nor even from the words of a statement of practice agreed between Parliament and government. Parliament will, almost inevitably, wish to assert the continuing vitality of the doctrine. It is in the government's political interest to assert its own constitutional accountability[18], whether or not supported by the facts. There is, however, nothing new in suggesting that ministers owe a responsibility which is, at least, shared between Parliament and public. Nor is it new to suggest that the BBC's 'Question Time' (or indeed 'Newsnight') has a higher political prominence than Parliament's own. But today it is perhaps truer to say that the hugely greater political power of the mass media combined with a more subservient and less autonomous role for Parliament have redrawn the constitutional lines of responsibility. Winning and maintaining media support on key issues and scoring highly in opinion polls[19], rather than support in Parliament, are seen as the truer tests of governmental performance. Praise or blame in Parliament may be an insecure guide to fortunes in the country. Ministerial accountability is ultimately more a state of mind and a political fact than a constitutional doctrine.

Whatever the real condition of ministerial responsibility to the UK Parliament, it was, in name at least, the equivalent doctrine which was received into Scottish practice. In language similar to the UK Code, the *Scottish Ministerial Code*[20] states that 'Ministers have a duty to the Parliament to account, and be held to account, for the policies, decisions and actions taken within their field of responsibility'[21]. Later, it is stated that 'Ministers should seek to uphold and promote' the key principles which guided the work of the Consultative Steering Group', including that 'the Scottish Government should be accountable to the Scottish Parliament and the Parliament and Government should be accountable to the people of Scotland'[22]. One of the *Code*'s highest obligations is to 'give accurate and truthful information to the Parliament.' Ministers who knowingly mislead Parliament are expected to resign[23]. The wording of the Scottish Code may, however, be intended to produce, or to reflect a somewhat different relationship between ministers and the Scottish Parliament from that at Westminster. Not confined to one or other Parliament. The tendency to coalition or minority government can produce a different balance between executive and Parliament and different relationships of accountability. The fact that there is not, in the practice of the Scottish Government, a direct alignment between the distribution of functions of ministers and departments or directorates[24] may dilute the idea of the responsibility of one for the other. The starting point, however, is one of assumed equivalence. Although powers are vested in the Scottish Ministers and, for instance, parliamentary questions are addressed to the Scottish Government as a whole[25], individual accountabilities among the members of the Government are, as indicated in the *Code*, plain enough. Scottish practice is also acquiring its own portfolio of high-profile cases. The resignation of Dr Richard Simpson MSP as a deputy minister was forced on 26 November 2002 after it had been revealed that he had spoken of the striking firefighters in highly disparaging tones[26]. That was a matter of personal behaviour but, as a matter of departmental responsibility, there was no doubt, when severe problems occurred at the Scottish Qualifications Authority, about the ministerial accountability of Sam Galbraith MSP, the Minister for Education. He was exposed to the first vote of no confidence in the Parliament and, although that challenge was unsuccessful and the minister did not resign, he was subsequently removed from his position[27].

---

1   *Civil Service Code (2010)* para 2. And civil servants are accountable to ministers.
2   *Ministerial Code: A Code of Conduct and Guidance on Procedures for Ministers* (Sept 2010) para 1.2(b). For 'next steps' or 'executive' agencies, see para 7.24. The principle is repeated in *The Cabinet Manual* (Oct 2011) para 5.6.
3   Sometimes a civil servant sheds anonymity, as was the case in the high-profile appearance of Alastair Campbell before the House of Commons Foreign Affairs Committee on 25 June 2003. More routinely, in his capacity as Principal Accountable Officer, the permanent secretary of the Scottish Administration appears before the Scottish Parliament's Public Audit Committee. For accountable officers, see ch 11.
4   See para 11.18.
5   Although this does not protect such officials from parliamentary appearances. See eg the Scottish chief constable at the Scottish Parliament's Justice Sub-Committee on Policing, 31 Oct 2013; and Lord Smith, chair of the Environment Agency at the House of Commons Environment, Food and Rural Affairs Committee (on flooding), 2 Apr 2014.
6   Nicely illustrated in the House of Commons Northern Ireland Affairs Committee on 13 January 2015, when former Prime Minister Tony Blair accepted full responsibility for the 'On the Runs' policy of his government.

7 *Ministerial Code* para 27. See House of Lords Communication Committee report, Government Communications, 26 January 2009, First Report of Session 2008–09, HL Paper 7).
8 This is made explicit in relation to the Scottish Parliament by the Scotland Act 1998 (SA 1998), ss 45(2), 47(2), 48(2) and 49(4)(c).
9 On collective responsibility, see para 7.11.
10 A cause of embarrassment to James Prior in 1983 and Michael Howard in 1995 and in 2009 to First Minister Alex Salmond and Cabinet Secretary for Justice Kenny McAskill.
11 HC Debs, 20 July 1954, cols 1285–1287.
12 For a discussion of this and other terminological distinctions, see D Woodhouse 'The Reconstruction of Constitutional Accountability' [2002] PL 73.
13 For executive agencies, see para 7.24.
14 For example, Treasury and Civil Service Committee *The Role of the Civil Service* (HC Paper 27 (1993–94)).
15 Woodhouse [2002] PL 73.
16 For some further useful analysis, see R Mulgan (2000) 78 Public Administration 555.
17 (1956) 34 Public Administration 377.
18 In the Scottish Executive *Partnership Agreement* of May 2003 it was declared: 'We will support robust parliamentary arrangements to hold the Executive to account.'
19 See D Woodhouse 'Ministerial responsibility in the 1990s: when do ministers resign?' (1993) 46 Parl Aff 277.
20 Reissued Dec 2011.
21 Para 1.2(b).
22 Para 3.1.
23 Note the ministerial apology for inaccurate information inadvertently provided on 4 Feb 2009; and the apologies of Mr Salmond (15 Nov 2012) and Mr Russell (20 Nov 2012) for inaccurate statements about college funding.
24 See para 7.25 above.
25 See para 10.6 below.
26 Perhaps for related reasons, he lost his seat in the May 2003 elections.
27 See also para 10.7 below.

PARLIAMENTARY MECHANISMS

10.3   It is valuable to carry forward this preliminary consideration of ministerial responsibility as we now turn to the actual mechanisms established in both Parliaments to hold ministers to account. We should keep in mind the flexibility and even ambiguity in the concept of responsibility and the question whether it is best seen as responsibility to the people, with the relevant Parliament acting simply as the agent of the people, albeit formally the most important agent, in holding the executive to account; or whether the Parliament is better seen as the primary accountee. The actual function of parliamentary mechanisms will, in any event, depend on political conditions of the time – the balance of parties in the Parliament, the political vulnerability of the government (especially if a minority government) and whether the government is drawn from a single party or is the product of a coalition or partnership. The effectiveness of parliamentary scrutiny may also depend on the structures of government adopted, including the use, or not, of executive agencies. It will depend too upon quite practical considerations such as the availability of time. The Scottish Parliament maintains an emphasis upon a strong committee system. But committees quickly devour the time of members and the strains of squeezing committee meetings into three half days of the parliamentary week have had to be accommodated. A related question is the divided loyalty of back-bench members. They are interested in the scrutiny of the executive but it is an interest which usually has to be combined with loyalty to their party (whether or not it is in government); ambition for personal advancement which is usually seen in terms of advancement in a party; and the need for most members to maintain a high profile in their own locality. Members are fighting the next election as well as a scrutinising the executive. If an MP or MSP appears to be pressing the government with questions in either the chamber or a committee, he or she will also have an eye on the party whip, as well as on what will appear on the parliamentary website and in the national or local newspapers.

Issues of accountability may arise in virtually all aspects of parliamentary business. Whatever the business, ministers are aware that they are subject to the scrutiny of their parliamentary colleagues and, although a line is often drawn between scrutiny of law-making and of executive action, ministers are as vulnerable to critical examination of their proposals in both. It is, however, possible to identify certain parliamentary procedures as devoted principally to executive scrutiny, and these may usefully be divided into three: parliamentary questions; debates on the initiative of opposition parties or of individual members; and the work of select or subject committees.

Parliamentary questions

10.4   Probably the most distinctive and potentially the most incisive mechanism for demonstrating the accountability of ministers to MPs and MSPs is the parliamentary question. Questions have historically been prominent at Westminster and, if the record of the first four sessions of the Scottish Parliament is anything to go by, MSPs at Holyrood have shown an enthusiasm for questions which has expanded the answering function of the Scottish Government far beyond that of the Scottish Office in the pre-devolution period.

Questions at Westminster

10.5   In the House of Commons[1], question time has established itself as central to ministerial accountability. A government statement has agreed that 'questions are a highly effective means of holding the executive to account. A well-aimed question can benefit a Member simply by enabling them to obtain information. It can also benefit the Government, perhaps by requiring attention to a detail, which had been insufficiently considered, perhaps by allowing the Government to put its case across'[2]. On a rota basis, questions are put to departmental ministers for about an hour on sitting days except Fridays, and to the Prime Minister for half an hour on Wednesdays. The practice of the House, policed in the first instance by its Clerks, confines questions to matters within the departmental responsibility of ministers and acknowledges that ministers cannot be compelled to answer questions which would entail the disclosure of information when this is not in the public interest[3] or where the cost of obtaining information would be excessive. The limits of responsibility exclude questions about institutions outwith central government, such as local authorities. Current practice on questions about the work of (executive) agencies has shifted from an earlier practice of leaving chief executives to respond by letter to ministerial answers. Special rules were adopted by resolution of the House in October 1999[4] to ensure that UK ministers may not, in general, be required to answer questions on matters devolved to the Scottish Parliament or to the National Assembly for Wales[5]. Ministers are expected to answer questions purely on devolved matters by making it clear that such questions should be addressed to the relevant devolved administration. It is, however, acknowledged that a clear dividing line cannot always be drawn where, for instance, a question relates to a reserved matter which is executively devolved to the Scottish Ministers[6]. It is, in practice, often the case that issues overlapping the division of competences arise in questions to the Secretary of State for Scotland, including, commonly, questions about meetings between the Secretary of State and the First Minister.

The effectiveness of questions depends only in part upon their formally permitted scope but much more on matters of procedure and style. Pressures on parliamentary time make it necessary to ration access by MPs who may put down no more than two questions for oral answer which are then subject to a draw ('shuffle') for priority status while the opportunity for important supplementary follow-up questions is regulated by the Speaker. MPs are often unhappy about 'evasive or unhelpful replies' letting ministers 'off the hook'[7]. As the *Ministerial Code* stipulates, 'it is of paramount importance that Ministers give accurate and truthful information to Parliament' and ministers should refuse information only in the public interest and in accordance with relevant statutes and the Freedom of Information Act 2000[8] (although for the difficulties which can arise where questions are answered by reference to the Freedom of Information Act see *Office of Government Commerce v Information Commissioner*[9]). Changes to the rules on the submission of questions have enabled questions for oral answer to be submitted as little as two sitting days beforehand (four days in the case of questions to the Secretaries of State for Scotland, Wales and Northern Ireland, to enable information to be gathered from the devolved administrations) to ensure greater immediacy of impact[10]. Unanswered oral questions join other 'unstarred' questions for written answer. Such written answers, published in Hansard and often replete with the facts and figures of governmental performance, are a rich source of information and, despite their low political profile, are a significant further indicator of accountability.

1   Similar arrangements operate in the House of Lords.
2   Cm 5628, 2002, para 2.
3   And see *Scottish Ministerial Code* para 1.2(d).
4   HC Debs 25 October 1999 col 774. A similar practice was adopted in relation to the 'Stormont' government in Northern Ireland.
5   Devolution Guidance Note 1: 'Common Working Arrangements'.
6   See also Devolution Guidance Note 13: 'Handling of Parliamentary Business in the House of Lords'.
7   HC Paper 622 (2001–02), para 48.
8   Para 1.2(d).
9   [2010] QB 98.
10 HC Debs, 29 October 2002 cols 813–814. See HC SOs 22(5).

Questions at Holyrood

10.6   In the Scottish Parliament the standing orders make provision for questions to the Scottish Government[1]. Questions must be in writing (in English) and lodged with the Clerk of the Parliament. They must relate to a matter for which the First Minister, the Scottish Ministers or the Scottish Law Officers have general responsibility and must be brief, clearly worded and address specific points. They must not, however, express a point of view; they must not contain offensive language; they must not breach any enactment or rule of law or be contrary to the public interest. Nor may they be in breach of the general '*sub judice*' rule of the Parliament – questions may not refer to any matter in relation to which legal proceedings are active[2] except to the extent permitted by the Presiding Officer[3]. To be admissible, a question must comply with these requirements but will be inadmissible if the information it seeks has been provided in response to a similar question in the previous six months. Disputes as to admissibility are to be determined by the Presiding Officer. A question must specify whether it is an oral question or a written question.

Written questions are published in the Parliament's Business Bulletin and must usually be answered within 14 days. A question concerning a matter for which he or she is alone responsible must be answered by the First Minister; similarly in respect of the Law Officers. All other questions may, in terms of the standing orders, be answered by any member of the Scottish Government but, in practice, questions will be answered by the minister with direct responsibility. Answers (along with questions) are published in the Official Report. Oral questions are answered at the weekly periods of question time (usually held on Thursdays) – with 30 minutes for First Minister questions and with questions to the Scottish Government divided between 'portfolio' questions (40 minutes, normally on Wednesdays) focused on specific topics rotating from week to week and 'general' questions (20 minutes, normally on Thursdays) and 'topical' questions (normally on Tuesdays) – subject to prescribed timetables for the lodging of questions and to selection procedures to bring questions down to manageable numbers. Questions may also be asked of the Scottish Parliamentary Corporate Body[4].

At First Minister's question time, a question must usually, of course, be answered by the First Minister but provision is made for another member of the Government to answer if the First Minister is unable to attend. Supplementary questions (required to be on the same subject matter and to be brief) from any MSP may follow, at the discretion of the Presiding Officer. Often this is used to enable senior opposition leaders to intervene. At the 'general' and 'themed' question times, relevant members of the Scottish Government (Cabinet Secretaries) and (junior) ministers answer questions[5]. A supplementary question may follow from the MSP who put the question and, at the discretion of the Presiding Officer, from other members as well. Special provision is made for emergency questions[6]. An oral question 'of an urgent nature' may, if lodged by an MSP by 10 am on a day when the Parliament is meeting, be referred to the Presiding Officer who, if he or she thinks it sufficiently urgent, will allow the question to be put and answered at some appropriate point in the meeting. In the course of the first session of the Parliament, the process of parliamentary questions had established itself at the heart of the Parliament's procedures. The volume of questions quickly reached a high level. During 2013–14, the total number of oral questions (combining general, portfolio and topical questions) was 1135, written questions (including inspired questions) 5202, and, to the First Minister, 215. The volume of business has, however, produced problems for both the Government and the Parliament. There is a limit of ten days for a response to a written question but ministers may initially offer 'holding answers'. As an alternative to a formal question MSPs may contact officials directly in order to pursue points of information. But, of course, simply obtaining the information requested may not be the sole motivation of a parliamentary question: the opportunity to apply political pressure on ministers and publication in the official record may be important. Another issue in the Scottish Parliament, as at Westminster, has been that of the question 'inspired' or 'planted' by the Government. It is required that all questions initiated by the Government are identified as such.

1 SOs, rr 13.3–13.8. The Parliament also publishes *Guidance on Parliamentary Questions* (2nd edn (of session) March 2014).
2 For the purposes of the Contempt of Court Act 1981, s 2.
3 SOs, r 7.5.
4 SOs r 13.9.
5 The Law Officers are usually required to answer questions within their responsibility.
6 SOs, r 13.8. To Dec 2014, only nine emergency questions had been submitted.

Debates on the initiative of opposition parties (including motions of no confidence) and of individual members

10.7   At Westminster, opposition parties are anxious to use opportunities available to them to debate issues of their choosing and in a way designed to hold the government to account. Rarely used but potentially of high political profile is the motion of no confidence in the government[1]. More routinely, there are regular debates in both the main Commons chamber and, since November 1999, the parallel chamber in 'Westminster Hall', on matters proposed by the opposition parties. Away from these relatively high-profile debates and sometimes late at night, individual MPs have the opportunity to initiate short 'adjournment debates' in which they raise matters of more specific concern – frequently of relevance to their own constituency – and elicit a ministerial response.

At Holyrood, similar opportunities are available. Standing order provision is made for motions of no confidence – whether in relation to the Scottish Government as a whole, or an individual member of the Government, or a junior minister[2]. To be included in the business programme of the Parliament, such a motion must have the support of at least 25 members. Two such motions were debated in the first and second sessions of the Parliament. In the fourth session, there has been one. None has been successful[3]. It is also the specific responsibility of the Parliamentary Bureau to ensure that the business programme includes debates initiated by persons and bodies other than the Government[4]. There must be at least 12 half-sitting days in each parliamentary year in which priority is given to the business of committees; there must be at least 16 half-sitting days devoted to business chosen by opposition political parties and groups; and, at the end of each meeting of the Parliament, there is a period of up to 45 minutes for any members' business.

On general debates in the chamber, it was the observation of the (then) Procedures Committee[5] that, while these provided the opportunity for challenging the Government, debates tended to be highly predictable because they were structured around motions and amendments which reinforced party differences. The Committee proposed that there might, in addition, be 'subject-based debates' in the Parliament in which there would be no specific motion and no vote. General debates in the chamber have, in the main, focused, as would be expected, on matters devolved to the Parliament and Government, although important opportunities have also been taken to debate reserved matters such as, on 16 January 2003, the possibility of an attack on Iraq and on 6 August 2014, the Trident programme and the removal of nuclear weapons from Scotland. As well as providing an opportunity for discussion of the topic under debate, these occasions have been used to air differences as to whether reserved matters are suitable for debate in the Parliament[6] and whether the formal scope of the Parliament's powers should be extended.

Debates on members' business have provided an opportunity for the discussion of motions which are non-controversial and on topics which usually raise either local constituency and regional issues or general campaigns or causes in which the sponsoring MSP is interested[7]. As the Procedures Committee has noted, the debates pass without a vote and attendance is usually small. The level of attendance does not, however, undermine the rationale for such business. The debates provide opportunities to raise important local issues with the Government, or to press very specific issues which might otherwise not be capable of being pursued. They often attract specific audiences to the public gallery and, since they are rarely of a party political nature, they tend to be free of partisanship. The Procedures Committee thought that, perhaps as a result, these debates frequently attain a quality and freshness which general debates lack[8]. The Committee proposed that the value of members' business might be enhanced by removing the selection of motions from the Parliamentary Bureau (perhaps by substituting a ballot) and, on some occasions at least, by holding the debates at a more popular time in the parliamentary day.

1 On 28 March 1979, the Callaghan government failed to repel a motion of no confidence and was forced into the dissolution of Parliament.
2 SOs, r 8.12.
3 The first (on 13 December 2000) was directed at Sam Galbraith for his handling of the SQA examinations affair and the second (on 15 February 2001) at Sarah Boyack for her handling of road transport policy. In the second session, Malcolm Chisholm faced a confidence motion on health service provision (30 Sept 2004). It was reported in May 2009 that, when Cabinet Secretary Kenny MacAskill came under threat of a no confidence vote following a prison escape, the First Minister in turn threatened that the whole Government would instead resign (Times, 23 May 2009). On 21 May 2014 Alex Neil faced a vote of no confidence in relation to the management of cuts in health services in his constituency. On 9 Oct 2014, Kenny MacAskill faced a (lesser) motion calling for his resignation. He survived that but was subsequently a victim of new First Minister Nicola Sturgeon's first Cabinet reshuffle. For the consequences for ministers of a resolution that the Government no longer enjoys the confidence of the Parliament, see para 7.16.
4 SOs, r 5.6.
5 *CSG Inquiry* paras 486–497.

6 SP OR, 16 January 2003, col 17013.
7 *CSG Inquiry* paras 498–506.
8 *CSG Inquiry* para 499.

Select and subject committees

10.8   Whatever the strengths and weaknesses of the parliamentary mechanisms so far considered, it is in scrutiny by committee that first Westminster and now Holyrood have invested most trust and resources in recent times. The general structure of parliamentary committees has been noted in Chapter 5 and, in particular, the provision made in the House of Commons for the post-1979 system of departmental select committees and then, at Holyrood, the setting up of the 'subject' committees of the Parliament with remits intended to combine the functions of both the Commons select committees and its public bill committees.

Select committees at Westminster

10.9   Despite early reservations about the potential of House of Commons select committees to fail because of their political domination by the governing party or because of their lack of resources, there is today no doubting their high level of productivity in the use of their powers 'to call for persons, papers and records' to conduct serious inquiries in their areas of focus. Through their reports, much information is put into the public domain. The only major targets of criticism have been, since devolution in 1999, the committees tracking the 'territorial' departments – the Northern Ireland Affairs, Scottish Affairs[1] and Welsh Affairs Committees. Individual inquiries continue to be held[2] but questions hang over these committees, as they have done over their related departments. Although a standing committee rather than a select committee and, therefore, not a committee to hold inquiries, the Scottish Grand Committee has held occasional debates on Scottish matters since devolution but has not met since 2002/03[3].

It is difficult to assess the overall contribution of select committees in seeking to secure the accountability of the executive to Parliament. An exchange of views between the Liaison Committee of the House of Commons – a committee consisting of the chairman of all select committees – and the Government nicely illustrates the issues. The Committee entitled a report issued in 2000 *Shifting the Balance: Select Committees and the Executive*[4]. In it, it took as its starting point the proposition that, despite the best efforts of select committees, in practice governmental power has always outstripped parliamentary control. Prior to 1979 and the creation of the new committees, it had been an unequal struggle and governments had always had the upper hand. The new system had been a success. Independent scrutiny of government had been achieved. Ministers and civil servants had been questioned and forced to explain policies. On occasion, short-sighted policies and wrongdoing had been exposed. The system had been a source of unbiased information, national debate and constructive ideas. The political process had been made less remote and more accessible to the citizen. The system had shown the House of Commons at its best: working on the basis of fact, not supposition or prejudice; and with constructive co-operation rather than routine disagreement. On the other hand, success had not been unalloyed and questions had arisen about the overall effectiveness of the system. After two decades – and especially in the present climate of constitutional change – it was time for some further reform and modernisation.

The Committee prefaced its proposals with a statement of what it called the 'realities of select committee work'. It is an interesting list (some points have already been touched on) which is as relevant to the consideration of the work of committees at Holyrood as it is to those at Westminster:

(1)   Select committees have to operate within a constitutional framework in which, unlike the position in the United States, there is no separation of powers, and a stronger party system. Ministers are also members of Parliament, and are sustained in office by Parliament. The relationship is thus more subtle, the Liaison Committee said, but there is no reason why select committees should not call ministers to account.

(2)   Select committees are affected by party loyalty and organisation, which structure the way in which Parliament and its institutions work. In turn, careers have generally been shaped by party service and the floor of the House rather than by work on select committees.

(3)   Because select committees are bodies created by and subordinate to the House itself, the exercise of their formal powers is eventually subject to the will of the House, in which the government of the day is likely to have a majority. A particular application of this is the powers committees have to ensure the attendance of those they wish to interview, especially civil servants. A general agreement on access to civil servants has been made under the 'Osmotherley rules'[5] but, in the case of a refusal supported by ministers, a committee would need the backing of an order of the House as a whole which, because of the government's majority, would be very unlikely to be forthcoming[6].

(4)   There is no easy route to success. A determined and hard-working committee, in which members are prepared to devote substantial effort and put the interests of the citizen and taxpayer first, can be extraordinarily effective.

(5)   Within their powers, and subject to any instruction from the House, committees are entirely independent. It is up to them to decide how to do their job, set their priorities, and select and run inquiries.

(6)   The scarcest resource in the committee system is members' time. The credibility of the system depends upon members being fully involved in the work of committees, being prepared to put in the necessary preparation and study as well as taking part in the committee's programme. Additional staff resources may improve the quality of a committee's work, but should not be the means of increasing a committee's output at the cost of member involvement.

Against that background, the Committee made a number of reforming proposals. The Liaison Committee itself should be reconstituted as the Select

Committee Panel with an important new task of proposing the membership of select committees, rather than the Committee of Selection which is more readily dominated by party whips. The functions of select committees should be extended and strengthened, especially in relation to the scrutiny of secondary legislation, draft Bills and treaties. Committees should hold 'confirmation hearings' for major public appointments. Steps should also be taken to improve attendance at select committees and also the status of the committee chairman who might be paid a salary or receive additional financial allowances. Select committee reports should be given a higher priority for debate by the House of Commons, and the quality of government replies to reports should be improved. There should be a relationship of constructive co-operation between committees and the government. There should be more use of joint working between committees. 'Joined-up government' must be scrutinised by joined-up committees. Committee staffing should be strengthened. Committee reports should be made more attractive and should be given wider publicity.

Although the government gave a formal welcome to the Liaison Committee's report and affirmed the success of the select committee system – it was indeed 'an entrenched part of our constitutional arrangements' – it also recorded a number of robust reservations[7]. The government initially rejected the Committee's call for new procedures for the appointment of select committee members. However, in 2008–10 there was a return to the issue of committee reform. A Select Committee on the Reform of the House of Commons published two (Wright) reports on Rebuilding the House[8] the most significant consequences of which are that select committee chairs are elected by the House as a whole and members are elected by their party groups. In January 2013, the House adopted (on the proposal of the Liaison Committee)[9] a revised list of 'core tasks' for select committees, including scrutiny of the strategy, policy and performace of their department, scrutiny of draft Bills, assist in the consideration of Bills and orders, post-legislative scrutiny and the scrutiny of major appointments and the holding of pre-appointment hearings, where appropriate. One innovation in select committee practice has been the thrice-yearly appearances now made by the Prime Minister for questioning by the Liaison Committee of the Commons[10]. Has the balance shifted? Has the balance of power changed between select committees on behalf of Parliament as a whole and the executive departments they scrutinise? Certainly activity has increased and well-publicised investigations such as that of the Foreign Affairs Committee into *The Decision to go to War in Iraq*[11] in June 2003 do much to raise the profile and, therefore, perhaps the influence of committees as a whole. Similarly, there is no doubting the influence of the Treasury Select Committee in its work on a series of reports on the Banking Crisis in 2009[12]. But the overriding constraints imposed by the political underpinnings of parliamentary government will always loom large. Committees often appear to land more critical blows when witnesses other than ministers are in their sights[13]. And, of course, there is again a different relationship when it is ministers of the Scottish Government (and other MSPs) who are subject to questioning[14].

Important areas of activity in which Westminster committees have made a significant contribution and, joining the Public Accounts Committee[15] in which party politics are less prominent, have been investigations by the Constitution

Committee of the House of Lords and the Political and Constitutional Reform Committee of the Commons. The Joint Committee on Human Rights has been especially active in its critique of Governments.

1   For the role of this Committee during the referendum debate, see para 4.11.
2   For the role of the Scottish Affairs Committee during the referendum debate, see para 4.11.
3   In 2002–03, the Committee debated the Scottish Fishing Industry (10 December 2002) and the Scottish Economy. For the demise of its legislative role, see para 9.5.
4   HC Paper 300 (1999–2000).
5   Guidance is published by the Cabinet Office as 'Departmental evidence and response to select committees' (July 2005).
6   For problems with securing the attendance of Lord Birt, the PM's Strategy Adviser, see Public Administration Select Committee (2005–06) HC 690.
7   The Government's Response to the First Report from the Liaison Committee on Shifting the Balance: Select Committees and the Executive (Cm 4737, 2000).
8   HC 1117 (2008–09) and HC 372 (2009–10). See also the Political and Constitutional Reform Committee's report on the Wright reforms HC 82 (2013–14).
9   HC Debs 31 Jan 2013, col 1125.
10 See eg HC 647, 939, 1254 (2013–14).
11 HC Paper 813 (2002–03).
12 See 2008–09 HC 402, 416, 519, 656.
13 See eg the Culture, Media and Sports Committee's report on *News International and Phone-hacking* HC 903 (2010–12).
14 See the HL Economic Affairs Committee's *The Implications for the United Kingdom of Scottish Independence* HL Paper 152 (2012–13).
15 See para 11.18.

Subject committees at Holyrood

10.10   At Holyrood, many of the same questions are also relevant since many of the same constraints on committee activity apply. On the other hand, the Holyrood committees have been created in a parliamentary environment deliberately designed to give them a strong role from the start. The subject committees of the Parliament have a standing obligation to examine matters within their remit and to report to the Parliament. As well as their legislative duties, they are to 'consider the policy and administration of the Scottish Administration'[1]. For each committee, the scope of its powers is then further defined – generally in such a way as to map on to the responsibilities of the sector of the Scottish Government to which it relates. As to their investigative powers, a committee may *invite* any person to attend its proceedings for the purpose of giving evidence or to produce documents in that person's custody or control[2]. In addition the power of the Parliament to *require* persons to attend to give evidence and to produce documents, conferred by SA 1998, s 23, has been extended to committees[3]. That power is, however, confined to evidence and documents concerning subjects 'for which any member of the Scottish Government has general responsibility'. Special provision is made in respect of persons 'outside Scotland'[4]. Such persons may be required to attend or to produce documents only in connection with the discharge by that person of functions of the Scottish Administration or of a Scottish public authority[5] or a cross-border public authority and again only where those functions are within the general responsibility of a member of the Scottish Government[6]. The intention is to narrow accountability to the Scottish Parliament to those matters which do not also attract accountability at Westminster. To similar effect, UK ministers (or former ministers) and civil servants (or former civil servants) may be summoned only in respect of matters within the general responsibility of a member of the Scottish Government and expressly *not* in the case of matters where responsibility is shared with the Scottish Ministers, ie the relevant member of the Scottish Government should be the principal target of the committee. Requirements to attend may not be imposed on judges or tribunal members[7]. No witness may be obliged to answer questions or to produce documents in circumstances where in judicial proceedings a court would permit a refusal to do so[8] – for example, where there would be a risk of self-incrimination.

The Scottish Government and the Parliament have agreed in a protocol[9] the ground rules (equivalent to the Osmotherley Rules) according to which ministers and officials submit written and oral evidence to committees. It includes the instruction: 'Where a committee takes oral evidence from officials, particularly when they are not accompanying a Minister, committee members should take into account in questioning the limits imposed on officials by the nature of their role.'

In the course of the first session of the Parliament, UK ministers were called upon to give evidence on several occasions, the first being the European Committee's questioning of Peter Hain MP in November 2001[10]. Since then UK ministerial appearances have been sparse but have included Anne McGuire MP[11] and Vera Baird MP[12]. In guidance issued by the UK government[13], it has been stressed that, while circumstances in which a UK minister may be required to attend a committee of the Scottish Parliament will be rare and while a minister's overriding responsibility is to Westminster, any invitation to attend 'should be treated with as much care and courtesy' as an invitation to attend a Westminster select committee. During 2012–14 the Parliament's Welfare Reform Committee encountered particular difficulties in their efforts to persuade UK ministers to give evidence to the Committee[14].

For the first time, in September 2013, the Conveners Group[15] held a meeting at which the First Minister answered questions[16]. In the early sessions of the Parliament subject committees conducted a number of inquiries leading to the publication of important reports[17]. The Local Government Committee investigated possible reform of local government finance and this led, inter alia, to the Executive's agreement to modify the 'capital consents' regime[18]; the Health and Community Care Committee recommended that personal care for the elderly should be free[19]; the Justice 1 Committee's report on prison estates was influential in the eventual decision not to close Peterhead Prison[20] and the Health and Community Care Committee reported critically on the Executive's risk assessment procedures in relation to the planting of genetically modified crops[21]. Perhaps of highest profile were the investigations carried out by the Enterprise and Lifelong Learning Committee[22] and the Education, Culture and Sport Committee[23] into the calamitous conduct of the Higher examination procedures by the Scottish Qualifications Authority which led to the 'no confidence' debate in the chamber on 13 December 2000.

As already noted in Chapter 5, the work of the subject committees figured prominently in the '*CSG Inquiry*' conducted by the Procedures Committee.

The committees had made a substantial impact although concerns had been expressed about some aspects of their work, including complaints of too much secrecy, instability caused by changes of membership and general time pressures. On the other hand, at least one committee, the Justice 2 Committee was able to comment in generally favourable terms on its scrutiny work in the first session. Members believed that the relationship between the Committee and ministers had matured. The rigour of its questioning had produced a more open-minded response from ministers[24].

Although there were some notable committee reports in the second and third sessions[25] their prominence seems to have declined. It is true, of course, that during the fourth session of the Parliament MSPs had other things on their minds but, reports on Bills referred to them apart, there has been very little sign of inquiry activity by the subject committees. At the end of the third session, the 'legacy paper' published by the Parliament's Conveners Group contained many critical comments on subject committee performance and noted that, despite the other claimed advantages of the combined role, the time devoted to legislation was squeezing out other work[26].

There was some recognition of weaknesses in the Parliament's oversight mechanisms through its committee system in the Report of the Smith Commission in November 2014[27]. In his personal recommendations Lord Smith referred to the reforming initiatives of the Presiding Officer and urged that she should build on that work 'by undertaking an inclusive review which will produce recommendations'[28]. On 1 December 2014, the Parliament's Standards, Procedures and Public Appointments Committee, responding to a specific request from the Presiding Officer[29] launched an inquiry into the election of committee conveners.

1   SOs, r 6.2.2(a).
2   SOs, r 12.4.1.
3   SOs, r 12.44.14.1 and see SA 1998, s 23(8).
4   A phrase not further explained in SA 1998.
5   See para 8.11.
6   SA 1998, s 23(2).
7   SA 1998, s 23(7). A protection is also extended to procurators fiscal. Members of the judiciary are, of course, free to attend committee hearings if they wish, as the Lord President and others did at Justice Committee hearings on the Judiciary and Courts (Scotland) Bill in 2008. On the other hand, the Lord President declined to attend meetings of the Public Petitions Committee in 2014 when it considered a petition calling for the declaration of financial interests by judges (PEO 1458). See para 10.15 below.
8   SA 1998, s 23(9).
9   *Protocol between the Scottish Parliament and the Scottish Government in relation to the handling of Committee business* (2009).
10 SP EU OR 5 November 2001, col 1275. Another was the appearance of Eliot Morley MP before the Rural Development Committee on 18 Feb 2003 (col 4330).
11 Procedures Committee 1 March 2005.
12 Equal Opportunities Committee, 2 Dec 2008.
13 Devolution Guidance Note 12 'Attendance of UK Ministers and Officials at Committees of the Devolved Legislatures'.
14 See eg Interim Report on the *New Benefit Sanctions Regime: Tough Love or Tough Luck?* SP Paper 552 (2014).
15 A group consisting of committee conveners and chaired by the Presiding Officer (or a deputy) which superintends the working of the committee system.

16 See http://www.scottish.parliament.uk/Committeeconvenersgroup/20130912_Transcript_of_ the_Conveners_Group_meeting_with_the_First_Minister.pdf.
17 A list of successes to that point was set out in the Presiding Officer's Constitution Unit lecture of 29 January 2003.
18 *Sixth Report* (2002) SP Paper 551.
19 *Sixteenth Report* (2002) SP Paper 219.
20 *Sixth Report* (2002) SP Paper 612.
21 *First Report* (2002) SP Paper 743.
22 *Sixth Report* (2002) SP Paper 225.
23 *Eleventh Report* (2002) SP Paper 234.
24 Justice 2 Committee, Session 1 Legacy Paper 200.
25 See eg the Report on Child Poverty by the Local Government and Communities Committee, 2009, SP Paper 267.
26 See http://www.scottish.parliament.uk/Committeeconvenersgroup/Conveners_Group_legacy_ paper_-_Session_3.pdf.
27 See para 4.21.
28 *Report*, Foreword.
29 By letter of 31 October.

PARLIAMENTARY AND OTHER OMBUDSMEN[1]

10.11   Fifty years on, it is puzzling to recall how difficult it was in the 1960s to make the case, against its more conservative opponents, for establishing a United Kingdom parliamentary ombudsman. In the period since the Parliamentary Commissioner Act 1967 (PCA 1967) was brought into effect, however, that case has become more familiar and, with experience of the actual operation of the office of the parliamentary ombudsman, it has been given greater strength. The principal reason for the creation of the ombudsman was the weakness of the other parliamentary mechanisms for accountability. These served some useful purposes but they tended to fail where individuals had specific complaints about mistreatment by civil servants. The complaints might be about serious injustices done or they might be about quite minor flaws in administrative behaviour, such as delay or rudeness, which nevertheless caused offence or inconvenience. Collectively such failings, great or small, have been grouped together as 'maladministration'. Often, however, they do not readily lend themselves to resolution by either the courts or Parliament. The courts deal only with alleged illegality, whether in judicial review proceedings or in ordinary actions, and often only rather inefficiently and at some considerable expense. Many complaints of maladministration do not actually involve illegality and, even if they do, the prospects for successful resolution by litigation are not good. Nor are such complaints always susceptible to resolution by parliamentary means. While an MP or MSP may ask a parliamentary question or write to a minister on behalf of a constituent, this is rarely appropriate where the circumstances are complex or contested or both and a systematic inquiry into all the circumstances is necessary. It is not satisfactory to have such an inquiry carried out by civil servants who will have considerable advantages over the complainant in terms of access to information held on files or by other civil servants and whose impartiality will obviously be doubted by the aggrieved complainant. The ministerial response to a complaint will often fail to satisfy the complainant for these reasons. Equally, other parliamentary mechanisms, while appropriate for other purposes, are not well designed to handle the individual complaint. Select committees of the House of Commons and committees at Holyrood may be successful in addressing complaints of general policy failure but they are less well equipped to conduct inquiries into complaints by individuals. Nor do they have the resources to do so[2].

At Westminster in the 1960s, these arguments led to the creation of the parliamentary ombudsman by PCA 1967 and, because the arguments have been judged to remain sound, have led to a general strengthening of the office – though not going as far as some would wish – in subsequent years. They are arguments which were adapted to produce the case for the creation of local government ombudsmen[3]; health service ombudsmen[4]; and more recently the Scottish Public Services Ombudsman. SA 1998, required the Scottish Parliament to make provision for the investigation of complaints made to MSPs in respect of action taken by or on behalf of a member of the Scottish Executive or any other office-holder in the Scottish Administration. On a permissive basis, the Parliament could extend the scope of any provision it made to other public bodies, and, indeed to the Parliamentary corporation. Initially, temporary provision was made for the creation of the office of Scottish Parliamentary Ombudsman[5], very much along the lines of the Westminster counterpart and, indeed, with the offices held by the same person. This was followed by the Scottish Public Services Ombudsman Act 2002 (SPSOA 2002), creating for Scotland an ombudsman whose jurisdiction includes not only the Scottish Government and Administration but also Scottish local government and the health service. In this brief account of the work of the parliamentary ombudsmen, we start with the UK Parliamentary Commissioner for Administration and move on to the Scottish Ombudsman.

1 For a major review of ombudsman practice see Time for a People's Ombudsman Service, HC 655 (2013–14).
2 For the handling of petitions by committees of the Scottish Parliament, see para 10.15 below.
3 In Scotland, by the Local Government (Scotland) Act 1975, Pt II.
4 By the National Health Service (Scotland) Act 1972 and later the Health Service Commissioners Act 1993.
5 Scotland Act 1998 (Transitory and Transitional Provisions) (Complaints of Maladministration) Order 1999, SI 1999/1351.

UK Parliamentary Commissioner for Administration

10.12   The ombudsman's constitutional contribution depends on four main characteristics of the office: (1) its independence; (2) the investigatory powers; (3) the quality of investigations carried out; and (4) the supporting contributions of a parliamentary committee. With these in place, the ombudsman has the potential to ensure the righting of individual wrongs; the potential too to achieve the wider reform of administrative systems where her[1] investigations may have exposed systemic deficiencies; and the important deterrent role of the scrutineer whose invisible presence may often be felt by administrators as they make decisions affecting the interests of individuals. Just as the knowledge that the powers of courts may be invoked to expose illegality may encourage decision-making within the law, so too the ombudsmen may have a similarly encouraging effect.

The independence of the ombudsman is secured in her appointment by the Crown and security of tenure resembling that of senior judges. She holds office during good behaviour but may be removed, like senior English judges only following an address from each House of Parliament[2]. Her salary is, again like judicial salaries, a charge on the Consolidated Fund[3]. The function of the ombudsman is to investigate complaints by individuals (or a body of persons, but not a public authority) who claim to have suffered 'injustice in consequence of maladministration' by any of the government departments or public bodies listed in PCA 1967, Sch 2[4]. With effect from the implementation of devolution in 1999, the list of departments was amended to remove the Scottish Government and devolved public bodies[5]. They became instead subject to investigation by the Scottish Ombudsman. Just as courts are, in principle, confined to legal issues when involved in judicial review and are not in general, permitted to stray into broader policy matters[6], so too the ombudsman is statutorily confined to questions of maladministration. Certain types of administrative function are excluded from investigation[7], sometimes controversially. Many would accept that action affecting relations with foreign governments should be excluded and so too the commencement or conduct of civil or criminal proceedings. But the exclusion of action relating to commercial transactions or action in respect of civil service personnel matters define the ombudsman's jurisdiction in ways which make it unnecessarily narrow. Another restriction normally prevents the ombudsman from conducting an investigation where a legal remedy is available[8] and the ombudsman may not question the merits of a decision taken without maladministration[9].

Procedurally, a complaint must reach the ombudsman in writing and by way of an MP[10]. This requirement that access be via an elected member has both a practical and a more broadly constitutional aspect. It provides the opportunity for complaints to be scrutinised prior to their submission to the ombudsman, and for incompetent or frivolous complaints to be filtered out. It also ensures that MPs are integrated into the constitutionally significant process of the investigation of complaints against executive bodies on behalf of Parliament. On the other hand, ombudsmen themselves have joined those who criticise the restriction because of the tendency to deter individuals from pursuing their complaints. Considering the range of public bodies against which complaints may be made, numbers of complaints are small and they should not be discouraged by procedural barriers[11].

The investigations themselves are conducted by the ombudsman's staff in private, with powers in reserve to compel the production of evidence[12]. The outcome is a report which may, if appropriate, recommend a remedy but the ombudsman has no direct power to enforce a recommendation. The report is to Parliament and there may be a special report if an injustice has not been remedied[13]. The ombudsman is a *parliamentary* commissioner whose independent powers of investigation have greatly extended the reach of Parliament's function to scrutinise administrative activity. She remains dependent, however, for the implementation of her recommendations, upon the status and influence of her parliamentary support. For this purpose, the specific support of a parliamentary committee has been crucial for the UK ombudsman. This, at least, was the case until 1997 when the Parliamentary Commissioner

Select Committee had a remit dedicated to the office. Until recently, it was not so clear that the Public Administration Select Committee (PASC) which now embraces the ombudsman's work in a wider remit was having the same supportive effect. However, 2014 brought a fresh approach which (despite the lack of any legislative amendment) has already had a major impact on the ombudsman's practice. In April the PASC published *Time for a People's Ombudsman Service*[14]. It appears that, nearly 50 years after the institution was created, radical change in terms of access to the ombudsman and then complaints-handling has arrived. In an ancillary (but important) section of the report, the PASC acknowledged[15] that any future reform of the principally 'English' ombudsman services would need to take continuing account of the ombudsman's present UK dimension (especially that relating to non-devolved services in Scotland).

1   The current ombudsman is Dame Julie Mellor.
2   PCA 1967, s 1.
3   PCA 1967, s 2 (as amended). For the Consolidated Fund, see para 11.2.
4   PCA 1967, s 5(1).
5   Scotland Act 1998 (Consequential Modifications) (No 2) Order 1999, SI 1999/1820.
6   See para 14.9.
7   PCA 1967, s 5(3), Sch 3.
8   PCA 1967, s 5(2).
9   PCA 1967, s 12(3).
10 PCA 1967, s 5(1).
11 The Annual Report of the PCA for 2013–14 recorded a huge increase in the number of investigations completed as a result of work practice changes. See HC 536 (2014–15).
12 PCA 1967, s 8.
13 PCA 1967, s 10. See, for example, *Equality under the law? The treatment of widowers by the Inland Revenue and the Department for Work and Pensions* (HC Paper 122 (2002–03)); *The Prudential Regulations of Equitable Life* (HC Paper 809 (2002–03)); *Tax Credits: Getting it wrong?* (HC Paper 1010 (2006–07)); *Trusting in the Pensions Promise* (HC Paper 984 (2005–06)). More recently, significant reports have included *Sexual Assault Abroad* HC 837 (2013–14) and *Handling Allegations of Corruption* HC 1074 (2013–14).
14 HC 655 (2013–14). See also *More Complaints Please!* HC 229 (2013–14) and note 11 above for apparent impact.
15 Paras 100–105.

Scottish Public Services Ombudsman

10.13   As far as Scotland is concerned, the UK parliamentary ombudsman's role continues in relation to 'reserved' departments such as HMRC and the Department for Work and Pensions. In relation to the devolved areas, early consultations by the Scottish Executive indicated a preference for consolidating into a single ombudsman office the transitional Scottish Parliamentary Ombudsman, the health service ombudsman and the local government ombudsman as well as the housing association ombudsman[1]. The principal objective was to merge the different offices into a 'one-stop shop', headed by a single ombudsman, with substantially integrated powers of investigation, and the SPSOA 2002[2], passed by the Scottish Parliament and brought into effect on 23 October 2002, made the new provision. Apart from the merger of the offices, the model of PCA 1967 is broadly maintained with the exception that:

(a)   The ombudsman is appointed by the Queen, for a non-renewable period of up to eight years, on the nomination of the Scottish Parliament[3] rather than simply on the nomination of the government[4]. Dismissal would require a resolution of the Parliament to that effect to be passed by a two-thirds majority of the total number of the MSPs[5].

(b)   The scope for investigations has been extended to include not only action taken by an authority but also any 'service failure' ie any failure in a service provided or failure to provide a service[6].

(c)   Complaints to the ombudsman are not subject to any 'MSP filter' and may be made whenever a person claims to have sustained injustice or *hardship* in consequence of maladministration or service failure[7]. In circumstances where an 'internal' complaint may be made or review requested, the ombudsman must not normally investigate unless that internal procedure has been exhausted[8].

(d)   Investigations may also be carried out pursuant to a request by the public authority affected[9] but only when it has been alleged publicly that one or more members of the public have sustained injustice or hardship and the authority has taken all reasonable steps to deal with the matter[10].

(e)   All reports on investigations must be sent, in addition to the person aggrieved and authority affected, to the Scottish Ministers, whether or not it was a member of the Scottish Government against whom the complaint was made, and must be laid before the Parliament[11]. In the case of a failure to remedy any injustice or hardship, a special report may follow[12]. In this respect the Scottish ombudsman follows the (UK) style of non-enforceable recommendations – although s 4 of the (current) Welfare Funds (Scotland) Bill would give the ombudsman a power of review (of local authority decisions) whose outcome is an enforceable direction.

The impact of this integrated ombudsman model has been interesting to observe. Despite the involvement, perhaps only formal or symbolic, of the Parliament in the ombudsman's appointment, the broad span of the jurisdiction and the loss of the MSP filter has tended to disengage the office from any specifically parliamentary lines of accountability. The ombudsman has become more free-floating, as may be appropriate for someone receiving complaints from a wide range of sources. On the other hand, the system of reporting to the Scottish Ministers and the Scottish Parliament may have had oddly centralising consequences in relation to complaints against local authorities. It would cut sharply across existing lines of accountability[13]. Since 2006, the ombudsman has appeared before the Local Government and Regeneration Committee (previously the Local Government and Communities Committee and, before that, the Local Government and Transport Committee) to discuss the annual report[14]. On one occasion, however, this was an opportunity for abrupt questioning about the case of *Argyll and Bute Council v SPSO*[15]. There has been some critical discussion of the accountability of the SPSO to the Parliament in the light of the SPCCA 2010 but suggestions that the review of SPSO special reports and the scrutiny of the SPSO are inadequate have been rejected[16]. Since April 2011, the SPSO has been required to produce a four-year strategic plan setting out his objectives and priorities[17].

The 2013–14 Annual Report of the SPSO revealed a total of 4456 complaints lodged (up by 8% on 2012–13) with complaints from local authorities on 39% of the total and from the health service on 31%, although the health services had a much higher number of complaints wholly or partially upheld following investigation[18]. The title of that report, *Transforming Scotland's Complaints Culture,* gives a clue to a shift in the emphasis of the SPSO's work since changes introduced by the Public Services Reform (Scotland) Act 2010 (PSR(S)A 2010). The SPSO now has a duty to promote and oversee the adoption of complaints-handling procedures by public authorities[19].

1   See *Modernising the Complaints System* (SE 2000/84, 2000) and *A Modern Complaints System* (SE/2001/139, 2001). See also B Thompson 'The Scottish Public Services Ombudsman: Revolution or Evolution?' in A McHargand T Mullen (eds) *Public Law in Scotland* (2006).
2   Subject to approval by the Scottish Parliament, the scheduled list of bodies subject to investigation may be amended by Order in Council. See, for example, SSIs 2002/468, 2012/43, 2012/85.
3   On 27 June 2002, the Parliament nominated Professor Alice Brown as the first holder of the office. From April 2009, the ombudsman has been Mr Jim Martin.
4   SPSOA 2002, s 1 and Sch 1 (as amended by the Scottish Parliamentary Commissions and Commissioners etc Act 2010 (SPCCA 2010)).
5   SPSOA 2002, Sch 1, para 4.
6   SPSOA 2002, s 5(1), (2).
7   SPSOA 2002, s 5(3).
8   SPSOA 2002, s 7(9),(10).
9   SPSOA 2002, s 2(2).
10 SPSOA 2002, s 5(5).
11 SPSOA 2002, s 15.
12 SPSOA 2002, s 16.
13 But see the suggestion made by the ombudsman that the Parliament might hold to account a defaulting local authority – Local Government and Transport Committee 5 Dec 2006 col 4389.
14 See eg 11 Dec 2013.
15 2008 SC 155 and see para 10.14 below.
16 See letter from the Chair of the Standards, Procedures and Public Appointments Committee to the SPSO of 4 April 2014 at http://www.scottish.parliament.uk/S4_ StandardsProceduresandPublicAppointmentsCommittee/Inquiries/Letter_to_SPSO_-_ April_2014.pdf and Petitions Committee 14 Jan 2014, in response to petition PEO 1489.
17 SPSOA 2002 as amended by SPCCA 2010.
18 *Transforming Scotland's Complaints Culture*, 2014 pp 11, 57.
19 SPSOA 2002, ss 16A–16G.

Ombudsman decisions in the courts

10.14   Despite the rules which are intended to prevent ombudsmen from encroaching on issues which are appropriately decided by courts, there is no doubt that there are points at which illegality and maladministration overlap and that, in any event, ombudsmen and courts become partners in the broader goal of checking administrative misbehaviour. On the other hand, it is sometimes the case that the decisions of ombudsmen are themselves challenged in the courts. A succession of English cases has established that ombudsmen are indeed susceptible to judicial review[1] and the case of *Argyll and Bute Council v SPSO*[2] made it clear that, where the ombudsman misinterprets statutory provisions (here, the Community Care and Health (Scotland) Act 2002), a decision and recommendation flowing from that misinterpretation must be struck down. The case of *R (Bradley) v Secretary of State for Work and Pensions*[3] explored the question of whether the rejection by a public authority of an ombudsman's finding of maladministration or subsequent recommendation is challengeable. The English Court of Appeal held that successful challenge would be confined to those extreme situations where *Wednesbury* unreasonableness[4] could be established.

1 See *R v Parliamentary Commissioner for Admininstration, ex p Dyer* [1984] 1 All ER 375; *R (Cavanagh) v Health Service Commissioner* [2004] EWHC 1847; *R (Parish) v Pensions Ombudsman* [2009] EWHC 32.
2 2008 SC 155.
3 [2009] QB 114.
4 See para 14.9 below.

PUBLIC PETITIONS

10.15   The right of citizens to petition one or other of the Houses of the Westminster Parliament, principally the House of Commons, has an important history and a symbolic constitutional significance. Public petitions may range over diverse subject matter and 'may pray for an alteration of the general law or the reconsideration of a general administrative decision, and they may also pray for redress of local or personal grievances'[1]. Provision is made in the standing orders of both Houses for the presentation of a petition by a member of the relevant House, in the case of the Commons normally at the adjournment. Procedural restrictions have, however, produced a low profile for petition procedures at Westminster. On the other hand, a vigorous system for the direct e-petitioning of the Government has been established which, if there are 100,000 signatories, can lead to a petition being considered (by the Commons Backbench Committee) for debate in the House. The House of Commons itself responded on 8 May 2014 with a motion: That this House supports the establishment, at the start of the next Parliament, of a collaborative e-petitions system, which enables members of the public to petition the House of Commons and press for action from Government. In December 2014, the Procedure Committee produced a report which proposed an e-petition system overseen by a new Petitions Committee[2].

The position in Scotland has been very different. When the Scottish Constitutional Convention came to make its proposals for establishing the Scottish Parliament, it insisted on the need for the Parliament to encourage the greatest possible involvement by the people of Scotland and for arrangements to be put in place to ensure that the Parliament remained responsive to their wishes and values. It made a specific recommendation that standing orders should be adopted to enable electors directly to petition the Parliament[3]. This was a theme taken up by the Consultative Steering Group who declared it to be an important principle that the Scottish people should be able to petition the Parliament. Public petitions should be encouraged and there should be clear and simple rules as to form and content. The Parliament should accept all petitions for which the remedy sought would be within its competence. A decision on the action to be taken should depend on the strength and depth of support for the petition and not simply on the number of signatories. A Committee for Petitions should be established to decide, in the first instance, how each petition should be processed[4].

These recommendations were carried forward into the standing orders of the Scottish Parliament and these provide for a Public Petitions Committee to be established[5] and for its procedures[6]. A petition may be brought by an individual person, a body corporate or an unincorporated association in a form determined by the Public Petitions Committee. The Committee has two functions in respect of any petition lodged. It must first decide whether the petition is admissible. It will be inadmissible if it requests the Parliament to do anything which, in the opinion of the Committee, the Parliament clearly has no power to do. Although a test of admissibility based on the competence of the Parliament seems appropriate, this version adopted in the standing orders is curiously phrased. The Parliament's own powers are, of course, primarily legislative and many petitions will not be directly aimed at a change in the law. This is not a merely technical matter. It reflects an ambiguity inherent in the purpose of petition procedures in a modern Parliament. It is unclear how a Parliament should respond to petitions, given the relative sophistication of other procedures for the handling of the complaints and concerns of citizens. Should a petition procedure merely operate as a channel towards those other procedures – designed mainly to secure a response from the Government rather than the legislature – or should it offer some quite separate response?

The standing orders of the Parliament offer a number of procedural options for the Petitions Committee as it exercises its second function, that of deciding what action should be taken on a petition judged to be admissible. Following consideration of the petition, the Committee may (a) refer the petition to the Scottish Ministers, any other committee of the Parliament or any other person or body for them to take such action as they consider appropriate; or (b) report to the Parliamentary Bureau or to the Parliament itself; or (c) take any other appropriate action. The Committee has issued its own web-based guidance on the submission of public petitions which, in addition to explaining the mechanics of how petitions are to be made, explains some of the limitations of the process. The Parliament does not have the power to interfere with or overturn the executive decisions of other public bodies in Scotland, such as the decisions of local authorities on planning applications or school closures. Nor can the committee recommend action in relation to cases which are or have been subject to court or tribunal proceedings. Petitions must be in the public interest and should not, for instance, ask the Parliament to do something which may be unlawful. As with much of the work of the Parliament, it is difficult to form a concluded view of the petition work handled so far[7]. Certainly petitioning has proved popular and receipt of the 1000th petition was recorded in October 2006. By the end of 2013, the total had reached 1500 petitions.

Petitions have been lodged by a wide variety of individuals and organisations including residents' associations, community councils, local authorities, political parties and pressure groups. Issues raised have been personal, local and national. Many have had a sympathetic reception and many petitioners appear personally before the Committee. At other points the Petitions Committee has expressed concern about the burdens imposed by petitions and the undue expectations raised. Committee members have been apprehensive about the risks of manipulation by professional or other powerful interest groups. There was also early frustration about individuals who bombarded the Parliament with strings of petitions: one petitioner had lodged over 30 petitions by June 2000.

In 2006 the Public Petitions Committee commissioned a report on the operation of the system to that point[8]. This confirmed the popularity of the procedure. Most (53%) of petitions had been from individuals, with five accounting for 11% of all petitions. 30% of all petitions had over 100 signatures. Petitioners were disproportionately older, male and middle class. 58% were graduates. In its consideration of petitions, the Committee had shifted from a concentration on questions of admissibility to a concentration on merits. Rather than referring petitions to other committees, it was investigating many more itself. No substantial proposals for reform were made, except some rather tentative suggestions for a form of 'appeal' to a reviewing panel.

In the meantime, it is the case that the process has revealed some substantial concerns and prompted substantial inquiries by the Committee[9]. In January 2014, the Public Petitions Committee published a report[10] of its inquiry, deriving from a petition by Barnardo's[11], into child sexual exploitation in Scotland. Also in 2014, a constitutionally significant petition was lodged calling on the Parliament to urge the Scottish Government to create a register of pecuniary interests for judges[12]. In a Chamber debate on 9 October 2014, the Government made clear its own hostile position and further progress for the petitition seemed unlikely.

It will be interesting to see how the petitions process develops. Despite the generally positive reaction so far, the early experience raises questions about the value to the parliamentary system as a whole of a mechanism which may turn out to add little to the procedural resources already available to MSPs. Legitimate complaints will probably be directed to the same destination in the end. Some less worthy concerns, or those already fully aired in the political process, may receive undeserved attention. In the meantime, however, there can be little doubt that the best-known petition ever was that supported by 43,000 signatures to retain acute services at Stobhill Hospital in Glasgow[13]. It was on the strength of her own support for this cause that the independent MSP Dr Jean Turner secured election to the Parliament for the Strathkelvin and Bearsden constituency on 1 May 2003.

1   *Erskine May's Parliamentary Practice* (24th edn 2011) ch 24.
2   *E-petitions: a collaborative system* HC 235 (2014–15).
3   *Scotland's Parliament, Scotland's Right* pp 24 and 26.
4   *CSG Inquiry*, s 3.6, paras 13–18.
5   SOs, r 6.10.
6   SOs, rr 15.4–15.6.
7   For an early review, see P Lynch and S Birrell 'Linking Parliament to the People' (2001) 37 Scottish Affairs 1.
8   CJ Carman, *Assessment of the Scottish Parliament's Public Petitions System 1999–2006*. SP Paper 654.
9   See, for instance, its investigation into the availability on the NHS of cancer treatment drugs – SP Paper 133 (2008).
10   SP Paper 449.
11   PEO 1393.
12   PEO 1458. For the general rules about judicial impartiality, see para 12.13.
13   PEO 354.

Chapter 11

Public Finance

INTRODUCTION

11.1   Financial issues retain a centrality and vitality in any modern constitutional account. Sometimes they become hidden behind a veil of technicality and complexity which serves to distort their significance, but financial matters are frequently of concern not only to those in government but also to ordinary citizens in their relations with governments. Individuals have an acute interest in the taxes and charges imposed on them as well as in the financial benefits which may come their way. Financial questions are also very important in the shaping of relations between the executive and the legislature and relations between devolved and central institutions. A chapter on 'Financing Devolution' was prominent in the 2003 report of the House of Lords Select Committee on the *Constitution on Devolution: Inter-Institutional Relations in the United Kingdom*. They have been at the heart of the recent modification of the Scottish devolution settlement by the Scotland Act 2012 (SA 2012) and, as we saw in Chapter 4, financial issues loomed very large in the independence referendum debate and continued to be significant in its aftermath. The most important recommendations of the Smith Commission Report published in November 2014[1] were contained in the Commission's 'Pillar 3' on 'strengthening the financial responsibility of the Scottish Parliament'. In particular, the limited arrangements discussed below (in paras 11.10–11.12) for the Scottish Parliament's powers to set income tax levels in Scotland (with effect from April 2016) would be expanded to include complete control of income tax on earned income. There would be two new 'devolved taxes' (air passenger duty and aggregates levy); the 'block grant' to the Scottish Government, using the Barnett formula would be retained (but with adjusted levels to be agreed[2]); and the borrowing power of the Government would be strengthened.

In the meantime, this chapter focuses on the law as it currently is (taking account of SA 2012). United Kingdom-level issues and Scotland-level issues are considered in parallel under five broad headings. In the first place, paras 11.2–11.4 on the UK level of government take a brief look at the annual cycle of financial decision-making by government and Parliament, as to both the raising and the spending of public money. There are the procedures leading to the passing of the annual Finance Act which contains proposals for new or amended taxes and then the decisions made by governments on their expenditure plans and the parliamentary procedures available for their scrutiny and approval. At Westminster, procedures for both types of decisions have been progressively refined over many years and they remain under review. They are procedures in which the House of Commons has its clearest pre-eminence over the House of Lords and in which it also claims to assert its strongest controls over the executive – there can be no imposition of taxation nor any expenditure without statutory authority. However, it is also an area in which the executive asserts a powerful right of initiative and does, in practice, maintain substantial overall control. The rules governing the equivalent processes in Scottish government require rather different treatment. Thus, at paras 11.5–11.8, the system by which the annual grant of funds is made by the Secretary of State is considered and then, at paras 11.9–11.16, the changing powers of the Scottish Parliament to fix the rates of income tax and to impose other devolved taxes payable by Scottish taxpayers. At para 11.17, the system by which the Scottish Government proposes and the Scottish Parliament approves expenditure on an annual basis is outlined. Finally, at para 11.18, a mainly Scottish consideration is given to procedures for the audit of accounts and the parliamentary supervision of those procedures at both levels of government.

1 See para 4.21.
2 Including taking into accout assigned levels of VAT.

FINANCIAL PROCEDURES: WHITEHALL AND WESTMINSTER[1]

11.2   Discussion of financial procedures is apt to become very complex and technical. It starts, however, from two elementary propositions. The first is that governments need financial resources to do the job of governing and that, subject to economic constraints which will vary from time to time, they must, by one means or another be given these resources. Governments have statutory duties to perform: they have political programmes to which they are committed and on which they must deliver. Secondly, however, it is constitutionally important that governments' access to and use of resources are subject to appropriate forms of scrutiny and control. These two phenomena interact but at their centre is *parliamentary control*, exercised almost exclusively by the House of Commons rather than the House of Lords[2] and deriving from Parliament's successful claims to control asserted in the seventeenth century. The Crown and the Crown's ministers must be financially accountable to Parliament and Parliament insists that it controls both the income (by taxation) and expenditure of governments. This quickly links with the second form of *control by the courts*. The courts will strike down as invalid any attempt by the executive either to raise or to spend money which does not have the authority of an Act of Parliament[3]. The third form of control is that performed by the independent operations of the Comptroller and Auditor General, the National Audit Office and the accounting officers in individual government departments. These are carried out under the authority and supervision of Parliament but under conditions which are substantially free from political control. At the points where the House of Commons authorises taxation or expenditure it inevitably behaves in a way which reflects the close political alliance between a government and its Commons majority. When officials appointed to be independent of both government and Parliament perform their tasks of financial scrutiny, they should, and it seems do, operate quite differently.

The focus for any study of the process of government financing and its control is what is known as the Consolidated Fund. The Consolidated Fund is held at the Bank of England and is managed by the Treasury, the government department headed by the Chancellor of the Exchequer which co-ordinates the financial affairs of all other departments and formally initiates all financial decision-making. Most income to the Fund derives from taxation and all taxation requires the authority of an Act of Parliament. All expenditure from the Fund requires authority by an Act of Parliament, almost all of it by authority of an annual Act of Parliament – the Appropriation Act – passed in the year to which the expenditure relates. It is by the need for parliamentary assent to these statutes authorising both taxation and expenditure that the most direct forms of parliamentary control are, at least in theory, assured. At the same time, it should be borne in mind that there are other opportunities for scrutiny available. When new legislation is passing through Parliament as a Bill, one of the issues for consideration will be the cost of the new proposals. This is formally recognised in the need for the passing of a money resolution on the motion of a minister, following the Bill's second reading, but questions about the financial resources which the Bill's proposals will require – whether they are thought to be too much or too little – will often be relevantly discussed at all stages. The other point at which financial matters are constantly raised is in select committee investigations into the activities of ministers and their departments. Questions of extravagance and waste may be the principal targets but underspending may equally be an issue.

1 This is necessarily a highly simplified summary of some very complex material. *Managing Public Money* (July 2013) contains accessible commentary despite its primary function as a Treasury guide for government departments. See also Erskine May, *Parliamentary Practice* (ed M Jack) (24th edn, 2011) chs 32–36.
2 An adjustment to this position has been the annual scrutiny (from April 2003) of the Finance Bill by a sub-committee of the House of Lords Economic Affairs Committee. The Committee's approach is intended to be wholly technical and not 'to challenge Commons financial privilege' – see *Third Report* (HL Paper 121 (2002–03)).
3 *A-G v Wilts United Dairies* (1921) 37 TLR 884. See also *O'Brien v Independent Assessor* [2007] UKHL 10, [2007] 2 AC 312 at para 66 (Lord Rodger).

Taxation

11.3   Statutory authority is required for all forms of taxation. Much of that authority derives from statutes which remain in force over long periods, with the need only for authority for changes in the tax rates from time to time. Other taxes, including, above all, income tax, require the rate to be stipulated for each financial year (1 April to 31 March). Sometimes entirely new forms of taxation are proposed and the vehicle for establishing any new regime and for achieving the other categories of change is the annual Finance Act. Only a minister, on behalf of the Crown, may propose a new tax or level of tax[1].

The Finance Bill incorporates proposals first announced by the Chancellor of the Exchequer in the Budget speech which is currently delivered in the

House of Commons in March each year. The Budget, preceded by a pre-Budget statement in November, is the occasion for the Chancellor to publish[2] not only proposals for new taxes and for changes in tax rates but also, as a background to the proposals, substantial information on the state of the UK economy. Because some tax changes must come into effect immediately, they are announced before the Finance Bill can be debated and enacted into law, and authority for the collection of tax at the new rates is given in the form of resolutions, approved by the House of Commons, whose own authority derives from a statute passed for this purpose, currently the Provisional Collection of Taxes Act 1968[3].

1 The same applies to expenditure proposals. See *Erskine May's Parliamentary Practice* (24th edn, 2011) ch 34. Both taxation and expenditure involve 'charges, whether as a charge upon the people or a charge upon public funds, the initiative for which must come from the Crown'.
2 In the speech itself but also in a range of additional Budget documents.
3 The need for such statutory authority, rather than a simple reliance upon the resolutions themselves, was established in the landmark case of *Bowles v Bank of England* [1913] 1 Ch 57. Normally, preparatory work in advance of the launch of a new tax does not require specific statutory authority.

Expenditure

11.4   Just as statutory authority must be given for the raising of taxes paid into the Consolidated Fund, so also must there be statutory authority for expenditure by departments out of the Fund. For the most part, this is the process historically known as 'supply' for the government's purposes and then the 'appropriation' (ie allocation) of the total amount to the several departments. Exceptions to the standard route to parliamentary approval are those payments which, mainly for 'separation of powers' reasons, but in some cases on more technical grounds, are protected from the need for direct annual approval. The most prominent payments to be 'charged on the Consolidated Fund'[1] are judicial salaries and pensions but others include the salaries of the Speaker of the House of Commons, the Comptroller and Auditor General, and of the Parliamentary Ombudsman[2]. These cases apart, the processes of supply and appropriation operate formally on an annual cycle and involve the submission of proposals of estimated expenditure by departments and the Treasury in the light of current spending guidelines which are, under present practice, published pursuant to a spending review[3]. The estimates are scrutinised by select committees and approved by resolution of the House of Commons, following 'estimates day' debates. The spending proposals are then carried forward into a Consolidated Fund (Appropriation) Bill which, on enactment, becomes an Appropriation Act[4].

1 Designated 'Consolidated Fund standing services'.
2 Also charged on the Fund in this way are payments of interest on the national debt and payments to the European Union.
3 Most recently in June 2013 (to 2015–16).
4 That procedure is supplemented each year by the passing of a further Act – a (confusingly named) Consolidated Fund Act – whose main purpose is to make initial spending provision for the next following financial year, effective before that next year's Appropriation Act can be passed.

FUNDING OF SCOTTISH GOVERNMENT BY WESTMINSTER

11.5   In *Scotland's Parliament*, the White Paper which preceded the Scotland Bill in 1997, the UK government set out its proposals for the funding of devolved Scottish government[1]. With one significant change – the introduction of the Scottish Parliament's limited power of tax variation discussed at para 11.9 below – it was to be business as usual. Funding would come from the UK government itself and would be allocated on an annual basis according to the same principles on which funds were allocated to the Scottish Office prior to devolution. Since 1978–79, immediately prior to the aborted introduction of devolution under the Scotland Act 1978 (SA 1978), there had been in place a scheme for the distribution to Scotland (and also to Wales and to Northern Ireland) of annual grants – 'block' grants – to provide for domestic services within the remit of the Scottish Office[2]. The amounts to be allocated to Scotland (and the other territories) were made in accordance with a formula which initially took account of the relative assessed 'needs' of the territories (largely population-based but also encompassing factors such as poverty and sparcity of population) but which, in subsequent years, was adjusted in accordance with the percentage increase (or decrease) in resources allocated for parallel services in England. That adjustment was made by the application of a population-based formula (the 'Barnett' formula[3]) to enable expenditure in Scotland, Wales and Northern Ireland to grow proportionately.

Although the principles for funding allocations could be broadly carried forward to apply to devolved Scottish government, the mechanisms for making the allocation had to be changed. Instead of being simply an accounting device for the division of resources internally within the UK governmental machine, it had to be a mechanism for the transfer of funds from one government to the other. This was very simply done, as far as the Scotland Act 1998 (SA 1998) is concerned, in s 64(1) and (2). Section 64(1) establishes a separate Scottish Consolidated Fund[4]. Then SA 1998, s 64(2) provides: 'The Secretary of State shall from time to time make payments into the Fund out of money provided by Parliament of such amounts as he may determine.' Nothing is said in SA 1998 itself about the amount that should be paid annually nor what relation it should bear to amounts paid, for example, to Wales or Northern Ireland. No mention is made of the Barnett formula. All of that has been left to less formal documentation issued by HM Treasury[5], setting out the principles of public expenditure allocation across the United Kingdom, the working of the formula and other practical matters.

These procedures established for the funding of Scottish devolved government have not gone uncriticised and this was especially acute during the independence referendum period. There are three main complaints:

1 Cm 3658, Ch 7.
2 See *Scotland's Parliament*, Annex B, para 4.
3 Named after the late Lord (Joel) Barnett, former Chief Secretary to the Treasury.
4 Subsequent provisions deal with payments into and out of the Fund – SA 1998, ss 64, 65. See para 11.7 below for expenditure from the Fund.
5 The arrangements launched in 1999 are comprehensively and authoritatively described in the Treasury document *Funding the Scottish Parliament, National Assembly for Wales and Northern Ireland Assembly: A Statement of Funding Policy* (6th edn, Oct 2010).

(a) Reliance on the block grant

11.6   The near-total reliance of the Scottish Parliament and Government upon grant aid from the UK government has been criticised. Unless and until the Scottish Parliament makes use of its own limited tax-varying power, Scottish government depends almost entirely for its income upon what the UK government, in its discretion, decides to provide – the other principal sources being income derived from non-domestic rates and council tax collected by local authorities[1], as well as a small amount in charges for services provided. Some might say that there should be no problem with that, provided that the funds provided are sufficient – on which, see below. Others, not necessarily of a nationalist persuasion, argue differently. There *is* something inherently wrong about a model of democratic government which has no control, or virtually no control, over the resources available to it. Accountability is undermined because politicians will tend to pass the blame for their failures in government to those who, they claim, are underfunding them. This was a complaint made about the Scotland Act 1978 (SA 1978) model. It was a complaint addressed, to an extent, by the former tax-varying power (see para 11.9 below). But some have gone much further in asserting the need for a 'fiscal autonomy' which would enable the Scottish Government and Parliament to raise funds from a range of sources and at levels which they themselves can determine. Because of the challenge it might present to the economic and fiscal integrity of the United Kingdom[2], and thus to the principles underpinning the devolution settlement, a strong form of autonomy has not been conceded and, for the time being at least, there will be a continuing substantial dependence upon grant aid.

This was all considered by the Calman Commission which reported in June 2009[3]. The Commission's recommendations on 'strengthening accountability in finance' were at the core of their report. They proposed that the Scottish budget's near-total reliance on the block grant and the Barnett formula should be reduced. The then-existing tax-varying power should be replaced by a new Scottish rate of income tax, applicable to both the basic and higher rates of tax. The rates levied by the UK government should be reduced by 10 pence in the pound (with a consequential reduction in the block grant), leaving the Scottish Parliament to substitute a rate of its own choosing[4]. In addition, certain other taxes – stamp duty land tax, the aggregates levy, landfill tax and air passenger duty – should be devolved to the Scottish Parliament and the Parliament should be empowered to introduce further new taxes with the agreement of the UK Parliament. In response to calls from many quarters, the borrowing powers of the Scottish Ministers should be extended to enable an increase in capital investment. These proposals did not meet with universal approval but their (partial) adoption by the 'Unionist' parties for discussion was immediate[5].

1 See para 8.5.
2 See HL Committee on the Constitution *Devolution: Inter-Institutional Relations in the United Kingdom* (HL Paper 28 (2002–03)) (*Inter-Institutional Relations*) para 105.
3 See para 3.20 above.
4 Income tax on savings and distributions would not be devolved but half of the yield would be assigned to the Parliament's budget.
5 The funding of devolution has been under investigation by other bodies. In July 2009, the House of Lords ad hoc Barnett Formula Committee issued its report – (2008–09), HL 139. Also in July

2009 the (Holtham) Independent Commission on Funding and Finance for Wales made its first report to the Welsh Assembly Government and in July 2010 it issued its final report, *Fairness and accountability: a new funding settlement for Wales*, July 2010. The Barnett formula and its consequences for the different parts of the United Kingdom were a focus of attention during the independence referendum period.

(b) The system of grant allocation

11.7   The lack of transparency and impartiality in the determination of amounts of grant payable to Scotland and the other territories[1] has also been questioned. One change which might have been introduced at the time of devolution was some form of independent board or commission to oversee the process of grant distribution[2]. In a constitutional environment which has become similar to that in federal countries, there would be an advantage in having such an independent body to make recommendations for grant distribution according to relatively objective economic criteria rather than leaving distribution to the hidden judgment of politicians. Disputes between different parts of the United Kingdom might be lessened as a result.

1 The use of 'territories' may be unfamiliar but it is the terminology adopted in UK government official documents.
2 See Constitution Unit *Scotland's Parliament: Fundamentals for a New Scotland Act* (1996), ch 5; and *Inter-Institutional Relations* paras 102 and 107.

(c) The amount of funding

11.8   It is certainly true that, whether or not because of the lack of an independent grants commission, disputes have arisen[1]. On the one hand, it is argued by some in Scotland that the distribution formula which once favoured Scotland because it deliberately recognised its greater funding needs now discriminates against Scotland because the formula for *amending* levels of expenditure operates, as was intended (or was, at least, wholly predictable), to reduce differentials between territories and thus to leave Scotland without the advantage it once had. There is a 'Barnett squeeze' on Scottish expenditure which arguably should be remedied by a new needs assessment which would find in favour of a greater allocation to Scotland in future. There is, on the other hand, an argument mainly associated with London and the north-east of England to the effect that some at least of the English regions are already being *underfunded* in comparison with Scotland. Poignant comparisons have been drawn between the funding of schools in Northumbria and the Scottish Borders[2]. And adverse comparisons have also been made from a Welsh perspective[3]. Such disputes would be likely to increase if regional government in England is extended and pressure to revise Barnett will grow[4]. In the meantime, the commitment in the 'Vow' of September 2014[5] and the recommendation of the Smith Commission to continue with Barnett[6] provoked friction in other parts of the United Kingdom.

1 Nicely documented in the memorandum by I McLean published as evidence to the HL Committee on the Constitution (*Inter-Institutional Relations*).
2 *Inter-Institutional Relations* para 3.2.

3 See report of the (Silk) Commission on Devolution in Wales, *Empowerment and Responsibility: Financial Powers to Strengthen Wales* (Nov 2012).
4 A recommendation to review the system was made by the House of Commons Select Committee on the Office of the Deputy Prime Minister. See *Reducing Regional Disparities in Prosperity* (HC Paper 492 (2002–03), para 75).
5 See para 4.13.
6 See para 4.21.

THE SCOTTISH PARLIAMENT'S TAXING POWERS

11.9   This chapter is not, in general, one in which specific forms of taxation at the UK level are discussed, even in outline. The principles of parliamentary control over taxation at Westminster are of constitutional significance but the actual taxes imposed are beyond the scope of a constitutional study. In the case of the Scottish Parliament, however, its powers to tax, as a part of its overall funding arrangements, are important.

As explained in the last section, Scottish government is largely financed by grant paid by the UK government. Under SA 1998 it is not within the legislative competence of the Parliament to enact new general powers to tax[1] and if it were not for the specific powers of taxation conferred by the Act as amended, the Parliament and Government would be compelled to operate within the financial limits of the block grant. It is true that there might be scope for adjusting the charges made for some services provided – proposals for road tolls/parking charges are an example. And there might also be scope for the Scottish Government to reduce the grant it makes to local authorities and force the local authorities to make up the shortfall by increasing levels of council tax, although that has not been at all attractive to recent governments[2]. The financial and political limitations on the use of such measures are, in practice, likely to keep their effect very marginal.

It is a principle of some constitutional importance that bodies established to be democratically accountable to their electorates – whether they are states in a federal system of government or local authorities – should also have a form of financial accountability. As the Scottish Constitutional Convention put it: 'In the Western democracies all principal levels of national and local government have powers over taxation'. While the Parliament's income will be principally based on totals of expenditure set at UK level, the power to vary the rate of tax is vital if the Parliament is to be properly accountable. Critics of the proposal to establish a Parliament in Scotland repeatedly state that such a power is essential for an effective Parliament'[3]. A tax-raising or tax-varying power had not been included in SA 1978 but it was proposed in the 1997 White Paper that 'the Scottish Parliament should be able to raise limited income at its own hand by means of a defined but limited power to vary income tax in Scotland'[4]. The power was included as Part 4 of SA 1998.

A little paradoxical in these circumstances was the Scottish Labour Party's own commitment, prior to the Scottish Parliament elections in 1999, not to make use of the tax-varying power in the course of the first Parliament. This was an undertaking reconfirmed in 'Partnership for Scotland', the statement which formed the basis of the coalition agreement between the Scottish Labour Party and the Scottish Liberal Democrats in May 1999. The undertaking was further reconfirmed in the second coalition agreement, *A Partnership for a Better Scotland*, in May 2003. And this remained the policy of the SNP Government after 2007. As a practical matter, therefore, the original provisions in SA 1998 are never to be implemented.

However, the publication of the Calman Commission Report in June 2009; the adoption of its principal recommendations in the UK Government's White Paper *Strengthening Scotland's Future* in November 2010; and their enactment in the Scotland Act 2012 (SA 2012) have all ensured that, in the name of the enhancement of the financial accountability of the Parliament, provision was made for four principal initiatives. In order of the time-tabling of their introduction, from April 2013, the Scottish Government has had increased powers to borrow (with others to follow from 2015)[5]. Secondly, the Scottish Parliament has used new powers to legislate for two taxes (effective from April 2015) formerly levied by the UK Treasury – the land transactions tax and the landfill tax[6]. Thirdly and most significantly, from April 2016, the Scottish Parliament will have a new power to set Scottish rates of income tax. And, fourthly, for potential use in the future, provision has been made[7] for additional 'devolved taxes'[8] to be specified by Order in Council, subject to the affirmative approval of both Parliaments[9].

1 SA 1998, Sch 5, Pt II, S A1.
2 See para 8.7.
3 *Scotland's Parliament: Scotland's Right* (1995) p 27.
4 *Scotland's Parliament* (Cm 3658) para 7.1.
5 See para 11.5 below.
6 See para 11.13 below.
7 SA 1998, s 80B, inserted by SA 2012, s 23(2).
8 A devolved tax is one so specified in Pt 4A of SA 1998, ie starting with the land transactions tax and the landfill tax.
9 SA 1998, Sch 7, as amended by SA 2012, s 23(6).

The Scottish Rate of Income Tax

11.10 Of these new 'income streams', much the most significant in political terms is the new power to set Scottish rates of income tax. From April 2016, four changes are to be introduced[1]:

1 The old power to vary the income tax rate will be repealed[2].
2 The amount provided to the Scottish Government by way of the 'block grant' will become subject to downward adjustment.
3 The rates (basic, higher and additional) of income tax[3] imposed on 'Scottish taxpayers' (see para 11.12 below) by the UK tax authorities will be reduced by ten percentage points[4].
4 The new Scottish Parliament power to set tax rates will commence.

1 For the policy background, see *Strengthening Scotland's Future*.
2 SA 2012, s 35(4), providing for Pt 4 of SA 1998 to be 'omitted'.
3 Except on savings income.
4 Income Tax Act 2007, s 6(2B) (as inserted by SA 2012, s 26(2)).

The Resolution of the Scottish Parliament

11.11 It will be for the Scottish Parliament by resolution (a 'Scottish rate resolution') to 'set the Scottish rate for the purposes of calculating the rates of income tax to be paid by Scottish taxpayers' on the motion of a member of the Scottish Government[1]. In contrast with the old tax-varying power which was confined to the adjustment of only the basic rate of income tax, the new power applies to all bands. The resolution may apply to one year only and the rate specified must be a whole number or half a whole number[2].

1 SA 1998, s 80C(1), (8) inserted by SA 2012, s 25(3).
2 SA 1998, s 80C(3)–(6).

The 'Scottish taxpayers'

11.12 As was the case with the tax-varying power, the new legislation is largely devoted to the potentially fraught issue of the identification of the taxpayers liable to pay (additional tax) at the Scottish rates[1]. The details are a little complex and may prove difficult to apply. In summary, however, there are four principal rules:

1   In any tax year, to be a Scottish taxpayer one must first be an individual (dubbed 'T' in the Act) resident in the United Kingdom for income tax purposes (s 80D(1)).
2   If T is also an MP, or MEP or MSP for the whole or part of the year, T is a Scottish taxpayer.
3   If, much more commonly, T instead has a 'close connection' with Scotland, T is a Scottish taxpayer.
4   If T does not have a 'close connection' with any part of the United Kingdom other than Scotland and spends more days of the year in Scotland in any other part of the United Kingdom, T is also a Scottish taxpayer.

Elected representatives apart, these rules require further specification of the meaning of 'close connection' with a part of the United Kingdom and this is done (s 80E) by reference to T's 'place[2] of residence' and living at that place for at least part of the year; or, in the case of T having two or more places of residence in the United Kingdom, T's *main* place of residence being in that part of the United Kingdom, calculated by reference to the days spent in the year at that residence[3].

1 SA 1998, ss 80D, 80E, 80F inserted by SA 2012, s 25(3).
2 Which may include a place on board a boat or other means of transport.
3 There are additional rules defining 'days spent'. See SA 1998, s 80F.

Land Transactions Tax and Landfill Tax

11.13 The significance of defining a tax as a 'devolved tax' (see para 11.9 above) is that SA 2012 has created a new exception (the other being local taxes) to the reservation to the UK Parliament by Sch 5 to the 1998 Act of the power to tax[1]. 'Devolved taxes, including their collection and management' are that new exception. Thus the only further provisions required in SA 2012 are to specify that a 'tax on transactions involving interests in land' and a 'tax on disposals to landfill' are indeed devolved taxes[2] and to make appropriate adjustments (to exclude Scotland) to the existing UK stamp duty land tax and landfill tax regimes[3]. It was then for the Scottish Parliament to use its new powers and the Land and Buildings Transaction Tax (Scotland) Act 2013[4] and the Landfill Tax (Scotland) Act 2014 were passed in anticipation of the introduction of the new taxes from April 2015.

1 SA 1998, Sch 5, para SA1.
2 SA 1998, Pt 4A, Chs 3 and 4, inserted by SA 2012, ss 28, 30.
3 SA 2012, ss 29, 31.
4 The rates of tax proposed from April 2015 were announced by Mr Swinney on 9 October 2014. Rates on lower valued properties (to £250,000) would be reduced (from UK stamp duty levels) but others raised, a situation complicated from 3 December 2014 when UK stamp duty rates on most properties were suddenly lowered.

Tax Collection

11.14   In addition to the legislation for the two new devolved taxes, the Scottish Parliament passed the Revenue Scotland and Tax Powers Act 2014 to create the new tax authority for their 'collection and management'[1]. Revenue Scotland is a body corporate and designated as a nonministerial office in the Scottish Administration[2]. It is empowered to delegate functions to the Keeper of the Registers of Scotland (with respect to the land and buildings transaction tax) and to the Scottish Environment Protection Agency (landfill tax) (s 4). Part 4 of the Act creates a new structure of tax tribunals. At the time of the debates on the Bill[3], the point was not lost on SNP MSPs that they might have been legislating for structures relevant to the management of a much wider range of tax powers in the future.

1 Commissioners for Revenue and Customs Act 2005.
2 SA 1998, s 126(8).
3 See eg Stage 3 at SP OR 19 Aug 2014.

The Scottish Government's powers to borrow

11.15   With effect from 2013 and then 2015, the powers of the Scottish Government to borrow to fund current and capital spending have been substantially increased[1].

1 SA 2012, s 32 in implementation of *Strengthening Scotland's Future*, pp 36–40.

Intergovernmental relations

11.16   It was foreseen in *Strengthening Scotland's Future*[1] that the SA 2012 reforms would require a new joint response by the Scottish and UK Governments to the process of their implementation, at both ministerial and official level. The Act itself imposes duties on the two governments to produce annual reports on the implementation and operation of the financial reforms until final reports are produced after April 2020[2]. In addition, however, a Joint

Exchequer Committee (of ministers from both governments) has been meeting periodically to discuss 'key milestones' of implementation and matters of joint concern including block grant adjustment. There is a Memorandum of Understanding[3] on the Scottish Rate of Income Tax between the Scottish Government and HMRC.

1 Pages 40–42 and Ch 3.
2 SA 2012, s 34.
3 For the general MoU, see para 7.26.

THE AUTHORISATION OF EXPENDITURE BY THE SCOTTISH GOVERNMENT

11.17   As we turn to expenditure by the Scottish Government, the parallels between the procedures which operate at the United Kingdom level and the procedures which have now been established in Edinburgh are quite close. At their centre is the authority for payments to be made from the Scottish Consolidated Fund.

SA 1998, s 65 provides that sums may be paid out of the Fund under two main forms of authority. The first is where sums have been statutorily charged on the Fund and it is by this means that judicial salaries, as with their UK equivalents, are made payable without the need for further parliamentary approval year by year[1].

The other authority for payments conferred by SA 1998 is for sums paid out for the purposes of meeting the expenditure of the Scottish Administration (or other statutory purpose) in accordance with rules made by or under an Act of the Scottish Parliament[2]. Those rules have been laid down by the Public Finance and Accountability (Scotland) Act 2000 (PFA(S)A 2000)[3]. This provides that the use of resources for any purpose by the Scottish Administration and by other bodies reliant upon the Scottish Consolidated Fund must be authorised by a Budget Act passed by the Parliament[4]. Such authorisations relate to a particular financial year and the use of resources must not exceed the amount authorised for the year and purpose[5]. Thus the principal authority for expenditure is the annual Budget Act but PFA(S)A 2000 also authorises emergency funding arrangements at the beginning of a financial year if a Budget Act has not yet provided routine authorisation. Pro rata expenditure may be incurred on the basis of the previous year's figures[6]. There is also provision for the exceptional funding of 'contingencies' not otherwise authorised. Such funding is permitted only on the authority of the Scottish Ministers and then only where it is necessarily required in the public interest and reasons of urgency make the use of standard procedures not reasonably practicable. There are also strict financial limits. Any use of the power must be reported to the Parliament[7].

The adoption of the use of an annual Budget Act as the standard means of authorisation of expenditure followed discussion of alternatives[8]. The possibility of setting budgets to cover more than a year at a time had been considered but rejected because this might prejudice parliamentary scrutiny and would not dovetail well with UK requirements for financial control. Another possibility had been a procedure for approval of expenditure by secondary rather than primary legislation. It had, however, been accepted that the importance of this function demanded primary legislation and that an annual Budget Act should be required. On the other hand, the case for the use of secondary legislation for budget revisions later in the course of a financial year was accepted. It would be unnecessarily burdensome to insist on repeated recourse to primary legislation and, despite the model of successive Appropriation Bills at Westminster, the use of revising orders would be simpler[9].

The Parliament's standing orders provide the procedure for Budget Bills[10]. In line with practice at Westminster, a Budget Bill may be introduced only by a member of the Scottish Government and it need not be accompanied by a financial memorandum, explanatory notes or a policy memorandum[11]. At Stage 1 the Bill must be referred immediately to the Parliament for consideration of its general principles without the need for a committee report and Stage 2 must then be taken in the Finance Committee. Certain of the other standard procedural provisions on Bills are then suspended but it is specifically provided that (a) Stage 3 may begin no earlier than 20 days after the introduction of the Bill; but (b), if Stage 3 is not completed within 30 days from introduction, the Bill falls. Amendments to a Budget Bill may be moved only by a member of the Scottish Government. Specific provision is also made for the possibility that a Budget Bill is itself dependent upon the Parliament's passing a tax-varying resolution as the source of additional revenue. If, in those circumstances, the tax-varying resolution is rejected, the Budget Bill falls[12]. If, for any reason, a Budget Bill falls or is rejected, a replacement Bill in the same or similar terms may be introduced at any time[13].

To take a recent example, the Budget (Scotland) Act 2014 (B(S)A 2014) – made provision for the authorisation of expenditure in 2014–15 in respect of both the Scottish Administration and other bodies. Specific amounts were attributed to 15 itemised 'purposes' for which resources could be used by the Scottish Administration[14] and to four direct-funded bodies – the Forestry Commissioners, the Food Standards Agency, the Scottish Parliamentary Corporate Body and Audit Scotland[15]. Then B(S)A 2014, s 7 provided for its own amendment to enable the amounts of authorised expenditure to be revised. Subject to prior approval of a draft of the order by the Parliament, the Scottish Ministers may amend the amounts specified in the Act[16]. The procedures just described relate to the formal stage at which the Parliament gives its approval by statute to the Government's proposals for forward spending. However, it is important to recognise that those procedures come at the end of a much longer annual process which starts with the Government's publication of its spending proposals produced on a three-year cycle in line with the UK spending reviews. The Scottish Budget Spending Review 2011 covered the financial years to 2014–15 and, in non-review years, the Government simply publishes a draft budget in respect of the one year following and concludes with the publication of the Budget Bill by 20 January. That is a timetable agreed between the Parliament and the Scottish Ministers in 2005[17]. As well as the overall timetable, the agreement deals with the content of the two stages of the process prior to the introduction of the Budget Bill[18]. Following proposals originally made by FIAG[19] and the CSG[20], the intention has been to provide the Parliament's Finance Committee, subject committees and the Parliament in plenary session the opportunity to scrutinise the budget proposals. At Stage 1 the general expenditure proposals are available; at Stage 2, during October and November, detailed proposals can be scrutinised, concluding with a chamber debate based on a report produced by the Finance Committee, after consultation with subject committees.

Quite apart from the annual budget process, it is also a function of the Finance Committee to scrutinise the financial memoranda which accompany Bills introduced into the Scottish Parliament. This is intended to ensure that the Parliament is in full possession of relevant financial information in advance of taking decisions on the general principles of Bills.

1   See SA 1998, s 119(3) – a provision which is itself 'entrenched' in relation to judicial salaries by SA 1998, Sch 4, paras 4(3), 5(a). See Scottish Consolidated Fund Account , SG/2014/222 (Nov 2014) ('note' 6). See also para 12.10 below.
2   SA 1998, s 65(1)(c).
3   Temporary provision was made for the period up to 31 March 2000 by the Scotland Act 1998 (Transitory and Transitional Provisions) (Finance) Order 1999, SI 1999/441. The passing of the Act followed a period of consultation on the (Scottish Office) Financial Issues Advisory Group (FIAG) Report *Principles of the Scottish Parliament's Financial Procedures* (November 1998). See *Consultation Paper on a Financial Framework for the Scottish Parliament* (July 1999).
4   PFA(S)A 2000, s 4.
5   PFA(S)A 2000, s 1(3) defines 'the use of resources' as 'their expenditure, consumption or reduction in value'. PFA(S)A 2000 has incorporated the UK terminology of resource accounting – see Government Resources and Accounts Act 2000, s 27.
6   PFA(S)A 2000, s 2. These arrangements may be adjusted by a Budget Act – see, for example, the B(S)A 2014, s 6.
7   PFA(S)A 2000, s 3. Additional authority for contingency funding and for provisional emergency funding at the start of the following year may also be made in a Budget Act – see the B(S)A 2014, ss 5, 6.
8   For a summary, see the policy memorandum which accompanied the Public Finance and Accountability Bill.
9   See Subordinate Legislation Committee, 1 Feb 2000.
10 SOs, r 9.16. The introduction of the Budget Bill is preceded by (draft) budget scrutiny procedures (below).
11 For standard procedure on Bills, see para 9.9.
12 SOs, r 9.16.7.
13 SOs, r 9.16.8.
14 B(S)A 2014, s 1 and Sch 1.
15 B(S)A 2014 , s 2 and Sch 2. Provision was also made for for certain capital expenditure and borrowing, see B(S)A 2014, s 3 and sch 3.
16 For an order amending B(S)A 2014, see SSI 2014/363.
17 As updated in the *Written Agreement between the Finance Committee and the Scottish Government on the Budget Process in Session 4 of the Scottish Parliament* (Revised version, Dec 2013).
18 See also SOs, r 5.8.
19 See above.
20 *CSG Report* s 3.4 and Annex 1.

GOVERNMENT ACCOUNTING AND AUDIT

11.18   The detailed rules of government accounting are well beyond the scope of this work. There are, however, some aspects of the rules on accounting and audit which are of the highest constitutional importance. These rules operate in support of the appropriation procedures already considered and they add an important further dimension to the parliamentary procedures for the scrutiny and control of government action dealt with in Chapter 9. They involve the work of significant independent scrutineers of government in the form of the Comptroller and Auditor General and the National Audit Office at the United Kingdom level and, in Scotland, the Auditor General for Scotland and Audit Scotland; the specialised functions of the Public Accounts Committee of the House of Commons and the Public Audit Committee of the Scottish Parliament; and the work of 'accounting' (UK Government) and 'accountable' (Scottish Government) officers who, while senior civil servants whose loyalties are usually channelled through ministers, owe a special loyalty to their respective auditors. In this account the focus is on the Scottish arrangements introduced by SA 1998 and PFA(S)A 2000[1].

Although the UK Parliament deliberately left to the Scottish Parliament the task of making detailed provision in this area, SA 1998 does contain certain of the core rules[2]. SA 1998, s 69 provides for the appointment of an Auditor General for Scotland by the Queen, on the nomination of the Parliament[3]. Like the Comptroller and Auditor General, the Auditor General for Scotland enjoys formal security of tenure equivalent to that of a senior judge in that no recommendation may be made to the Queen for removal from office unless the Parliament approves by a two-thirds majority[4]. The independent operation of the Auditor General is sought to be further assured by a provision that he or she must not be subject to the direction or control of any member of the Scottish Government or of the Parliament[5].

The duties of the Auditor General are laid down in outline by SA 1998[6] and then in more detail by PFA(S)A 2000. There are two main functions. The first is the approval of any payment from the Scottish Consolidated Fund, on the request of the Scottish Ministers. Such payments are approved only if authorised[7]. In this way the Auditor General is acting as the independent scrutineer and enforcer of the rules on expenditure approval.

Secondly, the Auditor General is responsible for the audit of the accounts of the Scottish Ministers, the Lord Advocate and other persons and bodies to whom sums are paid out of the Scottish Consolidated Fund[8]. For this purpose, the staff of a body known as Audit Scotland assist the Auditor General. Audit Scotland consists of the Auditor General, the Chairman of the Accounts Commission for Scotland[9] and three other members appointed jointly by the first two[10]. The audit process has a dual aspect. On the one hand, it is an examination of whether accounts have been properly kept. A report on such audits must be submitted to the Scottish Ministers who, in turn, must publish the report and lay a copy before the Parliament[11]. On the other hand, the Auditor General may initiate examination into the economy, efficiency and effectiveness (value for money audit) of any of the bodies subject to scrutiny. In determining whether to carry out such an examination, the Auditor General must take into account any proposals made by the Parliament and he may report the results to the Parliament[12]. For the purposes of discharging these functions the Auditor General is entitled to all documents and information reasonably required[13]. In addition, the work of the Auditor General is assisted by the contribution required of the principal accountable officer for the Scottish Administration, the 'most senior member of the staff of the Scottish Administration' ie the Permanent Secretary[14]. Accountable officers are stated to be answerable to the Parliament for the exercise of their functions which, in addition to ensuring the general propriety and regularity of the finances of their part of the Administration, include special obligations if they consider that something inconsistent with the proper performance of their functions is being required of them by ministers. In such an event accountable officers must obtain written authority from ministers before taking the action, and send a copy to the Auditor General[15]. These arrangements and the personal responsibilities they impose place accountable officers in a special relationship with ministers which is quite different from their usual position as civil servants[16].

In the Parliament, it is the responsibility of the Public Audit Committee to consider and report on accounts and reports by the Auditor General which are laid before the Parliament[17]. At Westminster, the Public Accounts Committee of the House of Commons has achieved a reputation as the most powerful and independent of select committees. It is, by convention, always chaired by an opposition MP. At Holyrood, standing orders provide that the convener of the Public Audit Committee must not be an MSP who represents a political party represented in the Scottish Government. No minister may be a member of the Committee[18].

1   For arrangements at the UK level, see *Erskine May's Parliamentary Practice* (24th edn, 2011).
2   Under SA 1998, transitional provision was made, pending the passing of the necessary further legislation by the Scottish Parliament, for the period to 31 March 2000 by the Scotland Act 1998 (Transitory and Transitional Provisional) (Finance) Order 1999, SI 1999/441.
3   SA 1998, s 69(1). Provision for the salary and pension of the Auditor General is to be made by the Parliament: PFA(S)A 2000, s 13.
4   For the procedure to dismiss a Court of Session judge, see para 12.7 below.
5   SA 1998, s 69(4).
6   SA 1998, s 70(1)(c), (2).
7   PFA(S)A 2000, s 5.
8   SA 1998, s 70(1), (2), (9) and PFA(S)A 2000, ss 21–22. Accounts themselves are required by SA 1998, s 70(1) and PFA(S)A 2000, s 19.
9   The body responsible for the audit of the accounts of Scottish local authorities under the Local Government (Scotland) Act 1973. The composition and functions of the Accounts Commission were modified by PFA(S)A 2000 to transfer responsibility for the audit of bodies, including the Health Service, to the Auditor General.
10 PFA(S)A 2000, ss 10–11 and sch 2. Audit Scotland's own accounts are audited by the Scottish Commission for Public Audit, a body consisting of the convener of the Parliament's Public Audit Committee and four other MSPs: PFA(S)A 2000, ss 12, 19 and 25.
11 PFA(S)A 2000, ss 21, 22.
12 PFA(S)A 2000, s 23.
13 PFA(S)A 2000, s 24.
14 PFA(S)A 2000, s 14. The Clerk of the Parliament is principal accountable officer for the Parliamentary corporation: PFA(S)A 2000, s 16.
15 PFA(S)A 2000, s 15(8).
16 See *Scottish Ministerial Code* (Dec 2011) paras 6.4–6.8.
17 SOs, r 6.7.
18 SOs, r 6.7.2.

Chapter 12

Courts and the Independence of the Judiciary

INTRODUCTION

12.1

'An independent judiciary is a feature of every democracy which is worth the name.'[1]

'The role of the courts as resolver of disputes, interpreter of the law and defender of the Constitution requires that they be completely separate in authority and function from all other participants in the justice system.'[2]

'A judge shall exercise the judicial function independently on the basis of the judge's assessment of the facts and in accordance with a conscientious understanding of the law, free of any extraneous influences, inducements, pressures, threats or interference, direct or indirect, from any quarter or for any reason.'[3]

There is something striking and compelling about these statements. They contain a direct appeal to the doctrine of the rule of law and the importance of judges in sustaining it. Coming from Scottish, Commonwealth and United Nations sources, there is an assertion of universality. The first, as a statement about the United Kingdom, which has not, historically, in its system of parliamentary government made strong claims to sustain the principle of the separation of powers[4], it is a very bright reassertion of one aspect of that principle. The judiciary should be independent. What this means (and how far it is advanced) is the main focus of this chapter. In Chapter 14, consideration is given to the principal constitutional functions of the Scottish judiciary, with a particular focus on the processes of public law and constitutional adjudication.

For reasons to be explained, the main focus here will be upon the higher judiciary. They have a special significance in the constitutional order but it is valuable also to recognise that (a) the judicial system of Scotland extends to include the lower courts upon which, in quantitative terms, the main burdens fall[5]; (b) the judges in the courts of the system as a whole are discharging a wide variety of different functions; and (c) on the other hand, there are many other persons and bodies who would not be included in the 'judiciary' but who are undoubtedly carrying out functions of a judicial character. It is a reminder of the limitations of a crude application of the idea of the separation of powers[6].

1 Lord Cullen of Whitekirk 'The Judge and The Public' 1999 SLT (News) 261.
2 *Beauregard v Canada* [1986] 2 SCR 56 at 73 per Dickson CJ.
3 The Bangalore Principles of Judicial Conduct, 2002, as endorsed by the United Nations Human Rights Commission, 2003.

4 Although see the discussion of the Constitutional Reform Act 2005 at paras 12.18 and 12.20 below.
5 And will fall more heavily when the Courts Reform (Scotland) Act 2014 (CR(S)A 2014) is brought into force, most particularly as a result of the increase in the privative jurisdiction (or, now, the 'exclusive competence') of the sheriff court in civil cases to £100,000 (s 39).
6 See para 2.5.

The judicial system and judicial functions

12.2 As to the judicial system proper, this is taken to include the full range of civil and criminal courts from the Justice of the Peace (JP) courts of very limited criminal jurisdiction and staffed in the main by lay justices[1]; the sheriff courts organised across the six sheriffdoms[2] and with very extensive civil and criminal jurisdictions; the sheriff appeal court to be established under CR(S)A 2014; through to the Court of Session whose civil jurisdiction is both original (mainly before a single judge in the Outer House) and appellate (in the Inner House constituted in Divisions – the First Division presided over by the Lord President, the Second by the Lord Justice Clerk and Extra Divisions appointed by the Lord President and usually under the chairmanship of the most senior of the judges comprised in the Division[3]). Civil cases may be taken on appeal (since October 2009) to the UK Supreme Court whose membership of 12 Justices has included two Scottish judges who will both normally sit in Scottish cases. Broadly the role of the Supreme Court replicates that of the former Appellate Committee of the House of Lords and in particular, there is provision that the creation of the Supreme Court is not to affect the 'distinctions between the separate legal systems of the parts of the United Kingdom'[4] and that a decision of the Court[5] is 'to be regarded as the decision of a court of that part of the United Kingdom'[6]. The senior criminal jurisdiction is vested in the High Court of Justiciary, sitting at first instance or, under the presidency of the Lord Justice General or more usually the Lord Justice Clerk, on appeal. There is no further general right of appeal in criminal cases.

Since devolution in 1999, however, special forms of appeal have been created under which, in all civil cases and in some criminal cases, the determination of a 'devolution issue' may be appealed or referred from the Court of Session to the Supreme Court and in some other criminal cases a 'compatibility issue' may be so referred[7].

Although all these courts must be included in a full description of the Scottish judicial system, it is not difficult to see that the courts and those who preside over them are carrying out a huge range of functions. There is the broad distinction to be drawn between criminal business, in which the Crown will almost always be the prosecuting party, and civil business usually involving private parties but including cases where public bodies are involved. This latter portion of civil business, in turn, includes contractual disputes or reparation cases arising, for instance, out of the alleged negligence of a public authority or its employees. Also included in civil cases are those arising in the Court of Session as petitions for judicial review in the exercise of the court's supervisory jurisdiction[8] or in the form of statutory appeals in the sheriff court or Court of Session against decisions made by public bodies[9]. While cases at all levels and of all types demand certain standards of fairness and impartiality it is clear that, from the point of view of their constitutional significance, the many activities carried on by those collectively known as the judiciary vary greatly. Low-level trials of minor traffic and other regulatory offences in JP courts, mainly involving the resolution of disputes over facts, bear little resemblance to the hearing of appeals on difficult points of law in the Inner House or the Supreme Court. Sentencing in criminal cases, although treated as a judicial function, bears little relation to most other forms of judicial activity and merges more into the administration of penal policy largely undertaken by other authorities. Sheriffs, although mostly involved in civil and criminal cases, are also required to undertake functions which clearly straddle the boundary between judicial and executive and are administrative in character. They make licensing decisions and hear administrative appeals in matters such as child welfare and mental health[10].

This mix of functions is also reflected on the administrative side of the divide between judicial and executive institutions. Historically, so-called 'administrative tribunals' have varied greatly in function and mode of operation but they are as much involved in adjudication as courts themselves. Some include judges and other lawyers in their membership. Others have an entirely lay membership but they have an adjudicative role and their work involves many of the same problems of doing justice between individuals or between an individual and a public authority. The reorganisation of devolved Scottish tribunals by the Tribunals (Scotland) Act 2014 will bring a more coherent structure to the tribunals system but the essential role will remain the same[11].

This mix of functions extends right into central government itself. Civil servants as planning reporters decide most appeals from local authorities to the Scottish Ministers on planning matters, holding, if necessary, public local inquiries in the process[12]. Some of the most important planning appeals fall to be decided by the relevant member of the Scottish Government, currently the Minister for Local Government and Planning, and the Scottish Ministers also retain the power to call in particularly important appeals which would otherwise be dealt with by a reporter[13]. Such decisions are undoubtedly judicial (or 'quasi-judicial') in character.

Even though it is easy to see, therefore, that those whom we correctly regard as part of the judiciary, broadly defined, are often discharging functions of no great constitutional significance and sometimes not of a judicial nature at all and, on the other hand, many judicial tasks are carried out by members of the executive, there *is* good reason for paying special attention to the situation of the senior judiciary, by which is principally meant the judges of the Court of Session and of the Supreme Court. They have a direct responsibility for the most important tasks of adjudication where the interpretation of the powers of the executive and the legislature are most at issue. This adjudicative role is the principal subject matter of Chapter 14. In addition, the senior judiciary have a supervisory responsibility, exercised through procedures of appeal and review, over the standards of adjudication by inferior courts and by ministers and other administrative bodies. This is done partly on the basis of standards generated by the courts themselves but increasingly also by the application of standards derived from the European Convention on Human Rights (ECHR)[14]. The Court of Session and, in England, the High Court also assume responsibility for seeking to keep open access to the courts. They will, for instance, interpret narrowly statutory language intended to restrict access[15]. They will treat, equally critically, delegated legislation which, without specific authority, restricts access to the courts[16] and have held unlawful (as thwarting the intention of the Scottish Parliament) the failure by Ministers to bring into 'effective operation' legislation intended to provide access to a tribunal to certain mental health patients[17].

1   Criminal Proceedings etc (Reform) Scotland Act 2007 as amended. For an account of the origins and history of justices of the peace in Scotland, see the opinion of Lord Hope of Craighead in *Clark v Kelly* 2003 SLT 308.
2   CR(S)A 2014 confers new powers on the Scottish Ministers to abolish and alter the boundaries of sheriffdoms and the sheriff court districts within them. The power may be exercised in response to a proposal made by the Scottish Courts and Tribunals Service (as the Scottish Court Service will be renamed) where that proposal has the agreement of the Lord President of the Court of Session.
3   Judiciary and Courts (Scotland) Act 2008 (JS(S)A 2008), s 46.
4   Constitutional Reform Act 2005, s 41(1).
5   Other than a decision on a devolution matter. See para 14.32.
6   Constitutional Reform Act 2005, s 41(2).
7   See ch 14. The distinction between 'devolution issues' and 'compatibility issues' was introduced by the Scotland Act 2012. Prior to the creation of the Supreme Court, devolution issues in both criminal and civil cases were dealt with by the Judicial Committee of the Privy Council (JCPC) to which appeals from certain professional bodies still go, along with appeals from a limited number of Commonwealth countries.
8   See ch 14.
9   See ch 14.
10 For a general introduction see I D Macphail *Sheriff Court Practice* (3rd edn by T Welsh, 2006) vol 1, ch 27.
11 See para 14.5.
12 Town and Country Planning (Scotland) Act 1997, sch 4 and Town and Country Planning (Determination of Appeals by Appointed Persons) (Prescribed Classes) (Scotland) Regulations 2010, SSI 2010/467.
13 See, for example, *Lafarge Redland Aggregates Ltd v Scottish Ministers* 2000 SLT 1361.
14 Particularly art 6 ECHR, which has, as its central concern, the requirements of due process or procedural fairness.
15 *Watt v Lord Advocate* 1979 SC 120, applying *Anisminic Ltd v Foreign Compensation Commission* [1969] 2 AC 147. See also, however, *Eba v Advocate General for Scotland* 2012 SC (UKSC) 1 discussed at para 14.11 below.
16 *Singh v Home Secretary* 1993 SC (HL) 1.
17 *RM v Scottish Ministers* 2013 SC (UKSC) 139.

The importance of judicial independence

12.3   If the higher judiciary are to continue to discharge the functions already allocated to them and to take on others, it is necessary that the right conditions for high-quality decision-making are created and maintained. In this context 'quality' refers only partly to ideas of accuracy or technical sophistication in the application of the law. There is an expectation that judges will have the knowledge and skills required but also that they will be enabled to deploy these skills, both individually and collectively, in conditions which protect decision-makers from inappropriate influences or pressures and which enable the judiciary to maintain their legitimacy within the constitutional and political system as a whole. These conditions are often referred to, in shorthand, as 'judicial independence'.

As the reference to 'legitimacy' suggests, the importance of judicial independence does not rest merely on the extent to which it actually protects judges from inappropriate influences or pressures or ensures quality decision-making. At least as important in this context is the impact which the principles of judicial independence – and the degree to which these are maintained – have on public confidence in the judicial system. That such confidence is considered to be a key value is evidenced by the now famous maxim, repeated in various different guises over the years, that 'justice must not only be done but must manifestly be seen to be done'. Indeed, in practice, complaints of a lack of judicial independence are invariably accompanied by a concession that there has been no actual prejudice or bias on the part of the judge involved but simply that the circumstances provide the opportunity for unfairness or the appearance of bias[1]. Confidence in the judiciary is not a 'one-way' process: 'A litigant is entitled to expect integrity of the judge, but he in turn must give the judge his trust. That is the only basis on which litigation can be conducted in an atmosphere of confidence rather than suspicion.'[2]

Views on exactly what *in fact* is required to ensure judicial independence change over time. They change in the light of changes in the duties assigned to judges and as a consequence of diminishing deference to the judiciary and more exacting scrutiny of the judicial system. The issue of judicial independence has become more prominent in recent years as the judiciary are increasingly being asked to determine disputes which are perceived as having an overtly 'political' dimension. This is particularly true in the field of human rights where, in the implementation of the Human Rights Act 1998 (HRA 1998) and devolution legislation in Scotland, Wales and Northern Ireland, there has been regular criticism of the courts by the media, and increasingly by government ministers[3]. The threats to maintaining independence also vary, although there is a recurring assumption that the most persistent threat comes from the executive branch of government[4]. This is not merely because of the seventeenth-century inheritance but because central government, in the exercise of its very substantial powers, will often wish to press those powers to their limits. It is a frequent litigant in the courts and usually in cases where the rights of weaker parties are at stake. The Crown is also the prosecutor in virtually all criminal cases.

Historically, the expression 'judicial independence' has been treated by the Scottish courts as a reference to all those safeguards – institutional and jurisprudential – put in place to ensure high-quality decision-making. However, there has been increasing recognition of a distinction between the concepts of judicial *independence* and judicial *impartiality*[5]. The emergence of this distinction can be seen in domestic case law under the influence of both evolving Commonwealth standards and the interpretation and application of art 6 ECHR, which guarantees that, in the determination of his or her civil rights and obligations or of any criminal charge against him or her, an individual is entitled to a 'fair and public hearing within a reasonable time by an independent *and* impartial tribunal established by law'. In the context of the Canadian Charter of Rights and Freedoms, the distinction between independence and impartiality has been illuminated in this way:

> 'Although there is obviously a close relationship between independence and impartiality, they are nevertheless separate and distinct values or requirements. Impartiality refers to a state of mind or attitude of the tribunal in relation to the issues and the parties in a particular case. The word "impartial" ... connotes absence of bias, actual or perceived. The word "independent" ... reflects or embodies the traditional constitutional value of judicial independence. As such, it connotes not merely a state of mind or attitude in the actual exercise of judicial functions, but a status or relationship to others, particularly to the Executive Branch of government, that rest on objective conditions or guarantees.'[6]

Crudely put, the idea of judicial *independence* may be thought to refer to external, institutional or systemic safeguards to protect the judiciary as a whole from inappropriate influences while judicial *impartiality* concerns, much more directly, the circumstances of the individual decision-maker in any given case and personal, subjective factors which may influence the decision-maker in a way which is considered to be illegitimate. This concept of judicial impartiality accords most closely with that protected by the well-established common law rule against bias[7].

It is clear, though, that while it may be possible to separate the *concepts* of judicial independence and judicial impartiality, in *practice* one is very much dependent upon the other and indeed the Scottish judiciary have been equivocal about whether they consider the distinction to have value even as an analytical tool[8]. In a lecture in 2002 on the topic of 'judicial independence'[9], Lord Hope of Craighead, former Deputy President of the Supreme Court and former Lord of Appeal in Ordinary and Lord President of the Court of Session, addressed three principal questions: (1) What purpose does judicial independence serve? (2) Is our judicial independence at risk of being compromised? (3) How can judicial impartiality be preserved? In answer to his first question, Lord Hope said that judicial independence serves the one very specific purpose of preserving the judge's impartiality. On the question of the risks of compromising judicial independence, he referred to the centrality of security of tenure as a way of ensuring impartiality[10] and acknowledged that security's vulnerability to erosion at the hands of the executive. As to how judicial impartiality might be preserved, Lord Hope's starting point was the Commonwealth's *Latimer House Guidelines*[11]. They are described as 'Guidelines on good practice governing relations between the Executive, Parliament and the Judiciary in the promotion of good governance, the rule of law and human rights' and they address, in turn, questions of judicial autonomy, funding and judicial training.

1 See paras 12.14–12.16 below.
2 *Robbie the Pict, Petitioner* 203 SCCR 299 per the Lord Justice Clerk Gill at para 8.
3 Two decisions of the UK Supreme Court in October 2010 (*Cadder v HMA* 2011 SC (UKSC) 13) on the incompatibility with art 6 of the Scottish approach to interviewing suspects in the absence of legal representation) and May 2011 (*Fraser v HMA* 2011 SC (UKSC) 113 on non-disclosure of evidence in a murder trial) provoked the particular ire of the then Scottish Cabinet Secretary for Justice, Kenny MacAskill and then First Minister Alex Salmond, both of whom criticised the approach of the Supreme Court (and indeed a prominent Scottish human rights

lawyer). Their comments led the President of the Law Society of Scotland and the Dean of the Faculty of Advocates to issue a joint public statement exhorting ministers to respect the independence of the judiciary and the rule of law. For a brief summary of events see SP OR 27 October 2011 Col 2874. The approach of the Supreme Court was characterised, in particular, as failure to understand and respect the distinctiveness of the Scottish criminal justice system: see SP OR, 27 October 2010 Col 29571 (First Minister) and SP OR Scotland Bill Committee 8 February 2011, Col 479 (Lord Advocate). For the response of Lord Hope of Craighead see (2012) 16 Edin LR 58 and see, also, A Paterson *Final Judgement: The Last Law Lords and the Supreme Court* (2013) at p 244.

4 'Threats to judicial independence usually come from governments irked by a judiciary fulfilling its traditional role of standing between the executive and the citizen': Lord Steyn 'Democracy Through Law' [2002] EHRLR 723 at 726.

5 See eg *Gillies v Secretary of State for Work and Pensions* 2006 SC (HL) 71 para 38 (per Lady Hale of Richmond).

6 *Valente v The Queen* (1985) 24 DLR (4th) 161 per Le Dain J.

7 As to which see para 12.14 below.

8 For example, in *Starrs v Ruxton* 2000 JC 208 Lord Prosser expressed the view that while independence and impartiality were concepts which were 'inextricably interlinked', nevertheless the requirement of independence was an additional substantive requirement and was wider than impartiality (at 232). By contrast, in *Clancy v Caird* 2000 SC 441 Lord Sutherland described the Canadian approach as unnecessarily analytical (at 445) and Lord Coulsfield was of the view that independence and impartiality are so closely related as to be difficult to distinguish (at 459–460).

9 'Judicial Independence' 2002 SLT (News) 195.

10 Citing Lord Fraser of Tullybelton 5 *Stair Memorial Encyclopaedia*, paras 663–665.

11 So called because they were the product of a colloquium which was held at Latimer House in June 1998 and attended by lawyers and judges from 20 Commonwealth countries. The Guidelines were subsequently annexed to the Commonwealth Principles and reissued (with an Edinburgh Plan of Action) in 2009 and the commitment of the Commonwealth to the Latimer House Principles was reaffirmed in the preamble to the Commonwealth Charter of 2013 (Cm 8572).

JUDICIAL INDEPENDENCE

12.4   In the United Kingdom the conditions of judicial independence, as well as varying over time, are only in part the result of direct legal intervention. Much depends instead on constitutional practice with only the sporadic intrusion of legal rules many of which have, over time, lost the significance they once had.

However, the administrative and operational independence of the Scottish judiciary has been reinforced in recent years by the Judiciary and Courts (Scotland) Act 2008 (JC(S)A 2008)[1] and CR(S)A 2014 which confer substantial powers and duties on the Lord President of the Court of Session and on sheriffs principal. The reforms may also be regarded as a step towards further separation of the executive and judiciary in Scotland, consigning to history many of the powers over the Scottish judiciary which had been exercisable first by the Secretary of State and then, on devolution, by the Scottish Ministers under the Sheriff Courts (Scotland) Act 1971 (SC(S)A 1971).

A bold new and explicit statement is now provided by s 1 of JC(S)A 2008. Without seeking to define what is meant by 'independence', the section[2] imposes on the First Minister, the Lord Advocate, the Scottish Ministers, MSPs and other persons responsible for matters relating to the judiciary or the administration of justice an obligation to 'uphold the continued independence of the judiciary'. In particular, the First Minister, the Lord Advocate and the Scottish Ministers must not seek to influence particular judicial decisions through any special access to the judiciary and must have regard to the need for the judiciary to have the support necessary to enable them to carry out their functions. Some may doubt whether these declaratory statements will have any practical effect. They do, however, have an undoubted symbolic impact.

JC(S)A 2008 also confirms the Lord President as Head of the Scottish Judiciary, and renders him responsible for making and maintaining arrangements for securing the efficient disposal of business in the Scottish courts. Delivery of those arrangements is in practical terms the work of the Scottish Court Service (which following implementation of CR(S)A 2014 will become the Scottish Courts and Tribunal Service). The Lord President is also responsible for representing the views of the Scottish judiciary to the Scottish Parliament and the Scottish Ministers and has appeared before the Scottish Parliament on several occasions[3].

CR(S)A 2014 restates the duty of sheriffs principal to ensure the efficient disposal of business within their sheriffdom and the powers (originally introduced by JC(S)A 2008) for the Lord President to exercise the administrative functions of the sheriff principal where he considers that the sheriff principal's exercise of those functions is prejudicial to the efficient disposal of business in the sheriffdom, is prejudicial to the efficient organisation or administration of those courts, or is otherwise against the interest of the public[4].

As to the more specific rules relating to the manner in which judicial independence is safeguarded, the subject is divided into two parts: first, the appointment of judges; and second, the creation of conditions conducive to high-quality and independent decision-making by the judiciary as a whole. Thereafter, under the head of 'Judicial impartiality' there is a discussion of the legal principles, developed almost entirely by the courts themselves, which seek to ensure that in any specific case the parties involved can have confidence in the neutrality of the decision-maker involved.

1 For discussion of the background to the Act as well as of its provisions in detail, see the Current Law Statutes Annotations by J Harrison and C Himsworth.
2 Following a similar rule in s 3(1) of the Constitutional Reform Act 2005.
3 However, in April and May 2013 the Lord President declined a repeated invitation to give oral evidence to the Scottish Parliament's Petitions Committee on the proposal for a register of interests for members of the Scottish judiciary, citing the need to protect the independence of the judiciary as his reason for doing so (PE1458/J 13 May 2013). In January 2014 he agreed to meet informally with members of the Committee, and the notes taken by the clerk to the Committee of that informal meeting on 21 January 2014 are available on the Committee's webpage. The Committee's consideration of this petition has been wide ranging, extending into judicial complaints and oaths, and remains ongoing. See SP OR 9 October 2014, col 60.
4 CR(S)A 2014, s 29.

Judicial appointments

12.5   Judicial appointments are made formally by the Crown. Members of the Supreme Court (including the Scottish judges) are appointed on the recommendation of the Prime Minister[1]. Below that level, the rules have been changed in line with the broader arrangements for devolution under the Scotland Act 1998 (SA 1998). Except to ensure the 'continued existence' of the High Court of Justiciary and the Court of Session, SA 1998 does not, in general, make the judicial system of Scotland a reserved matter[2] but s 95 does make special provision for the appointment and removal of judges. Thus it is for the Prime Minister to make recommendations for appointment to the two most senior judicial positions in the Court of Session and the High Court of Justiciary: the Lord President and the Lord Justice Clerk[3]. However, a recommendation may be made only of a person nominated by the First Minister and the First Minister is, in turn, required first to consult the Lord President and the Lord Justice Clerk (unless either office is vacant)[4]. In the case of other judges of the Court of Session, sheriffs principal and sheriffs, it is for the First Minister (again after consultation with the Lord President) to make recommendations on appointments[5]. In respect of both nominations for the two most senior posts and recommendations for the others, the First Minister is required to comply with any requirements imposed by another enactment. Such requirements have been laid down by the JC(S)A 2008 and by CR(S)A 2014.

Recommendation for appointment as a Court of Session judge cannot be made unless the individual concerned has, in turn, been recommended by the Judicial Appointments Board for Scotland (the JAB) (JC(S)A 2008, s 11(1)). Originally established on a non-statutory basis in 2002 to replace an appointments process which was left very much in the hands of the Lord Advocate[6] the JAB has a membership of ten, divided into three categories. The three 'judicial members', appointed by the Lord President are a Court of Session judge, a sheriff principal and a sheriff[7]. The two 'legal members' appointed by the Scottish Ministers are a practising advocate and solicitor and there are five 'lay members' (one of whom is designated the Chairing Member) also appointed by the Scottish Ministers[8]. Using procedures including public advertisement and interview, the JAB must have regard to the need to encourage diversity – one of the principal reasons for establishing the JAB at all was to seek to draw the judiciary from a broader base – but tempered also by the need to assess legal knowledge, skills and competence and, as the Act expressly stipulates, to select 'solely on merit' (JC(S)A 2008, ss 12–16). Both the Scottish Ministers and the Lord President may issue procedural guidance to the JAB[9]. The CR(S)A 2014 confers on the JAB the power to appoint legal and lay assistants (in each case for a maximum term of three years) to help it carry out its functions[10].

The JAB's task of balancing the need for diversity with the obligation to select on merit is not a simple one[11]. A prior requirement for any appointment, however, is legal qualification. Article 19 of the Treaty of Union originally required that candidates be advocates of at least five years standing – a position modified to include sheriffs and solicitor advocates[12].

In addition to Court of Session judges, the JAB's remit includes most temporary judges (except those who hold or have held certain judicial offices), sheriffs principal and sheriffs[13]. In respect of the two last offices, the formal prerequisite for appointment is legal qualification for at least ten years[14]. JP recommendations are not within the Board's remit.

Recommendations to the First Minister for nomination to the Prime Minister for appointment as Lord President or Lord Justice Clerk are made not by the JAB but by a smaller ad hoc panel established for the purpose, chaired by the JAB's Chairing Member, another lay member of the JAB and two judges[15].

Evaluation of the effectiveness of the JAB has in practice been left as a matter for the JAB itself. It commissioned in 2009 an external evaluation of the judicial appointments process which involved a survey of the legal profession in Scotland with the aim of providing more information about the pool of individuals in Scotland eligible to apply for judicial office and to identify those factors which might encourage or discourage those individuals in applying and it also formed a diversity working group in 2007 which reported in 2010[16] and which, amongst other things, noted a downward trend in applications from women.

1   Constitutional Reform Act 2005 s26. Initially the Court comprised the then serving Lords of Appeal in Ordinary (s 24). Prime ministerial recommendations follow processes involving the participation of a selection commission and the Lord Chancellor (ss 26–31).
2   SA 1998, Sch 5, Pt I, para 1. But see SA 1998, Sch 5, Pt II, S L1, which does reserve the determination of judicial remuneration, and para 12.10 below.
3   The Lord President, carrying the title of Lord Justice-General when sitting in the High Court of Justiciary.
4   SA 1998, s 95(1)–(3). The wording of SA 1998, s 95(3), which refers to 'persons' nominated by the First Minister, was quite deliberate draftsmanship: it enables the First Minister to identify two or three candidates for consideration by the Prime Minister (HL Debs, 6 October 1998, col 403).
5   SA 1998, s 95(4). In the case of nominations under SA 1998, s 95(2) and recommendations under SA 1998, s 95(4), the First Minister is also to comply with any requirement imposed by any enactment.
6   The scheme adopted in the 2008 Act followed consultation on a succession of reforming proposals from the Scottish Executive (both Labour/Liberal Democrat and SNP): Judicial Appointments: An Inclusive Approach (2000); Strengthening Judicial Independence in a Modern Scotland (2006); Proposals for a Judiciary (Scotland) Bill (2007); and the Judiciary and Courts (Scotland) Bill itself. For discussion, see the Annotations referred to at para 12.4, n 1 above.
7   The JAB also makes recommendations for shrieval office – see below.
8   JC(S)A 2008, sch 2.
9   JC(S)A 2008, ss 15–16.
10 CR(S)A 2014, s 120.
11 See eg the evidence of JAB members to the Parliament's Justice Committee – SPJCOR 5 May 2009.
12 Law Reform (Miscellaneous Provisions) (Scotland) Act 1990 as amended.
13 JC(S)A 2008, s 10. It will also include the new tier of 'summary sheriffs' to be created under CR(S)A 2014.
14 Previously SCSA 1971, s 5(1), to be replaced, when in force, by CR(S)A 2014, s 14.
15 JC(S)A 2008, ss 19–20 and sch 3. A similar panel was convened prior to the appointment of Lord Hamilton as Lord President in 2005.
16 Both reports are available on the Board's website: www.judicialappointmentsscotland.org.uk. On the issue of diversity see para 12.17 below.

Safeguarding independent adjudication

12.6   These recent developments apart, there has been little about the process of *appointing* judges that has been designed to guarantee their 'independence'. Much more attention, however, has been paid to rules, whether or not strictly rules of law, which are intended to protect judges from inappropriate pressures while carrying out their functions. Some operate as restrictions on the behaviour of others; some on their own behaviour. Some are aimed at the conduct of individual cases; some at a judge's position in general. In many instances, the purpose of the protective rules does not differ greatly from that of the rules designed to protect the independence of many other officials or employees. It is, for instance, usually considered appropriate that university teachers should be able to perform their functions of research, teaching and examining without the sort of influences which might affect the independence of their research or cause them to be unfair in their examining decisions. Security of tenure may be considered important but so too are codes of behaviour, whether externally or self-imposed. A degree of accountability both to students and to a wider public is important and most would agree that a teacher who is too incapacitated, by illness or otherwise, should not continue in office. Although some of the rules concerning judges are more formalised, the comparison with such other positions is easily made. In the case of judges, as with others, there is a substantial reliance upon their behaviour and the behaviour of others being regulated without the need for legal intervention at all. In almost all cases, there is room for reasonable disagreement as to whether the lines which mark the limits of acceptable behaviour have been drawn at the right place.

Security of tenure

12.7   There is a cluster of rules and practices, which may be described as 'constitutional' in the broadest sense, which are designed to protect a judge's independence while in office. Traditionally most prominent among these has been the assurance of security of tenure. There is no more inappropriate influence than the threat of loss of office and it has been considered important, since the Claim of Right 1689, that the tenure of Court of Session judges has been *ad vitam aut culpam*: for life or until fault[1]. Since 1959 that position has been qualified by provisions for compulsory retiral at age 70, but extendable to 75[2].

REMOVAL OF COURT OF SESSION JUDGES Important provisions concerning the dismissal of Court of Session judges are contained in SA 1998. As noted above, this Act amended appointment procedures to adapt to the introduction of devolved government. For dismissals, rather more was required because, in contrast with the position in other parts of the United Kingdom, formal procedures for dismissal had never been laid down[3]. It was presumed that dismissal would have been by the Crown on the advice of ministers and *culpa* would have had to be established. But there was not, for instance, the protective mechanism originally provided by the Act of Settlement 1700 and latterly by the Senior Courts Act 1981, that a judge in England and Wales or Northern Ireland cannot be dismissed without an address presented to the Crown by both Houses of Parliament[4].

SA 1998 now requires that a judge may be removed from office only by the Queen, on the recommendation of the First Minister, and such a recommendation may be made only if the Scottish Parliament, on a motion by the First Minister, resolves that such a recommendation should be made[5]. If the motion is in respect of the Lord President or the Lord Justice Clerk, the First Minister must first have consulted the Prime Minister[6]. A motion to dismiss a judge may be made only if the First Minister has received a written report from an independent tribunal appointed under SA 1998 which concludes that 'the person in question is unfit for office by reason of inability, neglect of duty or misbehaviour' and gives reasons for that conclusion[7]. 'Neglect of duty' and 'misbehaviour' continue the old test of *culpa* but it will be noticed that dismissal for 'inability' – presumably on the grounds of severe illness or other incapacity – is added[8].

As to the constitution and operation of the tribunal itself, some rules are laid down by SA 1998[9] but others are provided by ch 5 of JC(S)A 2008. A tribunal must be established by the First Minister when he or she is requested by the Lord President to do so and may be formed in such other circumstances as the First Minister thinks fit. The tribunal must be chaired by a member of the JCPC. The second member must be another senior judge; the third is someone qualified as an advocate or solicitor for at least ten years; the fourth must be a person who is not, and never has been, legally qualified. Provision is made for the suspension from office of a judge who is subject to investigation by the tribunal.

This quite detailed statutory procedure to be followed before the removal of a Court of Session judge can be effected may be viewed as a safeguard of judicial independence and a necessary protection for the judiciary against arbitrary removal. It also sends an important message about the accountability of the judiciary to Parliament and to the public at large.

REMOVAL OF SHERIFFS The existing machinery for terminating the appointment of a sheriff provided by SC(S)A 1971 will be replaced by an almost identical process set out in CR(S)A 2014. CR(S)A 2014, s 25 provides that a sheriff, summary sheriff or sheriff principal may be removed from office by the First Minister by order, subject to annulment by the Scottish Parliament. The Scottish Ministers may, however, act only in response to a report in writing following investigation by a tribunal similar to that required for a Court of Session judge, save that the second judicial member must be a sheriff principal or sheriff. A report justifying dismissal must be to the effect that the sheriff is unfit for office by reason of inability, neglect of duty or misbehaviour.

Two sheriffs were removed under an earlier procedure which involved investigation by the Lord President and the Lord Justice Clerk and an order by the Secretary of State. The first was Sheriff Peter Thomson in 1977 for associating himself with a Scottish Plebiscite campaign. In 1992 Sheriff Ewen Stewart was dismissed on grounds of inability based on a report focusing on his behaviour in court. He had, for instance, constantly interrupted proceedings and this indicated an underlying defect of character which had continued despite prior warnings. Sheriff Stewart's petition for judicial review of the Secretary of State's order[10] on the grounds that he was not subject to an 'inability' in the narrow sense of physical or mental infirmity and that his investigation had not been in accordance with the rules of natural justice was rejected in the Court of Session[11] and in the House of Lords[12].

TEMPORARY SHERIFFS AND SECURITY OF TENURE The unfortunate circumstances which have led to the use of the powers to dismiss sheriffs are likely to remain rare occurrences and the provisions made by SA 1998 for the dismissal of Court of Session judges are likely to be even more rarely invoked. In both cases they preserve security of tenure – which itself safeguards the judiciary against the threat of loss of office – in all but the most extreme conditions. The safeguard of security of tenure *ad vitam aut culpam* was not extended, however, to the temporary sheriffs who were introduced in 1971 and were, until 1999, widely used in the Scottish courts. Under SC(S)A 1971 the Secretary of State could appoint temporary sheriffs in circumstances where a sheriff was ill or otherwise unable to perform his duties; when there was a vacancy; or when, for any other reason, it appeared expedient to do so to avoid unnecessary delays[13]. Although not much used in its early years, this apparently restricted power came to be relied on to provide extensive support for the permanent sheriffs. By 1985 there were 88 permanent sheriffs and 61 temporary sheriffs and by 1999 the corresponding numbers were 110 and 129 respectively. The proportion of work, in terms of total sheriff court days, carried out by temporary sheriffs was nearly 25 per cent[14]. SC(S)A 1971 provided that the appointment of a temporary sheriff would subsist 'until recalled by the Secretary of State',[15] although in practice the Secretary of State developed a policy whereby temporary sheriffs were appointed for a fixed, but renewable, one-year term[16].

The use of temporary sheriffs came under challenge from two directions. The principal challenge arose in *Starrs v Ruxton*[17] in which the Appeal Court of the High Court of Justiciary was asked to consider whether the relative lack of security of tenure enjoyed by temporary sheriffs gave rise to difficulties under art 6 ECHR. Specifically, the court was invited to rule on whether the Lord Advocate – in pursuing the prosecution of the two accused before a temporary sheriff – was acting in a manner which was incompatible with the rights of the accused to trial before an 'independent and impartial tribunal'[18]. While the court focused on the question of a temporary sheriff's security of tenure it was, nevertheless, presented with a good deal of information about the practical operation of the appointment of temporary sheriffs, a process in which the Lord Advocate's leading role was obvious despite the formal allocation of the statutory powers to the Secretary of State and, from 1 July 1999, the Scottish Ministers[19]. The most prominent feature of the system that had operated in the preceding years was that virtually all temporary sheriffs were appointed for a period of a calendar year. In holding that, for the purposes of the Convention, a temporary sheriff was not an independent and impartial tribunal, the court made clear that it was not objectionable that temporary sheriffs were, like their permanent counterparts and Court of Session judges, appointed by the Executive but that their tenure was too precarious to satisfy the requirements of art 6(1) ECHR. The provision in SC(S)A 1971 that a temporary sheriff's appointment subsisted only 'until recalled by the Secretary of State'[20] conferred a power of recall which appeared 'to be exercisable at pleasure'[21] and 'the use of the one year term suggests a reservation of control ... [which] reinforces the impression that the tenure of office by the individual temporary sheriff is at the discretion of the Lord Advocate'[22]. It should be repeated that the fact that temporary sheriffs were, like other members of the judiciary, appointed by the Executive and, in particular, effectively on the nomination of the head of the prosecution system, was not relied on by the court, although these issues had been raised in argument[23]. Lord Reed accepted that issues of perception in this area were important. There was a risk, in any situation where judges were appointed by the Executive, that they might be perceived as having attained their position as a result of the Executive's favour, and therefore as being obligated to the Executive. But perceptions, he said, 'are of course relevant only if they have some objective justification, rather than being the product of mere cynicism'[24].

The impact of the decision in *Starrs v Ruxton* was immediate. The use of temporary sheriffs was ended with the Deputy First Minister confirming to the Scottish Parliament just a few hours after the decision that he had 'asked the Justice Department to suspend the availability of temporary sheriffs for new civil or criminal business'[25]. Additional permanent sheriffs were rapidly recruited. The decision also raised doubts about appointments to district courts and practice was changed there too. In a second challenge concerning temporary sheriffs, an issue was raised not as to their impartiality but as to whether the widespread use of temporary sheriffs already noted in *Starrs* went so far beyond the scope anticipated and permitted by SC(S)A 1971 as to be an abuse of the powers of appointment and therefore *ultra vires*. If such a challenge had been upheld, the consequences for the validity of judgments over many years – much longer than the period since the 'incorporation' of the ECHR in May 1999 – might have been considerable. In *Gibbs v Ruxton*[26], however, the Appeal Court held that the power to appoint temporary sheriffs was not one which was confined to situations of illness, vacancy of office or short-term emergencies but could be used to provide a long-term and large pool of temporary sheriffs for deployment as needs arose. Their Lordships reserved their opinion on whether, had they found the appointment of a temporary sheriff to have been *ultra vires*, the consequence would have been that the acts and decisions of those temporary sheriffs would be held to be invalid.

Related doubts extended to the appointment of temporary judges in the Court of Session and the High Court but in *Clancy v Caird*[27] it was held by an Extra Division, on report from a case conducted by T G Coutts QC, sitting as a temporary judge, that temporary judges appointed for three-year terms[28] were to be regarded as sufficiently independent and impartial for the purposes of art 6 ECHR[29]. Then in *Kearney v HM Advocate*[30] the Judicial Committee of the Privy Council held that there could be no grounds for challenge to the conduct of a criminal trial by a temporary judge. The case provided the opportunity for Lord Hope of Craighead to conduct a substantial review of both the history and modern practice of the appointment of temporary judges, including his own involvement as Lord President (paras 10–54).

The provisions of CR(S)A 2014 which allow for appointment of a temporary sheriff principal and for, as a transitional measure, appointment of Senators of the Court of Justice as Appeal Sheriffs do not raise the same concerns as the holders of each of those appointments will, in any event, be a permanent holder of judicial office.

1　*Mackay and Esslemont v Lord Advocate* 1937 SC 860.
2　See the Judicial Pensions Act 1959, the Judicial Pensions Act 1981, and the Judicial Pensions and Retirement Act 1993, s 26(7) and Sch 5. For a discussion, see W Finnie 'Judicial Tenure and Judicial Pensions' 1993 SLT (News) 213. In 2012 the ECJ declared Hungary to be in breach of its obligations under the Equal Treatment Directive (Council Directive 2000/78) in passing new legislation reducing the compulsory retirement age of judges, prosecutors and notaries from 70 to 62. Hungary's aim of establishing a more balanced age structure to encourage access for young lawyers to the professions of judge, prosecutor and notary could be legitimate but the measure was disproportionate given the 'abrupt' and 'significant' impact on the individuals concerned: *European Commission v Hungary* [2013] 1 CMLR 44.
3　See C M G Himsworth 'Securing the tenure of Scottish Judges: A somewhat academic exercise?' [1999] PL 14.
4　Act of Settlement 1700, s 3 and Senior Courts Act 1981, s 11(3).
5　SA 1998, s 95(6), (7).
6　SA 1998, s 95(10)(b).
7　SA 1998, s 95(10)(a).
8　For the English rule on permanent infirmity, see Senior Courts Act 1981, s 11.
9　SA 1998, s 95(8), (9).
10　Until 1999 and devolution, removal orders were made by the Secretary of State, subject to annulment by resolution of either House at Westminster.
11　*Stewart v Secretary of State for Scotland* 1996 SC 271.
12　*Stewart v Secretary of State for Scotland* 1998 SC (HL) 81.
13　SC(S)A 1971, s 11(2).
14　These figures were supplied to the court by the Solicitor General in *Starrs v Ruxton* 2000 JC 208 at 216–217.
15　SC(S)A 1971, s 11(4).
16　In *Starrs v Ruxton* 2000 JC 208, it was suggested that, as there was nothing in SC(S)A 1971, s 11 to empower the Lord Advocate to impose any term or condition on the appointment of a temporary sheriff, the adoption of such a policy may raise questions of vires (at 227–228 per Lord Justice General Rodger). That specific point was not argued before the court and their Lordships reserved their opinion on it.
17　*Starrs v Ruxton* 2000 JC 208.
18　The accused were in fact, and as one would expect in the sheriff court, prosecuted at the instance of the local procurator fiscal but in the course of the proceedings in the High Court it was accepted on behalf of the Lord Advocate that in both solemn and summary proceedings he is represented by the procurator fiscal. That the challenge was taken against the prosecutor at all – rather than against the temporary sheriff concerned – was a consequence of the rather disjointed way in which the ECHR was given effect in Scotland. HRA 1998 – in terms of which a court is a public authority and is bound itself to act in a manner which is compatible with Convention rights – came into force throughout the United Kingdom on 2 October 2000. However, as a member of the Scottish Executive, the Lord Advocate had been required (by virtue of SA 1998, s 57) to act compatibly with the Convention rights with effect from 20 May 1999 (SI 1998/3178). Characterising the challenge in *Starrs v Ruxton* 2000 JC 208 (which was taken in July 1999) as a challenge to the Lord Advocate as a means of addressing the position of temporary sheriffs was a tactic employed by a defence team keen to employ Convention rights arguments as soon as possible.
19　An interesting side-issue was explored briefly by Lord Reed when he questioned (*Starrs v Ruxton* 2000 JC 208 at 251) whether the transfer of authority to the Scottish Ministers had been effective. If the powers exercisable under SC(S)A 1971, s 11 were held to be incompatible with the Convention rights they could not be within 'devolved competence'; could not be transferred to the Scottish Ministers; and had, therefore, been retained by the Secretary of State.
20　SC(S)A 1971, s 11(4).
21　*Starrs v Ruxton* 2000 JC 208 at 226.
22　*Starrs v Ruxton* 2000 JC 208 at 228.
23　*Starrs v Ruxton* 2000 JC 208 at 241.
24　*Starrs v Ruxton* 2000 JC 208 at 241.
25　SP OR 11 November 1999, col 574.
26　*Gibbs v Ruxton* 2000 JC 258.
27　*Clancy v Caird* 2000 SC 441. See also, approving *Starrs v Ruxton* 2000 JC 208, *Millar v Dickson* 2002 SC (PC) 30.

28 Under the Law Reform (Miscellaneous Provisions) (Scotland) 1990, s 35(3).
29 As a preliminary issue the court had also held that the case raised a 'devolution issue' (see para 14.19 below) because the Scottish Executive's provision of judicial resources amounted to an 'act' for the purposes of SA 1998, s 57(2) (Lord Penrose at 473).
30 2006 SC (PC) 1.

Judicial Incapacity

12.8   Quite distinct from questions of dismissal, JCSA 2008 provides for the circumstances in which the office of Lord President is vacant or the Lord President is incapacitated or suspended[1]. His or her functions become exercisable by the Lord Justice Clerk. Similar provision is made for the Lord Justice Clerk to be replaced, in the same circumstances, by the senior Inner House judge.

1 JC(S)A 2008, Part 2, Ch 2. These provisions replace the Senior Judiciary (Vacancies and Incapacity) (Scotland) Act 2006 which was passed hurriedly in case of the need to respond to the Lord President's absence through illness.

Judicial Conduct

12.9   Until recently the Scottish legal system lacked any formal rules applicable in cases of judicial misconduct short of behaviour which might warrant dismissal. Normal procedures for the appeal or review of decisions in individual cases might provide a remedy in some circumstances. And doubtless informal interventions by senior judges or even the Lord Advocate were other possibilities. But it is a sensitive area. Important questions of the individual and institutional autonomy of judges are at stake. There is a tension between autonomy and accountability.

The passing of JC(S)A 2008, however, and, in particular, its formal designation of the Lord President as the Head of the Scottish Judiciary brought an opportunity to introduce a new approach (ss 28–34). The Lord President may make rules (to be published) for the investigation and determination of matters concerning the 'conduct' (a term not defined in the Act) of judges (including sheriffs)[1]. Following any such investigation, the Lord President may give the judge formal advice, a formal warning or a reprimand[2]. Somewhat controversially, these processes are overseen by a Judicial Complaints Reviewer, appointed by the Scottish Ministers with the consent of the Lord President[3]. Another conduct-related provision added by JC(S)A 2008 gives the Lord President (or, if unavailable, the Lord Justice Clerk or other senior judge) the power to suspend a judicial office holder (judge or sheriff) if he considers that it is 'necessary for the purpose of maintaining public confidence in the judiciary' (s 34).

1 JC(S)A 2008, s 28 and see the Complaints about the Judiciary (Scotland) Rules 2013.
2 In April 2009 the Lord Justice General publicly criticised a temporary judge who had summarily jailed a rape witness.
3 The first appointee as Judicial Complaints Reviewer was Ms Moi Ali who stood down in August 2014 and who had voiced concerns about the relatively narrow scope of her powers and the inadequacy of the resources allocated to her (an annual budget of £2000). She was replaced by Ms Gillian Thompson on 1 September 2014: www.judicialcomplaintsreviewer.org.uk. See also J Harrison 'Judging the judges: the new scheme of judicial conduct and discipline in Scotland' (2009) 13 Edin LR 427.

Judicial salaries

12.10   Historically, at least, an important further condition of judicial quality and independence has been the assurance of substantial salaries for judges and their protection from the need for annual parliamentary debate and approval. The *Latimer House Guidelines* emphasise the importance of protection of judicial funding from political interference: 'funds, once voted for the judiciary by the legislature, should be protected from alienation or misuse. The allocation or withholding of funding should not be used as a means of exercising improper control over the judiciary.'[1]

The determination of the salaries of judges of the Court of Session, sheriffs and sheriffs principal is a reserved matter under SA 1998[2] and is made formally by the Treasury[3] but on the recommendation of the Senior Salaries Review Body[4]. CR(S)A 2014 creates the office of summary sheriff and in so doing appears to escape the terms of the relevant reservation: s 16(3) of CR(S)A 2014 provides that summary sheriffs shall be paid such remuneration as the Scottish Ministers determine[5].

It has been considered appropriate that the funding of judicial salaries should not be the subject of parliamentary (and, therefore, potentially party political) debate. At Westminster this meant ensuring that judges should be paid out of the Consolidated Fund without the need for specific appropriation[5]. The same mechanism has been extended to apply in the Scottish Parliament[6] albeit by virtue of CR(S)A 2014 the salaries of judges and sheriffs (and a number of other judicial office holders) will be paid by the new Scottish Courts and Tribunals Service and then charged to the Scottish Consolidated Fund. While the provision of substantial salaries should ensure that the judiciary are less vulnerable to corruption than they otherwise might be, it remains a criminal offence to attempt to bribe a judge and, of course, an offence to accept such a bribe[7].

Judges have not however been entirely immune from the effects of constraints on public sector budgets, there having recently been a degree of conflict between the senior English judiciary and the Lord Chancellor over changes to judicial pensions arrangements[8].

1 *Guidelines* I, 2.
2 SA 1998, Sch 5, Pt II, S L1.
3 Administration of Justice Act 1973, s 9. For the sheriff court, see Sheriff Courts (Scotland) Act 1907, s 14, which is repealed and replaced by s 16 of the CR(S)A 2014 when CR(S)A 2014 comes into force.
4 See Review Body on Senior Salaries 36th Report 2014, Cm 8822.
5 Section 16 of the CR(S)A 2014 also empowers the Scottish Ministers to set the salaries of part-time sheriffs and part-time summary sheriffs, again apparently avoiding the relevant reservation.
5 For the Consolidated Fund and Scottish Consolidated Fund see ch 11.
6 See SA 1998, s 119(3), Sch 4, para 5(a) and Sch 8, para 9(b).
7 See G H Gordon *The Criminal Law of Scotland* (3rd edn, 2001) (hereafter Gordon) vol II, para 49.04. Bribery of a judge would also amount to an offence under the Bribery Act 2010.
8 See Review Body on Senior Salaries, 35th Report 2013, Cm 8569 and G Gee, 'What are Lord Chancellors for?' [2014] PL 11.

Liability of judges

12.11   The very considerable weight which is attached to providing judges with
security of tenure and with financial security is a recognition of the importance
of ensuring their independence from the executive. That independence should
enable the judiciary to decide even politically controversial matters without
fear of or favour from the government of the day. But judges, in order to
remain 'independent', must also be protected from the threat of reprisals from
those who are directly affected by their acts or decisions. It is a longstanding
principle of Scots law that a judge enjoys absolute immunity from civil liability
for anything done by him in the exercise of his judicial office[1], even if his
actions would otherwise give rise to a claim for damages for, for example,
defamation or wrongful imprisonment[2].

This common law principle has been supplemented in relation to damages for
infringement of Convention rights under HRA 1998 with a distinction being
made between damages for judicial acts done in good faith and those which
are not[3].

1 See *Haggart's Trs v Lord President Hope* (1824) 2 Sh App 125.
2 There appears to be just one statutory exception to this general rule: the Criminal Procedure
   (Scotland) Act 1995, s 170(1) provides for damages to be payable to any person who has
   been wrongfully imprisoned by a justice of the peace (or stipendiary magistrate) in summary
   proceedings and it is proved that the justice or magistrate acted maliciously and without
   probable cause. The immunity of sheriffs was questioned by temporary judge T G Coutts QC
   in *Russell v Dickson* 1997 SC 269: 'It does ... seem to be inequitable by today's standards that
   a man can spend five days in prison unreasonably and improperly without compensation from
   some quarter being awarded to him' (at 278).
3 HRA 1998, ss 8, 9. In the case of judicial acts done in good faith damages are only available in
   cases involving a breach of art 5(5) ECHR (unlawful arrest or detention).

Public criticism of judges

12.12   In addition to being protected from civil liability for the decisions
which they make, judges are also protected to a limited extent by the
criminal law from undue public criticism of themselves and their decisions.
It is a common law crime to slander or 'murmur' a judge[1] (although the last
successful prosecution for such an offence was more than a century ago[2]) and
criticism of a judge or of a court may amount to contempt of court. This is
undoubtedly a difficult area: it is not easy to assess precisely what might today
amount to murmuring[3], particularly when the need to protect the judiciary from
criticism must be balanced against the rights of individuals and of the media to
comment upon the justice system. The prosecution of a genuine offence should
not 'degenerate into an oppressive or vindictive abuse of the Court's powers'[4]
and this is also an area in which the ECHR is of some relevance. The European
Court of Human Rights (ECtHR) 'has repeatedly emphasised the importance
of freedom of expression for democracy'[5] and will scrutinise domestic laws
which prevent or simply discourage criticism of the state and those who
represent it. While the Court has, understandably, focused on the freedom to
criticise politicians it has also been willing to assess the compatibility with art
10 ECHR (freedom of expression) of penalties imposed on those who publicly

question or disparage the judiciary[6]. A special instance of this arises in relation to the law of contempt whose purpose is the maintenance of the authority and impartiality of the judiciary and the prevention of wilful challenge or affront to the authority of the court[7].

By convention, members of the Westminster Parliament, and to a greater extent UK ministers, sought to avoid public criticism of the judiciary and the decisions made in individual cases and this is reflected in parliamentary practice[8]. Notwithstanding that convention, criticisms have been made from time to time. Those criticisms have in recent years, both at Westminster and at Holyrood, tended to focus on the outcome of cases involving human rights issues in areas such as criminal justice, immigration and terrorism and have been directed at courts as a whole rather than individual judges[9]. And it would appear that, following devolution, members of the Scottish Government and Scottish Parliament have been somewhat less restrained than their UK counterparts. While the First Minister rather mildly remarked that a decision of Sheriff Gimblett concerning the legality of the UK's Trident programme had come as 'a surprise', more robust Scottish parliamentary criticism of judges has addressed such matters as the interpretation by a High Court judge of the Scots law of rape[10] and the approach of the Inner House to questions of the validity of Skye Bridge tolls[11]. There was particularly virulent and public debate in September 2007 arising out of the abrupt ending by Lord Clarke of the murder trial in the infamous 'World's End' case. Public criticism of the Crown Office brought a defence from the Lord Advocate which, in turn, was interpreted as a criticism of Lord Clarke. A letter from the Lord President expressed concerns about the need for judicial independence to be protected – attracting, in turn, a response from the First Minister at question time in the Scottish Parliament[12].

1 See *SME Reissue* Constitutional Law para 603 and Gordon vol II, para 50.03.
2 *HM Advocate v Robertson* (1870) 42 SJ 336.
3 In *HM Advocate v Robertson* (1870) 42 SJ 336, the offence was committed by the sending of letters to the Lord Chancellor and the Home Secretary complaining of the official and personal conduct of a sheriff including allegations to the effect that the sheriff involved had misused his official powers and had engaged, amongst other things, in following Mr Robertson home and trying to pick a fight with him.
4 Gordon vol II, para 50.03.
5 J McBride 'Judges, Politicians and the Limits to Critical Comment' (1998) 23 EL Rev (HRS) 76.
6 See *Anwar* 2008 JC 409.
7 *De Haes v Belgium* (1998) 25 EHRR 1.
8 *Erskine May's Parliamentary Practice* (24th edn, 2011), pp 396 and 443–444.
9 See para 12.3, n 3 for recent criticism of the Supreme Court by the Scottish Government and which did, unusually, involve criticism of Lord Hope personally. In an article in a Sunday newspaper in February 2013 Home Secretary Theresa May accused judges of ignoring the wishes of Parliament in failing (on Convention rights grounds) to order the deportation of non-nationals who had been convicted of criminal offences.
10 During a debate on the matter Dr Winnie Ewing MSP declared that she was 'happy to murmur Lord Abernethy in this particular matter' and that she had no doubt that 'Lord Abernethy has made a fool of himself' (SP OR 25 April 2002 col 73). Lord Abernethy's ruling was reviewed, and the law on this matter restated, by an Appeal Court bench of seven: *Lord Advocate's Reference (No 1 of 2001)* 2002 SLT 466.
11 See the proceedings of the Public Petitions Committee of the Scottish Parliament (SP OR 5 February 2002, col 1559 ff).
12 SPOR 27 Sept 2007, col 2227. The accused was retried following the enactment of the Double Jeopardy (Scotland) Act 2011: see para 12.16 below.

JUDICIAL IMPARTIALITY

Introduction

12.13   The issues raised in *Starrs v Ruxton* and the other cases discussed above concerning the ways in which the circumstances of a judge's appointment and tenure of office may be treated as detracting from his or her independence form part of a wider concern about the maintenance of judicial impartiality. It has been reaffirmed at the highest level that: 'One of the cornerstones of our legal system is the impartiality of the tribunals by which justice is administered.'[1]. This principle manifests itself in the common law rules of natural justice, and in particular the 'rule against bias'[2], and has been added to by the requirements of art 6 ECHR. Where this principle is infringed by a judge then his or her decision may be challenged[3] and, ultimately, overturned.

1 *R v Bow Street Metropolitan Stipendiary Magistrate, ex parte Pinochet Ugarte (No 2)* [2000] 1 AC 119 at 140 per Lord Hope of Craighead.
2 There is a very substantial body of case law and scholarship about the content and application of the rules of natural justice which cannot be treated fully here. See further at paras 14.9 below.
3 By way of appeal or judicial review (as to which, see ch 14).

The rule against bias

12.14   The rule against bias requires, as a fundamental principle, that a person may not be a judge in his or her own cause. If such a clash of interest arises, a judge[1] is disqualified from sitting and the judge should disclose the conflicting interest and, unless all parties waive any objections, they might have, withdraw ('recuse' himself or herself) from the case[2]. If there is no such disclosure, the decision in the case cannot stand. The application of the principle that a person should not be a judge in his or her own cause is not at all confined to those situations where a judge is actually biased and wrongly brings improper considerations to bear when hearing or deciding the particular case before him or her. Such behaviour would plainly be unlawful. The significance of the principle is in its extension to include circumstances where there is an *appearance* of bias. The use of the language of 'appearance' or 'perception' is not unproblematic[3] but it has usually been the practice of the courts to identify two main forms of *apparent bias*. As explained by Lord Browne-Wilkinson in *ex parte Pinochet Ugarte (No 2)*[4], the principle may be applied literally – where the judge is in fact a party to the litigation or has a financial or proprietary interest in its outcome. In this case, the mere fact that the judge is involved in one of these ways is sufficient to cause *automatic* disqualification. The second application of the principle is where the circumstances – for example the judge's conduct or behaviour or, for instance, friendship with one of the parties – may give rise to a suspicion that the judge is not impartial. In these cases there is no automatic disqualification. Instead an assessment has to be made – either by the individual judge when the case comes before him or by an appeal court after the event – as to whether the circumstances are sufficiently serious to warrant the judge's disqualification. The formulation of the test to be applied by the courts in making that assessment has been the subject of recent cases which are discussed below.

1 Or, indeed, in arbitrations an arbiter/arbitrator (cf *Sellar v Highland Rly Co* 1919 SC (HL) 19).
2 *R v Bow Street Metropolitan Stipendiary Magistrate, ex parte Pinochet Ugarte (No 2)* [2000] 1 AC 119 at 140.
3 See also *Starrs v Ruxton* 2000 JC 208.
4 *R v Bow Street Metropolitan Stipendiary Magistrate, ex parte Pinochet Ugarte (No 2)* [2000] 1 AC 119 at 143.

Automatic disqualification

12.15 Historically, cases of 'automatic' disqualification have arisen where the judge has had a direct financial interest in the case: the classic, oft-cited, example being where the judge was found to be a shareholder in a company which was one of the parties to the case[1]. Where such an interest was present it was irrelevant how small the interest actually was[2]. The concept of 'automatic disqualification' was further developed in *Pinochet*, a case itself famous as that in which the House of Lords set aside an earlier decision of the House itself on the grounds that one of the judges in the case, Lord Hoffmann, had a disqualifying interest by virtue of his undisclosed links with Amnesty International, an organisation which had intervened in the proceedings[3]. It was held that these links with Amnesty International brought Lord Hoffmann within the first head of disqualification. The Lords were clear that he could not be regarded as a party to the proceedings[4], nor could he be said to have had a financial or proprietary interest in the outcome – but then, in the peculiar circumstances of these criminal proceedings to determine the susceptibility to extradition of General Pinochet, nor did Amnesty International[5]. Through his involvement in the organisation, however, Lord Hoffmann shared its interest in the promotion of its cause[6]. That was sufficient to establish the circumstances of automatic disqualification[7].

1 *Dimes v Grand Junction Canal Proprietors* (1852) 3 HL Cas 759. The judge involved was the Lord Chancellor. See also *Sellar v Highland Rly Co* 1919 SC (HL) 19.
2 *Wildridge v Anderson* (1897) 25 R (J) 27.
3 Lord Hoffmann was not a member of Amnesty International itself but was an unpaid director and chairman of an associated charity. For a detailed comment on the case, see T H Jones *'Judicial bias and disqualification in the Pinochet case'* [1999] PL 391.
4 *R v Bow Street Metropolitan Stipendiary Magistrate, ex parte Pinochet Ugarte (No 2)* [2000] 1 AC 119 at 134.
5 *R v Bow Street Metropolitan Stipendiary Magistrate, ex parte Pinochet Ugarte (No 2)* [2000] 1 AC 119 at 134.
6 *R v Bow Street Metropolitan Stipendiary Magistrate, ex parte Pinochet Ugarte (No 2)* [2000] 1 AC 119 at 135.
7 The extension of the long-standing principle in *Dimes v Grand Junction Canal Proprietors* (1852) 3 HL Cas 759, to include the 'promotion of a cause' interest in *ex parte Pinochet (No 2)* was later considered in *Locabail (UK) Ltd v Bayfield Properties Ltd* [2000] QB 451 discussed below.

Disqualification on other grounds

12.16 Because *ex parte Pinochet (No 2)* was decided on the basis of automatic disqualification, the House of Lords was not required to examine closely the other category of disqualification beyond noting that it was, for the English courts, based on the test laid down in *R v Gough*[1]: 'is there in the view of the court a *real danger* that the judge was biased?'. There was, however, an acknowledgment that a review of that decision might be needed in the light of the reopening of a gap between the 'real danger' test in *Gough* and, on the other hand, decisions in other jurisdictions where the question was 'whether the events in question give rise to *a reasonable apprehension or suspicion* on the part of a fair-minded and informed member of the public that the judge was not impartial'[2]. Lord Hope, in particular, explained that, in Scotland, the courts had applied the 'reasonable suspicion' test[3] but he also observed that, although the tests were described differently, their application by appellate courts was likely in practice to lead to results which were so similar as to be indistinguishable. They were founded on the same broad principle. The judge must be seen to be impartial[4].

Whichever test is adopted, there will obviously be some uncertainty as to how it is to be applied in the circumstances of particular cases and this was an issue addressed in an important decision in the English Court of Appeal intended to provide guidance for other courts and tribunals. In *Locabail (UK) Ltd v Bayfield Properties Ltd*[5] the court started with the requirement of art 6 ECHR; moved on to the 'automatic disqualification' test of *Dimes* and *Pinochet*; but then acknowledged the much greater importance in practice of the 'real danger' test in *Gough*. Surveying the authorities, the court concluded:

'It would be dangerous and futile to attempt to define or list the factors which may or may not give rise to a real danger of bias. Everything will depend on the facts, which may include the nature of the issue to be decided. We cannot, however, conceive of circumstances in which an objection could be soundly based on the religion, ethnic or national origin, gender, age, class, means or sexual orientation of the judge. Nor, at any rate ordinarily, could an objection be soundly based on the judge's social or educational or service or employment background or history, nor that of any member of the judge's family; or previous political associations; or membership of social or sporting or charitable bodies; or Masonic associations; or previous judicial decisions; or extra-curricular utterances (whether in textbooks, lectures, speeches, articles, interviews, reports or responses to consultation papers); or previous receipt of instructions to act for or against any party, solicitor or advocate engaged in a case before him; or membership of the same Inn, circuit, local Law Society or chambers (see *KFTCIC v Icori Estero SpA* (Court of Appeal of Paris, 28 June 1991, International Arbitration Report, vol 6, 8/91)). By contrast, a real danger of bias might well be thought to arise if there were personal friendship or animosity between the judge and any member of the public involved in the case; or if the judge were closely acquainted with any member of the public involved in the case, particularly if the credibility of that individual could be significant in the decision of the case; or if, in a case where the credibility of any individual were an issue to be decided by the judge, he had in a previous case rejected the evidence of that person in such outspoken terms as to throw doubt on his ability to approach such person's evidence with an open mind on any later occasion; or if on any question at issue in the proceedings before him the judge had expressed views, particularly in the course of the hearing, in such extreme and unbalanced terms as to throw doubt on his ability to try the issue with an objective judicial mind (see *Vakauta v Kelly* (1989) 167 CLR 568); or if, for any other reason, there were real ground for doubting the ability of the judge to ignore extraneous considerations, prejudices and predilections and bring on an objective judgment to bear on the issues before him. The mere fact that a judge, earlier in the same case or in a previous case, had commented adversely on a party or witness, or found the evidence of a party or witness to be unreliable, would not without more found a sustainable objection. In most cases, we think, the answer, one way or the other, will be obvious. But if in any case there is real ground for doubt, that doubt should be resolved in favour of recusal. We repeat; every application must be decided on the facts and circumstances of the individual case. The greater the passage of time between the event relied on as showing a danger of bias and the case in which the objection is raised, the weaker (other things being equal) the objection will be.'[6]

This statement concerning the factual circumstances which may or may not lead to a judge's disqualification for apparent bias appears to be comprehensive. It does not, however, eliminate all difficulty. For one thing, it does not make any clear distinction – in terms of their relative significance – between the various factors listed as potentially relevant or irrelevant to disqualification. Are we to take it that the judge's own Masonic associations are to be weighed equally with his brother's previous employment background? Another difficulty is that the lists of the irrelevant factors suggested by the court are qualified in an important way: they apply only 'ordinarily' and this, of course, leaves open the possibility that such factors will be important in an 'extraordinary' case. Very little guidance is given to assist in identifying such a case.

What *Locabail* demonstrates, however, is the desire to see questions of bias move away from 'subjective' personal and private attributes of the judge's character, his or her opinions and his or her family and social connections to issues more directly relevant to how he or she has behaved while fulfilling his or her judicial role. Nevertheless, the bottom line is that every case will turn very much on its own facts. So, for example, in Scotland a sheriff was disqualified where he made, at a social occasion, disparaging remarks about striking miners and afterwards did not recuse himself from hearing cases involving such miners[7]. While *Locabail* suggests that a judge's 'extracurricular utterances' will not normally give rise to apparent bias, it was held that Lord McCluskey's published remarks about the ECHR 'would create in the mind of an informed observer an apprehension of bias on the part of Lord McCluskey against the Convention and against the rights deriving from it'[8]. And in an interesting series of cases the Inner House held that, where it was suggested that a judge's membership of a private society gave rise to apparent bias, it was appropriate for such a judge to recuse himself from deciding whether it did give rise to such bias[9]. Ultimately, however, it was held that no such bias had been established[10].

The decision in *Locabail* focused on this lengthy narration of the factors which may or may not give rise to a 'real danger' of bias (subject, of course, to the proviso that 'everything will depend on the facts'). It did not revise the wording of the test itself. In *Porter v Magill*[11] the House of Lords (and, in particular,

Lord Hope of Craighead) revisited that question. The difference between the English 'real danger' test and the 'reasonable apprehension' test applied in Scotland and beyond had been commented upon in *ex parte Pinochet Ugarte No 2* and Lord Hope noted that the latter test placed more emphasis on the perceptions of the reasonable member of the public looking at all the facts of the case than on those of the reviewing court. Drawing on the decision of the Court of Appeal in *In re Medicaments and Related Classes of Goods (No 2)*[12], he recommended the 'modest adjustment' of the *Gough* test which had been suggested there. In Lord Hope's view, to resolve any conflict between England, Scotland and the Commonwealth, the test of apparent bias should be restated as being 'whether the fair-minded and informed observer, having considered the facts, would conclude that there was a real possibility that the tribunal was biased'[13]. Whether this does, in fact, resolve the tensions between the 'real danger' and 'reasonable apprehension' tests remains to be seen[14]. In *Davidson v Scottish Ministers (No 2)*[15] the House of Lords held that where Lord Hardie had decided an issue on the basis of his interpretation of s 21 of the Crown Proceedings Act 1947, having earlier, as Lord Advocate, having expressed a view on the matter, there was, applying *Porter v Magill*, a risk of apparent bias. In *Helow v Home Secretary*[16] it was held that the Lord Ordinary's membership of the International Association of Jewish Lawyers (whose publication *Justice* included fervently pro-Israeli articles) should not disqualify her from hearing an asylum appeal brought by a Palestinian activist. The 'fair-minded observer' is someone who always reserves judgement until both sides of the argument are fully understood. She is not unduly sensitive or suspicious. She is not to be confused with the complainant but is someone with a measure of detachment[17]. Most recently, the Appeal Court of the High Court of Justiciary concluded that the Lord Justice Clerk should not recuse himself from the task of determining an application by the Crown under the Double Jeopardy (Scotland) Act 2011 to have an acquittal set aside and authority granted for a fresh prosecution 'upon the flimsy ground that he had, many years ago, presided over a trial at which a jury found the respondent guilty [of other offences of rape and murder] and, as a result, the Lord Justice Clerk had been required to pass sentence'[18].

1   *R v Gough* [1993] AC 646. For discussion of the emergence of the test, see *Locabail (UK) Ltd v Bayfield Properties Ltd* [2000] QB 451 at 475–476.
2   *R v Bow Street Magistrate, ex parte Pinochet Ugarte (No 2)* [2000] 1 AC 119 at 136, citing, as an example the Australian case *Webb v R* (1994) 181 CLR 41.
3   See *Bradford v McLeod* 1986 SLT 244; *Doherty v McGlennan* 1997 SLT 444.
4   *R v Bow Street Magistrate, ex parte Pinochet Ugarte (No 2)* [2000] 1 AC 119 at 142.
5   *Locabail (UK) Ltd v Bayfield Properties Ltd* [2000] QB 451.
6   *Locabail (UK) Ltd v Bayfield Properties Ltd* [2000] QB 451 at 480.
7   *Bradford v McLeod* 1986 SLT 244.
8   *Hoekstra v HM Advocate (No 2)* 2000 SLT 602.
9   *Robbie the Pict v HM Advocate* 2003 SCCR 99.
10 *Robbie the Pict, Petitioner* 2003 SCCR 299.
11 *Porter v Magill* [2002] 2 AC 357.
12 *In re Medicaments and Related Classes of Goods (No 2)* [2001] 1 WLR 700.
13 *Porter v Magill* [2002] 2 AC 357 at 494.
14 Some subsequent Scottish cases have referred both to the test in *Porter v Magill* [2002] 2 AC 357 and also to the test set out by Lord Hope in *Millar v Dickson* 2002 SC (PC) 30: 'grounds which would be sufficient to create in the mind of a reasonable man a doubt about the judge's impartiality' (at 54). See *Mellors, Petitioner* 2003 SLT 479 and *Robbie the Pict, Petitioner* 2003 SCCR 299.

15 [2005] 1 SC (HL) 7.
16 2009 SC (HL) 1.
17 Ibid. Lord Hope of Craighead, para 2. See also *Johnson v Johnson* (2000) 201 CLR 488; *Gillies v Secretary of State for Work and Pensions* 2006 SC (HL) 2.
18 *HMA v Sinclair* 2014 SLT 1087 at para 24.

A brief assessment

12.17   The law relating to automatic disqualification for apparent bias, and the formulation of the test for disqualification where the judge does not have a pecuniary interest and is not 'promoting a cause' in the sense which arose in *ex parte Pinochet Ugarte (No 2)* have been the subject of much scrutiny in recent years. Despite this, and despite the subtle reworkings of the tests to be applied, questions remain.

Is the dichotomy between the tests for automatic disqualification and the remaining grounds sustainable? There have been suggestions of a '*de minimis*' exception to automatic disqualification[1]; there is a blurring of the interest of the judge with that of a spouse, partner or family member[2]; and there must be an underlying doubt now about which interests in which entities should disqualify automatically. The circumstances of the *Pinochet* case – the extremely unusual position of Lord Hoffmann and his involvement in the promotion of the cause of Amnesty International and the court's desire to ensure that, in a case of such political sensitivity, it should be beyond reproach – may have extended the 'automatic' test too far. It might have been more difficult to have established a 'real danger' of bias on the part of Lord Hoffmann[3].

Separately, the ECtHR has thrown further light on the question of judicial impartiality, this time in the situation where a judge's position may be compromised by prior involvement in some aspect of the case while performing some other role in government. In *McGonnell v UK*[4] the Bailiff of Guernsey had presided over the Royal Court in an appeal on a planning matter and the Strasbourg Court held that the Bailiff's prior involvement in the making of the rules which had to be applied in the case was capable of casting doubt on his impartiality. He had presided, as Deputy Bailiff (a government office), over the States of Deliberation (a legislative body) when the measure was adopted. The court noted that there was no suggestion that the Bailiff was subjectively prejudiced or biased but held that he lacked the required 'appearance' of independence or 'objective' impartiality[5]. The applicant had legitimate grounds for fearing that the Bailiff may have been influenced by his prior participation in the adoption of the measure: that doubt in itself, however slight its justification, was sufficient to vitiate the impartiality of the Royal Court[6]. In its defence of Mr McGonnell's application, the UK pointed to previous case law of the Strasbourg court which indicated that the ECHR did not require 'compliance with any particular doctrine of separation of powers'[7]. The Court was careful to agree with this submission, emphasising that states were not obliged to 'comply with any theoretical constitutional concepts as such'. But for Mr McGonnell the question was not a theoretical one: the Bailiff had, in fact, been directly involved in his case in a manner which cast doubt on the objective impartiality of the court[8]. The point arose in the domestic context in

Davidson v Scottish Ministers (No 2) in which the House of Lords concluded that where a Scottish judge had, in his previous capacity as Lord Advocate, been involved in the passage of SA 1998 there was a real risk of apparent bias should he be involved in determining a case about the proper application of that Act[9].

If the modern cases have indeed provided reasons to question the division between the supposedly distinct categories of apparent bias, they have also quite explicitly reopened the debate between those who favour the 'real danger' test and those who prefer that of the 'reasonable suspicion'. It may be that, in some cases at least, the tests will produce similar results but there *is* a conceptual difference nicely captured by the fear that the reliance on 'real danger' impinges on the requirement that justice should appear to be done[10]. There is a link here with *Starrs* and also with *McGonnell*. As Lord Reed said in *Starrs*, the importance of a court being perceived to be independent is that it must command public confidence[11]. But is it the perception of the judge of a 'real danger' or is it the judge's perception of a public suspicion reasonably held? If an analogy may be drawn here with decision-making in the face of scientific uncertainty, there is a division between those who would rely on the scientific analysis of the judge and those who would insist on the application of a precautionary principle.

Finally, deeper philosophical questions remain about the relevance of the personal characteristics, background and connections of a judge to his or her role. *Locabail* and subsequent cases suggest that such factors are in the main to be disregarded when considering the question of apparent bias: the premise being that they are not to be thought likely to have a significant (or at least not adverse) impact on day to day adjudication. That premise might be viewed as being in contrast with the premise which underpins the desire to see greater diversity in the judiciary[12]: that the personal characteristics, commitments and views of a judge will inevitably (and positively) influence their professional practice.

1 *Locabail (UK) Ltd v Bayfield Properties Ltd* [2000] QB 451 at 473.
2 *Locabail (UK) Ltd v Bayfield Properties Ltd* [2000] QB 451 at 473, but see the robust approach taken in *Jones v DAS Legal Expenses Insurance Co Ltd & Ors* [2003] EWCA Civ 1071.
3 *R v Bow Street Metropolitan Stipendiary Magistrate, ex parte Pinochet Ugarte (No 2)* [2000] 1 AC 119 at 135.
4 *McGonnell v UK* (2000) 30 EHRR 289.
5 Adopting the test applied in *Findlay v UK* (1997) 24 EHRR 221.
6 *McGonnell v UK* (2002) 30 EHRR 289 at 308.
7 *McGonnell v UK* (2000) 30 EHRR 289 at 307, and see, in particular, the concurring opinion of Sir John Laws sitting as an ad hoc judge.
8 See also *Procola v Luxembourg* (1996) 22 EHRR 193.
9 *Davidson v Scottish Ministers (No 2)* 2005 1 SC (HL) 7.
10 *R v Bow Street Metropolitan Stipendiary Magistrate, ex parte Pinochet Ugarte (No 2)* [2000] 1 AC 119 at 142.
11 *Starrs v Ruxton* 2000 JC 208 at 252.
12 See (in the context of England and Wales) 'The Report of the Advisory Panel on Judicial Diversity 2010'. In a 2012 lecture on the relative lack of gender balance on the UK Supreme Court, Baroness Hale opined: 'You can only think that it is a bad thing to bring different experiences and perspectives to the business of judging if you think that the only valid experience which can shape the law is the experience of one half of the human race – that that is the only real experience, and it results in a neutral, unbiased view of the law, whereas anything else is unreal and results in a partial, biased view of the law.' (Norfolk Law Lecture 2012 'It's a Man's World: Redressing the Balance', University of East Anglia, Norwich, 16 February 2012).

JUDGES AND POLITICS

12.18   The previous sections of this chapter have considered the legal rules which have been put in place to ensure that individual judges are protected, collectively and individually, from inappropriate influences which might otherwise affect the way in which they exercise their judicial functions. We have also seen the important consequences of judicial impartiality for the individuals whose rights and obligations are determined by those judges. However, the significance of judicial independence goes beyond the need to guarantee dispassionate adjudication of disputes brought before the courts: there are wider constitutional considerations which must be satisfied. We have referred elsewhere[1] to the importance of the separation of powers and – perhaps more relevant in the United Kingdom – to the need, in ensuring the accountability of any one branch of government, to maintain the autonomy of those other individuals or institutions who must exercise that control. Particularly in the context of constitutional adjudication, therefore, it is important that the judiciary enjoy sufficient independence from the legislature whose laws they must interpret and apply and from the executive whose actions they must review and sometimes overturn.

These wider considerations are recognised partly in rules imposed by law but also, in the British constitutional tradition, by conventions observed by members of the judiciary themselves. Again, in the traditional British way, current arrangements are perhaps more the product of piecemeal evolution than of principled and deliberate design. Thus, members of the judiciary are disqualified by law from membership of the House of Commons and the Scottish Parliament[2] but while there is no bar to their membership of political parties as such, by convention, members of the judiciary do avoid associating themselves publicly with a particular political party[3] and overt support for a political campaign may constitute grounds for removal under the statutory procedures described earlier[4]. The Statement of Principles of Judicial Ethics for the Scottish Judiciary[5], issued by the Judicial Office for Scotland explains that 'it is a cardinal feature of judicial independence that a judge should have no party political involvement of any kind, other than the exercise of his or her right to vote'[6] and that 'a judge should do nothing which could give rise to any suggestion of political partisanship, such as involvement in party political controversy'[7]. Equally, 'a judge should take care about the place at which and the occasion on which he or she speaks publicly, so as not to cause the public to associate the judge with, or create the perception of partiality towards, any particular organisation, group, or cause'[8]. The English judiciary are exhorted to exercise their freedom to talk to the media, with 'the greatest circumspection'[9] and they are similarly expected to take care with contributions to public debate in general[10]. Nevertheless, it is increasingly common for members of the judiciary to contribute to debates on law reform, the legal system and matters of constitutional importance. Indeed, many of their contributions are referred to in this book.

Interestingly, it seems that while the independence of the judiciary is promoted by a deliberate distance from party political activity, judges are also protected against the imposition of penalties for expressing criticism of the legislature or the executive. In *Wille v Liechtenstein*[11] the ECtHR held that the refusal by Prince Hans-Adams II of Liechtenstein to reappoint the applicant to judicial office following their disagreement over the interpretation of the constitution and the jurisdiction of the Liechtenstein Constitutional Court amounted to a violation of the applicant's art 10 ECHR right to freedom of expression.

As to the judiciary's formal separation from Parliament and the executive, until recently, the issue was dominated in the United Kingdom by, (a) the former constitutional position of the Lord Chancellor and (b) the status of the former Law Lords and (c) the appointment of senior judges to conduct inquiries into matters of political controversy or great public interest. The reform of the position of the Lord Chancellor (the combination of the office with that of Secretary of State for Justice; the separate creation of the Lord Speaker of the House of Lords and the designation of the Lord Chief Justice as head of the English judiciary under the Constitutional Reform Act 2005) and the creation of the UK Supreme Court have removed the first two concerns from the constitutional agenda. Item (c) retains its vitality.

1   At para 2.5.
2   House of Commons Disqualification Act 1975, Sch 1, para 1 and SA 1998, s 15; and see para 5.7 In terms of the Scottish judiciary this covers judges of the Court of Session, the chairman of the Scottish Land Court, sheriffs principal, sheriffs and stipendiary magistrates. It may be anticipated that summary sheriffs will, in due course, be similarly disqualified.
3   Guidance for judges published by the English Judges' Council makes clear that: 'A Judge must forego any kind of political activity and on appointment sever all ties with political parties' (*Guide to Judicial Conduct*, 2013, para 3.3).
4   See para 12.7.
5   Originally published in 2010 and revised in 2013.
6   Para 4.5.
7   Ibid.
8   Para 5.1.
9   *Guide to Judicial Conduct* para 8.1.1. The English rules were formerly promulgated as the 'Kilmuir rules'.
10 Ibid para 8.2.
11 *Wille v Liechtenstein* (2000) 30 EHRR 558; and see 'Freedom of Expression: Disqualification from Public Office' (2000) EHRLR 196.

Judicial inquiries

12.19   The Law Lords, as we have seen, were previously both members of the legislature and members of the judicial branch of government. In that former capacity they were involved, by virtue of their membership of a House of Lords select committee for example, in scrutiny and perhaps criticism of the work of government. Somewhat analogous to this scrutinising role – but with important differences – is the involvement of senior judges in what may broadly be described as 'judicial inquiries'. These may take a number of different forms and go by a variety of different names. Royal Commissions are frequently chaired by judges[1], public inquiries may be permitted by statutes dealing with particular subject areas[2], and judges may be appointed to chair inquiries under the Inquiries Act 2005[3]. In recent years inquiries involving Scottish judges have included Lord Cullen's inquiries into the shootings at Dunblane Primary School in March 1996[4] and the Paddington rail crash[5], Lord

Clyde's inquiry into the removal from children from Orkney following claims of child abuse[6] and inquiries by Lords Coulsfield[7] and Bonomy[8] respectively into aspects of civil and criminal procedure. Lord Gill's inquiry into civil justice[9] was the genesis of CR(S)A 2014.

The desirability of judicial involvement in such inquiries and the implications of that involvement for judicial independence are not easy to assess. On the one hand it is clear that there is a public appetite for 'judicial' scrutiny of the executive. There is a perception that in relation to issues of intense political controversy – particularly where doubts have been cast as to the probity of government action – the 'truth' is more likely to come out at the hands of a judge than at those of elected politicians. So, for example, in July 2003 when the House of Commons Select Committee on Foreign Affairs published its report on the use of military intelligence by the government in the lead-up to the Iraq war[10] the leader of the Liberal Democrats, Charles Kennedy, criticised the report as incomplete and demanded that an 'independent judicial inquiry' be appointed[11]. Indeed, the establishment of a judicial inquiry can become, itself, a campaigning objective: the establishment of the Saville Inquiry into 'the events of Sunday, 30th January 1972 which led to loss of life in connection with the procession in Londonderry on that day'[12] followed one such campaign.

There is no doubt that such inquiries can provide much-needed scrutiny[13] and may be a useful addition to the various mechanisms for accountability of the executive which are explored elsewhere in this book[14]. However, this method of scrutiny does not fall squarely within our traditional understanding of the judicial role – while evidence is heard and conclusions are reached, such an inquiry is not a 'court case' and does not produce any legally binding decision or order – and is more akin to the kind of political inquiry which is ordinarily carried out by parliamentary committees. Certainly, their work can have serious political ramifications. The publication of the Saville Inquiry report was, for example, followed immediately by a statement by the Prime Minister David Cameron in the House of Commons in which he accepted the Inquiry's conclusion that the British Army had unjustifiably opened fire on the civilians who were killed and injured: 'the conclusions of this report are absolutely clear. There is no doubt. There is nothing equivocal. There are no ambiguities. What happened on Bloody Sunday was both unjustified and unjustifiable. It was wrong.'[15] Although the involvement of a judge may appear to add 'legitimacy' to an investigation[16], this legitimacy may be more apparent than real and sceptical observers may see the appointment of a judge as an attempt to 'pass the buck'. From the perspective of independence of the judiciary we should remain alert to the potential difficulties of involving judges in a process which may lead them to criticise government or to propose legislative or administrative changes. Their status as judges inevitably gives such proposals weight but it may also bring them dangerously close to overstepping the bounds of their constitutional role and to finding themselves in conflict with politicians. This was particularly evident in the case of the Hutton inquiry[17] and, more recently, the Leveson Inquiry[18].

More prosaically, an inquiry can become a burden both for the judge leading it and for the public purse. The Penrose Inquiry (into Hepatitis C/HIV acquired infection from NHS treatment in Scotland with blood and blood products) and the Vale of Leven Hospital Inquiry (into the occurrence of C. difficile infection at the Vale of Leven Hospital and chaired by Lord MacLean) were established in 2005 and 2009 respectively. The former has not yet concluded its work, with the latter reporting only in November 2014[19]. The Saville Inquiry was reported to have involved costs of around £200m.

1   For example, the Royal Commission on Local Government in Scotland 1966–69 was chaired by Lord Wheatley.
2   For example, the Public Inquiry into the Piper Alpha Disaster, chaired by Lord Cullen, was established in terms of the Offshore Installations (Public Inquiries) Regulations 1974, SI 1974/338. See Cm 1310.
3   Formerly the Tribunals of Inquiry (Evidence) Act 1921. In November 2014 it was announced that the Edinburgh Tram Inquiry – into the delivery of the Edinburgh Trams project – had been converted, at the request of the Chair Lord Hardie, from a non-statutory inquiry to an inquiry governed by the 2005 Act. The notice of conversion, issued under s 15 of the 2005 Act, is available at http://www.edinburghtraminquiry.org.
4   Cm 3386.
5   The *Ladbroke Grove Rail Inquiry*. Lord Cullen was appointed by the Health and Safety Executive, with the consent of the Deputy Prime Minister (the minister responsible for transport), under the Health and Safety at Work etc Act 1974, s 14.
6   *Report of the Inquiry into the Removal of Children from Orkney in February 1991* (HMSO).
7   *Report by Working Party on Court of Session Procedure* (2000).
8   Lord Bonomy *Improving Practice – The 2002 Review of the Practices and Procedure of the High Court of Justiciary*.
9   The Report of the Scottish Civil Courts Review 2009.
10 *The Decision to go to War in Iraq* (HC Paper 813 (2002–03)).
11 Reported by the BBC on 8 July 2003. A public inquiry into the death of David Kelly was later established under Lord Hutton. This reported ((2003–04) HC 247) in Feb 2004 amidst great controversy.
12 Better known as the 'Bloody Sunday Inquiry'. The terms of reference for the inquiry were announced by Prime Minister Blair on 29 January 1998 (HC Debs, cols 501–503). Although chaired by a Lord of Appeal in Ordinary, the two other Members of the inquiry were senior members of the Canadian (Hon W Hoyt) and Australian (Hon J L Toohey) judiciary. The inquiry reported to Parliament on 15 June 2010: Report of the Bloody Sunday Inquiry HC 29-I (2010–12)
13 See M Flinders 'Mechanisms of judicial accountability in British Central Government' (2001) 54 *Parl Aff* 51.
14 See especially chs 9 and 10. 15 HC Debates 15 June 2010 col 739.
16 See G Drewry 'Judicial inquiries and public reassurance' [1996] PL 368.
17 See note 11 above.
18 An Inquiry into the Culture, Practices and Ethics of the Press, Report, November 2012. For a discussion see D McKie 'Leveson: the implications for Scotland's media' (2013) 17 Edin LR 229–234.
19 The Vale of Leven Hospital Inquiry Report, 2014.

AN APPRAISAL

12.20   It should be apparent from even a brief consideration of the issues discussed in this chapter that the concepts of judicial independence and impartiality raise difficult questions. The variety of legal rules and institutional mechanisms which have been put in place to preserve the independence of the judiciary do not always present a coherent picture. Senior judges themselves disagree not only on what is required to preserve judicial independence but on how to express the requirements: a point illustrated by the recent cases, discussed at para 12.16 of this chapter, concerning the common law test for apparent bias. In a quite different environment, judges have encountered difficulties in defining exactly what judicial independence demands in terms of sentencing practice. In proceedings on the Criminal Justice and Licensing (Scotland) Bill the Lord Justice General and the Lord Justice Clerk raised 'constitutional' objections to the creation of a Sentencing Council for Scotland with a power to issue sentencing guidelines for use by the judiciary[1]. Whilst the issue of statutory guidelines by the Parliament would be acceptable, the issue of guidelines by a quango (or at least one without a judicial majority) was not. The power of the Scottish Sentencing Council to issue guidelines survived but the Bill was amended to require the approval of such guidelines by the High Court of Justiciary[2].

Perhaps one reason for the difficulties which surround this topic is that, at least on the face of it, judicial independence is an umbrella under which a number of competing, and even contradictory, concerns attempt to shelter. There is the recognition that the judiciary requires to be protected from undue influence, principally from government but also from the parties before them. However it is also acknowledged that those affected by judicial decision-making need some protection from the judiciary. They are entitled to expect that determinations about their legal rights and obligations – affecting their liberty, personal status, family and property – are not affected by what might be described as 'non-legal' and irrelevant considerations such as a judge's personal views about race, religion or politics. At a more fundamental constitutional level, it is understood that the independence of the judiciary is essential to preserve the rule of law by controlling, where necessary, the exercise of legislative and executive power and by upholding the rights of individuals and minority groups. Yet this desire to ensure government 'according to law' is tempered by a further concern that the judiciary themselves ought not to overstep the bounds of their role by interfering unnecessarily with the work of government.

Again, while it is accepted that reform of the judicial system may be necessary to deal with threats to judicial independence and to preserve public confidence – by, for example, completely removing senior judges from the legislature as was done by the Constitutional Reform Act 2005 – it is equally important to the preservation of public confidence that judges are seen to be robust and that the work of the courts is not disrupted by frequent, sometimes trivial, accusations of bias. Over-zealous pursuit of an absolutely impartial tribunal is not only futile but is damaging if it is allowed to go too far and concern for impartiality must be considered in light of the problems caused by delays and the perceived advantages to be gained by individuals who may stall legal proceedings by raising objections to an adjudicator's independence.

1 See SP JC OR 12 May 2009.
2 Criminal Justice and Licensing (Scotland) Act 2010, ss 3 and 5(1): 'Sentencing guidelines have no effect unless approved by the High Court of Justiciary'.

Chapter 13

Citizen and State

INTRODUCTION

13.1   Any constitution has to define not only the different institutions of the state[1] and their interrelationships but also the relationships between the state and the members of its population. The state exercises powers over its people, some of which may be very burdensome, but it also confers benefits. Individuals have rights to those benefits and must, to an extent, enjoy protection from state powers. Equally, however, they have responsibilities to both the state and to each other. It is, therefore, necessary for constitutions to define the extent of the powers exercisable by the state against the individual and then the extent to individuals may be protected from the use of those powers. In very large measure those protections are conferred, in the modern law, in the form of the rights deriving from the European Convention on Human Rights (ECHR), and these are discussed below, along with an analysis of a selection of the principal powers exercisable by the police and authorities which impinge most acutely on individual liberty. Before doing so, however, we should consider the concept of citizenship and, in summary form, some elements of the closely-related law of immigration control.

1 Although the state is the entity to which citizenship normally relates, the European Union also attributes rights to its citizens (TFEU Art 20).

CITIZENSHIP

13.2   We have referred so far to the relationship of 'individuals' to the state but we quickly find that individual persons have to be differentiated one from another to produce a variety of different relationships which vary according to the status of each individual and the area of state activity with which we are concerned. Different degrees of connection with the state define different rights and responsibilities. We shall find that it is, in principle, mere presence within the United Kingdom which determines access to the general rights under the ECHR[1]. For the purposes of specific areas of law, however, whilst specific rights are defined by the legislation concerned, general rules as to equality and non-discrimination[2] otherwise apply without special regard to citizenship and art 14 ECHR which prohibits discrimination has been held to have similar effect[3]. It was indeed on this ground that in *A v Home Secretary*[4] the House of Lords held that, despite the closely entwined immigration aspects of the case, discriminatory distinctions between UK national and foreign terrorist suspects could not be sustained. But in the United Kingdom, as in other countries, the core concept of citizenship serves to define a degree of connection or belonging to the country which then serves as a common framework for determining the rights and responsibilities of those classed as

359

citizens. To an extent, the need for a definition of citizenship is driven by the demands of international law. States are, however, free to determine their own rules[5].

In the United Kingdom[6] the process of defining citizenship has followed a complex historical pattern which has produced some difficult modern rules which are badly in need of reform[7]. The historical complexity derives from the slow emergence of the legal concept of citizenship, as opposed to that of being a 'British subject', and the fluctuating pressures (both opportunities and constraints) of disengagement from the British Empire. These led, in particular, to rules which, since the British Nationality Act 1948, have been required to decouple rights to citizenship of the United Kingdom from the rights to settle ('right of abode') in the country[8]. The British Nationality Act 1981 which, in its time, attempted to simplify the law but has since been frequently amended[9] now provides for six different categories of citizens[10]: British citizen, British overseas territories citizen, British overseas citizen, British national (overseas), British protected person and British subject. All but the first two are, however, 'residual' in the sense that they are transitional categories to which no new members can be admitted and are, therefore, in decline. The principal way in which British citizenship may be acquired under the 1981 Act is by birth in the United Kingdom where the mother is a British citizen[11] or adoption where the adopter is a citizen. Alternatively, citizenship may be acquired by registration (by right or by decision of the Secretary of State)[12] or by naturalisation[13]. Citizenship may be renounced by declaration to the Home Secretary, a step required by any citizen who wishes to apply for citizenship of a country whose laws deny the option of dual citizenship – not a position adopted by the United Kingdom. It is, however, possible for the Home Secretary to deprive a person of British citizenship where the Home Secretary is satisfied that deprivation would be conducive to the public good and (normal) provided that the deprivation would not render the person stateless[14].

A separate source of ambiguity in relationship to citizenship is the tendency to use the term to define *political* as opposed to legal rights and responsibilities. The Conservative Government's *Citizen's Charter* of 1991 and then the Labour Government's focus from 2006 on 'Britishness' were illustrations of the promotion of political rather than strictly legal purposes. Reforms proposed by the Goldsmith review[15] of 2008 sought a simplification of the law but also, as a part of the political strengthening of citizenship, proposed a group of measures designed to 'enhance the bond of citizenship', such as citizenship education and citizenship ceremonies.

In the meantime, however, the existing legal rights and responsibilities of citizenship may be summarised[16]:

Right of abode and free movement
- Right of abode and freedom of movement in the UK;
- Freedom of movement within the Common Travel Area and the European Economic Area;
- Expectation of issue of a British passport

Right of protection – and duty of allegiance

- Entitled to request that the State exercises diplomatic protection where they have suffered a wrong at the hands of another State;
- Entitled to request consular assistance when abroad;
- Entitled to domestic protection;
- Duty of allegiance to the Crown;
- Duty to obey the law when in the UK – liable for certain offences in the UK even if committed abroad

Civic rights

- Right to vote where registered as resident in Westminster and European Parliamentary elections, and in local and devolved elections;
- Right to vote in Parliamentary and European Parliamentary elections where valid overseas declaration made (contingent upon UK residence and registration in preceding 15 years[17]);
- Right to stand in elections, subject to residence requirements in local elections;
- Duty to provide information for purpose of electoral registers on request;
- Right to campaign in referendum if resident in UK or appearing on one of the electoral registers

The reforms of the substantive categories of citizenship proposed by Goldsmith have not been undertaken but the Borders, Citizenship and Immigration Act 2009 made a number of minor amendments including reform of the law on naturalisation.

1 See paras 13.7–13.13. In some cases, indeed, presence within territory under the effective authority and control of the United Kingdom is sufficient: cf *Smith v Ministry of Defence* [2013] UKSC 41, [2014] AC 52.
2 See the Equality Act 2010.
3 See *int al Belgian Linguistics Case (No 2)* (1968) 1 EHRR 252.
4 [2005] 2 AC 68.
5 *Nottebohm* Case (*Liechtenstein v Guatemala*) ICJ Reports 1955, 4.
6 During the independence referendum campaign, consideration was given by the Scottish Government to the question of future Scottish citizenship. See *Scotland's Future* (para 4.8) p 271; *The Scottish Independence Bill* s 18 (para 4.14).
7 For brief account of the history and the current rules, together with proposals for reform, see Lord Goldsmith, *Citizenship: Our Common Bond* 2008 (Goldsmith).
8 The Commonwealth Immigrants Act 1962 and the Immigration Act 1971.
9 British Nationality (Hong Kong) Act 1997, British Overseas Territories Act 2002; Nationality, Immigration and Asylum Act 2002.
10 Goldsmith paras 17, 18, 27 and Annex C.
11 Or 'settled' in the UK ie 'ordinarily resident' without immigration restrictions.
12 1981 Act, s 1(3), (4).
13 Ibid s 6.
14 British Nationality Act 1981, s 40(2) as amended by the Immigration, Asylum and Nationality Act 2006, s 56 and the Immigration Act 2014. The 2014 Act permitted removal of citizenship from certain categories of citizen despite resulting statelessness. Citizenship acquired by registration may also be revoked on grounds of fraud or concealment of a material fact.
15 See note 7 above.
16 Goldsmith 5, 6 – the source of this informal summary.
17 See para 5.6.

IMMIGRATION CONTROL[1]

13.3   It has already been noted that the development of the law of citizenship has been closely entwined with the development of the right to enter and live in the United Kingdom – the right of abode. There has been a declared need for controls – still contained in the Immigration Act 1971, as amended – to be imposed on all those who, in terms of the British Nationality Act 1981, lack British citizenship and, therefore, the right of abode.

As also already noted, however, there are two categories of non-citizen which receive special treatment – a special treatment which extends to their position under immigration law. These are citizens of the Republic of Ireland[2] and citizens of other EU states[3] and of Iceland, Liechtenstein, Norway and Switzerland[4]. Though liable to deportation, these categories are not subject to the normal immigration controls.

Previously in the hands of the UK Border Agency, immigration control has been, since 2013, primarily in the hands of the UK Visas and Immigration division of the Home Office. The division implements and enforces an elaborate and complicated code of regulations contained in the Immigration Act 1971 (as comprehensively amended) and the Immigration Rules made (and, again, frequently amended) under s 3(2) of the Act for application by immigration officers at ports and airports of entry. The Act and Rules create different categories of would-be entrants to the country, by reference to their need (or not) for a visa and the purpose of their visit – as short-term visitor, student, au pair, employee or (on a 'points-based' system) as highly skilled migrants, entrepreneur migrants, investor migrants and some others[5]. Under this system, minimum points totals must normally be achieved, by reference to levels of education, other qualifications, age, previous earnings and wealth.

Separately, the Act and Rules (Parts 11, 11A and 11B) make provision for applications made by those who seek admission as refugees claiming protection under the Geneva Convention 1951 ie on the grounds of a well-founded fear of being persecuted for reasons of race, religion, nationality, membership of a particular social group or political opinion but is unable or unwilling to see protection in his or her own country. Decisions made by immigration officers may be taken on appeal to the Asylum and Immigration Chamber of the First-tier Tribunal[6] and thereafter, on statutory review, to the Upper Tribunal and to the Inner House of the Court of Session – with some matters, eg a refusal of leave to appeal by the Upper Tribunal, subject to common law judicial review[7] – but, since *Eba v Advocate General for Scotland*[8] on only a restricted basis[9]. If the original decision was made on the grounds of national security, the appeal lies to the Special Immigration Appeals Commission[10], with a further review by the Court of Session.

1   For a comprehensive introduction, see, though a little out of date, RM White *Immigration* SME Reissue 2003.
2   1971 Act, s 2 as amended.
3   Immigration Act 1988, s 7.
4   Switzerland, although not a member of the European Economic Area (cf Iceland, Liechtenstein and Norway which are), is defined as an 'EEA State' by the Immigration (EEA) Regulations 2006, SI 2006/1003.

5 Special, controversial, provision is made for former members of the Brigade of Gurkhas.
6 Asylum and Immigration (Treatment of Claimants etc) Act 2004 and SI 2005/230 (as much amended) and the Tribunals, Courts and Enforcement Act 2007. Appeals to the Tribunal are decided by one or more Tribunal members including an 'immigration judge'.
7 In *Tehrani v Home Secretary* 2007 SC (HL) 1 the House of Lords held that, in the judicial review of decisions of the then Asylum and Immigration Tribunal, both the Court of Session and the English Administrative Court had jurisdiction.
8 2012 SC (UKSC) 1.
9 See also *A v Home Secretary* 2013 SLT 1132; *EP v Home Secretary* 2014 SC 706 and para 14.11 below.
10 Special Immigration Appeals Commission Act 1997.

DEPORTATION, REMOVAL AND EXTRADITION

13.4   Just as British citizenship carries with it the right to enter and reside in the United Kingdom[1], British citizens are not subject to powers to remove or deport them. Non citizens, however, have no such immunity. They are subject to two principal powers. First, the regime of immigration control itself necessarily incorporates a power to remove those in breach of the rules as a means of their enforcement. Secondly, they are subject to a power of the Home Secretary to deport when this would be conducive to the public good or where a trial court has recommended deportation after conviction of an offence punishable with imprisonment[2]. In the latter case, such recommendations may, like other sentencing decisions, be appealed to the High Court of Justiciary[3]. Once an order to remove or deport has been made, the decision may be appealed to the Asylum and Immigration Chamber (as above).

Quite different considerations arise where a person physically present (and whatever their citizenship or residence status) in the United Kingdom may be subjected to extradition proceedings designed to ensure his or her removal to another country for the purpose either of standing trial for a criminal offence or for punishment in respect of conviction of an offence.

The modern law is in the Extradition Act 2003 and this contains two distinct statutory schemes. Part 1 of the Act relates to 'category 1' countries, defined as those which are EU member states[4]. Part 2 relates to 'category 2' countries, which are all those other countries designated for extradition purposes. The principal difference between the two is that proceedings under Part 1 are almost entirely judicial but that proceedings under Part 2 also involve the intervention of the Scottish Ministers[5]. Part 1 proceedings begin with the submission by the appropriate judicial authority of the other country of an arrest warrant to, for Scotland, the Crown Office[6] which then ensures its execution and the commencement, by the Lord Advocate[7], of proceedings before the sheriff of Lothian and Borders[8]. The Act requires the sheriff to decide whether the offence specified in the warrant is an extradition offence[9]; whether any specified 'bars to extradition' (eg double jeopardy or the passage of time or conviction in absence) apply[10]; and whether the person's extradition would be compatible with Convention rights[11]. If satisfied on all counts, the sheriff must order the person's extradition. There is a right of appeal to the High Court of Justiciary[12]. Meanwhile, extradition to category 2 countries is handled rather differently under Part 2 of the Act. The principal modification is that, as with the earlier treaty-based regimes, the Scottish Ministers have a significant role. In the first place, it is they who initiate the procedure by certifying the incoming request as valid[13] and forward it (once again to a sheriff in Lothian and Borders) for consideration. More importantly, the judicial stage ends not with an order to extradite but, subject to an appeal to the High Court Justiciary, with the return of the case to the Scottish Ministers for further consideration[14] including the issue of whether the death penalty might be imposed in the receiving state[15]. In the absence of specified factors requiring them not to do so, the Scottish Ministers must order the person to be extradited. The Supreme Court in *BH (AP) v Lord Advocate*[16] and in *Kapri v Lord Advocate*[17] reconfirmed the lack of any further general appeal under the 2003 Act but nevertheless affirmed a separate right of appeal to the Supreme Court on the 'devolution issue'[18] of the Lord Advocate's (or other member of the Scottish Government's) compliance with SA 1998 s 57(2)[19].

1   But powers contained in a the Counter-terrorism and Security Bill published in Nov 2014 might enable the seizure of the passports of certain terrorist suspects.
2   Immigration Act 1971, s 3.
3   See eg *Alili v HMA* 2008 SCCR 566.
4   All EU states have ratified the European Council Framework Decision of 13 June 2002, which Part 1 of the 2003 Act transposes into UK law.
5   2003 Act, s 141.
6   Section 2.
7   Section 191.
8   Section 67(1)(b) interpreted as *any* sheriff of the sheriffdom.
9   Section 10.
10 Sections 11–20.
11 Section 21.
12 Sections 26, 216(9). See below for appeals to the UKSC.
13 Section 70.
14 2003 Act, s 92.
15 Section 94.
16 2012 SC (UKSC) 308.
17 2013 SC (UKSC) 311.
18 Not a 'compatibility issue' – see *Kapri* at paras 14–23. For discussion of the two categories, see para 14.9.
19 See para 7.19 above.

LIMITATIONS ON STATE POWER AND PROTECTION OF THE INDIVIDUAL

13.5   It has been noted above that the overarching concept of citizenship does much to define the relationship between individuals (both citizens and non-citizens) and the state. In particular, citizenship in large measure determines a person's right to reside permanently in the United Kingdom and whether he or she could be required to leave. But, even if the current law of citizenship were to be reformed, it could never provide a detailed account of all the rules which determine the relationship between state power and individual freedoms. For the most part, in the law of Scotland, we look to the particularities of the extent of state power and individual freedom, as defined in specific rules contained mainly in statute, but also in the common law. A selection of some of the higher-profile instances of such power-freedom contexts is provided in paras 13.18–13.19 of this chapter. However, those specific instances have to be understood within the context, on the one hand, of the ECHR and the Human Rights Act 1998 (HRA 1998) (paras 13.7 and 13.10 et seq) and, on the other, of the statutory 'information' rights of individuals (paras 13.20–13.25). The law across the entire scope of this chapter remains in flux – especially, in recent years, because of the enactment of substantial terrorist (or anti-terrorist) legislation by the Westminster Parliament. The principal components are the Terrorism Act 2000, the Anti-Terrorism, Crime and Security Act 2001, the Terrorism Act 2006, the Counter-Terrorism Act 2008, the Terrorist Asset-Freezing etc Act 2010, and the Terrorism Prevention and Investigation Measures Act 2011. The detailed content of this legislation cannot be considered here. However, the impact of terrorism legislation is taken into account at relevant points of this chapter[1].

1 See C Walker, *Terrorism and the Law* (2011). There is now a new Counter-Terrorism and Security Bill in the Westminster Parliament.

HUMAN RIGHTS

13.6   When describing in Chapter 1 our 'model' constitution, we suggested it would be natural to include within that constitution a list of rights and freedoms which were to be regarded as 'fundamental', to be enjoyed by citizens and others to whom the state has responsibility, and which were enforceable in the courts, against the state itself. However, one consequence of the absence of a written constitution in the UK has been the concomitant absence of a 'Bill of Rights' in the sense understood in other democracies around the world. The traditional doctrine of the supremacy of Parliament (see para 6.5) to which the courts have given effect has in practice precluded the striking down of Westminster legislation on any grounds, including on grounds of interference with individual rights. Similarly, so far as executive (rather than legislative) action is concerned, historical explanations are grounded in an assertion that the state is generally free to act in whatever manner it sees fit, unless it is expressly prohibited from particular conduct by the legislature[1]. As we have seen (para 6.5) the higher courts have in recent years suggested that parliamentary supremacy may not be absolutely unqualified – particularly where individual rights and freedoms are at risk. This new approach may be viewed by some as little more than a change of tone or shift of emphasis but, as we will see, it has been accompanied by the use by the courts of still relatively new mechanisms for the protection of human rights.

In this chapter we discuss the institutional framework created following the incorporation of the ECHR by the HRA 1998 and describe the substantive rights conferred by HRA 1998. Our treatment of this area is necessarily brief: there is significant literature available elsewhere[2] which we do not attempt to replicate. In Chapter 14 we describe in more detail the manner in which human rights issues come to be adjudicated upon in the British courts and the approach which the courts have adopted to their determination. We have, elsewhere, described the manner in which the 'Convention rights' also place limits on the legislative competence of the Scottish Parliament[3] and the devolved competence of Scottish Ministers[4] and, again in Chapter 14, we consider the way in which this further 'incorporation' of the ECHR – and the interplay between the Scotland Act 1998 (SA 1998) and HRA 1998 – has been dealt with by the courts.

1 See, for example, *Malone v Commissioner of Police of the Metropolis (No 2)* [1979] Ch 344 discussed below in the context of wire taps.
2 See in particular, R Reed and J Murdoch *A Guide to Human Rights in Scotland* (3rd ed, 2011); A Lester, D Pannick and J Herberg (eds *Human Rights Law and Practice* (3rd ed, 2009); R Clayton and H Tomlinson *The Law of Human Rights* (2nd ed, 2009); A Boyle et al (eds) *Human Rights and Scots Law* (2002).
3 See para 6.20.
4 See para 7.19.

The European Convention on Human Rights

13.7   The prominence that we and others give to HRA 1998 is quite understandable in light of its particular role within the UK legal order. But the drafters of HRA 1998 did not, of course, begin with a blank canvas. The Act is, and was quite deliberately intended to be, a vehicle by which certain rights contained in an international agreement to which the United Kingdom is a party – the European Convention on Human Rights (ECHR)[1] – become enforceable at a domestic level in the British courts.

As has been described elsewhere[2] the ECHR was one product of the European movements which had arisen 'simultaneously and spontaneously' in western European democracies 'in response to the threat to fundamental human rights and to political freedom which had all but overwhelmed the European continent in the [Second World] War and which reappeared after the War in new forms of totalitarianism'[3]. The United Kingdom signed the ECHR in 1950 and ratified it in 1951 and in doing so committed itself, as a matter of international law, to compliance with the ECHR in its treatment of individuals – citizens and others – over which it had jurisdiction. As an international treaty, however, the ECHR did not confer rights or obligations as a matter of the domestic law of the United Kingdom[4] and the principal mechanism available to individuals who believed their rights had been infringed by the United Kingdom, and wished to vindicate those rights, was an application to the European Court of Human Rights in Strasbourg (ECtHR)[5]. While a relatively large number of such applications were made to the ECtHR by British citizens, and in many of those the United Kingdom was found to have breached the Convention, success for an applicant could represent a pyrrhic victory: while binding in international law, a favourable decision from the ECtHR did not automatically result in a remedy being afforded the applicant at a domestic level. In some cases, of course, such decisions did lead to changes in domestic law with the express purpose of giving effect to the ECtHR's interpretation of the ECHR[6].

The ECHR was the product of work carried out by the Council of Europe, and the Council has continued to play an important role in promoting observance of the ECHR. While the ECtHR is concerned with the adjudication of individual disputes, the Council has a much wider role in raising awareness of human rights issues, engaging in public education projects, encouraging cultural exchange and participating in activities designed to assist in the development of emerging democracies through, for example, election monitoring.

The rights protected by the ECHR reflect the concerns of those who drafted it: civil and political rights and freedoms drafted predominantly in 'negative' language, requiring governments and state apparatus to refrain from interfering with those rights and freedoms. Those rights are described in more detail below.

The ECHR is not, of course, the only international human rights instrument to which the United Kingdom is a party and other such instruments adopt a more expansive approach to the rights they seek to protect. The Universal Declaration of Human Rights[7], for example, provides that everyone has the 'right to work, to free choice of employment, to just and favourable conditions of work and to protection against unemployment' (art 23) as well as a right to 'rest and leisure, including reasonable limitation of working hours and periodic holidays with pay' (art 24). Perhaps unsurprisingly, the Universal Declaration is not binding, per se, even in international law and has not been 'incorporated' in the domestic law of the United Kingdom. By contrast, although it does not say so explicitly on the face of the Act, the Children (Scotland) Act 1995 was intended, amongst other things, to give effect in Scots law to a number of the principles set out in the 1989 United Nations Convention on the Rights of the Child[8], as was the more recent Children and Young People (Scotland) Act 2014. Space does not permit a more detailed discussion of these and other treaties to which the United Kingdom is party but special mention should be made of one further human rights instrument: the Charter of Fundamental Rights of the European Union.

1 Formally the Convention for the Protection of Human Rights and Fundamental Freedoms of 4 November 1950.
2 See Lester, Pannick & Herberg, op cit, pp 4–8 and Rainey, Wicks and Ovey, op cit, p 4.
3 B Rainey, E Wicks and C Ovey, Jacobs, White and Ovey *The European Convention on Human Rights* (6th edn, 2014), pp 1–8.
4 For discussion of the limited use made of the ECHR by English and Scottish courts prior to the passing of HRA 1998 see para 14.16.
5 The right of individual petition to the ECtHR was accepted by the United Kingdom in 1966 and for a discussion of the timing of that acceptance see Lester, Pannick & Herberg, op cit, pp 8–9. The ECtHR has been the subject of reform by virtue of both the 11th and 14th to 16th Protocols to the ECHR with the aims of enabling the Court to deal more efficiently with its large and ever growing caseload and to respond to some of the concerns about subsidiarity and the relationship between Strasbourg and members of the Council of Europe which are discussed below. See, for example, L Caflisch, 'The Reform of the European Court of Human Rights: Protocol No 14 and Beyond' (2006) 6 HRL Rev 403 and K Dzehtsiarou and A Greene, 'Restructuring the European Court of Human Rights: preserving the right of individual petition and promoting constitutionalism' [2013] PL 710.
6 For example, in *Campbell and Cosans v United Kingdom* (1982) 4 EHRR 165 the applicants, both parents of children in Scottish schools, complained that the possibility of their children being subject to corporal punishment represented a breach of art 3 ECHR (inhuman and degrading treatment) and of art 2, protocol 1, ECHR (rights of parents to have their children educated in conformance with their own religious and philosophical convictions). The ECtHR rejected the art 3 complaint but upheld that under art 2, protocol 1 and this judgment led to the abolition of such corporal punishment in state schools: see s 48A of the Education (Scotland) Act 1980.
7 Adopted by the United Nations General Assembly in 1948.
8 The Convention was ratified by the United Kingdom on 16 December 1991. For discussion of the Convention and the 1995 Act, see K M Norrie, *Children (Scotland) Act 1995* (2nd revised edition, 2004) and A Cleland and E Sutherland, *Children's Rights in Scotland* (3rd edn, 2009).

Charter of Fundamental Rights of the European Union

13.8   The Charter was drafted by a Convention established by European Council in 1999 and the text of the draft Charter was approved by the Council, the European Parliament and the European Commission in 2000. The Charter sets out a range of civil, political, economic and social rights and freedoms which are intended to be enjoyed by all those resident within the EU (whether as citizens of the EU or otherwise): including, for example, a right to 'protection of personal data' (article 8), a freedom to 'conduct a business in accordance with Community law and national laws and practices' (article 16), and an obligation on the EU to 'respect cultural, religious and linguistic diversity' (article 22). The text borrows extensively and deliberately from the ECHR but is intended to reflect not only the ECHR but, amongst other things, the 'constitutional traditions and international obligations common to the Member States' (preamble). The Charter forms part of the Lisbon Treaty (see para 3.3).

The applicability and the status of the Charter within the United Kingdom has been the topic of some controversy and considerable debate[1]. In 2007, the then Prime Minister Tony Blair reported to the House of Commons on the European Council summit which agreed the main elements of the Lisbon Treaty. In doing so he stated that it was 'absolutely clear that we [ie the UK] have an opt-out from...the Charter'[2]. The 'opt out' was thought to have been secured through Protocol 30 to the Charter. The preamble to Protocol 30 records, amongst other things, that the member states of the EU were 'Desirous... of clarifying the application of the Charter in relation to the laws and administrative action of Poland and of the United Kingdom and of its justiciability within Poland and within the United Kingdom'. It goes on to provide as follows:

'Article 1

1.   The Charter does not extend the ability of the Court of Justice of the European Union, or any court or tribunal of Poland or of the United Kingdom, to find that the laws, regulations or administrative provisions, practices or action of Poland or of the United Kingdom are inconsistent with the fundamental rights, freedoms and principles that it reaffirms.

2.   In particular, and for the avoidance of doubt, nothing in Title IV of the Charter creates justiciable rights applicable to Poland or the United Kingdom except in so far as Poland or the United Kingdom has provided for such rights in its national law.

Article 2

To the extent that a provision of the Charter refers to national laws and practices, it shall only apply to Poland or the United Kingdom to the extent that the rights or principles that it contains are recognised in the law or practices of Poland or of the United Kingdom.'

It has become clear that the description of Protocol 30 as an 'opt out' was inaccurate and any perception that it prevented reliance upon the Charter in the United Kingdom's courts misguided. The European Court of Justice was asked in 2011 to consider preliminary references from the English Court of Appeal and the Irish High Court concerning asylum seekers[3]. In the British reference, the UK government argued that the Secretary of State was not bound, when exercising her discretion to order the removal of an asylum seeker to Greece, to observe EU fundamental rights. In rejecting that contention the ECJ held that the wording of the Protocol 'does not call into question the applicability of the Charter in the United Kingdom or in Poland...Thus, according to the third recital in the preamble to Protocol (No.30), art.6 TEU requires the Charter to be applied and interpreted by the courts of Poland and of the United Kingdom strictly in accordance with the explanations referred to in that article. In addition, according to the sixth recital in the preamble to that protocol, the Charter reaffirms the rights, freedoms and principles recognised in the Union and makes those rights more visible, but does not create new rights or principles.' As the House of Commons European Scrutiny Committee explained it, 'Protocol 30 is deceptive in looking to a non-lawyer as if it provides an opt-out, when it does not'[4]. The Protocol does nothing more, it seems, than confirm that the Charter does not create any new rights or obligations beyond those contained in the Charter itself.

The question remains when the Charter rights can be enforced in the domestic courts of the United Kingdom, which itself turns on the meaning of Article 51(1) of the Charter which provides that 'The provisions of this Charter are addressed to the institutions, bodies, offices and agencies of the Union with due regard for the principle of subsidiarity and to the Member States only when they are implementing Union law.' Both at an EU level and a domestic UK level, a relatively expansive approach has been taken thus far. So, in *Åklagaren v Åkerberg Fransson*[5], concerning criminal charges for certain tax offences, the ECJ held that domestic legislation which fell 'within the scope of EU law' was susceptible to challenge on the grounds that it breached EU fundamental rights while in *Rugby Football Union v Viagogo Ltd*[6] (delivered some months before *Fransson*) the UK Supreme Court considered itself bound to act in accordance with the Charter whenever it was acting 'within the material scope of EU law'[7]. The precise bounds of the Charter's influence remains to be seen but, particularly given its impact on private disputes such as that in *Viagogo*, it has the potential to have at least as much impact as the ECHR[8].

1 A fascinating exposition of the history of the United Kingdom's involvement in its negotiation and of Protocol 30 to the Charter, together with a discussion of its legal effect is to be found in the March 2014 report of the House of Commons European Scrutiny Committee 'The application of the EU Charter of Fundamental Rights in the UK: a state of confusion', HC 979 (2013–14).
2 HC Deb, 25 June 2007, col 37.
3 *NS v Secretary of State for the Home Department* [2012] 2 CMLR 9.
4 HC 979, op cit, at paragraph 17.
5 [2013] 2 CMLR 46.
6 [2012] UKSC 55, [2013] 1 All ER 928.
7 See also *R (on the application of Zagorski) v Secretary of State for Business, Innovation and Skills* [2010] EWHC 3110 (Admin) and *R (on the application of Sandiford) v Secretary of State for Foreign and Commonwealth Affairs* [2013] EWCA Civ 581, [2013] 1 WLR 2938 (CA (Civ Div)).
8 See B van Bockel and P Wattel 'New wine into old wineskins: the scope of the Charter of Fundamental Rights of the EU after *Åkerberg Fransson*' (2013) 38 EL Rev 866 and R Clayton and C Murphy 'The emergence of the EU Charter of Fundamental Rights in UK law' (2014) 5 EHRLR 469.

The move to incorporation of the ECHR

13.9   HRA 1998 was a flagship policy for the first Blair government. The enactment of a Bill of Rights by the 'incorporation' of the ECHR had been forecast by the Labour Party prior to the 1997 general election[1] and then in the White Paper *Rights Brought Home*[2]. The government saw incorporation as an integral part of its 'comprehensive programme of constitutional reform' which was aimed at increasing individual rights, decentralising power, opening up government and reforming Parliament. The White Paper described the continuing effect on the British people of non-incorporation as 'a very practical one. The rights, originally developed with major help from the United Kingdom, are no longer actually seen as British rights. And enforcing them takes too long and costs too much'[3]. The elimination of the delay and of the expense involved in enforcing rights protected by the ECHR in Strasbourg was seen as one of the many benefits of incorporation. Other advantages included the fact that 'the rights will be brought much more fully into the jurisprudence of the courts throughout the United Kingdom and their interpretation will thus be far more subtly and powerfully woven into our law' and that 'British judges will be enabled to make a distinctively British contribution to the development of the jurisprudence of human rights in Europe'[4]. Perhaps most important, in the view of the government, was what it perceived to be evidence of the failure of the then existing arrangements: the number of cases in which the United Kingdom had been found to have violated rights protected by the Convention. While such violations could not be attributed to one single cause, an important factor was the lack of any 'framework within which the compatibility with Convention rights of an executive act or decision can be tested in the British courts'[5].

As was made clear in *Rights Brought Home*[6], the Human Rights Bill which became HRA 1998 was the successor to a line of (private members') Bills which from 1987 onwards had unsuccessfully sought to incorporate the Convention. All had failed in Parliament because of the lack of governmental support. The two main political parties had previously resisted incorporation and it was a resistance which extended beyond politicians. Many commentators opposed the trend towards what they saw as the transformation of matters of social and political debate into issues about rights; and their transfer from political fora, above all Parliament, into the courts for resolution[7]. The general arguments for and against incorporation provided a platform for a more specific debate about which bodies or authorities should be bound, in domestic law, by the terms of the Convention. In the view of the protagonists, much would be gained by making ministers, local authorities and other public bodies subject to the Convention. But what about the Westminster Parliament itself? Should Parliament enact a Bill of Rights which would restrict future Parliaments, requiring them always to enact laws which complied with the Convention? Some would say that this was essential if the risks of 'elective dictatorship'[8] were to be overcome: Parliament itself represented the biggest threat to human rights and should be restrained. But could Parliament restrain future Parliaments by passing a new Human Rights Act or did the doctrine of legislative supremacy[9] prevent this? Could the difficulty be overcome by the use of a device similar to that used in ECA 1972, s 2(4)[10]? Would the courts treat a provision which required them to apply the terms of HRA 1998 (and of ECHR) in preference to the terms of a later Act with the same respect as they now accorded ECA 1972?

1 In particular by a 1996 consultation document entitled '*Bringing Rights Home*'.
2 Cm 3782.
3 Cm 3782, para 1.14.
4 Cm 3782, para 1.14.
5 Cm 3782, para 1.16.
6 Cm 3782.
7 See KD Ewing 'The Human Rights Act and Parliamentary democracy' (1999) 62 MLR 79; N Lyell 'Whither Strasbourg? Why Britain should think long and hard before incorporating the European Convention on Human Rights' (1997) 2 EHRLR 132; KD Ewing and C A Gearty 'Rocky Foundations for Labour's new rights' (1997) 2 EHRLR 146.
8 See Lord Hailsham *The Dilemma of Democracy* (1978) ch XX.
9 See para 6.5.
10 See para 3.12. Such a device was included in a draft Bill promoted by Lord Lester: see 'The Mouse That Roared: The Human Rights Bill 1995' [1995] PL 198.

The Human Rights Act 1998

13.10   In the event, HRA 1998 steered a new path of some ingenuity through this difficult area. It sought to compel future legislative compliance with the terms of the Convention, while (as is discussed in the following chapter) also acknowledging the continuing force of the Westminster Parliament's legislative supremacy.

The 'Convention rights'

13.11   HRA 1998 sets out (most but not all of) the rights guaranteed by the articles and protocols of the ECHR; names them 'the Convention rights'; and provides that they are to have effect for the purposes of the Act[1]. The Convention rights which by virtue of HRA 1998 are to have effect are (in summary):

THE RIGHT TO LIFE (art 2): Everyone's right to life is to be protected by law. However, causing a person's death will not be regarded as a breach of art 2 where that is the result of defending another person from unlawful violence, making a lawful arrest or preventing the escape of a detained person, or taking lawful action to quell a riot or insurrection. This article has been interpreted as not only requiring the state to refrain from taking life unlawfully but as requiring positive measures to be put in place to enable, for example, the review by the courts or other bodies of the use of lethal force by the state and to take effective operational measures to protect the lives of those in the care of the state[2].

THE PROHIBITION OF TORTURE (art 3): No one is to be subjected to torture or to inhuman or degrading treatment or punishment[3].

THE PROHIBITION OF SLAVERY AND FORCED LABOUR (art 4): No one is to be held in slavery or servitude or required to perform forced labour[4].

THE RIGHT TO LIBERTY AND SECURITY (art 5): Everyone has the right to liberty and security of the person and deprivation of liberty is permitted only in specific circumstances (for example after conviction by a competent court, for the purpose of bringing a suspect before a court or, in the case of a minor, for the purpose of educational supervision) and so long as the detention is in accordance with procedures set down by law[5].

THE RIGHT TO A FAIR TRIAL (art 6): In the determination of his civil rights and obligations or of any criminal charge against him, everyone is entitled to a fair and public hearing within a reasonable time by an independent and impartial tribunal established by law. Article 6 goes on to make provision in relation to accessibility of legal proceedings, the presumption of innocence in criminal cases and, again in relation to charges of criminal offences, the giving of adequate time and facilities for the preparation of a defence, availability of legal advice, cross-examination of witnesses and access to an interpreter where necessary. It is one of the most cited and litigated articles of the ECHR and is frequently pled in tandem with claims of breach of common law standards of fair process (see para 14.9)[6].

THE PROSCRIPTION OF PUNISHMENT WITHOUT LAW (art 7): No one is to be held to be guilty of a criminal offence in relation to conduct which was not an offence when the conduct was committed. This article is concerned with the particular unfairness which arises from retrospective application of the criminal law[7].

THE RIGHT TO RESPECT FOR PRIVATE AND FAMILY LIFE (art 8): Everyone has the right to respect for his private and family life, his home and his correspondence albeit that this right may be interfered with by the state so long as the interference is lawful and necessary 'in the interests of national security, public safety or the economic well-being of the country, for the prevention of disorder or crime, for the protection of health or morals, or for the protection of the rights and freedoms of others'. There is extensive domestic and Strasbourg case law on the proper interpretation of the various different elements of art 8 – what is private life, family life, what amounts to a person's[8] home[9] and their correspondence[10] – and as is discussed below (para 13.24) art 8 has been a significant driver in the development of the common law of confidence so as to give greater protection to individual privacy.

THE RIGHT TO FREEDOM OF THOUGHT, CONSCIENCE AND RELIGION (art 9): Everyone has the right to freedom of thought, conscience and religion including the freedom to change a religion or belief and to manifest[11] that religion or belief in 'worship, teaching, practice and observance'. Again this freedom may be subject to limitations provided those are prescribed by law and are necessary in the interests of public safety, protection of public order, health or morals or for the protection of the rights and freedoms of others[12].

FREEDOM OF EXPRESSION (art 10): Everyone has the right to freedom of expression, including the right to hold opinions, receive and impart information and ideas without interference by public authority and regardless of frontiers. This article does not prevent the licensing of broadcasting, television or cinemas and the exercise of the freedoms conferred by art 10 'since it carries with it duties and responsibilities, may be subject to such formalities, conditions, restrictions or penalties as are prescribed by law and are necessary in a democratic society, in the interests of national security, territorial integrity or public safety, for the prevention of disorder or crime, for the protection of health or morals, for the protection of the reputation or rights of others, for preventing the disclosure of information received in confidence, or for maintaining the authority and impartiality of the judiciary'[13].

FREEDOM OF ASSEMBLY AND ASSOCIATION (art 11): Everyone has the right to freedom of peaceful assembly and association with others including the right to form and join trade unions. The freedom should not be restricted except as prescribed by law and where necessary in the interests of national security, public safety, protection of health or morals or protection of the rights and freedoms of others. Article 11 does not prevent restrictions being imposed on the exercise of these rights by members of the armed forces, the police or the 'administration of the State'.

THE RIGHT TO MARRY AND FOUND A FAMILY (art 12): Men and women of marriageable age have the right to marry and to found a family, according to the national laws governing the exercise of this right[14].

THE PROHIBITION OF DISCRIMINATION (art 14): The enjoyment of the Convention rights is to be secured 'without discrimination on any ground such as sex, race, colour, language, religion, political or other opinion, national or social origin, association with a national minority, property, birth or other status. This prohibition of discrimination is not 'free standing' – it applies only where another Convention right is engaged – and does not, therefore, provide general protection against discrimination on grounds of sex, race or sexuality in employment in the manner provided for by EU legislation[15].

PEACEFUL ENJOYMENT OF POSSESSIONS (art 1 of protocol 1): Every natural or legal person is entitled to the peaceful enjoyment or his possessions. No one shall be deprived of their possessions except in the public interest and subject to the conditions provided for by law and by the general principles of international law. Article 1 of protocol 1 does not, however, prevent laws being put in place to control the use of property in accordance with the general interest or to secure the payment of taxes, contributions or penalties[16].

THE RIGHT TO EDUCATION (art 2 of protocol 1). No one is to be denied the right to education and in making provision relating to education and teaching the state must respect the right of parents to ensure that such education and teaching conforms with their own religious and philosophical convictions[17].

THE RIGHT TO FREE ELECTIONS (art 3 of protocol 1). States are to hold free elections at reasonable intervals by secret ballot and under conditions which will ensure the free expression of the people in the choice of the legislature[18].

ABOLITION OF THE DEATH PENALTY (arts 1 and 2 of protocol 6). The death penalty is abolished, albeit that states may continue to make provision for the death penalty in respect of acts 'committed in time of war or of imminent threat of war'.

1   HRA 1998, s 1(1)–(3), Sch 1. The Convention rights have effect subject to any designated derogation or reservation from ECHR which has been entered into properly by the United Kingdom – see HRA 1998, ss 1(2), 14, 15 and Sch 3. Such a derogation, from art 5(1) ECHR (liberty and security of the person), was intimated to the Secretariat General of the Council of Europe by the United Kingdom on 18 December 2001 in relation to the extended power to detain contained in the Anti-terrorism, Crime and Security Act 2001. The derogation was implemented at a domestic level by the Human Rights Act 1998 (Designated Derogation) Order 2001, SI 2001/3644. Derogations must, however, be justified by reference to art 15 ECHR which provides that such a derogation may be made 'in time of war or other public emergency threatening the life of the nation' and must be limited to 'the extent strictly required by the exigencies of the situation'. The United Kingdom's derogation was held by the House of Lords (*A v Secretary of State for the Home Department* [2005] 2 AC 68) and by the ECtHR (*A & Others v United Kingdom* (2009) 26 BHRC 1) not to have been justified inasmuch as it represented a disproportionate and discriminatory (in treating nationals and non-nationals differently) response to the admitted public emergency faced by the United Kingdom. The 2001 Order was quashed by the House of Lords and the United Kingdom withdrew its derogation on 16 March 2005.

2   See *R (Sacker) v HM Coroner for West Yorkshire* [2004] 2 All ER 487; *R (Gentle) v Prime Minister* [2008] 1 AC 1356; and *Smith v Ministry of Defence* [2014] AC 52. There have been failed attempts in the United Kingdom and before the ECtHR to argue that art 2 confers a positive right (which must be protected by the state) to choose to end one's life, for example by assisted suicide or euthanasia (see *R (Pretty) v DPP (Secretary of State for the Home Department intervening)* [2001] 1 AC 800; and *Pretty v United Kingdom* (2002) 35 EHRR 1) although if the state chooses to make provision for such a right that will not necessarily amount to a breach of the article. The question of assisted suicide also engages art 8 ECHR: see *R (Nicklinson) v Ministry of Justice* [2013] UKSC 38, [2014] 3 All ER 843.

3   This is one of the most 'absolute' rights guaranteed by the ECHR and is not limited by any exceptions in the way in which, for example, arts 8, 10 and 12 are limited. It is intended to prevent the state from engaging in, or permitting, the use of force or ill-treatment, particularly in relation to detained persons. Cases involving the United Kingdom have concerned, for example, interrogation techniques used by the security forces in Northern Ireland (*Ireland v United Kingdom* (1978) 2 EHRR 25) and the use of corporal punishment on the Isle of Man (*Tyrer v United Kingdom* (1978) 2 EHRR 1). The success of Scottish prisoners in arguing that the practice of 'slopping out' amounted to degrading treatment and a breach of art 3 has been one of the most significant Scottish examples of the use of the Convention since the incorporation of the ECHR by the HRA (and by SA 1998, see para 6.20: *Napier v Scottish Ministers* 2005 1 SC 229 and see A Lawson and A Mukherjee 'Slopping out in Scotland: the limits of degradation and respect' 2004 6 EHRLR 645. While slopping out amounted to a breach of art 3, use of a chemical rather than flushing toilet did not: *Greens, Petitioner* 2011 SLT 549.

4   In 2005, the Joint Committee on Human Rights expressed concerns that certain provisions of the Children and Adoption Bill – which became the Children and Adoption Act 2006 – relating to the imposition of unpaid work as a penalty for breach of a contact order were likely to breach art 4. See Joint Committee on Human Rights, Fifth Report of Session 2005–2006, Legislative Scrutiny: Second Progress Report, HL 90/HC 767. The Supreme Court held in 2013 that a legislative requirement imposed on claimants of a social security benefit – Jobseeker's Allowance – that such claimants participate in unpaid work came 'nowhere close to the type of exploitative conduct at which art 4 is aimed': *R (Reilly) v Secretary of State for Work and Pensions* [2013] UKSC 68, [2014] AC 453 at para 83. The subordinate legislation in question was, though, defective on other grounds.

5   The compatibility of this article with aspects of the United Kingdom's anti-terrorism laws has been particularly controversial and has brought the courts into direct conflict with the UK Government and Parliament. As noted above (n 1), the derogation from art 5 which was felt by the UK government to be required by provisions of the Anti-terrorism, Crime and Security Act 2001 was found not to be justified by reference to art 15 ECHR. The offending provisions

themselves – allowing for indefinite detention without trial of certain non-nationals – were held, as had been anticipated by the government, to breach the art 5 rights of those detained (*A v Secretary of State for the Home Department* [2005] 2 AC 68). Parliament responded to this ruling by introducing a system of 'control orders' – effectively house arrest – under the Prevention of Terrorism Act 2005. The procedure by which these control orders were made was the subject of successful challenge in 2009 on the grounds that they breached the art 6 rights of the individuals concerned: *Secretary of State for the Home Department v F* [2010] 2 AC 269. Control orders were replaced by Terrorism Prevention and Investigation Measures under the Terrorism Prevention and Investigation Measures Act 2011. See the Second Report of the Independent Reviewer on the operation of the Terrorism Prevention and Investigation Measures Act 2011 at https://terrorismlegislationreviewer.independent.gov.uk.

6   See in particular Lester, Pannick & Herberg op cit pp 277–348 for much more detailed treatment than could be given here.

7   For an example of the court declining to find a breach of art 7 see *R (McFetrich) v Secretary of State for the Home Department* [2003] 4 All ER 1093 concerning differences in sentencing policy affecting a prisoner transferred from Scotland to England. On sentencing guidelines produced after the date of the relevant criminal offence see *R v Bao* [2008] 2 Cr App R (S) 10.

8   The ECtHR has made it clear that art 8 rights can in some circumstances be enjoyed by legal persons such as companies as well as by individuals: see *Société Colas Est v France* (2004) 29 EHRR 373 and *Wieser v Bicos Beteiligungen GmbH v Austria* (2008) 46 EHRR 54.

9   Which may include business premises: see *Niemietz v Germany* (1992) 16 EHRR 97.

10 Interference with the correspondence and other communications of prisoners has been the subject of particular litigation in the Scottish courts: see *Beggs v Scottish Ministers* 2006 SC 649 and *Potter v Scottish Ministers* 2007 SLT 1019. Segregation of a prisoner has also been held not to infringe his art 8 rights: *Shahid v Scottish Ministers* 2014 SC 490.

11 There has been a great deal of debate about the extent to which external, physical symbols of religious belief are 'manifestations' of religious belief. Even where they are, it may be lawful to place restrictions on the wearing or exhibiting of those symbols: see *R (SB) v Governors of Denbigh High School* [2007] 1 AC 100 (a jilbab (headscarf) worn by a Muslim schoolgirl was such a manifestation but it was not a breach of her art 9 rights to require her to adhere to the school's dress code which excluded the jilbab); *R (Playfoot) v Governing Body of Millais School* [2007] HRLR 34 (a 'purity ring' was not a manifestation of Christian belief and art 9 not engaged by a school dress code which forbade the wearing of it); and *R (Watkins-Singh) v Governing Body of Aberdare Girls' High School* [2008] ELR 561 (a religious bangle worn by a Sikh schoolgirl was a manifestation of her religious beliefs). These cases (albeit in the education context) must now be read in the context of the decision of the ECtHR in *Eweida v United Kingdom* (2013) 57 EHRR 8 in which the Strasbourg Court considered the complaints of four individuals that they had each, in the context of different jobs and different employers, suffered the breach of their art 9 rights. So, for example, the first applicant, Ms Eweida, worked for an airline and had been forbidden to wear a crucifix while in uniform, as had the second applicant who was a Christian nurse. In holding, inter alia, that there had been a disproportionate interference with the art 9 rights of the first applicant (but not of the other applicants) the Court departed from the previously understood position that a person complaining of a breach of art 9 in the workplace could negate the interference by leaving their job: rather the possibility of accommodating the person's beliefs should be weighed in the overall assessment of the proportionality of a restriction.

12 The protections afforded by art 9 are enjoyed principally by individuals although in some cases churches or other 'collective' entities may act on behalf of individual members of the church in claiming a breach of art 9 rights. See the discussion in Reed and Murdoch, op cit pp 872 to 874. A series of recent cases have addressed the conflict between art 9 rights and anti-discrimination law: see in particular *R(E) v JFS Governing Body* [2009] UKSC 15, [2010] 2 AC 728 and *Hall v Bull* [2014] 1 All ER 919.

13 Art 10 is concerned with, amongst other things, rights to engage in the expression of views which may be unpalatable or offensive to 'majority' or 'mainstream' views. This includes the expression of racist opinions or opinions which might provoke religious division (*Jersild v Denmark* (1995) 19 EHRR 1); expressions of support for unlawful activity including terrorism (*Norwood v United Kingdom* (2005) 40 EHRR SE11); political speech (*R v BBC, ex parte ProLife Alliance* [2004] 1 AC 185); and advertising (*Stambuk v Germany* (2003) 36 EHRR 1059). See the discussion below (para 13.24) concerning those provisions of HRA 1998 which seek to balance art 8 rights with the freedom of the press protected by art 10.

14 States are entitled to exclude same sex couples from the right to marry (*Rees v United Kingdom* (1986) 9 EHRR 56) but not transsexual persons (*Goodwin v United Kingdom* (2002) 35 EHRR 447). See also *MB v Secretary of State for Work and Pensions* [2014] EWCA Civ 1112, [2014] ICR 1129 and *Hämäläinen v Finland* (Application No 37359/09) 16 July 2014.

15 And for discussion of the concept of 'other status' see *Kjelsden, Busk Madsen and Pedersen v Denmark* (1976) 1 EHRR 711; and *R (S) v Chief Constable of Yorkshire Police* [2004] 1 WLR 2196.

16 Art 1 of protocol 1 is concerned with rights of property and with the interference with or deprivation of property by the state. Obvious examples concern confiscation or compulsory acquisition of property – which may be permissible provided proper procedures are followed (and art 1, protocol 1 claims are frequently combined with claims about breaches of art 6) and appropriate compensation is paid. *AXA General Insurance, Petitioners* 2012 SC (UKSC) 122 (discussed in detail at para 14.26 below) was an unsuccessful attempt to strike down an Act of the Scottish Parliament on grounds of its incompatibility with Article 1 of Protocol 1 while in *Salvesen v Riddell* 2013 SC (UKSC) 236 (also discussed at para 14.27 below) certain provisions of the Agricultural Holdings (Scotland) Act 2013 were held to be incompatible with art 1 of Protocol 1. A breach can give rise to a claim for damages calculated on a commercial basis: *R (Infinis Plc) v Gas and Electricity Markets Authority* [2013] JPL 1037.

17 See *Campbell and Cosans v United Kingdom* (1982) 4 EHRR 293.

18 See *Hirst v United Kingdom (No 2)* (2006) 42 EHRR 41 and para 5.6.

Public Authorities and Convention Rights

13.12   HRA 1998, s 6(1) provides that it is unlawful for a public authority to act in a way which is incompatible with a Convention right[1]. The definition of 'public authority' for the purposes of HRA 1998, s 6 is not straightforward and has been the subject of considerable debate and partial reform. Firstly, it provides that 'public authority' includes any 'court or tribunal'[2]. By requiring courts themselves to comply with Convention rights – and not just to enforce compliance by others – it is argued that HRA 1998 has what is described as 'horizontal effect'[3]. Thus, in developing and applying the common law, even in disputes involving only private parties, the courts must do so in a manner which is compatible with the Convention rights of the parties before them[4]. Secondly, HRA 1998 provides that a public authority also includes 'any person certain of whose functions are functions of a public nature'[5] but qualifies this definition with the proviso that even where a person has some public functions 'in relation to a particular act, a person is not a public authority ... if the nature of the act is private'[6]. This part of the definition of 'public authority' has been a cause of difficulty for the English courts in particular[7]. Decisions about what constitutes a 'public function' and, as a consequence, which bodies should be bound to act compatibly with the Convention rights inevitably involve judgments by the courts in areas which are close to the boundary between law and politics. In response to concerns in some quarters about the interpretation of 'public authority' by the courts and the impact which that might have on the protection of individual rights, the Joint Committee on Human Rights has on a number of occasions called for amendment of the definition so as to ensure an expansive rather than restrictive application of HRA 1998[8]. Very specific provision was made by the Health and Social Care Act 2008 which does not amend the definition of public authority in HRA 1998 but which does provide that a person 'who provides accommodation, together with nursing or personal care, in a care home for an individual under arrangements made with [the person] under the relevant statutory provisions is to be taken for the purposes of subsection (3)(b) of section 6 of the Human Rights Act 1998 to be exercising a function of a public nature in doing so'[9].

The question of whether a public authority has acted unlawfully in terms of HRA 1998, s 6(1) may be raised in proceedings in 'the appropriate court or tribunal'[10], for instance in an application for judicial review[11]. Breach of Convention rights has, therefore, become a very important new ground for judicial review.

1   This general rule is subject to a number of exceptions and qualifications. For instance, in line with HRA 1998, ss 3, 4 (see below) there is an exception in the case of acts unavoidably required by 'primary legislation'.
2   HRA 1998, s 6(3)(a).
3   For discussion, see M Hunt, 'The 'Horizontal' Effect of the Human Rights Act' [1998] PL 423; D Oliver 'The Human Rights Act and Public Law/Private Law Divides' (2000) 4 EHRLR 343; R Buxton 'The Human Rights Act and Private Law' (2000) 116 LQR 48; N Bamforth 'The true "horizontal effect" of the Human Rights Act 1998' (2001) 117 LQR 34; A L Young 'Remedial and substantive horizontality: the common law and *Douglas v Hello! Ltd*' [2002] PL 232; K Hughes 'Horizontal privacy' (2009) 125 LQR 244; K Visser and E Reid (eds), *Private Law and Human Rights: Bringing Rights Home in Scotland and South Africa* (2013).
4   Similarly, the obligation imposed on the courts by HRA 1998, s 3 to interpret primary and subordinate legislation in a manner compatible with Convention rights is relevant in even 'private' disputes.
5   HRA 1998, s 6(3)(b). Excluded from this part of the definition of 'public authority' are 'either House of Parliament or a person exercising functions in connection with proceedings in Parliament'.
6   HRA 1998, s 6(5).
7   See, in particular, *Poplar Housing and Regeneration Community Association v Donoghue* [2002] QB 48; *R (Heather) v Leonard Cheshire Foundation* [2002] 2 All ER 936; *Marcic v Thames Water Utilities* [2002] QB 929; *Aston Cantlow and Wilmcote with Billesley Parochial Church Council v Wallbank* [2004] 1 AC 546 and *L v Birmingham City Council* [2008] 1 AC 95.
8   Joint Committee on Human Rights, Seventh Report of Session 2003–04, 'The Meaning of Public Authority under the Human Rights Act', HL Paper 39/HC 382; Joint Committee on Human Rights, Ninth Report of Session 2006–07, 'The Meaning of Public Authority under the Human Rights Act', HL Paper 77/HC 410.
9   Health and Social Care Act 2008, s 145.
10 HRA 1998, s 7(2). For Scotland, see the Human Rights Act 1998 (Jurisdiction) (Scotland) Rules 2000, SSI 2000/301, r 3 of which provides that for the purpose of this section the appropriate court is 'any civil court of tribunal which has jurisdiction to grant the remedy sought'; and Act of Adjournal (Criminal Procedure Rules Amendment No 2) (Human Rights Act 1998) 2000, SSI 2000/315.
11 In all cases, proceedings are subject to the applicant's being a 'victim' for the purposes of the ECHR and subject also to restrictions as to remedies: see HRA 1998, ss 7(1), (3) and 8.

Territorial extent of the Human Rights Act

13.13   Particularly, though not exclusively, as a consequence of the United Kingdom's recent involvement in conflicts in the Middle East, questions have arisen about the extent to which the United Kingdom – through its armed forces – is bound to act compatibly with HRA 1998 where it is operating overseas. It has been held that the application of HRA 1998 depends on the extent to which the United Kingdom exercises 'effective control' of a territory and that, even where effective control of a particular territory is absent, HRA 1998 does apply to activity within British embassies, military bases and the like[1]. It also applies to protect members of the armed forces themselves when conducting operations overseas[2].

1 See *R (Quark Fishing Ltd) v Secretary of State for Foreign and Commonwealth Affairs* [2006] 1 AC 529; *R (Al-Skeini) v Secretary of State for Defence* [2008] 1 AC 153; *R (Al-Jedda) v Secretary of State for Defence* [2008] 1 AC 332; *R (Hassan) v Secretary of State for Defence* [2009] EWHC 309 (Admin); *Mohammed v Ministry of Defence* [2014] EWHC 1369 (QB).
2 *Smith v Ministry of Defence* [2014] AC 52.

Commissions, Commissioners and Others

13.14 HRA 1998 is concerned predominantly with the imposition of an obligation on public authorities to act compatibly with Convention rights. The natural arena within which debates about the scope and meaning of those rights will take place is the courts and the approach of the courts to determining disputes about the rights conferred by HRA 1998 is discussed in Chapter 14. It can be, and is, argued by many, however, that the protection of human rights is about much more than the legal enforceability of those rights and the determination of individual disputes in an adversarial contest. Rather, respect for individual rights requires changes in culture within public authorities, public education and awareness-raising about the importance of rights and the application of political pressure to the legislature and the executive to ensure an ongoing focus on the protection of rights.

The perceived need for an official 'flagbearer' for human rights at a domestic level, with a role perhaps comparable to that of the Council of Europe at the European level, led to the creation of commissions and commissioners with broad remits in relation to the promotion and protection of human rights[1]. The Scottish Commission for Human Rights Act 2006 (SCHRA 2006) created the Scottish Commission for Human Rights which now 'trades as' the Scottish Human Rights Commission[2]. The Commission is a statutory corporation comprising a chair (currently Professor Alan Miller) and up to four other members[3]. It has a 'general duty…through the exercise of its functions under this Act, to promote human rights and, in particular, to encourage best practice in relation to human rights', which rights include but are not limited to the Convention rights[4]. To enable it to fulfil this general duty, the Commission has a range of powers including the power to review and recommend changes to 'any area of the law of Scotland' and 'any policies or practices of any Scottish public authorities'[5]. It may also publish information, provide advice, conduct research and provide education and training[6] and it may consult, act jointly with, co-operate with or assist any other person[7]. SCHRA 2006 makes quite careful provision about the manner in which the Commission can become involved in legal proceedings. It is expressly prohibited from providing assistance (which includes advice, guidance and grants) to or in respect of any person in connection with any claim or legal proceedings to which that person is or may become a party[8]. However, the Commission may, with the leave, or at the invitation, of the court[9], intervene in legal proceedings for the purpose of making a submission to the court on an issue arising in the proceedings. The provision of SCHRA 2006 which confers this power removes any doubt about the '*vires*' of an attempt by the Commission to intervene in relevant proceedings but does not give the Commission a right of intervention: it will continue to be a matter for the court to decide whether or not to allow such an intervention. The power conferred on the Commission relates to civil proceedings only and excludes children's hearings proceedings[10]. The extent of the Commission[er]'s power to intervene in proceedings was the subject of considerable debate at Stage 1 of the Bill's passage[11].

Because not all aspects of human rights protection in Scotland are devolved under SA 1998 (see para 6.16), the Great Britain Commission for Equality and Human Rights (EHRC) also has a role to play in Scotland. The EHRC was created by the Equality Act 2006 (EA 2006)[12] and took over the responsibilities formerly discharged by the Equal Opportunities Commission, the Commission for Racial Equality and the Disability Rights Commission. It was given new powers and duties in relation to human rights, with specific provision being made for Scotland to take account of the 'reserved/devolved' boundary. So, EA 2006 provides that the 'Commission shall not take human rights action in relation to a matter if the Scottish Parliament has legislative competence to enable a person to take action of that kind in relation to a matter'[13]. 'Human rights action' is defined by reference to a list of other provisions of EA 2006 but includes the promotion of the understanding of the importance of human rights, encouraging good practice in relation to human rights and encouraging public authorities to comply with s 6 of HRA 1998. In addition, despite its general duty to take account of 'any relevant human rights' in discharging certain of its functions, the EHRC shall not, in the course of discharging those functions 'consider the question whether a person's human rights have been contravened if the Scottish Parliament has legislative competence to enable a person to consider that question'[14]. The potentially unhelpful consequences of these provisions are intended to be ameliorated by provisions which permit the EHRC to take action with the consent of a person 'established by Act of the Scottish Parliament' and whose 'principal duties relate to human rights and are similar to any of the Commission's duties under section 9'[15] and to act jointly or cooperate for a purpose relating to human rights and connected with Scotland[16]. The EHRC has somewhat wider powers in relation to legal proceedings than does the Scottish Commission for Human Rights, being entitled to 'institute or intervene in legal proceedings, whether for judicial review or otherwise, if it appears to the Commission that the proceedings are relevant to a matter in connection with which the Commission has a function'[17]. To avoid any doubt about the EHRC's title and interest/locus standi to raise proceedings, it is provided explicitly that it is to be 'taken to have title and interest in relation to the subject matter of any legal proceedings in Scotland which it has capacity to institute, or in which it has capacity to intervene, by virtue of subsection (1)'[18]. A summary of the EHRC's intervention activity is available on its website[19].

Amongst a range of other provisions of EA 2006 relating to Scotland, those concerning the constitution of the EHRC are particularly noteworthy. The Commission is to be comprised of between 10 and 15 Commissioners including at least one who has been appointed with the consent of the Scottish Ministers and who 'knows about conditions in Scotland'[20]. The current 'Scotland Commissioner is Ms Kaliani Lyle. In addition, the EHRC is required to establish a 'Scotland Committee' the role of which is to advise the EHRC about the exercise of its functions so far as they affect Scotland and with whom the EHRC is obliged to consult before it exercises a function in a manner likely to affect persons in Scotland[21].

Finally, mention should also be made of the Scotland's Commissioner for Children and Young Persons (SCCYP[22]). The SCCYP's general function is to promote and safeguard the rights of children and young people[23] and he has a wide range of powers in the exercise of which she must have regard, amongst other things, to any relevant provisions of the United Nations Convention on the Rights of the Child[24]. The current commissioner is Tam Baillie who took office in May 2009, replacing the first commissioner Professor Kathleen Marshall. In addition to the role to be played by the commissions described above, there are a number of other bodies, formal and informal, which play a role in generating public debate and discussion about human rights protection and in providing mechanisms of political accountability. At a parliamentary level, the Scottish Parliament has a cross-party group on human rights which meets on a regular basis but which, in terms of status and output, cannot match the Westminster Parliament's Joint Committee on Human Rights. That Committee has proved influential in provoking debate and holding the Westminster Parliament and UK government to account in relation to the impact of both legislation and executive action human rights.

1   In addition to the Scottish and Great Britain Commissions discussed below, the Northern Ireland Human Rights Commission was established in 1999 by the Northern Ireland Act 1998 following the Good Friday Agreement. For discussion of the power of the NIHRC to intervene in legal proceedings see *R (Northern Ireland Human Rights Commission) v Greater Belfast Coroner* [2002] HRLR 35 and for criticism of the Commission in using its powers to intervene in legal proceedings in the public interest see *Re E (A Child)* [2009] 1 AC 536 per Lord Hoffmann at p 542.
2   See www.scottishhumanrights.com. The Bill which became SCHRA began life as the Scottish Commissioner for Human Rights Bill.
3   There are three other members currently: Professor Kay Hampton, Ms Shelagh McCall and Mr Matt Smith.
4   SCHRA 2006, s 2.
5   SCHRA, s 4.
6   SCHRA, s 3.
7   SCHRA, s 5.
8   SCHRA, s 6.
9   Which in this context means only the Sheriff Court, Court of Session and Land Court: SCHRA, s 14(9). Section 14(8) provides that this specific power is 'without prejudice to the Commission's capacity to intervene in any proceedings before any court or tribunal under an enactment or in accordance with the practice of the court or tribunal'.
10 SCHRA, s 14.
11 See Stage 1 Report, SP Paper 508, 23 February 2006.
12 EA 2006 was principally concerned with reform of the institutional arrangements for protection of rights and preventing discrimination. The substantive law of discrimination for which the CEHR has responsibility is contained in the Equality Act 2010.
13 EA 2006, s 7(1).
14 EA 2006, s 7(3) as amended.
15 EA 2006, s 7(4)
16 EA 2006, s 7(5).
17 EA 2006, s 30(1).
18 EA 2006, s 30(2).
19 http://www.equalityhumanrights.com/legal-and-policy/our-legal-work/strategic-litigation. For example, the EHRC intervened in the Supreme Court in *North v Dumfries and Galloway Council* 2013 SC (UKSC) 298 on an equal pay question.

20 EA 2006, s 2 and Sch 1, para 2(3). Similar provision is made for the appointment of a Commissioner with the consent of the Welsh Ministers and who knows about conditions in Wales.
21 See EA 2006, s 2 and Sch 1, paras 16 to 23. Again, similar provision is made for a Wales Committee.
22 Created by the Commissioner for Children and Young People (Scotland) Act 2003.
23 EA 2006, s 4(1).
24 Ibid, s 5(2).

Human Rights, Politics and Possible Reforms

13.15   At the outset of this chapter we referred to the importance of relationships between the state and individual: to the benefits which individuals can derive from the exercise of state power and to the importance of providing protections for the individual against the abuse of power by the state. In the years since the incorporation of the ECHR by the HRA 1998 there have developed (at least) two separate but often conflated debates about the protection of human rights in the United Kingdom which sit alongside those which concern rights and protections against state power. The first is a debate about responsibilities owed by individuals to one another and to the state itself and the extent to which the enjoyment of fundamental rights is conditional upon the discharge by individuals of those responsibilities. The second, broadly, is a debate about the relationship between the United Kingdom's courts and the European Court of Human Rights in Strasbourg (often confused with the Court of Justice of the European Union) and the extent to which human rights protection within the United Kingdom is or should be the result of decisions of a 'foreign' court.

The cruder versions of both debates play out fairly regularly in the pages of the tabloid press, usually in response to a decision of the courts which is perceived to have put the interests (and Convention rights) of an undeserving individual – perhaps a delinquent youth, a hardened criminal or a terrorist suspect – before those of the wider community. At the level of national politics, the discussion has led to proposals from some quarters for repeal of the Human Rights Act and withdrawal of the United Kingdom from the Council of Europe.

Rights and Responsibilities

13.16   In its 2007 Green Paper 'The Governance of Britain'[1], the UK Government announced that it wanted to 'forge a new relationship between government and citizen'. A range of issues were discussed in the Green Paper but a chapter was dedicated to the 'citizen and the state' and canvassed a number of options which, if implemented, might convey to individuals 'a better sense of their British identity in a globalised world'[2]. Options included offering to everyone within the United Kindgom 'an easily understood set of rights and responsibilities when they receive citizenship', the launch of a Youth Citizenship Commission and greater investment in education and integration of new citizens to the United Kingdom. In addition, the government asked Lord Goldsmith QC to carry out a review of citizenship, 'looking both at legal aspects and other issues including civic participation and social responsibility'[3]. The outcome of that review was the 2008 report '*Citizenship: Our Common Bond*' ('the Goldsmith report', also discussed above at para 13.2), the predominant focus of which was identifying the distinctions between citizens and other non-citizen residents (such as, for example, those seeking asylum) and seeking to analyse whether those distinctions were rational and defensible. A persistent theme was the importance of identifying responsibilities as well as rights of citizens and Lord Goldsmith recommended that the government consider the formulation of a statement of rights and responsibilities 'which is not intended to be justiciable but will draw on existing rights and duties and rely on those other laws and enactments for their force'[4].

This consideration was to take place as part of the government's wider project of examining the case for a 'British Bill of Rights' which had been adverted to in the Green Paper and by Prime Minister Brown in 2007 when the Green Paper was published[5]. In fact, the initiative so far as discussion about a Bill of Rights was concerned was taken from the government fairly forcefully by the Joint Committee on Human Rights which launched its own inquiry into the need, if any, for such a Bill of Rights. It took evidence from a range of sources – including on one occasion sitting in a Committee Room of the Holyrood Parliament[6] – and in August 2008 produced a comprehensive report in which it concluded that the United Kingdom should adopt a Bill of Rights[7] which would go further than HRA 1998 in conferring a number of new rights including certain social and economic rights but which would not result in a constitutional revolution by giving powers to the courts to strike down primary legislation. So far as responsibilities were concerned, the Joint Committee was clear: 'rights cannot be contingent on performing duties or responsibilities. We recommend that a Bill of Rights and Freedoms should not include directly enforceable duties. However, we acknowledge that responsibilities are implicit in human rights instruments. On that basis, and to that end we suggest that the language of responsibilities could have a role to play in a Bill of Rights and Freedoms, perhaps in the Preamble to the Bill'[8]. Although not described as such, the further Green Paper published by the government in March 2009 – 'Rights and Responsibilities: developing our constitutional framework'[9] – was in large part a response to the Joint Committee's work.

In the last edition of this book we described that Green Paper as something of a 'retrenchment' but, as it turned out, the question of a bill of rights remained firmly on the agenda. David Cameron, having been appointed Prime Minister following the general election of 2010, took steps to fulfil an earlier commitment to replace HRA 1998 with a British Bill of Rights. A Commission on a Bill of Rights, under the chairmanship of Sir Leigh Lewis[10] was established by the Government in March 2011. It was charged with investigating the creation of a UK Bill of Rights that 'incorporates and builds on all our obligations under the European Convention on Human Rights, ensures that these rights continue to be enshrined in UK law, and protects and extend our liberties.' It was to examine the operation and implementation of these obligations, and consider ways to promote a better understanding of their true scope and provide interim advice to the Government on the ongoing Interlaken process to reform the Strasbourg court ahead of and following the United Kingdom's Chairmanship of the Council of Europe[11]. It was also to consult with the public, judiciary and devolved administrations and legislatures, and aim to report no later than by the end of 2012.

The Commission's life was not a particularly happy one. Its membership comprised (amongst others) several individuals who were very publicly on record as supporting HRA 1998 and the regime created by it and several individuals who were very publicly 'against'. In March 2012 one of the eight commissioners, Dr Michael Pinto-Duschinsky resigned from the Commission following reports that the chairman and several other commissioners had written to the government to complain that Dr Pinto-Duschinsky was impeding progress. It did fulfil its mandate to provide interim advice to the government on reform of the ECtHR and published its final report in December 2012[13]. Even then it was clear that there had been difficulty in reaching agreement on the conclusions reached by the Commission: the final report recorded, for example, the regret of some members of the Commission that its terms of reference had presupposed the United Kingdom's continuing adherence to the ECHR and ECtHR. The conclusions themselves were relatively weak: 'As a minimum none of us considers that the idea of a UK Bill of Rights in principle should be finally rejected at this stage. We all consider that, at the least, it is an idea of potential value which deserves further exploration at an appropriate time and in an appropriate way'[14]. The majority on the Commission went further in saying that on balance there was a strong argument in favour of a Bill of Rights but two of the seven – Baroness Helena Kennedy and Professor Philippe Sands – dissented[15]. On 22 January 2013, Damian Green, the Minister for Policing and Criminal Justice, announced that no formal response to the Commission's report would be made by the Government[16] – a position explicable by reference to the divergent views held within the coalition on the importance of preserving HRA 1998 and accession to the ECHR. The issue does, however, remain very live in advance of the 2015 general election. In October 2014 the Conservative Party published its own proposals[17] which include 'repealing Labour's Human Rights Act', limiting the use of human rights laws to the 'most serious cases' and 'limiting the reach of human rights cases to the UK'. Some of the proposals concerned the second debate mentioned above: the relationship between the UK courts and Strasbourg.

1   Cm 7170, 2007.
2   Ibid, para 185.
3   Ibid, para 193.
4   The Goldsmith report, para 31.
5   HC Deb 3 July 2007 col 819.
6   On 10 March 2008.
7   29th Report of Session 2007–08, A Bill of Rights for the UK?, HL Paper 165, HC 150.
8   Ibid, p 6.
9   Cm 7577, 2009.
10 A former Permanent Secretary at the Department for Work and Pensions.
11 The process which led to adoption of the 15th and 16th Protocols discussed above.
12 Letter from Sir Leigh Lewis to the Deputy Prime Minister Nick Clegg and Lord Chancellor Kenneth Clarke 28 July 2011.
13 A UK Bill of Rights? The Choice Before Us.
14 Para 67.
15 Para 88 et seq. See, for discussion, H Fenwick, *'The Human Rights Act or a British Bill of Rights: creating a down-grading recalibration of rights against the counter-terror backdrop?'* [2012] PL 468; and F Klug and A Williams, *'The choice before us? The report of the Commission on a Bill of Rights'* [2013] PL 459.
16 HC Hansard, 22 January 2013, cols 215–6W.
17 *'Protecting Human Rights in the UK'*.

Strasbourg and London

13.17   The Conservative Party's proposals document expressed a desire for reforms which would mean that 'The European Court of Human Rights is no longer binding over the UK Supreme Court' and that 'The European Court of Human Rights is no longer able to order a change in UK law and becomes an advisory body only'. Neither premise may quite accurately reflect the existing legal position but each reflects a wider debate about the quality of the judgments of the ECtHR and the extent to which those judgments should influence the determination of human rights cases by the British courts. Relatively unusually, a number of judges have been outspoken in their criticism of the current approach. So, for example, Lord Justice Laws in a 2013 Hamlyn Lecture entitled 'The Common Law and Europe' (addressing both the ECHR and the EU) criticised the approach taken by the House of Lords and subsequently the Supreme Court which, in his view, accorded greater weight to the decisions of the Strasbourg court than was required or justified by HRA 1998, s 2[1].

This lecture was followed later in 2013 by another delivered by Supreme Court Justice Sumption in Kuala Lumpur entitled 'The Limits of Law'[2]. Lord Sumption was highly critical of what he considered to be illegitimate judicial law-making by Strasbourg in developing and extending the scope of the rights conferred by the ECHR: 'The treatment of the Convention by the European Court of Human Rights as a 'living instrument' allows it to make new law in respects which are not foreshadowed by the language of the Convention and which Parliament would not necessarily have anticipated when it passed the Act. It is in practice incapable of being reversed by legislation, short of withdrawing from the Convention altogether. In reality, therefore, the Human Rights Act involves the transfer of part of an essentially legislative power to another body.' Lord Sumption also pursued a related theme which has been taken up with some energy recently by the UK Supreme Court; the importance of the British common law in protecting individual rights. So, for example, in *R (Sturnham) v Parole Board*, Lord Reed emphasised that the 'starting point' for analysis should be 'our own legal principles rather than the judgments of an international court'[3]. Space does not permit a full discussion of the question of the appropriate role of the Strasbourg Court or of the competing voices participating in that debate or of their motivations[4]. Such a discussion would have to address, amongst other issues, the extent to which the reassertion by the Supreme Court of the common law might itself be viewed as a pre-emptive attempt to defuse political momentum against a move towards repeal of HRA 1998 or withdrawal from the Council of Europe. Precisely how the United Kingdom's relationship with the ECHR and its enforcement mechanisms might change will not become clear, if it all, until after the next general election. It seems unlikely, though, that the issue will go away.

1 Referencing, in particular, the cases of *R (Ullah) v Special Adjudicator* [2004] UKHL 26, [2004] 2 AC 323, *R (Osborn) v The Parole Board* [2013] UKSC 61 and *R (Chester) v Secretary of State for Justice* [2013] UKSC 63.
2 The lecture is available on the Supreme Court's website: www.supremecourt.co.uk.
3 [2013] 2 AC 254 , para 29.

4 See, by way of example, Judge JP Costa, 'The relationship between the European Court of Human Rights and the national courts' (2013) 3 EHRLR 264 and P Mahoney, 'The relationship between the Strasbourg court and the national courts' (2014) 130 LQR 568.

POLICE POWERS OF DETENTION AND ARREST

13.18   Reflected in art 5 ECHR are the threats to individuals of the powers of public authorities to deprive them of their personal liberty. Inevitably, the extent of these powers, their limits, and the protections afforded to individuals are a matter of concern, especially since, in the modern law, these powers range widely. A selection may, however, be made under the headings of police powers to detain and arrest, with associated powers to search the person and property and to question suspects. These are treated in the pages which follow. At para 13.19 below, we move on to the powers of the police and other authorities to maintain public order (including restraints on behaviour in public and the conduct of processions).

But first a word on the police service itself. Many of the powers to be discussed in this section and that which follows are exercisable by public bodies – in the main, ministers at the Scotland or UK level (or civil servants on their behalf) or local authorities – which are established, organised, and accountable in familiar ways[1]. The police service, however, is a special case and one which has recently undergone a profound change. Until March 2013, it could be described as having a tripartite structure. Policing in Scotland was organised at a local level in that local authorities, acting through joint boards to produce eight police authorities, provided decentralised provision of premises, equipment and pay for the forces in their areas. The police authorities had the important task of appointing the chief constable – the second element in the overall structure. From that point, however, police management diverged from that of other services. Instead of council control over policy and practice in the force, with the local democratic accountability which that implies, it was the chief constable on whom those responsibilities were directly conferred. One obligation retained by the police authority was that of meeting the cost of any damages awarded against the chief constable where a member of the force was held liable in a civil action[2].

The third element in the constitutional structure of the police was the Scottish Ministers who had significant powers of central control over police authorities and chief constables. In particular, police funding was very largely a matter for ministerial control, as well the size of forces and the general regulation of police organisation[3].

From April 2013, however, the tradition of avoiding a national police force was abruptly abandoned – ostensibly in the interests of efficiency and financial savings. The Police and Fire Reform (Scotland) Act 2012 (PFR(S)A 2012) abolished the eight local police forces and replaced them with a single police service – Police Scotland – headed by a chief constable[4]. The Act created a single Scottish Police Authority, appointed by the Scottish Ministers, which appoints the chief constable (with the approval of the Scottish Ministers) and discharges other functions inherited from its eight predecessors[5]. Arrangements for the handling of complaints against the police are made by the Authority and the chief constable, subject to the supervision of the police investigations and review commissioner. A measure of local accountability is maintained through the requirement of the appointment of local commanders (s 44). There have, however, been complaints about an inappropriate insistence on uniformity of policing provision across the country and there are emerging doubts about the financial savings achieved by the reforms.

Although the governance of the police service as a whole is in the hands of the Scottish Ministers, Police Scotland and the chief constable, most police powers are vested in individual officers[6] and, in so far as constables exercise powers which may affect individual liberty, they do so against the background of two important principles. The first is the rule of law[7] itself which seeks to ensure that no invasion of individual rights at the hand of a public official is permitted unless authorised by law which may have its source either in statute or in common law. We shall find that, in the modern law, statute dominates but the police also have some remaining common law powers. We should also note, however, that, when obtained, the consent of the individual affected normally removes the need for specific legal authority. For instance, the police need legal authority for a search of premises or of a person. A search conducted with consent, however, is lawful in itself.

The second informing principle derives from art 5 ECHR which, subject to specified exceptions, provides that 'everyone has the right to liberty and security of person'. Any laws which confer powers on the police must themselves be compatible with the Convention's requirements.

As we turn to specific police powers, these are dominated by the powers of detention and arrest. In the absence of legal authority, a purported arrest or detention leaves a person free to resist, short of force involving 'cruel excess'[8], any physical constraint and absolves that person from any vulnerability to prosecution for assaulting or impeding the police.[9]

The principal statutory powers to detain are contained in ss 13–14 of the Criminal Procedure (Scotland) Act 1995 (CP(S)A 1995)[10]. The Act prescribes the circumstances in which the powers may be exercised, the extent of the core and ancillary powers, and the restrictions attached to their exercise. Section 13 provides that where a constable has reasonable grounds for suspecting that a person has committed or is committing an offence at any place he or she may require *that person* (at that place or at any place where the constable is entitled to be) to give his (or her) name and address and may ask for an explanation of the suspicious circumstances; and require *any other person* whom the constable believes to have relevant information to give their name and address (subs (1)). A suspect may be required (with reasonable force) to remain with the constable while the name and address are verified (if that can be done quickly) and the explanation noted (subss (2)–(4)). A person in either category is guilty of a criminal offence if, without reasonable excuse, they fail to comply and may be arrested without warrant (subss (6), (7)). There is also, however, a requirement that the constable informs a suspect of his or her suspicion and of the general nature of the offence and of why the suspect is being asked to remain. A witness must be informed of the suspicion and why the constable requires a name and address. Both must be informed that a failure to comply may be an offence (subs (5)).

Whilst the powers under s 13 are quite limited, those under s 14 are much more intrusive. Where a constable has reasonable grounds for suspecting[11] that a person has committed or is committing a serious offence (an offence punishable by imprisonment), the constable may, for the purpose of facilitating investigations, detain the suspect and take him (or her) as quickly as is reasonably practicable to a police station or other premises or place (subs (1)). It seems clear that a detention may be effected in either a public place or on private property. If on private property, however, entry on the property in the absence of a warrant must be done with consent[12]. Once detained, a person may be questioned and may be searched – using powers applicable also to an arrest (see below) (subs (7)). Reasonable force may be used (subs (8)).

Five protections for the person detained are prescribed:

(1)   At the time of detention the suspect must be informed of the suspicion, the general nature of the offence and the reason for detention (subs (6)).

(2)   Although the suspect may be questioned, he or she is under no obligation to answer a question beyond provision of name and address – and the suspect must be so informed (subs (9)).

(3)   The suspect is entitled to have intimation of the detention sent to a solicitor (s 15) and also access to a solicitor, a new right introduced following the controversial case of *Cadder v HMA*[13] when emergency legislation (Criminal Procedure (Legal Assistance, Detention and Appeals) (Scotland) Act 2010 (CPLADA(S)A 2010)) was passed[14].

(4)   The police are obliged formally to record details of the detention (times, places, suspected offence, details of intimation under s 15) (s 14(6)).

(5)   And, most importantly, a detention is normally limited to a maximum period of 12 hours – extended from six hours by CPLADA(S)A 2010– but with the possibility of extension for a further 12 hours by a (senior) custody review officer. A detention must be terminated if the person is arrested[15]; detained under another enactment (there can be no redetention under s 14); or there are no longer any grounds for detention (subss (2)–(5).

Whilst the powers exercisable under ss 13 and 14 of CP(S)A 1995 are the most commonly exercised statutory powers of detention, they do not stand alone. There are many other specific statutory powers of arrest , the most prominent of which are those under s 24 of the Misuse of Drugs Act 1971, s 59 of the Civic Government (Scotland) Act 1982 (in respect of *inter alia* drunkenness), s 6D of the Road Traffic Act 1988 (drink driving), and s 41 of the Terrorism Act 2000[16].

In addition to all of these, however, police officers have common law powers of arrest. Statutory powers of detention were introduced to plug gaps in the common law powers but not to replace them entirely. Common law powers of arrest divide into the power to arrest under the authority of a warrant issued by a competent court[17] and the power to arrest without a warrant. Few problems arise in the execution of a warrant to arrest, normally accompanied by a warrant to search persons and premises. On the other hand, arrest without warrant at common law is more problematic. As with the statutorily conferred powers, however, the key components are the power of arrest itself, ancillary powers (especially the power to search), procedural requirements, and protections afforded to individuals[18].

As to the power itself, on the authority of the mid-nineteenth century case of *Peggie v Clark*[19] which has received consistent support to the present day, the exceptional circumstances which justify an arrest without seeking a warrant are that there are reasonable grounds to suspect that the person has committed an offence but *also* that a prompt arrest is justified by the seriousness of the crime (eg murder) and/or the risk that the offender may abscond[20].

Whatever the source of authority to make an arrest or detention, the arrest or detention is not effective without both an appropriate statement of intention to arrest or detain on the part of the police officer and, as necessary, the use of an appropriate degree of physical restraint. As to the words to be used, no precision is required but they must make clear that the person's freedom is being curtailed[21]. On the physical aspect, there too the rules are applied flexibly. It is plain, however, that a degree of physical restraint is required[22]. There is not an effective detention under s 14 of CP(S)A 1995 if the words of detention are shouted to an escaping potential detainee but not accompanied by any actual physical restraint[23].

Once a lawful detention or arrest *has* been effected certain consequences follow. In particular, the police may undertake a personal search of the suspect[24] and 'relevant physical data' may be taken – a term which includes fingerprints, skin records and other samples[25]. Premises may also be searched – normally under authority of a warrant, in which case lawful search will be confined to the subject matter of the warrant save where plainly incriminating evidence of another crime is 'stumbled across'[26].

Also very important to the circumstances of arrest and detention is the power to question the suspect. Apart from the specific obligation already mentioned to inform a suspect of the right to contact a solicitor and a general rule that police questioning must cease at the point of a formal charge, there is no prescribed code for police behaviour during a period of vulnerability (especially to misplaced admissions of guilt) of suspects under arrest or detention. In a long series of cases, the Scottish courts insisted, perhaps unhelpfully, simply on a general test of 'fairness' to the accused[27]. It had been assumed that the admissibility of evidence resulting from questioning in the absence of a solicitor was subject to the same general test of fairness[28] – but this situation was overtaken by the amendments made by CPLADA(S)A 2010 above. Such formulations of a test for lawfulness of police actions arise in the context of subsequent criminal trials in which the admissibility of evidence against the accused may be challenged. Only if the questioning was 'fair', will the evidence, which may be crucial to the prosecution case, be admissible. This reminds us that questions of the lawfulness of police action, not just in relation to questioning but also to other powers of arrest, detention and search, usually arise in this context. It is at least formally possible that a civil action might be raised (including a petition for judicial review) or a complaint lodged under the police complaints procedure in relation to an alleged breach of the rules but, in practice, most such issues are resolved as questions of admissibility in subsequent trials[29]. Such cases frequently turn, sequentially, on the lawfulness of the arrest or detention; the lawfulness of any subsequent search[30]; and, if *prima facie* unlawful, whether that can be excused in all the circumstances, despite the countervailing arguments based on the rule of law and individual liberty, on grounds of the technicality of the breach or the good faith (rather than, for instance, an unfair trick) on the part of the police[31].

There is currently (January 2015) a Bill in the Scottish Parliament – the Criminal Justice (Scotland) Bill – which may, if enacted, make substantial changes to the law on arrest, rights in custody, and police powers of questioning and search. The Bill reached Stage 2 but was then put on hold[32]. The Bill contains high-profile provision to abolish corroboration and is to await the report of the (Bonomy) review of 'post-corroboration safeguards', expected by April 2015. The Bill contains *inter alia* new statutory powers of arrest (s 1), the apparent abolition of many existing powers of arrest (s 50), and the creation of new (but also the preservation of old) powers of search (ss 39, 40).

1   See chs 8 and 10.
2   Police (Scotland) Act 1967, s 39.
3   *Ibid* s 26.
4   A single Scottish Fire Service was also established.
5   Including PFR(S)A 2012, s 24 liability, via the Chief Constable, for the wrongful acts of constables.
6   PFR(S)A 2012, s 19.
7   See ch 2.
8   *Wither v Reid* 1980 JC 7. See also *Gillies v Ralph* 2008 SLT 978.
9   See PFR(S)A 2012, s 90 which is the successor to the Police (Scotland) Act 1967, s 41.
10 Originally enacted as ss 1, 2 of the Criminal Justice (Scotland) Act 1980.
11 *Wilson v Robertson* 1986 SCCR 700; *Houston v Macdonald* 2000 SLT 333.
12 *Gillies v Ralph* 2008 SLT 978. But see also *Paton v Dunn* [2012] HCJAC 49.
13 2010 SC (UKSC) 13.
14 CPLADA(S)A 2010, s 1.
15 In *Jones v HMA* 2008 JC 78 it was held that the arrest need not be for the same offence as the detention.
16 And Sch 8. See also s 44 for powers to 'stop and search'.
17 CP(S)A 1995, ss 34 and 135.
18 There is a presumption that common law powers are to be interpreted restrictively. See *Gillies v Ralph* 2008 SLT 978.
19 1868 7M. 89.
20 Ibid. See, in particular, Lord President Inglis and Lord Deas.
21 *Forbes v HMA* 1990 SCCR 69.
22 *Muir v Magistrates of Hamilton* 1910 1 SLT 164.
23 *Gillies v Ralph* 2008 SLT 978.
24 *Adair v McGarry* 1933 JC 72.
25 CP(S)A 1995, s 18(2)–(7B).
26 *HMA v Hepper* 1958 SLT 160.
27 See eg *Chalmers v HMA* 1954 SLT 177; *Miln v Cullen* 1967 SLT 35; *Codona v HMA* 1996 SLT 1100; *Peebles v HMA* 2007 SLT 197.
28 *Paton v Ritchie* 2000 JC 271; *HMA v McLean* 2010 SLT 73.
29 See, in addition to the cases cited in, *HMA v Hepper* 1958 SLT 160; *Jones v HMA* 2008 JC 78.
30 See eg *Paton v Dunn* [2012] HCJAC 49, *Freeburn v HMA* 2013 SLT 70.
31 *Lawrie v Muir* 1950 SLT 37. And see *Henderson v HMA* 2005 1 JC 301.
32 SPOR 23 April 2014.

THE MAINTENANCE OF PUBLIC ORDER

13.19   As with the police powers regime in general, the development of the powers of the police and other public authorities to maintain public order (mainly on the streets but also in places to which the public may have access) has been a story of successive stages of statutory intervention, whilst never wholly ousting the residual availability of common law powers. Once again, the starting point is that, in the absence of powers deriving from one or other source, members of the public, whether acting individually or collectively, are broadly free to behave as they please in public places and, subject to the private rights of landowners and others, in private places as well. Restraint of that freedom requires specific legal authority. And this is an historic approach to liberty which has been reinforced by the ECHR, arts 10 (freedom of expression) and 11 (freedom of assembly and association).

In the modern law, the range of restraining powers available may usefully be divided into those which impose controls *in anticipation* of the possibility of disorder and those, on the other hand, which enable a response to *an immediate threat of or actual* disorder.

It is in the realm of anticipatory controls that the contribution of statute has been particularly important. The common law offers little, although the early case of *Deakin v Milne*[1] is perhaps authority for a police intervention to restrain a peaceful march in circumstances where those targeted are well intentioned but where, nevertheless, there has been a tendency for disorder to result – at the hand of others. The legitimacy of such precautionary measures taken against people who have not (or have not yet) disturbed the peace was also considered in cases such as *O'Kelly v Harvey*[2], *Duncan v Jones*[3] and *Thomas v Sawkins*[4] but the law has been recently reviewed and restated in *Austin v Metropolitan Police Commissioner*[5] where the English Court of Appeal held, following police action to contain demonstrators in Oxford Circus in London, that containment was lawful in the circumstances because necessary to prevent an imminent breach of the peace by others. It was subsequently held by the House of Lords[6] that the containment did not amount to a breach of art 5 ECHR. It was a question to be measured by the degree of intensity of the restriction but, in those particular circumstances, the containment did not amount to a deprivation of liberty[7].

The decisions in *Austin* join that in *R (Laporte) v Chief Constable of Gloucestershire*[8] where the preventative action taken had been the stopping by the police of a bus load of would-be protestors 5 kms short of their destination of a US air base. It was held that, since there was not, at the time, any reasonable apprehension that an actual breach of the peace was imminent, the bus was not lawfully stopped. Only if the means adopted were the only practicable way of preventing an imminent breach of the peace would restraint of an innocent party be justifiable[9].

The Civic Government (Scotland) Act 1982[10] imposes controls on the holding of processions in public[11]. With some exceptions, such processions require local authority permission in advance (subject to appeal to the sheriff) and offences are committed by those who act in breach of this requirement or in breach of conditions laid down in a permission granted. A person proposing to hold a procession in public must give at least 28 days written notice to the local authority and to the chief constable, specifying date, time, route[12], likely number of participants, arrangements for control and the person's name and address (s 63(3)). This requirement does not normally apply to 'processions commonly or customarily held'[13] and local authorities may themselves modify the requirements (subss (4), (11)).

In response to the notice the local authority must deliver (at least two days before the proposed procession) an order either prohibiting the procession or imposing conditions as to date, time, duration, route and prohibiting its entry into a public place – defined as a public road or any place to which the public has access (as of right or with permission) on payment or otherwise[14]. There is an appeal to the sheriff against the local authority's order (s 64). Those who hold or take part in an unauthorised procession or act in breach of a condition commit a criminal offence (s 65).

In addition to these anticipatory measures, statutory powers are also available to the police under the Public Order Act 1986, s 12 to take measures 'on the day'. In relation to a public procession already being held or where people are already assembling with a view to taking part, the most senior police officer present at the scene is given certain powers of control[15]. If, having regard to the time, place or circumstances in which the procession is being held (or intended) and to its proposed route, that officer 'reasonably believes' that either it may result in serious public disorder, serious damage to property or serious disruption to the life of the community or the purpose of the organisers is to intimidate others, that officer may 'give directions' imposing conditions on the organisers and those taking part or prohibiting entry into any specified public place (subs (1)). Knowingly to fail to comply is a criminal offence, unless because of circumstances beyond the control of the organiser or participant (subss (4), (5)). Incitement to commit such an offence is also an offence (subs (6)). Persons suspected of these offences may be arrested.

Under the same circumstances (of anticipated serious disorder etc.) the senior police officer may give directions (as to place, maximum duration or maximum number of persons) in the case of organisers of and participants in a public assembly – defined as an 'assembly of 20 or more persons in a public place (defined as above) which is wholly or partly open to the air.'[16]

A later addition to the Public Order Act 1986 was another power to plug the gap left by the earlier focus on 'public' places, because of increasing resort by demonstrators to private land[17]. This power has an anticipatory aspect to it in that it enables the chief constable to apply to the local authority to order the prohibition of 'trespassory assemblies' in its area. Such an application may be made if the chief constable reasonably believes that an assembly (of 20 or more persons) is proposed to be held without permission on private land (in the open air) to which the public has no right (or a limited right) of access[18] and may result either in serious disruption to the life of the community or significant damage to a site of historical, architectural or scientific importance (s 14A). An order made by the local authority must be in writing (or recorded in writing as soon as practicable) and may apply to a period of no more than four days or to an area greater than a circle with a radius of five miles from a specified centre (subss (6), (8)). It may, however, be revoked or varied (subs (7)). Breach of an order is a criminal offence (s 14B(1), (2)) and a constable in uniform may arrest suspected offenders (s 14B(4)). A constable in uniform may also direct a person reasonably believed to be on his or her way to a prohibited assembly not to proceed with the direction of the assembly, with the same consequences as to committing an offence for non-compliance and power of arrest (s 14C). In the circumstances of a demonstration at Stonehenge it was held in *DPP v Jones*[19] that the public's right of access to a public road nearby was not a 'limited right of access' to which the section could apply. The public's rights included that of use of the roadway for peaceful assembly.

Section 1 of the Public Order Act 1936 makes it an offence for any person (in a public place or at a public meeting) to wear uniform signifying association with any political organisation or with the promotion of any political object. The term 'uniform' is not defined but *O'Moran v DPP*[20] made clear that a full uniform was not required but that items such as dark berets, dark glasses and dark clothing (though perhaps not merely a lapel badge), taken together and in the circumstances, suffice. The 1936 Act also created a number of offences relating to the organising and equipping of paramilitary forces (s 2). Those offences remain on the statute book but have largely been overtaken by the Terrorism Act 2000, Part II of which enables the proscription of terrorist organisations (listed in Sch 2 to the Act to include various Ireland-related organisations and many others including Al-Qa'ida). A number of related offences are created including those of membership of and support for such organisations (ss 11–12) and wearing items of clothing (s 13) in public in such circumstances as to arouse reasonable suspicion of membership or support. In *Rankin v Murray*[21] it was held that neck chains, pendants or rings with a prominent 'UVF' symbol would suffice.

Accompanying the core provisions directed towards public processions and meetings are a variety of other statutory provisions:

(1) Related to the 'trespassory assemblies' above, there is additional provision for the regulation of 'raves' (100 or more persons)[22].
(2) It is an offence to act in a disorderly manner at election meetings[23] or at public meetings in general[24].
(3) It is an offence to stir up racial hatred (in public or in private)[25].
(4) It is an offence to publish a statement encouraging terrorism[26].
(5) It is also an offence to engage in certain forms of 'offensive behaviour' at football matches[27].

Historically, an additional important weapon in the common law armoury of the police has been the offence of breach of the peace. In its modern application, the basis of the offence is doing anything which is 'genuinely alarming and disturbing in its context, to any reasonable person'[28]. Latterly, however, s 38 of the Criminal Justice and Licensing (Scotland) Act 2010 has made it an offence for a person to behave in a threatening or abusive manner if the behaviour would be likely to cause a reasonable person to suffer fear or alarm and the person intends by the behaviour, to cause fear or alarm, or is reckless as to whether the behaviour would cause fear or alarm. Broadly, this replicates the common law offence and is widely deployed by prosecutors in its place[29]. In *Paterson v Harvie*[30] the High Court resolved a problem in the interpretation of s 39[31] to confirm that the statutory test is an objective one and that it was no defence merely to show that fear and alarm were not actually caused.

1 (1882) 10R. (J.) 22. But see the English case of *Beatty v Gillbanks* (1881–82) LR 9 QBD 308 to contrary effect.
2 (1883) 14 LR 1R 105.
3 [1936] 1 KB 218.
4 [1935] 2 KB 249.
5 [2008] QB 660; [2008] 1 All ER 564.
6 [2009] 1 AC 564.
7 Lord Hope of Craighead at para 18.
8 [2006] UKHL 55; [2007] 2 All ER 529.
9 See eg Lord Rodger of Earlsferry at para 90.
10 As amended, esp by the Police, Public Order and Criminal Justice (Scotland) Act 2006.
11 A public procession means a procession in a public place – defined by the Public Order Act 1986, s 16 as a public road or any place to which at the material time the public has access on payment or otherwise, as of right or by virtue of express or implied permission.
12 The case of *Kay v Metropolitan Commissioner* [2009] 2 All ER 935 raised doubts (in relation to the Public Order Act 1986, s 11) about whether processions (in that case, a mass cycle rally) which lack organisers and a route are 'processions' which can be regulated at all.
13 Subs (7).
14 See note 11 above.
15 Public Order Act 1986, ss 12(1), (2), (11).
16 Public Order Act 1986, ss 14, 16.
17 Criminal Justice and Public Order Act 1994, s 70, inserting ss 14A–14C into the 1986 Act.
18 Such a right of access does not include access rights (the right to roam) under the Land Reform (Scotland) Act 2003.
19 [1999] 2 AC 240.
20 [1975] QB 864.
21 2004 SLT 1164.
22 Criminal Justice and Public Order Act 1994, ss 63–66.
23 Representation of the People Act 1983, s 97.
24 Public Meeting Act 1908, s 1.
25 Public Order Act 1986, s 18.
26 Terrorism Act 2006, s 1.
27 Offensive Behaviour at Football and Threatening Communications (Scotland) Act 2012. Such behaviour joins other forms of antisocial behaviour for which a fixed penalty notice may be issued under the Antisocial Behaviour etc. (Scotland) Act 2004.
28 *Smith v Donnelly* 2002 JC 65; *Miller v Thomson* 2009 SLT 59.
29 See P Ferguson *Breach of the Peace* (DUP, 2013).
30 2014 SLT 857.
31 See *Jolly v HMA* 2014 JC 171; *Rooney v Brown* [2013] HCJAC 57.

INFORMATION LAW

13.20   A rapidly developing area of law in recent years has been the regulation – by legislation and by the courts – of access to, and use of, information. That regulation can pull in different directions depending on the nature of the information involved: an increased emphasis on openness and access to *official* information is matched by recognition of the importance of protecting *private* information. In the former case, greater access to information is founded upon the belief that information is essential to accountability and, equally, that accountability is essential to the wider project of an informed population. In the latter case, development has been accompanied, and to some extent caused, by heightened public anxiety about the security of personal information and fears about the increasingly sophisticated surveillance and information gathering techniques used by law enforcement agencies[1].

1 For comprehensive treatment see P Coppel *Information Rights* (4th edn, 2014) and (although now a little out of date) J Macdonald, R Crail and C Jones (eds) *The Law of Freedom of Information* (2nd edn, 2009). For a Scottish perspective on freedom of information see K Dunion *Freedom of Information in Scotland in Practice* (2011).

Official Secrets

13.21 In matters of public access to official information, the United Kingdom had a notoriously bad record. It has been said that the twentieth century saw the growth of a secrecy culture which was unfavourably compared with more liberal regimes elsewhere, including the United States. Such comparisons are not easily or accurately made but they produced a critique of the British position which, by the end of the century, saw the beginnings of substantial change.

Two principal legal characteristics were associated with the growth of secrecy. The first was the severity with which the secrets of government were protected by the Official Secrets Act 1911 and, latterly in a modified form, by the Official Secrets Act 1989 (OSA 1989). The latter protects from disclosure without lawful authority any information about security and intelligence (OSA 1989, s 1), defence (OSA 1989, s 2), international relations (OSA 1989, s 3) and criminal investigations (OSA 1989, s 4). To make a 'damaging disclosure by a member of the security and intelligence services' is a criminal offence. Secondly, there was lacking in the United Kingdom any general right of access to official information. Some types of documents and information held by local authorities were required to be put into the public domain[1] and certain types of personal information could be demanded by individuals[2]. But, until the passing, by the Westminster Parliament of the Freedom of Information Act 2000 (FOIA 2000) and, by Holyrood, of the Freedom of Information (Scotland) Act 2002 (FOI(S)A 2002), there was no generally assured right of access to information.

1 Local Government (Scotland) Act 1973, Pt IIIA.
2 For example, Access to Personal Files Act 1987.

Freedom of Information

13.22 FOIA and FOI(S)A came into effect fully on 1 January 2005 and make very similar – though not identical – provision to ensure a substantial degree of statutorily guaranteed access to information held by public authorities exercising, on the one hand, reserved functions and, on the other, devolved functions in Scotland. In summary, FOI(S)A 2002 creates a broad right to information by providing that any person who requests information from a Scottish public authority which holds it is entitled to be given it by the authority (FOI(S)A 2002, s 1(1)[1]). Scottish public authorities are defined to include the Scottish Ministers, the Scottish Parliament (and the Parliamentary Corporate Body[2]), non-ministerial office holders in the Scottish Administration (including, for example, the Chief Inspector of Prisons and procurators fiscal), local authorities, National Health Service bodies, educational institutions such as colleges and universities, the chief constable and a long list of Scottish quangos (FOI(S)A 2002, s 3 and sch 1).

With that general entitlement in place, the most important remaining sections of FOI(S)A 2002 are those which (a) grant exemptions from the general entitlement and (b) provide for the enforcement of the duty to supply information. The exemptions in Part 2 extend to information reasonably accessible by other means (FOI(S)A 2002, s 25); information whose disclosure is prohibited by law (FOI(S)A 2002, s 26[3]); information being held for publication within 12 weeks and certain information deriving from programmes of research (FOI(S)A 2002, s 27); information whose disclosure would, or would be likely to, 'prejudice substantially relations between' governments (including devolved governments) in the United Kingdom (FOI(S)A 2002, s 28); information held by the Scottish Administration and relating to the formulation or development of government policy, ministerial communications, advice by any of the Law Officers or the operation of any ministerial private office (FOI(S)A 2002, s 29). 'Ministerial communications' means any communications between ministers (members of the Scottish Government and junior Scottish Ministers) and includes, in particular, communications relating to proceedings of the Scottish Cabinet or of its committees. Other exemptions extend to information which would be likely to prejudice substantially the maintenance of the convention of the collective responsibility of the Scottish Ministers[4], inhibit the free and frank provision of advice or otherwise prejudice substantially the effective conduct of public affairs (FOI(S)A 2002, s 30[5]); information required for the purpose of safeguarding national security (FOI(S)A 2002, s 31); information which would prejudice substantially international relations (FOI(S)A 2002, s 32) or certain commercial interests (FOI(S)A 2002, s 33). And further exemptions apply to information relating to certain public investigations (FOI(S)A 2002, s 34[6]), law enforcement (FOI(S)A 2002, s 35), certain confidential communications (FOI(S)A 2002, s 36), court records (FOI(S)A 2002, s 37), personal data (FOI(S)A 2002, s 38[7]), certain audit functions (FOI(S)A 2002, s 40) and communications with the Queen (FOI(S)A 2002, s 41). Special arrangements have been made for the provision of environmental information[8].

Whenever one of the exemptions applies, the duty to give information to a person requesting it applies only to the extent that the exemption is not one of those that is 'absolute' (ie those exemptions contained in FOI(S)A 2002, s 25 (information otherwise accessible), s 26 (disclosure prohibited), s 36(2) (entailing breach of confidence), s 37 (court records), and s 38 (personal data)) and 'in all the circumstances of the case, the public interest is disclosing the information is not outweighed by that in maintaining the exemption' (FOI(S)A 2002, s 2)[9]. There is also provision for the refusal of information if its provision would entail excessive cost (FOI(S)A 2002, s 12)[10] or if a request is vexatious or repeated (FOI(S)A 2002, s 14).

Essential to the process of enforcing the provisions of FOI(S)A 2002 is the Scottish Information Commissioner, an officer appointed by the Queen on the nomination of the Scottish Parliament[11] and with the same security of tenure as the Public Services Ombudsman (FOI(S)A 2002, s 42)[12]. The Commissioner has certain general functions including the promotion of good practice under FOI(S)A but her most important function has been the making of decisions on applications from anyone dissatisfied with the response from an authority to a request for information (FOI(S)A 2002, s 47). The Commissioner may issue enforcement notices requiring an authority to take action (FOI(S)A 2002, s 51) and the Commissioner's decisions are appealable on a point of law to the Court of Session (FOI(S)A 2002, s 56)[13].

The Freedom of Information (Amendment) (Scotland) Act 2013 (FOIA(S)A 2013) addressed some limited and quite specific issues which had arisen during the first years of FOI(S)A 2002's operation.

First, it made changes to s 5 of FOI(S)A 2002 which confers power on the Scottish Ministers[14] to extend the coverage of FOI(S)A 2002 to persons not already listed as public authorities in sch 1 to the Act by designating such a person as a public authority for the purposes of FOI(S)A 2002. That power is exercisable only where the person appears to the Scottish Ministers to exercise functions of a public nature or is providing, under a contract made with a Scottish public authority, any service whose provision is a function of that authority. The potential use of s 5 was the subject of debate from a very early stage in the life of FOI(S)A 2002[15] with particular concern that where public services were being delivered 'at arms' length' it should be possible to 'follow' this expenditure of public money and that there should be appropriate transparency[16]. Despite extensive discussion, s 5 has been used only once, to designate what are commonly referred to as 'leisure trusts': (normally charitable) companies established by local authorities to deliver cultural, sports or social facilities[17]. The amendments made by FOIA(S)A 2013 concern the persons with whom the Scottish Ministers must consult when considering the exercise of the s 5 power and place a new obligation on the Ministers to report to Parliament on the use of the power[18].

Second, FOIA(S)A changes the time limit within which a prosecution can be brought in respect of the offence created by s 65 of FOI(S)A 2002 (altering, concealing or destroying information with the intention of preventing its disclosure). As originally drafted, s 65 permitted the bringing of a prosecution only within six months of the offence having been committed – even if the offence came to light much later than that. Section 65A of FOI(S)A 2002, added by FOIA(S)A 2013, s 5, allows for a prosecution 'within the period of 6 months beginning with the date on which evidence that the prosecutor believes is sufficient to justify the proceedings came to the prosecutor's knowledge' but subject to an overriding three year time limit[19].

Third, FOIA(S)A 2013 amended the provisions of FOI(S)A 2002 which concern 'historical records'. Where information is contained in a 'historical record' the number of exemptions on which a public authority can rely to prevent disclosure is significantly reduced: the aim being to facilitate the disclosure of older (assumed to be less sensitive) material. The amendments confer on the Scottish Ministers powers to reduce the period after which records become historical records from 30 years to a lesser period, with flexibility to specify different periods for different kinds of records[20]. The new powers have been used to reduce to 15 years the period after which a range of information becomes a historical record[21].

Fourth, relatively minor amendments have been made to the provisions on refusal notices and the exemption under s 25 of FOI(S)A 2002 for information which is otherwise reasonably accessible.

A provision contained in the Bill introduced in the Scottish Parliament but which did not survive its passage concerned royal communications. Section 41 of FOI(S)A 2002 provides that information is exempt from disclosure if it relates to communications with Her Majesty, with other members of the Royal Family or with the Royal Household or to the exercise by Her Majesty of Her prerogative of honour. The exemption is, however, a qualified one and application of the s 2 public interest test in any particular case may result in a conclusion that such information should be released. It had been proposed, to mirror amendments of FOIA made by the Constitutional Reform and Governance Act 2010[22] to carve out communications with the monarch and the first and second in line to the throne and to render these communications absolutely exempt under FOI(S)A 2002. The amendment was opposed by the Scottish Information Commissioner and by the (lead) Finance Committee in its Stage 1 report on the Bill: it was dropped at Stage 2.

It may fairly be said that over the past ten years freedom of information law has had a significant impact on public attitudes to access to official information and, through its use by the media, has contributed to (some would say generated) a number of high profile political 'scandals'. In particular, access to information about amounts of money claimed by MSPs at Holyrood and by MPs at Westminster led to the resignation of individual politicians[23] and, at least indirectly, to the resignation of the Speaker of the House of Commons in May 2009[24]. More recently, during the Scottish independence referendum campaign the Scottish Government lodged and then abandoned at the eleventh hour an appeal to the Court of Session against a decision by the Scottish Information Commissioner (in response to a request for information made by the Labour MEP Catherine Stihler) that the Government should confirm whether it had taken legal advice on the question of an independent Scotland's entitlement to membership of the European Union[25].

1   For the extent of the entitlement and discussion of a number of technical provisions of FOI(S)A 2002 see *Glasgow City Council v Scottish Information Commissioner* 2010 SC 125.
2   See, for example, Decisions 008/2005 and 09/2005 (Scottish Parliament) and 125/2009 and 094/2014 (Scottish Parliamentary Corporate Body) of the Scottish Information Commissioner, available at www.itspublicknowledge.info/home/ScottishInformationCommissioner.asp
3   See *Dumfries and Galloway Council v Scottish Information Commissioner* 2008 SC 327. Section 64 of FOI(S)A 2002 empowers the Scottish Ministers to amend or repeal statutory provisions which prevent the disclosure of information so as to relax the relevant prohibition. The Freedom of Information (Relaxation of Statutory Prohibitions on Disclosure of Information) (Scotland) Order 2008, SSI 2008/339 relaxed prohibitions contained in the Factories Act 1961, the Offices, Shops and Railway Premises Act 1963, the Medicines Act 1968, the Health and Safety at Work etc. Act 1974, and the Diseases of Fish Act 1983.
4   For collective responsibility, see para 7.11.
5   See *Scottish Ministers v Scottish Information Commissioner* 2007 SC 330; 2007 SLT 274.
6   *Beggs v Scottish Information Commissioner* [2014] CSIH 10.
7   *The Common Services Agency v Scottish Information Commissioner* 2008 SC (HL) 184; *Craigdale Housing Association v Scottish Information Commissioner* 2010 SLT 655; *South Lanarkshire Council v Scottish Information Commissioner* 2014 SC (UKSC) 1.
8   FOI(S)A 2002, ss 39 and 62 and the Environmental Information (Scotland) Regulations 2004, SSI 2004/520 (as amended). The 2004 Regulations implement Directive 2003/4/EC of

the European Parliament and of the Council on public access to environmental information which itself gave effect at an EU level to parts of the Aarhus Convention (The United Nations Economic Commission for Europe Convention on Access to Information, Public Participation in Decision-Making and Access to Justice in Environmental Matters of 1998). For Aarhus and protective expenses orders in environmental litigation see ch 14.

9   See *Beggs v Scottish Information Commissioner* [2014] CSIH 10.

10 As to which see the Freedom of Information (Fees for Required Disclosure) (Scotland) Regulations 2004, SSI 2004/467. Fees can be charged for the provision of information in certain circumstances: see FOI(S)A 2002, s 13 and the Freedom of Information (Fees for Disclosure under Section 13) (Scotland) Regulations 2004, SSI 2004/376.

11 Ms Rosemary Agnew (who followed the first holder of the post, Mr Kevin Dunion who served between 2002 and 2012) was nominated by the Parliament on 1 February 2012.

12 See para 10.13 above.

13 And ultimately to the House of Lords (*The Common Services Agency v Scottish Information Commissioner* 2008 SC (HL) 184) and now the Supreme Court (*South Lanarkshire Council v Scottish Information Commissioner* 2014 SC (UKSC) 1).

14 A similar power is conferred on Ministers of the Crown by s 5 of FOIA 2000.

15 One Year On: A consultation on the operation of the Act after one year in force, December 2005; Scottish Government Discussion Paper: Coverage of the Freedom of Information (Scotland) Act 2002, November 2008; Scottish Government Consultation on extending the coverage of the Freedom of Information (Scotland) Act 2002, 2010; Scottish Government Consultation on proposals for a Freedom of Information (Amendment) (Scotland) Bill, 2011.

16 See Audit Scotland, *Arm's-length external organisations (ALEOs): are you getting it right?*, 2011.

17 Freedom of Information (Scotland) Act 2002 (Designation of Persons as Scottish Public Authorities) Order 2013, SSI 2013/278.

18 FOIA(S)A 2013, s 1.

19 Similar amendments have been made to the Environmental Information (Scotland) Regulations to allow for prosecution in relation to environmental information: Environmental Information (Scotland) Amendment Regulations 2013, SSI 2013/127.

20 FOIA(S)A 2013, s 4 amending FOI(S)A 2002, s 59.

21 Freedom of Information (Scotland) Act 2002 (Historical Periods) Order 2013, SSI 2013/365.

22 The amendments were widely recognised as a response to requests made by journalist Rob Evans for what have been called 'the Black spider memos': letters and memos written by Prince Charles to UK Government ministers and politicians. Those requests have generated significant and controversial litigation, concluding with a hearing in the Supreme Court in November 2014, the result of which is awaited. See *R (Evans) v Attorney General* [2014] 3 All ER 682; *Department for Business, Innovation and Skills v Evans* [2014] EWCA Civ 253.

23 David McLetchie, MSP resigned as leader of the Scottish Conservative Party in October 2005 in the face of criticism of expenses claims which related to taxi journeys between the Holyrood Parliament and the Edinburgh law firm at which he worked (see Decision 033/2005 of the Scottish Information Commissioner at www.itspublicknowledge.info).

24 The Westminster Parliament resisted in the courts the UK Information Commissioner's direction that expenses claims made by MPs should be made public. Ultimately defeated (see *Corporate Officer of the House of Commons v Information Commissioner* [2009] 3 All ER 403, MPs first contemplated changes to FOIA to exempt their expenses information from disclosure before accepting that publication was inevitable. Scheduled for July 2009, disclosure by Parliament was pre-empted by the leaking to, and publication by, the Telegraph Newspapers over a number of weeks in May and June, of highly damaging revelations about the types of claims made by MPs of all parties. Speaker Martin's failure to maintain the confidence of the House in connection with potential reform of the expenses and allowances system resulted in his resignation (see HC Debs, 19 May 2009, col 1323).

25 See ch 4.

Data Protection

13.23   While freedom of information legislation confers rights on individuals to obtain official information, the focus of data protection law is on the rights of individuals to obtain – and to regulate the use of – their own personal information.

The Data Protection Act 1998 (DPA 1998), an Act of the Westminster Parliament, is the vehicle by which the UK gives effect to the requirements of the EC Data Protection Directive[1]. As the Directive acknowledges, the European internal market requires that 'personal data should be able to flow freely from one Member State to another, but also that the fundamental rights of individuals should be safeguarded'. Those fundamental rights include rights protected by the Charter of Fundamental Rights of the European Union[2] and the ECHR and the Directive can be seen, in part, as further developing principles first recognised by the Council of Europe's 1981 Convention for the Protection of Individuals with regard to Automatic Processing of Personal Data[3].

The Convention's title reveals one of the key preoccupations which informed the drafting of the Convention and, in due course, the Directive: the exponential growth of electronic storage and automated processing of personal information over the last four decades. As a consequence of this preoccupation, DPA 1998 focuses on personal information which is (or is intended to be), 'processed by means of equipment operating automatically in response to instructions given for that purpose' or is 'recorded as part of a relevant filing system'[4]. DPA 1998 is a lengthy and complex Act but its key elements involve (1) providing a definition of the concept of 'personal data'; (2) conferring rights on individuals to obtain access to their own personal data; and (3) imposing duties on those 'data controllers' who process personal data.

Personal data is defined as data which 'relate to a living individual who can be identified (a) from those data or (b) from those data and other information which is in the possession of, or is likely to come into the possession of, the data controller' (DPA 1998, s 1(1)). The definition 'includes any expression of opinion about the individual and any indication of the intentions of the data controller or any other person in respect of the individual' (DPA 1998 s 1(1)). A subset of personal data is 'sensitive personal data' to which more stringent requirements apply. Sensitive personal data is personal data consisting of information as to an individual's racial or ethnic origin, political opinions, religious beliefs or other beliefs of a similar nature, trade union membership, physical or mental health or condition, sexual life, and history of criminal conduct or prosecution.

Domestic litigation about data protection has been relatively rare but is increasing. In one of the few Scottish cases, the House of Lords considered the definition of personal data in *Common Services Agency v Scottish Information Commissioner*[5]. The key issue addressed by the court was when an individual can be 'identified' from information held by a data controller. Their Lordships holding that where sufficient steps can be taken by the data controller to anonymise data in its own hands – for example, in the case of statistical information, by making it difficult to 'unravel' statistics internally so as to identify the individuals represented by those statistics – then the data may cease to be 'personal data' at all[6].

DPA1998 is chiefly concerned with the protection of 'data subjects': the individuals who are the subject of personal data (DPA 1998, s 1(1)). Data subjects have a variety of rights relating information about them which are set out in the Act's 'subject information provisions' (DPA 1998, s 27(2)). A data subject is entitled to be informed by any data controller, in response to a properly constituted request, whether any of his personal data are being processed by or on behalf of that data controller, and if so to be given a description of the personal data concerned, the purposes of the processing and the recipients or classes of recipients to whom the data are or may be disclosed. The data subject is also entitled to have communicated to him in 'intelligible form' the personal data held by the data controller and any information available to the data controller as to the source of those data (DPA 1998, s 7). Importantly, individuals are entitled not only to know what information is held about them but also how that information may be used: a data subject is entitled, where his personal data is processed by automatic means for 'the purpose of evaluating matters relating to him such as, for example, his performance at work, his creditworthiness, his reliability or his conduct, has constituted or is likely to constitute the sole basis for any decision significantly affecting him', to be informed of the 'logic involved in that decision-taking' (DPA 1998, s 7).

The rights of individuals to access their own personal data are not absolute. There are a variety of exemptions contained in DPA 1998 itself – for example, personal data which has been processed for the purposes of assessing suitability for judicial office or appointment as a QC are exempt from the subject information provisions (DPA 1998, Sch 7, para 3) – and others have been added by statutory instrument[7].

In addition to these rights to obtain information, DPA1998 also seeks to protect individuals by placing obligations on data controllers in relation to their use of data. A data controller is defined for most purposes as 'a person who (either alone or jointly or in common with other persons) determines the purposes for which and the manner in which any personal data are, or are to be, processed' (DPA 1998, s 1). Data controllers include government and public authorities but the definition extends far beyond the public sector. The definition of processing is extremely wide and includes obtaining, recording or holding the information or data and carrying operations on the information or data, including organising or altering of the information or data, consulting or using the data, and disclosing and destroying the data (DPA 1998, s 1). Importantly, a data controller must comply with the "data protection principles" in relation to all personal data with respect to which he is the data controller (DPA1998, s 4(4)). The requirements of the data protection principles include the fair and lawful processing of personal data, that personal data which is held is 'accurate and, where necessary, kept up to date' and that appropriate steps are taken to prevent the unauthorised use or accidental loss or destruction of personal data.

While DPA 1998 does confer some rights which can be enforced by individuals through the courts[8], the Act is chiefly policed by the UK Information Commissioner. The Commissioner is appointed by the Queen[9] for a term of up to five years (which may be renewed but is subject to an overall maximum of 15 years' service) and has wide ranging powers of investigation and enforcement.

These include powers to issue fines ('monetary penalty notices') for serious breaches of the data protection principles – a response to concerns raised by a number of high profile incidents of the loss or inadvertent disclosure of large amounts of personal data by government departments, financial institutions and others[10]. The Commissioner has used those powers extensively. Appeals against decisions of the Information Commissioner may be taken to the Information Tribunal (also established by DPA 1998, s 6) and thereafter to the courts[11].

The European Union has recognised that the Directive no longer meets the increasing challenges of privacy and data protection presented by the digital age, and the internet in particular. The ECJ has recently considered the extent to which the Directive, for example, should be interpreted as conferring what has been described as a 'right to be forgotten': entitlement to require an internet search engine to remove personal data so that it no longer appears in search results[12]. There have also been concerns that the Directive has failed to achieve a sufficient degree of harmonisation of data protection laws within member states and that a more prescriptive approach by the EU is needed. The EU Commission has therefore proposed a new General Data Protection Regulation, with a draft proposal released in March 2012. Progress in agreeing the terms of the Regulation (using the 'co-decision' or ordinary legislative procedure) has been relatively slow, with the European Parliament adopting a compromise text in March 2014 but with the Council of Ministers having agreed, in May 2014, a position only on part of the draft. The terms of the final Regulation are not expected to be known until later in 2015.

1   Directive 95/46/EC of the European Parliament and of the Council of 24 October 1995 on the protection of individuals with regard to the processing of personal data and on the free movement of such data. Data Protection is reserved to Westminster (see 128) by SA1998, s 30 and Sch 5, Pt II, S B1.
2   For a discussion of the Charter and its domestic application where the disclosure of personal data is in issue, see the decision of the Supreme Court in *Rugby Football Union v Viagogo Ltd* [2013] 1 All ER 928 discussed at para 13.8 below.
3   The 1981 Convention refers to the potential adverse effects which unfettered processing might have on rights of privacy, non-discrimination and fair trial and on other 'legitimate interests' such as employment and consumer credit.
4   DPA 1998, s 1(1).
5   2008 SC (HL) 184. This was an appeal against a decision of the Scottish Information Commissioner directing the release of information about the occurrence of leukaemia in children living in Dumfries and Galloway. The decision was resisted by the CSA on the grounds that the information was exempt under s 38 of FOI(S)A 2002, being personal data the release of which would breach the data protection principles. FI(S)A incorporates the definition of personal data in DPA1998 for the purposes of the s 38 exemption and the case is therefore of relevance to the interpretation of DPA1998 notwithstanding its roots in a freedom of information request.
6   See also *Craigdale Housing Association v Scottish Information Commissioner* 2010 SLT 655 and *Department of Health v Information Commissioner* [2011] EWHC 1430, [2011] ACD 97, both concerned with the question of whether information was truly 'anonymised' and therefore not personal data. See also *Durant v Financial Services Authority* [2003] EWCA Civ 1746, [2004] FSR 28 in which the Court of Appeal considered the meaning of the words 'relate to a living individual' which appear in the definition of personal data and the subsequent treatment of *Durant* by the Court of Appeal in *Edem v Information Commissioner* [2014] EWCA Civ 92. As all these cases demonstrate, arguments about this definition can be highly technical, if not to say esoteric.
7   See, for example, the Data Protection (Subject Access Modification) (Health) Order 2000, SI 2000/413; the Data Protection (Subject Access Modification) (Social Work) Order 2000, SI 2000/415 (as amended); the Data Protection (Subject Access Modification) (Education)

Order 2000, SI 2000/414; the Data Protection (Miscellaneous Subject Access Exemptions) Order 2000, SI 2000/419 (as amended).

8 See, for example, DPA 1998 s 13 which entitles an individual to compensation in some circumstances if they have suffered damage and/or distress as a consequence of a contravention of the Act by a data controller. For an unsuccessful attempt to pursue a s 13 claim see *Lyons v Chief Constable of Strathclyde* 2014 SCLR 281.

9 DPA 1998, s 6. The current Commissioner, Christopher Graham, replaced Richard Thomas in June 2009. The UK Commissioner has additional responsibilities for enforcement of UK – rather than Scottish – freedom of information law.

10 See the Criminal Justice and Immigration Act 2008, s 144.

11 In 2013 Scottish Borders Council appealed to the First-tier Tribunal a decision of the Information Commissioner to impose a monetary penalty of £250,000 in respect of a data security breach which involved pensions records being found in a paper recycling bank outside a supermarket. The Council argued successfully that the breach was not one which was likely to cause substantial damage or distress for the purposes of s 55A of the DPA (*Scottish Borders Council v Information Commissioner* 21 August 2013). See also *Central London Community Healthcare NHS Trust v Information Commissioner* [2013] UKUT 551 (AAC).

12 Case C131/12 *Google Spain SL v Agencia Espanola de Proteccion de Datos* [2014] 3 CMLR 50.

Privacy Rights

13.24 Historically, the British courts have not recognised any general right of privacy or any presumption against the intrusion by the state – or by others such as the press – into the private affairs of individuals. This is in contrast to the constitutional protection of privacy which exists in states such as France, Canada or the USA. As we have seen, specific protections are now offered by the DPA 1998 in relation to the processing of personal data, and we describe below (para 13.25) the role of Regulation of Investigatory Powers legislation in relation to surveillance and intelligence gathering. In addition, there have been two separate (but related) developments over the last decade or so which have significantly extended the legal protection of privacy within the United Kingdom.

The first was the incorporation of the ECHR by HRA 1998 (see para 13.9). As noted above, art 8 provides that 'Everyone has the right to respect for his private and family life, his home and his correspondence'. A qualified right, interference with it is permitted where that is 'in accordance with the law and is necessary in a democratic society in the interests of national security, public safety or the economic well-being of the country, for the prevention of disorder or crime, for the protection of health or morals, or for the protection of the rights and freedoms of others'. The component parts of the protection – relating to private life, family life, home and correspondence – may be infringed individually or cumulatively. Article 8 has been held by British courts to be breached by the taking, and retaining by the police, of photographs of an individual who was engaged in wholly lawful activity[1] but not necessarily by different approaches to parental rights and responsibilities taken by the law in relation to married and unmarried fathers[2] or by a practice of attaching to all external telephone calls from prisoners a pre-recorded message making it clear to the recipient that the call was coming from within a prison[3].

As may be expected, the particular 'rights or freedoms of others' which most frequently collide with those protected by art 8 – and which are relied upon by the media in particular to justify the publication of personal information – are those referred to in art 10 ECHR: rights to freedom of expression, including the freedom to 'hold opinions and to receive and impart information and ideas without interference by public authority and regardless of frontiers'. For many of the same reasons as justify freedom of information laws – the importance of scrutinising and holding to account those who exercise the powers of the state – special significance is attached to the rights of journalists to bring to public attention information which public officials and politicians might prefer to keep secret. The potential risks to democracy of limitations on those rights are recognised by s 12 of HRA 1998. Section 12 applies 'if a court is considering whether to grant any relief which, if granted, might affect the exercise of the Convention right to freedom of expression' – the most obvious example of which would be a court considering an application for an interdict to prevent publication or broadcast. In such circumstances the court is required to take steps to ensure that the person against whom the order is sought is given the opportunity to put their case[4]. The court is also under a duty to have 'particular regard to the importance of the Convention right to freedom of expression and, where the proceedings relate to material which the respondent claims, or which appears to the court, to be journalistic, literary or artistic material', the extent to which the information concerned is already (or about to be) in the public domain and whether it is in the public interest for it to be published[5].

The fact that the ECHR has been incorporated in domestic law does not, of course, preclude applications to the European Court of Human Rights (ECtHR) by individuals who believe the UK has failed to give proper respect to their art 8 rights. The United Kingdom has been found guilty of such failure in relation to, for example, the release to the public of CCTV pictures of a man who attempted suicide in a public place[6] and the long-term retention by the police of DNA samples taken from individuals who had not been convicted of any crime[7]. The extent to which the holding and disclosure of information by the police – whether that is the DNA samples just mentioned or historic data relating to convictions for relatively minor offences – has been the subject of a good deal of recent 'dialogue' between the ECtHR in Strasbourg and the UK courts[8].

The second recent development in the protection of individual privacy has been the extension, particularly by the English courts, of the common law of confidence: that the law which recognises and enforces duties to keep information confidential either because such a duty has been set out expressly (for example in a contract) or because the it is to be implied from the nature of the information and the circumstances in which it has been communicated by one person to another. Traditionally concerned with the rights of commercial parties to maintain the confidentiality of business information, the last ten years have seen breach of confidence being used by individuals, particularly 'celebrities', to restrain the publication of personal information about, and photographs of, them. This development of the law of breach of confidence, following the incorporation of the ECHR, is not coincidental and may be viewed as an example – sometimes more or less explicit – of the 'horizontal' application of the Convention described above (para 13.12). Many recent cases involve not only breach of confidence and of Convention rights through publication of personal information but breach of art 8 in acquisition of that information by the media[9].

1 *Wood v Commissioner of Police of the Metropolis* [2009] EWCA Civ 414.
2 *D v Children's Reporter* 2008 GWD 1-10.
3 *Potter v Scottish Prison Service* 2007 SLT 1019. It was conceded that art 8 rights were engaged but not that they had been infringed.
4 HRA 1998, s 12(2). For a recent, long running but unsuccessful attempt by BBC Scotland to overturn a reporting restriction made by the Lord Ordinary in terms of s 11 of the Contempt of Court Act 1981 and a discussion by the Supreme Court of the competing interests of privacy and press freedom see *A (Respondent) v British Broadcasting Corporation* [2014] UKSC 25.
5 See, for example, *Attorney General's Reference No 3 of 1999*: Application by the British Broadcasting Corporation to set aside or vary a Reporting Restriction Order 2010 1 AC 145.
6 *Peck v United Kingdom* (2003) 36 EHRR 41.
7 *S v United Kingdom; Marper v United Kingdom* (2009) 48 EHRR 50.
8 Limits of space preclude a full discussion but see in particular *R(T) v Chief Constable of* Greater Manchester [2014] 4 All ER 159; *MM v United Kingdom*, Times, January 16, 2013; *R (L) v Comr of Police of the Metropolis* (Secretary of State for the Home Department intervening) [2010] 1 AC 410; *Gillan v United Kingdom* (2010) 50 EHRR 45.
8 See *Douglas v Hello! Ltd (No 1)* [2001] QB 967; *Campbell v Mirror Group Newspapers Ltd* [2004] 2 AC 457; and *Mosley v News Group Newspapers Ltd* [2008] EMLR 20 (and for the follow up application to the ECtHR: *Mosley v United Kingdom* [2012] EMLR 1 . For discussion, see N A Moreham 'Privacy in the common law' (2005) 121 LQR 628.

Surveillance and Data Retention

13.25 Finally, one further area in which there has been statutory intervention is in the field of surveillance and intelligence gathering by law enforcement agencies. As has been noted, interference with the rights to private life, family and home protected by art 8 ECHR is permissible provided certain conditions are met. Amongst those conditions are that the interference is 'in accordance with the law'. One difficulty which the United Kingdom faced in complying with this condition was the absence of any general legal regime governing the circumstances in which public authorities might engage in activity such as telephone tapping, interception with correspondence or electronic communications and the gathering of information using 'informants'. This absence, together with an approach to individual rights which held that so long as the state was not expressly prohibited by law from engaging in a particular activity it was free to do so[1] left individuals with little real protection against covert surveillance activity by the state.

The incorporation of the ECHR rendered the need for reform more pressing and resulted in the passing of the Regulation of Investigatory Powers Act 2000 (RIPA 2000) and the Regulation of Investigatory Powers (Scotland) Act 2000 (RIP(S)A 2000)[2]. As the policy memorandum to the Scottish Bill explained, in order for an interference to be 'acceptable in ECHR terms…(a) a framework of controls must have a basis in law; (b) the law must define the scope and manner of the exercise of a public authority's functions with sufficient clarity to protect the individual from arbitrary interference and to ensure that it is the subject of effective control; (c) the law must be sufficiently accessible and precise; [and] (d) the exceptions which allow interference should be construed narrowly and interference with those rights should be necessary and proportionate to any offence". RIPA 2000 and RIP(S)A 2000 are designed to meet these criteria.

RIP(S)A 2000 applies to Police Scotland, the Scottish Administration, Scottish health service bodies, Scottish local authorities, SEPA and provides a scheme for the authorisation and control of directed surveillance activity (for example, using CCTV cameras to monitor the activity of specific individuals in a street or public park) intrusive surveillance (for example the use of a listening device placed in a car or in someone's home) and the use of 'covert human intelligence sources' (i.e. informants or 'undercover' investigators). RIPA 2000 regulates these activities in the remainder of the UK and also contains further provisions which apply in the whole of the United Kingdom including Scotland (for example in relation to interception of communications).

Compliance with the requirements of RIPA 2000 and RIP(S)A 2000 is chiefly the responsibility of the Surveillance Commissioners appointed under each Act, although the Secretary of State and the Scottish Ministers, respectively, also issue codes of practice explaining how they expect public authorities to discharge their duties under the Acts. Complaints about the use of surveillance powers may be made by aggrieved individuals to the Investigatory Powers Tribunal, established under s 65 of RIPA 2000. Perhaps more importantly, if an individual is able to demonstrate that surveillance activity has been carried out which is not in accordance with the requirements of RIPA 2000 or RIP(S)A 2000 this may enable him to prevent the use, in criminal proceedings against him, of any evidence obtained through that activity[3].

Communications data – particularly information about electronic communications – has presented a particular challenge at an EU and at a domestic level with increasing state and supra state regulation being justified by reference to goals of crime and terrorism prevention but challenged on grounds of its disproportionate interference with privacy rights. So, for example, the ECJ declared unlawful the Data Retention Directive which required member states to impose obligations on providers of electronic communications services to retain for a minimum period significant amounts of data including data necessary to trace and identify the source of a communication and its destination, to identify the date, time, duration and type of a communication, to identify users' communication equipment, and to identify the location of mobile communication equipment, data which consisted, inter alia, of the name and address of the subscriber or registered user, the calling telephone number, the number called and an IP address for internet services. This was held to be a disproportionate interference of the fundamental rights of data protection and privacy that were protected by the EU Charter of Fundamental Rights[4].

The UKGovernment reacted to the Digital Rights case, somewhat controversially, by introducing emergency legislation: the Data Retention and Investigatory Powers Act 2014 was passed in April 2014 and authorises (amongst other things) the Secretary of State to issue a 'retention notice' requiring a public telecommunications operator to retain relevant communications data if that is thought by the Secretary of State to be 'necessary and proportionate' for one or more of the purposes falling within paragraphs (a) to (h) of s 22(2) of the RIPA 2000 (purposes for which communications data may be obtained)[5]. The Act, very unusually, provides for its own repeal on 31 December 2016 but it seems unlikely not to survive in some shape or form given the first reading in the House of Commons in November 2014 of the Counter-Terrorism and Security Bill which includes provision for the amendment of the 2014 Act to extend its scope to include 'relevant internet data' (that is, subject to certain limitations, communications data which relates to an internet access service or an internet communications service and which may be used to identify, or assist in identifying, which internet protocol address, or other identifier, belongs to the sender or recipient of a communication).

1 See *Malone v Commissioner of Police of the Metropolis (No 2)* [1979] Ch 344.
2 There had been limited earlier reform: see the Police Act 1997 and the Intelligence Services Act 1994.
3 See, for general discussion by the House of Lords of the range of issues raised by covert surveillance, *Re C's Application for Judicial Review* [2009] 1 AC 928 and, for a Scottish example of exclusion of evidence obtained not in accordance with the requirements of RIP(S) A 2000, see *HMA v Higgins* 2006 SLT 946. See also, B Goold *'Liberty and others v United Kingdom*: a new chance for another missed opportunity' [2009] PL 5 and M H Murphy, 'A shift in the approach of the European Court of Human Rights in surveillance cases: a rejuvenation of necessity?' [2014] EHRLR, 507–518.
4 *Digital Rights Ireland Ltd v Minister for Communications, Marine and Natural Resources* [2014] 3 CMLR 44.
5 Data Retention and Investigatory Powers Act 2014, s 1.

Chapter 14

Public Law Adjudication

INTRODUCTION

14.1   A typical but not inevitable characteristic of a country which has a written constitution is a constitutional court. The constitution itself generates questions and disputes which must be resolved at the very highest level by a court of the highest prestige and authority. There may be an entrenched Bill of Rights whose guarantees must be upheld and, more generally, the status of the constitution as the supreme law within the state may require the ordinary laws enacted by the legislature to be measured against its precepts[1]. Equally, in countries with a federal system of government in which the constitutional rights of the states or provinces must be sustained, it is usually assumed that the task must fall to a constitutional court. There must be an umpire to decide between the claims of the state and federal governments and that will usually be a court[2]. What distinguishes courts performing functions such as these is not their name. They may or may not be designated 'constitutional courts'. The jurisdiction of the German Federal Constitutional Court is broadly paralleled by that of the Supreme Courts of the United States and Canada and of the High Court in Australia. The parallels are not exact. The German court has a more specialised role. It is competent to resolve disputes about the validity of legislation not only on the basis of 'concrete' facts after the legislation has been enacted but also 'abstract' disputes before legislation reaches the statute book[3]. In this respect it could be contrasted with the French Constitutional Council (Conseil Constitutionnel) which previously had powers to consider challenges to legislation *only* at the pre-enactment stage[4]. Both of these courts are, however, to be contrasted with the highest courts of the United States, Canada and Australia[5] which, while much occupied with constitutional matters, operate also as final courts of general jurisdiction. Similarly, in these jurisdictions constitutional issues are not the exclusive preserve of the single highest court but, at least some of the time, arrive there only after they have been first raised, and provisionally answered, in courts below[6]. The task of constitutional adjudication is, in those systems, dispersed across the courts as a whole.

In the United Kingdom there has been no constitutional court on either of these models: its absence no doubt a consequence of Britain's constitutional tradition and, in particular, the lack of a written constitution. The sovereignty of Parliament and the problem which this presents for any claim to entrenchment of rules against interference by Parliament, whether in the form of a federal structure or of a Bill of Rights, have tended to restrict the 'constitutional' role for courts to the preservation of the will of Parliament and little more[7]. The claims to supremacy made on behalf of the Treaty of Union 1707 have, whatever their other strengths, never been sufficient to make the case for a new court[8]. The supremacy of EU law[9] has created, since 1 January 1973, a special role for UK courts (alongside courts in other member states) and has given rise to the argument that the ECJ should itself be regarded as a 'constitutional court' for the European Union[10] but never that a new court to handle EU issues should be created for the United Kingdom.

Paradoxically, the London-based Judicial Committee of the Privy Council (JCPC) did, for many years, perform the functions of a surrogate constitutional court for countries of the Empire and Commonwealth and, to an increasingly limited extent, continues to do so[11]. Although the JCPC has also discharged certain functions as a court for the United Kingdom[12] and was indeed available to perform a constitutional role during the period of the Stormont Government in Northern Ireland[13], it did not achieve the status of a final court of appeal for either constitutional or general business and seems destined never to do so given the transfer to the UK Supreme Court of the tasks previously assigned to it under the Scotland Act 1998 (SA 1998)[14], the Government of Wales Act 2006 (GWA 2006)[15] and the Northern Ireland Act 1998 (NIA 1998)[16] and we consider these below.

At the end of this chapter (at para 14.31) we return to the subject of constitutional courts to consider why, for other reasons, a case has been increasingly strongly made for the creation of a constitutional court for the United Kingdom and whether the new Supreme Court – as a final court of appeal of general jurisdiction – has answered calls for a separate constitutional court.

In the meantime, it is acknowledged that, even in the absence of a single specialised court, there are functions which UK courts certainly are required to perform which are appropriately regarded as constitutional in character and which, in turn, attract many of the concerns about the need to create and sustain judicial independence which were considered in Chapter 12. Among such functions to be treated as constitutional in character are adjudication under the Human Rights Act 1998 (HRA 1998) and under the devolution legislation for Scotland, Wales and Northern Ireland. But they also include decision-making deriving from the European Communities Act 1972 (ECA 1972) and, of much longer standing, civil liberties and administrative law adjudication. The linking feature is the challenge in the courts of the decisions, whether administrative or legislative, of public bodies of all sorts – often, but not inevitably, in litigation initiated by individuals to protect rights they believe have been or may be infringed.

As in other forms of litigation, the task of the courts in such cases is to establish the facts, if these are disputed, and to apply the law. Facts are not often the main focus of dispute in the superior courts. On the other hand, the application of the law, a process which may at first sound merely technical or mechanistic, is frequently very difficult. Three principal factors contribute to different degrees to make constitutional or public law adjudication problematic.

There is, first, the nature of the disputes which arise. They involve the challenge to decisions made by public bodies and public officials, often at the highest level and often involving bodies claiming a special legitimacy of their own deriving from their elected status. Sometimes they involve disputes between different public bodies[17] and, almost always, the outcome of the litigation will be politically (as well as legally) damaging to at least one of the parties. In some jurisdictions, and for some purposes, the acute political sensitivities involved have led courts to decline to adjudicate upon such essentially political questions. The courts have been unwilling to enter the 'political thicket' and have declared those issues non-justiciable[18]. This is not, however, an option for most courts most of the time. There is no avoiding the decision to be made, despite its political context: 'the courts should not be too eager to relinquish their judicial review function simply because they are called upon to exercise it in relation to weighty matters of state'[19].

This combines with the second characteristic – the flexibility of many of the rules to be applied. The political context would cause little difficulty for courts if the rules they applied were clear and unproblematic. This, however, is rarely the case. Whether they derive from common law or statutory sources, the rules which define the legal limits of the acts of public authorities are often open-textured and in need of interpretation as they are applied to particular facts. Courts are seen, therefore, to have a choice as to which interpretation to adopt. Judges may disagree publicly with other judges as to the decision to be reached and, against a background of political controversy, this inevitably makes the process more problematic and potentially fraught.

The third characteristic is the finality of much constitutional adjudication. A prominent feature of decision-making by a constitutional court or supreme court is that the court's decision is the last word on the matter at issue. Unless the procedures for formal constitutional amendment are invoked – and, given the difficulties of doing so, this is rare[20] – a court's decision on a matter of constitutional interpretation will be final and, where this is in effect a decision about the law-making competence of the country's legislature, may raise particularly acute questions about the power of unelected courts to 'trump' decisions of elected parliaments. The role of the courts appears to be 'countermajoritarian', and as such may be viewed as undemocratic and illegitimate[21]. There are different responses to this. On the one hand, there is the robust defence of the courts with the argument that it is wholly proper for them to uphold the protective mechanisms of the constitution – often designed to shelter weak minorities – against the oppression of a, sometimes temporary, majority in a legislature or indeed in wider society[22]. Another defence of the finality of the courts' role is that it is designed not to undermine a narrow version of majoritarian democracy but positively to sustain a broader rights based democracy, in particular by monitoring and keeping open the processes of democracy themselves[23]. Whatever view is taken, however, there is no doubt that, when courts are placed in such a position of final decision-making, their constitutional status becomes much more contested. Until relatively recently, this has not been an issue which has arisen in the UK constitutional order. The absence of the 'higher law' of a written constitution and the power of the Westminster Parliament, in theory at least, to undo almost any imaginable decision of any court have left 'final' power with Parliament[24]. To a significant degree, however, the impact of the supremacy of EU law has undermined this position and, although the unlimited legislative powers of the Westminster Parliament have been explicitly retained in the terms of SA 1998[25], courts do now have the power to make decisions about the limits of the powers of the Scottish Parliament – a role which is, at least, analogous to that of a constitutional court[26]. Likewise, the powers given to superior courts by HRA 1998 to declare that provisions in Acts of the Westminster Parliament are incompatible with the Convention rights[27] are, while formally lacking the finality of much constitutional adjudication in other countries, similar in effect.

It is with these considerations in mind that we turn to the various categories of constitutional or public law adjudication in which courts may be involved. At para 14.2, the courts' common law jurisdiction is discussed; then, at paras 14.3–14.13, the control of administrative action by administrative tribunals and by the courts, including the process of judicial review followed, at para 14.14, by the use of judicial review in relation to delegated legislation. Paragraphs 14.15–14.18 address the issues raised by HRA 1998 and paras 14.19–14.30 the resolution of 'devolution issues' under SA 1998 and of 'compatibility issues' in Scottish criminal cases. The chapter concludes, at para 14.31, with a return to the question of a constitutional court.

1   The remit and powers of a constitutional court in this context depend on the particular legal system in question. The Australian High Court, for example, is empowered to declare invalid Acts of a state legislature or of the Commonwealth Parliament if they conflict with the constitution, whereas the Swiss Federal Tribunal may declare invalid legislation emanating from the provincial ('cantonal') legislatures but has no such power in respect of laws passed by the Federal Assembly. See K C Wheare *Federal Government* (4th edn, 1963), especially ch IV.

2   But, for a contrary view, see, for example, P C Weiler *In the Last Resort: A Critical Study of the Supreme Court of Canada* (1974) ch 6.

3   See L Mammen 'A Short Note on the German Federal Constitutional Court and its Power to Review Legislation [2001] EHRLR 433.

4   See M Hunter-Henin 'Constitutional Developments and Human Rights in France' (2011) 60 ICLQ 167-188.

5   For the United States see L H Tribe *American Constitutional Law* (3rd edn, 2000); for Canada see P W Hogg *Constitutional Law of Canada* (5th edn, 2007); and for Australia see J Clarke *Hanks Australian Constitutional Law* (9th edn, 2013) (hereafter *Hanks*).

6   For example, the Australian High Court has original jurisdiction in respect of those matters specified in the Commonwealth constitution, ss 75 and 76 (for example all matters arising under any treaty and all matters in which a writ of mandamus or prohibition or an injunction is sought against an officer of the Commonwealth) but also hears appeals on constitutional matters from state supreme courts and from the Australian Federal Court. For an example of the latter type of appeal, see *Eastman v The Queen* [2000] HCA 29.

7   See para 6.5. And for discussion of a recently ignited debate on the possibility of 'entrenching' the Scottish Parliament see para 4.21.

8   Although, interestingly, the Treaty provisions on the location of Scottish business gave rise to comments, made in the context of the UK government's announcement in June 2003 of its intention to create a new supreme court, concerning the need for a separate court building. See para 14.32.

9   See para 3.12.

10 For discussion, see para 3.15.

11 The JCPC continues to hear appeals on constitutional matters from a number of independent states including Jamaica, Barbados and St Lucia and from certain UK overseas territories and Crown dependencies. The JCPC also hears appeals 'by proxy' on behalf of the Sultan of Brunei from the Court of Appeal of Brunei to whom (rather than Her Majesty) the Committee report their opinion: see *Bolkiah v Brunei Darussalam* [2007] UKPC 63. Appeals from New Zealand have ceased as a consequence of the New Zealand Supreme Court Act 2003, and the last appeal from Belize was heard in 2011: *The Belize Bank Limited v Attorney General of Belize* [2011] UKPC 36. Until October 2009 the JCPC sat in Downing Street but now shares Middlesex Guildhall with the Supreme Court. It also, occasionally, sits overseas.

12 For example, as the final court of appeal in relation to disqualification for election to the House of Commons, see *Re MacManaway* [1951] AC 161 (concerning the now repealed House of Commons (Clergy Disqualification) Act (1801)) and the House of Commons Disqualification Act 1975, s 7.

13 See para 14.22 below.

14 SA 1998, ss 32–34, 98 and Sch 6 (and in relation to 'compatibility issues' s 288ZA of the Criminal Procedure (Scotland) Act 1995 (CP(S)A 1995)) and see paras 14.19–14.21 below.

15 GWA 2006, s149 and Sch 9 (previously the Government of Wales Act 1998, s 109 and Sch 8), although the JCPC was not called upon to determine any 'devolution issues' under either Act before the transfer of its devolution jurisdiction to the Supreme Court.

16 NIA 1998, ss 11, 79, 82 and Sch 10. Again, the JCPC had not been asked to determine any 'devolution issues' under this Act before the jurisdiction was transferred to the Supreme Court.

17 See, for example, *Scottish Ministers v Scottish Information Commissioner* 2007 SC 330 discussed at para 13.22; *Argyll and Bute Council v Scottish Public Services Ombudsman* 2008 SLT 168 discussed at para 10.14; and more recently *Comhairle Nan Eilean Siar v Scottish Ministers* 2013 SC 548 (concerning a school closure decision).

18 For a discussion of the definition and scope of 'political questions' under the United States Constitution, see *Baker v Carr* 369 US 186 (1962). However, constitutional courts have often displayed an unwillingness to relinquish jurisdiction over a dispute simply because it raises issues of political controversy. The Supreme Court of Canada has, for example, been prepared to rule on the constitutionality of the Canadian government's decision to permit testing of US cruise missiles within its territory (*Operation Dismantle v The Queen* [1985] 1 SCR 441). By contrast, in *Gibson v Lord Advocate* 1975 SLT 134, Lord Keith was of the view that the question whether UK legislation, in this case ECA 1972, s 2, which altered Scots private law, was not 'for the evident utility' of the Scottish people (as required by the Act of Union 1707, Art XVIII) was not a justiciable issue for the court.

19 *Operation Dismantle v The Queen* [1985] 1 SCR 441 per Wilson J at 471.

20 For example, the Commonwealth Constitution of Australia may be altered only by a law passed by the Australian Parliament and approved by both a majority of electors throughout Australia and by a majority of the electors in a majority of the states (Commonwealth Constitution, s 128). Only eight alterations to the Commonwealth Constitution were approved between 1906 and 1977.

21 The most sustained debate on this has been in the United States. For some of the most prominent contributions, see H Wechsler 'Towards Neutral Principles of Constitutional Law' (1959) 73 Harv LR 1; AM Bickel *The Least Dangerous Branch* (1962); and JH Ely *Democracy and Distrust* (1980) (hereafter Ely).

22 One famous example of such protection being the decision of the US Supreme Court in *Brown v Board of Education* 347 US 483 (1954) in which it rejected the racial segregation of public schools on the ground that such segregation breached the constitutional right of those black children affected to 'equal protection of the laws'.

23 See, especially, Ely and Lord Steyn 'Democracy through Law' (2002) 6 EHRLR 723.

24 While the courts have asserted the right to declare unconstitutional Acts of the Westminster Parliament on grounds of fundamental constitutional principle they have not in any case gone so far as to make such a declaration: see *R (Jackson) v Attorney General* [2006] 1 AC 262 and *AXA General Insurance Ltd, Petitioners* 2012 SC (UKSC) 122 and the discussion at para 14.26.

25 SA 1998, s 28(7).

26 See, for example, the comments of Lord President Rodger in *Whaley v Watson* 2000 SC 340 at 348, 349 and of Lord Brodie in *Whaley v Lord Advocate* 2004 SC 78 at 98, 99. Both cases are discussed below at para 14.24.

27 HRA 1998, s 4 and see para 14.17 below. Such a declaration of incompatibility does not affect the validity, continuing operation or enforcement of the legislation in question, nor is it binding on the parties to the proceedings in which it is made (HRA 1998, s 4(6)).

COURTS AND THE COMMON LAW

14.2   It is now 130 years since Dicey wrote his *Introduction to the Study of the Law of the Constitution* and, for many purposes, his work has to be regarded as largely overtaken by the political and constitutional events of the last century. Certainly the developments affecting the constitutional role of the courts, to be discussed in the later sections of this chapter, would have surprised (and probably dismayed) him. The growth of administrative law would perhaps have seemed the greatest shock.

There is, however, one aspect of the role of the courts, as Dicey described it, which remains residually in place. It was part of his version of the doctrine of the rule of law that the general principles of the British constitution are the result of judicial decisions determining the rights of private persons in particular cases brought before the courts[1]. They are inductions or general propositions based on particular decisions pronounced by the courts[2]. Even statutes 'being passed to meet special grievances, bear a close resemblance to judicial decisions, and are in effect judgments pronounced by the High Court of Parliament'[3]. This was all to be sharply contrasted with the situation in most other states where it was the written constitution itself that laid down general principles. Dicey regarded this as a 'merely formal difference' which did not, necessarily, have any impact on those whose rights were protected in this way. It was not that liberty was less well secured in Belgium, for instance: it was simply that it was differently secured[4]. Historically it was almost entirely to decided cases that, in the United Kingdom, one looked for the law and it was there that the landmark principles of civil liberties and the limits to public power were to be found.

By the beginning of this century, practically all of this had changed. For the protection of the rights and liberties of individuals, we now look primarily to statutes – for instance, anti-discrimination legislation[5] – and, above all, to the rights protected by the European Convention on Human Rights (ECHR) and secured under HRA 1998. There are, however, four ways in which an important common law jurisdiction survives. The *first* is in relation to all those areas in which, despite the general encroachment of statute, public bodies invoke common law powers in the exercise of their authority and it falls to the courts to determine the limits of those powers. Good examples of this arise where ministers use powers deriving from the royal prerogative, such as the prerogative of mercy[6] or, until the passing of the Constitutional Reform and Governance Act 2010[7], the power to regulate the civil service[8]. Such powers are usually subject to regulation under judicial review procedures[9]. *Secondly*, subject to specific statutory exceptions, and, in the case of the Crown, the Crown Proceedings Act 1947, public authorities are generally subject to common law rules on the extent of their civil liability in contract or delict when they are alleged to have acted in breach of contract or, for instance, negligently. The interpretation of the statutory powers of authorities in such cases will always be relevant but the courts have been forced to evolve common law principles of liability against the statutory background. It is a process which continues to prove uncomfortable for the courts as they try to develop general rules as to how far statutory powers and duties will, on the one hand, create the conditions of civil liability or, on the other hand, provide immunity from it[10]. Questions of how far public bodies should be liable in damages when injuries (or physical damage) are caused by a failure to clear snow from roads[11]; or to extinguish properly a fire in a neighbouring property[12]; to protect local authority tenants from the violent conduct of neighbours[13]; or to ensure that a disabled person wears a seatbelt on a return from day care services[14] have exercised judicial minds. The traditional approach of the English courts to questions of negligence by public authorities – in terms of which some latitude was afforded to those public bodies and restrictions were placed on the circumstances in which, in the exercise of public functions, a duty of care was owed to individuals – was successfully challenged in the European Court of Human Rights (ECtHR) as an infringement of the rights of such individuals to a 'fair trial' under art 6 ECHR[15]. Although the Strasbourg Court has now effectively conceded that its decision in *Osman v United Kingdom* was based on a misunderstanding of English law, the case has had lasting effects, encouraging arguments for a more generous (from the point of view of the claimant) approach to claims against public authorities[16]. *Thirdly*, it can reasonably be argued that, except for some procedural and remedial aspects regulated under statute, the whole of the law of judicial review developed by the Court of Session in the exercise of its inherent supervisory jurisdiction is a creation of the common law. Judicial review is dealt with separately at para 14.7. *Fourthly*, the wider claim is sometimes made that it is an aspect of the inherent powers of the courts and, therefore, of the common law when they claim to be the guardians of the unwritten constitution. They, and not Parliament, are, it has been argued, the ones to determine the ultimate powers of Parliament; they are the ones to determine the legitimate limits of institutional reform of the central constitutional relationship; they are the final guardians of the fundamental rights of citizens. These are claims which have been addressed at other points in this book[17].

1 AV Dicey *Law of the Constitution* (10th edn, 1959) (hereafter Dicey) p 195. For discussion of the rule of law see para 2.6.
2 Dicey p 197.
3 Dicey p 197.
4 Dicey p 198.
5 Now mostly consolidated in the Equality Act 2010: see para 13.14.
6 *R v Secretary of State for the Home Department, ex parte Bentley* [1994] QB 349 (cf the comments of Lord Roskill in *Council of Civil Service Unions v Minister for the Civil Service* [1985] AC 374 at 418); *McDonald v Secretary of State for Scotland* 1996 SLT 16. For discussion of potential for the reform of prerogative powers see para 7.2.
7 For further discussion see para 7.23 and for partial regulation of a limited category of civil servants see The Civil Service (Special Advisers) Act (Northern Ireland) 2013.
8 Council of *Civil Service Unions v Minister for the Civil Service* [1985] AC 374.
9 See para 14.7 et seq below.
10 See A Mason 'Negligence and the Liability of Public Authorities' (1998) 2 Edin LR 3; D Fairgrieve 'Pushing Back the Boundaries of Public Authority Liability' [2002] PL 288; C Booth and D Squires *The Negligence Liability of Public Authorities* (2006); D Brodie 'Public authority liability: the Scottish approach' (2007) 11 Edin LR 254; and WJ Stewart 'Fundamentally reconsidering statutory duty in delict' 2009 SLT (News) 99.
11 *Syme v Scottish Borders Council* 2003 SLT 601; *Goodes v East Sussex CC* [2000] 3 All ER 603. In relation to road signage see *MacDonald v Aberdeenshire Council* 2014 SC 114.
12 *Burnett v Grampian Fire and Rescue Service* 2007 SLT 61.
13 *Mitchell v Glasgow City Council* 2009 SLT 247.
14 *Murphy v East Ayrshire Council* 2012 SLT 1125.
15 *Osman v United Kingdom* (2000) 29 EHRR 245.
16 *TP v UK* (2002) 34 EHRR 2; *Z v UK* (2002) 34 EHRR 3; and see A Lidbetter and J George 'Negligent Public Authorities and Convention Rights – The Legacy of *Osman*' (2001) 6 EHRLR 599. See also K Starmer 'Human rights and victims: the untold story of the Human Rights Act' (2014) 3 EHRLR 215.
17 See paras 14.16, 14.26.

JUDICIAL CONTROL OF ADMINISTRATIVE ACTION

14.3   One of Dicey's best-known stances, deriving from his conception of the proper role of the ordinary courts in the application of the ordinary law, was his antipathy to what he called 'administrative law'. By this he meant the *'droit administratif*' applied by the Conseil d'Etat to officials of the French state. His objection was that the application of special law by special courts or tribunals to officials was an automatic breach of (his version of) the rule of law. Any special treatment meant unacceptable concessions and a compromise of one of the constitution's highest principles.

A full account of the development of administrative law in the United Kingdom during the 20th century, despite these inauspicious beginnings, cannot be given here[1]. However, the ideological clouding of Dicey's assessment of the changing condition of the British state – and its effects on the law and the role of the courts – lifted eventually, to reveal a strong system of administrative law. The last century saw the emergence of state institutions with expanded powers. The state became more interventionist, initially broadly in the direction of establishing the 'welfare state' but also in *consequence* of the state's role as promoter or regulator of many forms of economic activity. Such intervention brought inevitable disputes between public authorities and those affected by their decisions and the task of managing and resolving these disputes has fallen both to the ordinary courts and to specially created tribunals of limited jurisdiction. Challenges to the administrative decisions of public bodies are generally dealt with in one of two different ways:

1 See, for example, PP Craig *Administrative Law* (7th edn, 2012) ch 2; Lord Clyde and DJ Edwards *Judicial Review* (2000) ch 2; H Woolf et al *De Smith's Judicial Review of Administrative Action* (7th edn, 2013) ch 1.

(a) Statutory appeals

14.4   First, the 20th century saw a substantial growth in procedures, provided by statute, for challenging decisions made by government officials. In situations where many thousands of decisions are being made annually by such officials, considerations both of fairness to each individual affected and also of efficiency and consistency of provision demand that those initial decisions should not be absolutely final. Mistakes of fact may have been made by the original decision-maker or the relevant statutory rules may have been misinterpreted or misapplied. Parliament responded to these risks by establishing a wide variety of mechanisms for appeal and review.

Administrative Tribunals

14.5   The UK Government remains for the moment, notwithstanding devolution, responsible for the vast majority of tribunals operating in Scotland while the Scottish Government and Parliament exercise power in relation to tribunals which fall wholly within devolved competence[1]. The last decade has seen significant reform of the UK tribunals system, while similar reform of the

Scottish tribunals system is currently underway. That latter process of reform is expected to facilitate, in due course, the proposal (set out most recently by the Smith Commission) to further devolve responsibility for 'reserved' tribunals where those affect Scotland[2]. In addition to administrative rationalisation and reorganisation, tribunal reform is also concerned with the mechanisms of appeal available to those who are affected by the decisions of tribunals.

UNITED KINGDOM: At the UK level, HM Courts and Tribunals Service was created in April 2011, merging what had been HM Courts Service (responsible for the courts of England and Wales) and the Tribunals Service – which had itself been created in 2006 to provide a centralised and unified system of administrative support for most non-devolved UK tribunals. HM Courts and Tribunals Service is an executive agency of the Ministry of Justice. The Framework Document which governs the Service describes its aim as being to 'run an efficient and effective courts and tribunals system, which enables the rule of law to be upheld and provides access to justice for all' and its objectives include providing the supporting administration for a fair, efficient and accessible courts and tribunal system; supporting an independent judiciary in the administration of justice; continuous improvement of performance and efficiency across all aspects of the administration of the courts and tribunals; effective collaboration with other justice organisations and agencies to improve access to justice; and working with government departments and agencies to improve the quality and timeliness of their decision making in order to reduce the number of cases coming to courts and tribunals[3]. The Service is headed by a Chairman[4] who is to be distinguished from the Senior President of Tribunals – the most senior member of the tribunals judiciary (see below).

The Tribunals Service has its origins in the Leggatt Review. Sir Andrew Leggatt was appointed in 2000 to conduct a review of the then existing tribunal structure for which the UK government was responsible. His terms of reference were wide ranging: he was to 'review the delivery of justice through tribunals other than ordinary courts of law, constituted under an Act of Parliament by a Minister of the Crown or for purposes of a Minister's functions' and to review whether in resolving disputes, tribunals ensured '…fair, timely, proportionate and effective arrangements for handling those disputes, within an effective framework for decision-making which encourages the systematic development of the area of law concerned, and which forms a coherent structure, together with the superior courts, for the delivery of administrative justice;…[that] administrative and practical arrangements for supporting those decision-making procedures meet the requirements of the European Convention on Human Rights for independence and impartiality;' and whether proper arrangements for funding and performance management were in place and whether tribunals 'overall constitute a coherent structure for the delivery of administrative justice'[5]. Sir Andrew's report was published in August 2001[6] and contained a large number of recommendations for reform. Some of those related to concerns over judicial independence – a recommendation that there should be separation between the minister or other authority whose policies and decisions are tested by a tribunal, and the minister who appoints and supports the tribunal itself[7] – while many more focused on the importance of modernising and unifying the tribunal system. In addition, Tribunals for Users made specific recommendations in relation to individual tribunals including the Criminal Injuries Compensation Appeals Panel, Employment Tribunals, the Pensions Appeal Tribunal and the Social Security and Child Support Commissioners.

THE TRIBUNALS, COURTS AND ENFORCEMENT ACT 2007. Establishing the Tribunals Service was a precursor to more significant structural reform of the tribunal system itself by the Tribunals, Courts and Enforcement Act 2007 (TCEA 2007). TCEA 2007 created a new framework into which many existing UK tribunals have already moved and with scope for further expansion to accommodate other tribunals which have remained outside that framework[8]. That framework involves a two-tier structure: a First-tier Tribunal and an Upper Tribunal, with the Upper Tribunal being described as a 'superior court of record', i.e. that its decisions are binding on tribunals and chambers below[9]. The First-tier and Upper Tribunals are then[10] sub-divided into 'Chambers' which are intended to deal with matters of a broadly similar nature. Currently, the First-tier Tribunal is divided into seven such Chambers: the General Regulatory Chamber, the Social Entitlement Chamber, the Health, Education and Social Care Chamber, the Immigration and Asylum Chamber, the Property Chamber, the War Pensions and Armed Forces Compensation Chamber and the Tax Chamber. The Upper Tribunal is divided into four Chambers: an Administrative Appeals Chamber, an Immigration and Asylum Chamber, a Finance and Tax Chamber and a Lands Chamber. The jurisdiction of each First-tier and Upper Tribunal Chamber is set out in some detail in the order establishing the Chambers. So, for example, the First-tier Social Entitlement Chamber has assigned to it functions relating to financial support for asylum seekers, criminal injuries compensation, social security benefits and a number of other areas including industrial accidents[11].

Of particular interest is the jurisdiction of the Administrative Appeals Chamber of the Upper Tribunal. That Chamber has jurisdiction to hear appeals against decisions of all of the First-tier Chambers except the Tax Chamber (which appeals, as might be anticipated, are heard by the Finance and Tax Chamber of the Upper Tribunal) and the Immigration and Asylum Chamber (heard by the Immigration and Asylum Chamber of the Upper Tribunal). The Administrative Appeals Chamber also has jurisdiction to hear appeals against the decisions of other tribunals which are not comprised within a First-tier Chamber (for example, decisions of the Pensions Appeal Tribunal in Scotland[12]) and, perhaps most unexpectedly, enjoys first instance jurisdiction over certain matters which would previously have been dealt with by way of petition for judicial review in the Court of Session[13]. That jurisdiction is discussed in more detail below (para 14.7).

In addition to establishing the First-tier and Upper Tribunals, TCEA 2007 also makes provision relating to the tribunals judiciary. It firstly extends the 'guarantee' of judicial independence conferred by s 3 of the Constitutional Reform Act 2005 (see para 12.4) to members of a range of tribunals[14]. It also creates a new office of Senior President of Tribunals and confers on the Senior President a number of powers and functions including, for example, a power to make representations to Parliament about matters 'that appear to him to be matters of importance relating (a) to tribunal members, or (b) otherwise to the administration of justice by tribunals'[15].

Finally, TCEA 2007 abolished the Council on Tribunals (and its Scottish Committee) and replaced it with the Administrative Justice and Tribunals Council (AJTC) the role of which was to keep the whole system of administrative justice under review, to consider ways in which to make that system more accessible, fair and efficient and to make recommendations for change or for further research[16]. Somewhat controversially, the AJTC was itself abolished in 2013[17], in order to 'reduce duplication'[18].

SCOTTISH TRIBUNALS[19] The Leggatt review acknowledged the potential difficulties created by devolution in achieving a consistent approach to tribunal organisation where certain tribunals dealt with matters which are wholly reserved, others were concerned with matters which are wholly devolved (for example the Crofters Tribunal) and others which were formally cross-border public authorities (see para 8.9)[20]. The Scottish Committee of the AJTC was, until its abolition, concerned with all administrative tribunals with a Scottish role and produced its own annual report for laying before the Scottish Parliament. In addition, in 2006 the then Scottish Public Services Ombudsman, Professor Alice Brown, established an Administrative Justice Steering Group to report on, amongst other things, the likely impact of TCEA 2007 on Scotland. Its report was published in June 2009 and included proposals for 'rationalising' tribunal provision in Scotland and for further exploration of the potential for a unified Scottish tribunals service[21]. This was followed in 2012 by publication of 'Scottish Government's Proposals for a New Tribunal System for Scotland: Consultation Report', the key features of which have been enacted in the Tribunals (Scotland) Act 2014[22] which is expected to be brought into force by the end of 2016. In the interim, the Scottish Government also established (in December 2013) a non-statutory Scottish Tribunals and Administrative Justice Advisory Committee to fulfil the role previously undertaken by the Scottish Committee of the AJTC.

THE TRIBUNALS (SCOTLAND) ACT 2014: T(S)A 2014, when implemented, will in many respects replicate in the devolved Scottish context the structure created by TCEA 2007. There will be both a First-tier Tribunal and an Upper Tribunal which will be referred to collectively as 'the Scottish Tribunals'[23]. The Lord President is the Head of the Scottish Tribunals and in that capacity has the functions exercisable by him by virtue of T(S)A 2014[24] which role is to be separate from that of the newly created office of President of the Scottish Tribunals[25]. The President of the Scottish Tribunals must be a Court of Session judge 'assigned' to the office by the Lord President and the precise division of responsibilities between the Lord President and the President of the Scottish Tribunals will depend to a significant degree on how the Lord President exercises his powers under ss 8 and 9 of the T(S)A 2014 to delegate functions and to direct the President of the Scottish Tribunals as to the exercise of the latter's functions.

The First-tier Tribunal is to be organised into a number of chambers, having regard to the different subject-matters falling within the Tribunal's jurisdiction, and any other factors relevant in relation to the exercise of the Tribunal's functions[26]. Each chamber will have one or two Chamber Presidents who will be appointed by the Scottish Ministers. The Upper Tribunal will be organised into different divisions, following the same principles[27] and each will be led by one or two Vice Presidents.

The transfer of tribunals into the new framework created by T(S)A 2014 is to take place on a phased basis, with the functions of each of the listed tribunals 'to become the functions of the Scottish Tribunals at such time and in so far as the Scottish Ministers consider appropriate'[28], it then being made explicit that this might involve the transfer of functions to the First-tier Tribunal only, to the Upper Tribunal only or to both the First-tier and Upper Tribunals.

T(S)A 2014 includes, again mirroring TCEA 2007, the power to remit judicial review cases from the Court of Session to the Upper Tribunal in certain circumstances[29] and provision is made for appeals from the Upper Tribunal to the Court of Session.

1   For example the Scottish Charity Appeals Panel, the Crofting Commission and the Mental Health Tribunal for Scotland.
2   The Smith Commission (see paras 4.20 and 4.21) has proposed that all powers over the management and operation of all reserved tribunals be devolved to the Scottish Parliament other than the Special Immigration Appeals Commission and the Proscribed Organisations Appeals Commission.
3   Cm 8882, July 2014.
4   Currently Robert Ayling.
5   The terms of reference were announced on 18 May 2000 by the then Lord Chancellor Lord Irvine of Lairg in a speech to the Council on Tribunals Conference.
6   *Tribunals for Users – One System, One Service* (2001), hereafter *Tribunals for Users.*
7   Tribunals for Users, para 2.23.
8   At the time of writing those tribunals include the Employment Tribunal and Employment Appeal Tribunal, the Proscribed Organisations Appeal Commission and the Special Immigration Appeals Commission.
9   TCEA 2007, s 3.
10 By order made by the Lord Chancellor but with the concurrence of the Senior President of Tribunals: TCEA 2007, s 7 and see the First-tier Tribunal and Upper Tribunal (Chambers) Order 2010, SI 2010/2655 (as amended).
11 SI 2010/2655, art 6.
12 Ibid, arts 10(a)(iii). 7(a)(iii).
13 See TCEA 2007, ss 20, 21 and SI 2010/2655, art 10(b)(ii).
14 TCEA 2007, s 1.
15 TCEA 2007, s 2 and Sch 1, para 13.
16 TCEA 2007, s 44 and Sch 7.
17 By the Public Bodies (Abolition of Administrative Justice and Tribunals Council) Order 2013, SI 2013/2042. See, for discussion, the AJTC's last publication *'Future Oversight of Administrative Justice'*, July 2013.
18 'Consultation on reforms proposed in the Public Bodies Bill: Reforming the Public Bodies of the Ministry of Justice', Consultation Paper CP10/2011.
19 For the position pre-TCEA 2007 see S Craig, 'Tribunals in Scotland' in A McHarg and T Mullen (eds), *Public Law in Scotland* (2006).
20 Tribunals for Users, ch 11.
21 *Administrative Justice in Scotland – The Way Forward* (2009).
22 For a summary of the history leading to the 2014 Act see T Mullen 'Tribunals (Scotland) Bill' (2013) SPEL 79-80.
23 T(S)A 2014, s 1.
24 T(S)A 2014, s 2.
25 T(S)A 2014, s 4.
26 T(S)A 2014, s 20.
27 T(S)A 2014, s 23.

28 T(S)A 2014, s 28.
29 T(S)A 2014, s 57.

Appeals to the Courts

14.6   Although the powers of most 'administrative' tribunals relate to decision-making by central (including devolved) government, decisions by local authorities and other bodies also attract statutory appellate procedures, sometimes involving a first stage appeal to the Scottish Ministers. The best example of such an appeal is that available to applicants for planning permission who are aggrieved by decisions made in the first instance by local authorities[1]. In other cases, rights of appeal are direct to the courts. Appeals from decisions of the Scottish Information Commissioner, for example, are to the Court of Session (see para 13.22). A special feature of Scottish practice at this level has been the role of the sheriff as, in effect, a statutory appellate tribunal[2]. The powers of the sheriff vary from one form of appeal to another. Sometimes those powers are cast in quite narrowly defined terms leaving the sheriff with only questions of law to decide[3] but sometimes the statutory formulae which are used give the sheriff a much wider range of decision-making over matters of fact, law and even of policy. This dimension of the sheriff's jurisdiction raises interesting questions about the appropriateness of the use of judges to determine the issues allocated to them. Are sheriffs, whose expertise derives from their training in the law, the people who can best decide whether a child should be admitted to a particular school or a house should be demolished because of its poor condition? This is an area in which the principle of the separation of powers seems to be largely ignored[4].

Whatever form they take, statutory appeals have some characteristics in common. The circumstances in which an appeal may be lodged are defined (for example, when an adverse decision has been issued by an official). So too are the categories of person permitted to make the appeal (for example, the person in respect of whom the decision has been made); the period within which an appeal must be made; the tribunal or court to whom the appeal must go; the permitted grounds of appeal; the powers of the relevant tribunal including the procedures it must follow and its powers to grant remedies, whether interim or final; and the availability of any further appeal against the decision. The rules on these matters vary from one statutory scheme to another and sometimes they are themselves cast in statutory language which is imprecise and in need of interpretation by a tribunal or court.

There is, however, a sharp contrast between, on the one hand, all the statutorily defined procedures for appeal to a tribunal or court and, on the other, the second type of challenge referred to above – the procedure known as judicial review in the Court of Session.

1 Town and Country Planning (Scotland) Act 1997, ss 47–48 (as amended by the Planning etc (Scotland) Act 2006). See also appeals against decisions of the Scottish Environment Protection Agency (SEPA) under the Pollution Prevention and Control (Scotland) Regulations 2012 (as amended), SSI 2012/360, reg 58.
2 See para 12.2.
3 Firearms Act 1968, s 44 and Sch 5, Part III, para 4.

(b) Judicial review[1]

14.7   Judicial review provides, like statutory appeals, a procedure by which the decision of a governmental authority or official may be challenged. However, unlike statutory appeals which are available, by definition, only where the UK or Scottish Parliament by statute has made specific provision for them[2], judicial review is a procedure which has simply been asserted as a power of the Court of Session by the court itself. It is claimed to be inherent; to be of very long standing; and the rules concerning its availability have been the subject of development by the court. The origins and history of this supervisory jurisdiction were outlined by Lord President Hope in the leading case of *West v Secretary of State for Scotland*[3] which is discussed in more detail below.

What makes the development of judicial review interesting is the way in which the courts have sought to define their role in the supervision and control of public bodies. It is often suggested that this role has expanded and certainly the numbers of decided cases did grow substantially during the twentieth century and especially in the second half of the century. At the same time, the courts have sought to place this expansion within a principled framework which, while permitting and justifying growth, also explains the limits to that growth. Sometimes, however, these principles have been indistinct because they are not expressly and coherently articulated by the judges. Indeed, it is not so very long ago that judicial review was described as a 'wilderness of single instances'[4]. Latterly, however, greater efforts have been made to articulate the conceptual basis of judicial review.

A good starting point is the early twentieth-century case of *Moss' Empires Ltd v Glasgow Assessor*[5] in which Lord Kinnear stated that '[w]herever any inferior tribunal or any administrative body has exceeded the powers conferred on it by statute to the prejudice of the subject, the jurisdiction of the court to set aside such excess of power as incompetent and illegal is not open to dispute'[6]. The reviewing power of the court is, in principle, triggered whenever it is claimed that an 'administrative body' has exceeded its powers.

The essential preconditions for the exercise of this supervisory power of review by the courts are four:

1 For fuller discussion of judicial review in Scotland, see Lord Clyde and DJ Edwards *Judicial Review* (2000); *SME Reissue* Administrative Law; A O'Neill *Judicial Review in Scotland* (1999); CMG Himsworth, 'Judicial Review in Scotland' in H Fenwick, M Supperstone, J Goudie and P Walker (eds), *Judicial Review* (5th edn, 2014) and S Blair *Scots Administrative Law: Cases and Materials* (1999). Leading English works include HWR Wade and CF Forsyth *Administrative Law* (11th edn, 2014); PP Craig *Administrative Law* (7th edn, 2012); and H Woolf et al, *De Smith's Judicial Review of Administrative Action* (7th edn, 2013).
2 Occasionally by statutory instrument, for example the (now repealed) Licensing of Venison Dealers (Application Procedures etc) (Scotland) Order 1984, SI 1984/922.
3 *West v Secretary of State for Scotland* 1992 SC 385.

4 See HWR Wade and CF Forsyth *Administrative Law* (10th edn, 2009) at p 14, quoting Tennyson *Aylmer's Field*, line 441.
5 *Moss' Empires Ltd v Glasgow Assessor* 1917 SC (HL) 1.
6 *Moss' Empires Ltd v Glasgow Assessor* 1917 SC (HL) 1 at 6.

Scope

14.8   There must have been conferred on the administrative or other body under review a power to act or a power to decide – described by Lord President Hope in the leading case of *West v Secretary of State for Scotland* as a 'jurisdiction'[1]. Typically, this jurisdiction will have been conferred – in primary or secondary legislation – by the Westminster or Scottish Parliament but it may also have derived from a prerogative source, and perhaps from elsewhere. It is possible that the 'jurisdiction' may have been conferred by an arrangement which does not involve a Parliament or any public authority at all. For example, Lord Hope referred to the decision in *St Johnstone FC v SFA*[2] in which the Court of Session considered that it was competent to review decisions of the Council of the Scottish Football Association to fine or expel member clubs in accordance with the SFA's articles of association. Lord Hope, in citing this case, also sought to emphasise that in Scots law the availability of judicial review did not depend on the existence of some 'public law' element in the decision-making process, as is the case in England[3]. That being said, purely contractual disputes – such as that between Mr West and his employers, the Scottish Prison Service – were not amenable to judicial review. What was absent from the relationship between those parties was the necessary 'tripartite relationship'[4] in which (1) power is conferred (2) on a party 'to whom the taking of the decision is entrusted' and (3) whose decision affects the rights and obligations of another person[5].

1 *West v Secretary of State for Scotland* 1992 SC 385.
2 *St Johnstone FC v SFA* 1965 SLT 171. For a more recent example of a successful judicial review of the SFA, in the context of the insolvency of Glasgow Rangers FC, see *Rangers Football Club PLC, Petitioner* 2012 SLT 1156.
3 There is a large body of case law and scholarship on the need for a 'public law' element in English judicial review proceedings. For general discussion, see the references cited at para 14.7 and, in particular, *O'Reilly v Mackman* [1983] 2 AC 237; *Cocks v Thanet District Council* [1983] 2 AC 286; *Roy v Kensington and Chelsea Family Practitioner Committee* [1992] 1 AC 624; *Boddington v British Transport Police* [1999] 2 AC 143; and, as a more recent example, *R (McIntyre) v Gentoo Group* [2010] EWHC 5 (Admin), [2010] 2 P & CR DG6.
4 For the difficulties of this terminology, see W Finnie 'Triangles as Touchstones of Review' 1993 SLT (News) 51 and CMG Himsworth 'Further *West?* More Geometry of Judicial Review' 1995 SLT (News) 127 and for further judicial consideration of the '*West* test' see *Blair v Lochaber DC* 1995 SLT 407; *Wm Fotheringham & Son v British Limousin Cattle Society Ltd* 2004 SLT 485; *Magnohard Ltd v United Kingdom Atomic Energy Authority* 2004 SC 247 and *D Petitioner* 2011 SLT 101. Most recently, a company director's petition for judicial review in respect of disciplinary proceedings was refused on the grounds that the relationship between the petitioner and the company was essentially bilateral rather than tripartite: *G v Watson* 2014 SLT 1030.
5 Referring to *St Johnstone FC v SFA* 1965 SLT 171, Lord Hope described the case as 'a clear example of the tripartite relationship to which we referred earlier, by which a decision making body – in this case the council – has been entrusted by an enabling body with a limited jurisdiction for decision taking in regard to others to which it must adhere' (*West v Secretary of State for Scotland* 1992 SC 385 at 400). There have been several petitions for judicial review taken against sports clubs in recent years, leading some to question whether the availability of the supervisory jurisdiction in such cases is in the interests of the parties or the administration

of justice. See *Irvine v Royal Burgess Golfing Society of Edinburgh* 2004 SCLR 386; *Crocket v Tantallon Golf Club* 2005 SLT 663; *Smith v Nairn Golf Club* 2007 SLT 909 and *Foley v Glen Golf Club* 2012 GWD. 32-636. For discussion, see S Thomson 'Golf Clubbing Judicial Review to Death' 2008 SLT (News) 221.

Grounds

14.9   Second, there must be an alleged excess or abuse in the exercise of this power or jurisdiction. In *West v Secretary of State for Scotland*, Lord Hope reaffirmed that there was 'no substantial difference' between English law and Scots law as to the grounds which the process of decision-making may be open to review[1]. A helpful restatement of the grounds of review was developed in *CCSU v Minister for the Civil Service* (the '*GCHQ*' case)[2] at the hand of Lord Diplock. There he noted that 'the English law relating to judicial control of administrative action has been developed upon a case to case basis' but that this development had reached the stage where 'one could conveniently classify under three heads the grounds upon which administrative action is subject to judicial review. The first ground I would call "illegality", the second "irrationality" and the third "procedural impropriety"'[3].

It must be borne in mind that this summary of the grounds of judicial review was indeed a *restatement*: Lord Diplock identified three seemingly straightforward labels under which a number of different – but well established – principles could be grouped. These are principles which have been, by and large, developed on an incremental basis by the courts themselves on a case-by-case basis. Indeed, Lord Diplock adverted to the possibility of further such development not only of these three categories, but potentially, of altogether new heads:

> 'That is not to say that further development on a case by case basis may not in course of time add further grounds. I have in mind particularly the possible adoption in the future of the principle of "proportionality" which is recognised in the administrative law of several of our fellow members of the European Economic Community[4]'.

A full account of those principles cannot be given here[5] but an outline may give a flavour of the complexity which Lord Diplock's labels disguise.

ILLEGALITY Illegality is arguably the broadest of the three categories identified by Lord Diplock as giving rise to a claim for judicial review. Indeed, at one level – and illustrating immediately the difficulties of terminology which are inescapable in this area – all three categories represent illegality (or 'unlawfulness') of one sort or another. Lord Diplock described the ground as follows:

> 'I mean that the decision-maker must understand correctly the law that regulates his decision-making power and must give effect to it. Whether he has or not is par excellence a justiciable question to be decided, in the event of dispute, by those persons, the judges, by whom the judicial power of the state is excercisable'[6]

The concept of 'illegality' encompasses ultra vires, by which is meant that a decision-maker must act within the four corners of the statutory powers under which he or she acts, but it also extends beyond that straightforward principle. So, for example, where statute clearly empowers a public body to provide 'ferry services' across the River Tay that public body may not use those powers to carry on profit-making tourist trips[7]. More than that, though, even where legislation appears to confer very wide decision-making powers – 'discretion' – on a public body or government minister, the courts have asserted their right to regulate the manner in which those powers may be exercised. They must be used for proper and not improper purposes[8]; the public body must take account of relevant and not irrelevant considerations[9]; and it must not act with malice or bad faith[10]. Where one person or body is charged with making a decision or taking action they must not delegate their responsibilities to another body or person[11] (although there are a number of exceptions to this general rule[12]) and they must not abdicate their responsibilities altogether by refusing or failing to make any decision at all[13].

One area of complexity which falls within the broad ambit of 'illegality' but which is often discussed as a free standing ground of judicial review is that of 'error of law'. This concerns circumstances in which it is claimed that in the exercise of administrative discretion by a public authority, or in the determination of disputes by an adjudicator such as a tribunal or arbiter, the decision-maker has failed to apply properly the law which governs the decision-making process. This is one area in which the grounds of review north and south of the border had fallen out of step[14]. In England, it had been held that all errors of law are capable of being challenged by way of judicial review whereas the Scottish approach had been to distinguish between errors of law which are 'intra vires' – that is permissible for the original decision-maker to make without being challenged – and those which are 'ultra vires' – impermissible and giving rise to the possibility of the decision being struck down[15]. This difference of approach was recently disapproved of by the Supreme Court in *Eba v Advocate General for Scotland*[16] in which Lord Hope made it plain that he considered *Watt v Lord Advocate* to have been wrongly decided and that 'once again it must be stressed that there is, in principle, no difference between the law of England and Scots law as to the substantive grounds on which a decision by a tribunal which acts within its jurisdiction may be open to review'[17]. *Anisminic*, as subsequently interpreted, therefore sets out the correct test. Errors of law are all reviewable.

IRRATIONALITY Judicial review is frequently characterised by the courts as an exercise in assessing the legality rather than the merits of the decisions of public bodies, ensuring that they act within their lawful powers. However, of the three grounds identified by Lord Diplock 'irrationality' comes closest to a test of the substantive merits of a decision. Lord Diplock viewed irrationality as simply another term for what had come to be known as '*Wednesbury* unreasonableness'[18] albeit described in slightly different language. In *Wednesbury*, Lord Greene MR explained that 'if a decision on a competent matter is so unreasonable that no reasonable authority could ever have come to it then the courts will interefere'[19] whereas Lord Diplock's characterisation was that:

'By "irrationality" I mean what can by now be succinctly referred to as '*Wednesbury* unreasonableness... It applies to a decision which is so outrageous in its defiance of logic or of accepted moral standards that no sensible person who had applied his mind to the question to be decided could have arrived at it. Whether a decision falls within this category is a question that judges by their training and experience should be well equipped to answer, or else there is something badly wrong with our judicial system'.

However described, traditionally, the courts have treated this as a very difficult test for a petitioner to meet, requiring to be satisfied that the decision-maker's judgment is quite obviously flawed before substituting their own[20].

PROCEDURAL IMPROPRIETY Finally, the courts have been concerned to ensure not only that a decision-maker acts within the parameters of their lawful powers but also that the manner in which those powers are exercised meets certain minimum standards. The third ground of judicial review identified by Lord Diplock – that of a 'procedural impropriety' – has been characterised as imposing a 'duty to act fairly'[21] on those exercising discretionary powers:

'I have described the third head as "procedural impropriety" rather than failure to observe basic rules of natural justice or failure to act with procedural fairness towards the person who will be affected by the decision. This is because susceptibility to judicial review under this head covers also failure by an administrative tribunal to observe procedural rules that are expressly laid down in the legislative instrument by which its jurisdiction is conferred, even where such failure does not involve any denial of natural justice.'[22]

It requires them both to observe any relevant statutory procedural requirements but also to comply with the precepts of 'natural justice', that is the common law rules of fair process which have been developed by the courts themselves. So far as procedural requirements contained in legislation are concerned, one question which arises is whether a failure to follow such a procedural requirement should have the consequence that the action taken by the public authority – which might but for the procedural failure be quite lawful – should be treated as being wholly invalid or whether it may survive. Sometimes the legislation under scrutiny will make express provision about what is to happen if procedural hurdles are not cleared but, where it does not, historically one way in which the courts have answered the question is by categorising statutory procedural requirements as being of one of two kinds: mandatory or directory. In the case of mandatory requirements a failure will result in the nullity of the public body's act whereas in the case of directory requirements a failure will not automatically lead to that result. Doubt has been case on the usefulness of this distinction[23] and though it continues to feature[24] other approaches have also found favour. In particular, the seriousness of the breach and the impact of the breach on the person(s) affected by the public body's action will influence the attitude of the courts[25].

In addition to such statutory requirements there are also, of course, the principles of natural justice which may be summarised as follows.

Firstly, the rule against bias – *nemo iudex in sua causa* – concerns the impartiality of the decision-maker himself. This concept is discussed in much fuller detail in Chapter 12 and involves, for example, a requirement that a decision-maker should not have any personal pecuniary interest in the outcome of the decision-making process[26], should not make a decision directly involving someone, such as a family member, with whom he has a close personal relationship[27], or having a direct impact on a company of which he is a director[28]. The rule against bias goes beyond a prohibition against the decision-maker actually acting in a partial manner towards one or other of the parties. Reliance is often placed on the dictum that 'justice must not only be done but must manifestly be seen to be done'[29] and decisions may be struck down where the circumstances are such that a 'fair-minded and informed observer, having considered the facts, would conclude that there was a real possibility that the tribunal was biased'[30].

Secondly, the right to a hearing – *audi alteram partem* – focuses on the rights of a party involved in a dispute or affected by an administrative decision to put their case fully and effectively to the court, tribunal or public body entrusted with decision-making powers. Although many cases have concerned the very specific issue of whether a party is entitled to an oral hearing before a decision is made, the right to a hearing encompasses wider concerns with fair procedure. Consideration has been given, for example, to the circumstances in which a person may be entitled to legal representation[31], to lead witnesses[32] and to test the evidence of an opponent whether by cross-examination or otherwise[33]. Questions have also concerned the right of a party to have appropriate notice of any case against him and to have access to evidence which may be used by his opponent or by the decision-maker in forming a view on the merits of his case[34].

Closely linked to these two main principles of natural justice are rules which concern when and to what extent a party is entitled to be furnished with the reasons for any decision which is made[35]. In addition, art 6 ECHR concerns procedural fairness and a breach of that article (or indeed any other of those incorporated by HRA 1998) now provide grounds for judicial review[36].

Indeed, it is now fair to describe breach of Convention rights as a fourth ground of review to be added to the three grounds identified by Lord Diplock. Lord Diplock's grounds were each rooted in the common law, while breach of Convention rights is a ground which flows from the incorporation of the ECHR by HRA 1998 but the latter is now at least as prevalent a ground of challenge in the courts as the common law grounds. The courts' treatment of Convention rights claims is discussed at para 13.12 above.

1   The position having been taken earlier by Lord Fraser in *Brown v Hamilton District Council* 1983 SC (HL) 1 at 42.
2   *CCSU v Minister for the Civil Service* [1985] AC 374.
3   *CCSU v Minister for the Civil Service* [1985] AC 374 at 410.
4   Ibid, and for discussion of proportionality see para 14.13.
5   See the works cited at para 14.7.
6   Ibid.
7   *Dundee Harbour Trustees v Nicol* 1915 SC (HL) 7. Nor, where a statute requires a local authority to provide a 'pure supply of wholesome water' will that permit the proactive fluoridation of the water supply as a purported public health measure: *McColl v Strathclyde Regional Council* 1983 SC 225.

8 *Highland Regional Council v British Railways Board* 1996 SLT 274; *Congreve v Home Office* [1976] QB 629; *Bromley London Borough Council v Greater London Council* [1983] 1 AC 768.

9 *Gerry Cottle's Circus Ltd v City of Edinburgh District Council* 1990 SLT 235; *Cunningham v East Lothian Council* 2011 GWD 39-792.

10 *Pollok School Co Ltd v Glasgow Town Clerk* 1946 SC 373; *R v Secretary of State for the Environment, ex parte Ostler* [1977] QB 122.

11 *Young v Fife Regional Council* 1986 SLT 331; *Dalziel School Board v Scotch Education Department* 1915 SC 234.

12 *Carltona v Commissioners of Works* [1943] 2 All ER 560; *R v Home Secretary, ex parte Oladehinde* [1991] 1 AC 254; Local Government (Scotland) Act 1973, s 56; and cf *R v Race Relations Board, e xp Selvarajan* [1976] 1 All ER 12; *Somerville v Scottish Ministers (No 2)* 2008 SC (HL) 45.

13 *Kilmarnock Magistrates v Secretary of State for Scotland* 1961 SC 350; *British Oxygen Co Ltd v Minister of Technology* [1971] AC 610.

14 See SME Reissue, Administrative Law, paras 47 to 51.

15 See *Watt v Lord Advocate* 1979 SC 120.

16 2012 SC (UKSC) 1.

17 Ibid, at para 34.

18 *Associated Provincial Picture Houses Ltd v Wednesbury Corpn* [1948] 1 KB 223.

19 In *Associated Provincial Picture Houses Ltd v Wednesbury Corpn* [1948] 1 KB 223, Lord Greene MR referred to a decision 'so unreasonable that no reasonable authority could ever have come to it' ([1948] 1 KB 223 at 230). See the discussion at para 14.26 below.

20 *Secretary of State for Education and Science v Tameside Metropolitan Borough Council* [1977] AC 1014; *K v Scottish Legal Aid Board* 1989 SC 21; *Woods v Secretary of State for Scotland* 1991 SLT 197; *McTear v Scottish Legal Aid Board* 1995 SCLR 611; *Rooney v Strathclyde Police Joint Board* 2009 SC 73.

21 *Re HK (an infant)* [1967] 2 QB 617; *Errington v Wilson* 1995 SC 550.

22 Ibid.

23 *London and Clydeside Estates Ltd v Aberdeen District Council* 1980 SC (HL) 1 and *Wang v Commissioner for Inland Revenue* [1995] 1 All ER 367.

24 See, for example, *McInnes v Forth Ports Ltd* [2014] CSOH 92; *R v Birmingham City Council, ex parte Ireland* [1999] 2 All ER 609 and *Robinson v Secretary of State for Northern Ireland* [2002] NI 390.

25 See, for example, *Mitchell v North Lanarkshire Council* 2007 SLT 765 in which a petition for judicial review of a demand notice for Council Tax – on the grounds that the notice failed to refer to the recipient's right of appeal or to a colour pamphlet which ought to have been sent with the notice – was dismissed. Lord McEwan held that 'it would be astonishing if Parliament having laid out a careful scheme for taxation then legislated in subordinate rules for the frustration of the scheme if the collection documents were not a model of clarity' (para 16).

26 *Dimes v Grand Junction Canal Proprietors* (1852) 3 HL Cas 759; *Sellar v Higland Railway Co* 1919 SC (HL) 19.

27 *Moncrieff v Lord Moncrieff* (1904) 6 F 1021.

28 *R v Bow Street Metropolitan Stipendiary Magistrate, ex parte Pinochet Ugarte (No 2)* [2000] 1 AC 119.

29 See *Barrs v British Wool Marketing Board* 1957 SC 72.

30 *Porter v Magill* [2002] 2 AC 357 per Lord Hope of Craighead at 494.

31 *Abbas v Home Secretary* 1993 SLT 502; *R v Home Secretary, ex parte Tarrant* [1985] QB 251.

32 *R v Hull Board of Prison Visitors, ex parte St Germain (No 2)* [1979] 3 All ER 545.

33 *R v Hull Board of Prison Visitors, ex parte St Germain (No 2)* [1979] 3 All ER 545; *Errington v Wilson* 1995 SC 550.

34 *Inland Revenue Comrs v Barr* 1956 SC 162; *Moore v Clyde Pilotage Authority* 1943 SC 457; *R v Criminal Injuries Compensation Board, ex parte Ince* [1973] 3 All ER 808; *R v Home Secretary, ex parte Fayed* [1997] 1 All ER 228.

35 *R v Civil Service Appeal Board, ex parte Cunningham* [1991] 4 All ER 310; *R v Higher Education Funding Council, ex parte Institute of Dental Surgery* [1994] 1 WLR 242; *Lloyds Pharmacy Ltd v National Appeal Panel for Entry to the Pharmaceutical Lists* 2012 GWD 8-137.

36 *Anderson v Scottish Ministers* 2002 SC (PC) 63; *M v Law Society of Scotland* 2013 SLT 462.

Standing

14.10 Third, there must be someone (whether a natural or artificial person or group of persons) who has the necessary standing to sue. Of the four preconditions for a successful petition to the supervisory jurisdiction of the Court of Session it is this which has undergone the most significant development since the last edition of this book; that development having been heralded by the decision of the Supreme Court in the case of *AXA General Insurance Ltd, Petitioners*[1].

Historically, the courts in both Scotland and England have been keen to insist that they are not simply available to all and sundry in judicial review proceedings. Judicial review may not be sought by someone with a merely academic interest in, or who is otherwise unaffected by, the act or decision of the public authority. In England, since 1981, a person has been statutorily required to have 'sufficient interest' in the case[2]. In Scotland, until the passing of the Courts Reform (Scotland) Act 2014, there was no statutory definition of *locus standi* and, before the decision in *AXA,* the Court of Session insisted on the need for both *title* – deriving from 'some legal relation' which gives the petitioner some right which the person against whom he or she raises the action infringes or denies[3] – and an *interest* which, will usually derive from the petitioner's pecuniary rights or status[4]. The practical consequences of the need to establish both title and interest may not have, for the most part, been very great – of those motivated to raise the issue in the courts, there was usually be *someone* who satisfied the tests – but an increasingly urgent question of concern was the standing of representative voluntary organisations such as pressure groups. While in England, the courts took a relatively generous view[5], a more restrictive regime applied in Scotland. That regime was exemplified by the Scottish *Age Concern* case[6] in which Age Concern Scotland was held not to have the 'interest' necessary to challenge the legality of administrative guidance concerning the payment of cold weather allowances to elderly people. In reaching this view Lord Clyde took account of a number of factors including the fact that it had not been argued that 'the association or any of its members have claimed the benefit in question or are intending to do so … [they] are not suing as a body of potential claimants but as a body working to protect and advance the interests of the aged'[7].

The question whether the Scottish approach to title and interest in judicial review should be revised came before the Supreme Court in *AXA* in a somewhat roundabout way. There was little doubt that the *petitioners* (insurance companies who would face claims as a result of the passing of the Damages (Asbestos-related Conditions) (Scotland) Act 2009) had the requisite standing[8] to challenge that legislation. The petitioners, however, disputed the entitlement of individuals who stood to benefit from the 2009 Act to enter the proceedings to defend the legislation. Eight such individuals sought to become involved, not as interveners in the public interest (see below) but as *respondents*, relying on a rule of court[9] which entitles any person on whom a petition for review has not been served – but who contends that they are 'directly affected' by any issue raised in the review – to apply for leave to enter the process. Their right to do so was upheld at first instance[10] but rejected by the Inner House on appeal[11], setting the stage for a debate on the issue in London[12].

Lords Hope and Reed, the two Scottish judges sitting as part of a panel of seven justices, took the opportunity to make clear their views that the Scottish approach to title and interest was outdated and did not reflect or serve the purposes for which judicial review existed: to hold public authorities to account and to preserve the rule of law. In doing so they acknowledged the distinction between public and private law which, so far as the scope of judicial review is concerned, has not otherwise played a prominent role in Scottish cases[13]. So far as Lord Hope was concerned:

> 'I think that the time has come to recognise that the private law rule that title and interest has to be shown has no place in applications to the court's supervisory jurisdiction that lie in the field of public law. The word 'standing' provides a more appropriate indication of the approach that should be adopted. I agree with Lord Reed (see para 170) that it cannot be based on the concept of rights, but must be based on the concept of interests.'[14]

Lord Reed, in a fuller discussion, sought to explain the origins and reasons for distinctions between private law cases and those, like judicial review, concerned with public law issues. He concluded that a test of 'title and interest' as the gateway to the supervisory jurisdiction of the court was one which failed to recognise the essential nature of judicial review:

> '169...There is thus a public interest involved in judicial review proceedings, whether or not private rights may also be affected. A public authority can violate the rule of law without infringing the rights of any individual: if, for example, the duty which it fails to perform is not owed to any specific person, or the powers which it exceeds do not trespass upon property or other private rights. A rights-based approach to standing is therefore incompatible with the performance of the courts' function of preserving the rule of law, so far as that function requires the court to go beyond the protection of private rights: in particular, so far as it requires the courts to exercise a supervisory jurisdiction. The exercise of that jurisdiction necessarily requires a different approach to standing.

> 170 For the reasons I have explained, such an approach cannot be based upon the concept of rights, and must instead be based upon the concept of interests. A requirement that the applicant demonstrate an interest in the matter complained of will not however operate satisfactorily if it is applied in the same way in all contexts. In some contexts, it is appropriate to require an applicant for judicial review to demonstrate that he has a particular interest in the matter complained of: the type of interest which is relevant, and therefore required in order to have standing, will depend upon the particular context. In other situations, such as where the excess or misuse of power affects the public generally, insistence upon a particular interest could prevent the matter being brought before the court, and that in turn might disable the court from performing its function to protect the rule of law. I say 'might', because the protection of the rule of law does not require that every allegation of unlawful conduct by a public authority must

be examined by a court, any more than it requires that every allegation of criminal conduct must be prosecuted. Even in a context of that kind, there must be considerations which lead the court to treat the applicant as having an interest which is sufficient to justify his bringing the application before the court. What is to be regarded as sufficient interest to justify a particular applicant's bringing a particular application before the court, and thus as conferring standing, depends therefore upon the context, and in particular upon what will best serve the purposes of judicial review in that context.

171 The supervisory jurisdiction has developed almost entirely through judicial decisions. One of the responsibilities of the courts is to ensure its continuing development, on an incremental basis, so as to meet the needs of the time. In my opinion, the time has come when it should be recognised by the courts that Lord Dunedin's dictum pre-dates the modern development of public law, that it is rooted in private law concepts which are not relevant in the context of applications to the supervisory jurisdiction, and that its continuing influence in that context has had a damaging effect on the development of public law in Scotland. This unsatisfactory situation should not be allowed to persist. The time has also come when the courts should cease to use the inappropriate terminology of title and interest in relation to such applications, and should refer instead to standing, based upon a sufficient interest.'[15]

The consequence of these 'potentially revolutionary comments suggesting a major relaxation of the rules on standing in judicial review actions before the Scottish courts'[16] has not thus far been a glut of new public interest litigation by pressure groups and voluntary associations[17]. Nevertheless, while the Supreme Court felt compelled to reiterate its views on sufficient interest in the face of perceived hesitation by the Court of Session[18], title and interest has now been laid firmly to rest. By virtue of s 89 of the Courts Reform (Scotland) Act 2014[19], the Court of Session will not be entitled to grant permission for an application for judicial review to proceed unless it is satisfied that 'the applicant can demonstrate a sufficient interest in the subject matter of the application'.

Alongside this fresh approach to standing, pressure groups, voluntary associations and NGOs have also been able to take advantage of the still relatively new rules concerning 'public interest intervention' in judicial review proceedings. Since 2000[20] it has been possible for a party who believes that proceedings for judicial review (which have been initiated by someone with sufficient interest) raise a matter of 'public interest' to apply for leave to intervene in those proceedings. Before leave is granted the court must be satisfied that a matter of public interest is at stake, that the applicant has relevant arguments to make and that the intervention will not 'unduly delay or otherwise prejudice the rights of the parties, including their potential liability for expenses'. Where intervention is allowed the intervener's submissions are normally to be made in writing, although an oral hearing may be held. The first reported public interest intervention in Scotland was made not in the context of a judicial review: in 2008 the NGO Liberty was given leave to intervene in the public interest in proceedings for contempt involving a Scottish solicitor who had criticised a trial judge following his client's conviction for terrorist offences. Notwithstanding that the rules of court applicable to such proceedings contain no express provision for intervention, Liberty was permitted to make written and oral submissions in relation to the implications of the proceedings for the solicitor's rights to freedom of expression under art 10 ECHR[21]. Since then there have been a number of interventions in judicial review proceedings, including in challenges to Acts of the Scottish Parliament[22], and indeed in other proceedings for which no specific provision has been made in the rules of court[23].

1 2012 SC (UKSC) 122.
2 Senior Courts Act 1981, s 31(3).
3 *Dundee Harbour Trustees v D Nicol* 1915 SC (HL) 7 at 12, 13 (per Lord Dunedin).
4 *Swanson v Manson* 1907 SC 426 at 429 (per Lord Ardwall).
5 See, for example, *R v HM Inspectorate of Pollution, ex parte Greenpeace Ltd (No 2)* [1994] 4 All ER 329 (challenge to grant of permission for discharge of radioactive waste) and *R v Secretary of State for Foreign and Commonwealth Affairs, ex parte World Development Movement Ltd* [1995] 1 All ER 611 (successful challenge by pressure group to government's decision to grant aid for construction of Malaysian hydro-electric dam).
6 *Scottish Old People's Welfare Council, Petitioners* 1987 SLT 179.
7 *Scottish Old People's Welfare Council, Petitioners* 1987 SLT 179 at 187. See also *Rape Crisis Centre v Secretary of State for the Home Department* 2000 SC 527 and Lord Hope of Craighead 'Mike Tyson comes to Glasgow – a question of standing' [2001] PL 294.
8 Although the point was taken against them by the respondents at first instance: 2010 SLT 179.
9 RCS 58.8(2).
10 2010 SLT 179.
11 2011 SC 662.
12 At which stage in the proceedings Friends of the Earth Scotland was permitted to intervene in the public interest to address, specifically, the issue of title and interest in judicial review proceedings in Scotland.
13 See para 14.8 above.
14 2012 SC (UKSC) 122 at para 62.
15 Ibid.
16 C T Reid 'Fundamental change to the rules about standing' (2011) SPEL 133.
17 Indeed, in January 2015 Lord Pentland refused the petition for judicial review of the Children and Young People (Scotland) Act 2014 in which the seven petitioners included four 'corporate' petitioners: The Christian Institute, Family Education Trust, The Young ME Sufferers Trust and CARE (Christian Action Research & Education). The Lord Ordinary held that those four corporate petitioners did not have sufficient interest entitling them to bring the judicial review: 'these petitioners are not in any realistic sense directly affected by Part 4 of the Act'. See *The Christian Institute, Petitioners* [2015] CSOH 7.
18 *Walton v Scottish Ministers* 2013 SC (UKSC) 67. See also *MacReath, Petitioner* 2012 SLT 1195.
19 Introducing new ss 27A to 27D of the Court of Session Act 1988.
20 Act of Sederunt (Rules of the Court of Session Amendment No 5) (Public Interest Intervention in Judicial Review) 2000, SSI 2000/317 (as amended); and see R Charteris 'Intervention – in the Public Interest' 2000 SLT (News) 87. Third party interventions in public law proceedings, particularly in the Supreme Court, have been the subject of considerable debate: see Lady Hale 'Who guards the guardians' 2014 CJICL 3(1) 100; M Fordham 'Public Interest interventions in the Supreme Court; ten virtues' (2010) 15 JR 18. Equally, there has been a degree of judicial criticism of interveners who have, in the court's view, failed to fulfil their proper role: *E (A Child) v Chief Constable of the Royal Ulster Constabulary* [2008] UKHL 66, [2009] 1 AC 536.
21 See *Anwar,* 2008 JC 409 and JP Marshall 'Liberty to intervene beyond judicial review' 2008 SLT (News) 187.
22 As mentioned above, Friends of the Earth Scotland intervened (under the Supreme Court's rules) in *AXA*, while Alcohol Focus Scotland was permitted to intervene in the Outer House in the judicial review of the Alcohol (Minimum Pricing) (Scotland) Act 2012 (*The Scotch Whisky Association, Petitioners* 2012 GWD 33-659). Having declined, however, to participate in the Inner House appeal proceedings, AFS was unable to persuade the court to treat it as a 'party'

to the proceedings for the purposes of a preliminary reference to the Court of Justice of the European Union: see the opinion of the court at 2014 GWD 24-444.
23 In *IA* 2011 SC 625 the United Nations High Commission for Refugees was given leave to intervene in an appeal to the Court of Session against a decision of the Asylum and Immigration Tribunal on the question of the meaning and effect of recognition by the UNHCR that a person has 'mandate refugee status'.

Access to the courts

14.11   The final core prerequisite for judicial review is that access to the courts has not been prohibited or curtailed by statute. Judicial review is a power asserted by the courts but its scope and availability are open to manipulation by parliaments. This may take two principal forms, sometimes in combination. The first is where there has been provision for a statutory remedy – typically an appeal to a court or tribunal – which may be used, as described above, by specified persons to challenge the administrative act or decision. The courts have, in general, taken the view that where such a statutory appeal has been provided, Parliament has impliedly excluded the residual option of judicial review[1]. The second form of statutory intervention has been where Parliament has gone further and has explicitly excluded review. In most cases, this has been in circumstances where statute has deliberately provided an appeal but restricted access to the appeal to a specified period of, for example, six weeks and then excluded any form of legal challenge thereafter[2]. In a few cases, the Westminster Parliament has simply excluded review, without access to any form of statutory appeal. Considerations of secrecy and state security have been used to justify some such use of provisions to 'oust' the jurisdiction of the courts in this way[3].

Another oft-cited example was the statutory attempt to close off all challenges to decisions ('determinations') made by a body known as the Foreign Compensation Commission. The Foreign Compensation Act 1950 provided that '[t]he determination by the commission of any application made to them under this Act shall not be called in question in any court of law'[4]. However in the leading case of *Anisminic Ltd v Foreign Compensation Commission*[5] the House of Lords showed great ingenuity, if not defiance, in holding that even such clear statutory rules did not exclude review of a determination which was demonstrably invalid through the legal error of the Commission. Despite a general attitude of deference to the will of Parliament – an attitude which the courts have extended to the Scottish Parliament – the courts are apt to respond more robustly when their own powers are at stake[6]. The courts' wish, and indeed obligation, to secure their powers of review against statutory intervention is strengthened by the terms of art 6 ECHR, especially since its incorporation by HRA 1998 and – with heightened impact on the Scottish Parliament – by SA 1998[7].

New issues concerning access to the courts for the purposes of judicial review are raised by TCEA 2007[8] which for the first time empowers a court other than the Court of Session to consider first instance applications for judicial review. The Court of Session must in some cases and may in others transfer petitions for judicial review to the new Upper Tribunal (and specifically to the

Administrative Appeals Chamber) to be heard there. An application *must* be transferred if all that is sought is an exercise of the supervisory jurisdiction of the Court of Session and if the application is of a type specified by an Act of Sederunt made with the consent of the Lord Chancellor. The first type of application so specified was an application which challenges a procedural decision or a procedural ruling of the First-tier Tribunal[9]. That was followed in 2010 by the transfer of the functions of the Asylum and Immigration Tribunal[10]. An application *may* be transferred if, again, all that is sought is an exercise of the supervisory jurisdiction, the application relates to matters which are not devolved and it does not fall within a class specified in an Act of Sederunt described above. The powers of the Upper Tribunal in relation to such cases are the same as the powers of review of the Court of Session in an application to the supervisory jurisdiction[11] and the Upper Tribunal is bound to apply the same principles of judicial review as would be applied by the Court of Session[12].

Another related but different problem has been raised by TCEA 2007 in relation to certain decisions of the Upper Tribunal. In terms of TCEA 2007, s 13(8), certain decisions of the Upper Tribunal are defined as 'excluded decisions'. There is no statutory right of appeal against any such 'excluded decision': might such decisions nevertheless be subject to challenge by judicial review? The question was addressed by the Supreme Court following a conjoined hearing in the cases of *R(Cart) v Upper Tribunal*[13] and, in relation to Scotland, *Eba v Advocate General for Scotland*[14]. Perhaps unsurprisingly, the Supreme Court held in *Cart* that the absence of a right of appeal against 'excluded' decisions did not preclude altogether an application for judicial review. However, the circumstances in which such review would be available should be limited in such a way as to balance the need to avoid the courts being overburdened by applications for judicial review with the importance of ensuring that 'important errors'[15] of law can be corrected. That balance would be achieved by limiting the grounds on which such an excluded decision might be judicially reviewed to those which applied to 'second appeals' from the Upper Tribunal to the Inner House of the Court of Session or to the English Court of Appeal, namely that an important point of principle or practice was raised or there was some other compelling reason for the case to be heard. In *Eba*, the Supreme Court held that the same approach should be taken in relation to applications for judicial review of excluded decisions in Scotland. On the question of what might amount to a 'compelling reason' Lord Hope said that he would leave it to the Court of Session to give further guidance on that point but went on to say, by reference to *Anisminic*, that 'The court must then distinguish between errors of law that raise an important issue of principle or practice, or reasons that are compelling, and those that do not answer to this description'[16]. He also suggested that a Court of Session judge presented with a petition for judicial review of an excluded decision might scrutinise that petition more carefully than might be the case in the general run of judicial review cases before agreeing to grant a first order[17]: the Lord Ordinary should at that stage address the question whether the petitioner had made out an 'arguable case'[18].

Access to the courts may also, practically rather than legally speaking, be cut off by inadequate resources or by the fear that failure will lead to an adverse award of expenses running to tens or potentially hundreds of thousands of pounds. Where legal aid may not be available, first the English and then the Scottish courts have been prepared in limited circumstances to make a 'protective costs' or 'protective expenses' order, respectively: in essence an order which provides an 'insurance policy' to a litigant by making it clear that they will not be required to meet the other party's expenses if their case ultimately fails.

Protective costs orders were developed first by the English High Court in the context of judicial review cases which were thought to raise issues of 'general public importance'[19]. The Scottish courts followed somewhat tentatively, first by expressing a preparedness in principle to make a protective expenses order (PEO)[20] and then by agreeing to make such an order, notwithstanding the absence of any specific rules of court governing PEOs[21]. This area of procedure has developed much more rapidly over the last several years in the area of environmental law, particularly as a result of the EU's implementation (via Council Directive 2003/35/EC) of the Aarhus Convention[22]. NGOs and others questioned the adequacy of the United Kingdom's rules on protective costs and expenses, in particular the question whether they were sufficiently clear and precise to meet the obligation that pursuing environmental law remedies should not be 'prohibitively expensive'[23]. This debate was one of the key drivers for the introduction into the Court of Session rules of a new chapter governing protective expenses orders in environmental appeals and judicial reviews[24]. A body of caselaw is now developing in Scotland on the circumstances in which PEOs should be granted[25].

Finally, and on the other side of the 'access' coin, persons aggrieved by the decision of a public authority are normally expected to exhaust all statutory remedies which they may have before pursuing a petition for judicial review[26].

1 See, for example, *O'Neill v Scottish Joint Negotiating Committee for Teaching Staff* 1987 SC 90.
2 For such time limits in a planning context, see *Hamilton v Secretary of State for Scotland* 1972 SC 72 and *Pollock v Secretary of State for Scotland* 1993 SLT 1173.
3 See, for example, the Prevention of Terrorism Act 2005, s 11 concerning appeals against certain decisions relating to the 'control orders' (as to which see para 13.11, n 5).
4 Foreign Compensation Act 1950, s 4(4).
5 *Anisminic Ltd v Foreign Compensation Commission* [1969] 2 AC 147.
6 See para 14.14.
7 See para 6.20.
8 See para 14.5 above.
9 See Act of Sederunt (Transfer of Judicial Review Applications from the Court of Session) 2008, SSI 2008/357.
10 Act of Sederunt (Rules of the Court of Session Amendment) (Transfer of Functions of the Asylum and Immigration Tribunal) Order 2010, SSI 2010/16.
11 TCEA 2007, s 21(2).
12 TCEA 2007, s 21(3).
13 [2011] UKSC 28, [2012] 1 AC 663.
14 2012 SC (UKSC) 1.
15 Lady Hale at para 57.
16 Lady Hale at para 57.
17 The order required by a petitioner before he or she can initiate the judicial review and serve it on the respondent(s)).
18 For discussion of the application of *Eba* in the Scottish courts see C Himsworth 'Doing judicial review in the post-*Eba* era: *A v Secretary of State for the Home Department*' (2014) 18 Edin LR 395.

19 See *R (Corner House Research) v Secretary of State for Trade and Industry* [2005] 1 WLR 2600.

20 *McArthur v Lord Advocate* 2006 SLT 170.

21 *McGinty, Petitioner* [2010] CSOH 5.

22 Convention on Access to Information, Public Participation in Decision-Making and Access to Justice in Environmental Matters.

23 Challenges which led to the EU Commission taking action: *European Commission v United Kingdom* [2014] 3 CMLR 6. See also *R (Edwards) v Environment Agency (No 2)* [2013] UKSC 78.

24 Rules of the Court of Session, Ch 58A.

25 See *Carroll v Scottish Borders Council* 2014 SCLR 532 , *Friends of Loch Etive, Petitioner* 2014 GWD 25-471 , *John Muir Trust, Petitioner* 2015 GWD 1-20.

26 See *British Railways Board v Glasgow Corporation* 1976 SC 24. Failure to utilise a non-statutory complaints process (and thereafter recourse to the Scottish Public Services Ombudsman) may result in a petition for judicial review being refused: *McCue v Glasgow City Council* 2014 SLT 891. See also *Wallace v East Lothian Council* 2013 GWD 2-84.

The Gill reforms and judicial review

14.12   Mention has been made elsewhere of the Gill review of civil justice[1] and the reforms which will result from implementation of some of the recommendations of that review. Some of those reforms relate specifically to judicial review and while they may be characterised in some respects as 'merely' procedural, their impact could be significant.

Section 89 of the Courts Reform (Scotland) Act 2014 (CR(S)A 2014) amends the Court of Session Act 1988 (CSA 1988) by introducing new provisions on time limits and on permission for applications for judicial review: mirroring to a degree similar but much more longstanding requirements in England and Wales. The date of commencement of these new provisions is expected to be in Autumn 2015.

TIME LIMITS. As a matter of common law there was no fixed time limit within which a petition for judicial review must be brought. Instead, it was open to a respondent who felt aggrieved by delay on the part of a petitioner in raising proceedings to include, within its answers to the petition, a plea of 'mora, taciturnity and acquiescence'[2]. Despite only 20 per cent of responses to its consultation exercise advocating the introduction of a time limit, the Gill review concluded that 'the common law plea of mora, taciturnity and acquiescence is not particularly well suited to a procedure designed to provide a speedy and effective remedy to challenge the decisions of public bodies. In such cases there is a public interest in challenges being made promptly and resolved quickly. Accordingly, we are of the view that a time limit should be introduced within which petitions for judicial review must be presented. If there is good reason for delay in making an application, or where the court is satisfied that injustice would result if a petition presented outwith the time limit was not allowed to proceed, the court should have discretion to allow a late petition to proceed'[3]. Gill advocated, in line with the time limit then applicable to English judicial review proceedings, that a three month time limit would be appropriate. The Scottish Government agreed and s 89 of the CR(S)A 2014 introduces a new s 27A into the CSA 1988 which provides:

'Time limits

(1) An application to the supervisory jurisdiction of the Court must be made before the end of –

(a) the period of 3 months beginning with the date on which the grounds giving rise to the application first arise, or

(b) such longer period as the Court considers equitable having regard to all the circumstances.

(2) Subsection (1) does not apply to an application to the supervisory jurisdiction of the Court which, by virtue of any enactment, is to be made before the end of a period ending before the period of 3 months mentioned in that subsection (however that first-ending period may be expressed).'

The issue of time limits for the bringing of judicial review proceedings has been the subject of controversy in England, being viewed in many quarters as a mechanism to exclude otherwise meritorious claims. The English time limit has included a more onerous 'promptly' requirement which has in practice significantly reduced the three month longstop[4], which longstop has itself now been reduced to six weeks in relation to certain planning decisions[5].

PERMISSION: There has not been in Scotland any need to obtain the permission or leave of the court to raise a petition for judicial review. While it is possible for the Lord Ordinary to refuse a petition at the first order stage, that is very rarely done[6]. The Gill review recommended the introduction of a leave or permission stage, apparently on the grounds of the pressure of business placed on the Court of Session by judicial review applications and an assumption that a failure to appeal against a refusal of permission was evidence that the challenge had in any event been without merit: 'There has been a steady increase in numbers of petitions for judicial review. They occupy a disproportionate amount of sitting days. We also note the impact of the recent change in the rule relating to the granting of first orders. In England and Wales the introduction of a pre-action protocol for judicial review and a procedure, by which a respondent may oppose the granting of permission, has resulted in around a third of all applications for judicial review being resolved before the permission stage is reached. Of those cases which proceed to the permission stage, permission is refused in a relatively high percentage; in only a small minority of cases is there an appeal against refusal of permission. Research suggests that these procedures work well in filtering out unmeritorious applications and in prompting early concessions where claims are well founded'[7].

Sections 27B to 27D of CSA 1988 contain the new provisions on permission. No proceedings may be taken in respect of an application to the supervisory jurisdiction of the Court unless the Court has granted permission for the application to proceed[8] and the Court may grant permission only if it is satisfied that the applicant can demonstrate a sufficient interest in the subject matter of the application, and the application has a real prospect of success[9]. For judicial reviews of relevant decisions of the Upper Tribunal the new provisions incorporate the requirements set out in *Eba* and discussed above that the application would also raise an important point of principle or practice, or that there is some other compelling reason for allowing it to proceed. The new provisions also permit a petitioner to request an oral hearing before a different judge where permission has been refused or has been granted only in part or subject to conditions[10]. There is also provision for an appeal to the Inner House against a further refusal after an oral hearing[11].

1   See para 12.19.
2   See *Somerville v the Scottish Ministers* 2007 SLT 96; *CWS v Highland Council* [2008] CSOH 28; *Pocock's Trustee v Skene Investments (Aberdeen) Ltd & Others* 2012 GWD 27-562; *Hendrick v Chief Constable of Strathclyde* 2014 SLT 382.
3   Report of the Scottish Civil Courts Review, Vol 2, para 38.
4   See, for example *R v Cotswold District Council* (1998) 75 P & CR 515. The promptness requirement has, however, been held to be incompatible with the principle of legal certainty in cases involving the application of EU law: see *Uniplex (UK) Ltd v NHS Business Services Authority* [2010] 2 CMLR 47. There is no reference to promptness in the new Scottish provision.
5   Civil Procedure (Amendment No 4) Rules 2013, SI 2013/1412.
6   For an example see *Unison, Petitioners* 2006 [CSOH] 193.
7   Report of the Scottish Civil Courts Review, Volume 2, para 50.
8   CSA 1988, s 27B(1).
9   CSA 1988, s 27B(2).
10 CSA 1988, s 27C.
11 CSA 1988, s 27D.

Judicial review and the constitution

14.13   The constitutional significance of judicial review hardly needs to be stated. It enables and indeed compels courts to determine whether the acts and decisions of public authorities are legally valid and thus whether they are, or can become, enforceable. The courts are there both for the protection of individuals (frequently also companies, other businesses and sometimes public bodies themselves) from unlawful activity by public authorities and also, where appropriate, to uphold the lawful acts of those authorities as they implement powers conferred by statute[1]. In so doing, the courts are, in either event, implementing the will of Parliament[2] and upholding the rule of law: a function simply described but sensitive in its operation.

It is sensitive because the striking down of decisions made by executive bodies – especially those such as local councils and ministers who are democratically elected and directly accountable to the electorate – is a serious matter. It reconfirms the need for a robust and independent judiciary but, in order to maintain their legitimacy, it also requires the judiciary to remain within their allocated domain. They must be seen to confine themselves to deciding the issues before them on legal and not political grounds. They must be seen not merely to substitute their views on how executive decisions should be made for the views of those whom a Parliament has designated for the task. This is a position frequently restated by the courts themselves[3] as a shield from criticisms that might otherwise be launched against them. However, two particular features of judicial review can still make the courts' task controversial. Both relate to the grounds of review.

The first is the problem of statutory interpretation and the evaluation, often in the light of loosely constructed criteria such as 'fairness' and 'reasonableness', of the lawfulness of administrative action. It might be thought, for instance, that Lord Diplock's 'procedural impropriety' would be relatively easy to detect. A decision-maker has either followed the statutory procedures laid down or he or she has not. But it is not as simple as that[4]. The courts have, in addition, adopted and applied their own standards of procedural propriety. They have applied tests of 'natural justice' (incorporating the need for impartiality of the decision-maker and the need to hear both sides before deciding), 'fairness' and, latterly, the obligation of decision-makers to respect the 'legitimate expectation' of a hearing prior to decision[5]. Much flexibility attaches to the interpretation of all those terms and indeed to the concept of 'unreasonableness'. On the one hand, unreasonableness may be viewed as synonymous with Lord Diplock's 'irrationality', itself a term giving a broad interpretative freedom to the courts. As we have seen, in the earlier classic English case of *Associated Provincial Picture Houses Ltd v Wednesbury Corporation*[6] Lord Greene referred to the sort of decision caught by this test as one 'so unreasonable that no reasonable authority could ever have come to it'[7]. But, while that case provided Lord Greene with the opportunity to warn against the intrusion by courts into the decision-making of bodies on whom Parliament has conferred the power to decide, it also enabled him to broaden the scope of reviewable unreasonableness to include cases where public bodies were claimed to have taken into account 'irrelevant considerations', failed to take into account 'relevant considerations' or used their powers for an 'improper purpose'. Once again, tests cast in such terms provide much freedom for courts.

In addition to such interpretative difficulties and the apparent threats to the legitimacy of the process of judicial review that they produce, there is a wider debate about expanding the grounds of judicial review. In his speech in the GCHQ case, Lord Diplock not only set out the existing grounds of review but also speculated that they might, in due course, be joined by others. In particular, he mentioned a test of 'proportionality'[8]. There are a number of different understandings of what such a test demands of decision-makers. One widely deployed is that the decision-maker should not 'use a sledgehammer to crack a nut'[9]. More prosaically, in the context of EU law, the test has been formulated as allowing a decision-maker to take measures which interfere with fundamental rights only so far as 'necessary and appropriate'[10]. Now, no one would deny, of course, that proportionality so defined is a desirable quality in decision making. The question, as with tests of reasonableness and fairness, is whether the arbiter of these standards should be administrative bodies – who should be politically accountable for the proportionality of their decisions – or whether their judgment should be second-guessed by courts. For some, the extension of the reviewing courts' jurisdiction to embrace proportionality would be unproblematic. Either it would involve the same processes as deciding questions of 'irrationality' or be only a small extension of them; the obligation of UK courts to apply EU law[11] already requires the courts to use the proportionality tests and it would be logical to extend that use into non-EU issues; and, similarly, the need for courts to apply the terms of the ECHR involves the 'balancing' of individual rights against the public interest – a process which, again, closely resembles recourse to proportionality[12].

Against this, it is reasoned that the tests of rationality and proportionality involve quite different techniques. Judges are equipped to recognise a decision which is 'outrageous in its defiance of logic or of accepted moral standards'[13] when they see it. However, they have neither the skills nor the resources to undertake the balancing exercise demanded by the proportionality test[14]. The fact that EU law requires a particular response does not demand its extension. And the same applies to the ECHR: the obligation to balance rights does not carry with it the competence to balance wider policy issues. The concept of proportionality, and its relevance in a domestic rather than EU or ECHR context has been the subject of considerable recent discussion by the UK Supreme Court, the consequence of which might fairly be said to be that if a distinction between rationality and proportionality remains, that distinction is a relatively narrow one. The House of Lords took a firm negative stance on proportionality in *R v Home Secretary, ex parte Brind*[15] but a more sympathetic approach began to develop at the beginning of this century, for example in *Daly*[16] and *Alconbury*[17]. One of the most significant discussions of the origins and conceptual underpinnings of proportionality is contained the opinion of Lord Reed in *Bank Mellat v Her Majesty's Treasury (No 2)*[18]. The case concerned the making by the Treasury of an Order under the Counter-Terrorism Act 2008 which prohibited all persons operating in the UK financial sector from doing business with Bank Mellat, a major commercial Iranian bank. The Treasury made the Order on the grounds that it believed that Iran's nuclear weapons programme presented a major threat to the United Kingdom's national interests and that disrupting Iran's banking sector would contribute to the disruption of that nuclear weapons programme. The particular provisions of the 2008 Act under which the Order was made required such an Order to be proportionate: this was not then a case in which the Supreme Court had to consider whether the common law would have allowed for an attack on the measure's proportionality. Nevertheless, in his otherwise dissenting judgment on the merits, Lord Reed described the statutory test of proportionality under the 2008 Act as reflecting 'a principle which has roots in the common law: there are a number of cases where administrative acts of an oppressive or penal character have been quashed as being disproportionate'[19]. He also explained in some detail why, in his view, the application of the proportionality test by the UK courts, even, in ECHR and EU cases did not directly mirror the approach taken, for example, by the Strasbourg Court but, instead, involved 'a more clearly structured'[20] analysis. Some months later, in *Kennedy v Charity Commission*[21] Lord Mance also referred to the value of a structured approach, in a judgment which suggested that proportionality and rationality were broadly interchangeable terms: 'both reasonableness review and proportionality involve considerations of weight and balance, with the intensity of the scrutiny and the weight to be given to any primary decision maker's view depending on the context. The advantage of the terminology of proportionality is that it introduces an element of structure into the exercise, by directing attention to factors such as suitability or appropriateness, necessity and the balance or imbalance of benefits and disadvantages. There seems no reason why such factors should not be relevant in judicial review even outside the scope of Convention and EU law.'[22]. Despite this apparent narrowing of the gap between irrationality and proportionality, it remains fair to say that proportionality has not yet been generally accepted by the courts as a free standing ground of judicial review at common law and some resistance remains[23].

The debate about the proper limits of the grounds of judicial review is one which has been further complicated by a separate but related discussion about the more fundamental constitutional basis of judicial review. There has been a (perhaps rather contrived) tussle between those who see the function of judicial review as to uphold Parliament's will and those, on the other hand, who see the courts' authority to undertake judicial review as grounded not simply in obedience to Parliament but in the common law[24]. It may be that there is less at stake in this debate than meets the eye and, in any event, a truce seems to have been called around a compromise position. If, however, there really is an important disagreement here, it is one which would produce different views of the desirability and indeed the competence of the courts to extend their review jurisdiction into new areas. At the heart of all debates about the proper jurisdiction of courts of law – whether in relation to the expansion of judicial review into proportionality or the adoption of more pervasive human rights adjudication – is the question of whether greater trust and reliance should be placed in political or judicial accountability.

1   Advocates of each of these sometimes competing interests – protection of individual liberty versus facilitating the work of government – have been described, respectively as 'red light'and 'green light' theorists: C Harlow and R Rawlings *Law and Administration* (3rd edn, 2009).
2   But see para 14.16 below.
3   See *Associated Provincial Picture Houses Ltd v Wednesbury Corpn* [1948] 1 KB 223 and, in the planning context, Lord Hoffmann in *Tesco Stores Ltd v Secretary of State for the Environment* [1995] 2 All ER 636: 'If there is one principle of planning law more firmly settled than any other, it is that matters of planning judgment are within the exclusive province of the local planning authority or the Secretary of State' (at 657).
4   See eg para 14.9 above.
5   This 'legitimate expectation' can arise in a variety of ways, for example where a public authority gives an undertaking that a hearing will be held before a given decision is taken (see *A-G of Hong Kong v Ng Yuen Shiu* [1983] 2 AC 629) or where the individual involved has enjoyed the benefit of some right or licence and it is proposed that this be withdrawn or revoked by a public body (see *McInnes v Onslow-Fane* [1978] 3 All ER 211).
6   *Associated Provincial Picture Houses Ltd v Wednesbury Corpn* [1948] 1 KB 223.
7   *Associated Provincial Picture Houses Ltd v Wednesbury Corpn* [1948] 1 KB 223 at 230.
8   *CCSU v Minister for the Civil Service* [1985] AC 374 at 410.
9   See *R v Secretary of State for the Home Department, ex parte Brind* [1991] 1 AC 696 per Lord Ackner at 759.
10 See *R v Chief Constable of Sussex, e xp International Trader's Ferry Ltd* [1999] 2 AC 418 and *Commission v France* [1997] ECR I-6959.
11 See para 3.12.
12 See para 14.18 below.
13 *CCSU v Minister for the Civil Service* [1985] AC 374 per Lord Diplock at 410.
14 In *R v Secretary of State for the Home Department, ex parte Brind* [1991] 1 AC 696, Lord Lowry expressed the view that the fact that proportionality was not an established principle of English law was 'no cause for regret' because, amongst other things '[t]he judges are not, generally speaking, equipped by training or experience, or furnished with the requisite knowledge and advice, to decide the answer to an administrative problem where the scales are evenly balanced, but they have a much better chance of reaching the right answer where the question is put in a *Wednesbury* form' ([1991] 1 AC 696 at 767).
15 *R v Home Secretary, ex parte Brind* [1991] 1 AC 696.
16 *R (Daly) v Home Secretary* [2001] 2 AC 532. 'The infringement of prisoners' rights to maintain the confidentiality of their privileged legal correspondence is greater than is shown to be necessary to serve the legitimate public objectives already identified' (per Lord Bingham of Cornhill at 543).
17 *R (Holding & Barnes plc) v Secretary of State for the Environment, Transport and the Regions* [2001] UKHL 23, [2001] 2 All ER 929: 'I consider that even without reference to the 1998 Act

the time has come to recognise that this principle is part of English administrative law, not only when judges are dealing with Community acts but also when they are dealing with acts subject to domestic law' (per Lord Slynn of Hadley at 976). The House of Lords disposed of a number of separate applications in this case, one of which had been raised by Alconbury Developments Ltd.

18 [2014] AC 700.
19 Lord Reed at para 82.
20 Lord Reed, para 72.
21 [2014] 2 All ER 847.
22 Lord Mance, para 54.
23 See for example *Eastwood v The Royal Borough of Windsor and Maidenhead* [2014] CA C1/2013/3375.
24 See C Forsyth (ed) *Judicial Review and the Constitution* (2000) and, for other contributions, PP Craig 'Constitutional Foundations, the Rule of Law and Supremacy' [2003] PL 92; C Forsyth and M Elliot 'The Legitimacy of Judicial Review' [2000] PL 286; TRS Allan 'Doctrine and Theory in Administrative Law: An Elusive Quest for the Limits of Jurisdiction' [2003] PL 429; A Lever 'Is Judicial Review Undemocratic?' [2007] PL 280. For the discussion of fundamental common law rights as a limit on the powers of parliaments and executives see para 14.16.

JUDICIAL REVIEW OF DELEGATED LEGISLATION

14.14   As already seen, an important characteristic of judicial review is the breadth of its application across the full extent of decision-making by ministers, local authorities and other public bodies and officials. One aspect of its coverage is that it extends to include not only the 'administrative' decision making of public bodies but also their law-making. When ministers, including the Scottish Ministers, make delegated legislation in the form of statutory instruments[1] or local authorities make byelaws, the validity of such delegated legislation may be questioned in judicial review proceedings[2]. If it fails the tests laid down by the Court of Session discussed at para 14.19, the court may intervene. It is unsurprising, however, that the review of delegated legislation does raise some special questions which have required a response from the courts.

The relative generality of the scope of legislative rules rather than of specific decisions may prompt different problems of *locus standi*[3] – who is or might be relevantly affected by them? In addition, many rule-making powers are extremely widely drafted and this has caused the courts to take a view of the purposes for which the use of the powers was intended[4]. Courts have adopted a restrictive interpretation of powers to insist that the rights of individuals should not be adversely affected, unless clear language in the empowering statute justifies this[5]. Thus, the courts will tend to take a narrow view of rules purporting to rely on a merely implied power to impose a tax or charge[6]; or to restrict professional freedom with retrospective effect[7]; or to restrict access to the courts[8]. In the absence of express statutory language, the courts will presume that it was not the legislature's intention to enact such intrusions into individual liberty. Another difference in the interpretation of powers of delegated law-making is that questions of fairness and natural justice[9] may take a different form. Nevertheless important issues about, for instance, the scope and thoroughness of consultation prior to rules being made have proved important[10].

Three other special characteristics of the review of delegated legislation deserve particular mention. One is the robust defence by the courts of their power to review a statutory instrument despite the fact that the instrument under review may previously have been approved under the affirmative resolution procedure by the relevant Parliament[11] or, by default, under the negative procedure. The courts have sometimes suggested that they should be even more sparing in making a finding of irrationality in respect of an instrument approved not only by a minister but also by Parliament itself. A measure of additional deference is called for because of the constitutional relationship involved[12]. But it is clear that the deference accorded to Acts of the UK Parliament by virtue of the doctrine of the sovereignty of Parliament is not, in principle, extendable to other rules approved by Parliament[13]. A second special feature of the review of delegated legislation is that, if a challenge to the validity of an instrument is upheld, a question may arise as to whether the court is obliged to strike down the whole of the instrument, leaving it of no legal effect whatever, or whether the court may instead strike down the instrument only to the extent of its defective part or parts, leaving the rest of the instrument intact. Here the courts have taken the view that a finding of partial validity and partial invalidity is a legitimate outcome. Where it can be assumed that the rule-making authority would still have wished to issue the remaining rules if it had known in advance that others would be nullified, then a remedy incorporating a finding of partial invalidity is appropriate. If that interpretation of the will of the law-maker in that hypothetical situation *cannot* be made, then the whole document should be struck down[14].

The third special feature of the review of delegated legislation is that, in addition to its being challengeable in the ordinary way by application for judicial review, the validity of delegated legislation may also be challenged by way of defence to a criminal prosecution brought under the delegated legislation itself[15]. No one should be vulnerable to prosecution under rules which are themselves invalid, and a defence based on such invalidity may be raised in whatever court the prosecution is brought.

The reason for spelling out the court's approach to delegated legislation is that an obvious comparison may be drawn between, on the one hand, the judicial review of delegated legislation made by ministers under primary legislation (of both the Westminster and Scottish Parliaments) and, on the other, the review of primary legislation made by the Scottish Parliament under SA 1998. Both are reviewable on the grounds that the law-maker has gone beyond the limits of the powers laid down. As we shall see, however, such comparison has proved to be of relatively limited value.

1 Including Scottish statutory instruments. See para 6.24.
2 See, generally, *SME Reissue* Administrative Law para 93 ff; HWR Wade and CF Forsyth *Administrative Law* (11th edn, 2014) ch 22; PP Craig *Administrative Law* (7th edn, 2012).
3 See *Scottish Old People's Welfare Council, Petitioners* 1987 SLT 179; *Air 2000 Ltd v Secretary of State for Transport (No 1)* 1989 SLT 698.
4 See, for example, *R (Spath Holme Ltd) v Secretary of State for the Environment and Transport* [2000] 1 All ER 884.
5 Including where unfairness results from a failure by the executive to make the relevant subordinate legislation: *RM v Scottish Ministers* 2013 SC (UKSC) 139.
6 *A-G v Wilts United Dairies* (1921) 37 TLR 884; *Scottish Milk Marketing Board v Ferrier* 1936 SC (HL) 39.

7   *Malloch v Aberdeen Corpn* 1973 SC 227.
8   *Kerr v Hood* 1907 SC 895; *Leech v Secretary of State for Scotland* 1993 SLT 365.
9   See, for example, *Bates v Lord Hailsham of St Marylebone* [1972] 3 All ER 1019; *Bank Mellat v HM Treasury (No 2)* [2014] AC 700.
10 *Agricultural, Horticultural and Forestry Industry Training Board v Aylesbury Mushrooms* [1972] 1 All ER 280; *R v Secretary of State for Social Services, ex parte AMA* [1986] 1 All ER 164; *Neizer v Johnston* 1993 SCCR 772; *MacGillivray v Johnston (No 2)* 1994 SLT 1012; *R (O'Callaghan) v Charity Commission for England and Wales* [2007] EWHC 2491 (Admin) 10.
11 See *F Hoffmann-la Roche & Co AG v Secretary of State for Trade and Industry* [1975] AC 295. This case arose, of course, in relation to an instrument subject to procedures in the Westminster Parliament but there is no doubt that the same principle would apply (to even stronger effect) to an instrument approved by Holyrood. See also, more recently, *R (Javed) v Home Secretary* [2002] QB 129.
12 *East Kilbride District Council v Secretary of State for Scotland* 1995 SLT 1238, following *R v Secretary of State for the Environment, ex parte Hammersmith and Fulham London Borough Council* [1991] 1 AC 521; *cf R v Secretary of State for the Environment, ex parte Nottinghamshire County Council* [1986] AC 240.
13 And, in principle, even less deference is to be shown to prerogative legislation which is not the product of a 'democratic' parliamentary process but is in substance an exercise of executive power: see *R (Bancoult) v Secretary of State for Foreign and Commonwealth Affairs* [2009] 1 AC 453. In fact, in this case, a significant degree of latitude was afforded the government in deciding not to allow resettlement of former inhabitants of the Chagos Islands and the courts have also declined to review the exercise of some prerogative powers such as that to commit troops to armed conflict: *R (Gentle) v The Prime Minister* [2008] 1 AC 1356.
14 *DPP v Hutchinson* [1990] 2 AC 783; *Dunkley v Evans* [1981] 1 WLR 1522.
15 *MacGillivray v Johnston (No 2)* 1994 SLT 1012; *Robbie the Pict v Hingston (No 1)* 1998 SLT 1196; *Boddington v British Transport Police* [1999] 2 AC 143.

HUMAN RIGHTS ADJUDICATION

14.15   It is undoubtedly the case that HRA 1998, fully implemented from 2 October 2000[1], has had a substantial effect upon the courts of the United Kingdom[2]. Related provisions in SA 1998[3] took effect over a year earlier as part of the rules defining the competence of the Scottish Parliament and the (then) Scottish Executive[4] and their impact was significant[5]. In Chapter 13 we discussed the process by which HRA 1998 was enacted and described the 'Convention rights' incorporated by the HRA 1998. We also explained the political and administrative structures which have been put in place which are intended to foster and maintain a 'rights culture' in Scotland and throughout the United Kingdom. Those aspects of human rights protection should not be underplayed but it nevertheless remains true that in any discussion of constitutional law and the legal protection of individual rights it is the work of the courts which demands most attention.

We have already described how Convention rights have become a new ground on which to seek judicial review and suggested the difficulties which face the courts in resolving human rights questions (para 13.12). In this section we discuss the approach of the courts to human rights questions before and after the passing of HRA 1998.

1 SI 1998/2882; SI 2000/1851.
2 See R Reed and J Murdoch *A Guide to Human Rights Law in Scotland* (3rd ed, 2011); D Hoffman (ed) *The Impact of the UK Human Rights Act on Private Law* (2011); S Shah and T Poole 'The impact of the Human Rights Act on the House of Lords' [2009] PL 347; M Hunt

'The impact of the Human Rights Act on the legislature: a diminution of democracy or a new voice for Parliament?' 2010 EHRLR 601.

3 SA 1998, ss 29(2)(d), 54, 57, 101 and 129(2). See also the GWA 2006, ss 81, 108 and Sch 9, and NIA 1998, ss 6, 7, 24, 71, 79 and Sch 10.

4 See paras 6.20 and 7.19 above.

5 See, for example, the discussion of *Starrs v Ruxton* 2000 JC 208 at para 12.7.

The pre-incorporation approach to fundamental rights

14.16 Although the pre-incorporation period has passed into history, it retains interest, for better or for worse, as one of great judicial creativity in the face of legislative and executive inactivity. The courts, especially in England, were energetic in their efforts to subject ministers and others to scrutiny on grounds of compliance with human rights[1]. There were two channels for this. The first was to insist that, despite the lack of formal incorporation of the ECHR, its terms could be used as an interpretative aid, especially in circumstances of statutory ambiguity. Parliament could be presumed to have wished to comply with the United Kingdom's international obligations[2]. The English courts were willing to adopt such an approach quite early on. In Scotland, though, the position which prevailed for many years was that taken by Lord Ross in *Kaur v Lord Advocate*[3], to the effect that the courts would not have regard to the Convention even in cases of statutory ambiguity. Scots law was brought into line with the English approach only very shortly before incorporation of the Convention[4].

Secondly, it was argued that 'fundamental rights', even though secured (only) in the common law rather than in the ECHR, could be deployed to similar interpretative effect[5]. This led, in particular, to an insistence on a high degree of scrutiny in judicial review when the fundamental rights of individuals were at stake. Public decision-making should be subject to anxious scrutiny[6] in such circumstances. In a 'balancing' process familiar in the process of interpretation of the ECHR at Strasbourg (and latterly in UK courts themselves), the courts insisted that the need for a particular decision or rule be weighed against the countervailing rights of the individual.

The role of common law fundamental rights – in addition to or (for some commentators) as an alternative to those protected by the ECHR – remains an area of interest and, in some quarters, controversy. The debate is related to those other debates on a British Bill of Rights and the role of the Strasbourg Court discussed at paras 13.15–13.17 above but is not coterminous with it. So, for example, in *AXA General Insurance, Petitioners*[7] (discussed more fully below), Lord Reed expressed the view that the Scottish Parliament was bound not only by the limit on its legislative competence contained in SA 1998 that it cannot legislate in breach of Convention rights but that the Parliament might also be subject to challenge on grounds of interference with common law fundamental rights: 'Parliament did not legislate in a vacuum: it legislated for a liberal democracy founded on particular constitutional principles and traditions. That being so, Parliament cannot be taken to have intended to establish a body which was free to abrogate fundamental rights or to violate the rule of law'[8].

1 See M Hunt *Using Human Rights Law in English Courts* (1997).

2 See *R v Secretary of State for the Home Department, ex parte Brind* [1991] 1 AC 696 per Lord Bridge of Harwich at 747, 748.
3 *Kaur v Lord Advocate* 1980 SC 319.
4 *T, Petitioner* 1997 SLT 724.
5 See *Derbyshire County Council v Times Newspapers Ltd* [1993] AC 534. For the difficulties of defining the scope of such 'fundamental rights' and their relevance post-enactment of HRA 1998 see Lord Rodger of Earlsferry's observations in *Watkins v Secretary of State for the Home Department and others* [2006] UKHL 17 at paras 58 to 64.
6 *Singh v Secretary of State for the Home Department (No 1)* 1998 SLT 1370.
7 2012 SC (UKSC) 122.
8 Ibid at para 153. See also Lady Hale 'UK Constitutionalism on the March' Keynote address to the Constitutional and Administrative Law Bar Association Conference, 12 July 2014 and R Clayton 'The empire strikes back: common law rights and the Human Rights Act' [2015] PL 3.

HRA 1998 and Legislation

14.17   We have discussed elsewhere (para 6.5) the potential difficulties, in the context of the United Kingdom's constitutional history, of attempts to 'entrench' human rights against infringement by a sovereign Westminster Parliament. HRA 1998 acknowledges those difficulties directly in the way in which it provides for adjudication of human rights disputes by the courts: principally by denying the courts any power to strike down as invalid an Act of the Westminster Parliament and, instead, permitting at most a declaratory judgement that such an Act breaches Convention rights.

Section 3(1) of HRA 1998 provides that '[s]o far as it is possible to do so, primary legislation and subordinate legislation must be read and given effect in a way which is compatible with the Convention rights'. As well as assisting in the interpretation of Convention rights for the purposes of HRA 1998, s 6, this provision links with the other principal power conferred on the courts – the making of a declaration of incompatibility in relation to primary legislation.

The scheme of HRA 1998 is to make unlawful and, therefore, invalid any act of a public authority which is incompatible with a Convention right and this includes the making of what HRA 1998 defines as 'subordinate legislation'. Thus delegated legislation made by ministers and, importantly, Acts of the Scottish Parliament[1] are to be held invalid to the extent of their incompatibility. Section 3(1) may assist in saving some such legislation where it is possible to read it as compatible with the relevant Convention right. How this provision applies in any individual case in practice is not always easy to predict[2]. It provides a starting presumption of compatibility but with unclear limits[3].

The same presumption is applied by HRA 1998, s 3(1) to the interpretation of 'primary legislation', ie Acts of the Westminster Parliament[4]. They too must be read as compatible if possible. If, however, that is not possible, the consequences are difficult. The court must continue to treat HRA 1998 as wholly valid and binding on the parties to the case[5]. This applies whether the Act was passed before or after the enactment of HRA 1998 and it is by this means that that Act is seen to uphold the principle of the supremacy or sovereignty of Parliament. What HRA 1998 does allow, however, is that senior courts (including the Supreme Court, the High Court of Justiciary sitting otherwise than as a trial court (ie on appeal), and the Court of Session) may make a 'declaration of incompatibility' where incompatibility with a Convention right is held to occur, HRA 1998, s 3(1) notwithstanding[6]. Declarations have been made relating to mental health[7], the legal status of transsexuals[8], the Home Secretary's involvement in fixing life sentences in England and Wales[9] and the denial of voting rights to prisoners[10]. Contrary to the contention of the Advocate General for Scotland, the Court of Session has confirmed that it is competent to bring a petition for judicial review for the sole purpose of obtaining a declaration of incompatibility[11].

All UK government Bills introduced since 24 November 1998 have had to be accompanied (prior to second reading) by a ministerial statement of compatibility with the Convention rights (or a statement that the government intends to proceed despite any incompatibility)[12]. Statements admitting incompatibility are unusual but have been made and the possibility reconfirms the freedom of Parliament to enact legislation of its choosing[13].

If a declaration of incompatibility is made, it is open to the Westminster Parliament to rectify the position by making the necessary legislative modification. In the case of provisions which do not affect reserved matters and are otherwise within its competence, the Scottish Parliament has the same powers. HRA 1998 does, however, also provide a 'fast-track' mechanism for a relevant UK minister or, as the case may be, the Scottish Ministers to make such a necessary modification by means of a 'remedial order' where there are 'compelling reasons' to do so. Such orders must be approved in draft by either both Houses of the Westminster Parliament or (again, as the case may be) by the Scottish Parliament[14]. Parallel provisions are contained in the Convention Rights (Compliance) (Scotland) Act 2001 enabling the Scottish Ministers to make remedial orders. Such remedial orders may address the incompatibility with Convention rights not only of an Act of the Westminster Parliament (which cannot be struck down by virtue of that incompatibility) but also of an Act of the Scottish Parliament or of subordinate legislation.

The fact that a declaration of incompatibility is the only remedy available to an individual whose rights have been breached by an Act of the Westminster Parliament has itself been challenged as being incompatible with the ECHR. Although the Strasbourg Court has cast doubt on the adequacy of such a declaration and has held that an individual need not pursue a declaration of incompatibility at a UK level before making an application to Strasbourg, it has also said that it may be open to persuasion that declarations of incompatibility are an effective remedy if there is evidence that they lead, invariably, to changes in the law to remedy the incompatibility[15].

1   HRA 1998, s 21(1).
2   See *Advocate General for Scotland v MacDonald* 2002 SC 1; *Adam v HMA* 2013 JC 221; *HM's Application for Judicial Review* [2014] NIQB 43. For Rules falling outside the HRA definition of subordinate legislation see *B, Petitioner* 2010 GWD 20-385.
3   For the similar provision contained in SA 1998, s 101, see para 14.22.
4   HRA 1998, s 21(1). The definition of 'primary legislation' also includes Measures of the General Synod of the Church of England and any Order in Council made in exercise of Her Majesty's Royal Prerogative. See in particular *Ghaidan v Godin-Mendoza* [2004] UKHL 30, [2004] 2 AC 557.
5   HRA 1998, ss 3(2), 4(6).

6 HRA 1998, s 4.
7 *R (H) v Mental Health Review Tribunal North & East London Region* [2002] QB 1, in consequence of which a remedial order was made to amend the Mental Health Act 1983, ss 72 and 73.
8 *Bellinger v Bellinger* [2003] 2 AC 467.
9 *R (Anderson) v Home Secretary* [2003] 1 AC 837.
10 *Smith v Scott* 2007 SC 345 For the court's reluctance to grant further declarations of incompatibility where the issue was under active consideration by Parliament see *R (Chester) v Secretary of State for Justice* [2014] AC 271.
11 *M's Guardian v Advocate General for Scotland* 2009 SC 643.
12 HRA 1998, s 19 and SI 1998/2882.
13 When the Communications Bill – now the Communications Act 2003 – was introduced in November 2002 it was accompanied by a statement under HRA 1998, s 19(2) to the effect that the government was unable to state that the Bill's provisions were compatible with the Convention rights but that it, nevertheless, wished to proceed with the Bill: see HC Debs, 3 Dec 2002, col 785 ff. A similar statement was made on the introduction in 2004 of the Civil Partnership Bill which became the Civil Partnership Act 2004. In 2012, the Explanatory Notes to the (subsequently abandoned) Lords Reform Bill contained a statement made by the Deputy Prime Minister Nick Clegg: 'I am unable to make a statement of compatibility under section 19(1)(a) of the Human Rights Act 1998 in respect of the House of Lords Reform Bill. This is only because of clause 6, which applies to House of Lords elections the laws on entitlement to vote at House of Commons elections, including the rules which prevent prisoners serving sentences from voting. The Government nevertheless wishes the House to proceed with the Bill.' The concern about incompatibility concerned a blanket ban on voting by peers convicted of offences: see para 5.6 above. Such a ban was included in the more modest private member's bill which became the House of Lords Reform Act 2014.
14 HRA 1998, s 10 and Sch 2. Special provision is made for urgent orders to be made, in the first instance, without the need for such approval (HRA 1998, Sch 4, paras 2(b) and 4). A number of remedial orders have been made so far at Westminster (including the Terrorism Act 2000 (Remedial) Order 2011, SI 2011/631); but none have been made under HRA 1998 at Holyrood. Three such orders have however been made in terms of the Convention Rights (Compliance) (Scotland) Act 2001: the Sexual Offences Act 2003 (Remedial) (Scotland) Order 2010, SSI 2010/370 which was repealed and replaced with the Sexual Offences Act 2003 (Remedial) (Scotland) Order 2011, SSI 2011/45 and the Agricultural Holdings (Scotland) Act 2003 Remedial Order 2014, SSI 2014/98 which addressed the incompatibility identified in *Salvesen v Riddell* discussed below.
15 *Burden v United Kingdom* (2007) 44 EHRR 51.

The Human Rights Act and the significance of Strasbourg jurisprudence

14.18 We described in Chapter 13 the approach which the courts have taken to the definition of 'public authority' in HRA 1998 in considering challenges to government (and in some cases private) action based on Convention rights arguments. We also discussed there the development of the common law by the courts – as public authorities themselves – in a manner which reflects the Convention rights of those whose rights are being determined. In determining when and to what extent there has been a breach of Convention rights, HRA 1998 provides some guidance to the courts in how to approach that task. That guidance has in recent times become increasingly politically controversial, with the senior judiciary itself somewhat divided on the issue.

Section 2 of HRA 1998 provides that a court or tribunal, when determining a question which has arisen in connection with a Convention right, must take into account any judgment, decision, declaration or advisory opinion of the ECtHR[1].

This is logical in the light of the general aims of ECHR and HRA 1998: a degree of uniformity of interpretation of the Convention rights across all the 47[2] member states of the Council of Europe is desirable and it would do nothing to limit the number of UK applications to Strasbourg[3] if UK courts were known to be interpreting the Convention very differently from the ECtHR[4]. But 'taking account' of Strasbourg jurisprudence is not itself easy. The ECtHR's decisions range widely across many types of proceedings and, of course, across many national jurisdictions. They have now been decided over many years and not always consistently. Strasbourg jurisprudence has also developed interpretative principles of its own which may or may not be of much assistance to UK courts. The Court has, for instance, developed the concept of the 'margin of appreciation' designed to give a sort of 'benefit of the doubt' to national authorities. They are afforded some latitude in deciding the manner in which, and the extent to which, individual rights are protected in light of their own assessment of local conditions and of the needs of their 'democratic society'[5].

This issue is one of some controversy[6]. It is argued by some commentators that there is no need – and no justification – for national courts to accord the same respect to decisions of domestic governments as is appropriate where the adjudicator is an international court. However, since HRA 1998 came into force, the British courts have developed a concept, justified at least notionally by reference to the principle of the separation of powers, described initially as one of 'due deference' to a decision of the legislature or of the executive in areas where they have a 'discretionary area of judgment'. This concept was explained by Lord Hope of Craighead in *R v DPP, ex parte Kebilene*[7] in which he commented that in 'some circumstances it will be appropriate for the courts to recognise that there is an area of judgment within which the judiciary will defer, on democratic grounds, to the considered opinion of the elected body or person whose Act or decision is said to be incompatible with the Convention'[8]. There has been, since *Kebilene*, a move away from the language of 'deference', Lord Hoffmann expressing the view in *R (ProLife Alliance) v BBC*[9] that the word itself was inapposite:

> 'I do not think that its overtones of servility, or perhaps gracious concession, are appropriate to describe what is happening. In a society based upon the rule of law and the separation of powers, it is necessary to decide which branch of government has in any particular instance the decision-making power and what the legal limits of that power are. That is a question of law and must therefore be decided by the courts.'[10]

and that what is at the heart of the issue is which branch of government is best suited to the particular task at hand:

> 'The principles upon which decision-making powers are allocated are principles of law. The courts are the independent branch of government and the legislature and executive are, directly and indirectly respectively, the elected branches of government. Independence makes the courts more suited to deciding some kinds of questions and being elected makes the legislature or executive more suited to deciding others. The allocation of these decisionmaking responsibilities is based upon recognised principles. The principle that the independence of the courts is necessary for a proper

decision of disputed legal rights or claims of violation of human rights is a legal principle. It is reflected in article 6 of the Convention. On the other hand, the principle that majority approval is necessary for a proper decision on policy or allocation of resources is also a legal principle. Likewise, when a court decides that a decision is within the proper competence of the legislature or executive, it is not showing deference. It is deciding the law.'[11]

The limits of the 'discretionary area of judgment' in any given case will, of course, fall to be determined by the courts themselves but in deciding just where the line should be drawn – particularly, in recent years, in relation to issues of national security – the courts have been criticised by some as being too deferential and by others as insufficiently so[12].

Another feature of the Strasbourg Court's decisions has been the adoption of a principle of 'proportionality' in the balancing of rights of individuals against the policy needs of state authorities[13]. As has already been mentioned[14], this principle is playing an increasing role in UK jurisprudence, not only because of human rights arguments raised prior to HRA 1998[15] because of the adoption of the principle in EU law[16] but as a result of judicial creativity in domestic cases.

1   Indeed it must also take into account certain opinions and decisions of the (now abolished) European Commission on Human Rights and the Committee of Ministers.
2   As at December 2014.
3   The right to apply to Strasbourg, once proceedings under HRA 1998 (or, in relation to Convention rights, proceedings under SA 1998, GWA 2006 or NIA 1998) are completed, is not formally excluded by HRA 1998 and remains available under the Convention. Recent examples include (partially) successful applications by individuals who considered that their rights to freedom of religion/conscience were infringed by employer-imposed restrictions on manifestation of their beliefs (*Eweida v United Kingdom* (2013) 57 EHRR 8); a finding that the law concerning retention and disclosure of historic information on criminal convictions had a disproportionate impact on article 8 rights (*MM v United Kingdom* 24029/07); and repeated challenges to the UK's approach to prisoner voting (*Hirst v United Kingdom* (2006) 42 EHRR 41; *Greens v United Kingdom* (2011) 53 EHRR 21).
4   For fuller discussion of the ongoing debate on the relationship between the Strasbourg Court and domestic courts see paras 13.17 above.
5   *Handyside v UK* (1976) 1 EHRR 737; *James v UK* (1986) 8 EHRR 123.
6   See, for example, S Atrill 'Keeping the executive in the picture' [2003] PL 41; Lord Irvine 'The Impact of the Human Rights Act: Parliament, the Courts and the Executive' [2003] PL 308; I Leigh 'Taking rights proportionately: judicial review, the Human Rights Act and Strasbourg' [2002] PL 265; D Pannick 'Principles of interpretation of Convention rights under the Human Rights Act and the discretionary area of judgment' [1998] PL 545.
7   *R v DPP, ex parte Kebilene* [2000] 2 AC 326.
8   *R v DPP, ex parte Kebilene* [2000] 2 AC 326 at 381. A similar respect for the 'discretionary area of judgment' of the legislature appears to be emerging in relation to the disposal of devolution issues under SA 1998. This is discussed at para 14.24 below.
9   [2004] 1 AC 185.
10 [2004] 1 AC 185 at 240.
11 Ibid.
12 See for example KD Ewing 'The futility of the Human Rights Act [2004] PL 829; KD Ewing and JC Tham 'The continuing futility of the Human Rights Act' [2008] PL 668; and, in reply, A Kavanagh 'Judging the judges under the Human Rights Act: deference, disillusionment and the "war on terror"' [2009] PL 287.
13 See *Handyside v UK* (1976) 1 EHRR 737; *Jersild v Denmark* (1995) 19 EHRR 1.
14 See para 14.13.
15 See para 14.16.
16 See para 14.13.

THE SCOTLAND ACT 1998, DEVOLUTION ISSUES & COMPATIBILITY ISSUES

14.19   That the Scottish Parliament is a Parliament of defined legislative competence is by now familiar. It may make laws only within the limits specified in SA 1998, ss 29–30 and Schs 4 and 5[1]. We have also noted that a number of devices are built into the law-making process and which are designed to ensure that the Parliament does, in practice, operate within the limits laid down. For example, the minister in charge of a Government Bill is required to state that the Bill's provisions are within the Parliament's competence[2]. Similarly, the Presiding Officer must state whether, in his or her view, the Bill's provisions are competent[3] Then, finally, SA 1998 provides for an interval of up to four weeks between the passing of a Bill and its submission for royal assent to give the opportunity to one or more of the Law Officers to refer the Bill to the Supreme Court if they suspect that its provisions are outside the Parliament's legislative competence[4]. If the Supreme Court considers that a provision in the Bill would not be within the Parliament's legislative competence, the Bill cannot proceed further without amendment[5].

It would have been possible for those who drafted the Scotland Bill to draw a line at that stage. They might have considered that these controls on the validity of legislation would have been sufficient and that SA 1998 could then provide that 'no provision in an Act of the Scottish Parliament may be challenged in any court' or words to that effect. Such a formula might, however, have been the cause of difficulty. It could not have protected a provision found later to be incompatible with EU law[6] or with a Convention right[7] and it would have raised difficult questions about the validity of a provision seen clearly to be trespassing upon reserved matters, especially where an individual claimed that an injustice was being done[8].

In the event, no such finality clause was included in SA 1998 and, by contrast, specific provision is made for dealing with legal challenges which may be made to the validity of an ASP after it has been enacted. These might be thought are most likely to arise in litigation in which the validity of a decision made by a member of the Scottish Government depends in turn upon the validity of a provision of an ASP under which it purports to be made. By this route the validity of the provision conferring the power on the minister becomes an issue in the case. The most likely type of action in which this might arise (and in practice has arisen) is an application for judicial review but it has also arisen in the course of the court's consideration of a petition for adoption[9] and in the exercise of its power to issue directions to a liquidator[10]. The issue might arise in an action brought by an individual to recover money or property or as a defence to such an action brought by a public body. It might also arise as a defence to a criminal prosecution when a person seeks to establish that the provision under which he or she is charged was itself beyond the Parliament's competence[11] (albeit the manner in which certain challenges are brought in criminal proceedings has been changed by the Scotland Act 2012 (SA 2012)).

It is also possible that a devolution issue may arise in proceedings which involve a dispute between the Scottish and UK administrations. This is facilitated by

SA 1998, s 99 which makes provision for a 'division' of the Crown in certain circumstances. Thus, '[r]ights and liabilities may arise between the Crown in right of Her Majesty's Government in the United Kingdom and the Crown in right of the Scottish Administration by virtue of a contract, by operation of law or by virtue of an enactment as they may arise between subjects'[12]. The section also provides for the transfer of property and liabilities between the Crown in these two capacities.

It is also possible to raise proceedings with the sole purpose of challenging the validity of an ASP. However, interestingly, it seems that in such circumstances the appropriate party against whom such proceedings should be raised is not the Parliament (or more precisely the Scottish Parliamentary Corporate Body (SPCB)) itself. In *Adams v Scottish Ministers*[13] – which is discussed in more detail below – Lord Nimmo Smith held that the SPCB was not the 'appropriate contradictor' of a petition for judicial review of an Act of the Parliament. In his view it was clear from SA 1998 (and the structure of s 28 in particular) that, following royal assent, an ASP 'has a specific character such that its enactment is not merely an Act of the Parliament. The Act has passed out of its hands.'[14] In such a case the Lord Advocate was the appropriate respondent[15].

In addition to litigation in which the legislative competence of the Parliament is challenged, SA 1998 also creates the possibility of challenging decisions of and subordinate legislation made by the Scottish Ministers where it is their own devolved competence which is at issue, rather than the validity of an ASP. A member of the Scottish Government may be challenged on the use of powers claimed to be transferred to the Scottish Ministers under SA 1998, ss 53 and 54[16].

As explained below, it is now also clear that it is possible to attack the validity of an Act of the Scottish Parliament on common law grounds, albeit such an attack will be bound to fail in all but the most exceptional circumstances[17].

1 See paras 6.11–6.12.
2 SA 1998, s 31(1); and see para 9.10.
3 SA 1998, s 31(2); and see para 9.10.
4 SA 1998, ss 32–34 and para 9.18.
5 SA 1998, s 32.
6 See para 3.12.
7 Because of the designation by HRA 1998 of ASPs as 'secondary legislation'.
8 For consideration of this issue, including discussion of a finality clause included in the Scotland Bill of 1987 (introduced as a private member's Bill by Donald Dewar), see *Scotland's Parliament* (Constitution Unit, 1996) para 127.
9 *S v L* 2012 SC 8.
10 *Scottish Environment Protection Agency v Joint Liquidators of the Scottish Coal Co Ltd* 2014 SC 372.
11 See *Martin v Most* 2010 SC (UKSC) 40 which concerned a challenge to sentencing provisions.
12 SA 1998, s 99(1).
13 *Adams v Scottish Ministers* 2003 SLT 366.
14 *Adams v Scottish Ministers* 2003 SLT 366 at 377.
15 Lord Nimmo Smith's decision on this point has some practical importance. The Advocate General had suggested that the proceedings ought to have been against the SPCB and, had she been correct, as a consequence of SA 1998, s 40(3), the remedy of reduction of the Act would not have been available. The most which the petitioners could have obtained would have been a declarator to the effect that the ASP provision was 'not law'. For discussion of additional 'respondents' being permitted to enter proceedings to defend the validity of an ASP see para 14.10.

16 See para 7.19.
17 *AXA General Insurance Ltd, Petitioners* 2012 SC (UKSC) 122.

Definition of 'devolution issues' and 'compatibility issues'

14.20   It has, therefore, to be envisaged that in a large number of situations, deriving in one way or another from the devolution of powers under SA 1998, there will be the potential for legal challenge to legislation or decisions made. However, SA 1998 does not seek to regulate the manner in which individual litigants may initiate their proceedings and, as already mentioned, this may often be by way of application for judicial review. But it does identify certain types of 'devolution issue' and then makes special provision for how these are to be handled by the courts. This includes a power of the law officers to raise such issues, on their own initiative, for resolution by the courts including, if necessary, by the Supreme Court.

The detailed provisions on devolution issues are provided by SA 1998, Sch 6, Pt I which starts by defining what is meant by a 'devolution issue' and then identifies six categories. The first relates to the powers of the Parliament itself:

(a)   a question whether an ASP or any provisions of an ASP is within the legislative competence of the Parliament.

The other five, in different ways, raise issues of executive competence, starting with:

(b)   a question whether any function (being a function which any person has purported, or is proposing, to exercise) is a function of the Scottish Ministers, the First Minister or the Lord Advocate;

(c)   a question whether the purported or proposed exercise of a function by a member of the Scottish Government is, or would be, within devolved competence.

And then two relating to compatibility with Convention rights and EU law:

(d)   a question whether a purported or proposed exercise of a function by a member of the Scottish Government is, or would be, incompatible with any of the Convention rights or with EU law;

(e)   a question whether a *failure to act* by a member of the Scottish Government is incompatible with any of the Convention rights or with EU law.

Then, finally:

(f)   any other question about whether a function is exercisable within devolved competence or in or as regards Scotland and *any other question* arising by virtue of this Act about reserved matters.

The list of defined devolution issues is qualified by the statement that a devolution issue shall not be taken to arise 'merely because of any contention of a party to the proceedings which appears to the court or tribunal ... to be frivolous or vexatious'[1]. Frivolity or vexatiousness apart, it will, in the first instance, be for the court in which a devolution issue is claimed to arise to

decide whether it satisfies one of the definitions laid down[2] before going on
to determine the issue itself. One question which may yet have to be resolved
is the scope of paragraph (b). The question of whether or not a function is a
function of the Scottish Ministers might raise issues of statutory interpretation,
for example of the ASP which is claimed to confer the function, which have
nothing at all to do with the devolution settlement established by SA 1998
and do not have the 'constitutional' flavour one would expect of such issues.
Would it nevertheless be a 'devolution issue' attracting the special procedural
provision made by SA 1998, Sch 6? The answer may be a formal 'yes' but
producing a situation in which a court would, in the exercise of its discretion,
decline to make any special order in relation to an appeal or reference[3].

There has been a further important addition to the SA 1998 mechanisms for
determining questions of legislative and executive competence: the creation by
SA 2012 of the new category of 'compatibility issues'.

Paragraph 1 of Sch 6 now provides:

> 'But a question arising in criminal proceedings in Scotland that would,
> apart from this paragraph, be a devolution issue is not a devolution issue
> if (however formulated) it relates to the compatibility with any of the
> Convention rights or with EU law of –
>
> (a)   an Act of the Scottish Parliament or any provision of an Act of the
>   Scottish Parliament,
>
> (b)   a function,
>
> (c)   the purported or proposed exercise of a function,
>
> (d)   a failure to act.'

The effect of this addition to Sch 6 is to remove from the scope of the general
procedural provisions for determination of devolution issues (discussed below)
certain questions relating to legislative or executive competence where those
arise in a criminal case. The carve out is limited: should a question arise in
criminal proceedings as to whether a statutory provision is outside of legislative
competence by virtue of relating to reserved matters[4] that continues to be
categorised as a devolution issue.

The introduction of 'compatibility' issues – or rather the elimination of
Convention rights and EU questions in criminal cases from the scope of the
'standard' devolution issue procedure – resulted from a somewhat peculiar
series of distinct but related events during 2010 and 2011. The underlying
issue was the (seemingly unexpected) substantial use to which the devolution
issue mechanism had been used by defence lawyers in Scottish criminal cases.
A very large number of such cases were making their way to the Supreme
Court for determination and there was a growing view, within the Scottish
Government and the Crown Office in particular, that the devolution issue
procedure was becoming costly and burdensome, as well as delaying the
outcome of a large number of criminal trials. To this general concern about
the bureaucracy generated by devolution issues in criminal cases was added
a degree of high political drama: the cases of *Cadder v HMA*[5] and *Fraser v*

HMA[6], in which the Supreme Court overturned decisions of the High Court in relation to the right to legal representation during police questioning and suppression of evidence respectively, led to highly personalised criticism by Scottish politicians of individual justices of the Supreme Court[7]. The cases also led to a debate about the role of the Supreme Court in Scottish criminal devolution issues cases, which role was characterised in some quarters as an inappropriate 'English' intrusion into the Scottish criminal law. All of this took place against the background of the ongoing work of the Calman Commission[8] on the operation of Scottish devolution and the raising with the Calman Commission by the Scottish judiciary of concerns about the operation of the devolution issues process in criminal cases. The UK and Scottish Governments responded by establishing expert groups. In September 2010 the Advocate General, Lord Wallace of Tankerness, appointed a group of five lawyers led by Sir David Edward[9]. That group summarised its remit as follows: 'Put very shortly, the question at issue is whether, and if so under what conditions, the Supreme Court of the United Kingdom should have jurisdiction to consider matters relating to the conduct of criminal proceedings in Scotland' and it concluded as follows:

'5.1. The existing statutory provisions whereby acts of the Lord Advocate in her capacity as head of the systems of criminal prosecution and investigation of deaths in Scotland are deemed to be 'devolution issues' are constitutionally inept because such acts fall within the retained functions of the Lord Advocate and have nothing to do with the devolution settlement.

5.2. The existing arrangements by which the jurisdiction of the Supreme Court can be invoked (except for the special reference procedure) are productive of delay and other serious problems for the Scottish court system, the Lord Advocate, the Advocate General and for victims, witnesses and others who are caught up in the court process.

5.3. The jurisdiction of the Supreme Court should be maintained both for reasons of constitutional propriety and, more importantly, to ensure that fundamental rights enshrined in international obligations are secured in a consistent manner for all those who claim their protection in the United Kingdom. That jurisdiction should, however, be clearly limited to ensuring compliance with the international obligations of the United Kingdom.

5.4. Acts of the Lord Advocate in her capacity as head of the systems of criminal prosecution and investigation of deaths in Scotland should therefore be removed from the purview of Section 57(2) of the Scotland Act and replaced by a self-standing provision defining the jurisdiction of the Supreme Court in relation to the criminal proceedings in Scotland.

5.5. Apart from the special reference procedure, recourse to the Supreme Court should be available only with leave of the High Court or special leave of the Supreme Court after determination of the relevant issue in the normal course of appeal proceedings in Scotland. The existing 'devolution minute' procedure should no longer apply. Intimation to the Lord Advocate and the Advocate General should not be required, but the Court should have power, where appropriate, to order intimation.

5.5.[10] The Supreme Court should continue to have power, but only in the context of appeal proceedings as recommended in the preceding paragraph, to make any order that it would be competent for the High Court of Justiciary to make.'

Provisions were introduced in the Scotland Bill (which became SA 2012) to give effect to the expert group's recommendations. Then, in June 2011, the Scottish Government appointed a review group 'to consider and assess the mechanisms created under the Scotland Act 1998 and the Human Rights Act 1998, and developed since then, for applying Human Rights law to criminal cases in Scotland, including particularly the regulation, subject matter and scope of appeals from the High Court of Justiciary to the Supreme Court of the United Kingdom...[and] to ensure Scotland's unique system of Criminal Law and Procedure is fully protected, within the context of the accepted need for that system to comply with the Human Rights Act.' The group was led by Lord McCluskey, a retired Scottish judge whose publicly expressed views on human rights legislation were well known[11] with three other members: Professor Neil Walker, Sir Gerald Gordon and Sheriff Charles Stoddart[12]. The review concluded[13] that the Supreme Court should continue to have an appellate jurisdiction in relation to Convention rights questions arising in Scottish criminal cases. That jurisdiction should, however, be limited and should not 'go beyond what is necessary to ensure that Convention rights are defined and understood by courts in the same way throughout the United Kingdom'[14]. The review made a number of specific proposals for reform of the existing process but did not address the manner in which questions of compatibility with EU law arising in Scottish criminal cases should be dealt with. The provisions which ultimately came to be enacted as part of SA 2012 represent a compromise between the UK and Scottish Governments and the recommendations of each expert group.

1   SA 1998, Sch 6, para 2.
2   In *Starrs v Ruxton* 2000 JC 208 it was conceded by the Crown that for a procurator fiscal to prosecute before a court that was claimed to be not impartial as required by art 6 ECHR, was an act of the Lord Advocate and, therefore, raised a devolution issue. That a prosecution by the Lord Advocate could give rise to a 'devolution issue' concerning the independence and impartiality of the court before which that prosecution was taken was affirmed in the JCPC by Lord Hope of Craighead in *Brown v Stott* 2001 SC (PC) 43. See also *Clancy v Caird* 2000 SC 441, especially Lord Penrose at 472.
3   See, for example, *Somerville v Scottish Ministers* (2008) SC (HL) 45 in which it was held by the House of Lords that Rule 80 of the Prisons and Young Offenders Institutions (Scotland) Rules 1994, SI 1994/1931, conferred functions on a prison governor which were distinct from those functions exercised by the Scottish Ministers.
4   See *Martin v Most* 2010 SC (UKSC) 40.
5   2011 SC (UKSC) 13.
6   2011 SC (UKSC) 113.
7   Discussed at para 12.3, n 3.
8   See para 3.20.
9   The other members being Professor Tom Mullen, Frances McMenamin QC, former Lord Advocate Lord Boyd of Duncansby and (the late) Paul McBride QC.
10 Sic.
11 See para 12.16.
12 Professor Walker had published in 2010 the results of a wider review of the appellate jurisdiction of the Supreme Court in Scottish cases which had also been commissioned by the Scottish Government: see N Walker *Final Appellate Jurisdiction in the Scottish Legal System* (January 2010).

13 Final Report of Review Group: Examination of the relationship between the High Court of
   Justiciary and the Supreme Court in criminal cases, September 2011.
14 Ibid, para 10.

Determination of devolution issues and compatibility issues

14.21   Such questions of definition apart, SA 1998, Sch 6 makes four forms
of special provision: (1) it ensures that, by way of the Advocate General or the
Lord Advocate, as appropriate, proceedings may be brought on behalf of either
the UK Government or the Scottish Government to resolve a devolution issue,
for example as to the legislative competence of the Scottish Parliament or the
devolved competence of the Scottish Government[1]; (2) it requires notice to be
given to both the Advocate General and the Lord Advocate of any devolution
issue raised in order to enable either or both to participate in the proceedings
if they wish to do so[2]; and then (3) the Schedule enables the reference of
devolution issues to be made by inferior courts to either the Court of Session
or the High Court of Justiciary and then for either a further reference or appeal
from either of those courts to the Supreme Court[3]. In addition, (4) the Lord
Advocate or Advocate General may *require* any court or tribunal to refer a
devolution issue direct to the Supreme Court and they may themselves refer a
devolution issue which is not the subject of proceedings[4].

SA 1998, Sch 6 also deals with certain ancillary, but practically important,
matters concerning questions of procedure and expenses in cases involving
devolution issues. SA 1998, Sch 6, para 37 permits the making of procedural
rules which prescribe the stage in legal proceedings at which a devolution
issue is to be raised or referred, which deal with the sisting of any proceedings
under Sch 6 and which prescribe the manner and timing of intimation or
notice of a devolution issues. Additionally, in recognition of the extra cost to
private parties which is likely to be incurred as a consequence of the regular
involvement of Law Officers in devolution issues cases, SA 1998, Sch 6, para
36 makes special provision for the award of expenses to take account of that
extra cost.

Compatibility issues, that is to say questions of compatibility of legislation or
executive action with EU law or Convention rights where those arise in criminal
proceedings, are dealt with not in terms of Sch 6 but under CP(S)A 1995[5]. The
relevant provisions of CP(S)A 1995 in many respects mirror those contained
in Sch 6 of the SA 1998. Specific provision is made for the participation of the
Advocate General for Scotland in proceedings in which a compatibility issue is
raised and for references from lower courts to the High Court and the Supreme
Court for determination of compatibility issues.

The principal points of difference with the devolution issues procedure relate,
however, to appeals. First, and in line with the procedure which applies to
devolution issues, the Advocate General may refer to the High Court any
compatibility issue which has arisen in a criminal case to which he has become
a party. That referral, and any opinion of the court which follows, cannot affect
the acquittal or conviction of the accused. Second, and in a change to the
devolution issue approach, an appeal on a compatibility issue by the accused

person from the High Court to the Supreme Court is now available only with the permission of the High Court.

The Supreme Court is now the final arbiter of devolution issues and compatibility issues. Section 41 of the Constitutional Reform Act 2005 (see below) provides that any decision of the Supreme Court on a devolution matter is not binding on the Supreme Court itself but is otherwise binding in all legal proceedings.

1 Para 4.
2 Paras 5–6.
3 Paras 7–12.
4 Paras 33–35. See *Clark v Kelly* 2003 SLT 308 and CM O'Neill 'Kirkcaldy to London via the Lord Advocate: Requiring a Reference to the Privy Council' 2001 SLT (News) 285.
5 CP(S)A 1995, ss 288ZA, 288B.

Questions of interpretation

14.22   On one view, however, the questions for the courts raised by devolution issues should not raise new difficulties. Questions about compatibility with EU law may not always be easy but they are not unfamiliar[1]. Disputes about compatibility with Convention rights are being dealt with by courts throughout the United Kingdom as they interpret HRA 1998[2]. As to the other issues which may arise, these should be largely resolved by the application of the normal principles of statutory interpretation with which the courts are familiar. Most judicial review of administrative action and of delegated legislation turns on statutory interpretation. It is, by no means, always easy but it is familiar. In some cases, the interpretation exercise involved – the comparison between what is prohibited by SA 1998 and what has been enacted in the ASP under review – may even be quite straightforward. With seeming precision, SA 1998, Sch 4 prohibits the modification of HRA 1998[3] and SA 1998, Sch 5 (to take one example among many) prohibits legislation on the subject matter of the Coastguard Act 1925[4]. Resolution of the question whether the Parliament has enacted law in either of these forbidden areas may, at least in some instances, not be difficult.

On the other hand, it was anticipated that the resolution of devolution issues would turn out to be fraught with difficulties. This was for two main reasons. Firstly, the language of SA 1998, especially in its definition of 'reserved matters' in Sch 5, is far from precise. On the contrary, the language is often very open-textured, imprecise and capable of a variety of meanings. This was, in large measure, deliberate: a very precise articulation of reserved matters was avoided for the very reason that it might cause difficulties for the Scottish Parliament and attract disputes in the courts. But general language has its own problems. Secondly, the division of the subject matter of legislation between devolved and reserved will always bring problems for the provisions of ASPs which quite evidently bridge the boundary. Are they to be treated as relating to reserved matters, and therefore unlawful, or not? In all constitutional systems which rely on the division of legislative powers on a functional basis, whether these are federal or devolved systems, there are bound to be difficulties in deciding whether legislation of mixed character should fall on one side of the line or the other. It has, of course, always to be remembered that disputes, when they arise, are quite likely to have consequences beyond the specific case to be decided. In particular, even if neither tier of government is directly involved in the litigation, the case may be politically very sensitive. It is one thing for a local authority or even a minister to be told that they have exceeded their powers. It may be quite another for a Parliament – the Scottish Parliament – to be told by a court that it has misbehaved. Political sensitivities will be even higher if the legislation under review had been passed by the Parliament in order directly to test the limits of its powers and of the devolution settlement.

SA 1998 does itself offer some assistance in the interpretation of legislation which appears to straddle the boundary of legislative competence[5]. Section 29(3) and (4) and Sch 4 have already been discussed in Chapter 6[6], especially the function of the 'purpose' test. Some further guidance is provided by SA 1998, s 101 which applies to the interpretation of provisions of Acts of the Scottish Parliament (or Bills for such Acts[7]) and provisions of subordinate legislation made or confirmed by a member of the Scottish Government. Where such a provision 'could be read in such a way as to be outside competence' the 'provision is to be read as narrowly as is required for it to be within competence, if such a reading is possible, and is to have effect accordingly'[8]. This section echoes the wording of HRA 1998, s 3(1) although it has been held that in the context of devolution and compatibility which concern Convention rights questions, s 3(1) should be applied rather than s 101 of the SA 1998[9]. It is less obvious what impact it may have on other aspects of legislative competence[10] but it seems fairly clear that, at the boundary between reserved and devolved matters, the intention is that the terms of a provision of an ASP are to be read as narrowly as is required to prevent its relating to reserved matters, if such a reading is possible. A provision which could be read as straying into the reserved area should not be so read, if that is possible. An example given by the Lord Advocate during debate on the Scotland Bill[11] was that of an ASP that might be passed to give a general power to the Scottish Ministers to hold referendums on matters of their choice. Without the inclusion of s 101 in SA 1998 the hypothetical Referendums (Scotland) Act might be held to be invalid simply because one of the many purposes for which it could be used would be the holding of a referendum on a reserved matter such as independence for Scotland or abolition of the monarchy. If, however, the Act were read 'narrowly' and confined in scope to its use for legitimate purposes, its validity could be saved[12].

It could not, of course, be guaranteed that the examples discussed and resolved in a particular way by ministers in Parliament would be approached by the courts in the same way. It would be open to them to place their own interpretation on the terms of the ASP (or subordinate legislation or decision of the Scottish Ministers) under challenge in the light of their interpretation of SA 1998 itself. In many respects, this is a process which may be compared with the more routine and more familiar forms of statutory interpretation. Two characteristics do mark out the adjudication of the validity of ASPs (although not necessarily of the validity of executive acts by members of the Scottish Government) as different. One general difficulty, which we have already mentioned, is the nonspecific nature of much of the language of SA 1998, Sch 5, upon which cases may turn. This is different from many 'ordinary' statutes which are, on the whole, designed to achieve a high degree of precision. SA 1998, Sch 5, while precise at some points, is quite deliberately cast in looser terms elsewhere. The idea is to create a more flexible framework within which the Parliament can do its work without the constant threat of being caught out exceeding its powers in minor, technical ways. However, the inevitable result of giving greater flexibility to the Scottish Parliament is also to give greater flexibility to the courts in the way they are to handle this 'constitutional' adjudication in comparison with their more routine decision-making.

Secondly, questions then arise as to how the courts should use this flexibility available to them. In particular, should the review of the validity of the Acts of a Parliament attract a response different in kind from that meted out to public bodies of a lesser order? Should the courts start out with a stronger presumption of validity in the case of the Act of a Parliament than in the case of decisions of a local authority? Should the courts permit a Parliament a greater 'margin of appreciation'? Should they be more sympathetic, more forgiving to a Parliament? Should they take a broader, more generous view of the powers of a Parliament?

Arguments in favour of such an approach derive from the greater democratic legitimacy of a Parliament than, say, a minister acting under statutory powers and comparisons here have been drawn with the attitude adopted by courts to legislatures under written constitutions. In the United States and Canada, for instance, the courts have taken the view that the review of legislation under a constitution *is* different from the review of administrative action under a statute and does demand a different response. Significantly, the courts were seen to adopt an analogous approach in the review of Acts of the Stormont Parliament in Northern Ireland[13]. In *Gallagher v Lynn*[14] Lord Atkin treated the questions raised by the Government of Ireland Act 1920 as entirely comparable with those involving the distribution of powers between Parliaments in a federal system and assumed, in particular, that relevant Canadian authority could be aptly invoked[15].

In the 15 years since the Scottish Parliament was established the courts have in fact been called on to tackle many of these questions[16].

1   See para 3.12.
2   See para 14.15.
3   SA 1998, Sch 4, para 1(2)(f).
4   SA 1998, Sch 5, Pt II, S E3(a).
5   For a detailed discussion of these provisions of SA 1998 and their potential limitations see the written evidence of Iain Jamieson to the Calman Commission (of 31 August 2008) which remains available at www.commissiononscottishdevolution.org.uk
6   See especially para 6.18.
7   Which may also fall to be adjudicated upon by the Supreme Court (SA 1998, s 33).
8   SA 1998, s 101(1), (2).
9   See *DS v HMA* 2007 SC (PC) 1; *Salvesen v Riddell* 2013 SC (UKSC) 236 and para 14.27.
10 For example, in relation to compatibility with EU law.
11 HL Debs, 28 Oct 1998, cols 1952–1956.
12 For the debate which in fact took place on the question whether a referendum on independence was within the Scottish Parliament's legislative competence see para 4.3 above.
13 See the works cited at paras 3.19–3.27.
14 *Gallagher v Lynn* [1937] AC 863.

15 *Gallagher v Lynn* [1937] AC 863 at 870. For discussion, however, of the dangers in drawing such parallels too closely, see H Calvert *Constitutional Law in Northern Ireland* (1968) ch 11 and B Hadfield *The Constitution of Northern Ireland* (1989) ch III.

16 As they have been in the context of Welsh and Northern Irish devolution. See, for example *Re P (A Child) (Adoption: Unmarried Couples)* [2009] 1 AC 173; *Attorney General v National Assembly for Wales Commission* [2013] 1 AC 792; *Attorney General for England and Wales v Counsel General for Wales* [2014] 4 All ER 789.

Challenges to Acts of the Scottish Parliament

14.23   Thus, it was inevitably a matter of interest from the start to see how the courts reviewing legislation made by the Scottish Parliament would approach their task under SA 1998. Comparisons with constitutional adjudication in other parts of the world had already been drawn[1]. It was expected that the Stormont experience would be called in aid[2].

But the starting point would always be the terms of SA 1998 itself, rather than guidance culled by analogy from elsewhere. The review of the Acts of a Parliament created by an Act of the UK Parliament is *not* the same as the review of the legislation of a Parliament created by a written constitution; and, especially where not only the interests of the UK government but also the interests of private individuals in Scotland are at stake it might have been thought that the courts would be disinclined to use the discretion available to them to make strong presumptions in favour of the legality of ASPs. In fact, as we will see, while the courts (including the Supreme Court) have declared themselves prepared in principle to interfere with the 'will' of the Scottish Parliament they have also shown a good deal of deference to the Parliament and to its legislative output. At the same time, the courts have in successive cases developed an increasingly rich and nuanced jurisprudence on the relationship between Holyrood and Westminster, the role of the common law in controlling the Parliament and the application of the more complex interpretative provisions of SA 1998.

In the paragraphs below we set out, broadly chronologically, an account of the challenges to Acts of the Scottish Parliament to date. By 2013, more than a decade after implementation of devolution in Scotland, Wales and Northern Ireland, Lord Hope, in the Welsh context, in *Attorney General v National Assembly for Wales Commission*[3] summarised the general principles to be adopted by the courts in determining questions of the legislative competence of the Scottish Parliament as follows:

'79 First, the question whether a Bill of the Assembly is within its legislative competence is a question of law which, if the issue is referred to it, the court must decide. The judicial function in this regard has been carefully structured. It is not for the judges to say whether legislation on any particular issue is better made by the Assembly or by the Parliament of the United Kingdom at Westminster. How that issue is to be dealt with has already been addressed by the United Kingdom Parliament. It must be determined according to the particular rules that section 108 of the 2006 Act and Schedule 7 have laid down. Those rules, just like any other rules, have to be interpreted. It is for the court to say what the rules mean and how, in a case such as this, they must be applied in order to resolve the issue whether the measure in question was within competence.

80 Second, the question whether the Bill is within competence must be determined simply by examining the provisions by which the scheme of devolution has been laid out. That is not to say that this will always be a simple exercise. But, as Lord Walker of Gestingthorpe JSC observed in *Martin v Most* 2010 SC (UKSC) 40 , para 44 when discussing the system of devolution for Scotland, the task of the United Kingdom Parliament in relation to Wales was to define the legislative competence of the Assembly, while itself continuing as the sovereign legislature of the United Kingdom. It had to define, necessarily in fairly general and abstract terms, permitted or prohibited areas of legislative activity. The aim was to achieve a constitutional settlement, the terms of which the 2006 Act was designed to set out. Reference was made in the course of the argument in the present case to the fact that the 2006 Act was a constitutional enactment. It was, of course, an Act of great constitutional significance, and its significance has been enhanced by the coming into operation of Schedule 7. But I do not think that this description, in itself, can be taken to be a guide to its interpretation. The rules to which the court must apply in order to give effect to it are those laid down by the statute, and the statute must be interpreted like any other statute. But the purpose of the Act has informed the statutory language, and it is proper to have regard to it if help is needed as to what the words mean.

81 Third, the question whether measures passed under devolved powers by the legislatures in Wales, Scotland and Northern Ireland are amenable to judicial review, and if so on what grounds, was considered in *AXA General Insurance Co Ltd v HM Advocate* [2012] 1 AC 868[4]. The court in that case had the benefit of submissions by the Counsel General. It was common ground that, while there are some differences of detail between the 2006 Act and the corresponding legislation for Scotland and Northern Ireland, these differences do not matter for that purpose. The essential nature of the legislatures that the devolution statutes have created in each case is the same. But it has not been suggested that the Bill is the result of an unreasonable, irrational and arbitrary exercise of the Assembly's legislative authority. This case is concerned only with the question whether the Bill is outside competence under the provisions laid down by the statute.'

1 See para 14.22.
2 Although, as the cases have developed, the courts – and in particular the Supreme Court – have expressed doubt about the ongoing value of authorities and interpretative principles which relate to quite different, and now historic, legislative regimes: see para 14.25 below.
3 [2013] 1 AC 792.
4 Cited elsewhere in this book as *AXA General Insurance Ltd, Petitioners* 2012 SC (UKSC) 122.

2000 to 2008: Early Challenges

14.24   In *Anderson v Scottish Ministers*[1] a challenge was made to the validity of the very first ASP, the Mental Health (Public Safety and Appeals) (Scotland) Act 1999 (MH(PSA)(S)A 1999). It was argued that a new power conferred on the Scottish Ministers by the Act to refuse to discharge a patient from hospital[2] if satisfied that detention is necessary to protect the public from serious harm was contrary to art 5 ECHR which guarantees liberty and security of the person. The Inner House[3] found little difficulty in upholding the validity of MH(PSA)(S)A 1999 on the basis of cases decided by the Strasbourg Court[4] but some of the dicta in the case are interesting. Lady Cosgrove remarked, for example, that it represented 'a significant milestone in the development of Scots law: for the first time in its history the Court of Session [was] asked to strike down the Act of a legislature, the power to do so having been conferred on it by s 29(1) of the Scotland Act'[5] Lord President Rodger noted that the balance which has to be struck, first by the Scottish Parliament and then by the court, on all major human rights issues under the ECHR, is between the general interest of the community on the one hand and individual rights on the other. In so doing, it was right, as previous authorities showed[6] that 'the court should give due deference to the assessment which the democratically elected legislature has made of the policy issues involved'[7] In the field of human rights jurisprudence this inclination to give 'due deference' to the views of the legislature reflects the Strasbourg Court's doctrine of 'margin of appreciation' or its equivalent, expressed in the domestic context as the 'discretionary area of judgment'[8].

In a case which did not itself relate to legislative competence, the former Lord President gave a sign of a more restrictive view. *Whaley v Watson*[9] concerned a pre-emptive challenge attempted to the member's Bill to outlaw certain blood sports which Lord Watson proposed to introduce in the Scottish Parliament early in its first session. The petition for interdict, on grounds of breach of the advocacy rules[10] for MSPs contained in SA 1998, was rejected by Lord Johnston and by the First Division. In doing so, however, different views were expressed about the relationship between the courts and the Scottish Parliament and in the Division Lord Rodger expressed some criticism of the earlier views in the Outer House.

Lord Johnston, conceding that challenges to the legislative competence of the Parliament might later occur[11], took the view that, as far as its internal rules were concerned, the Parliament should be entitled to make its own determination and that pressure groups should not be able to challenge such a determination in the courts[12]. Lord Rodger took a sterner line. Lord Johnston had given 'insufficient weight to the fundamental character of the Parliament as a body which – however important its role – has been created by statute and derives its powers from statute. As such, it is a body which, like any other statutory body, must work within the scope of those powers. If it does not do so, then in an appropriate case the court may be asked to intervene and will be required to do so, in a manner permitted by the legislation. In principle, therefore, the Parliament like any other body set up by law is subject to the law and to the courts which exist to uphold that law'[13]. These references to the Parliament's equivalence to any other statutory body suggested, at that relatively early stage, a potentially restrictive judicial approach to the interpretation not only of the Parliament's powers to regulate its internal procedures but also its legislative competence.

A different, more deferential, approach to political considerations was evident from the decision in *Adams v Scottish Ministers* discussed below and also from the Northern Ireland case of *Robinson v Secretary of State for Northern Ireland*[14]. This concerned the challenge by a member of the Northern Ireland Assembly to the election of a First Minister and Deputy First Minister of the Assembly in contravention, it was claimed, of the provisions of NIA 1998. The House of Lords was keen to emphasise that 'the 1998 Act does not set out all the constitutional provisions applicable to Northern Ireland'[15] and that it retained 'scope for the exercise of political judgment[16]'. NIA 1998 was not intended to 'constrain local politicians and the Secretary of State within ... a tight straightjacket'[17] and the court declined to interfere with the political compromise which had been reached.

There was a return to Lord Rodger's dicta in *Whaley* in the second case decided on the legislative competence of the Parliament. This was *Adams v Scottish Ministers*[18] which was a sequel to *Whaley* because it was a challenge to the validity of the legislation which Lord Watson's Bill eventually became: the Protection of Wild Mammals (Scotland) Act 2002 (PWM(S)A 2002). This challenge was launched shortly before PWM(S)A 2002 was due to come into effect on 1 August 2002[19].

Mr Adams, the first petitioner, was a self-employed manager of foxhounds for the Buccleuch Hunt. He was joined in his challenge to PWM(S)A 2002 by three other individual petitioners and a variety of associations including a hunt supporters' club and a campaigning organisation, the Countryside Alliance[20]. The petitioners claimed that PWM(S)A 2002 was outside the competence of the Scottish Parliament because it breached their Convention rights under arts 8 (respect for private life) and 14 (freedom from discrimination) and art 1, protocol 1 ECHR (protection of property and possessions). They also argued that in passing PWM(S)A 2002 the Parliament had been guilty of procedural impropriety and of *Wednesbury* unreasonableness[21]. Lord Nimmo Smith summarised the petitioners' complaints under this head as being that

'the Act is not a bona fide or reasonable exercise of limited legislative powers; it is unnecessary for the good government of Scotland; it involves oppressive or gratuitous interference with rights; it will have damaging and disproportionate economic and social effects; it is based on incompletely informed views as to the moral desirability or appropriateness of criminalising certain types of conduct; proceedings on the Bill were vitiated by procedural impropriety, especially owing to reformulation of its scope at stage 2; and the Scottish Parliament failed to take account of limitations on its legislative powers. They aver that the legislative powers of Parliament are limited because it can only enact legislation that is reasonable and necessary for the legitimate aims of good government in Scotland.'[22]

The petitioners sought reduction of PWM(S)A 2002 and, more immediately, an interim order disapplying the operation of the Act's commencement order pending final determination of the petition[23].

In rejecting the petition, Lord Nimmo Smith concentrated on the interpretation of the relevant Convention rights but also dealt with the other aspects of the challenge. In particular he held that it was incompetent to attempt to judicially review an ASP on traditional common law grounds. In coming to this view, his Lordship considered the nature of Acts of the Scottish Parliament. Notwithstanding the comments made by the Lord President in *Whaley* and notwithstanding the classification of Acts of the Scottish Parliament, by HRA 1998, as secondary legislation, his opinion was that such an Act is 'of a character which has far more in common with a public general statute than with subordinate legislation'[24]. What was significant for his Lordship was that 'the Scotland Act is clearly intended to provide a comprehensive scheme, not only for the Parliament itself, but also for the relationship between the courts and the Parliament' and that 'ss 28, 29, 100, 101 and 102 and Sch 6 are definitive of the extent of the court's jurisdiction and of the procedure to be followed when a devolution issue is raised. It necessarily followed that traditional common law grounds of judicial review were excluded, and that there was no room for the implication of common law concepts in considering the legislative competence of the Parliament'[25]. This was clearly contrary to the dicta of Lord Johnston in *Whaley v Watson* to the effect that 'fundamental irrationality' might invalidate an ASP and was revisited in *AXA*, discussed below.

The petitioners appealed to the Inner House but did not pursue their irrationality argument there[26]. So far as the Convention rights challenge to PWM(S) A 2002 was concerned, the Inner House endorsed the conclusions reached by Lord Nimmo Smith that there was no breach of the petitioners' Convention rights[27]. Their Lordships addressed directly the scope of the Scottish Parliament's 'discretionary area of judgment'[28] and were of the view that the key factors relevant to that issue were '(1) whether the Parliament had before it any proper factual basis for the conclusion that mounted foxhunting with dogs was cruel per se; and whether, if it had, it was entitled to make the judgment that the infliction of such cruelty by such means for the purpose of sport and recreation should be proscribed by law; and (2) whether the likely impacts of the legislation would be such that it should not be enacted.'[29]. On the question of the factual basis for the legislation, their Lordships were keen to distinguish the legislative from the judicial process:

> 'The factual basis upon which a legislature decides to enact a specific provision is not governed by the rules of admissibility and sufficiency of evidence that would apply in a court of law. A legislator is entitled to bring to bear on his decision his personal knowledge gained from his experience of life and from the representations that he may receive on current political topics from informants, pressure groups, committee witnesses, and so on. It is entirely for the judgment and experience of the individual legislator to decide which competing factual account he prefers. He is entitled to accept any account that in his judgment is reliable, no matter that it may be contradicted from other sources.'[30]

The court was satisfied that the competing views for and against the legislation had been fully canvassed before the Parliament, including views about the social and economic impacts of PWM(S)A 2002 and views about the extent to which it could be said fox-hunting was cruel. On the question of the Parliament's 'moral judgment' in this area, the Court considered that the Act 'represents a considered decision by the Parliament on a long-standing and highly charged public controversy. In our view, any judgment on that controversy is pre-eminently one for MSPs[31]....MSPs are elected on their policies on matters such as this.'[32]

A further challenge to PWM(S)A 2002 has also been disposed of. In *Whaley v Lord Advocate*[33], two party litigants sought judicial review of it on the grounds not only of breach of Convention rights (including, in this case, arts 9 (freedom of conscience), 10 (freedom of expression), and 11 (freedom of assembly and association) ECHR) but also on the grounds that certain of its provisions did not comply with the United Kingdom's international obligations. In particular, it was argued that PWM(S)A 2002 breached the Rio Declaration on Environment and Development (1992), the Rio Convention on Bio Diversity (1992), the Final Act of the Helsinki Conference on Security and Co-operation in Europe (1975), the UN International Covenant on Economic, Social and Cultural Rights (1966), the UN International Covenant on Civil and Political Rights (1966) and the UN Declaration of Human Rights (1948).

In dismissing the petition at first instance, Lord Brodie referred to Lord President Rodger's opinion in *Adams v Scottish Ministers*, reiterating his comments to the effect that the Scottish Parliament is not a sovereign body. With reference to the submissions of the second petitioner (Mr Friend), Lord Brodie's view was that he was 'correct to say that the Scottish Parliament is governed by what is, in effect, a mini-constitution' by which was meant that, 'in the Scotland Act, the Convention and Community law, there are written sources of law which have primacy over what the Scottish Parliament may purport to enact'[34]. However, while the Convention and Community law were specifically referred to by SA 1998, s 29 as placing restrictions on the Parliament's legislative competence, similar limitations were not imposed in relation to the other international obligations to which the petitioners had referred. With respect to those measures the traditional approach of the courts, set out by Lord Dunedin in *Mortensen v Peters*[35] remained valid: they had no jurisdiction to set aside Acts of Parliament on the grounds of incompatibility with international law[36]. The second petitioner appealed against Lord Brodie's decision. So far as the Convention rights arguments were concerned, the court accepted that those issues had, by the time of this appeal, been considered and disposed of appropriately by the Inner House in *Adams* and they endorsed Lord Brodie's reasoning in relation to the appellant's arguments based on international law[37]. The House of Lords – to which the further appeal had gone rather than to the Judicial Committee of the Privy Council – also dismissed Mr Friend's complaints about the validity of PWM(S)A 2002 and rejected his contention that by refusing his petition for judicial review without hearing evidence the Lord Ordinary had breached his right under art 6 ECHR to a fair trial[38].

1   *Anderson v Scottish Ministers* 2002 SC 1. See B K Winetrobe 'Scottish devolved legislation in the courts' [2002] PL 31 and I Jamieson 'Challenging the validity of an Act of the Scottish Parliament: some aspects of *A v The Scottish Ministers*' 2002 SLT (News) 71.
2   The State Hospital at Carstairs.
3   *Anderson v Scottish Ministers* 2001 SC 1. The decision of the Inner House was upheld in the JCPC which restricted itself to consideration of art 5 ECHR and did not make more general comments on the principles to be applied in considering a challenge to an ASP.

4   *Guzzardi v Italy* (1981) 3 EHRR 333; *Winterwerp v The Netherlands* (1979) 2 EHRR 387.
5   *Anderson v Scottish Ministers* 2001 SC 1 at 36.
6   Lord Rodger cited, in particular *Soering v UK* (1999) 11 EHRR 439; *R v DPP, ex parte Kebilene* [2000] 2 AC 326; *Murray v UK* (1995) 19 EHRR 193; and *A-G of Hong Kong v Kwong-Kut* [1993] AC 951.
7   *Anderson v Scottish Ministers* 2001 SC 1 at 21.
8   See *R v DPP, ex parte Kebilene* [2000] 2 AC 326 per Lord Hope at 380 and the discussion at para 14.18 above.
9   *Whaley v Watson* 2000 SC 125, 340.
10 See para 5.21.
11 Including the possibility of a challenge on the grounds of some 'fundamental irrationality' in the Parliament's approach to the legislation it passes (*Whaley v Watson* 2000 SC 125 at 134).
12 *Whaley v Watson* 2000 SC 125 at 134.
13 *Whaley v Watson* 2000 SC 125 at 348.
14 *Robinson v Secretary of State for Northern Ireland* [2002] NI 390. The claimant in these proceedings, Peter Robinson, is now First Minister of Northern Ireland.
15 *Robinson v Secretary of State for Northern Ireland* [2002] NI 390, per Lord Bingham of Cornhill at para 11.
16 *Robinson v Secretary of State for Northern Ireland* [2002] NI 390, per Lord Bingham of Cornhill at para 12.
17 *Robinson v Secretary of State for Northern Ireland* [2002] NI 390, per Lord Bingham of Cornhill at para 14.
18 *Adams v Scottish Ministers* 2003 SLT 366.
19 Protection of Wild Mammals (Scotland) Act 2002 (Commencement) Order 2002, SSI 2002/181.
20 For Lord Nimmo Smith's comments concerning the standing of these bodies, see 2003 SLT 366 at 386–389.
21 See para 14.19.
22 *Adams v Scottish Ministers* 2003 SLT 366 at 384.
23 Lord Nimmo Smith did not, as matters turned out, require todetermine the application for interim orders. For discussion of the approach of Lord Glennie, and then of Lord Emslie, to that issue in the context of the ongoing challenge to the Damages (Asbestos-related Conditions) (Scotland) Act 2009, see below.
24 *Adams v Scottish Ministers* 2003 SLT 366 at 385.
25 *Adams v Scottish Ministers* 2003 SLT 366 at 385, 386.
26 The question of the Parliament's susceptibility to challenge on traditional common law grounds has however been raised again in the most recent challenge to an ASP (see below) in which the petitioners argue that Lord Nimmo Smith's analysis is wrong.
27 *Adams v Scottish Ministers* 2004 SC 665.
28 Noting, by reference to Lord Hoffmann's comments in *R v BBC, ex parte ProLife Alliance* 2004 1 AC 185 (see p 394 above) that the 'vocabulary of "deference" is no longer seen as appropriate. It is a question of the court's deciding if the Parliament has complied with the Convention'.
29 2004 SC 665 at 674.
30 2004 SC 665 at 675.
32 Citing *R v DPP e xp Kebilene* [2002] 2 AC 326, per Lord Hope of Craighead at pp 380–381 and *Brown v Stott* 2001 SC (PC) 43 per Lord Bingham of Cornhill at pp 58–59.
32 2004 SC 665 at 676.
33 *Whaley v Lord Advocate* 2004 SC 78.
34 *Whaley v Lord Advocate* 2004 SC 78 at p 107.
35 *Mortensen v Peters* (1906) 8 F (J) 93; and see para 6.5.
36 *Whaley v Lord Advocate* (20 June 2003, unreported) OH, Lord Brodie at paras 43, 44.
37 *Friend v Lord Advocate* 2006 SC 121.
38 *Friend v Lord Advocate* 2008 SC (HL) 107.

Reserved Matters Challenges

14.25   There has now been a number of challenges to Acts of the Scottish Parliament in which it has been contended by the petitioners that the legislation in question is outside legislative competence because it 'relates to reserved matters'. In none of those cases has the challenge succeeded and the approach of the courts (as it has been in analogous cases under the Government of Wales Act 2006 (GoWA 2006)) has been to adopt a generous – and pragmatic – approach to the legislative competence of the devolved legislature[1].

That approach begins by recognising that in considering whether a provision or provisions 'relate to' reserved matters it is possible to characterise the provision in question in different ways:

> 'a degree of trespass into reserved areas was inevitable…it was intended that any argument as to whether a provision in an Act of the Scottish Parliament "relates to" a reserved matter must be decided by reference to its "pith and substance" or its purpose and if its purpose is a devolved one it is not to be outside legislative competence merely because it affects a reserved matter'[2].

The language of 'pith and substance' was, in *Martin v Most*, deprecated as being not entirely apt in relation to SA 1998: 'The question whether [the legislative aim] has been achieved must be determined by examining the provisions of the Scotland Act in which the scheme is laid out. While the phrase "pith and substance" was used while these provisions were being debated, it does not appear in any of them. The idea has informed the statutory language, and the rules to which the court must give effect are those laid down by the statute. As to what they mean, the Scotland Act provides its own dictionary.' (Lord Hope at para 15); 'Parliament established the Scottish Parliament and the Scottish Executive and undertook the challenging task of defining the legislative competence of the Scottish Parliament, while itself continuing as the sovereign legislature of the United Kingdom. That task is different from defining the division of legislative power between one federal legislature and several provincial or state legislatures (as in Canada or Australia, whose constitutional difficulties the Judicial Committee of the Privy Council used to wrestle with, often to the dissatisfaction of those dominions). The doctrine of "pith and substance" mentioned by Lord Hope in his judgment is probably more apt to apply to the construction of constitutions of that type. But both have to face the difficulty of defining (necessarily in fairly general and abstract terms) permitted or prohibited areas of legislative activity.' (Lord Walker at para 44).

It has also been acknowledged that the rules on the allocation of powers to devolved legislatures should be interpreted in a manner designed to uphold the intention of the UK Parliament that the relevant devolution scheme should be stable and workable: 'The best way of ensuring that a coherent, stable and workable outcome is achieved is to adopt an approach to the meaning of a statute that is constant and predictable. That will be achieved if the legislation is construed according to the ordinary meaning of the words used.'[3]

The first reserved matters challenge under SA 1998 was *Martin v Most*[4] in which it was contended that s 45 of the Criminal Proceedings etc. (Reform)

Scotland Act 2007 (CPR(S)A 2007) related to the reserved matter of the Road
Traffic Offenders Act 1988 (RTOA 1988). Section 45 increased the maximum
sentence which could be imposed for certain offences under RTOA 1988. The
court considered not only s 29(2)(b) of SA 1998 – the general prohibition
against legislation which 'relates to reserved matters' – but also s 29(3) (whether
legislation relates to reserved matters is to be determined by reference to its
purpose and effect); s 29(4) (concerning provisions which do not otherwise relate
to reserved matters, but which modify Scots private law or Scots criminal law as
it applies to reserved matters) and are to be treated as relating to reserved matters
unless their purpose is to make the law in question apply consistently to reserved
matters and otherwise; para 2 of Sch 4 (the prohibition against modification of
the law on reserved matters) and the meaning in that paragraph of the expression
'special to a reserved matter'. The decision of the Supreme Court is complex,
indeed too complex to be done justice to here[5]. The justices found the contested
provision within the Parliament's legislative competence. In Lord Hope's view
the issue could be disposed of fairly shortly. Having summarised the policy
background and history of the legislation he concluded that 'this material shows
conclusively that the purpose of sec 45 of the 2007 Act was to contribute to the
reform of the summary justice system by reducing pressure on the higher courts.
An increase in the sentencing powers of sheriffs when they were dealing with
statutory offences was seen as a necessary part of this process. The jurisdiction
of the sheriff sitting summarily is defined by reference to the penalties that the
sheriff can impose. These are pre-eminently matters of Scots criminal law (see
1998 Act, s 126(5)). As it was to a rule of Scots criminal law that the provision
was directed, I would hold that it does not relate to a reserved matter within the
meaning of sec 29(2)(b)'[6]. The justices divided 3 to 2 on the Sch 4 question,
Lord Hope concluding that the rule of Scots law which was being modified by
CPR(S)A 2007 was a rule of procedure which was not a rule which was 'special'
to the reserved matter of RTOA 1998 and Lord Rodger taking the contrary view:
'I conclude that the rule of Scots criminal law prescribing the maximum term of
imprisonment for a summary conviction of a contravention of sec 103(1)(b) of
the [Road Traffic Act 1988], in Pt I of sch 2 to the RTOA [1998], is 'special' to
that reserved matter, in the sense that Parliament has chosen it specifically for
that offence. So, by virtue of para 2(1) of Pt I of sch 4 to [SA 1998], the Scottish
Parliament has no power to modify it'[7]. For that reason Lord Rodger was of the
view that the provision was outside competence.

Subsequent reserved matters challenges have met with no greater success. So,
for example, in *Imperial Tobacco Ltd, Petitioner*[8] the Supreme Court held that
the provisions of the Tobacco and Primary Medical Services (Scotland) Act
2010 prohibiting the display of tobacco products and the use of tobacco vending
machines did not relate to the reserved matters of the sale and supply of goods to
consumers or to product safety: the purpose of the (health related and therefore
devolved) provisions was to make cigarettes less readily available, particularly to
children and young people, with a view to reducing smoking. In *Joint Liquidators
of Scottish Coal v SEPA*[9] the Inner House of the Court of Session was satisfied
that, while the Water Environment (Controlled Activities) (Scotland) Regulations
2005 and 2011 undoubtedly had a practical effect on the liquidators of companies,
their purpose was environmental protection and not modification of the (reserved)

law on insolvency. Perhaps most surprisingly, the Supreme Court also held that the Agricultural Sector (Wales) Bill 2013 which established a regime setting minimum terms and conditions of employment for agricultural workers, including minimum wages, did not 'relate to' employment or industrial relations but rather to agriculture: its purpose was 'to regulate agricultural wages so that the agricultural industry in Wales would be supported and protected.'[10].

1   For discussion of the question whether a referendum on Scottish independence was a reserved matter see para 4.3 and see also N Aroney, 'Reserved matters, legislative purpose and the referendum on Scottish independence' [2014] PL 422. However, on 9 February 2015 the Supreme Court issued its decision in the reference by the Counsel General for Wales of the Recovery of Medical Costs for Asbestos Diseases (Wales) Bill ([2015] UKSC 3) in which it held for the first time that provisions of a Welsh Assembly Bill were outside the legislative competence of the Assembly. Time did not permit a full analysis of the judgment to be included in this book.

2   *Martin v Most* 2010 SC (UKSC) 40, per Lord Hope at para 14 et seq, citing Lord Sewel during the passage of SA 1998. See also *In re Agricultural Sector (Wales) Bill* [2014] 1 WLR 2622, per Lord Reed at para 67: 'Provided that the Bill fairly and realistically satisfies the test [of falling within a devolved area] it does not matter whether in principle it might also be capable of being classified as relating to a subject which has not been devolved. The legislation does not require that a provision should only be capable of being characterised as relating to a devolved subject'.

3   *Imperial Tobacco Limited, Petitioner* 2013 SC (UKSC) 153 per Lord Hope of Craighead at para 14 and see *In re Agricultural Sector (Wales) Bill* [2014] 1 WLR 2622 at para 66.

4   2010 SC (UKSC) 40. Lord Hope described *Imperial Tobacco Ltd v Lord Advocate* 2013 SC (UKSC) 153 as being the first 'in which provisions of an Act of the Scottish Parliament have been challenged on the ground that they relate to specific reservations listed in Pt II of sch 5 as reserved matters' (para 6).

5   For fuller discussion see C Himsworth 'Nothing special about that? *Martin v HM Advocate* in the Supreme Court' 2010 14 Edin LR 487. Lord Rodger was himself critical of the complexity of approach in relation to Sch 4 SA 1998 and lack of practical guidance which he considered was provided by the reasoning of the majority: 'Until now, judges, lawyers and law students have had to try to work out what Parliament meant by a rule of Scots criminal law that is 'special to a reserved matter'. That is, on any view, a difficult enough problem. Now, however, they must also try to work out what the Supreme Court means by these words. It is a new and intriguing mystery.' (para 149).

6   Para 31.

7   Para 141.

8   2013 SC (UKSC) 153.

9   2014 SC 372.

10 *In re Agricultural Sector (Wales) Bill* [2014] 1 WLR 2622.

AXA General Insurance Ltd, Petitioners

14.26   The case of *AXA General Insurance Ltd, Petitioners*[1] may be regarded as perhaps the most significant to date of the challenges to Acts of the Scottish Parliament, notwithstanding the eventual failure in the Supreme Court of the petitioners' case. The importance of the case to the law of standing in judicial review in Scotland has been discussed above but the case is at least as important for its discussion of the constitutional position of the Scottish Parliament and its relationship with Westminster and with the common law.

The case involved a challenge to the Damages (Asbestos-related Conditions) (Scotland) Act 2009 (DAC(S)A 2009). DAC(S)A 2009 was passed by the Scottish Parliament in response to the decision of the House of Lords in the case of *Rothwell v Chemical & Insulating Co Ltd*[2] in which their Lordships held that a particular physical condition, asymptomatic pleural plaques (a type of scarring of the lungs), was not 'damage' for which the law of tort or delict would allow recovery of compensation[3]. The Act provides that asymptomatic pleural plaques (and two other asymptomatic conditions which also result from exposure to asbestos) are 'a personal injury which is not negligible'[4] and that accordingly 'they constitute actionable harm for the purposes of an action of damages for personal injuries'[5]. These provisions are retrospective and are to be treated as 'for all purposes as having always had effect'[6]. The petitioners, five insurance companies who expected to bear the cost of meeting compensation claims under employers' liability insurance policies, claimed that DAC(S)A 2009 infringed their Convention rights under art 6 and art 1 of protocol 1 ECHR. They also argued – tackling head on Lord Nimmo Smith's finding in *Adams* at first instance (see above) that SA 1998 provided a comprehensive and exclusive framework within which challenges to Acts of the Scottish Parliament could be brought – that the Parliament was guilty of irrationality and arbitrariness in legislating to compensate individuals for a condition which Parliament appeared to have accepted was not itself harmful to health.

The petitioners first sought interim interdict to prevent the Scottish Ministers making a commencement order to bring DAC(S)A 2009 into force pending the outcome of the judicial review. That application was refused by the Lord Ordinary, Lord Glennie, on 27 April 2009[7] who was prepared to accept that the petitioners had made out a prima facie case but that it was not a sufficiently strong prima facie case[8] as to warrant interference 'with the acts of a democratically elected body'[9].

When it became clear in early June of 2009 that the first hearing of the judicial review would not be completed before DAC(S)A 2009 came into force, a further application was made, this time for interim suspension of the commencement order. This was also refused by the Lord Ordinary, Lord Emslie, who was hearing the substantive argument in the case, essentially on the grounds that the petitioners would not be prejudiced by the coming into force of the Act given the apparent willingness of the Scottish courts to sist individual actions for damages pending the outcome of the judicial review.

The Lord Advocate entered the process to respond to the petition in the public interest and, as noted above, a number of individuals who would benefit from the provisions of DAC(S)A 2009 were given leave to participate as respondents to the judicial review and to defend the Act's validity.

The petitioners failed at first instance[10] but, importantly, Lord Emslie did not find that the petitioners' common law challenge was incompetent. Rather, 'while s 29 of the Act plainly does not include irrationality among the specified limits on legislative competence I do not regard that as in any way fatal to the petitioners' position'[11]. He considered it significant that there was no attempt by SA 1998 to oust the jurisdiction of the courts on common law grounds: 'If the Scottish Parliament was intended to be the first UK statutory body for two centuries or more to be wholly immune from judicial review on traditional common law grounds, it would (assuming the competency of such a measure) have been easy for SA 1998 to spell that out in clear and unambiguous terms. Had the intention been for the new devolved legislature to enjoy all or even part of the immunity traditionally attaching to the sovereign Parliament at

Westminster, this could equally have been made the subject of explicit provision. But that did not happen. SA 1998 contains no hint of an express provision bearing to exempt Acts of the new statutory Parliament from the possibility of judicial review on the ground of irrationality.'[12] While his ultimate conclusion was that the petitioners had not made out a case which justified striking down DAC(S)A 2009 on common law grounds he went on to observe that 'I would still not have been prepared to close the door on the possibility that, if extreme circumstances were ever to arise in the future, the courts would require to intervene in defence of the rule of law and the fundamental rights and liberties of the subject. In today's climate there is of course no reason to fear any such development, but if, hypothetically, a Scottish Parliament were ever to legislate in a manner which could be described as a flagrant and unconstitutional abuse of power, it is to my mind unthinkable that the courts should have no option but to hold themselves powerless to intervene.'[13]

Lord Emslie's approach to the possibility of common law challenge to Acts of the Scottish Parliament provoked the Advocate General – who had not participated at first instance – to enter the proceedings at the stage of the Inner House appeal. The submissions made on behalf of the Advocate General in essence endorsed the approach taken by Lord Emslie (to the effect that the Holyrood Parliament did not enjoy sovereignty in a manner comparable with Westminster) while the Lord Advocate maintained the position that the limits of the Scottish Parliament's legislative powers were set by SA 1998 and by SA 1998 alone. The Inner House[14] accepted that a challenge to an Act of the Scottish Parliament on common law grounds might be competent but was concerned by the scope of review beyond the limits of legislative competence set out in SA 1998, s 29. Their analysis was critically dependent on how Acts of the Scottish Parliament were to be categorised – were they primary or secondary legislation or were they neither?

'We, like the Lord Ordinary…are inclined to agree with Lord Nimmo Smith's description…in *Adams v Advocate General*[15] … of legislation enacted by the Scottish Parliament as sui generis. Notwithstanding its classification for the purposes of the Human Rights Act 1998 as "subordinate legislation" (s 21(1)), it is "law" essentially of a primary nature. The processes which lead to its enactment include parliamentary procedure which involves scrutiny at various stages by democratically elected representatives who ultimately vote on whether the Bill in question should be enacted and, if so, in what terms. Having passed through these stages the Bill then receives the Royal Assent. These procedures, taken together, distinguish legislation so enacted from acts or instruments subject to judicial review on traditional grounds, including from executive acts of the Scottish Ministers and from subordinate legislation – even subordinate legislation or other instruments which have been approved by the Westminster Parliament. They are much more proximate to Acts passed at Westminster. Other features of the Scotland Act support that proximity: the exclusion of procedural challenge (s 28(5)) and the provision for judicial notice (s 28(6)). On the other hand, there is nothing, in our view, either expressly or impliedly in the Scotland Act which gives to enactments of the Scottish Parliament the status of Acts of the Parliament of the United Kingdom. That is not to ignore the significance of the Scotland Act as of real constitutional importance. But it is to recognise that, however wide-ranging the powers conferred on the Scottish Parliament, its establishment did not involve the ceding to it of 'sovereignty' (whatever precisely that may mean) even within its restricted statutory field of competence: its legislation is open to abrogation or supersession by Acts of the Westminster Parliament (s 28(7)).

The recognition that Acts of the Scottish Parliament are sui generis calls, in our view, for a new approach to these novel instruments. The traditional grounds of common law judicial review are not, without modification, apt for them. It is acknowledged that, while they are open to review on the grounds of "illegality" (by reason of infringement of the restrictions imposed by s 29), they are not apt for review on the ground of "procedural irregularity" (s 28(5)). The notion of "irrationality", even in the extreme sense of being "so absurd that [the legislature] must have taken leave of [its] senses" is not, in our view, apt – at least in the context of the legislation here under discussion....

That does not mean, in our view, that there are no circumstances in which the Court of Session could strike down on common law grounds legislation of the Scottish Parliament. The three categories identified by Lord Diplock in *Council of the [sic] Civil Service Unions v Minister for the Civil Service* (essentially for review of administrative action) are not exhaustive. A fourth category ("proportionality") was contemplated. In the Nottinghamshire case Lord Scarman spoke also of "bad faith" and "improper motive". These latter grounds are not, in our view, truly aspects of irrationality but of deliberate misuse of power. The restriction which Lord Scarman formulated (and in which all the other members of the Appellate Committee concurred) was endorsed by Lord Bridge (and all his colleagues) in *Hammersmith*. If a case were to be made out on such grounds the court might well hold itself entitled to intervene. Likewise, if the Scottish Parliament were to take an exceptional measure of the kind contemplated by Lord Steyn in *R (on the application of Jackson)* – such as a purported abrogation of the citizen's right to challenge unlawful executive action by judicial review – we do not exclude the possibility that any such enactment would be challengeable at common law.'[16].

The petitioners maintained their challenge on common law grounds in the Supreme Court. In its rejection of that challenge – and of the petitioners' challenge based on art 1 of Protocol 1 ECHR – the Court, through Lords Hope and Reed in particular, embarked on a detailed discussion of the Scottish Parliament's constitutional status which, while holding open in theory the possibility of a successful common law challenge to an Act of the Scottish Parliament, made it clear that such a challenge would succeed only in exceptional circumstances. The Court was clearly keen to balance two competing imperatives: respect for the democratic legitimacy of the Parliament's legislative process with an appreciation that the overarching requirements of the rule of law may, on occasion, conflict with majoritarian politics:

'The Scottish Parliament takes its place under our constitutional arrangements as a self-standing democratically elected legislature. Its democratic mandate to make laws for the people of Scotland is beyond question. Acts that the Scottish Parliament enacts which are within its legislative competence enjoy, in that respect, the highest legal authority. The UK Parliament has vested in the Scottish Parliament the authority to make laws that are within its devolved competence. It is nevertheless a body to which decision-making powers have been delegated. And it does not enjoy the sovereignty of the Crown in Parliament that, as Lord Bingham said in *R (Jackson and ors) v Attorney-General* (para 9), is the bedrock of the British constitution. Sovereignty remains with the UK Parliament. The Scottish Parliament's power to legislate is not unconstrained. It cannot make or unmake any law it wishes. Section 29(1) declares that an Act of the Scottish Parliament is not law so far as any provision of the Act is outside the legislative competence of the Parliament....

Against this background, as there is no provision in the Scotland Act which excludes this possibility, I think that it must follow that in principle Acts of the Scottish Parliament are amenable to the supervisory jurisdiction of the Court of Session at common law. The much more important question is what the grounds are, if any, on which they may be subjected to review...

The dominant characteristic of the Scottish Parliament is its firm rooting in the traditions of a universal democracy. It draws its strength from the electorate. While the judges, who are not elected, are best placed to protect the rights of the individual, including those who are ignored or despised by the majority, the elected members of a legislature of this kind are best placed to judge what is in the country's best interests as a whole. A sovereign Parliament is, according to the traditional view, immune from judicial scrutiny because it is protected by the principle of sovereignty. But it shares with the devolved legislatures, which are not sovereign, the advantages that flow from the depth and width of the experience of its elected members and the mandate that has been given to them by the electorate. This suggests that the judges should intervene, if at all, only in the most exceptional circumstances. As Lord Bingham of Cornhill said in *R (Countryside Alliance and ors) v Attorney-General and anr* (para 45) the democratic process is liable to be subverted if, on a question of political or moral judgment, opponents of an Act achieve through the courts what they could not achieve through Parliament...

Can it be said, then, that Lord Steyn's endorsement of Lord Hailsham's warning about the dominance over Parliament of a government elected with a large majority has no bearing because such a thing could never happen in the devolved legislatures? I am not prepared to make that assumption. We now have in Scotland a government which enjoys a large majority in the Scottish Parliament. Its party dominates the only chamber in that Parliament and the committees by which bills that are in progress are scrutinised. It is not entirely unthinkable that a government which has that power may seek to use it to abolish judicial review or to diminish the role of the courts in protecting the interests of the individual. Whether this is likely to happen is not the point. It is enough that it might conceivably do so. The rule of law requires that the judges must retain the power to insist that legislation of that extreme kind is not law which the courts will recognise.'[17]

Lord Reed addressed the specific question of the scope (rather than competence) of any common law challenge to Acts of the Scottish Parliament. In his view, 'It cannot however be assumed that the grounds upon which the lawfulness of an Act of the Scottish Parliament may be reviewed include all, or any, of the grounds upon which the Court of Session may exercise its supervisory jurisdiction in other contexts'[18]. Emphasising that in any case of judicial review the grounds on which that review is available depends on the nature of the power whose exercise is under review, he noted that judicial review at common law is 'based upon an understanding of the respective constitutional responsibilities of public authorities and the courts. The constitutional function of the courts in the field of public law is to ensure, so far as they can, that public authorities respect the rule of law. The courts therefore have the responsibility of ensuring that the public authority in question does not misuse its powers or exceed their limits. The extent of the courts' responsibility in relation to a particular exercise of power by a public authority necessarily depends upon the particular circumstances, including the nature of the public authority in question, the type of power being exercised, the process by which it is exercised, and the extent to which the powers of the authority have limits or purposes which the courts can identify and adjudicate upon.'[19]. He considered the background to the establishment of the Scottish Parliament and concluded:

> 'it appears to me that it must have been Parliament's intention, when it established the Scottish Parliament, that that institution should have plenary powers within the limits upon its legislative competence which were created by sec 29(2) . Since its powers are plenary, they do not require to be exercised for any specific purpose or with regard to any specific considerations. It follows that grounds of review developed in relation to administrative bodies which have been given limited powers for identifiable purposes, and which are designed to prevent such bodies from exceeding their powers or using them for an improper purpose or being influenced by irrelevant considerations, generally have no purchase in such circumstances, and cannot be applied. As a general rule, and subject to the qualification which I shall mention shortly, its decisions as to how to exercise its law-making powers require no justification in law other than the will of the Parliament. It is in principle accountable for the exercise of its powers, within the limits set by sec 29(2), to the electorate rather than the courts.'[20].

The qualification to which Lord Reed alluded to was that it would be open to the courts to strike down an Act of the Scottish Parliament if such an Act was contrary to fundamental rights or the rule of law. There was no suggestion, in Lord Reed's view, that the Scottish Parliament had behaved in such a manner in passing DAC(S)A 2009.

1 2012 SC (UKSC) 122. See for discussion A McHarg, (2012) Edin LR 224 and CM O'Neill and CD Livingstone 'Rewriting the rules: the Supreme Court and the Scottish Parliament' (2012) 17 JR 11.
2 [2008] 1 AC 281.
3 See, for a critical view of the draft Bill which became DAC(S)A 2009, M Hogg 'Asbestos related conditions and the idea of damage in the law of delict' 2008 SLT (News) 301.
4 DAC(S)A 2009, s 1(1).
5 DAC(S)A 2009, s 1(2).

6 DAC(S)A 2009, s 4(2). DAC(S)A 2009 received Royal Assent on 17 April 2009 and a petition
   for judicial review was lodged almost immediately afterwards.
7 *AXA General Insurance, Petitioners* [2009] CSOH 57.
8 The test being, in Lord Glennie's view, as set out by Lord Goff of Chieveley in *R v. Secretary
   of State for Transport, ex parte Factortame (No 2)* [1991] AC 603: 'In the end, the matter is
   one for the discretion of the court, taking into account all the circumstances of the case. Even
   so, the court should not restrain a public authority by interim injunction from enforcing an
   apparently authentic law unless it is satisfied, having regard to all the circumstances, that the
   challenge to the validity of the law is, *prima facie*, so firmly based as to justify so exceptional
   a course being taken'. Lord Glennie also referred to *Infant and Dietetic Foods Association Ltd,
   Petitioners* 2008 SLT 137.
9 [2009] CSOH 57, para 19.
10 2010 SLT 179.
11 At para 125.
12 At para 131.
13 At para 144.
14 2011 SLT 439.
15 This is a reference to *Adams v Scottish Ministers* 2003 SLT 366 discussed above. One of
   the particular issues which arose at first instance was whether the appropriate respondent to
   a challenge to the vires of an Act of the Scottish Parliament was the Lord Advocate or the
   Advocate General for Scotland (the latter being the UK Government's Scottish law officer: see
   para 7.8 above.
16 At paras 87 to 89. See *Council of Civil Service Unions v Minister for the Civil Service* [1985]
   AC 374; *Nottinghamshire County Council v Secretary of State for the Environment* [1986]
   AC 240; *R v Secretary of State for the Environment, ex p Hammersmith and Fulham London
   Borough Council* [1991] 1 AC 521; *R (Jackson) v Attorney General* [2006] 1 AC 262.
17 Lord Hope at paras 46 to 52.
18 2012 SC (UKSC) 122, para 140.
19 Ibid at para 142.
20 Ibid at para 147.

A successful challenge: Salvesen v Riddell

14.27   A finding that provisions of an Act of the Scottish Parliament were
outside legislative competence was, finally, made in *Salvesen v Riddell*[1]. The
Inner House of the Court of Session, endorsed by the Supreme Court, concluded
that s 72 of the Agricultural Holdings (Scotland) Act 2003 was incompatible
with the Convention rights (specifically, the right to peaceful enjoyment of
possessions conferred by art 1, protocol 1 ECHR) of certain landlords of
agricultural holdings.

Of particular significance was the fact that the challenge to s 72 came several years
after the 2003 Act had come into force and in circumstances in which landlords
and tenants had organised their affairs relying on the validity of that provision.
A declaration, in April 2013, that s 72 was 'not law' had the potential to cause
significant disruption. In light of that potential disruption, the Supreme Court
invoked s 102 of SA 1998[2] which provides that where a court finds that an Act of
the Scottish Parliament, or part of it, is outside legislative competence: 'The court
or tribunal may make an order (a) removing or limiting any retrospective effect
of the decision, or (b) suspending the effect of the decision for any period and
on any conditions to allow the defect to be corrected.' Lord Hope was unwilling
to limit the retrospective effect of the decision – 'Any adverse effect on rights
arising from tenancies…will need to be provided for'[3] – but considered that it was
for the Parliament to determine precisely how that should be done. He accepted

that any resolution would require time and consultation with those affected and concluded that 'the court should do what it can to enable it to be conducted in as fair and constructive a manner as possible. So I would suspend the effect of the decision that sec 72(10) is not law for a period that will be sufficient to enable the defect to be corrected.'[4]. In the event, the relevant remedial provisions were contained in the Agricultural Holdings (Scotland) Act 2003 Remedial Order 2014, SSI 2014/98.

1 2013 SC (UKSC) 236.
2 See para 14.31 below.
3 2013 SC (UKSC) 236 at para 57.
4 Ibid.

Ongoing litigation

14.28   At the time of writing two Acts of the Scottish Parliament remain subject to 'live' legal challenge: the Alcohol (Minimum Pricing) (Scotland) Act 2012 (AMP(S)A 2012) and the Children and Young People (Scotland) Act 2014 (CYP(S)A 2014).

AMP(S)A 2012: This Act, if brought into force, would allow the Scottish Ministers, by subordinate legislation, to set a minimum price at which a unit of alcohol could be sold by retailers in Scotland. The Scottish Government has published a draft order in terms of which the proposed initial price set in terms of the legislation would be fifty pence per unit. AMP(S)A 2012 has been challenged by the Scotch Whisky Association and by European spirits and wine producers on the grounds that it constitutes a breach of EU law (and is therefore outside legislative competence in terms of SA 1998, s 29(2)(d))[1] because it contravenes art 34 of the Treaty on the Functioning of the European Union (TFEU), being an unjustifiable interference with free movement of goods. The petitioners' challenge was dismissed at first instance[2], the Lord Ordinary concluding that minimum pricing could be justified in terms of art 36 TFEU, being a measure which had a legitimate aim (tackling alcohol misuse and overconsumption) and which was proportionate. On appeal, the Inner House was persuaded, in the course of the hearing of the appeal, that the EU law questions raised by the challenge justified the making of a preliminary reference to the ECJ[3]. That reference is expected to be dealt with by the ECJ in the course of 2015.

CYP(S)A 2014: In January 2015 the Lord Ordinary dismissed a challenge brought to the validity of Part 4 of CYP(S)A 2014 which provides for the appointment of a 'named person' (in most cases a health visitor or school teacher) to every child in Scotland. When the legislation is brought into force (expected to be in 2016) the named person will have a range of functions in respect of each child, including the gathering and in some cases sharing of information which is likely to be relevant to the child's wellbeing.

The seven petitioners comprised four 'corporate' petitioners – the Christian Institute, the Family Education Trust, the Young ME Sufferers Trust and CARE (Christian Action Research & Education) – and three individuals (all parents of children to whom a named person would be appointed).

The petitioners contended that the named person provisions of CYP(S)A 2014 were incompatible with the Convention rights of the three parents[4], arguing breaches of arts 8 (private life, family and home), 9 (freedom of thought, conscience and religion) and art 2 of Protocol 1 (right to respect for parents' religious and philosophical convictions in the delivery of education). In addition, it was argued that the information sharing provisions of CYP(S)A 2014 were contrary to the Data Protection Act 1998 and the Data Protection Directive and, as such, constituted an unlawful trespass into the reserved matter of data protection[5]. Finally, the petitioners claimed that the fundamental constitutional rights of the fifth to seventh petitioners had been infringed.

As noted above (para 14.10, n17), Lord Pentland concluded that the first to fourth petitioners lacked sufficient interest entitling them to bring a judicial review of Part 4 of CYP(S)A 2014. On the substance of the challenge, he concluded that the fifth to seventh petitioners' case 'fails on all points'[6], in essence because their complaint about the legislation was premature given that it was not yet in force and no 'named person' had in fact been appointed or had exercised any of the functions conferred by CYP(S)A 2014. In addition, the provisions of Part 4 of CYP(S)A 2014 'do not constitute a free-standing scheme in terms of which the named person service can be established and operated. Part 4 contains merely the basic legislative framework under which the named person system will work, but it will be filled out in important respects by subordinate legislation, statutory guidance and advice from appropriate agencies'[7]. Only when these other elements are in place would it be possible to make a proper assessment of the compatibility of CYP(S)A 2014 with Convention rights. The Lord Ordinary also concluded that the information sharing provisions of CYP(S)A 2014 would have to be operated in a manner compatible with both the Data Protection Act 1998 and the Data Protection Directive and that those provisions did not make any modification of the law on reserved matters. The petitioners are, according to media reports, considering an appeal.

1 It is also contended that the making of an order imposing a fifty pence minimum price would breach EU law and therefore constitute a breach of SA 1998, s 57. An additional ground of complaint, that AMP(S)A 2012 infringed the Articles of Union between Scotland and England, was dropped after the first instance hearing of the challenge.
2 *The Scotch Whisky Association, Petitioners* 2013 SLT 776.
3 [2014] CSIH 38. Although not specifically referred to by the Court, such a reference is provided for in terms of SA 1998, s 34. See para 9.18.
4 The four corporate petitioners did not argue that they had any relevant Convention rights.
5 The reservation, set out in SA 1998, Sch 5, para B2, is 'The subject-matter of (a) the Data Protection Act 1998, and (b) Council Directive 95/46/EC (protection of individuals with regard to the processing of personal data and on the free movement of such data).'
6 *The Christian Institute, Petitioners* [2015] CSOH 7, para 98.
7 Ibid, para 50.

Challenges to acts or decisions of the Scottish Government

14.29   While there have been relatively few challenges to Acts of the Scottish Parliament, a much greater number of devolution issues have been raised concerning the activities of the Scottish Government. Disappointingly, perhaps, from the perspective of the constitutional lawyer, these continue to have focused on Convention rights matters[1] rather than on wider questions of devolved competence.

Nevertheless, a few of these cases have raised interesting questions about the definition of 'devolution issues' under SA 1998, Sch 6. For example, in *HM Advocate v Campbell*[2] Lord Cameron of Lochbroom, in the High Court of Justiciary, was asked to rule on whether serving an accused person with a list of productions and witnesses referring to an identification parade – the circumstances of which identification parade were alleged to have infringed the accused's art 6 ECHR rights – was a 'purported or proposed exercise of a function by a member of the Scottish Executive' so as to constitute a devolution issue under SA 1998, Sch 6, para 1(d). Lord Cameron took the view that until the Lord Advocate took steps to introduce evidence in the accused's trial there was no 'act' of the Lord Advocate giving rise to a devolution issue[3].

Similarly, in *BBC, Petitioners*[4], the BBC complained that the refusal by the High Court of Justiciary to allow it to broadcast the trial of the men accused of the Lockerbie bombing constituted a devolution issue under SA 1998, Sch 6, para 1(d). It argued that this refusal breached its rights under art 10 ECHR (freedom of expression) and that the broadcasting restrictions which had been imposed were the result of action taken by the Lord Advocate because he had opposed the BBC's application for broadcasting rights. The Appeal Court of the High Court of Justiciary held that no devolution issue was raised because there had been no act or decision by the Lord Advocate. Although he had supported the application by the US government to have the trial broadcast on a limited basis for relatives of the victims, it was the court which made the decision.

1 See *County Properties Ltd v Scottish Ministers* 2002 SC 79; *Lafarge Redland Aggregates Ltd v Scottish Ministers* 2001 SC 298; *Clancy v Caird* 2000 SC 441.
2 *HM Advocate v Campbell* 1999 SCCR 980.
3 See also *Hoekstra v HM Advocate (No 5)* 2001 SC (PC) 37.
4 *BBC, Petitioners (No 2)* 2000 SLT 860.

Dual protection of human rights in Scotland

14.30 Special mention should be made of one particular issue which exercised the courts and which, ultimately, led to legislative reform: the overlapping protections for human rights contained in SA 1998 and HRA 1998. As noted elsewhere (para 13.12), HRA 1998 obliges public authorities – including the Scottish Parliament and the Scottish Government – to act in a manner which is compatible with Convention rights. Separately, by virtue of s 57 of SA 1998, a member of the Scottish Government 'has no power' to act in a way which is incompatible with Convention rights and further, in terms of s 54, the exercise of a function by the Scottish Ministers is outside of 'devolved competence' to the extent that such exercise of the function breaches Convention rights[1].

Questions arose in the courts about the way in which the SA 1998 and HRA 1998 were intended to interact in cases where it was claimed that the Scottish

Ministers were guilty of a human rights violation. Was the 'victim' of the breach required to pursue their claim under HRA 1998 or under SA 1998 or both? What time limits applied to the bringing of such a claim? And what remedies were available to the courts should it find that there had been a breach of Convention rights?

These questions were considered and determined by the House of Lords in the case of *Somerville v Scottish Ministers (No 2)*[2] which concerned claims by prisoners that their 'segregation' in terms of the Prisons and Young Offenders Institutions (Scotland) Rules 1994[3] breached their rights under art 8 ECHR. The House of Lords was not asked to determine the merits of the art 8 complaint: rather the appeal was taken part way through the first instance judicial review proceedings in relation to a number of specific issues[4].

One very significant question was whether a claim for damages for breach of Convention rights by the Scottish Ministers was subject to the time limit in s 7(5) of HRA 1998 which requires a person who claims that a public authority has acted in breach of s 6(1) of HRA 1998 (which itself requires the public authority to act compatibly with Convention rights) to bring proceedings with one year of the alleged breach[5]. This issue was of no small importance beyond the complaints of the four petitioners in this case: if the time limit did not apply then that exposed the Scottish Ministers to a much larger number of historic Convention rights claims (for example, in relation to 'slopping out' cases[6]). At first instance and on appeal to the Inner House the petitioners argued that they had no option but to raise their claim under SA 1998 and that the HRA 1998 time limit did not apply. The Scottish Ministers contended that the claim had to be brought under HRA 1998 and could not be brought under SA 1998 (and hence the one year time limit did apply). Their Lordships rejected the contention that only one of the two Acts was relevant:

> 'There can be no doubt that the Scottish Ministers are a public authority in terms of s 6(3) HRA and that, accordingly, under s 6(1) it is unlawful for them to act in a way that is incompatible with a Convention right. If the Ministers' decisions on the segregation of the appellants were indeed incompatible with the appellants' Convention rights, under s 6(1) the Ministers acted unlawfully in taking them. Equally, as already explained, under the Scotland Act, if the decisions were incompatible with the appellants' Convention rights, the Ministers acted ultra vires in purporting to take those decisions. Both Acts would apply in the circumstances.'[7]

That being the case, and subject to the one year time limit under HRA 1998, a victim of a breach of Convention rights was entitled to raise a claim under either Act or indeed under both. On the question of the one year time limit itself, on a plain reading of SA 1998, no time bar equivalent to that contained in s 7(5) of HRA 1998 applied to claims brought against the Scottish Ministers under SA 1998.

Tied into the arguments on this point was a contention on the part of the Scottish Ministers that there was no power to make an award of damages under SA 1998 where those damages were intended to provide 'just satisfaction' for a Convention rights violation. If that was correct, claims for the specific remedy of damages in the context of a Convention rights breach would have to be made under HRA 1998 (and would by that route be subject to the one year limitation period). This was based in part in the Ministers' construction of s 100(3) of SA 1998 which provides that: 'This Act does not enable a court or tribunal to award any damages in respect of an act which is incompatible with any of the Convention rights which it could not award if s 8(3) and (4) of the HRA 1998 applied'. It was argued that this wording indicated the UK Parliament's intention that damages should not be capable of being awarded under SA 1998. Lord Rodger dismissed this argument in the following way:

> 'If you tell a French girl visiting you on an exchange that she cannot go out to a club if her parents would not allow her to go to a similar club in France, you tell her two things: first, that she cannot go to the club if her parents would not permit her to do so in similar circumstances in France; but, secondly, that she can go to the club if they would permit it. Similarly, s 100(3) tells the court both what the Act does not enable it to do and what it does enable it to do. The court cannot award damages if it could not award them under s 8(3) and (4); but also the court can award damages if it could award them in respect of the act in question under s 8(3) and (4).'[8]

This part of the Lords' decision in *Somerville* led, ultimately, to the passing of the Convention Rights Proceedings (Amendment) (Scotland) Act 2009 (CRPA(S)A 2009. See para 6.19). The Act amended s 100 of SA 1998 to require (subject to limited transitional provisions) any proceedings (whether for damages or otherwise) in which it is claimed that the Scottish Ministers are guilty of a breach of Convention rights to be raised within a period of one year after the breach complained of. The court may waive that time limit where it is 'equitable having regard to all the circumstances'[9] and it does not apply at all where the breach complained of is the making of legislation[10]. The amendments to s 100 made by CRPA(S)A 2009 were repealed and re-enacted by s 14 of SA 2012.

1   SA 1998, s 54 provides that the exercise of a function is outside devolved competence to the extent that it would be outside the legislative competence of the Scottish Parliament to confer the function (or to confer it so as to be exercisable in that way) which includes, of course, conferring functions so as to be exercised in breach of Convention rights.
2   2008 SC (HL) 45. For discussion, see CMG Himsworth 'Conflicting interpretations of a relationship: damages for human rights breaches' 2008 12 Edin LR 321 and I Jamieson 'Remedies under the Scotland Act: implications of *Somerville* 2007 SLT (News) 289. Mr Jamieson's earlier article ('The *Somerville* Case' 2007 SLT (News) 111), in which he criticised the approach taken by the Inner House, was the subject of comment in the House of Lords. Lord Rodger noted that it had clearly influenced the arguments made on behalf of the petitioners and said that 'For my part, I would acknowledge the assistance that I have derived from it' (para 92).
3   SI 1994/1931.
4   These issues also included whether the exercise of functions by a prison governor under the applicable prison rules could be characterised as the exercise of those functions by the Scottish Ministers (see para 14.9) and the appropriate procedure to be adopted when a claim for public interest immunity was made in connection with documents which might be relevant to a litigation.
5   Section 7(5) provides that proceedings 'must be brought before the end of – (a) the period of one year beginning with the date on which the act complained of took place, or (b) such longer period as the court or tribunal considers equitable having regard to all the circumstances...'.

6   See para 13.11, n 3.
7   2008 SC (HL) 45 per Lord Rodger at para 107.
8   2008 SC (HL) 45 at para 124.
9   SA 1998, s 100(3B)(a) inserted by CRPA(S)A 2009, s 1.
10 Although it does apply to a claim that a breach has resulted from a failure to legislate: SA 1998, s 100(3D).

Consequences of a successful challenge

14.31   In recognition of the potentially serious consequences of a decision by the courts to invalidate all or part of an Act, or to strike down decisions or subordinate legislation of the Scottish Government, SA 1998 makes special provision for judicial and executive action deemed necessary as a result of such a decision.

First, SA 1998, s 102 applies where a court decides that all or part of an ASP is outside legislative competence or that a member of the Scottish Government does not have power to make, confirm or approve any provision of subordinate legislation which he or she has purported to make, confirm or approve. In those circumstances the court in question may make an order '(a) removing or limiting any retrospective effect of the decision, or (b) suspending the effect of the decision for any period and on any conditions to allow the defect to be corrected'[1]. Such an order could be used to protect, for example, third parties who have relied on legislation subsequently held to be invalid. The section requires a court, when considering whether or not to make an order, to 'have regard to the extent to which persons who are not parties to the proceedings would otherwise be adversely affected'[2] and to give notice to the Lord Advocate and, where a devolution issue is involved, to the appropriate Law Officers[3].

Secondly, SA 1998, s 107 confers power on the UK government to make subordinate legislation containing such provisions as it deems 'necessary or expedient in consequence of (a) an Act of the Scottish Parliament or any provision of an Act of the Scottish Parliament which is not, or may not be, within the legislative competence of the Parliament, or (b) any purported exercise by a member of the Scottish Government' which is or may not be an exercise or 'proper' exercise of their functions. This wide ranging power is similar to the power to make remedial orders conferred by HRA 1998[4]. It is to be noted that subordinate legislation made under this section may amend an ASP and may be made whether or not a court has been asked to rule on whether the Act is or is not within the legislative competence of the Parliament[5].

1   SA 1998, s 102(1).
2   SA 1998, s 102(3).
3   SA 1998, s 102(4)–(7).
4   See para 14.17.
5   See, for example, Scotland Act 1998 (Regulation of Care (Scotland) Act 2001) Order 2001, SI 2001/2478.

CONSTITUTIONAL ADJUDICATION AND THE SUPREME COURT

14.32   At the time when, in 1998, the Scotland Bill was being debated in the UK Parliament, the case was made for the creation of a new constitutional court for the United Kingdom[1]. The new business of devolution issues to be generated not only by SA 1998 but also by GWA 1998[2] and NIA 1998 needed a more radical response than that proposed by the use of the JCPC.

In essence this was an argument that, in acquiring the new devolved institutions, the British constitution had reached a new stage of maturity. The enhanced status accorded to the ECHR by HRA 1998 strengthened the case. At earlier stages of its development, the constitution was incapable – Northern Ireland in the Stormont years apart – of producing genuinely constitutional issues for resolution by courts. The supremacy of Parliament and the unitary nature of the state suppressed such issues. All that courts were empowered to do was to interpret and to apply the will of Parliament[3]. In legal, if not in political, ways, constitutional conflict was flattened. There was a need for a London-based court (the JCPC) to act as a final court of appeal and to resolve constitutional disputes in the Empire and Commonwealth but there was no such need for a court with a domestic jurisdiction. The United Kingdom's accession to the European Community in 1973 did not change this situation greatly because that brought with it a 'constitutional' court of its own – the European Court of Justice – although without doubt that accession has brought a new 'constitutional' dimension to the work of the ordinary courts. They must now determine the extent to which British law – including Acts of the UK Parliament – complies with the requirements of EU law and, in appropriate cases, may be faced with the task of disapplying an Act of the UK Parliament which contravenes those requirements[4]. The same courts are also frequently involved in interpreting and applying EU law in circumstances which are not explicitly constitutional in character.

But, it was argued, the arrival of devolution and of HRA 1998 produced a new situation and the case for a new court with a domestic jurisdiction. For its advocates, this jurisdiction would be quite separate from that of courts dealing with matters of 'ordinary' law. It would extend to 'difficult and controversial decisions about where state power ends and where personal liberty begins; decisions about striking a fair balance between competing human rights; decisions about the respective powers and duties of the Parliament of Westminster and central Government and of the devolved legislatures and administrations'[5]. The very nature of these decisions gave rise to the need for a specially constituted court: they were 'properly justiciable but they will sometimes be politically and ethically controversial. That is why it is especially important to ensure that the independence, authority and legitimacy of the final court are securely protected'[6].

This case was bolstered by both principled and more pragmatic objections to the continued reliance on existing institutions. It was, at the very least, a constitutional oddity that, in the 21st century, one final court should be formally part of the legislature (the House of Lords) and the other a part of the executive (the Privy Council). Nor was this merely a historical curiosity. The incorporation of the ECHR with its insistence upon the guarantee of the right to a hearing by 'an independent and impartial tribunal' brought a heightened awareness of the need for institutional distance between the judiciary and the other organs of government. There was growing unease, even among the Law Lords themselves[7], about the participation of the United Kingdom's most senior judges in the country's legislature. However restrained their political contribution may have been in that forum, their dual roles were undesirable. That concern was further heightened by their increasing involvement in cases of a political nature and there was an even more focused concern about the multiple roles of the Lord Chancellor. Once treated as little more than a matter of constitutional amusement, the capacity of that office seriously to infringe the rules of judicial impartiality could no longer be overlooked. The participation of the UK government's most senior member in the Upper House in cases, a large proportion of which have a governmental or human rights interest, had ceased to be justifiable[8]. The combined effect of these central questions of constitutional principle, the arrival of the new business under the Acts of 1998, together with more pragmatic reasons of case management in an overloaded system produced a strong imperative for new arrangements[9]. Proposals for a new constitutional court were rejected by the new Labour government during the passage of SA 1998, GWA 1998 and NIA 1998. The Lord Chancellor, in debate on the Scotland Bill, described the government's programme of constitutional reform as 'incremental'[10] and recalled that the government 'came down ... as a matter of policy against a constitutional court in ... the White Paper, *Rights Brought Home*'[11]. However, referring to not only the new devolution legislation but to the Human Rights Bill, the Freedom of Information Bill and provisions for locally elected mayors, Lord Irvine suggested that perhaps 'after all that legislation beds down, longer-term thought should be given to the appropriateness of a specialist constitutional court'. No reference to this issue appeared in the Labour Party's manifesto for the 2001 general election.

Nonetheless, on 12 June 2003 the UK government announced a number of measures billed as 'part of the continuing drive to modernise the constitution and public services'. These included abolition of the Lord Chancellor's Department, to be replaced with a Department for Constitutional Affairs which would also take on the responsibilities of the Scotland and Wales Offices[12]; abolition of the post of Lord Chancellor, to be replaced with a Secretary of State for Constitutional Affairs who would no longer act as Speaker of the House of Lords and who would neither sit as a judge nor have any involvement in judicial appointments[13]; establishment of a new Judicial Appointments Commission for England and Wales[14]; and the creation of a new Supreme Court to replace the Law Lords.

Undoubtedly this last proposal was driven principally by the perceived need to ensure the independence and impartiality of the UK's highest court by removing the senior judiciary from the legislature. Arguably, this difficulty could have been cured relatively simply by removing the rights of the Law Lords to sit and vote in the House of Lords. Little more would have been needed. However, following publication in July 2003 of the government's consultation paper

Constitutional Reform: A Supreme Court for the United Kingdom, it became clear that a number of other questions were to be asked about the arrangements for high-level adjudication – both constitutional and otherwise – in the United Kingdom and more far reaching reform has in fact been the result.

In setting out the case for reform, the consultation paper referred to the existing functions of both the Appellate Committee of the House of Lords and the JCPC, which functions raised 'questions about whether there is any longer sufficient transparency of independence from the executive and the legislature to give people the assurance to which they are entitled about the independence of the Judiciary'[15]. It noted that one consequence of the growth of judicial review in recent years has been that judges have been brought more into the 'political eye'[16] and that there was increased sensitivity to the 'anomaly of the position whereby the highest court of appeal is situated within one of the chambers of Parliament'[17]. The continuing role of the Lord Chancellor as head of the judiciary added to the perception that judicial independence might be compromised by the existing arrangements[18].

The government's proposals for reform were taken forward by the Bill which became the Constitutional Reform Act 2005 (CRA 2005) and the provisions of that Act concerning the independence of the judiciary, appointments to the new Supreme Court and modifications to the role and functions of the Lord Chancellor are discussed in other parts of this book. The remaining provisions of CRA 2005 appear less an attempt to create for the UK a more obviously 'constitutional' court than a reflection of a desire to streamline and modernise existing processes. So, in summary:

(1) With effect from 1 October 2009, the jurisdiction of the House of Lords within the United Kingdom's legal systems was abolished and the functions of the Appellate Committee vested in the Supreme Court. The Supreme Court may hear appeals from any order or judgment of the Court of Appeal in England and Wales in civil proceedings and in relation to Scottish appeals, an appeal 'lies to the Court from any order or judgment of a court in Scotland if an appeal lay from that court to the House of Lords at or immediately before the commencement of this section'[19].

(2) As a necessary consequence of the abolition of the House of Lords' judicial role, a large number of 'miscellaneous', and in some cases obscure, statutory jurisdictions formerly exercised by the Lords have been transferred to the Supreme Court including, for example, appeals which may involve the appointment of assessors under the Nautical Assessors (Scotland) Act 1894, appeals against decisions of disciplinary committees established under the Agricultural Marketing Act 1958 and appeals under the Extradition Act 1989[20].

(3) Also transferred to the Supreme Court was the jurisdiction formerly exercised by the JCPC in relation to devolution matters[21]. The JCPC's role as a final court of appeal for some Commonwealth jurisdictions has remained[22].

(4) CRA 2005 contains some explicit recognition of the distinct constituent legal systems of the United Kingdom and the importance of making

provision for those legal systems. So, 'a decision of the Supreme Court on appeal from a court of any part of the United Kingdom, other than a decision on a devolution matter, is to be regarded as the decision of a court of that part of the United Kingdom'[23]. In the appointment of Justices to the Supreme Court, the Judicial Appointments Commission must consult the Lord Chancellor, the First Minister for Wales, the Secretary of State for Northern Ireland and the Scottish First Minister[24]. The UK government's consultation paper acknowledged that the previous arrangements for devolution issues to be dealt with by the JCPC provided 'more opportunities to have Scottish and Northern Ireland judges sitting on devolution issues'[25] and in consequence it intended to make 'arrangements which enable additional Scottish and Northern Ireland judges to sit in cases raising devolution issues where that is appropriate'[26]. That has been done by allowing for the appointment, as 'acting' judges, a person who holds office as a 'senior territorial judge' which term includes Inner House judges in Scotland and judges of the English and Northern Irish Courts of Appeal[27]. The Supreme Court will not be quorate unless comprised of a majority of permanent judges[28] but nevertheless at least in theory the Supreme Court could constitute itself along more 'territorial' lines where that was thought appropriate in individual cases. There is no formal quota for Scottish and Northern Ireland judges but it was anticipated that the previous convention by which two Scottish judges were appointed to the House of Lords and sit on Scottish appeals would continue in the Supreme Court. In the event the convention has been honoured, with the appointments of Lords Reed and Hodge following, respectively, the death of Lord Rodger and retirement of Lord Hope.

In its 2003 consultation paper the government stated unequivocally that '[t]here is no proposal to create a Supreme Court on the US model with the power to overturn legislation. Nor is there any proposal to create a specific constitutional court, or one whose primary role would be to give preliminary rulings on difficult points of law'[29]. A court with the power to strike down Westminster legislation would not fit with the British tradition in which Parliament is supreme[30] and there is no need for an exclusively constitutional court because, in the UK, there 'is no separate body of constitutional law which takes precedence over all other law'[31]. CRA 2005 may, it seems, be as far as the United Kingdom is prepared, for now, to move in the direction of a constitutional court.

1   See HL Debs 28 Oct 1998, cols 1963–1986.
2   Now GWA 2006.
3   See para 6.5.
4   *R v Secretary of State for Transport, ex parte Factortame Ltd* [1991] 1 AC 603; *R v Secretary of State for Employment, ex parte Equal Opportunities Commission* [1995] 1 AC 1. For discussion, see para 6.9.
5   HL Debs, 28 October 1998, col 1969 (Lord Lester of Herne Hill).
6   HL Debs, 28 October 1998, col 1969 (Lord Lester of Herne Hill).
7   See Lord Bingham of Cornhill 'The Evolving Constitution' (2002) 6 EHRLR 1 and Lord Steyn 'The Case for a Supreme Court' (2002) 118 LQR 382.
8   See also para 11.17.

9 See, for example, A Le Sueur and R Cornes 'The Future of the United Kingdom's Highest
Courts' (Constitution Unit, 2001) and 'What Do the Top Courts Do?' (2000) 53 Current Legal
Problems 53.
10 HL Debs 28 October 1998, col 1982.
11 HL Debs 28 October 1998, col 1982.
12 See para 7.24.
13 See para 12.18.
14 See para 12.5.
15 Para 2.
16 Para 2.
17 Para 2.
18 Para 3.
19 CRA 2005, s 40.
20 See CRA 2005, s 40 and Sch 9, Pt I.
21 Devolution matters include both post-enactment devolution issues and any references under
SA 1998, s 33: see CRA 2005, s 40 and Sch 9, Pt II.
22 See para 14.1.
23 CRA 2005, s 41(2).
24 CRA 2005, s 27.
25 Para 19.
26 Para 21.
27 CRA 2005, s 38.
28 CRA 2005, s 42.
29 Para 8.
30 Para 23.
31 Para 23.

Index

[All references are to paragraph number]

Accountability of government
committees
introduction, 10.8
Scotland, in, 10.10
Westminster, at, 10.9
Crichel Down rules, 10.2
freedom of information, and, 10.1
introduction, 10.1
members' business debates, 10.7
ministerial responsibility
introduction, 10.2
mechanisms for holding ministers to
account, 10.3–10.14
no confidence motions, 10.7
opposition debates, 10.7
Parliamentary Commissioner for
Administration
effect of decisions in courts, 10.14
generally, 10.12
introduction, 10.11
parliamentary mechanisms
committees, 10.8–10.10
introduction, 10.3
ombudsmen, 10.11
opposition debates, 10.7
parliamentary questions, 10.4–10.6
select and subject committees,
10.8–10.10
parliamentary ombudsmen
effect of decisions in courts, 10.14
introduction, 10.11
Scotland, in, 10.13
Westminster, at, 10.12
parliamentary questions
introduction, 10.4
Scotland, in, 10.6
Westminster, at, 10.5
public petitions, 10.15
Scottish Ministerial Code, 10.2
Scottish Public Services Ombudsman
effect of decisions in courts, 10.14
generally, 10.13
introduction, 10.11
select committees, 10.9

Accountability of government – *contd*
subject committees, 10.10
UK Parliamentary Commissioner for
Administration
effect of decisions in courts, 10.14
generally, 10.12
introduction, 10.11
Accountability principle
standards of good governance, and, 2.4
Accounting and audit
public finance, and, 11.18
Additional member system (AMS)
voting systems, and, 5.8
**Administrative Justice and Tribunals
Council**
public law adjudication, and, 14.5
Administrative Tribunals
court system, and, 12.2
Advocate General for Scotland
UK government, and, 7.8
Amendment of the Scotland Act
law-making competences, and, 6.19
Apparent bias
automatic disqualification, 12.13
generally, 12.12
other grounds for disqualification,
12.14
overview, 12.15
Appeals
And see **Judicial review**
statutory appeals
Administrative Tribunals, 14.5
introduction, 14.4
Leggatt Review, 14.5
local authorities, 14.6
public bodies, 14.6
Arrest powers
generally, 13.18
Attorney-General
UK government, and, 7.8
Audit Scotland
public finance, and, 11.18
Auditor General for Scotland
public finance, and, 11.18

Barnett Formula
devolution, and, 3.19
public finance, and
amount of funding, 11.8
block grant, 11.6
funding by Westminster, 11.5
introduction, 11.1
Scottish Independence referendum,
and, 4.13, 4.21
Bias
automatic disqualification, 12.13
generally, 12.12
other grounds for disqualification,
12.14
overview, 12.15
Bill of Rights
human rights, and, 13.16
Bill of Rights 1689
unwritten constitution of the UK, and,
1.22
Block grant
allocation, 11.7
generally, 11.6
Borrowing
powers of Scottish Parliament, and,
11.15
Business programme
Scottish Government Bills, and, 9.10
Cabinet
UK government, and, 7.7
Cabinet government
collective responsibility, 7.11
generally, 7.10
role of Prime Minister, 7.12
Scottish Government, and, 7.18
Cabinet secretaries
Scottish Government, and, 7.17
Calman Commission
generally, 3.20, 5.18, 7.26, 9.13, 11.5
Canada
federal constitutions, and, 1.21
privacy rights, and, 13.24
public law adjudication, and, 14.1
territorial division, and, 1.11
Challenges
Acts of Scottish Government, to,
14.29
Acts of Scottish Parliament, to
AXA General Insurance Ltd, 14.26
between 2000 and 2008, 14.24
introduction, 14.23
ongoing (2014) litigation, 14.28
reserved matters, on, 14.25
Salvesen v Riddell, 14.27

Challenges – *contd*
Scottish Government Bills, to
introduction, 9.17
prohibition of submission for assent,
9.19
reference to the Supreme Court,
9.18
Charter of Fundamental Rights
See **EU Charter of Fundamental
Rights**
Citizens
arrest, 13.18
Bill of Rights, and, 13.16
citizenship, 13.2
civic rights, 13.2
Commission for Equality and Human
Rights, 13.14
Commissioner for Children and Young
Persons, 13.14
data protection, 13.23
data retention, 13.25
deportation, 13.4
detention and arrest, 13.18
European Convention on Human
Rights
citizenship, and, 13.2
generally, 13.7
incorporation, 13.9
extradition, 13.4
freedom of information, 13.22
human rights
Charter of Fundamental Rights of
the EU, 13.8
Commission for Equality and
Human Rights, 13.14
Commissioner for Children and
Young Persons, 13.14
Convention rights, 13.11
detention and arrest, 13.18
European Convention, 13.7–13.9
future reforms, 13.15–13.17
Human Rights Act 1998, 13.10–
13.13
introduction, 13.6
maintenance of public order, 13.19
public authorities, 13.12
Scottish Commission for Human
Rights, 13.14
territorial extent of the HRA, 13.13
immigration control, 13.3
information law
data protection, 13.23
data retention, 13.25
freedom of information, 13.22

Citizens – *contd*
 information law – *contd*
  introduction, 13.20
  official secrets, 13.21
  privacy rights, 13.24
  regulation of investigatory powers,
   13.25
  surveillance, 13.25
 introduction, 13.1
 limitations on state power
  human rights, 13.6–13.19
  information law, 13.20–13.25
  introduction, 13.5
 maintenance of public order, 13.19
 official secrets, 13.21
 police powers of detention and arrest,
  13.18
 privacy rights, 13.24
 regulation of investigatory powers,
  13.25
 removal, 13.4
 right of abode, 13.2
 Scottish Commission for Human
  Rights, 13.14
 surveillance, 13.25
Civic rights
 citizenship, and, 13.2
Civil service
 Scottish Government, and, 7.23
 UK government, and, 7.3
Collection of tax
 taxing powers of Scottish Parliament,
  and 11.14
Collective responsibility
 Scottish Government, and, 7.18
**Commission for Equality and Human
 Rights**
 generally, 13.14
**Commissioner for Children and Young
 Persons**
 generally, 13.14
Committee Bills
 law-making procedures, and, 9.24
**Committee of Permanent
 Representatives (COREPER)**
 European Union, and, 3.7
Committee stage
 Scottish Government Bills, and,
  9.12
 Westminster Bills, and, 9.6
Committees
 introduction, 10.8
 Scotland, in, 10.10
 Westminster, at, 10.9

Compatibility issues
 definition, 14.20
 determination, 14.21
 generally, 14.19
**Comptroller and Auditor General
 (UK)**
 generally, 11.18
 introduction, 11.2
Consolidated Fund
 See also **Scottish Consolidated Fund**
 expenditure, 11.4
 generally, 11.2
 judicial salaries, and, 12.10
 UK Parliamentary Commissioner for
  Administration, and, 10.12
Consolidation Bills
 Scottish Government Bills, and, 9.16
 Westminster Bills, and, 9.3
Constituencies
 boundaries, 5.9
 generally, 5.8
Constitution Treaty (2004)
 European Union, and, 3.15
Constitutional amendment
 structure of written constitution, and,
  1.12
Constitutional context
 devolution
  further evolution of the Constitution,
   3.20
  'home rule' movement, 3.17
  introduction, 3.16
  Scotland Act 1978, 3.18
  Scottish Constitutional Convention,
   3.19
 European Union
  Commission, 3.8
  Constitution Treaty (2004), 3.15
  constitutional significance, 3.11–
   3.15
  Council, 3.7
  Court of Justice, 3.10
  EU Charter of Fundamental Rights,
   3.14
  European Council, 3.6
  European Parliament, 3.9
  institutions, 3.5–3.10
  introduction, 3.3
  Lisbon Treaty, 3.15
  Ministerial accountability, 3.13
  primacy of EU law, 3.12
  relationship with Scotland, 3.15
  relationship with UK, 3.4
  treaties, 3.12

Constitutional context – *contd*
  formation of the United Kingdom, 3.2
  introduction, 3.1
Constitutional law
  accountability principle, 2.4
  individual liberty, 2.2
  introduction, 2.1
  justice, 2.8
  legality principle, 2.7
  overview, 1.1
  rule of law
    introduction, 2.6
    justice, and, 2.8
    legality principle, 2.7
  Scotland, in, 1.19–1.24
  separation of powers, 2.5
  standards of good governance
    accountability principle, 2.4
    introduction, 2.3
    separation of powers, 2.5
  United Kingdom, in, 1.20–1.24
  unwritten constitution of the UK,
    1.22–1.24
Constitutions
  See also **Written constitutions**
  functions, 1.14–1.18
  introduction, 1.13
**Convention of Scottish Local
  Authorities**
  generally, 8.6
Convention rights
  See **Human rights**
Council (of Ministers)
  European Union, and, 3.7
Council tax
  public finance, and, 11.6
Court of First Instance (CFI)
  European Union, and, 3.10
**Court of Justice of the European
  Union (ECJ)**
  European Union, and, 3.10
Court of Session
  court system, and, 12.2
Courts
  Administrative Tribunals, and, 12.2
  bias
    automatic disqualification, 12.13
    generally, 12.12
    other grounds for disqualification,
      12.14
    overview, 12.15
  Court of Session, 12.2
  functions, 12.2
  High Court of Justiciary, 12.2

Courts – *contd*
  House of Lords, 12.2
  immunity from suit of judges, 12.9
  introduction, 12.1
  judicial appointments, 12.5
  judicial conduct, 12.7
  judicial functions, 12.2
  judicial impartiality
    bias, 12.12–12.15
    conclusions, 12.20
    generally, 12.3
    introduction, 12.11
    politics, and, 12.16–12.19
  judicial incapacity, 12.7
  judicial independence
    appointments, 12.5
    conclusions, 12.20
    generally, 12.4
    immunity from suit, 12.9
    importance, 12.3
    politics, and, 12.16–12.19
    public criticism, 12.10
    safeguards and protection, 12.6–12.8
    salaries, 12.8
    security of tenure, 12.7
  judicial inquiries, 12.19
  judicial salaries, 12.8
  judicial system, 12.2
  justice of the peace courts, 12.2
  liability of judges, 12.9
  politics, and, 12.16–12.19
  public criticism of judges, 12.10
  security of tenure of judges, 12.7
  sheriff courts, 12.2
  Supreme Court, 12.2
  temporary sheriffs, 12.7
Crichel Down rules
  accountability of government, and,
    10.2
Cross-border public authorities
  generally, 8.12
  introduction, 8.9
Crown
  Scottish Government, and, 7.13
  UK government, and, 7.2
Currency
  Scottish Independence referendum,
    and, 4.17
Data protection
  information law, and, 13.23
Data retention
  information law, and, 13.25
Defence
  law-making competences, and, 6.15

Delegated legislation
control of exercise of powers, 9.31
control of legislation conferring
powers, 9.30
Interpretation and Legislative Reform
(Scotland) Act 2010, and, 9.32
introduction, 9.29
judicial review, and, 14.14
merits scrutiny, 9.34
Scotland Act 1998, under, 9.35
Statutory Instruments Act 1946, and,
9.32
technical scrutiny, 9.33
Departments
accountability, 2.4
expenditure, 11.4
financial procedures, 11.2
inter-governmental relations, and, 7.26
intermediate government, and, 8.8
introduction, 7.23
maladministration, 10.12
ministerial responsibility, and, 10.2
Scottish Government, 7.25
UK Government, 7.24
Deportation
generally, 13.4
Detention and arrest
police powers, and, 13.18
Devolved matters legislation
law-making competences, and, 6.22
Devolution
And see **Devolution issues;**
Independence referendum;
Scottish Parliament
administrative tribunals, and, 14.5
committee system, and, 5.18
constitutional relationship with the
UK, and, 3.2
deportation, and, 13.4
further evolution of the Constitution,
3.20
'home rule' movement, 3.17
independence referendum, and, 4.1
institutional framework of UK
Parliaments, and, 5.1
inter-governmental relations, and, 7.26
intermediate government, and, 8.8
introduction, 3.16
Ireland, and, 1.20
judicial system, and
appointments, 12.5
functions, 12.2
independence, 12.3
law-making procedures, and, 9.1

Devolution – *contd*
local authorities, and, 8.7
ministerial accountability, and, 3.13
public bodies, and, 8.9
public finance, and, 11.1
public law adjudication, and, 14.1
Scotland Act 1978, and, 3.18
Scotland Acts 1998 and 2012, and
further evolution of the Constitution,
3.20
'home rule' movement, 3.17
introduction, 3.16
Scottish Constitutional Convention,
3.19
Scottish Constitutional Convention,
3.19
separation of powers, and, 2.5
sources of executive authority, and,
7.19–7.24
subordinate legislation, and, 9.35
territorial division, and, 1.11
West Lothian, question, and, 5.9
Westminster legislation, and, 6.22
Westminster select committees, and,
10.9
Devolution issues
challenges to Acts of Scottish
Government, 14.29
challenges to Acts of Scottish
Parliament
AXA General Insurance Ltd,
14.26
between 2000 and 2008, 14.24
introduction, 14.23
ongoing (2014) litigation, 14.28
reserved matters, on, 14.25
Salvesen v Riddell, 14.27
definition, 14.20
determination, 14.21
effect of successful challenge, 14.31
generally, 14.19
human rights protection, 14.30
interpretation, 14.22
Dissolution of Parliament
Scottish Government, and, 7.15
UK government, and, 7.5
Edinburgh Agreement
Scottish Independence referendum,
and, 4.4
Elected chambers
composition, 5.2–5.4
members (MPs and MSPs), 5.3
Parliamentary sessions, 5.4
structure, 5.2–5.4

Elections
candidates
entitlement to be, 5.7
generally, 5.8
conduct, 5.11
constituency boundaries, 5.9
entitlement to be candidate and
member, 5.7
entitlement to vote, 5.6
introduction, 5.5
political parties, 5.12
system of voting, 5.8
tenure of members of parliament, 5.10
Emergency Bills
law-making procedures, and, 9.15
Employment
law-making competences, and, 6.16
Energy
law-making competences, and, 6.16
Enhanced devolution
Scottish Independence referendum,
and, 4.13
Ethical standards
public bodies, and, 8.17
EU Charter of Fundamental Rights
data protection, 13.23
generally, 13.8
introduction, 3.14
surveillance, 13.25
EU law
See also **European Union**
law-making competences, and, 6.20
EU membership
Scottish Independence referendum,
and, 4.16
**European Atomic Energy Community
(Euratom)**
generally, 3.3
**European Coal and Steel Community
(ECSC)**
generally, 3.3
European Communities Act 1972
law-making competences, and, 6.10
unwritten constitution of the UK, and,
1.22
European Union (EC)
generally, 3.3
European Union law
See also **European Union**
law-making competences, and, 6.20
**European Convention on Human
Rights**
See also **Human rights**
Administrative Tribunals, and, 14.5

**European Convention on Human
Rights** – *contd*
application and implementation, 2.1
citizenship, and, 13.2
generally, 13.7
incorporation, 13.9
parliamentary accountability, and, 10.1
public law, and
introduction, 14.15
legislative approach, 14.17
pre-incorporation approach, 14.16
significance of Strasbourg
jurisprudence, 14.18
rule of law, and, 2.8
European Council
European Union, and, 3.6
European Court of Justice (ECJ)
European Union, and, 3.10
**European Economic Community
(EEC)**
generally, 3.3
**European Governance (White Paper
2001, European Commission)**
application and implementation, 2.3
European Ombudsman
generally, 3.4
European Parliament
European Union, and, 3.9
European Union
Commission, 3.8
Committee of Permanent
Representatives, 3.7
Constitution Treaty (2004), 3.15
constitutional significance
Constitution Treaty (2004), 3.15
EU Charter of Fundamental Rights,
3.14
introduction, 3.11
Lisbon Treaty, 3.15
Ministerial accountability, 3.13
primacy of EU law, 3.12
treaties, 3.12
Council (of Ministers), 3.7
Court of First Instance, 3.10
Court of Justice, 3.10
EU Charter of Fundamental Rights,
3.14
European Council, 3.6
European Parliament, 3.9
institutions
Commission, 3.8
Council, 3.7
Court of Justice, 3.10
European Council, 3.6

European Union – *contd*
institutions – *contd*
European Parliament, 3.9
introduction, 3.5
introduction, 3.3
law-making competences, and, 6.25
Lisbon Treaty, 3.15
Ministerial accountability, 3.13
primacy of EU law, 3.12
relationship with Scotland, 3.15
relationship with UK, 3.4
treaties, 3.12
Executive
See **Scottish Government**
Expenditure
authorisation, 11.17
generally, 11.4
Explanatory notes
Scottish Government Bills, and,
9.10
Extradition
generally, 13.4
Finance
accounting and audit, 11.18
Audit Scotland, 11.18
Auditor General for Scotland,
11.18
block grant
allocation, 11.7
generally, 11.6
borrowing powers of Scottish
Government, 11.15
collection of tax, 11.14
Comptroller and Auditor General
generally, 11.18
introduction, 11.2
Consolidated Fund, 11.2
council tax, 11.6
expenditure
authorisation, 11.17
generally, 11.4
funding of Scottish Government
amount, 11.8
block grant, 11.6
council tax, 11.6
grant allocation, 11.7
introduction, 11.5
non-domestic rates, 11.6
intergovernmental relations, 11.16
introduction, 11.1
judicial control, 11.2
land transactions tax, 11.13
landfill tax, 11.13
local authorities, and, 8.5

Finance – *contd*
National Audit Office
generally, 11.18
introduction, 11.2
non-domestic rates, 11.6
parliamentary control, 11.2
procedures, 11.2
Public Accounts Committee, 11.18
Public Audit Committee, 11.18
rate of income tax, 11.10
'Scottish taxpayers', 11.12
taxing powers
borrowing powers of Scottish
Government, 11.15
'closest connection', 11.12
collection of tax, 11.14
generally, 11.9
intergovernmental relations, 11.16
introduction, 11.6
land transactions tax, 11.13
landfill tax, 11.13
resolution of Scottish Parliament,
11.11
Scottish rate of income tax, 11.10
'Scottish taxpayers', 11.12
taxation, 11.3
Financial and economic matters
law-making competences, and, 6.16
Financial memorandum
Scottish Government Bills, and,
9.10
First Minister
appointment, 7.15
functions, 7.16–7.17
First past the post (FPTP)
voting systems, and, 5.8
First reading
Westminster Bills, and, 9.4
Foreign affairs
law-making competences, and, 6.15
France
EU membership, and, 3.3
privacy rights, and, 13.24
public law adjudication, and, 14.1
role of head of state, and, 1.7
Scottish constitutional context, and,
3.1
Freedom of information
accountability of government, and,
10.1
generally, 13.22
Germany
EU membership, and, 3.3
federal constitutions, and, 1.21

Germany – *contd*
 public law adjudication, and, 14.1
 Scottish constitutional context, and,
  3.1
Gill Report (2009)
 judicial review, and, 14.12
 public inquiries, and, 12.19
Good governance
 accountability principle, 2.4
 introduction, 2.3
 separation of powers, 2.5
Government Bills (Scottish)
 accompanying documents, 9.10
 challenges to Bills pre-assent
  introduction, 9.17
  prohibition of submission for assent,
   9.19
  reference to the Supreme Court, 9.18
 consideration of details, 9.12
 consideration of principles, 9.1
 consolidation Bills, 9.16
 emergency Bills, 9.15
 final consideration, 9.13
 general, 9.9
 introduction of, 9.10
 Procedural Committee reviews, 9.20
 prohibition of submission for assent,
  and, 9.19
 reference to the Supreme Court, and,
  9.18
 royal assent, 9.17
 special forms, 9.14–9.16
 SPPA Committee reviews, 9.20
 Stage 1, 9.11
 Stage 2, 9.12
 Stage 3, 9.13
Government Bills (Westminster)
 distribution of business, 9.7
 committee stage, 9.6
 first reading, 9.4
 general, 9.2
 House of Lords, and, 9.7
 modernisation of procedures, 9.8
 procedure, 9.3
 second reading, 9.5
Government of Wales Act 2006
 devolution, and, 3.19
 European Communities Act 1972, and,
  6.10
 public law adjudication, and
  introduction, 14.1
  reserved matters challenges, 14.25
 unwritten constitution of the UK, and,
  1.22

Government statement of competence
 Scottish Government Bills, and,
  9.10
Head of state
 structure of written constitution, and,
  1.7
Health and medicines
 law-making competences, and, 6.16
High Court of Justiciary
 court system, and, 12.2
Home affairs
 law-making competences, and, 6.16
House of Commons
 accessibility, 5.23
 administration, 5.22
 committees
  generally, 5.17
  introduction, 5.16
 composition, 5.2–5.4
 elected chamber
  composition, 5.2–5.4
  members, 5.3
  Parliamentary sessions, 5.4
  structure, 5.2–5.4
 elections
  candidates, 5.8
  conduct, 5.11
  constituency boundaries, 5.9
  entitlement to be candidate and
   member, 5.7
  entitlement to vote, 5.6
  introduction, 5.5
  political parties, 5.12
  system of voting, 5.8
  tenure of members of parliament,
   5.10
 introduction, 5.1
 law-making competences, and
  European Communities Act 1972,
   6.10
  introduction, 6.3
  post-1 January 1973, 6.7–6.
  pre-1 January 1973, 6.4–6.6
  supremacy of EU law, 6.8–6.9
 management, 5.22
 members of Parliament (MPs)
  allowances, 5.20
  general, 5.19
  pay, 5.20
  privileges, 5.21
  standards, 5.21
 openness, 5.23
 sessions, 5.4
 structure, 5.2–5.4

Index

House of Lords
bicameralism in Scotland, and, 5.15
introduction, 5.13
law-making processes, and, 9.7
reform, 5.14
Scottish court system, and, 12.2
Human rights
adjudication
introduction, 14.15
legislative approach, 14.17
pre-incorporation approach, 14.16
significance of Strasbourg
jurisprudence, 14.18
Administrative Tribunals, and, 14.5
challenges to Acts of Scottish
Parliament
AXA General Insurance Ltd, 14.26
between 2000 and 2008, 14.24
Salvesen v Riddell, 14.27
Charter of Fundamental Rights of the
EU, 13.8
Commission for Equality and Human
Rights, 13.14
Commissioner for Children and Young
Persons, 13.14
Convention rights, 13.11
detention and arrest, 13.18
European Convention
Administrative Tribunals, and, 14.5
application and implementation,
2.1
citizenship, and, 13.2
generally, 13.7
incorporation, 13.9
parliamentary accountability, and,
10.1
rule of law, and, 2.8
future reforms, 13.15–13.17
Human Rights Act 1998, 13.10–13.13
introduction, 13.6
judicial review
access to the courts, 14.11
constitutional significance, 14.13
grounds, 14.9
locus standi, 14.10
maintenance of public order, 13.19
parliamentary accountability, and, 10.1
public authorities, 13.12
public law adjudication, and
adjudication, 14.15–14.18
common law, 14.2
rule of law, and, 2.8
Scottish Commission for Human
Rights, 13.14

Human Rights Act 1998
Convention rights, 13.11
introduction, 13.10
public authorities, 13.12
territorial extent, 13.1
unwritten constitution of the UK, and,
1.22
Illegality
judicial review, and, 14.9
Immigration control
generally, 13.3
Immunity from suit
judiciary, and, 12.9
UK government, and, 7.2
Impartiality of judges
bias, 12.12–12.15
conclusions, 12.20
generally, 12.3
introduction, 12.11
politics, and, 12.16–12.19
Incapacity
judiciary, and, 12.7
Income tax
taxing powers of Scottish Parliament,
and, 11.10
India
preamble to constitution, and, 2.1
Independence of judges
appointments, 12.5
conclusions, 12.20
generally, 12.4
immunity from suit, 12.9
importance, 12.3
politics, and, 12.16–12.19
public criticism, 12.10
safeguards and protection, 12.6–12.8
salaries, 12.8
security of tenure, 12.7
Independence referendum
Barnett Formula, and, 4.13, 4.21
campaigning
generally, 4.7
issues, 4.12–4.
participants, 4.8
publications, 4.8–4.11
constitutional design, 4.14
currency, 4.17
double-devolution, 4.15
Edinburgh Agreement, 4.4
enhanced devolution, 4.13
EU membership, 4.16
introduction, 4.1
issues
constitutional design, 4.14

Independence referendum – *contd*
  issues – *contd*
    currency, 4.17
    double-devolution, 4.15
    enhanced devolution, 4.13
    EU membership, 4.16
    introduction, 4.12
    local authorities, 4.15
    overview, 4.18
    Scottish Islands, 4.15
  legal authority, 4.3
  legislative basis, 4.5–4.6
  local authorities, 4.15
  participants, 4.8
  political context, 4.2
  publications, 4.8–4.11
  result, 4.19–4.21
  Scottish Islands, 4.15
  Sewel Convention, and, 4.21
  Smith Commission, and, 4.20–4.21
  'the Vow', 4.19–4.20
  'West Lothian Question', and, 4.20
India
  preamble to constitution, and, 2.1
Individual liberty
  constitutional law, and, 2.2
Information law
  data protection, 13.23
  data retention, 13.25
  freedom of information, 13.22
  introduction, 13.20
  official secrets, 13.21
  privacy rights, 13.24
  regulation of investigatory powers,
    13.25
  surveillance, 13.25
Interception of communications
  generally, 13.25
Intergovernmental relations
  generally, 7.26
  taxing powers of Scottish Parliament,
    and, 11.16
Intermediate government
  See also **Local authorities**
  accountability, 8.16
  appointments, 8.15
  bodies with mixed responsibilities,
    8.12
  bodies with responsibilities entirely
    connected with reserved matters,
    8.10
  bodies with responsibilities within
    competence of Scottish
    Parliament, 8.11

Intermediate government – *contd*
  control, 8.16
  cross-border public authorities, 8.9
  devolution, and, 8.9
  ethical standards, 8.17
  generally, 8.8
  introduction, 8.1
  need, 8.14
  reform proposals, 8.13
Intervention
  deportation, removal and extradition,
    and, 13.4
  European Parliament, and, 3.9
  foreign affairs, and, 6.15
  judicial control of administrative
    action, and, 14.3
  judicial review, and
    access to the court, 14.11
    standing, 14.10
  maintenance of public order, and,
    13.19
  rule of law, and
    introduction, 2.6
    legality, 2.7
  Scottish Government Bills, and,
    9.19
  sources of executive authority, and,
    7.19
  surveillance e and data retention, and,
    13.25
Irrationality
  judicial review, and, 14.9
**Judicial Committee of the Privy
  Council**
  public law adjudication, and, 14.1
Judicial impartiality
  bias, 12.12–12.15
  conclusions, 12.20
  generally, 12.3
  introduction, 12.11
  politics, and, 12.16–12.19
Judicial incapacity
  generally, 12.7
Judicial independence
  appointments, 12.5
  conclusions, 12.20
  generally, 12.4
  immunity from suit, 12.9
  importance, 12.3
  politics, and, 12.16–12.19
  public criticism, 12.10
  safeguards and protection, 12.6–12.8
  salaries, 12.8
  security of tenure, 12.7

Judicial inquiries
court system, and, 12.19
Judicial review
access to the courts, 14.11
constitutional significance, 14.13
delegated legislation, of, 14.14
generally, 14.7
Gill review of civil justice, and, 14.12
grounds, 14.9
illegality, 14.9
interest to sue, 14.10
irrationality, 14.9
locus standi, 14.10
procedural impropriety, 14.9
scope, 14.8
title to sue, 14.10
Judiciary
Administrative Tribunals, and, 12.2
bias
automatic disqualification, 12.13
generally, 12.12
other grounds for disqualification, 12.14
overview, 12.15
Court of Session, 12.2
functions, 12.2
High Court of Justiciary, 12.2
House of Lords, 12.2
immunity from suit of judges, 12.9
introduction, 12.1
judicial appointments, 12.5
judicial conduct, 12.7
judicial impartiality
bias, 12.12–12.15
conclusions, 12.20
generally, 12.3
introduction, 12.11
politics, and, 12.16–12.19
judicial incapacity, 12.7
judicial independence
appointments, 12.5
conclusions, 12.20
generally, 12.4
immunity from suit, 12.9
importance, 12.3
politics, and, 12.16–12.19
public criticism, 12.10
safeguards and protection, 12.6–12.8
salaries, 12.8
security of tenure, 12.7
judicial inquiries, 12.19
judicial salaries, 12.8
judicial system, 12.2

Judiciary – *contd*
justice of the peace courts, 12.2
liability of judges, 12.9
politics, and, 12.16–12.19
public criticism of judges, 12.10
security of tenure of judges, 12.7
sheriff courts, 12.2
structure of written constitution, and, 1.10
Supreme Court, 12.2
temporary sheriffs, 12.7
Junior Scottish ministers
Scottish Government, and, 7.17
Justice
rule of law, and, 2.8
Justice of the peace courts
court system, and, 12.2
Land transactions tax
taxing powers of Scottish Parliament, and, 11.13
Landfill tax
taxing powers of Scottish Parliament, and, 11.13
Law-making competences
European Communities Act 1972, 6.10
European Union, 6.25
external influences, 6.1
internal constraints, 6.1
introduction, 6.1
political parties, and, 6.1
post-1 January 1973
European Communities Act 1972, 6.10
generally, 6.7
supremacy of EU law, 6.8–6.9
pre-1 January 1973
generally, 6.4
legislative supremacy of UK Parliament, 6.5
Treaty of Union, 6.6
Scottish Parliament, and
devolved matters legislation, 6.22
generally, 6.11
limitations, 6.13–6.21
outline, 6.12
reserved matters, 6.14–6.18
Sewel convention, 6.22
subordinate legislation, 6.23–6.24
sources of law, and, 6.2
supremacy of EU law
EU perspective, 6.8
UK perspective, 6.9
Treaty of Union, and, 6.6

Law-making competences – *contd*
  Westminster Parliament, and
    European Communities Act 1972,
      6.10
    introduction, 6.3
    post-1 January 1973, 6.7–6.10
    pre-1 January 1973, 6.4–6.6
    supremacy of EU law, 6.8–6.9
Law-making competences of the
  Scottish Parliament
  amendment of the Scotland Act, and,
    6.19
  Constitution, and, 6.15
  Convention rights, and, 6.20
  defence, and, 6.15
  devolved matters legislation, 6.22
  employment, and, 6.16
  energy, and, 6.16
  EU law, and, 6.20
  European Communities Act 1972,
    6.10
  European Union, 6.25
  external influences, 6.1
  financial and economic matters, and,
    6.16
  foreign affairs, and, 6.15
  generally, 6.11
  health and medicines, and, 6.16
  home affairs, and, 6.16
  internal constraints, 6.1
  introduction, 6.1
  legislative consent motions, 6.22
  limitations
    amendment of the Scotland Act,
      6.19
    Convention rights, 6.20
    EU law, 6.20
    Lord Advocate's position, 6.21
    reserved matters, 6.14–6.18
    territory, 6.13
  Lord Advocate's position, 6.21
  media and culture, and, 6.16
  outline, 6.12
  political parties, and, 6.15
  powers of Westminster Parliament,
    and
    European Communities Act 1972,
      6.10
    introduction, 6.3
    post-1 January 1973, 6.7–6.
    pre-1 January 1973, 6.4–6.6
    supremacy of EU law, 6.8–6.9
  professional regulation, and, 6.16
  public service, 6.15

Law-making competences of the
  Scottish Parliament – *contd*
  reserved matters
    flexibility of Heads, 6.17
    general reservations, 6.15
    interpretation issues, 6.18
    introduction, 6.14
    specific reservations, 6.16
  Sewel convention, 6.22
  social security, and, 6.16
  sources of law, and, 6.2
  subordinate legislation
    general considerations, 6.23
    types of power in Scotland, 6.24
  supremacy of EU law, 6.8–6.9
  territory, and, 6.13
  trade and industry, and, 6.16
  transport, and, 6.16
  treason, and, 6.15
Law-making procedures
  introduction, 9.1
  Scottish Government, and
    And see **Law-making procedures**
      (Scotland)
    consolidation Bills, 9.16
    delegated legislation, 9.29–9.35
    emergency Bills, 9.15
    introduction, 9.1
    members' bills, 9.23
    post-legislative scrutiny, 9.28
    private legislation, 9.27
    public Bills, 9.9–9.20
    standing orders, and, 9.9
  Westminster government, and
    And see **Law-making procedures**
      (Westminster)
    introduction, 9.1
    private members' bills, 9.22
    private legislation, 9.26
    public Bills, 9.2–9.8
Law-making procedures (Scotland)
  committee Bills, 9.24
  consolidation Bills, 9.16
  delegated legislation
    control of exercise of powers,
      9.31
    control of legislation conferring
      powers, 9.30
    Interpretation and Legislative
      Reform (Scotland) Act 2010,
      and, 9.32
    introduction, 9.29
    merits scrutiny, 9.34
    Scotland Act 1998, under, 9.35

Law-making procedures (Scotland) – *contd*
delegated legislation – *contd*
Statutory Instruments Act 1946, and, 9.32
technical scrutiny, 9.33
emergency Bills, 9.15
introduction, 9.1
members' bills, 9.23
post-legislative scrutiny, 9.28
private legislation
generally, 9.27
introduction, 9.25
public Bills
accompanying documents, 9.10
challenges to Bills pre-assent, 9.17–9.19
consideration of details, 9.12
consideration of principles, 9.1
consolidation Bills, 9.16
emergency Bills, 9.15
final consideration, 9.13
general, 9.9
introduction of, 9.10
Procedural Committee revie s, 9.20
prohibition of submission for assent, and, 9.19
reference to the Supreme Court, and, 9.18
royal assent, 9.17
special forms, 9.14–9.16
SPPA Committee reviews, 9.20
Stage 1, 9.11
Stage 2, 9.12
Stage 3, 9.13
standing orders, and, 9.9
Law-making procedures (Westminster)
introduction, 9.1
private legislation, 9.26
private members' bills, 9.22
public Bills
distribution of business, 9.7
committee stage, 9.6
first reading, 9.4
general, 9.2
House of Lords, and, 9.7
modernisation of procedures, 9.8
procedure, 9.3
second reading, 9.5
Law Officers
Scottish Government, and
generally, 7.20
legal advice, 7.21
retained functions, 7.22

Law Officers – *contd*
structure of written constitution, and, 1.8
UK government, and, 7.8
Legality principle
rule of law, and, 2.7
Legislative consent motions
law-making competences, and, 6.22
Legislature
structure of written constitution, and, 1.9
Liability of judges
generally, 12.9
Liberty of individuals
constitutional law, and, 2.2
Lisbon Treaty
European Union, and, 3.15
Local authorities
background, 8.2
central government relations, 8.6
devolution, and, 8.7
ethical standards, 8.17
finance and funding, 8.5
internal structure, 8.4
introduction, 8.2
judicial review, and, 14.14
organisation, 8.4
overview, 8.1
powers, 8.3
reorganisation, 8.2
reserved matters, and, 8.7
Scottish Independence referendum, and, 4.15
status, 8.1
statutory appeals, and, 14.6
structure, 8.4
written constitution, and, 1.11
Lord Advocate
generally, 7.20
law-making competences, and, 6.21
legal advice, 7.21
retained functions, 7.22
Magna Carta 1215
unwritten constitution of the UK, and, 1.22
Maintenance of public order
generally, 13.19
Media and culture
law-making competences, and, 6.16
Members' bills
Scottish Parliament, in, 9.23
Westminster, at, 9.22
Members' business
accountability of government, and, 10.7

Members of Parliament (MPs)
allowances, 5.20
disqualified persons, 5.6
elections, and
  candidates, 5.8
  conduct, 5.11
  constituency boundaries, 5.9
  entitlement to be candidate and
    member, 5.7
  entitlement to vote, 5.6
  introduction, 5.5
  political parties, 5.12
  system of voting, 5.8
  tenure of members, 5.10
filling vacancies, 5.10
general, 5.19
introduction, 5.3
pay, 5.20
privileges, 5.21
standards, 5.21
tenure, 5.10
**Members of the Scottish Parliament
(MSPs)**
allowances, 5.20
general, 5.19
introduction, 5.3
pay, 5.20
privileges, 5.21
standards, 5.21
Ministerial accountability
European Union, and, 3.13
Ministerial conduct
UK government, and, 7.9
Ministerial responsibility
introduction, 10.2
mechanisms for holding ministers to
  account, 10.3–10.14
Ministers
Scottish Government, and, 7.16
UK government, and
  appointment, 7.3
  collective responsibility, 7.11
  conduct, 7.9
  generally, 7.7
National Audit Office (UK)
generally, 11.18
introduction, 11.2
Nationality
structure of written constitution, and,
  1.6
No confidence motions
accountability of government, and, 10.7
Non-domestic rates
public finance, and, 11.6

Northern Ireland Act 1998
unwritten constitution of the UK, and,
  1.22
Official secrets
generally, 13.21
Ombudsmen
effect of decisions in courts, 10.14
funding, and, 11.4
introduction, 10.11
parliamentary accountability, and, 10.1
Scotland, in, 10.13
standards of good governance, and
  accountability, 2.4
  introduction, 2.3
  separation of powers, 2.5
Westminster, at, 10.12
Opposition debates
accountability of government, and,
  10.7
Parliament
structure of written constitution, and,
  1.9
Parliament Acts 1911 and 1949
House of Lords, and, 5.13
legislative supremacy, and, 6.5
parliamentary sessions, and, 5.4
passing Westminster Bills, and, 9.7
unwritten constitution of the UK, and,
  1.22
Parliamentary accountability
committees
  introduction, 10.8
  Scotland, in, 10.10
  Westminster, at, 10.9
Crichel Down rules, 10.2
freedom of information, and, 10.1
introduction, 10.1
members' business debates, 10.7
ministerial responsibility
  introduction, 10.2
  mechanisms for holding ministers to
    account, 10.3–10.14
no confidence motions, 10.7
opposition debates, 10.7
Parliamentary Commissioner for
  Administration
  effect of decisions in courts, 10.14
  generally, 10.12
  introduction, 10.11
parliamentary mechanisms
  committees, 10.8–10.10
  introduction, 10.3
  ombudsmen, 10.11
  opposition debates, 10.7

Parliamentary accountability – *contd*
  parliamentary mechanisms – *contd*
    parliamentary questions, 10.4–10.6
    select and subject committees,
      10.8–10.10
  parliamentary ombudsmen
    effect of decisions in courts, 10.14
    introduction, 10.11
    Scotland, in, 10.13
    Westminster, at, 10.12
  parliamentary questions
    introduction, 10.4
    Scotland, in, 10.6
    Westminster, at, 10.5
  public petitions, 10.15
  Scottish Ministerial Code, 10.2
  Scottish Public Services Ombudsman
    effect of decisions in courts,
      10.14
    generally, 10.13
    introduction, 10.11
  select committees, 10.9
  subject committees, 10.10
  UK Parliamentary Commissioner for
      Administration
    effect of decisions in courts,
      10.14
    generally, 10.12
    introduction, 10.11
**Parliamentary Commissioner for
    Administration**
  effect of decisions in courts, 10.14
  generally, 10.12
  introduction, 10.11
Parliamentary committees
  Holyrood, 5.18
  introduction, 5.16
  Westminster, 5.17
Parliamentary Liaison Officers
  Scottish Government, and, 7.17
Parliamentary ombudsmen
  effect of decisions in courts, 10.14
  introduction, 10.11
  Scotland, in, 10.13
  Westminster, at, 10.12
Parliamentary questions
  introduction, 10.4
  Scotland, in, 10.6
  Westminster, at, 10.5
Parliamentary Under-Secretaries
  UK government, and, 7.3
Parliaments
  accessibility, 5.23
  administration, 5.22

Parliaments – *contd*
  committees
    generally, 5.17
    introduction, 5.16
  composition, 5.2–5.4
  elected chamber
    composition, 5.2–5.4
    generally, 5.3
    Parliamentary sessions, 5.4
    structure, 5.2–5.4
  elections
    candidates, 5.8
    conduct, 5.11
    constituency boundaries, 5.9
    entitlement to be candidate and
      member, 5.7
    entitlement to vote, 5.6
    introduction, 5.5
    political parties, 5.12
    system of voting, 5.8
    tenure of members of parliament,
      5.10
  House of Lords
    bicameralism, 5.15
    introduction, 5.13
    reform, 5.14
  introduction, 5.1
  management, 5.22
  members of Parliament (MPs and
      MSPs)
    allowances, 5.20
    general, 5.19
    pay, 5.20
    privileges, 5.21
    standards, 5.21
  openness, 5.23
  sessions, 5.4
  structure, 5.2–5.4
Police powers
  detention and arrest, 13.18
Policy memorandum
  Scottish Government Bills, and, 9.10
Political parties
  generally, 5.12
  law-making competences, and, 6.15
Preamble
  structure of written constitution, and,
    1.3
**Presiding officer's statement of
    compliance**
  Scottish Government Bills, and, 9.10
Primacy of EU law
  European Union, and, 3.12
  law-making competences, and, 6.8–6.9

Prime Minister
appointment, 7.5
cabinet government, and, 7.12
conduct, 7.9
functions, 7.6
generally, 7.4
Principles of Good Administration (UK)
application and implementation, 2.3
Privacy rights
generally, 13.24
Private law
function of constitutions, and, 1.15
Private members' bills
generally, 9.22
Procedural impropriety
judicial review, and, 14.9
Professional regulation
law-making competences, and, 6.16
Prohibition of submission of Bill
Scottish Government Bills, and, 9.19
Public Accounts Committee (UK)
public finance, and, 11.18
Public Bills
Scottish Government
accompanying documents, 9.10
challenges to Bills pre-assent,
9.17–9.19
consideration of details, 9.12
consideration of principles, 9.1
consolidation Bills, 9.16
emergency Bills, 9.15
final consideration, 9.13
general, 9.9
introduction of, 9.10
Procedures Committee reviews, 9.20
prohibition of submission for assent,
and, 9.19
reference to the Supreme Court,
and, 9.18
royal assent, 9.17
special forms, 9.14–9.16
SPPA Committee reviews, 9.20
Stage 1, 9.11
Stage 2, 9.12
Stage 3, 9.13
Westminster
distribution of business, 9.7
committee stage, 9.6
first reading, 9.4
general, 9.2
House of Lords, and, 9.7
modernisation of procedures, 9.8
procedure, 9.3
second reading, 9.5

Public bodies
See also **Local authorities**
accountability, 8.16
appointments, 8.15
control, 8.16
cross-border public authorities
generally, 8.12
introduction, 8.9
devolution, and, 8.9
ethical standards, 8.17
generally, 8.8
introduction, 8.1
mixed responsibilities, with, 8.12
need, 8.14
reform proposals, 8.13
responsibilities entirely connected
with reserved matters, with,
8.10
responsibilities within competence
of Scottish Parliament, with,
8.11
judicial review, and, 14.14
statutory appeals, and, 14.6
Public finance
accounting and audit, 11.18
Audit Scotland, 11.18
Auditor General for Scotland, 11.18
block grant
allocation, 11.7
generally, 11.6
borrowing powers of Scottish
Government, 11.15
collection of tax, 11.14
Comptroller and Auditor General
generally, 11.18
introduction, 11.2
Consolidated fund, 11.2
council tax, 11.6
expenditure
authorisation, 11.17
generally, 11.4
funding of Scottish Government
amount, 11.8
block grant, 11.6
council tax, 11.6
grant allocation, 11.7
introduction, 11.5
non-domestic rates, 11.6
intergovernmental relations, 11.16
introduction, 11.1
judicial control, 11.2
land transactions tax, 11.13
landfill tax, 11.13
local authorities, and, 8.5

Public finance – *contd*
National Audit Office
generally, 11.18
introduction, 11.2
non-domestic rates, 11.6
parliamentary control, 11.2
procedures, 11.2
Public Accounts Committee, 11.18
Public Audit Committee, 11.18
rate of income tax, 11.10
'Scottish taxpayers', 11.12
taxing powers
borrowing powers of Scottish
Government, 11.15
'closest connection', 11.12
collection of tax, 11.14
generally, 11.9
intergovernmental relations, 11.16
introduction, 11.6
land transactions tax, 11.13
landfill tax, 11.13
resolution of Scottish Parliament,
11.11
Scottish rate of income tax, 11.10
'Scottish taxpayers', 11.12
taxation, 11.3
Public Audit Committee
public finance, and, 11.18
Public law adjudication
common law, 14.2
compatibility issues
definition, 14.20
determination, 14.21
generally, 14.19
devolution issues
challenges to Acts of Scottish
Government, 14.29
challenges to Acts of Scottish
Parliament, 14.23–14.27
definition, 14.20
determination, 14.21
effect of successful challenge,
14.31
generally, 14.19
human rights protection, 14.30
interpretation, 14.22
function of constitutions, and, 1.15
human rights
introduction, 14.15
legislative approach, 14.17
pre-incorporation approach, 14.16
significance of Strasbourg
jurisprudence, 14.18
introduction, 14.1

Public law adjudication – *contd*
Judicial Committee of the Privy
Council, 14.1
judicial control of administrative
action
introduction, 14.3
judicial review, 14.7–14.14
statutory appeals, 14.4–14.6
judicial review
access to the courts, 14.11
constitutional significance, 14.13
delegated legislation, of, 14.14
generally, 14.7
Gill review of civil justice, and,
14.12
grounds, 14.9
illegality, 14.9
interest to sue, 14.10
irrationality, 14.9
locus standi, 14.10
procedural impropriety, 14.9
scope, 14.8
title to sue, 14.10
statutory appeals
Administrative Tribunals, 14.5
introduction, 14.4
Leggatt Review, 14.5
local authorities, 14.6
public bodies, 14.6
Supreme Court, and, 14.32
Tribunals Service, 14.5
Public petitions
accountability of government, and,
10.15
Public service
law-making competences, and, 6.15
Quangos
accountability, 8.16
appointments, 8.15
bodies with mixed responsibilities, 8.12
bodies with responsibilities entirely
connected with reserved matters,
8.10
bodies with responsibilities within
competence of Scottish
Parliament, 8.11
control, 8.16
cross-border public authorities, 8.9
devolution, and, 8.9
ethical standards, 8.17
generally, 8.8
introduction, 8.1
need, 8.14
reform proposals, 8.13

Queen, the
Scottish Government, and, 7.13
Westminster government, and, 7.2
Questions in Parliament
introduction, 10.4
Scotland, in, 10.6
Westminster, at, 10.5
References to Supreme Court
Government Bills, and, 9.18
private Bills, and, 9.27
Regulation of investigatory powers
generally, 13.25
Report stage
Westminster Bills, and, 9.6
Reserved matters
flexibility of Heads, 6.17
general reservations, 6.15
interpretation issues, 6.18
introduction, 6.14
local authorities, and, 8.7
public bodies, with, 8.10
specific reservations, 6.16
Resolution of Scottish Parliament
taxing powers of Scottish Parliament,
and, 11.11
Right of abode
generally, 13.2
Right to a fair trial
rule of law, and, 2.8
Rights and freedoms
structure of written constitution, and,
1.5
Royal Assent
Scottish Government Bills, and,
9.17
Westminster Bills, and, 9.7
Rule of law
accountability, 2.4
Administrative Tribunals, and, 14.5
challenges to the Acts of the Scottish
Parliament, and, 14.26
judiciary, and, 12.1
introduction, 2.6
justice, and, 2.8
legality principle, 2.7
police powers, and, 13.18
protection of individual liberty, 2.2
public law adjudication, and, 14.2
questions to the Scottish Government,
and, 10.6
statutory instruments, and, 9.32
subordinate legislation, and, 6.23
Scotland Acts 1998 and 2012
amendment, 6.19

Scotland Acts 1998 and 2012 – *contd*
background
'home rule' movement, 3.17
introduction, 3.16
Scotland Act 1978, 3.18
Scottish Constitutional Convention,
3.19
compatibility issues, and, 14.19
constitutional context, 3.1
Convention rights, 6.20
devolution issues, and, 14.19
EU law, 6.20
further evolution of the Constitution,
3.20
Government Bills, and, 9.2
introduction, 1.20
judicial appointments, and, 12.5
local government, and, 9.1
position of Lord Advocate, 6.21
public bodies, and, 8.10
public finance, and, 11.1
public law adjudication, and, 14.1
reserved matters
devolved matters, 6.17
general reservations, 6.15
introduction, 6.14
problems of interpretation, 6.18
specific reservations, 6.16
role of Queen, and, 7.2
Scottish Constitutional Convention,
3.19
sources of law, and, 6.2
taxing powers of Scottish Parliament,
and, 11.9
unwritten constitution of the UK, and,
1.22
West Lothian question, and, 5.9
Scottish Law Commission Bills
Scottish Government Bills, and, 9.16
**Scottish Public Services Ombudsmen
(SPSO)**
effect of decisions in courts, 10.14
funding, and, 11.4
generally, 10.13
intermediate government, and
accountability of quangos, 8.16
generally, 8.8
introduction, 10.11
Parliamentary committees, and, 5.18
role of Queen, and, 7.2
separation of powers, and, 2.5
**Scotland's Parliament (White Paper,
1997)**
funding by Westminster, and, 11.5

Scotland's Parliament (White Paper, 1997) – *contd*
generally, 3.19
local authorities, and
bodies with responsibilities within competence of Scottish Parliament, 8.11
effect of devolution, 8.7
parliamentary accountability, and, 10.1
parliamentary committees, and, 5.18
public bodies, and
appointments, 8.15
responsibilities within competence of Scottish Parliament, 8.11
relations between St Andrew's House and Whitehall, and, 7.26
reserved matters, and, 6.14
Scotland's Parliament: Scotland's Right (Scottish Constitutional Convention, 1995)
generally, 3.19
Scottish Administration
Scottish Government, and, 7.25
Scottish Commission for Human Rights
generally, 13.14
Scottish Consolidated Fund
accounting and audit, 11.18
expenditure, 11.17
generally, 11.5
judicial salaries, and, 12.10
Scottish Government Bills, and, 9.12
Scottish Constitutional Convention
generally, 3.19
Scottish Government
accountability
And see **Accountability of government**
introduction, 10.1
ministerial responsibility, 10.2
no confidence debates, 10.7
ombudsmen, 10.11–10.14
opposition debates, 10.7
parliamentary mechanisms, 10.3
parliamentary questions, 10.4–10.6
public petitions, 10.15
select and subject committees, 10.8–10.10
administrative departments, 7.25
cabinet government, 7.18
Cabinet secretaries, 7.17
civil service, and, 7.23
collective responsibility, 7.18
Crown's role, 7.13

Scottish Government – *contd*
departments, 7.25
First Minister
appointment, 7.15
functions, 7.16–7.17
formation of government, 7.16
introduction, 7.14
junior Scottish ministers, 7.17
law-making procedures, and
And see **Law-making procedures (Scotland)**
consolidation Bills, 9.16
delegated legislation, 9.29–9.35
emergency Bills, 9.15
introduction, 9.1
members' bills, 9.23
post-legislative scrutiny, 9.28
private legislation, 9.27
public Bills, 9.9–9.20
Scottish Law Commission Bills, 9.16
standing orders, and, 9.9
Lord Advocate, 7.20
Ministers, 7.16
Parliamentary Liaison Officers, 7.17
public Bills, and
accompanying documents, 9.10
challenges to Bills pre-assent, 9.17–9.19
consideration of details, 9.12
consideration of principles, 9.1
consolidation Bills, 9.16
emergency Bills, 9.15
final consideration, 9.13
general, 9.9
introduction of, 9.10
Procedural Committees, 9.20
prohibition of submission for assent, and, 9.19
reference to the Supreme Court, and, 9.18
royal assent, 9.17
Scottish Law Commission Bills, 9.16
special forms, 9.14–9.16
SPPA Committee reviews, 9.20
Stage 1, 9.11
Stage 2, 9.12
Stage 3, 9.13
standing orders, 9.9
relations with Whitehall, 7.26
Scottish Administration, 7.25

Scottish Government – *contd.*
  Scottish Law Officers
    generally, 7.20
    legal advice, 7.21
    retained functions, 7.22
  Solicitor-General for Scotland, 7.20
  sources of authority, 7.19
  special advisers, and, 7.23
  the Queen, and, 7.13
  UK government departments, and,
    7.24
Scottish Government Bills
  accompanying documents, 9.10
  challenges to Bills pre-assent
    introduction, 9.17
    prohibition of submission for assent,
      9.19
    reference to the Supreme Court,
      9.18
  consideration of details, 9.12
  consideration of principles, 9.1
  consolidation Bills, 9.16
  emergency Bills, 9.15
  final consideration, 9.13
  general, 9.9
  introduction of, 9.10
  prohibition of submission for assent,
    and, 9.19
  reference to the Supreme Court, and,
    9.18
  royal assent, 9.17
  special forms, 9.14–9.16
  SPPA Committee reviews, 9.20
  Stage 1, 9.11
  Stage 2, 9.12
  Stage 3, 9.13
Scottish Independence referendum
  Barnett Formula, and, 4.13, 4.21
  campaigning
    generally, 4.7
    issues, 4.12–4.
    participants, 4.8
    publications, 4.8–4.11
  constitutional design, 4.14
  currency, 4.17
  double-devolution, 4.15
  Edinburgh Agreement, 4.4
  enhanced devolution, 4.13
  EU membership, 4.16
  introduction, 4.1
  issues
    constitutional design, 4.14
    currency, 4.17
    double-devolution, 4.15

Scottish Independence referendum –
  contd
  issues – *contd*
    enhanced devolution, 4.13
    EU membership, 4.16
    introduction, 4.12
    local authorities, 4.15
    overview, 4.18
    Scottish Islands, 4.15
  legal authority, 4.3
  legislative basis, 4.5–4.6
  local authorities, 4.15
  participants, 4.8
  political context, 4.2
  publications, 4.8–4.11
  result, 4.19–4.21
  Scottish Islands, 4.15
  Sewel Convention, and, 4.21
  Smith Commission, and, 4.20–4.21
  'the Vow', 4.19–4.20
  'West Lothian Question', and,
    4.20
Scottish Islands
  Scottish Independence referendum,
    and, 4.15
Scottish Law Commission Bills
  law making procedures, and, 9.16
Scottish Law Officers
  generally, 7.20
  legal advice, 7.21
  retained functions, 7.22
Scottish Ministerial Code
  accountability of government, and,
    10.2
Scottish Parliament
  accessibility, 5.23
  accountability
    And see **Accountability of**
      government
    introduction, 10.1
    ministerial responsibility, 10.2
    no confidence debates, 10.7
    ombudsmen, 10.11–10.14
    opposition debates, 10.7
    parliamentary mechanisms, 10.3
    parliamentary questions, 10.4–10.6
    public petitions, 10.15
    select and subject committees,
      10.8–10.10
  administration, 5.22
  bicameralism, and, 5.15
  committees
    generally, 5.18
    introduction, 5.16

Scottish Parliament – *contd*
composition, 5.2–5.4
elected chamber
composition, 5.2–5.4
members, 5.3
Parliamentary sessions, 5.4
structure, 5.2–5.4
elections
candidates, 5.8
conduct, 5.11
constituency boundaries, 5.9
entitlement to be candidate and
member, 5.7
entitlement to vote, 5.6
introduction, 5.5
political parties, 5.12
system of voting, 5.8
tenure of members of parliament,
5.10
introduction, 5.1
law-making competences
And see **Law-making competences**
devolved matters legislation, 6.22
European Union, and, 6.25
generally, 6.11
introduction, 6.1
limitations, 6.13–6.21
outline, 6.12
reserved matters, 6.14–6.18
Sewel convention, 6.22
sources of law, 6.2
subordinate legislation, 6.23–6.24
Westminster Parliament, and,
6.3–6.10
law-making procedures, and
And see **Law-making procedures
(Scotland)**
consolidation Bills, 9.16
delegated legislation, 9.29–9.35
emergency Bills, 9.15
introduction, 9.1
members' bills, 9.23
post-legislative scrutiny, 9.28
private legislation, 9.27
public Bills, 9.9–9.20
Scottish Law Commission Bills,
9.16
standing orders, and, 9.9
management, 5.22
members of the Scottish Parliament
(MSPs)
allowances, 5.20
general, 5.19
pay, 5.20

Scottish Parliament – *contd*
members of the Scottish Parliament
(MSPs) – *contd*
privileges, 5.21
standards, 5.21
tenure, 5.10
openness, 5.23
public Bills, and
accompanying documents, 9.10
challenges to Bills pre-assent,
9.17–9.19
consideration of details, 9.12
consideration of principles, 9.1
consolidation Bills, 9.16
emergency Bills, 9.15
final consideration, 9.13
general, 9.9
introduction of, 9.10
Procedural Committee reviews, 9.20
prohibition of submission for assent,
and, 9.19
reference to the Supreme Court,
and, 9.18
royal assent, 9.17
Scottish Law Commission Bills,
9.16
special forms, 9.14–9.16
SPPA Committee reviews, 9.20
Stage 1, 9.11
Stage 2, 9.12
Stage 3, 9.13
standing orders, 9.9
sessions, 5.4
structure, 5.2–5.4
Scottish Public Services Ombudsman
effect of decisions in courts, 10.14
generally, 10.13
introduction, 10.11
Scottish taxpayers
taxing powers of Scottish Parliament,
and, 11.12
Scottish Tribunals
public law adjudication, and, 14.5
Secondary legislation
control of exercise of powers, 9.31
control of legislation conferring
powers, 9.30
general considerations, 6.23
Interpretation and Legislative Reform
(Scotland) Act 2010, and, 9.32
introduction, 9.29
judicial review, and, 14.14
merits scrutiny, 9.34
Scotland Act 1998, under, 9.35

Secondary legislation – *contd*
Statutory Instruments Act 1946, and,
9.32
technical scrutiny, 9.33
types of power in Scotland, 6.24
Second reading
Scottish Government Bills, and, 9.11
Westminster Bills, and, 9.5
Secretaries of State
UK government, and, 7.3
Security of tenure
judiciary, and, 12.7
Select committees
accountability of government, and,
10.9
Separation of powers
standards of good governance, and, 2.5
structure of written constitution, and,
1.8
Sewel convention
generally, 6.22
Scottish Independence referendum,
and, 4.21
**Shaping Scotland's Parliament
(Consultative Steering Group,
1998)**
generally, 3.19
law-making procedures, and, 9.1
parliamentary accountability, and, 10.1
Sheriff Appeal Court
court system, and, 12.2
Sheriff courts
court system, and, 12.2
Single transferable vote (STV)
voting systems, and, 5.8
Smith Commission
administrative tribunals, and, 14.5
bicameralism, and, 5.15
committee system, and, 1.11
cross-border public authorities, and,
8.10
generally, 4.20–4.21
intergovernmental matters, and, 7.26
legislation on devolved matters, and,
6.22
legislative supremacy, and, 6.5
local government, and, 8.7
parliamentary accountability, and, 10.1
public finance, and, 11.1
reserved matters, and, 6.14, 6.17, 6.18
sources of executive authority, and,
7.19
Social security
law-making competences, and, 6.16

Solicitor-General
UK government, and, 7.8
Solicitor-General for Scotland
generally, 7.20
legal advice, 7.21
retained functions, 7.22
South Africa
preamble to constitution, and, 2.1
rule of law, and, 2.8
Scottish constitutional context, and,
3.1
Sources of law
law-making competences, and, 6.2
Special advisers
Scottish Government, and, 7.23
Standards of good governance
accountability principle, 2.4
introduction, 2.3
separation of powers, 2.5
**Standards, Procedures and Public
Appointments (SPPA) Committee**
election of committee conveners, and,
10.10
introduction, 5.18
review of legislative process, and
generally, 9.20
hybrid Bills, 9.27
post-legislative scrutiny, 9.28
standards and privileges, and, 5.21
Standing orders
law-making procedures, and, 9.9
Statement of competence
Scottish Government Bills, and, 9.10
Statement of compliance
Scottish Government Bills, and, 9.10
Status
structure of written constitution, and,
1.4
Statute of Westminster 1931
unwritten constitution of the UK, and,
1.22
Statutory appeals
Administrative Tribunals, 14.5
introduction, 14.4
Leggatt Review, 14.5
local authorities, 14.6
public bodies, 14.6
Subject committees
accountability of government, and,
10.10
Subordinate legislation
control of exercise of powers, 9.31
control of legislation conferring
powers, 9.30

Subordinate legislation – *contd*
general considerations, 6.23
Interpretation and Legislative Reform
(Scotland) Act 2010, and, 9.32
introduction, 9.29
judicial review, and, 14.14
merits scrutiny, 9.34
Scotland Act 1998, under, 9.35
Statutory Instruments Act 1946, and,
9.32
technical scrutiny, 9.33
types of power in Scotland, 6.24
Supremacy of EU law
law-making competences, and, 6.8–
6.9
Supreme Court
devolution issues, and, 14.20–14.21
generally, 12.2
human rights reforms, and, 13.17
judicial appointments, 12.5
legislative supremacy, and, 6.5
private Bills, and, 9.27
public law adjudication, and
devolution issues, 14.20–14.21
generally, 14.32
introduction, 14.1
role of Lord Advocate, and, 7.21
Scotland Act 1998, and, 6.15
Scottish Government Bills, and, 9.18
separation of powers, and, 2.5
Welsh devolution, and, 3.19
Surveillance
information law, and, 13.25
Taxation
public finance, and, 11.3
Taxing powers
borrowing powers of Scottish
government, 11.15
'closest connection', 11.12
collection of tax, 11.14
generally, 11.9
intergovernmental relations, 11.16
introduction, 11.6
land transactions tax, 11.13
landfill tax, 11.13
resolution of Scottish Parliament,
11.11
Scottish rate of income tax, 11.10
'Scottish taxpayers', 11.12
Temporary sheriffs
judiciary, and, 12.7
Territorial division
structure of written constitution, and,
1.11

Territory
law-making competences, and, 6.13
Third reading
Scottish Government Bills, and, 9.13
Westminster Bills, and, 9.6
**Towards Scotland's Parliament
(Scottish Constitutional
Convention, 1990)**
generally, 3.19
Trade and industry
law-making competences, and, 6.16
Transport
law-making competences, and, 6.16
Treason
law-making competences, and, 6.15
Treaties
European Union, and, 3.12
Territorial extent
structure of written constitution, and, 1.4
Tribunals Service
public law adjudication, and, 14.5
Tripartism
structure of written constitution, and,
1.8
UK Government
Advocate General for Scotland, 7.8
Attorney-General, 7.8
Cabinet, 7.7
cabinet government
collective responsibility, 7.11
generally, 7.10
role of Prime Minister, 7.12
civil service, and, 7.3
Crown's role
generally, 7.2
introduction, 7.1
dissolution of Parliament, 7.5
immunity from suit, and, 7.2
introduction, 7.3
Law Officers of the Crown, 7.8
ministerial conduct, 7.9
Ministers of State, 7.3
ministers of the Crown
collective responsibility, 7.11
conduct, 7.9
generally, 7.7
overview, 7.1
Parliamentary Under-Secretaries, 7.3
Prime Minister
appointment, 7.5
cabinet government, and, 7.12
conduct, 7.9
functions, 7.6
generally, 7.4

UK Government – *contd*
Secretaries of State, 7.3
Solicitor-General, 7.8
the Queen, and, 7.2
UK Government departments
Scottish Government, and, 7.24
UK government, and, 7.2
UK Parliament (Westminster)
accessibility, 5.23
administration, 5.22
committees
generally, 5.17
introduction, 5.16
composition, 5.2–5.4
elected chamber
composition, 5.2–5.4
members, 5.3
Parliamentary sessions, 5.4
structure, 5.2–5.4
elections
candidates, 5.8
conduct, 5.11
constituency boundaries, 5.9
entitlement to be candidate and
member, 5.7
entitlement to vote, 5.6
introduction, 5.5
political parties, 5.12
system of voting, 5.8
tenure of members of parliament,
5.10
House of Lords
bicameralism, 5.15
introduction, 5.13
reform, 5.14
introduction, 5.1
law-making competences, and
European Communities Act 1972,
6.10
introduction, 6.3
post-1 January 1973, 6.7–6.
pre-1 January 1973, 6.4–6.6
supremacy of EU law, 6.8–6.9
management, 5.22
members of Parliament (MPs)
allowances, 5.20
general, 5.19
pay, 5.20
privileges, 5.21
standards, 5.21
tenure, 5.10
openness, 5.23
sessions, 5.4
structure, 5.2–5.4

**UK Parliamentary Commissioner for
Administration/Ombudsman**
accountability of quangos, and, 8.16
effect of decisions in courts, 10.14
funding, and, 11.4
generally, 10.12
introduction, 10.11
role of Queen, and, 7.2
standards of good governance, and,
2.3
**United Kingdom of Great Britain and
Ireland**
formation, 3.2
United States of America
federal constitutions, and, 1.21
preamble to constitution, and,
2.1
privacy rights, and, 13.24
public law adjudication, and,
14.1
role of head of state, and, 1.7
territorial division, and, 1.11
Unwritten constitution
generally, 1.22–1.24
Voting systems
generally, 5.8
'Vow'
Scottish Independence referendum,
and, 4.19–4.20
'West Lothian Question'
generally, 5.9
Scottish Independence referendum,
and, 4.20
'Westminster model'
structure of written constitution, and,
1.8
Westminster Parliament (UK)
And see UK Parliament
generally, 5.1
Written constitutions
appointment of capital city, 1.4
constitutional amendment, 1.12
Executive, 1.8
head of state, 1.7
judiciary, 1.10
legislature, 1.9
nationality, 1.6
Parliament, 1.9
preamble, 1.3
rights and freedoms, 1.5
Scotland, for, 1.2
status, 1.4
territorial division, 1.11
territorial extent, 1.4